READINGS

IN

ICHTHYOLOGY

READINGS

IN

ICHTHYOLOGY

edited by

Milton S. Love

Research Associate
Department of Biology
Occidental College
Los Angeles, California

and

Gregor M. Cailliet

Associate Professor of Biology
Moss Landing Marine Laboratories
Moss Landing, California

Goodyear Publishing Company, Inc.
Santa Monica, California

Library of Congress Cataloging in Publication Data
Main entry under title:

Readings in ichthyology.
    Includes bibliographical references.
    1. Fishes—Addresses, essay, lectures.   I. Love,
Milton S.   II. Cailliet, Gregor M.
QL614.5.R42   597   78-16654
ISBN 0-87620-762-X

Current printing (last digit):
10 9 8 7 6 5 4 3 2 1

ISBN: 0-87620-762-X
Y-762X-6

Printed in the United States of America

Contents

Preface

In recent years, humans have become more aware of their natural surroundings. This increased awareness has resulted in more attention to such watery habitats as lakes, streams, estuaries and oceans. Ichthyology, the study of fishes, has become better known to the public, and courses in this field are common on most college and university campuses.

Since much of ichthyological knowledge comes from the ever-accumulating body of scientific literature, it is essential that students of fishes be aware of recent developments in the field. However, this literature is often difficult to obtain, especially when a large library is not available. It is our experience that many ichthyology or fish biology courses use reprints or copies of articles from the scientific literature, but this can constitute a hardship for the instructor, the library, and the student. We have long felt that a collection of readings would be valuable to both undergraduate and graduate students in courses dealing with such aspects of fish biology as systematics, morphology, phylogeny, ecology and physiology. That is, making some of the most interesting literature on "what makes a fish work" available in one volume. We have accumulated what we feel to be some of the most representative references in this diverse field with the idea that it could be either a strong supplement to existing textbooks, or a text by itself.

The topics we have covered are wide ranging, reflecting the diversity of approaches to studying fishes, the kind of information covered by various instructors in the field across the country, and our own personal experiences in teaching several levels of students about fishes. As can be seen from the lengthy list of articles, fishes have been the subject of numerous and varied investigations. We have attempted to cover this range as adequately as possible, without redundancy. Because of limitations on the size of this book, we have had to omit many pertinent papers, both classic and recent. Thus, to more completely cover each topic, we have included a list of additional references at the end of each chapter. Other ichthyologists would perhaps choose different papers on specific topics, but we have made a conscious effort to be comprehensive in our coverage, and would hope that this collection of readings is useful to those teaching courses in ichthyology. We welcome constructive criticism and comment.

ACKNOWLEDGEMENTS

We wish to thank the following individuals for their thoughtful and constructive review of our selections: M. Eric Anderson, Margaret Bradbury, George Barlow, Jeanne Davis, Alfred W. Ebeling, David Greenfield, Clark Hubbs, Richard Ibara, and Sanford Moss. We are especially grateful to Al Ebeling for his inspiration and guidance, and for stressing the importance of the literature in understanding the field of ichthyology. We would like to express appreciation to Regina Paull-Love for some of the typing and much of the encouragement, and the many students in our classes at the University of California, Santa Barbara, and at Moss Landing Marine Laboratories for their stimulating discussions of many of the articles considered. The Busy Bee Cafe in Pismo Beach, which is conveniently located approximately halfway between Santa Barbara and Moss Landing, provided pleasant facilities for extended periods of time for the mere price of breakfast and a cup of coffee. Finally, since this collection of readings would not have been possible without the considerable labors of the investigators who actually conducted the research cited, we would like to thank all of them for allowing us to present their interesting and stimulating findings. Their papers make it unnecessary for us to stress the great diversity and engrossing nature of the field of ichthyology.

Introduction

As Carl Hubbs has aptly pointed out (see Chapter 1), ichthyology has undergone "torrential growth" in the United States during the last half century, with the number of ichthyologists and their numerous approaches to studying fishes increasing exponentially. Much of this growth is a result of the evolution of ichthyology from an exploration, discovery and systematic phase (which is still very active), to other phases involving evolution, zoogeography, genetics, physiology, fishery biology, and ecology. This multitude of disciplines studying fishes, coupled with the wide variety of habitats that fishes occupy, has produced an extremely rich and interesting array of publications. In this collection of readings, we have attempted to adequately represent this overwhelming assemblage of knowledge so that others can become more aware of this exciting field.

We have organized *Readings in Ichthyology* so that the reader may be introduced to as large a spectrum of ichthyology as is possible in one volume. Subjects range from a presentation of the history of ichthyology and the protagonists involved, through discussions of the variety of habitats that fishes occupy, the kinds of fishes that occupy these habitats, and the evolutionary processes leading to the many adaptations that fishes have derived to function so successfully in their watery environments.

The cast of characters involved in studying fishes in the past (see Chapter 1), and present (see the remaining chapters), is extremely interesting. Ichthyologists come from varied backgrounds, including medicine and law, but all share one common interest: a fascination with fishes. Through the years, there have been many personal interactions, often controversial in nature, among ichthyologists. The net result, seen in the papers by G. S. Myers and C. L. Hubbs on the history of ichthyology, has been a stimulating and enjoyable body of literature, uncovering many interesting facts about fishes.

An analysis of the habitat utilization of the major fish groups is presented by D. M. Cohen and M. H. Horn (Chapter 2). Here, the areas where fish evolution occurred are itemized, citing possible mechanisms controlling the process. Fishes, especially teleosts, are often referred to as "the insects of the ocean," a phrase reflecting their numerical abundance and diversity. It is apparent from their success in both fresh and salt water that fishes have evolved in a way that has utilized available space very efficiently.

In the next two chapters, two papers are presented that deal with fish morphology, followed by four articles that discuss the possible pathways by which such morphological traits evolved. Some innovations in jaw morphology are covered by Karel Liem, while the processes leading to variation in meristics of fishes are discussed by R. K. Johnson and M. A. Barnett (Chapter 3). The early evolution of fishes is not represented in our readings, primarily because it is discussed commonly in general zoology texts. However, several articles listed in the Additional Readings section deal with this subject. The more controversial topic of teleostean phylogeny is represented by papers reflecting the opposing schools of thought (Chapter 4). The first two papers, by W. A. Gosline and by P. H. Greenwood, D. E. Rosen, S. H. Weitzman, and G. S. Myers, summarize the opposing positions. The other two papers present trends that have occurred as fishes evolved, in such things as feeding mechanisms and cellular DNA content. The voluminous literature on this subject alone can (and has) become the subject of a large book, thus making it impossible to present even the majority of representative articles. A more complete picture of the teleostean phylogeny controversy and the evidence on both sides can be found by reading some of the references listed at the end of Chapter 4).

One of the activities that fish do best is to propel themselves through their watery medium in a very efficient manner. Since fish as swimmers have been studied from a variety of angles, the articles that we have chosen to represent this field of study (Chapter 5) include discussions of the morphological and hydrodynamic aspects, metabolic considerations, and several physiological specializations that have allowed fishes to become very proficient at swimming. One of the more exciting recent discoveries in ichthyology has been that some fishes are not strictly poikilothermous, but, in such distantly related groups as sharks and tunas, they are capable of raising their body temperatures above ambient water temperatures, through a network of capillaries. They are able to regulate this body temperature, thus enabling more efficient muscle contractions to produce propulsion.

It is important to some fishes to be able to maintain neutral buoyancy in the water column. This can be accomplished in several ways. In one, a gas bladder is connected to the alimentary canal and gases can be exchanged between the surface air and the bladder. In another, there is no connection with the outside of the body, and, gases must be transported via the gills and blood stream and deposited at the bladder. The physiology of these two processes is discussed in the first three articles in Chapter 6. Yet another mechanism, often found in fishes from the deep-sea, in which the gas bladder either does not develop or is not filled with gases, is discussed in the paper by E. J. Denton and N. B. Marshall. Buoyancy in these fishes is often attained using high concentrations of low density compounds, such as lipids, combined with low density tissues.

Another task that fishes must accomplish is extracting oxygen for respiration out of the surrounding water. This is a much more difficult task in water than in air, since much more water must be passed by the respiratory organ to obtain sufficient oxygen. Therefore, fishes must have efficient mechanisms to move the water by the gills, while not interfering with other functions such as feeding. The elaborate and intricate series of muscle contractions which accomplish this task are discussed by C. M. Ballintijn and G. M. Hughes in Chapter 7. Once water is available to the gill surface, fish must extract oxygen from the water. They do this by a hairpin counter-current mechanism in which the oxygen-filled water is passed by blood vessels moving in the opposite direction in the gill lamellae, which enables them to concentrate gases in the blood for use by the fish in respiration. This mechanism, which is similar to that found in the heat-concentrating red muscles in tunas (Chapter 5), and in the gas-concentrating organ in the swimbladder (Chapter 6), is discussed by G. M. Hughes. Those fishes that constantly swim do not need to use respiratory muscles to force water over their gills but, rather, as pointed out by J. L. Roberts, can use their body propulsion to pass water over the gills via "ram gill ventilation." In the two additional articles, unique respiratory adaptations are presented. Air breathing and its relationship to buoyancy in a tropical fish is discussed by E. Todd, while G. F. Holeton introduces us to unusual Antarctic fishes that are capable of transporting oxygen throughout their bodies without the aid of blood hemoglobin.

Consumption of food is extremely important for all organisms and many morphological and behavioral adaptations have been derived to accomplish this chore. Fishes are certainly no exception to the rule and therefore exhibit many adaptations for capturing and processing food items (Chapter 8). R. McN. Alexander presents some experiments on fish feeding mechanics, and S. J. de Groot discusses the various morphological and behavioral adaptations found in flatfish alimentary systems. Further coverage of feeding behavior and food niche analysis can be found in the list of Additional Readings.

In order for fishes to know where they are, what to feed on, and perhaps detect what may desire to feed on them, they must be able to sense certain parameters of their environment. Since most fishes live in water, they have developed those senses that are most important in detecting aquatic stimuli. In Chapter 9 articles are presented that cover some of the important sensory mechanisms used by fish. F. W. Munz and W. N. McFarland discuss visual pigments in fishes from different habitats. J. E. Bardach, J. H. Todd and R. Crickmer present information on the sense of taste in catfishes, and T. H. Bullock explores the unique sense of electroreception in fish. The acoustico-lateralis system, which is an extremely important sensory mechanism in fishes, is not represented in this chapter, but an article by T. J. Pitcher, B. L. Partridge, and C. S. Wardle in Chapter 12 provides experimental evidence regarding the role of this sense in fish schooling. It is quite obvious that this chapter could be much enlarged, but lack of space prevents us from including many articles that should be made available. One very informative way to attain further insight into fish sensory mechanisms is to read several of the volumes of W. S. Hoar and D. J. Randall's edition of *Fish Physiology* (see Additional Readings).

Fishes live in both freshwater and seawater, and they must be able to regulate the ionic composition of their bodily fluids. G. Parry, in Chapter 10, evaluates the osmoregulation processes in migrating salmonid fishes, and J. W. Burger informs us of the function of the rectal gland in elasmobranchs for salt and water excretion.

Reproduction in fishes has been the subject of numerous articles, and the subject has recently been reviewed extensively by Breder and Rosen (1966), Hoar (1969), and Balon (1975) (see Additional Readings, Chapter 11). In our chapter on reproduction, we have attempted to present some informative articles representing the variety of reproductive strategies found among fishes. J. R. Burns discusses how environmental parameters are important in regulating reproductive activities, and L. Chen and R. L. Martinich evaluate the role of pheromones in controlling ovulation. D. R. Robertson discusses social aspects of sex reversal in a coral-reef fish. Internal fertilization occurs in several groups of fishes, and the young can develop in eggs inside the mother, or as embryos. The coelacanth has been found to be ovoviviparous, a fact just recently discovered by C. L. Smith, C. S. Rand, B. Schaeffer, and J. W. Atz. In another article, the way in which the surfperches (family Embiotocidae), a specialized group of viviparous marine fishes, transfer oxygen from the mother to the embryos is presented by P. W. Webb and J. R. Brett.

Since it was impossible to present chapters on each of the other subjects that ichthyologists study, we have combined several topics into Chapter 12, entitled "Behavior and Other Adaptations." Here we have chosen articles that cover fish schooling, homing and territoriality, symbiotic relationships, and behavioral interactions. One especially interesting article is by G. Barlow contrasting the social behavior of Central American cichlid fishes and coral-reef surgeon fishes. Several other articles discuss the ways in which fishes attempt to camouflage themselves. Another paper by G. Barlow analyzes the adaptive significance of fish eye-lines, while two articles concentrate on the function of bioluminescence in two unrelated groups of fishes. We realize that this "catch-all" chapter will not satisfactorily cover all of the specific topics that interest ichthyologists, but the literature is so voluminous that one must get completely involved with it to understand the breadth of the field. We encourage the reader to pursue some of the Additional Readings and to read even further on chosen subjects.

Hopefully, this assortment of readings in the field of ichthyology will prove interesting to those who sort through them. Ultimately, we hope that *Readings in Ichthyology* will serve to stimulate its readers to further investigate fishes, a group of organisms that we feel are among the world's most fascinating creatures.

1

The History
of Ichthyology

A Brief Sketch of the History of Ichthyology in America to the Year 1850[1]

George S. Myers

THE sciences developed chiefly in Europe, and if we were to cover all that was done in Europe on American fishes previous to 1850, there would be little time to say much about what happened in America. For this reason I refer to European events principally as a background. However, it is a very important background, because up to the year 1800, the sciences had barely begun to stir in colonial America, and almost everything that had been done in the New World was done primarily to advance the development of science in Europe.

Moreover, the memory of men still living reaches back to the time when ichthyology was relatively a rare discipline in American science. I recall Henry Fowler telling me at one time that he had shaken the hand of a man who had shaken hands with Rafinesque. Moreover, it shocked me not long ago to realize that I published my first fish paper only six years after the death of Albert Günther and Theodore Gill, the great 19th century leaders of our field. Science is young in America!

I was asked to end my paper with the year 1850. I was not told where to begin it! I thought of beginning it with the man we are told was the first namer of animals, but I doubt that Adam and the Garden of Eden were located in America. Then, too, were we concerned with ichthyology in general, there could be no pardon for failure to extend our history back to the time of Aristotle, or perhaps even to the clearly identifiable representations of *Tilapia nilotica* and other fishes of the Nile in Egyptian sculpture of some four thousand years ago. Nor, perhaps, should a historian of American ichthyology ignore Norse mention of the halibut and giant salmon found by the men of Leif and Thorwald Ericsson's explorations (*circa* 1000 AD) along the coast of their American *Vinland*, which, as the latest research has indicated, extended southward of Cape Cod. Finally, who can say that the American aborigines themselves were not observant students of fishes, when they applied specific names even to such insignificant fishes as the New England mummichog (*Fundulus heteroclitus*) and the Amazonian pirá caá (the leaf fish, *Monocirrhus*)? Indeed, a great deal could easily be written on preColumbian knowledge of fishes and their anatomy among the American Indians and Eskimos, but that is another story and we must adopt a starting point for ours.

According to the convention that I have adopted, the history of American ichthyology began at two o'clock in the morning of 12 October 1492, at approximately 24° north latitude, 74° 20′ west longitude. Dead ahead (due west) of the PINTA, the NIÑA, and the SANTA MARIA, the low, white sand cliffs of Guanahani, San Salvador, or Watlings Island, gleamed in the bright moonlight. To the Genoese navigator and *almirante*, Cristoforo Colombo, the moment must have been one of supreme and exquisite pleasure and relief—pleasure for the success of his stubborn quest and relief from the threats of mutiny that had become almost overwhelming only a single day before. After drifting SSW until dawn to avoid unknown reefs, the little squadron rounded Hinchinbroke Rocks and Southwest Point, sailed northward in the lee of the island, and anchored in the little bay protected by Gardiner Reef.

Appropriately for our history, the day was Friday. Surviving accounts are concerned principally with the landing, the naked Taino–Arowak inhabitants, and the lush vegetation. Both natives and vegetation are now gone, but we may be sure the sea-weary, pious, Spanish and Basque seamen became, on that Friday, the first Europeans to catch, cook, and taste the porkfish, *Anisotremus virginicus*. No doubt the *almirante* himself

[1] This paper is printed in the form in which it was presented orally at the annual meeting of the Society in Vancouver, June 1963.

dined on American fish that evening.[2]

Even had the catch been recorded, who could have said what the fishes were, save the Arowaks? Indeed, the naked savages of San Salvador were perhaps quite as able ichthyologists as any living European was in 1492. In that year, the first books ever printed in Europe were only 46 years old. The first Renaissance works of general importance on fishes (by Belon, Salviani, and Aldrovandi) were still 60 or more years in the future. Francis Bacon, Konrad Gesner, and William Harvey were not yet born. Indeed, save for the ancient works of Aristotle, Pliny, and a few others, ichthyology itself had not yet been born in the Europe of 1492.

We must omit mention here of most of the accounts of fishes given in the published works of a large number of Spanish, Portuguese, French, and English travelers during the two and a half centuries following the period of discovery. Many of them contributed interesting observations, but no real attempt was ever made to compile the information, and later contributions are of far more historical importance in ichthyology. However, it is interesting to note that the occurrence of a freshwater shark in Lake Nicaragua was recorded in print by Oviedo, only 25 years after Columbus' last voyage. Considering the time lag between geographical discovery and zoological exploration in more recent days, that was fast work on the part of the Spaniards. In fact, we may well credit Gonzalo Fernandez de Oviedo as the first naturalist–explorer of America and the first to record in print useful and accurate information on American fishes.

Jean de Lery, a French Calvinist minister belonging to the Huguenot colony founded in the bay of Rio de Janeiro in 1555, was perhaps the next, followed by José d'Acosta and other 16th century travelers. The first English man of science to visit America seems to have been Thomas Harriott of Oxford, who arrived at Sir Walter Raleigh's colony of Roanoke in North Carolina in 1585, whence he recorded and figured the garpike and other fishes.

The first important student of American ichthyology was unquestionably George Marcgrave of Liebstadt in Saxony, who, after his education, went to Leiden and Amsterdam. In 1638, he visited Brazil as physician with the expedition of Count Maurits of Nassau, who had temporarily conquered northeastern Brazil from the Portuguese. Marcgrave was apparently subordinate to the chief physician and scientist of the expedition, Willem Piso. Both men were interested in science, Piso more in medical matters, Marcgrave more in natural history. In Brazil, Marcgrave ingratiated himself with Count Maurits by his knowledge of military engineering, and Maurits rewarded him with opportunities for travel and collecting. In 1644, Maurits returned to the Netherlands, and Marcgrave also left, via Angola in West Africa. In Africa, he died at the age of 34 years. Marcgrave's manuscripts and drawings were finally edited and published by Piso in 1648 as *The Natural History of Brazil*—the most important early work on the fauna and flora of America. The woodcut engravers of the day reproduced the figures most crudely, but many of the fishes are recognizable, and Marcgrave's work was utilized by Linnaeus and other later writers.

No other book on America of such ichthyological importance as that of Marcgrave got into print until the appearance in England of Mark Catesby's great *Natural History of Carolina, Florida, and the Bahama Islands*, in the years 1731–1743. Despite the fact that the author was not a profound or particularly well-educated man, his work had the freshness of an original observer, and Catesby's fishes and other animals were figured in much better and finer style than those of the previous literature. Catesby's great folio, a result of extensive travels in the lands mentioned in its title, remained *the* great work on North American natural history for approximately 80 years, until superseded by the early 19th century works of Rafinesque, Say, LeSueur, Alexander Wilson, Audubon, De Kay, and other native American naturalists. However, the history of Mark Catesby and his great work have recently been recorded in detail, and we must pass on to other matters.

Because he also has received attention, we need barely to mention the work of Dr. Alexander Garden of Charleston, South Carolina, who, in the mid-18th century, supplied Linnaeus with specimens of many American fishes and other animals and was

---

[2] I venture gently but firmly to disagree with our Portuguese friends who insist on the preColumbian discovery of America by Portuguese navigators. Harvard's great naval historian, Admiral Samuel Eliot Morison, has disposed of such claims with the most crushing effectiveness.

rewarded by having the *Gardenia* named in his honor.

The first important European works of what can be called a modern type on fishes were those of Francis Willoughby, an Englishman (1686), and of Peter Artedi (1738), a Swede. It is interesting to note that in the case of each, the zoologist in whom we are interested was paired with another, usually a botanist, who long outlived him and who published his zoological colleague's manuscripts posthumously. Four such remarkable pairs appear in our history—Marcgrave and Piso, Willoughby and John Ray, Artedi and Linnaeus, and finally, Spix and Martius. Returning to Willoughby and Artedi, it may well be said that these two men, especially Artedi, were the founding fathers of ichthyology. Willoughby was the first to put fishes into a few anatomical groupings that are still generally recognized today. Artedi completed the classificatory system with great acumen and care, gathered the scattered literature and analyzed it in a modern way, and everywhere reduced confusion to order. There is some reason to believe that the somewhat elder Artedi was largely responsible for the younger Linnaeus' ideas and systems of biological classification. In later years, whenever Linnaeus attempted to improve on Artedi's fish classification, he usually fell into error. In any event, not until the publication of Artedi's work was the world in possession of a really useful treatise on fishes and their classification. No native American naturalist appears to have become familiar with Artedi's work until after it was superseded by Linnaeus' *Systema Naturae*. Even the latter was little known in America. Colonialism has rarely fostered native scientific investigation in any colony.

I pause at this point to narrate an interesting chain of events linking the royal house of Portugal with ichthyology—one that has never before been set forth anywhere. Because it provides perhaps the most interesting single result of my study, it seems worthwhile to present it here *in toto*. Moreover, it encompasses a great deal of the history of the study of American fishes.

In the 18th century, the Crown of Spain and the Crown of Portugal, between them, held practically all of South America in colonial status. Brazil comprised about half the area of South America and was held by Portugal, the ties of language, culture, and

history between the two being strong even today. Most of the rest of America, from Florida to Patagonia, and all of the Greater Antilles except Jamaica, were held by Spain.

Both monarchies, like most of them at that time, were secretive. Neither permitted colonial trade with any place but the mother country. Neither permitted foreigners to travel in their immense American colonies except by special royal permission. Neither wished other countries to find out anything really useful about the natural resources of its colonies.

It was a great day for science when, in 1799, Spain permitted the German scientist Alexander von Humboldt and the French botanist Aimée Bonpland to travel together in Venezuela and other Spanish American lands. Von Humboldt was the first European naturalist of real stature to collect, study, and publish papers on the fishes of Ecuador, Venezuela, and Mexico. His account of the electric eel in the Orinoco became a classic. Incidentally, Humboldt felt that the Portuguese were very backward when, upon his ascent of the Rio Orinoco and his arrival at a Brazilian frontier post on the upper Rio Negro, he was rudely arrested, confined, and then turned back by a Portuguese border commander as a meddling alien, and therefore undesirable. Humboldt visited the United States in 1804 on his way home from Spanish America at the invitation of Thomas Jefferson. His prodigious writings on America and the cosmos soon made his name a household word, not only in Europe but also the United States. I recall reverberations of his fame even in my own youth, over a century after his great journey.

However, considerably before Humboldt and Bonpland's journey of 1799–1804, the Portuguese Crown had become desirous of finding out more in regard to the natural riches of its immense Brazilian colony. The man selected to make the investigation was a native American, born in Bahia, Brazil, on 27 April 1756. His name was Alexandre Rodriguez Ferreira. At the age of 14, he was sent to Portugal for his education. Later, at the University of Coimbra, he came under the guidance of Professor Domingos Vandelli, an Italian naturalist and one of several Italian *savants* who had been imported to raise the tone of Portugal's foremost university. Later, the strangest Brazilian fish collected by Ferreira would be named *Vandellia*—the bloodsucking candirú catfish.

Vandelli proposed Ferreira as the man best qualified to investigate the fauna, flora, and minerals of Brazil. In 1783, at the age of 27, Dr. Ferreira, with his diploma in his pocket, set out for Brazil. He traveled throughout the Brazilian Amazon, Matto Grosso, and eastern Brazil, collecting specimens (including a number of fishes), notes, and drawings. After many vicissitudes, some medical, some caused by official red tape, he returned to Portugal in 1792 or 1793. There he was appointed Secretary of the Department of Marine and Colonies and was shortly also entrusted with the curatorship of the Royal Cabinet of Natural History.

In Portugal, Ferreira labored over his well-illustrated reports on the various animals, plants, and minerals collected, with Vandelli helping and guiding him. Apparently he classified his biological collections according to the Linnaean system, and gave them new generic and specific names. In fishes, at least, he was the only naturalist in Europe with a good collection of Brazilian specimens to work with, and into his manuscripts he was able to put firsthand accounts of the fishes as seen in the field, descriptions from actual specimens, and figures with the life colors taken from field sketches.

Ferreira could not properly classify some of his fishes, and approximately in the year 1800, Vandelli sent one of them to Lacépède in Paris—Vandelli being known in Paris whereas Ferreira was not. Lacépède seems to have ignored the fish, but many years later Valenciennes found it, with Vandelli's notes, and named it *Vandellia cirrhosa*. At least one generic name proposed in Ferreira's manuscripts still survives. It is the name *Osteoglossum*, proposed for the aruaná of the Amazon. Presumably the name got into the literature through a label ascribed to Vandelli accompanying Ferreira's type specimen.

However, the Portuguese court was still obsessed with secrecy about Brazil. Moreover, the events of the French Revolution and the rise of Napoleon had frightened the wits out of every monarch in Europe. Ferreira's manuscripts reposed on a shelf in Lisbon, mostly never to be published.

By 1807, Napoleon's armies were subjugating Europe, and one of them, under General Junot, was marching on Lisbon.

The Portuguese royal family fled in haste, on British men-of-war, and set up the Portuguese court in Rio de Janeiro—the first and, up to the 20th century, the last time that a ruling European monarch ever visited his American colonies. This also was of future importance to American ichthyology.

Ferreira was left in Lisbon to face the French. They appeared in the persons of General Junot and Geoffroy Sainte-Hilaire, who effectively cleaned out the Royal Cabinet and sent Ferreira's hard-won specimens to Paris as spoils of war. They paid little attention to his manuscripts!

Perhaps this was a good thing, due to Portuguese failure to publish Ferreira's papers. In any event, when Cuvier published his *Règne Animal*—the first edition in 1817, the second in 1829—Ferreira's specimens began to be noticed. A good many of the common Brazilian mammals, birds, reptiles, and fishes were named by Cuvier and his associates. With nearly all of these descriptions, it is noted that the type was a "gift of the Lisbon Museum," with no notice of the collector, Ferreira, whose very name seems to have been unknown to the French naturalists.

Among the fishes which we know to have been described from Ferreira's material in Paris were *Arapaima gigas*, the great pirarucú of the Amazon; *Osteoglossum bicirrhosum*, the aruaná; *Salminus brasiliensis*, the great dourado, largest of American characids; *Hydrolycus scomberoides*; *Myloplus rhomboidalis*, the great pacú; *Catoprion mento*; *Serrasalmus piraya*, the largest piranha; *Serrasalmus denticulatus*; *Boulengerella lucius*, the common pike–characid; *Chalceus macrolepidotus*; and perhaps a dozen others.

The types are still in Paris, although a later Portuguese, the herpetologist Barboza du Bocage, Director of the Lisbon Museum, made a valiant attempt to effect their return, in the 1850's or 1860's. One manuscript by Ferreira, on the pirarucú, was finally published in part, in Brazil in the mid-19th century.

Later, the Portuguese court made up for its previous remissness. When the king arrived in Rio in 1807, he found that the policy of restriction of trade and travel in regard to Brazil was harmful, not least to himself, and opened Brazil to foreign travelers. But nothing much could come of this until Napoleon was subdued and banished to St. Helena after Waterloo in 1815. Moreover, the Spanish colonies, led by Generals Bolívar and San Martín, had freed the Spanish-American mainland when Spain itself was taken by Napoleon in 1810, and the revolution and its aftermath persisted in Spanish America until 1823, when President Monroe effectively ended European attempts to regain the Spanish colonies by his promulgation of the Monroe Doctrine. Thus, a deluge of foreign travelers descended upon peaceful, unknown Brazil between 1816 and 1825, among them many naturalists, including Prince Maximilian of the small Rhenish principality of Wied–Neuwied, whose surviving collections are in the American Museum of Natural History in New York. Many mementos of the Brazilian and the later North American journeys of Prince Maximilian still survive in the castle of Wied–Neuwied.

However, the most important South American ichthyological explorers came in the wake of Karolina, Archduchess of Austria, who went to Brazil in 1817 as the bride of the Crown Prince of Brazil. With the large wedding party came three great naturalists, Johann Natterer, sent by the Imperial Museum of Vienna, and Spix and Martius, sent by the King of Bavaria. Natterer remained in Brazil for 18 years, sending tons of zoological and anthropological material to Vienna, where the numerous fishes were described in later years by Heckel, Kner, and Steindachner. Natterer's most important single fish discovery was the South American lungfish, *Lepidosiren*, but Fitzinger received credit for its naming because he published a brief preliminary notice before Natterer's memoir appeared. Johann Baptiste von Spix was a zoologist, Martius a botanist, founder, author, and editor of the gigantic work, *Flora of Brazil.* Unfortunately, Spix died soon after his three-year sojourn in Brazil. To Martius, Humboldt and others recommended a young Swiss naturalist to finish the fish volume. He was Louis Agassiz. The volume appeared in 1829, and Agassiz conceived a lifelong interest in Brazilian fishes.

Long after Agassiz's establishment at Harvard, he obtained funds from Nathaniel Thayer of Boston to spend a year collecting fishes in Brazil, in 1865–1866, together with a group of assistants. Among the student assistants were Charles Frederick Hartt, who was later to found the Brazilian Geological Survey; Joel Asaph Allen, later the well-known mammalogist; and, strangest of all, William James, who became America's great experimental psychologist and the builder of pragmatic philosophy. But this journey in Brazil would have accomplished far less than it did had it not been for the deep interest of another member of the Portuguese royal line—Dom Pedro the Second, Emperor of Brazil, himself a naturalist of sorts. He furnished Agassiz with a ship, assistants and guides, free passages, and every other kind of help he could. When he was called south by the sanguinary Paraguayan war, he personally had fish collections made in southern Brazil for Agassiz. Agassiz's other projects, and his death in 1873, prevented him from working on his immense Brazilian collection, and it was left to Steindachner, Eigenmann, and others to report on the fishes which are still preserved in the Museum of Comparative Zoology.

Finally, a still later member of the Portuguese royal house, Dom Carlos of Braganza, King of Portugal, became interested in the deep seas, made deep-sea investigations aboard the Royal Yacht AMELIA, and worked up and published many of the results himself during the early years of the present century.

Leaving now this saga of Portuguese royalty, it should be noted that almost nothing of a really scientific nature was contributed to North American zoology by native North Americans prior to the year 1800. Soon after that time, William Maclure and others in Philadelphia began to meet to discuss what were then coming to be called the natural sciences. By 1812, these men had formed the Academy of Natural Sciences of Philadelphia with Maclure and Thomas Say as its leaders.

To this institution soon gravitated two men, one a peculiar person from Naples, Sicily, and elsewhere in Mediterranean lands, named Constantine Samuel Rafinesque, the other one of the disciples of Cuvier, whom the latter called the finest zoological illustrator of the day, Charles Alexandre LeSueur. Both men were adventurous, but very different indeed. Rafinesque, who had spent much time studying Sicilian fishes, both alone and in the company of the English ornithologist and zoologist, William Swainson, was an erratic genius with much peasant cunning but little system to his enormous memory and active, voracious mind. It is indicative of his nature that he added Schmaltz to his name (Rafinesque-Schmaltz) solely because he found that Germans were well thought of in America. LeSueur was a polished Frenchman from LeHavre, an artist, explorer, and gentleman, who had accompanied Peron on his famous voyage to Australia. Between them, these two men, mostly on the then-primitive frontier along the Ohio and Wabash rivers, started North American freshwater ichthyology on its way.

Rafinesque's adventures on the Ohio are legendary, especially his visit to Audubon's log cabin, where Rafinesque battered Audubon's Cremona violin to pieces while using it to knock down bats in the cabin at midnight. Audubon later repaid him by giving Rafinesque drawings of imaginary Ohio fishes, which Rafinesque promptly described as new species and included in his famous *Ichthyologia Ohiensis*, published at Lexington, Kentucky, in 1820.

LeSueur described and beautifully illustrated a few Atlantic coast fishes and then migrated west to become a member of the ill-fated socialistic colony at New Harmony on the lower Wabash River, where he illustrated Say's *North American Conchology* and his own abortive monograph of North American fishes. In the 1830's, LeSueur traveled leisurely down the Mississippi, making sketches of colonial life and landscapes, and finally returned to LeHavre. Rafinesque returned to Philadelphia and a precarious life of peddling his plant and shell collections, and died there a pauper.

In the north, the principal ichthyological endeavors of this period were those of Sir John Richardson, the British naval surgeon who later contributed heavily to the ichthyology of China and Australia. Richardson's ichthyological work in northern America was summarized in his *Fauna Boreali–Americana* (1831–1837).

North American marine ichthyology began about the time the Philadelphia Academy was formed, with the publication of Samuel Latham Mitchill's little tract on *The Fishes of New York*. After Mitchill, LeSueur, and Rafinesque, there was a hiatus until the 1840's, when new things began to happen.

James De Kay, a Long Island zoologist, began his epic work, the *Natural History of New York*, including an excellently illustrated volume on the fishes and reptiles. In Ohio, Jared Potter Kirtland, who is recalled by modern zoologists through the silverside

genus *Kirtlandia* and by Kirtland's Warbler, began to untangle the confusion of Rafinesque's *Ichthyologia Ohiensis*. In New York, a man of one of the city's foremost families, James Carson Brevoort, became an ichthyological dilettante, whose most important ichthyological labor would become, in the 1850's, his sponsorship of a young protegé named Theodore Nicholas Gill, who wished to work at the Smithsonian. Brevoort's name survives in the generic name of the menhaden, *Brevoortia*. Also in the 1840's, in Charleston, South Carolina, a physician, John Edwards Holbrook, who had nearly completed his magnum opus, *North American Herpetology*, continued an interest in fishes which finally led to production of a beautifully illustrated *Fishes of South Carolina*.

In Boston, two ichthyologists appeared in the late 1830's and 1840's. David Humphries Storer, a physician who had presented a review of Massachusetts fishes, finally published a *Synopsis of the Fishes of North America*, which was, in the year 1850, the last word on the subject. Storer's Boston medical colleague, Dr. William O. Ayres, had then barely begun to distinguish himself in ichthyology as the first native American to publish important papers on exotic fishes. One was the description of *Polypterus palmas* Ayres from West Africa, one of the nine surviving species of the ancient family of bichirs. Another paper described one of the strangest of all deep-sea fishes, *Malacosteus niger* Ayres, from a specimen cast up on the deck of a transAtlantic ship. But Dr. Ayres was about to make a journey. The Forty-niners were stampeding to the California goldfields. In 1851, Ayres followed them, to become one of the first physicians in San Francisco, California's first ichthyologist, and one of the founders of the California Academy of Sciences.

In Carlisle, Pennsylvania, a young zoologist was coming to notice, mostly from his completely rewritten zoological volume in the *Iconographic Encyclopedia*, a German work translated by him and published in 1850. Spencer Fullerton Baird of Carlisle was selected for the Assistant Secretaryship of the Smithsonian Institution, and he and Charles Girard, a French pupil of Agassiz in Neufchâtel, would dominate North American ichthyology in the 1850's. Finally, the great Louis Agassiz himself had accepted a professorship at Harvard University and in 1850 made his entrance into American ichthyology with his well-known volume, *Lake Superior.*

Thus, we leave American ichthyology at the mid-century. It was not only in America that ichthyology would see new leaders. The era of Cuvier, the great classifier of the animal kingdom, was over. The ichthyological work of Lesson, Quoy, Gaimard, Guichenot, Valenciennes, John Richardson, Johannes Müller, Johann Jacob Heckel, and Hermann Schlegel was essentially finished. Within ten years, the active figures in world ichthyology would form an almost completely new group—Bleeker, Peters, Poey, Günther, Gill, and Kner, soon to be joined by Day, Lütken, Cope, Steindachner, Vaillant, Goode, and Jordan, all of whom would contribute heavily to rapidly expanding knowledge of fishes.

As the year 1851 dawned, it is notable that in only three minor areas of the earth had the greater part of the fish fauna been discovered, named, and described. One comprised the coastal seas and fresh waters of western Europe, where ichthyology was born. Another was the coastal part of New England and New York, where the work had been done by Mitchill, LeSueur, De Kay, and Storer. The third, almost unbelievably, was the valley of the Ganges, in India, where a remarkable Scotsman, Francis Buchanan Hamilton, had done the job with the help of no one, by 1822. If the ichthyologists of the 18th century founded the science, those between 1800 and 1850 were chiefly the regional pioneers. In the latter half of the 19th century the fishes of the world were made known, leaving to the 20th century the mopping up of the remainder and the consolidation of ichthyological knowledge. There is still much mopping up and consolidation to be done.

Professor Emeritus of Biology, STANFORD UNIVERSITY, STANFORD, CALIFORNIA.

History of Ichthyology in the United States after 1850[1,2]

Carl L. Hubbs

IT is my pleasure to flash some highlights from the history of ichthyology in the United States after the middle of the nineteenth century. Dr. Myers has illuminated the history of this science through the first half of that century in the United States and Latin America, and Dr. Dymond has given us a scholarly picture of the complete history of ichthyology in Canada. I am dealing with all research on the fishes of the United States without regard to the nationality of the researchers, and with all research by the ichthyologists of the United States, without regard to the part of the world covered by their investigations.

The century with which I am dealing has been one of extensive accomplishments by a large band of devoted workers, from among whom I have time, regretfully, to select only a few of the more outstanding and more picturesque. The vast amount of research published since 1850 makes the period seem long, but from other viewpoints the span of years seems very short—at least to an old-timer like me. My own ichthyological career covers about 45 percent of the period; my life, 60 percent. My father was already a husky lad at the inception of the period, and at the time of his death had lived through more than half of the history of the United States.

It has been my privilege to have known more or less intimately a large proportion of the ichthyologists with whom I am dealing, and to have had an indirect contact with most of the others, through my association with men who knew them personally. I am therefore privileged, I hope, to personalize to some degree the account that I am giving.

[1] Contribution from the Scripps Institution of Oceanography, University of California, San Diego.
[2] In the preparation of this paper I have been greatly aided by my wife, Laura C. Hubbs, who, with the aid of many, has obtained numerous birth and death dates and other information. Leonard P. Schultz has very kindly supplied many of the photographs (those reproduced on pp. 45–49) from the fine collection of portraits of ichthyologists in the Fish Division of the United States National Museum (for which additions are solicited). Three figures of British Museum ichthyologists were furnished by that museum, through the kindness of a later curator, our Honorary Foreign Member Ethelwynn Trewavas; the figure of George Albert Boulenger is from a photograph donated by another Honorary Foreign Member, Gaston F. de Witte.

The history of ichthyology in the United States after 1850 divides itself naturally into even quarter centuries: 1850–1875, 1875–1900, 1900–1925, and 1925–1950. The fourth quarter of the nineteenth century calls for the most expansive treatment. The most recent quarter century, 1925–1950, is treated with disproportionate and increasing brevity, largely because the activities and publications of this period are already best known to present-day workers. The period since 1950—virtually current events—is scarcely mentioned.

Some ichthyological activity in the United States continued from the first half of the nineteenth century into the second half. Thus, in 1850, David Humphreys Storer (1804–1891) was in the middle of his 30-year career, and his son Horatio Robinson Storer (1830–1922) was about to start a decade of research in the same area, that of the fish fauna of eastern North America. In 1850 John Edwards Holbrook (1796–1871) was in the midst of his treatises on the fishes of South Carolina, in preparation for his monograph on the Ichthyology of South Carolina (1855 and 1860).

FIRST QUARTER CENTURY, 1850–1875

In its exponential growth, characteristic of science in general, ichthyology in the United States had scarcely attained its marked upward inflection by 1850. That spur to penetrating biological research—the theory of evolution—had not yet been advanced. The great naturalist Cuvier, aided in ichthyology by Valenciennes, had completed his labors, leaving treatises of such magnitude and authority as to crystallize and even to some extent to deter fresh ichthyological thinking. Johannes Müller (1801–1858) had nearly completed his epochal work on fish classification and on the elasmobranchs. The commanding career of Albert Günther (1830–1914)—the last person able to cover the entire fish fauna of the whole world—was not yet, though soon to be, launched. In America, the vast western reaches had hardly been explored, the fish fauna scarcely touched, save for the tantalizingly imperfect descriptions by Constantine Samuel Rafinesque (1784–1842),

From *Copeia* 1964(1):42–60. Reprinted by permission.

Charles Alexander LeSueur (1780–1840), Jared Potter Kirtland (1793–1877), and a few others, of the fishes of the Ohio River and the Great Lakes. Already completed also was the work of other early American ichthyologists, notable among whom were Samuel Latham Mitchill (1764–1831) and James Ellsworth De Kay (1799–1851), William Dandridge Peck (1763–1822), and Samuel Stehman Haldeman (1812–1880). Nearly completed was the work on North American fishes by John Richardson (1787–1865) and Zadock Thompson (1796–1856).

The first decade of the third quarter of the nineteenth century encompassed the initial systematic exploration of the western half of the United States and of the Pacific Coast of North America, during the Mexican Boundary and Pacific Railroad surveys (followed by the Explorations of the Territories). The fishes obtained on the Boundary and Railroad surveys were largely described—some species repeatedly named as new—by Charles Frederic Girard (1822–1895), who had come from France and had begun his studies of American fishes with Louis Agassiz. His first contributions (1850–1852) dealt with the freshwater Cottidae. His first papers on the fishes collected on the western surveys were published in coauthorship with Spencer Fullerton Baird (1823–1887), who played a commanding role in the development of ichthyology and fisheries biology in America from early in the 1850's until his death in 1887 (soon after he had retired as Commissioner of Fisheries to become Secretary of the Smithsonian Institution). Jordan in 1905 paid Baird this tribute: "A large part of the work on fishes published by the United States National Museum and the United States Fish Commission has been made possible through the direct help and inspiration of Professor Baird." In 1871, Baird had brought into its early and vigorous beginning the United States Fish Commission, the forerunner of the Bureau of Fisheries and the Fish and Wildlife Service. In the same year, George Brown Goode (1851–1896) started his ichthyological career. Exploration of the deep sea, including its fish fauna—a field later promoted effectively by Goode — was only incipient during the 1850–1875 quarter century.

A prodigious role in the development of ichthyology in the United States between 1850 and 1875 was played by the masterful Swiss scientist Louis Agassiz (1807–1873). After his initial and brilliant career in Europe, marked particularly by researches on fishes of Brazil, on fish anatomy and embryology, on fossil fishes, and on glacial history, the elder Agassiz at the midturn of the century brought his powerful influence to bear on American science, with emphasis on ichthyology. He had begun to publish on fishes in 1828 and continued his fish studies until his death in 1873. In America, he promptly rose to leadership, through his public lectures and writings and through the pioneer establishments that he founded. Notable for ichthyology was his founding of the Museum of Comparative Zoology at Harvard College (with the then new policy of preserving large and random collections of fishes and other animals). Notable also was his founding of the Penikese Marine Laboratory, the forerunner of the Marine Biological Laboratory and its satellites at Woods Hole (Agassiz, if alive, would rejoice in learning that the MBL is beginning to return to studies of marine life as such). In addition to his promotional — almost missionary—activities, Agassiz himself contributed notably to the study of the freshwater and marine fishes of eastern North America and brought to scientific attention that remarkable and almost exclusively western North American viviparous perciform fish family to which he gave the name Embiotocoidae or Holconoti. At the time of his death Agassiz left a multitude of fishes, particularly of eastern North American fresh waters, bearing manuscript names on the shelves of MCZ—a tribute to his perspicuity and energy, and to his failure to recognize the limitations of time in general and of his own life-span in particular! Agassiz's most notable contribution to ichthyology was the inspiration he gave to one of his young summer-school students, when he weaned David Starr Jordan from studies on microbes and marine algae into ichthyology. Many of us, from the second to the nth generation of ichthyologists, owe a special and personal debt of gratitude to Louis Agassiz!

Louis Agassiz's son, Alexander (1835–1910), took over as director of the MCZ and carried on his father's traditions in several respects. Aided by profits from the copper mines his father had found on the famous trip to Lake Superior at the middle of the century, Alexander carried out some of the pioneering deep-sea explorations in the western North Atlantic Ocean (and later in the eastern Pacific). He greatly extended his father's work on the Embiotocidae and on the embryology of fishes, and did pioneering work on the larval development of eastern North American species. Alexander Agassiz's own ichthyological work, like that of Frederick Ward Putnam (1839–1915), also of the MCZ, was largely in the third quarter of the last century, but extended into the fourth period.

Louis Agassiz and Charles Girard were immigrants from Europe who came into prominence in the New World because science was relatively incipient there. Much further study of American fishes was done in Europe. Most notable of such work, I suppose, is the Catalogue of the Fishes of the British Museum, published 1859–1870, by Albert Günther (1830–1914), the last treatise purporting to cover the fishes of the entire world. During the period under discussion Auguste Duméril (1812–1870) started to replace the Histoire Naturelle des Poissons of Cuvier and Valenciennes with a new work of similar title (1865–1870), starting with the primitive fishes that the preceding treatise failed to encompass, but he died when only the second volume appeared. The one attempt to replace Günther's Catalogue, by George Albert Boulenger (1858–1937), did not pass beyond the first volume, issued in 1895. Günther published many papers on the fishes of Central America, including a monograph (1866), but the Pisces section of Biologia Centrali-Americana was not published until 1906–1908, by C. Tate Regan (1878–1943). Franz Steindachner (1834–1919) was one of the most prolific European contributors to New World ichthyology, beginning with descriptions of Mexican fishes in 1863 and continuing into the twentieth century; his work was characterized by (and was largely limited to) precise descriptions and magnificently detailed illustrations. Other European authors, particularly prior to the activity of Jordan and his school, contributed to knowledge of American fishes. Léon Louis Vaillant (1834–1915), one of these, attempted to review the "Etheostomatidae" in 1873. The ichthyological labors of Felipe Poey y Aloy (1799–1891) in Cuba are particularly pertinent.

Another great ichthyologist whose career overlapped the third and fourth quarters of the nineteenth century was Edward Drinker Cope (1840–1897), for whom our journal is named. His career in ichthyology, which extended from 1862 to 1897, also widely overlapped that of David Starr Jordan, with whom he, as one of the few of the time who did not do so, never directly collaborated. Perhaps the two were incompatible; both were strong-minded, but quite contrasting in many respects: Cope's ways with drink and women, for example, must have been abhorred by the strait-laced Jordan. But both were most able and productive as descriptive naturalists. Jordan's appraisal of Cope in his Guide to the Study of Fishes (1905) is revealing: "In breadth of vision and keenness of insight, Cope ranked with the first of taxonomic writers. Always bold and original, he was not at all times accurate in details, and to the final result in classification his contribution has been less than that of Dr. Gill." However, Cope's extensive work on fishes—though not so generally known as his researches in paleontology and in herpetology—I came to regard as of high quality during my early revisionary studies of the freshwater fishes of eastern North America: I resurrected a number of Cope's well-described species from the synonymy into which Jordan and his associates had buried them.

Another outstanding American authority was Cope's associate Theodore Nicholas Gill (1837–1914), who began to contribute to ichthyology early in the third quarter of the nineteenth century and continued his labors in this field beyond that quarter century. In fact, his ichthyological contributions date from 1853 to 1912—three score years. Like Cope, Gill did not actively collaborate with Jordan, but Jordan held Gill in very high regard: he dedicated his general treatise, Guide to the Study of Fishes, to Gill, as "Ichthyologist, Philosopher, Critic. Master in Taxonomy," and in the body of the text wrote that he could not too strongly express his own "obligation to this great teacher, his master in fish taxonomy," and characterized Gill as "the keenest interpreter of taxonomic facts yet known in the history of ichthyology." Though giving almost no indication of mastery in taxonomy at the species level, Gill was indeed highly endowed in respect to classifying the families and orders of fishes, particularly on the basis of their osteology. Jordan's classification, and through his arrangement to a considerable extent the systems of Regan and of Berg, were based to a very large degree on Gill's sophisticated conclusions. Gill also published extensively on the fishes of many regions. He was particularly strong in analysis, and broke down into units, largely still recognized, many of the excessively broad genera of Cuvier and other previous workers. He was also a master at synthesizing the literature on the general natural history of particular fishes, and spent his venerable declining years largely in this worthwhile enterprise.

Other American ichthyologists contributed independently to knowledge of the fishes of the United States over the years on either side of 1875. These included James Wood Milner (1841–1879) and Philo Romayne Hoy (1816–1892), who made pioneering studies on fishes of the Great Lakes, and like many others of the period, were also fish-culturists. More productive during this period was the New Jersey naturalist Charles Conrad Abbott (1843–1919).

I had wondered why Jordan did not collaborate with certain great naturalists somewhat his senior until I reread the following passage in an obituary of Charles Henry Gilbert written by Jordan in 1928: "In Washington, at the Smithsonian Institution, Gilbert first met Baird, Goode, Gill, Cope, Coues, and others [what a galaxy!] with whom, in later times, both of us had many relations. Dr. Coues then gave me an important piece of advice to the effect that I should not associate myself with any older naturalist (Dr. Gill or Dr. Cope, for example) but should rather select my best student and write my papers with his co-operation and assistance. Accordingly the ichthyological firm of 'Jordan and Gilbert' was soon established."

Second Quarter Century, 1875–1900

The final quarter of the nineteenth century may be thought of as a golden age of descriptive ichthyology in the United States, unmatched previously and unequaled thereafter for many years. And the wonder now is that this great advance was consummated before any major research subsidies were available; long before NSF, NIH, AEC, ONR, or other alphabetical agencies were created; when research positions were few and far between; when some of the promi-

nent ichthyologists (including David Starr Jordan, Barton Warren Evermann, and Charles Henry Gilbert) and other scientists had to start their career teaching grade schools or high schools and had to draw from pitifully low salaries their expenses to attend meetings or to engage in field work. No one then dreamed of proffering his failure to receive a research grant—as many disgustingly do today—as an excuse for lassitude in scientific endeavor. Collectors traveled by train and hired horse and wagon to reach collecting stations, or even hiked; and in the West often still had to keep one eye open for hostile Indians. Our predecessors were dedicated and stalwart men!

This period (1875–1900) was outstandingly characterized, though by no means restricted to:

(1) A very intensive descriptive study of the fishes of North and Middle America, with chief emphasis on those of the United States; dominated throughout by David Starr Jordan; passing through series of group revisions and faunal studies; culminating in the publication, in 1896–1900, of the Fishes of North and Middle America.

(2) The exploration of the deep-sea fauna of the western Atlantic and eastern Pacific oceans, chiefly during the second half of the quarter century and largely by the original ALBATROSS, a converted yacht operated by the Navy for the United States Fish Commission (later the Bureau of Fisheries). These early deep-sea operations culminated in the publication, in 1895 and 1896, of Goode and Bean's Oceanic Ichthyology.

(3) The early development and rapid expansion (at times and in places an over-expansion, at least in relative terms) of fish culture and of research oriented thereto. These areas occupied the time and labors of a large proportion—in full-time or part-time work perhaps the majority—of both professional and amateur fish workers of the time. And this not too healthy condition persisted through the next quarter century (1900–1925). The limit of time prevents me from discussing this phase of applied ichthyology.

(4) Continued extensive emphasis on the anatomy, embryology, and phylogeny of fishes. These were then still regarded as respectable fields of biological research, when systematics and natural history were downgraded. (We are common bedfellows

now.) European scientists, including John Beard (1858–1924), Walter Edward Collinge (1867–1947), Edwin Ray Lankester (1847–1929), and William Kitchen Parker (1823–1890), were active in these areas, and did much research on freshwater North American fishes, especially the relict genera *Lepisosteus* and *Amia*, but a number of Americans also participated during this quarter century (some continuing into the first quarter of the twentieth century). Among the Americans were: Louis Agassiz (1807–1873), Edward Phelps Allis (1851–1947), Howard Ayers (1861–1933), Bashford Dean (1867–1928), Charles Judson Herrick (1868–1960), Grant Sherman Hopkins (18— -1952), John Sterling Kingsley (1854–1929), William Albert Locy (1857–1924), Charles Freeman Williams McClure (1865–1955), Charles Sedgwick Minot (1852–1914), Julia Barlow Platt (1857–19—), George Clinton Price (1860–1950), Jacob Ellsworth Reighard (1861–1942), John Adam Ryder (1852–1895), William Berryman Scott (1858–1947), Charles Otis Whitman (1843–1910), Burt Green Wilder (1841–1925), and Henry Van Peters Wilson (1863–1939).

Throughout the final quarter of the nineteenth century David Starr Jordan—a man of massive frame and even vaster intellect—was the dominant figure in American ichthyology. I might rightly say, *has been* the dominant figure, for his leadership continued throughout and even beyond the following quarter century (he was born in 1851, started publishing on fishes in 1874, and continued so doing almost until his death in 1931); since then his students, and his students' students, and *their* students, and on for several academic generations, have carried on. Relatively few of the more active ichthyologists of the present day are unable to trace their lineage back to Jordan, and through him to Agassiz. Recounting one's scientific genealogy I recommend as a wholesome diversion. Jordan if alive today would, I am sure, delight in contemplating his many descendants. Very close to the end of his long career, in 1929, he dedicated the thirteenth and last edition of the Manual of the Vertebrate Animals "To five of my early students, 'brought up on the Manual of the Vertebrates,' . . . and to five others, equally gifted, who lost their lives while engaged in field work." He was ever proud of his students and associates, and they were rightly proud of him, from the

first to the last (as I well know, having myself been the last of the long line).

Jordan's vast knowledge of fishes is legendary, and was very real, as I pointed out some years ago (MS) in a symposium, of the Society of Systematic Zoology, on famous naturalists. Charles Henry Gilbert told me, almost 50 years ago and only a decade after the date of publication, that Jordan, around his endless other duties, included the presidency of Stanford University, dictated from memory the great bulk of his two-volume masterpiece, Guide to the Study of Fishes (1905). May we forgive some of the minor inaccuracies!

This truly great man was not content to restrict his writings to his hundreds of faunal papers, group revisions, shorter papers, and literature reviews, in his never abandoned prime-interest field of ichthyology. He authored hundreds of other articles and books in the areas of education, public affairs, evolution, and many other topics (a bibliography of Jordan's writings compiled by Alice N. Hays as Volume I of Stanford University Publications, University Series, Library Studies, lists 1,372 general writings and 645 ichthyological items). Mindful of the general public and of students, in addition to his scientific colleagues, he found time to put out the 13 editions of the Manual of the Vertebrates (alluded to above), and, with associates, a variety of other general treatises, notably the Synopsis of the Fishes of North America (1883), the more monumental Fishes of North and Middle America (1896–1900), and several other general works, noted below under the discussion of the 1900–1925 period.

Obviously no man, even one free of the almost endless other duties that Jordan carried out—not even one endowed with Jordan's all but superhuman capacities—could have done alone, or even as the major contributor in time and effort, all that Jordan did. Coauthor Charles Henry Gilbert I am sure did most of the detailed work on the "Synopsis," and the tremendous Fishes of North and Middle America was based largely on published revisions of families by Jordan and his many associates, or by these associates alone or in conjunction with still others; it was only through the help of this loyal and willing band that the description and analysis of the vast North American fish fauna was brought into a reasonable degree of order and completeness by 1900.

It now appears that Jordan, through the final quarter of the nineteenth century, may have continually planned his own work, and that of his associates, in preparation for the great monograph, through the initial, brief, and geographically limited Manual of the Vertebrates and the considerably expanded "Synopsis." Many families that had remained in 1883 without recent, or any, review were farmed out by Jordan to his associates, who prepared the accounts and thus became the anonymous authors of sections of the final monograph. Thus, as I heard long ago, Edwin Chapin Starks wrote at least most of the material on the mail-cheeked fishes, or Craniomi (other than *Sebastodes*, which was treated by Frank Cramer). Wilbur Wilson Thoburn (1859–1899) revised the Cottidae before he met his untimely death. Coauthor Barton Warren Evermann (1853–1932) must have done much of the coordination.

For those who may have entertained the idea that Jordan's reputation rests on his having taken unfair advantage of the labors of his associates, let me recall what I learned, through contacts with some of the men involved, about 50 years ago. It is true that Jordan's personal work on specimens (after his pioneering studies on eastern American freshwater fishes) was much less extensive than that of his coauthors, because of limited time and because of an allergy to preservatives, but he did polish the manuscripts and prepared many of the analytical comparisons; and, years later, he remembered much more of the contents of the joint papers than his hard-working colleagues did!

Jordan's students and his primary and secondary associates in ichthyology were indeed legion. Time will allow special comment on only a few of the more notable.

Most prolifically associated with Jordan in his early studies, chiefly on the freshwater and marine fishes of North America, beginning in 1877, was Charles Henry Gilbert (1859–1928), a man more meticulous, precise, and critical than his master. Jordan's strength lay more in comprehensive knowledge, truly marvelous memory, deep intuition, drive for rapid and major accomplishment, and commanding personality. The two men during their early association, at Butler University and Indiana University, made an effective team, complementing one another. Together, President Jordan and

Professor Gilbert laid much of the groundwork for the later Fishes of North and Middle America, culminating most of their joint efforts in the then monumental Synopsis of the Fishes of North America (1883). Not long after the "Synopsis" was published, Gilbert, on account of their fundamental differences in scientific approach, broke away from coauthorship with Jordan, and relented on only a few occasions. Despite this rupture in coauthorship relation, Gilbert, along with most of his contemporaries, held the master in respect and adulation so high as to approach hero worship. Jordan reciprocated a continuing feeling of high regard as is indicated both by the circumstance that he brought Gilbert to the new-born Stanford University to head the Zoology Department and by his appraisal of Gilbert in obituary notices. In 1928 Jordan wrote of Gilbert: "He was one of the most careful and accurate of scientific observers, the keenest and ablest critic in natural history I have ever known, and therefore a most helpful teacher." Jordan ended an obituary of Gilbert with this appreciation: *"A friend is one who knows all your faults and weaknesses, yet loves you just the same."* It was my great and rare good fortune to have had Gilbert as my major professor, and yet to have been chosen by Jordan as his last ichthyological associate.

Working alone, or with his own students, Gilbert, before and after the turn of the century, turned his critical eye chiefly to the demersal and pelagic fishes of the deep sea (particularly of the Pacific Ocean). He contributed also to the systematics and distribution of freshwater fishes of the Pacific drainage of North America, and in so doing laid the foundation for the later classical studies in this area by his staff member John Otterbein Snyder (1867–1943). In 1915, Gilbert published an important paper on deep-sea fishes collected by the ALBA-TROSS in California in 1904, but after 1911 he turned his attention chiefly to researches on the life history of the Pacific salmons, in which topic he was the very effective pioneer.

Better known to current workers as a major associate of Jordan was a scientist quite different from Gilbert, as both were quite different from their master. I speak of Barton Warren Evermann, who lived from 1853 to 1932—a life-span contemporaneous with that of Jordan—and published on ichthyology from 1886 almost until his death. Evermann joined Jordan's team quite early, but came into prominence as Gilbert was breaking away from his previously almost continuous collaboration with Jordan. Evermann, less meticulous and less critical than Gilbert, and withal less able as a systematist, retained coauthorship relation with Jordan to the end. Evermann's strength, contrasting with that of Gilbert, lay in a rather thorough compilation of synonymies and of the history of investigations, rather than in the critical study of specimens. It was these features of strength, along with Evermann's ability and opportunities in the logistics of preparing and publishing ichthyological treatises, that, combined with Jordan's vast insight, memory, and drive, led to the very effective collaboration of these two men, especially in the production of the Fishes of North and Middle America (1896–1900) and the two associated "Check Lists" (1896 and 1930). In addition to his collaboration with Jordan, Evermann, either alone or in conjunction with others, usually junior authors, published extensively, during the quarter centuries on either side of 1900, on North American and other freshwater and marine fishes. Through his many years of service in key positions with the United States Fish Commission and the California Academy of Sciences, Evermann was further effective in promoting ichthyological exploration and research. Like some other administrators he was a man of rather stern ways, and was proud too, as was illustrated by his adding an extra *n* to his name, to make it look more Germanic — as German science was then still generally emulated—whereas Garman dropped the final *n* from his originally German family name!

Carl H. Eigenmann (1863–1927) was another noteworthy American scientist, whom Jordan trained and inspired into a very active ichthyological career, and whose contributions to ichthyology spanned the half century centered at 1900. He collaborated with Jordan in a number of early regional studies and group revisions, and when Jordan left to assume the presidency of Stanford University in 1891, Eigenmann was appointed by Jordan as professor of zoology at Indiana University (in 1908 he became the first dean of the graduate school). From 1909 to 1918 he served also as Curator of Fishes in the Carnegie Museum. Toward the end of the nineteenth century, Eigenmann entered vigorously into a number of independent researches, most of which he continued with Teutonic diligence and attention to detail into or through the first part of the twentieth century. The topics included: the freshwater fish fauna of Indiana; the fish fauna of the Pacific coast; meristic variation in fishes; the embryology and larval development of fishes, and adaptations to viviparity; the structure, development, and systematics of blind cave fishes; and, the subject of most of his later work and his chief call to fame, the freshwater fish faunas of South America. Through persevering contacts he was successful in raising private funds for his expeditions and for the sumptuous publication of numerous faunal studies, as well as revisions of the catfishes and characins of South America.

Like many of the naturalists of his age, Eigenmann was a distinctive character (not many other types sacrificed themselves in those days for a life in science); he always retained, and I suspected that he cultivated, his German accent and certain other personal peculiarities (he was born in Germany and came to America at the age of 17). Eigenmann was notably successful in training and inspiring students, especially in ichthyology. In an obituary notice, his successor at Indiana University, the cold and critical Fernandus Payne, admitting that he had not worked in the same field, ventured the opinion that Eigenmann's researches "place him in the first rank of ichthyologists of all time." On Eigenmann's death, Jordan appraised him as "one of the most eminent workers in the field of systematic zoology and one of the ablest of natural history teachers, withal the most tireless of explorers."

Seth Eugene Meek (1859–1914) was another of Jordan's apostles, who, like Eigenmann, collaborated in various early group revisions and regional papers. Thereafter, during the 1880's and 1890's and to some extent later, when he focused his attention on the freshwater fishes of Middle America, Meek published independently and extensively on the freshwater fishes of the central United States.

Time does not permit recounting the ichthyological deeds of the many others who during the "golden age" of 1875–1900 collaborated with Jordan and with Evermann and other leading members of Jordan's team, mostly as students. I will merely list a series of names of these collaborators, and mention that their papers are listed in Dean's great Bibliography of Fishes (1916–1923): Willis Stanley Blatchley (1859–1940), Charles Harvey Bollman (1868–1889), Alembert Winthrop Brayton (1848–1926), Herbert Edson Copeland (1849–1877), Bradley Moore Davis (1871–1957), Charles L. Edwards (1863–1937), Bert Fesler (1866–1947), Morton W. Fordice, David Kopp Goss (*ca.* 1866–1904), James Alexander Gunn, Horace Addison Hoffman (1855–1950), Elizabeth G. Hughes, Oliver Peebles Jenkins (1850–1934), Philip H. Kirsch (1860–1900), Richard Crittenden McGregor (1871–1936), Charles Leslie McKay (1854–1883), Joseph Swain (1857–1927), Wilbur Wilson Thoburn (1859–1899), and Albert Jefferson Woolman (18— –1918).

Among the other ichthyologists who played a major role in pure and applied ichthyology in the United States during the eventful fouth quarter of the nineteenth century George Brown Goode (1851–1896) stands out boldly. His publications on fishes extended from 1871 until the year of his untimely death (1896). His ichthyological career thus widely overlapped that of Jordan, but the two did not publish together. However, they did cooperate effectively. Thus it was in connection with Goode's encyclopedic treatise on American fisheries that Jordan, with Gilbert, conducted the basic survey of the fishes of the Pacific Coast, in 1880. Later, Goode facilitated the publication of Jordan and Evermann's *magnum opus*. Goode's own career in ichthyology, furthermore, very nicely complemented that of Jordan, for his chief contributions were in the pioneer development of fisheries biology, in the intensive study of the biology of certain commercially important fishes (notably the menhaden, carangids, and scombroids), and in research on deep-sea fishes—in none of which topics was Jordan particularly active. The notable compilation by Goode and his associate Tarleton H. Bean on deep-sea fishes (Oceanic Ichthyology, 1895 and 1896) laid a basis for the rational inclusion of deep-sea fishes in the Fishes of North and Middle America. Goode was the protégé and disciple of Baird, whom he greatly aided in the establishment and in the vast initial activity of the United States Fish Commission. When Baird retired as Commissioner of

Fisheries to become, for a short time before his death, Secretary of the Smithsonian Institution, he took Goode along as Assistant Secretary, in charge of the United States National Museum. Goode, while continuing in this position under Secretary Langley, exercised a profound influence on the progress of ichthyology. He himself was an able scholar, as well as an effective administrator and promoter of pure and applied science.

In his own right, Tarleton H. Bean (1846–1916) was a major figure in the ichthyology of the United States during the fourth quarter of the nineteenth century. His ichthyological publications, which started in 1878 and continued into the twentieth century, thus fell within the career of Jordan, with whom Bean, like Goode, did not collaborate (in those days living on the two sides of the continent was like living in two worlds). One of Bean's earlier contributions was a book on the fishes of Pennsylvania (1893), which he supplemented during the first five years of the twentieth century by general accounts of the fishes of Long Island and of New York state as a whole. His ichthyological contributions dealt with deep-sea fishes of the Atlantic and other oceans (culminating in Goode and Bean's Oceanic Ichthyology), and with shore and freshwater fishes of various parts of eastern North America, Alaska, and elsewhere. Tarleton H. Bean's brother Barton A. Bean (1860–1947), who followed him as Curator of Fishes in the National Museum, led (let us be generous) a less productive and less illustrious scientific life (during slightly more than the last decade of the nineteenth century and the first two decades of the twentieth).

We can hardly escape mention of Samuel Garman (1843–1927), who came out of an obscure past in the Wild West to take over the ichthyological position at the Museum of Comparative Zoology at Harvard during the last quarter of the nineteenth century and the first half of the following quarter century. Louis Agassiz picked him up at San Francisco on the Hassler Expedition, and trained him in ichthyology (Garman and Jordan were fellow students under Agassiz at Penikese). In addition to publishing a considerable number of minor papers, he monographed the "Discoboli" (Cyclopteridae and Liparididae) in 1892, and the Cyprinodontes in 1895. From 1875 to 1908 he published numerous papers on elasmobranchs, but did not put forth his monographs thereon until 1911 ("The Chismopnea (chimaeroids)") and 1913 ("The Plagiostomi (sharks and rays)"). In 1899 appeared his sumptuously illustrated treatise on the deep-sea fishes collected by the ALBATROSS during an expedition led by Alexander Agassiz in the eastern tropical Pacific Ocean in 1891. Garman's work was characterized by much attention to anatomical detail ("Johannes Müller was his guiding genius"), but by rather mediocre systematic acuity. Garman was never a member of the Jordan school, nor was he indeed admired by Jordan, who once remarked to me, in characteristic aphorism, but in deprecation rare to his noble soul, "Garman dried up at forty." Garman indeed was an eccentric recluse; during his later years he took to locking himself into his ill-lit quarters at MCZ.

The 1875–1900 quarter century was notable among other ichthyological accomplishments for the elaboration of knowledge about the fish fauna of the Pacific Coast of the United States. Except for certain local and incidental studies, by Louis and Alexander Agassiz, Gill, William O. Ayres (1817–1891), James Graham Cooper (1830–1902), William P. Gibbons (1812–1897), and a few lesser lights, very little had been done there ichthyologically since the Pacific Railroad Survey of the 1850's until Jordan and Gilbert carried on their survey of 1880, in connection with George Brown Goode's exploration of the fisheries of the country (conducted jointly by the United States Fish Commission and the Census Bureau). They collected from British Columbia to San Diego, chiefly in the fish markets, which then, especially in California, contained a wide variety of inshore fishes. They took their samples to their hotel room to preserve, and rushed off quick descriptions of the many new species for prompt publication in a long series of short papers in the Proceedings of the United States National Museum for 1880 and 1881 (it would seem desirable for some of us to compromise between such dashing procedure and the long delays that we now often allow!). They also briefly annotated lists of their collections and tabulated the indicated geographical distributions. On a trip to Mazatlán and on two trips to Panamá, in 1881 and 1882, Gilbert made large fish collections that were

destroyed by fire before a monograph on The Fishes of the Pacific Coast of Tropical America could be written. "And practically every summer from 1882 to 1888 was devoted by one or both of us to explorations of the rivers of the United States" (Jordan 1928). William Neal Lockington (1842?–1902), at San Francisco, and Carl H. Eigenmann and Rosa Smith (1859–1947), later Mrs. Eigenmann, at San Diego, were working on the coast at that time, and Tarleton H. Bean, at the Smithsonian Institution, dealt with collections from the Northwest and Alaska.

The exploration of the deep-sea fauna of the eastern Pacific Ocean was inaugurated auspiciously by the ALBATROSS, which came around South America in 1887–1888 (incidentally, many of the collections obtained en route remain unworked; Will F. Thompson (1888–) treated those from Patagonia and Chile, in 1916, and in 1916–1917, I worked up at Stanford the more tropical series, but the manuscript has remained unpublished: a record I sincerely hope none of my younger colleagues will ever attempt to match!) Gilbert described in his careful way a very large proportion of the many novelties collected in the eastern Pacific Ocean from the tropical waters northward, but no one has ever reported on the entire collection.

The careers of a considerable number of productive American ichthyologists, barely or not at all mentioned elsewhere in this report, overlapped the 1900 boundary between two quarter centuries. Regretfully, I hardly more than list, alphabetically, a selection of them here: James Francis Abbott (1876–1926), fishes of Perú, Chile, and China; Theodore Dru Alison Cockerell (1866–1948), known for his rather uncritical work on the scales of fishes and on fishes of the Rocky Mountain region; Ulysses O. Cox, eastern North American freshwater fishes, including those of caves; Bashford Dean, anatomy, embryology, and phylogeny of primitive fishes, and (with special thanks from me in my present task the great Bibliography of Fishes); Charles Rochester Eastman (1868–1918), fossil fishes; Stephen Alfred Forbes (1844–1930), fishes of Illinois, especially their ecology; Simon Henry Gage (1851–1944), biology and systematics of lampreys; Oliver Perry Hay (1846–1930), eastern North American freshwater fishes and fossil fishes; James

Alexander Henshall (1836–1925), natural history of game fishes and freshwater fish faunas of eastern North America; Charles Frederick Holder (1851–1915), natural history of fishes, especially game fishes; Louis Hussakoff (1881–   ), fossil fishes; William Converse Kendall (1861–1939), various American and Pacific island fishes; Cloudsley M. Rutter (18—–1903), fishes of western North America, Alaska, China, etc.; Alvin Seale (1873–1958), fishes of eastern Asia and Pacific islands; Hugh McCormick Smith (1865–1941), fishes of eastern United States, eastern Asia, etc.; Edwin Chapin Starks (1867–1932), fishes of eastern Asia and western North America, and fish osteology.

Third Quarter Century, 1900–1925 (and Later)

The first quarter of the twentieth century contrasted sharply with the previous quarter century in the history of ichthyology in America. The publication of the Fishes of North and Middle America in 1896–1900 had brought to fruition the major efforts of American ichthyologists during the very active previous period. With this great work accomplished, Jordan and his colleagues turned to other fields. He now somehow found time to write his general treatise, A Guide to the Study of Fishes, which appeared in two volumes in 1905—later to be reissued as the single-volume Fishes. Jordan and Evermann could now produce their popular treatise on American Food and Game Fishes, which first appeared in 1902. Later in the quarter century, after his retirement and at an age when most men have slowed down to a halting walk, Jordan compiled two tremendously useful works, recently reprinted by Stanford University, The Genera of Fishes (1917–1920) and The Classification of Fishes (1923). Jordan's capacity to produce throughout his long life such general, largely compiled works, along with his many detailed ichthyological studies and multifarious other duties, is truly amazing.

In a way, "Jordan and Evermann" served as a stimulus for local faunal papers, in many of which the synonymies and species descriptions instead of being critically reviewed were lifted more or less bodily from the four-volume treatises—a ready way of adding pagination to one's bibliography. One such treatise was that of Evermann and Marsh on the Fishes of Porto Rico (1902).

The seeming completeness and the magnitude of "Jordan and Evermann" no doubt hampered progress, in respect to both faunal contributions and group reviews. For many years it was found to be so complete and so useful that some authors paid little attention to the literature that had intervened since 1900. Jordan himself was so impressed with the finality of the *magnum opus* as to advise his colleagues, as I was told half a century ago, to undertake the study of fishes of other lands, since the task for North American fishes had now been completed! Little did he realize how incomplete the systematics of North American fishes remained then; even now, we may add, five decades later!

Pursuing this delusion, Jordan, with John Otterbein Snyder as able assistant, set out for Japan in 1900 to collect material for a revision of the rich and varied fish fauna of that country. Characteristically, following his genius in producing compilations, he, with Snyder and Shigeho Tanaka (then the leading Japanese ichthyologist), put together, largely from the literature, and had published in Japan, in 1913, a list of the fishes known from the island empire. After returning to Stanford, Jordan and Snyder inaugurated a long series of revisions of Japanese fishes, group by group (published in the Proceedings of the United States National Museum). To the mental pain of Snyder, the ever-impetuous Jordan, overlooking the arrangement he had made with Snyder for them to complete the whole project, soon brought a young ichthyologist from the Philadelphia Academy, Henry Weed Fowler (1878–   ), to Stanford to collaborate on various groups, and added another Stanford man, Edwin Chapin Starks, to the team. Most of the groups were covered from 1901 to 1907; a few were completed later, by Jordan with Will F. Thompson and others. In 1906, the United States Bureau of Fisheries research ship Albatross, on a project promoted with President Theodore Roosevelt by Jordan, proceeded to Japan by way of Bering Sea, with a group of scientists under Gilbert as chief naturalist, primarily to explore the inshore and deep-sea fauna of Japan. I cut my teeth as a student at Stanford on the flatfishes of this expedition and, with Gilbert, studied the macrourids. Many groups remain untouched. Jordan returned to Japan in 1911 and in 1922, each time amassing, with the aid of hero-worshipping Japanese zoologists, further large collections, which Jordan promptly described in collaboration with Thompson and me, respectively.

Jordan had the ALBATROSS assigned to an ichthyological and fisheries survey of the Hawaiian Islands in 1901 and 1902 and in 1905 published with Evermann a definitive monograph on the shore fishes of the Archipelago, while Gilbert and Frank Cramer (1861–1948) treated the deep-sea fishes, and Oliver Peebles Jenkins (1850–1934), Snyder, Fowler, and others added papers on the shore fishes. Collections that came to America from various Asiatic countries, including Korea, China, Formosa, and the Philippines, were described by Jordan, Evermann, Alvin Seale (1871–1958), Albert W. C. T. Herre (1868–1962), and others, in various coauthorships. Jordan and Seale's monograph on the Fishes of Samoa (1906) was one of the more elegant of the published reports, though not ranking very high in taxonomic acumen.

After the Japanese cruise, the ALBATROSS proceeded to the Philippines, to conduct an extraordinarily long and intensive survey of the littoral and deep-sea waters. Hugh McCormick Smith (1865–1941) and Lewis Radcliffe (1880–1950) promptly proceeded to skim the cream off the fish collections, describing a host of new genera and species. That they failed notably even to discover all the new species became evident when Gilbert and I monographed the macrourids. Later, Fowler was employed by the Smithsonian as a consultant to describe the enormous fish collections as a whole, but most of his labors resulted only in filling cabinets full of unpublished manuscripts. What a wealth of material rests on Smithsonian shelves awaiting critical study!

The 1900–1925 quarter century encompassed also a major attack by ichthyologists of the United States on the freshwater fishes of Latin America. Eigenmann continued and energetically expanded the researches into the whole Latin American area that he had begun more than a decade previously, and earned top ranking. Jordan and Snyder, Tarleton H. and Barton A. Bean, Albert J. Woolman, and others contributed much of what we know regarding the fishes of México, but Seth Eugene Meek became the leading authority in that regard. Later, Meek continued his explorations through Central America, culminating his work with

the monographs on the fishes of Panamá, which were completed after Meek's death by his coauthor, Samuel F. Hildebrand (1883–1949).

During the first two decades of the twentieth century, critical work on the freshwater fishes of the country was largely confined to the basin-by-basin surveys of the western states, largely conducted by Snyder, though Eigenmann, Evermann, Meek, Cloudsley M. Rutter, Norman B. Scofield (1869–1958), and others contributed. Snyder's work was detailed and critical, though his conclusions were vitiated by his overemphasis on purely geographic (basin) rather than ecological speciation. He, and the other authors mentioned, completed studies of the fishes of many of the stream systems, but Snyder's field survey of the Bonneville Basin of 1915 (in which I assisted) resulted in little that was published, save for the description of the whitefishes that we discovered in Bear Lake.

In the area of eastern United States fresh waters, an ichthyological lull followed the completion of Jordan and Evermann's masterpiece in 1900. The chief exception was in Illinois, where the State Natural History Survey under Stephen Alfred Forbes carried on a major state fish survey, with strongest emphasis on ecological relations. This survey, which stemmed from earlier faunal studies in the state by Edward William Nelson (1855–1934) and by Jordan, culminated in the sumptuous monograph on The Fishes of Illinois by Forbes and Robert Earl Richardson (1877–1935). Some original work was done on freshwater fishes of some other eastern states, for example, in Michigan under Jacob Ellsworth Reighard (1861–1942), who studied the breeding behavior and development of fishes, in part in relation to fish culture.

Several other books on the fishes of individual states or regions — none matching The Fishes of Illinois in elegance of illustrations, bulk of information, or originality— were published during the early years of the twentieth century. Notable among these were The Fishes of North Carolina (1907) by Hugh M. Smith; Tarleton H. Bean's treatises on the fishes of New York (1901–1905), following one on Pennsylvania (1893); The Fishes of the Rocky Mountain Region (1908) by Theodore Dru Alison Cockerell; and others.

The first quarter of the twentieth century barely reached the upward swing on the exponential curve of ichthyological activity in America. When I came to the University of Michigan in 1920, after three rather frustrating years at the old Field Museum of Natural History in Chicago, I had as ichthyological associates only Jacob Reighard, rather spent, and one graduate assistant, Walter Koelz (1895–). This student, and, coming soon afterward John Van Oosten (1891–), were then the only subsidized investigators of Great Lakes fishes and fisheries. In contrast, a few months ago, during the social hour of a meeting of the Great Lakes Fish Commission in the same town of Ann Arbor, I encountered a large room overflowing with fishery biologists of the commission, of the dominion, provincial, federal, and state agencies, and of various universities.

Prior to 1920, Michigan had supported a modicum of ichthyological work (under Reighard), and gradually called on the University for more technical help in fishery affairs, in which I participated with a few students. In 1923, there was a call for the first state "fisheries expert," for which position I brought on Jan Metzelaar (1891–1929) from Holland. He and a few assistants, with help from us at the University (where he worked with us), carried on effectively until his tragic death by drowning in 1929. Soon thereafter, in 1930, I organized in the University, for the State Department of Conservation, as a pioneer enterprise, the Institute for Fisheries Research. With a few student assistants, on a budget fluctuating from about $5,000 to $30,000 per annum (in considerable part supplied by a private donor, Harry Harper), I carried on, and initiated in a humble way many of the future activities of such agencies. Behold now, a contrast, the relatively vast magnitude attained by this Institute since 1935, under the successive directorships of Albert S. Hazzard (1901–) and Gerald P. Cooper (1910–), not to mention the booming research organization of many other state fishery agencies.

Returning to the quarter century of 1900–1925, and looking over to the field of marine fisheries biology, may I recall that the California State Fisheries Laboratory was not established until 1917, when it was first occupied by only one scientist, the pioneering fishery biologist Will F. Thompson,

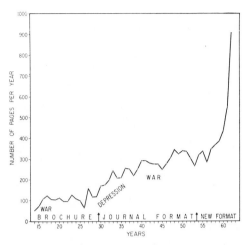

Fig. 1. Half century of growth of American ichthyology, as reflected in the annual pagination of this journal, COPEIA. Note slow growth for many years, changes in format (each markedly increasing volume of text per page), effects of wars, riding out of the great depression, and the very recent spectacular expansion.

aided during the first few years by a secretary and a few young assistants—including Elmer Higgins (1892–), Oscar Elton Sette (1900–), and others of later independent fame. Contrast this meager start, within the memory of some of us, with the small army of fishery biologists now busy at work in this expanded laboratory and in other state and federal laboratories and in universities and colleges up and down the Coast!

The torrential growth of ichthyology in the United States during the last half century is further exemplified—along with that of herpetology—by the growth of our Society. As M. Graham Netting has reminded you, the Society was founded in 1916. At the first meeting I attended, at Philadelphia in 1921, the total registration, as I recall, was 11. If you seek the present-day contrast, look about you!

The half century of growth of ichthyology in America is reflected in the ascending curve (Fig. 1) of annual pagination of COPEIA, which John Treadwell Nichols (1883–1958) started as a 4-page monthly brochure just 50 years ago; at first privately published by the founder; soon taken over by the Society, and transformed into a quarterly during the six-year editorial term of Emmett Reid Dunn; finally transformed into journal form in 1930 and enlarged by Helen Thompson Gaige and me and subsequently by other editors. The growth curve of pagination shows marked fluctuations and leveling off at times of war (though the great depression starting in 1929 was ridden out), but shows in general an accelerating rate of increase. The growth has been greater than is indicated by the graph, because at each major change in format much more material per page has been published. The spectacular increase during the last few years presumably reflects increasing interest in and support for science—and the increasing membership dues.

With this measure of growth, mindful of the limits on time and space, I close this history of ichthyology in the United States after 1850. To do so seems appropriate for a number of reasons. One reason (or should I say excuse) is that to continue would infringe on the domain of current events. Another reason is that to do so would call for a treatment of at least as many persons as I have already mentioned, or for an arbitrary and likely unjust omission of many who have contributed notably to ichthyology in America over the past quarter century or two. Still another reason is that I would prefer not to be so frank in evaluating my living colleagues, or their close associates, as I have been in picturing those who have passed on many years ago. And I have already used the personal pronoun too promiscuously. May someone complete the project!

SCRIPPS INSTITUTION OF OCEANOGRAPHY (UNIVERSITY OF CALIFORNIA, SAN DIEGO), LA JOLLA, CALIFORNIA.

Additional Readings
CHAPTER 1

NORRIS, K. S. 1974. To Carl Leavitt Hubbs, a modern pioneer naturalist on the occasion of his eightieth year. *Copeia* 3:581–610.

2

How Many Fishes Are
There, What Kind, and
Where Do They Live?

PROCEEDINGS

OF THE

CALIFORNIA ACADEMY OF SCIENCES

FOURTH SERIES

Festschrift for George Sprague Myers

Vol. XXXVIII, No. 17, pp. 341–346; 1 fig.   December 31, 1970

HOW MANY RECENT FISHES ARE THERE?

By

Daniel M. Cohen
Bureau of Commerical Fisheries
Washington, D. C.

It is a pleasure to dedicate this paper to Professor George S. Myers on the occasion of his 65th birthday. His interests in ichthyology have ranged widely and the topic of this paper seems especially appropriate, not least because he has been interested in this particular problem himself.

Estimates of the number of species of Recent fishes in the current ichthyological literature range from a low of 15,000–17,000 to a high of 40,000. Presented below is a brief list of some.

SOME PAST ESTIMATES OF NUMBER OF RECENT FISH SPECIES

Bailey (1960) gave 15,000 to 17,000, of which about 45 are Agnatha and about 575 are Chondrichthys. His estimate was apparently based on a group approach.

Marshall (1965) mentioned that, "We know more than twenty thousand living kinds, but our inventory is by no means complete." He gave no basis for his estimate.

Norman (1963) gave 25,000, with no mention of how the figure was reached.

Myers (1958) stated there are, ". . . .33,000 or more living species of teleosts." No mention of method of estimation was given.

Schultz and Stern (1948) gave a figure of 40,000; however, Schultz (1965) later lowered his estimate to 32,000. No basis was given for either figure.

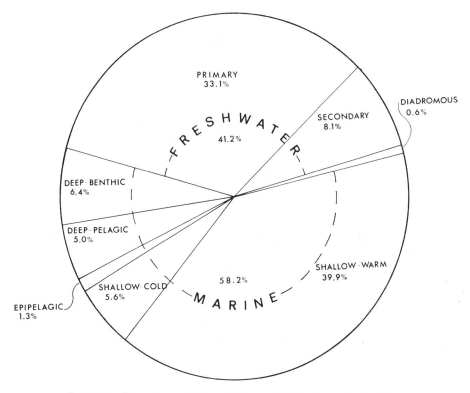

FIGURE 1. Percentages of Recent fish species living in various habitats.

MY ESTIMATE OF NUMBER OF RECENT FISH SPECIES

The wide range of figures suggests that a rational estimate, as opposed to an educated guess, is difficult for any one ichthyologist. With this in mind I compiled a list of fish families and began to solicit estimates from specialists and to consult recent revisions. Seven years have gone by since the initiation of the project, and this seems an appropriate time and place to present the results of my canvas. For the several groups for which neither colleagues nor recent revisions could supply information, I was obliged to consult several large faunal works and interpret the results in what I hope was a judicious manner.

Estimates are intended to be of the number of living species rather than described ones. Although approximately 75 to 100 species of Recent bony fishes are described each year (Zoological Record), we lack comparable information on how many species are placed in synonymy annually.

The final results of the present survey are: Agnatha about 50; Chondrichthyes 515 to 555; Osteichthyes 19,135 to 20,980. The figures given for bony fishes are two minimums rather than a maximum and a minimum. Most specialists who volunteered a single figure gave it as a minimum. Many colleagues, however, gave a range. The first figure, 19,135, is the sum of single estimates and the lower figures of ranges; therefore, it represents a bare minimum. The second figure is the sum of single estimates and the upper figures of ranges; therefore, it is a combination of minimum and maximum estimates.

I have attempted an ecological analysis of the data for Osteichthyes. The figures used for calculating percentages are averages of high and low estimates.

(1) Primary freshwater (Myers, 1949) 6650. *33.1 percent.* Approximately 6200 of this group belong to the Ostariophysi.

(2) Secondary freshwater (Myers, 1949) 1625. *8.1 percent.* Most of the species in this group belong to the families Cichlidae, Cyprinodontidae, and Poeciliidae.

Total freshwater 8,275. *41.2 percent.* If this astonishingly high percentage is valid it must be a reflection of the degree of isolation possible in the freshwater environment.

(3) Diadromous (including Complementary of Myers, 1949) 115. *0.6 percent.* As the systematics and life histories of tropical shore fishes become better known it seems likely that at least some species will be shifted from category 4 to this group.

(4) Marine shore and continental shelf to depths of approximately 200 meters—warm water 8000. *39.9 percent.* Perciform fishes and their derivatives are the major component of this category. Particularly important are percoid, blennioid, and gobioid fishes. Among nonperciforms, eels probably contribute the most species.

(5) Marine shore and continental shelf to depths of approximately 200 meters—cold water 1130. *5.6 percent.* A factor that may contribute to the substantially smaller size of this fauna as compared with that of group 4 is the smaller area occupied. Also, much of the region has had long-term, unstable climatic conditions so that many of the species must be fairly recent in their present habitats. There is no doubt, however, that a high degree of endemism prevails. Important components of this group are Gadidae, Zoarcidae, northern blennioids, and scorpaeniform fishes.

Total marine shore and continental shelf to 200 meters 9,130 *45.5 percent.*

(6) Continental slope and deep sea benthic below 200 meters 1280. *6.4 percent.* Important components of this group are Macruridae, and species of Brotulidae, Zoarcidae, Apodes, and Scorpaeniformes. Contrary to the opinion of Greenwood *et al.* (1966), I do not believe that this group or group 8 contains a great number of unknown species. Fishes of these groups occupy a vast amount of space; however, conditions are relatively so stable and uniform that niches are correspondingly few.

(7) Epipelagic (high seas) above 200 meters 255. *1.3 percent.* Important groups in this category are Scombroidei and Synentognathi. These fishes are mostly mobile, living in an environment that offers few niches. The small number of species is scarcely remarkable.

(8) Deep pelagic below 200 meters (including mesopelagic and bathypelagic) 1010. *5.0 percent.* Clupeiform and myctophiform fishes are the chief constituents of this category. Probably more space is occupied by this group than by any other, yet the number of species is small. The environment is poor in niches and in energy; it is surprising that the fauna is not smaller.

SOME CONCLUSIONS

The number of species in any one of the 8 categories seems to be chiefly related to the degree of isolation possible. Certainly tropical reefs, great river deltas, and major river drainages have contributed a great variety of habitats and ecological niches which are reflected in the high percentage of species found in freshwater and along tropical shores.

The most important regions economically (though not necessarily in terms of biological productivity) are the cooler water shelf areas and the epipelagic, both regions with relatively few species.

A final conclusion concerns the freshwater fishes. In view of the high percentage of fishes found in freshwater and man's increasing modification of this environment throughout the world, it is vital that research be drastically increased on the basic systematics of freshwater fishes while this is still possible.

ACKNOWLEDGMENTS

It is a pleasure indeed to acknowledge the cooperation that I have received from my colleagues. Whatever value this paper may have is due to their contributions. I thank R. Bailey, P. Bănărescu, R. Behnke, F. Berry, J. Böhlke, R. Bolin, M. Bradbury, J. Briggs, W. Burgess, D. Caldwell, B. Collette, E. Crossman, W. Davis, H. DeWitt, W. Eschmeyer, J. Garrick, R. Gibbs, W. Gosline, D. Greenfield, P. H. Greenwood, M. Grey, R. Haedrich, E. Herald, L. Knapp, E. Lachner, R. Lavenberg, N. B. Marshall, H. McCully, R. McDowall, G. Mead, A. G. K. Menon, G. Miller, G. S. Myers, T. Nalbant, N. Parin, J. Randall, W. Richards, L. Rivas, C. R. Robins, R. Rofen, D. Rosen, R. Rosenblatt, L. Schultz, W. B. Scott, V. Springer, R. Suttkus, A. N. Svetovidov, W. R. Taylor, J. Tyler, E. Trewavas, B. Walker, V. Walters, A. Wheeler, N. Wilimovsky, and L. Woods.

LITERATURE CITED

BAILEY, R. M.
  1960. Pisces (zoology), pp. 242–243 *in* McGraw-Hill Encyclopedia of Science and Technology. Vol. 10. New York, McGraw-Hill.

GREENWOOD, P. H. *et al*
  1966. Phyletic studies of teleostean fishes with a provisional classification of living forms. Bulletin of the American Museum of Natural History, vol. 131, pp. 339–456.

MARSHALL, N. B.
  1965. The life of fishes. London, Weidenfeld and Nicolson. 402 pp.

NORMAN, J. R.
  1963. A history of fishes. 2nd edition by P. H. Greenwood. New York, Hill and Wang. xxxi + 398 pp.

MYERS, G. S.
  1949. Salt-tolerance of fresh-water fish groups in relation to zoogeographical problems. Bijdragen tot de Dierkunde, vol. 28, pp. 315–322.
  1958. Trends in the evolution of teleostean fishes. Stanford Ichthyological Bulletin, vol. 7, pp. 27–30.

SCHULTZ, L. P.
  1965. Fishes and how they live, Chapt. 1 *in* Wondrous world of fishes. Washington
        D. C., National Geographic Society. 367 pp.
SCHULTZ, L. P. AND E. M. STERN
  1948. The ways of fishes. New York, Van Nostrand. xii + 264 pp.

THE AMOUNT OF SPACE AVAILABLE
FOR MARINE AND FRESHWATER FISHES

MICHAEL H. HORN

*Department of Biology
California State University
Fullerton, CA 92634*

Cohen (1970) has presented rather careful estimates of the total number of fish species in the world and in each of eight ecological groupings. He found that an "astonishingly high percentage" of bony fishes live in freshwater habitats. According to Cohen's analysis, 41.2% (8,275 species) of all fish species live in fresh water (includes both primary and secondary freshwater fishes). He indicates that this high percentage must reflect the degree of isolation possible in freshwater environments and refers to the great variety of habitats and ecological niches in fresh water and also along tropical shores.

The great number of freshwater fish species becomes even more striking if the volume of fresh water in the world is compared to the volume of the oceans. Indeed, the mode of speciation and the structure of the niche appear highly divergent between the two environments. The oceans account for 97% of all the water in the world whereas the amount of fresh water in lakes and rivers (that which would be available as fish habitat) approaches an almost negligible percentage—only 0.0093% of the world's water (van Hylckama, 1971) (Table 1). In this sense then, 41.2% of all fish species live in less than one one-hundredth of one percent of the available water. Table 2, which is based on Cohen's (1970) data and on the data presented in Table 1, shows the great disparity between freshwater and marine environments in terms of the number of species per unit volume of water. The calculations show that there are about 113,000 km³ of water per marine species but only about 15 km³ for each freshwater species, or approximately a 7,500-fold difference. It is, of course, true that a species does not occupy a particular parcel of water to the exclusion of other organisms; nevertheless, it seems conceptually possible and without undue loss of reality to consider that each species has available a certain volume of water which it can occupy. It is known, too, that marine habitats vary greatly from high diversity in tropical shore and coral reef regions to low diversity in open ocean areas (including the deep ocean which constitutes most of the volume of the oceans and in which numbers and biomass greatly decrease with depth).

Shore and shelf fishes have about 290 km³ of water per species compared with about 1,000,000 km³ for pelagic species (Table 2), or approximately a 3,400-fold difference. If the slope and deep-sea benthic species are added to the pelagic figure, the unit volume of water per species beyond the continental slope is reduced to about 500,000 km³, which is still a relatively very high figure. The volume of water per species of marine shore and shelf fishes is higher than the freshwater figure by about 20× (290 km³ vs. 15 km³). This reflects the similarity in the degree of partitioning in these two regions. Perhaps the number of species per unit volume in the richer tropical reefs exceeds that in a large percentage of freshwater habitats. Also, some marine habitats which are superficially similar to certain freshwater habitats may be expected to have species densities comparable to their freshwater counterparts. Examples might be 1) the deep parts of oceans and lakes (low species density), 2) kelp beds in coastal waters and the vegetated zones of lakes (high species density). It is the open ocean with its broad expanse and great depth that contributes most to the overall very low concentration of species and numbers (discussed below) of marine fishes.

TABLE 1.—Supply (km³) of water in the world available as fish habitat (from data by van Hylckama (1971)).

Item	Volume	Percent of total
Total water in the world	1,360,000,000	100.0
World oceans	1,320,000,000	97.0
Freshwater lakes	125,000	0.0092
Rivers (at any one time)	1,300	0.0001
(remainder of total is ice, groundwater, atmospheric water, etc.)		

TABLE 2.—Volume (km³) of water available per species in various habitats.

Type of species	Volume/species
Total marine	113,000
Marine shore and continental shelf to 200 m	290*
Marine pelagic beyond continental shelf	1,000,000
Marine pelagic + continental slope and deep sea benthic	500,000
Total fresh water	15

* The volume of water over the continental shelf was calculated by considering that the shelf underlies 7.5% of the ocean surface (Emery, 1969) and that the average depth over the shelf is about 100 m or 2.5% of the ocean's average depth of 4,000 m.

From *Fish. Bull.*, U.S. 70(4):1295-1297. Reprinted by permission.

While it is difficult to estimate the number of fish species in an environment, it is much more difficult to even speculate on the number of individuals per species in either marine or freshwater regions. Gadgil[1] arrived at a figure of 4×10^9 as the average number of individuals per fish species based largely on marine data. Certainly, different marine habitats support widely differing numbers of fishes. Pelagic species such as certain anchovies may attain population levels of 10^{12} whereas some rocky shore species may be several orders of magnitude lower in total numbers, perhaps near 10^6 individuals per species. A figure in the middle of the above two estimates would be 10^9, and in this discussion I have considered 10×10^9 to be the average number of individuals per species in the sea. It is fairly certain, I think, that there are fewer individuals per species among freshwater fishes than among marine fishes. The degree of difference in abundance is, however, difficult to estimate or even imagine. There are some very abundant freshwater species such as certain clupeids and cyprinids, but some are quite rare, most notably the desert cyprinodontids of the southwestern United States which may exist only in the thousands or even hundreds per species.

Two values were used for the average number of individuals per freshwater species—a high value (10×10^9), the same as the figure for marine species, and a low value (10×10^6) which I think is a conservative minimum. A range of values conveys more information in comparing the marine and freshwater situations. The calculations in Table 3 show that marine fishes have $10\times$ to $10,000\times$ more space available per individual than freshwater forms, depending upon which freshwater value is chosen. If the lower freshwater figure (10×10^6) is more nearly correct, then the degree of isolation and habitat partitioning in fresh waters becomes even more strikingly apparent. On the basis of total numbers per species, the difference per unit volume between the oceans and fresh water is only 10-fold whereas on the basis of species per unit volume, the difference is approximately 7,500-fold.

The above disparity would seem to be related not only to the degree of isolation but to the relative levels of productivity and biomass in the two environments. Table 4 shows net primary

TABLE 3.—Volume (km³) of water available per individual fish in the sea and in fresh water.

Type of species	Number of species	Individuals/ species	Volume/ individual
Marine	11,675	10×10^9	1.1×10^{-5}
Fresh water (1)	8,275	10×10^9	1.5×10^{-9}
Fresh water (2)	8,275	10×10^6	1.5×10^{-6}

productivity and plant biomass estimates for three major ecosystems: 1) lake and stream, 2) continental shelf, and 3) open ocean. Net primary productivity per unit area in fresh water is about $1.5\times$ to $4\times$ as high as in the sea, and plant biomass per unit area in fresh water is about $2\times$ to $7\times$ as high as in the sea. These figures are perhaps not in great discord with the estimate above that $10\times$ as many fishes occur per unit volume in fresh water as in the sea.

TABLE 4.—Net primary productivity and plant biomass per unit area in three major ecosystems (from data compiled by Whittaker (1970)).

Major ecosystem	Net primary productivity	Biomass
	dry g/m² /year (mean value)	*dry kg/m² (mean value)*
Lake and stream	500	0.02
Continental shelf	350	0.01
Open ocean	125	0.003

These data serve, I believe, to illustrate the quite astounding difference between the amount of space available for freshwater and marine fishes. As Cohen (1970) has emphasized, the calculations also make apparent the need for increased research on freshwater fishes since their habitats are being rapidly modified. In terms of conservation and economic policies, important studies should include those that compare numbers of species and individuals in different local and regional environments in relation to levels of productivity and other factors.

I thank Daniel M. Cohen for reading and offering valuable comments on the manuscript.

Literature Cited

COHEN, D. M.
1970. How many recent fishes are there? Proc. Calif. Acad. Sci., Ser. 4, 38:341-345.
EMERY, K. O.
1969. The continental shelves. *In* The ocean, p. 39-52. W. H. Freeman, San Franc.
VAN HYLCKAMA, T. E. A.
1971. Water resources. *In* W. W. Murdoch (editor), Environment, resources, pollution & society, p. 135-155. Sinauer Associates, Stamford, Conn.
WHITTAKER, R. H.
1970. Communities and ecosystems. Macmillan, N.Y., 162 p.

[1] Gadgil, M. On numbers of fish. (Unpublished manuscript) Biology Department, Harvard University, Cambridge, Mass. Present address: Maharashtra Association for the Cultivation of Science, Agarkar Road, Poona 4, India.

Additional Readings
CHAPTER 2

BRIGGS, J. C. 1974. *Marine Zoogeography.* New York: McGraw-Hill.

CROIZAT, L. 1964. *Space, time, form: the biological synthesis.* Caracas, Venezuela: Published by the author.

CROIZAT, L.; NELSON, G.; and ROSEN, D. E. 1974. Centers of origin and related concepts. *Syst. Zool.* 23 (2): 265–287.

DARLINGTON, P. J. Jr. 1957. *Zoogeography: the geographical distribution of animals.* New York: John Wiley & Sons, Inc.

EKMAN, S. 1967. *Zoogeography of the sea.* London: Sidgwick & Jackson.

HERALD, E. S. 1961. *Living fishes of the world.* New York: Doubleday.

HERALD, E. S. 1972. *Fishes of North America.* New York: Doubleday.

HUBBS, C. L. and LAGLER, K. F. 1964. *Fishes of the Great Lakes region.* Ann Arbor: University of Michigan Press.

LINDBERG, G. U. 1971. *Fishes of the world: a key to families and a checklist.* English translation 1974. New York: John Wiley & Sons.

NELSON, G. 1974. Historical biogeography: an alternative formalization. *Syst. Zool.* 23(4): 555–558.

NELSON, J. S. 1976. *Fishes of the world.* New York: John Wiley & Sons.

NIKOLSKY, G. V. 1961. *Special ichthyology.* Israel Program for Scientific Translations, Jerusalem. U.S. Department of Commerce, Washington, D.C.

STERBA, G. 1966. *Freshwater fishes of the world.* London: Studio Vista.

3

Morphology

EVOLUTIONARY STRATEGIES AND MORPHOLOGICAL
INNOVATIONS: CICHLID PHARYNGEAL JAWS

KAREL F. LIEM

Abstract

Liem, Karel F. (*Museum of Comparative Zoology, Harvard University, Cambridge, Mass.
02138*) 1974. *Evolutionary strategies and morphological innovations: Cichlid pharyngeal
jaws. Syst. Zool.* 22:425–441.—The percoid fish family Cichlidae possesses a phenomenal
ability to colonize lakes and to diversify to an extent unmatched by any other vertebrate
family in the presence of predator pressure and strong competition. The invading cichlids
successfully occupy contiguous and occasionally overlapping adaptive zones and specialize
progressively into diversified subzones, ramifying prodigiously and covering a breadth of
total adaptation that would have been entirely unpredictable if we were aware only of the
rudiments of the evolutionary process. This evolutionary avalanche can be attributed to the
cooccurrence of a wide range of prospective adaptive zones in the lacustrine environment,
and the presence of a unique morphological key innovation of maximum versatility. The
new adaptive complex has been revealed in this study by electromyographic analysis synchronized with cineradiography of the cichlid pharyngeal jaw apparatus. The morphological novelty characterizing the family Cichlidae involves the development of: a synarthrosis between the lower pharyngeal jaws, a strategic shift of insertion of the two fourth
levator externi muscles, and synovial joints between upper pharyngeal jaws and basicranium.
This specialized, highly integrated key innovation enables the cichlids not only to transport
(deglutination) but also to prepare food, freeing the premaxillary and mandibular jaws to
evolve numerous specializations dealing with the collection of dramatically diverse foods.
The functional integration of the innovation is so basic and its potential adaptive versatility
so rich that it is maintained throughout the adaptive radiation even though numerous nondisruptive evolutionary changes do take place, providing prodigious opportunities for explosive evolution during the exploitation of rich resources of food in the lacustrine environment.
The conversion of the preexisting elements into a new and significantly improved cichlid
adaptive complex of high selective value may have evolved by rapid steps under influence
of strong selection pressure acting on the minor reconstruction of the genotype which is
involved in evolutionary changes of the pertinent ontogenetic mechanisms. Such relatively
simple evolutionary processes are probably the cause for the general phenomenon that only
slight reconstructions of existing structures are necessary for successful and rapid adaptation
to drastic shifts of adaptive zones.

INTRODUCTION

Cichlid fishes have demonstrated a phenomenal ability to colonize lakes and to
diversify to an extent unmatched by any
other vertebrate family. In great African
lakes cichlids fulfil roles which elsewhere
are enacted by members of different families and orders (Greenwood, 1964). Cichlids have undergone their prodigious adaptive radiation in the presence of such
potentially competitive and highly successful families as the Cyprinidae, Characidae,
Bagridae, Mochocidae, and Clariidae. Their
evolutionary success seems to be due to the
perfection of their adaptations rather than
to the lack of either competition or predators (Fryer and Iles, 1972). However, the
exact nature of the refinements of cichlid
adaptations remains poorly known because
much attention has been focused on the

environmental factors, and the organism
tends to be lost from sight or sidetracked
as "black boxes" reacting in a mathemati-
cally predictable way to such factors as
abundance of food, lack of competition and
predatory pressures, etc. Why did the family Cichlidae undergo the most explosive
adaptive radiation among lacustrine fishes
and not the other successful fish families?
Recently Greenwood (1973) has dealt with
this question emphasizing the exceptional
"morphopotentiality" of cichlids as an important factor.

In general, adaptive radiations of organisms will not occur until after an evolutionary novelty has reached a certain degree
of development (Mayr, 1960; Bock, 1965).
Is there a special set of characteristics, i.e.,
key innovations, in cichlids enabling river-

From *Syst. Zool.* 20:425–441. Reprinted by permission.

ine forms to cope with the demands of the new lacustrine habitats? It is axiomatic that evolutionary adaptation (Bock, 1965) can be measured only in terms of function, regardless of how we employ the term (Schaeffer, 1965). Yet in most theoretical reviews no well documented examples are given and function is either superficially discussed in very broad general terms or inferred from form.

The focus of this paper is on key innovations in cichlids and how they have played a decisive role in giving the family a significant competitive advantage over other fish families in the rapid colonization of African lakes. Using detailed documentation and experimental analysis I will try to give a concrete case history of the emergence of an evolutionary innovation, and subsequently that of a higher level of organization and to discuss the findings in the light of the "modified saltationist theory" as interpreted by Davis (1949, 1964) and Frazzetta (1970) and the synthetic theory as proposed by Simpson (1953), Bock (1959, 1965), and Mayr (1960, 1963).

GENERALIZED PERCOID PHARYNGEAL JAW APPARATUS

In order to evaluate properly the change from the "generalized" to the "specialized" group, I will start with the functional analysis of the pharyngeal jaw apparatus of *Pristolepis fasciatus*, which is considered a generalized percoid (Rosen and Patterson, 1969).

Morphological pattern

Each upper pharyngeal jaw (Fig. 2:UB) is composed of three intimately articulated elements, i.e., the 2nd and 3rd infrapharyngobranchials with corresponding toothplates and the 4th toothplate, which function as one unit. The left and right upper pharyngeal jaws remain independent units. There are neither joints nor simple articulations between skull base and the upper pharyngeal jaws.

The lower pharyngeal jaws (Fig. 2:LB) are also paired each representing the fifth ceratobranchial provided with a corresponding toothplate (Fig. 1:CB5).

Each upper pharyngeal jaw is operated *directly* by (1) a retractor pharyngeus superioris (Fig. 1:RPH; Fig. 2:RP) muscle which originates from the first three verte-

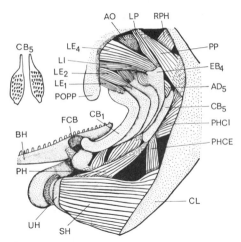

Fig. 1.—Lateral view of branchial apparatus and muscles of *Pristolepis fasciatus*. Opercular, suspensory apparatus, gills, gill rakers, and mucous membrane have been removed. AD5, adductor; AO, adductor operculi; BH, basihyal; CB1, first ceratobranchial; CB5, lower pharyngeal jaw (insert is dorsal view): CL, cleithrum; EB4, fourth epibranchial; FCB, fossa for hyoid ramus; LE1–4, levatores externi 1–4; LI, levator internus; LP, levator posterior; PH, pharyngohyoideus; PHCE, pharyngocleithralis externus; PHCI, pharyngocleithralis internus; POPP, postorbital process; PP, protractor pectoralis; RPH, retractor pharyngeus superior; SH, sternohyoideus; UH, urohyal.

brae and inserts on the posterodorsal surface of the upper pharyngeal jaw; (2) two levatores interni (Fig. 1:LI) originating from the anterodorsal corner of the prootic and inserting on the anterodorsal surface of the jaw; and *indirectly* by (3) levator externus 4 (Figs. 1, 2:LE4) originating from the anterodorsal corner of the prootic and inserting on a dorsal process of the 4th epibranchial (Fig. 1:EB4); (4) levator posterior (Figs. 1, 2:LP) originating from the ventral aspect of the pterotic and inserting on the dorsal aspect of the fourth epibranchial just posterior to the insertion of the fourth levator externus; (5) the fifth adductor (Figs. 1, 2:AD5) originating from the posterior rim of the fourth epibranchial and inserting on the superior aspect of the posteromedial corner of the lower pharyngeal jaw.

Each lower pharyngeal jaw is operated *directly* by (1) pharyngocleithralis internus (Figs. 1, 2:PHCI, PCI) originating from the cleithrum and inserting on the inferior aspect of the jaw; (2) pharyngocleithralis externus (Figs. 1, 2:PHCE, PCE) originat-

ing from the more distal part of the cleithrum and inserting on the ventrolateral
surface of the anterior corner of the jaw;
(3) pharyngohyoideus (Figs. 1, 2:PH) running between the anterior tip of the jaw and
the superior aspect of the urohyal; and *indirectly* by the fifth adductor (see (5)
above).

All generalized percoids exhibit the pattern described above. The salient features
are: the connection of the "dorsal" muscles
(i.e., levator externus 4 and levator posterior) with the dorsal branchial elements
(i.e., epibranchial 4), the absence of an
articulation between the upper pharyngeal
jaws and skull base and the paired, independent lower pharyngeal jaws.

Functional mechanisms

The sequence of muscle contractions has
been analysed electromyographically [using
the methods of Osse (1969) and Osse et
al. (1972)], while the movements of the
pharyngeal jaws have been determined by
successive X-ray pictures. Both procedures
were performed on unrestrained and unanesthetized *Pristolepis* feeding on live
crickets.

As shown in Fig. 3 we can distinguish two
phases:

Phase 1 ("retracted-adducted"), with activity in the levator posterior, geniohyoideus anterior, pharyngocleithralis internus
(PHAR CL I) and the retractor pharyngeus superior. The effect of the combined
activity of these muscles on the pharyngeal
jaws (UB, LB) is shown in Fig. 4 with bold
lines. Both jaws are retracted and rotated,
but occlusion of teeth does not occur. This
phase is initiated by the geniohyoideus anterior muscle which pulls the hyoid apparatus (Fig. 4:HY, UH) forwards and up and
is immediately followed by the retractor
pharyngeus superior, levator posterior and
finally the pharyngocleithralis internus muscles.

During *phase 2* ("protracted-abducted")
the fourth levator externus (Fig. 3:levator
ext 4), pharyngohyoideus and adductor
contract first, closely followed by the sternohyoideus and pharyngocleithralis externus muscles. The effect of the combined
activity of these muscles on the jaws is
shown in Fig. 4 in broken lines.

An important characteristic of this coor-

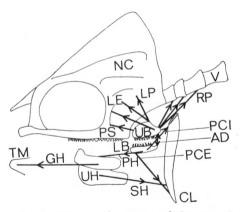

FIG. 2.—Diagram of position and direction of
major branchial muscles in the generalized percoid
fish *Pristolepis fasciatus*. Ad, adductor; CL, cleithrum; GH, geniohyoideus; LB, lower pharyngeal
jaw; LE, levator externus; LP, levator posterior;
NC, neurocranium; PCE, pharyngocleithralis externus; PCI, pharyngocleithralis internus; PH, pharyngohyoideus; PS, parasphenoid; RP, retractor
pharyngeus superior; SH, sternohyoideus; TM,
tip of mandible; UB, upper pharyngeal jaw; UH,
urohyal; V, vertebra.

dinated pattern is the three pairs of antagonist muscles: levator externus 4—levator posterior, pharyngocleithralis externus—
pharyngocleithralis internus, sternohyoideus
—geniohyoideus anterior. Paradoxically
the *fifth adductor* is only morphologically
an adductor. Electromyography of unrestrained and unanesthetized fish shows the
exact opposite function: the muscle *abducts*
the jaws. The movements of the pharyngeal
jaws of *Pristolepis* transport food into the
esophagus thus resembling the condition
in the nandid fishes (Liem, 1970). Food
preparation (or mastication) by pharyngeal jaws does not take place in either *Pristolepis* or other generalized percoids, Cottidae and some Blennidae (Vanden Berghe,
1928).

CICHLID PHARYNGEAL JAW APPARATUS

This description is based on *Haplochromis burtoni*, a generalized African
cichlid.

Morphological pattern

The upper pharyngeal jaws are paired
and slightly separated (Figs. 5, 6:UB).
Each consists of joined 2nd and 3rd infrapharyngobranchials with corresponding
toothplates and the fourth toothplate, functioning as a single unit. A distinct dorsal

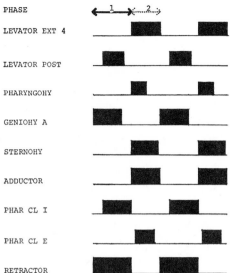

FIG. 3.—Diagram of active periods of branchial and hyoid muscles of unanesthetized and unrestrained *Pristolepis fasciatus* feeding on live crickets. GENIOHY A, geniohyoideus anterior; LEVATOR EXT 4, fourth levator externus; LEVATOR POST, levator posterior; PHAR CL E, pharyngocleithralis externus; PHAR CL I, pharyngocleithralis internus; PHARYNGOHY, pharyngohyoideus; RETRACTOR, retractor pharyngeus superior; STERNOHY, sternohyoideus.

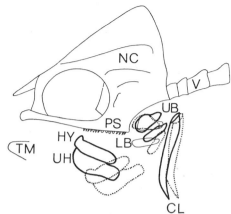

FIG. 4.—Diagram of movements of pharyngeal jaws as revealed by sequence of successive X-ray pictures in the generalized percoid fish *Pristolepis fasciatus*. CL, cleithrum; HY, hyoid; LB, lower pharyngeal jaw; NC, neurocranium; PS, parasphenoid; TM, tip of mandible; UB, upper pharyngeal jaw; UH, urohyal; V, vertebra.

articular process on the superior aspect of the third infrapharyngobranchial (Fig. 13: AS) articulates with a corresponding process, the pharyngeal apophysis, on the skull base (Fig. 9:A). This *basipharyngeal joint* between skull base and upper pharyngeal jaw is synovial, offering controlled mobility. Such a joint is absent in generalized percoids (Fig. 2).

In sharp contrast with the condition in generalized percoids, the lower pharyngeal jaws are suturally united, functioning as a single unit (Fig. 7). Each posterodorsal corner of the jaw is differentiated into a prominent process which serves as an insertion of the fourth levator externus and fifth adductor muscles. I, therefore, will refer to it as the *muscular process* of the lower pharyngeal jaw.

The muscles operating on the lower pharyngeal jaw directly resemble those of *Pristolepis* very closely with the remarkable exception that the fourth levator externus (Figs. 5, 6, 11, 16:LEV E4, LE4), which, although originally a "dorsal gill arch" muscle, bypasses the dorsal fourth epibranchial

element to insert on the muscular process of the lower pharyngeal jaw (i.e., the suturally united, ventral fifth ceratobranchials (Figs. 5, 7:CB5). The fourth levator externus muscle in the Cichlidae has become dissociated from the fourth epibranchial element and, consequently, also from the upper pharyngeal jaw, to assume a new and salient role in operating the lower pharyngeal jaw.

The muscles operating the lower pharyngeal jaw are essentially similar to those of *Pristolepis* but with the important difference of the addition of the fourth levatores externi muscles to the two muscular processes.

All Cichlidae exhibit the specialized morphological pattern described above. The characteristic specializations are: The appearance of two synovial basipharyngeal joints, the sutural connection of the two fifth ceratobranchials to form a single lower pharyngeal jaw provided with two muscular processes, and the shifts of insertions of the fourth levatores externi muscles from the fourth epibranchials to the lower pharyngeal jaw (this is at variance with the observations of Chardon and Vandewalle, 1971; Vandewalle, 1971; Vandewalle, 1972).

Functional mechanisms

The electromyographic recordings have been made in collaboration with Prof.

J. W. M. Osse at the University of Leiden, The Netherlands.

With the appearance of the basipharyngeal joint, the upper pharyngeal jaw is no longer a "freely-floating" complex (Fig. 6: UB; Fig. 9:A; Fig. 13:AS).

The pattern of muscle contractions in cichlids as revealed by electromyography differs significantly from that of *Pristolepis* (Fig. 8). A third phase (*phase 1a*, food preparation, or mastication) has been added to the two phases found in *Pristolepis* (Figs. 3, 8). This phase is initiated by full contraction of the geniohyoideus anterior, followed by the strongest activity of the fourth levator externus, full activity of the retractor pharyngeus superior towards the end of the phase and weak contraction of the levator posterior. The effect of the combined activity of these muscles during phase 1a is depicted in a simplified diagram in Fig. 9 with bold lines. Both jaws are protracted and strongly adducted. The protraction is carried over from phase 2 (Fig. 9, broken lines) during which the pharyngohyoideus (Fig. 6:PH) has pulled the lower pharyngeal jaw forwards. When the lower jaw is protracted, the strong contraction of the fourth levator externus results in a powerful adduction of the jaws.

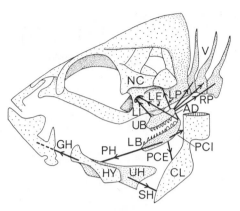

Fig. 6.—Diagram of position and direction of some major branchial muscles in a generalized cichlid fish. AD, adductor; CL, cleithrum; GH, geniohyoideus; HY, hyoid; LB, lower pharyngeal jaw; LE, fourth levator externus; LI, levator internus; LP, levator posterior; NC, neurocranium; PCE, pharyngocleithralis externus; PCI, pharyngocleithralis internus; PH, pharyngohyoideus; RP, retractor pharyngeus superior; SH, sternohyoideus; UB, upper pharyngeal bone; UH, urohyal; V, vertebrae.

In *phase 1b* three muscles are active: moderate contraction of the fourth levator externus, rapidly increasing activity of the levator posterior and full contraction of the retractor pharyngeus superior (Figs. 8, 10). The effect of the combined activity of the three muscles is a pronounced retraction of both upper and lower pharyngeal jaws by respectively strong contraction of the retractor pharyngeus superior and increasing activity of the pharyngocleithralis internus (Fig. 9). The levator posterior (Fig. 6:LP) rotates the upper jaw in such a way that its anterior tip moves down to approach its fellow from the lower jaw (Fig. 9:UB, LB), which rotates upwards as a result of the moderate activity of the fourth levator externus.

Phase 2 is the protracted-abducted condition in which the fourth levator externus, levator posterior, pharyngohyoideus, sternohyoideus, adductor, and pharyngocleithralis internus and externus muscles show considerable activity (Figs. 8, 10). During this phase the retractor pharyngeus superior stops its activity abruptly. The upper and lower pharyngeal jaws are pulled forward by respectively the levatores interni (although I have no electromyographic evidence for this) and the pharyngohyoideus (Fig. 6:LI, PH). The anterior tips of the

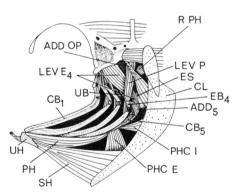

Fig. 5.—Lateral view of branchial apparatus and muscles of *Haplochromis burtoni* (Lake Tanganyika) after removal of opercular, suspensory apparatus, gills, gill rakers and mucous membrane. ADD5, fifth adductor; ADD OP, adductor operculi; CB1, first ceratobranchial; CB5, lower pharyngeal jaw; C, cleithrum; EB4, fourth epibranchial; ES, esophagus; LEV E 4, fourth levator externus; LEV P, levator posterior; PH, pharyngohyoideus; PHC E, pharyngocleithralis externus; PHC I, pharyngocleithralis internus; RPH, retractor pharyngeus superior; SH, sternohyoideus; UB, upper pharyngeal jaw; UH, urohyal.

upper and lower jaws move apart (Fig. 9:UB, LB) by the action of respectively the following groups of muscles: adductor—levator posterior (?), and fourth levator externus—pharyngocleithralis externus and internus.

The pattern of muscle contractions (Figs. 8, 10) associated with the pharyngeal jaws in cichlids can be characterized as follows: (1) The fourth levator externus is active *throughout* all stages of food preparation (mastication) and swallowing (deglutition), performing antagonistic functions in the various phases (Fig. 10); (2) the levator posterior is active during most of the three phases except for the initial stage of phase 1a; (3) the pharyngocleithralis internus is active during phases 1b and 2.

Phases 1a and b of cichlids (Fig. 8) represent both temporal and qualitative modifications of phase 1 of generalized percoids (Fig. 3). The ratio in duration of phase 1 and phase 2 in *Pristolepis* is 4:3 (Fig. 3), whereas in *Haplochromis burtoni* the ratio of phase 1a–b and phase 2 has changed to almost 3:1 (Fig. 8). This increase in ratio is caused by the interpolation of an additional interval of food preparation prior to deglutition. The qualitative differences involve the sequences of contraction of three muscles: (a) The pharyngocleithralis internus is active in phase 1b and 2 (Fig. 8). During phase 1b the muscle performs its original function of retracting the lower pharyngeal jaw (also see Liem, 1970),

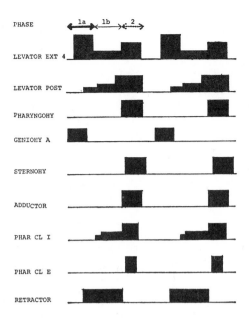

Fig. 8.—Diagram of active periods of muscles of unanesthetized and unrestrained *Haplochromis burtoni* feeding on *Gammarus* sp. Abbreviations as in Fig. 3.

while in phase 2 it acquires a new function in abducting the lower jaw once it has been pulled back; (b) the levator posterior plays a major role in stabilizing the superior pharyngeal jaws in phase 2, while during phase 1b (deglutition) it rotates the superior pharyngeal jaws (Fig. 9); (c) the role of the fourth levator externus has increased tremendously (Fig. 10), and changes with the shift in position of the lower pharyngeal jaw from an abductor (phase 2), to a rotator (phase 1b), and finally to an adductor (phase 1a).

THE CICHLID PHARYNGEAL JAW APPARATUS AS A KEY INNOVATION

All cichlids, whether riverine or lacustrine, from both the old world tropics and the neotropics, share the functionally integrated, highly specialized pharyngeal jaw apparatus described above. This clearly represents a major adaptive complex. Since this complex is unique among percoids, the Cichlidae can be defined on the basis of this unique evolutionary novelty, which represents strong evidence for the monophyletic origin of the family. The innovation (or novelty) emerged as a new functional and morphological reorganization and sub-

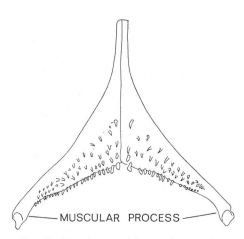

Fig. 7.—Dorsal view of lower pharyngeal jaw of the scale-eating *Plecodus paradoxus* from Lake Tanganyika.

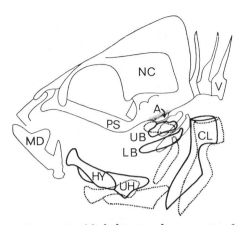

FIG. 9.—Simplified diagram of movements of the pharyngeal jaws of a generalized cichlid fish as revealed by successive X-ray pictures. Bold lines (phase 1a): food preparation (mastication); thin lines (phase 1b): food transport (swallowing, deglutition); broken lines (phase 2): protraction-abduction. A, pharyngeal process (apophysis); CL, cleithrum; HY, hyoid; LB, lower pharyngeal jaw; MD, mandible; NC, neurocranium; PS, parasphenoid; UB, upper pharyngeal jaw; UH, urohyal: V, vertebra.

and kinds of jaw movements, because the resulting synarthrosis will automatically double the number of muscle insertions without increasing the original ancestral number of muscles. In addition to this, another pair of muscles, the fourth external levatores (Figs. 5, 6, 16:LE4), which are originally "dorsal gill arch" muscles, bypass the dorsal element (fourth epibranchial) to insert on the muscular process of the ventral lower pharyngeal jaw. This shift produces an enormous range of possible functions that can be achieved by the total pharyngeal jaw apparatus. The new insertion site of the fourth levator externus makes it possible for the lower pharyngeal jaw to exert a strong adduction ("bite") against the upper one. Besides its new role as a potentially powerful adductor, the modified fourth levator externus is able to move the lower pharyngeal jaw in numerous ways. The lower pharyngeal jaw in cichlids is operated by ten muscles, whereas

sequent integration of existing branchial muscles, nerves and bones resulting in an ever increasing efficiency of function. The new adaptive complex originated by slight but significant shifts in positions, proportions and fusions of bones and muscles. However, this relatively simple innovation has produced an important change of function.

Let us review the structural and functional reorganization and integration of the cichlid pharyngeal apparatus: the development of the basipharyngeal joints between the cranial base and the upper pharyngeal jaws has furnished efficient Class I and Class II lever systems to such important muscles as the levatores interni (Fig. 6:LI), levator posterior (LP) and retractor pharyngeus superior (RP), and has cleared the way for many coordinated interactions (including powerful "occlusion") with the lower pharyngeal jaws. Without the basipharyngeal joints the upper jaws are free floating units with limited functional opportunities and no potential mechanism for occlusion and mastication (Liem, 1970). The fusion of the left and right fifth ceratobranchials (Fig. 1:CB5) into a single lower pharyngeal jaw (Fig. 7) provides a significant increase in the control, degree,

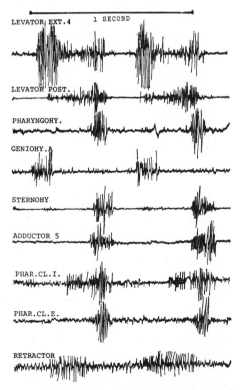

FIG. 10.—Electromyograms of branchial and hyoid muscles of unanesthetized and unrestrained *Haplochromis burtoni* feeding on frozen *Gammarus* sp. Abbreviations as in Fig. 3.

that of generalized percoids is operated by eight. Concomitantly with the osteological, arthrological and myological modifications, the pattern of sequences of muscle activity during food preparation and swallowing changes considerably (compare Figs. 3, 8).

The new adaptive complex has enabled the Cichlidae to penetrate numerous new adaptive zones, since it provided the organism with a highly efficient and versatile mechanism for food preparation. This innovation freed the mandibular and premaxillary jaw mechanisms from their dual tasks of food collecting and preparation by eliminating the latter function. Once this adaptive threshold was crossed, the premaxillary and mandibular jaw apparatus could concentrate on one major function only. The release of the restricting influence of a second major function resulted in the emergence of numerous specializations of collecting mechanisms dealing with dramatically diverse foods. Since the appearance of the adaptation of the pharyngeal jaw apparatus is central to the exploitation of new habitats, we can consider this specialization a key innovation (sensu Miller, 1949).

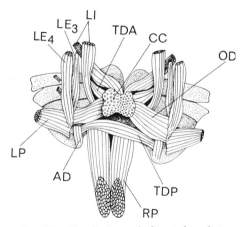

Fig. 12.—Dorsal view of dissected and isolated branchial muscles and apparatus of the generalized perciform *Badis badis*. Gills and mucous membranes have been removed. AD, adductor; CB5, lower pharyngeal jaw (fifth ceratobranchial); CC, cartilaginous cushion; LE3, 4, third and fourth levatores externi; LI, levatores interni; LP, levator posterior; OD, obliquus dorsalis; RP, retractor pharyngeus superior; TDA, transversus dorsalis anterior; TDP, transversus dorsalis posterior.

THE ORIGIN OF THE CICHLID PHARYNGEAL JAW ADAPTIVE COMPLEX

The most primitive state of this innovation is found in the neotropical species *Cichla ocellaris* (cf. Newsome, 1971). Although this species possesses a fully developed basipharyngeal joint, its lower pharyngeal jaw is composed of separate fifth ceratobranchial elements. The two bones have not formed a complete synarthrosis, and the muscular processes are only weakly developed. The fourth levator externus is moderately developed (Fig. 11:LE4) but it inserts on the lower pharyngeal jaw (CB5), although in a few specimens a lateral slip of the muscle is still attached to the dorsal aspect of the fourth epibranchial. Such an organization of the adaptive complex may be considered intermediate between the primitive state as found in such generalized percoids as *Pristolepis* (Fig. 1) and *Badis badis* (Fig. 12) and the derived state in more advanced cichlids (Figs. 5, 13, 14). The basipharyngeal joint may have evolved initially as a very simple contact between the dorsal surface of the upper pharyngeal jaw and the ventral surface of the cranial base. The rubbing and sliding of the two bony surfaces would require a cartilaginous cushion between the two

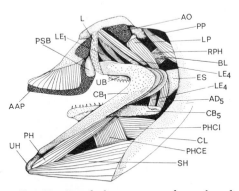

Fig. 11.—Branchial apparatus and muscles of *Cichla ocellaris* (Guyana) after removal of opercular, suspensory apparatus, gills, gill rakers and mucous membrane. AAP, adductor arcus palatini; AD5, fifth adductor; AO, adductor operculi; BL, Baudelot's ligament; CB1, first ceratobranchial; CB5, fifth ceratobranchial (lower pharyngeal jaw); CL, cleithrum; ES, esophagus; L, ligament; LE1, first levator externus; LE4, fourth levator externus; LP, levator posterior; PH, pharyngohyoideus; PHCE, pharyngocleithralis externus; PHCI, pharyngocleithralis internus; PP, protractor pectoralis; PSB, pseudobranch; RPH, retractor pharyngeus superior; SH, sternohyoideus; UB, upper pharyngeal jaw; UH, urohyal.

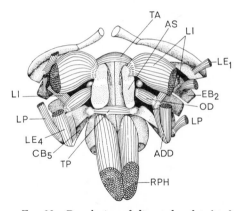

FIG. 13.—Dorsal view of dissected and isolated branchial apparatus and muscles of the scale-eating Lake Tanganyika cichlid *Plecodus paradoxus*. Gills and mucous membranes have been removed. ADD, adductor; AS, articular process of upper pharyngeal jaw; CB5, lower pharyngeal jaw; EB2, second epibranchial; LE1, first levator externus; LE4, fourth levator externus; LI, levator internus; LP, levator posterior; OD, obliquus dorsalis; RPH, retractor pharyngeus superior; TA, transversus dorsalis anterior; TP, transversus dorsalis posterior.

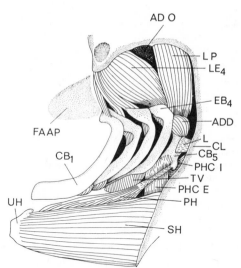

FIG. 14.—Lateral view of branchial apparatus and muscles of *Lamprologus tretocephalus* (mollusc feeder from Lake Tanganyika) after removal of opercular, suspensory apparatus, gills, gill rakers and mucous membrane. ADD5, fifth adductor; ADO, adductor operculi; CB1, first ceratobranchial; CB5, lower pharyngeal jaw; EB4, fourth epibranchial; FAAP, fossa for adductor arcus palatini; L, ligament; LE4, fourth levator externus; LP, levator posterior; PH, pharyngohyoideus; PHCE, pharyngocleithralis externus; PHCI, pharyngocleithralis internus; SH, sternohyoideus; TV, transversus ventralis; UH, urohyal.

bones as found in the generalized percoids *Badis* (Fig. 12:CC) and *Pristolepis*. It is known (Murray, 1937) that the development of such a simple contact between two bones into an amphiarthrosis and the subsequent change from an amphiarthrosis to a diarthrosis is a relatively simple and rapid ontogenetic process controlled by minor genetic changes.

The shift of the site of insertion of the fourth levator externus from the dorsal fourth epibranchial element to the ventral fifth ceratobranchial may have developed in one of two ways: (1) As found in some specimens of *Cichla ocellaris*, the fourth levator externus may have split into two heads, one inserting on the original site on the fourth epibranchial and the second on the fifth ceratobranchial. The latter hypertrophied under strong selection pressure, whereas the former's role diminished resulting in a reduction (occasional vestige in *Cichla*) or total loss of the muscle slip. (2) It is known that the levatores arcuum branchialium muscles in teleosts originate from muscle plates which are continuous dorsoventral structures (Edgeworth, 1935). The ventral parts of the muscle plates usually disappear leaving only their dorsal ends as the levatores. It is conceivable

that in cichlids, the fourth levator externus retains its continuous dorso-ventral extent throughout its development. Either of the two possible ontogenetic mechanisms may represent the results of relatively simple changes in the genotype.

The levator posterior in generalized percoids and *Cichla ocellaris* (Figs. 1, 11:LP) originates from the pterotic anterior to the origin of the protractor pectoralis and has an oblique relationship to the upper pharyngeal jaw complex, which results in a less than 90 degrees angle of pull, so that some of the muscle energy is dissipated. In most cichlids the muscle fiber direction of the levator posterior is at the optimum angle, i.e., perpendicular to the long axis of the upper pharyngeal jaw (Figs. 5, 14:LEV P, LP). This modification is accomplished by a caudal shift in the origin of the levator posterior from a point anterior to one posterior to the origin of the protractor pectoralis.

"Fusion" of the two fifth ceratobranchials

by means of a synarthrosis has evolved independently in several phylogenetically unrelated teleost fishes e.g., Anabantidae, some cyprinodonts, *Pogonias*, labroids and embiotocids (Liem, in preparation) indicating that the specialization plays such a highly significant trophic role that it has been exploited by the ever present pressure of selection.

Concomitant with these structural and functional changes, the pattern of nervous coordination of the branchial muscles changes significantly. The diphasic pattern is transformed into a triphasic one (compare Figs. 3 and 8). Such a change seems to have been brought about by the maintenance of the ancestral phase 2 (protraction and abduction) and an increase in relative duration and subsequent subdivision of phase 1 into phases 1a and 1b, respectively dealing with mastication and swallowing. The extension of the ancestral phase 1 may have been realized by the continuous firing of the nerve to the fourth levator externus throughout the feeding cycle, and the earlier firings of the nerves to the levator posterior and pharyngocleithralis internus muscles (Figs. 9, 10). Such changes can occur without major reorganization of the motor, proprioceptive, and sensory centers in the central nervous system

It is evident that the new adaptive complex took place without the emergence of a truly new structure. An intensification of the masticatory function has led to a transformation of the food transporting pharyngeal apparatus of a generalized percoid into the cichlid adaptive complex dealing with both food transport and preparation. The entire conversion has been accomplished by a modification of preexisting structural elements, which, when functionally integrated, give rise to a new and vastly improved character complex of high selective value. As Mayr (1960) so succinctly stated: "Perhaps most astonishing is the relative slightness of reconstruction that seems to be necessary for successful adaptation to rather drastic shifts of adaptive zones."

EVOLUTIONARY STRATEGIES

The emergence of the pharyngeal jaw apparatus as a key innovation in cichlids has resulted in an astonishingly dramatic episode of proliferation worthy of such snappy metaphors as "explosive evolution," "evolutionary avalanche" and "explosive speciation." For example, current conservative estimates of endemic cichlid species in Lakes Victoria, Malawi and Tanganyika are respectively 165, 200, and 126. Each of these large lakes has its own distinctive cichlid fauna exploiting most available food resources. Endemic cichlids are also well represented in smaller lakes, e.g., Barombi Mbo, a circular crater lake in West Cameroon with a diameter of 2.5 km. housing 11 endemic species (Trewavas et al., 1972). The spectacular diversity is especially manifested in the feeding specializations, which present the pharyngeal jaw apparatus with items as diverse as molluscs, fish scales, insects, whole fishes, higher plants, zooplankton, algae and phytoplankton.

The evolutionary patterns exhibited by the pharyngeal jaw apparatus illustrate most convincingly the ever ready opportunism of evolution. Correlated with the great diversity of food specializations a great number of distinctly different adaptive expressions evolve without changing the basic pattern of integration of the cichlid pharyngeal jaw apparatus. I will discuss some representative examples of adaptive expressions of cichlid pharyngeal jaws.

Adaptive strategies in dentition

The dentition of the pharyngeal jaws show considerable specializations not only among taxa but even in different fields of the same individual jaw.

In the mollusc-eating *Haplochromis placodon* (Fig. 15:B) the greatly enlarged central teeth are able to crush thick hard shells, whereas the (less modified) marginal teeth with the blunt hooklike pattern transport the crushed prey to the esophagus.

In the algae-eating *Labeotropheus fuelleborni* the teeth completely depart from the ancestral condition to form broad flat surfaces which can be used to compact the algal mass to facilitate subsequent swallowing (Fig. 15:D).

In the fish-eating *Ramphochromis macrophthalmus* the sharply-edged anterior margins of the pointed bladelike teeth are distinctly serrated (Fig. 15:C) to rasp flesh from its prey.

In the scale-eating *Corematodus taeniatus* of Lake Malawi (Fig. 15:A) the teeth

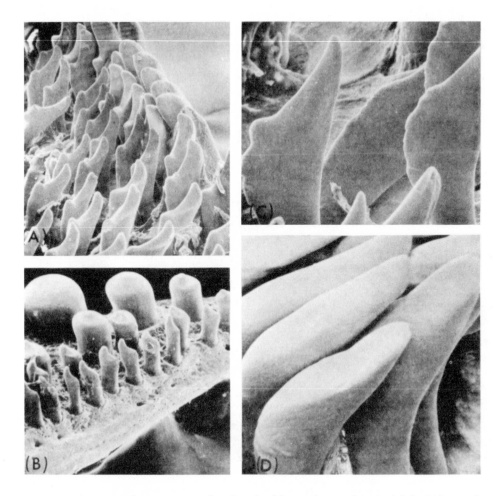

F<small>IG.</small> 15.—Scanning electron micrographs of teeth of lower pharyngeal jaws of Lake Malawi cichlids. A. *Corematodus taeniatus* (scale eater); B. *Haplochromis placodon* (mollusc eater); C. *Ramphochromis macrophthalmus* (fish eater); D. *Labeotropheus fuelleborni* (algae eater).

accentuate the ancestral condition by developing two "cusps" to enable the jaws to arrange the scales into packets so that they can be transported to the esophagus. An entirely different solution to the same problem is found in the Lake Tanganyika scale-eating species *Plecodus paradoxus* in which the dentition has been reduced to serve primarily as a transporting and manipulating system (Fig. 7).

Adaptive strategies of movements of upper pharyngeal jaws

Adaptive diversity is exhibited in the shape and size of the articular surfaces of the basipharyngeal joints (e.g., Fig. 13:AS). The movements in different adaptive types can be modified by varying not only the size of the articular surfaces but also the shape, i.e., elongate longitudinally or transversely, round or saddle-shaped. Natural selection has produced all possible types. In mollusc feeders, the hypertrophied pharyngeal apophysis also acts as a shock absorber (Greenwood, 1965). Variations in position of the basipharyngeal joints will result in significant changes of the moment arms of the levatores interni, levator posterior, and retractor pharyngeus superior muscles (Fig. 6:LI, LP, RP). All possible combinations between the position of the joint and insertion sites of the three muscles have been fully exploited during cichlid adaptive radiation.

Adaptive strategies of movements of lower pharyngeal jaw

The lower pharyngeal jaw varies in size and shape according to functional demands. Variations are also encountered in the size and shape of the muscular processes and in some cases new processes develop e.g., a special process for the insertion of the tendon of the pharyngohyoideus (Fig. 14:PH).

In several taxa, the lower pharyngeal jaw becomes firmly anchored to the cleithrum by a strong ligament (Fig. 14:L, CL, CB5). Such a fixation alters the biomechanical properties of the jaw significantly. The ligament in cooperation with some muscles may fix the lower pharyngeal jaw in such a way as to simulate a joint. With the appearance of this functional "joint" the lower pharyngeal jaw becomes a Class 1 lever. This specialization occurs in some of the taxa requiring a powerful "bite" during mastication.

Adaptive strategies of pharyngeal jaw muscles

The muscles operating the upper pharyngeal jaws do not change their relationships to each other, although coordinated shifts in relation to the basipharyngeal joint occur frequently. Both the fourth levator externus and the levator posterior vary in size but retain their long parallel fibered arrangement for which there is strong selection pressure because such an arrangement offers a longer range of movements than pinnate or shorter fibered muscles. In "hard-biting" taxa, the levator posterior is often subdivided into two heads, the anterolateral part having the original insertion on the fourth epibranchial and the posteromedial head inserted on the muscular process of the lower pharyngeal jaw (Fig. 16: LP, LPP).

Numerous functionally determined variations occur in relative numbers of fibers in all branchial muscles except the first three levatores externi.

Significant shifts occur in the position of muscles attaching to the lower pharyngeal jaw. The insertion of the pharyngocleithralis internus may shift posteriorly from a more cranial (Fig. 11:PHCI) to an intermediate (Fig. 5:PHCI) and finally to a more caudal position (Fig. 14:PHCI). The functional consequences are far-reaching: in the anterior position the muscle acts as

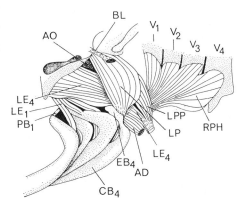

Fig. 16.—Lateral view of some branchial muscles in *Haplochromis vanderhorsti* (Luicha River, East Africa) after removal of lower pharyngeal jaw, which was attached to adductor (AD), fourth levator externus (LE4) and levator posterior (LP). AD, adductor; AO, adductor operculi; BL, Baudelot's ligament; CB4, fourth ceratobranchial; EB4, fourth epibranchial; LE4, fourth levator externus; LP, levator posterior; LPP, posteromedial head of levator posterior; PB1, first pharyngobranchial; RPH, retractor pharyngeus superior; V1–4, vertebrae.

an efficient abductor with a long power arm, whereas the posterior insertion reverses the function into an adductor of the lower pharyngeal jaw. It is important that the typical timing of activity of this muscle spanning both phase 1b and 2 (as revealed by electromyography in a generalized cichlid [Fig. 8:PHAR CL I]) is remarkably "preadapted" for this complete functional reversal. The evolutionary process has produced the best functional pattern to meet the demands of the specific trophic specialization in each taxon studied.

The insertion of the pharyngohyoideus also shifts from a more anterior (Figs. 5, 11:PH) to a more posterior site (Fig. 14: PH). Without electromyographic data it is premature to evaluate the adaptive significance of this change, but it is conceivable that a posterior insertion incorporates this muscle in the increasingly more important masticatory phase (1a).

The variations in the position of the pharyngocleithralis externus will alter the power arm and fiber length with subsequent changes in the range of movements.

The versatility of the pharyngeal jaw complex

It is clear from the above examples that

the functional integration of the cichlid pharyngeal jaw apparatus is so basic and its potential adaptive versatility so rich that it is maintained throughout the adaptive radiation even though numerous nondisruptive evolutionary changes do take place. Relatively simple, but seemingly endless, evolutionary variations on the basic "cichlid theme" provided prodigious opportunities for eruptive evolution during the exploitation of rich resources of food in the lacustrine environment. The noncichlid pharyngeal jaw apparatus, on the other hand, possesses very limited possibilities of adaptive expressions because its building blocks lack the necessary basic integration and versatility for evolving functional conversions by simple quantum shifts.

CONCLUSIONS AND GENERALIZATIONS

The cichlids possess a key prospective adaptive complex, i.e., the highly integrated pharyngeal jaw apparatus, which has given them a distinct selective advantage during the invasion and subsequent colonization of new lacustrine environments. The invading cichlids successfully occupy contiguous and occasionally overlapping adaptive zones and specialize progressively into diversified subzones, ramifying prodigiously and covering a breadth of total adaptation that would have been wholly unpredictable and incredible if we were aware only of the beginnings of the process. This extraordinary success can be attributed to a unique prospective adaptation of maximum potential with a wide range of prospective adaptive zones in the lakes. Ordinarily organisms do not undergo radiation until they possess prospective adaptations.

The preadaptive level of the evolutionary innovation is reflected in a rather advanced state in *Cichla*. The ancestral percoid pharyngeal jaw apparatus is a mechanism adapted purely for food transport with no provisions for extensive food manipulation, or preparation. Even when the fourth levator externus muscle made the all important shift of its insertion, the original deglutitionary function of the pharyngeal jaw apparatus was not changed. Once this morphological innovation had been established, however, the pharyngeal jaw apparatus became preadapted for a new function, i.e., food manipulation and preparation.

Under influence of new selection forces the novel adaptive complex acquired an extraordinarily distinctive biological role and the Cichlidae emerged as a new percoid family. The functional integration of the distinctive cichlid pharyngeal jaw complex seems so basic that it is rigidly maintained not only throughout the adaptive radiation but also in the many insectivorous *Haplochromis* species in which the fully specialized pharyngeal jaws function only for deglutition (Greenwood, personal communication). Among recent cichlids, only *Cichla* exhibits an intermediate level of integration, since its pharyngeal jaw apparatus seems to have somewhat limited capabilities for food manipulation and mastication, even though the rather weakly developed fourth levator externus has typical cichlid morphological characteristics. During adaptation, under control of the selection forces for food preparation and manipulation, the new adaptive complex is perfected (e.g., in many *Haplochromis* spp.) and becomes further specialized (e.g., in lacustrine cichlids). However, the original function of food transport is rigidly retained throughout the evolutionary process. This study supports Bock's theory (1959) that the emergence of most or all evolutionary novelties involves preadapted structures.

The crucial, primary morphological innovation in the development of the new adaptive type may have been the shift of insertion of the fourth levator externus muscle. As a response to this shift, secondary specializations, i.e., "fusion" of lower pharyngeal jaws and appearance of basipharyngeal joint, evolved. As discussed above the shift of the fourth levator externus can be accomplished by a very simple change in ontogenetic mechanism. Such a change requires a minor reconstruction of the genotype and will be under strong selection pressure. Although the saltationist theory as originally conceived by Goldschmidt (1940) must be rejected (cf. Simpson, 1953; Mayr, 1963), there is increasing experimental evidence that relatively simple genetic alterations could slightly affect the scheduling or velocity of ontogenetic events, which in turn are capable of producing adult phenotypic changes of rather profound but not monstrous dimensions (e.g., Waddington, 1962; Moss and Young, 1960; Hampé, 1959; Dubrul and Laskin, 1961; Klatt and Oboussier, 1951). Some recent proponents of the synthetic theory reject the possible occurrence of any saltatory changes, falsely maintaining that "saltationists" claim that the first bird quite literally hatched from a reptile egg and that the only way to achieve such a radical change is by polyploidy! A less extreme attitude toward some aspects of the saltationist theory may prove fruitful in our efforts to explain the evolutionary process by which new adaptive types emerge (cf. Frazzetta, 1970; Davis, 1949, 1964; Greenwood, 1973). Based on the data presented in this paper, I propose that the seemingly gradual emergence of the cichlid adaptive complex, i.e., shift of insertion of the fourth levator externus—development of basipharyngeal joint—"fusion" of lower pharyngeal jaws into one unit, took place by rapid saltatory steps under influence of strong selection pressure acting not on a single gene but on the minor reconstruction of the genotype which is involved in the necessary evolutionary changes of the controlling ontogenetic mechanisms. This hypothesis may apply to the evolution of almost all key innovations, and does not involve sudden, immense, "systemic mutations" producing "hopeful monsters" yet it does incorporate the wealth of ontogenetic raw materials on which natural selection can act as convincingly revealed by many experimental embryologists and morphologists.

ACKNOWLEDGMENTS

This project was supported by a generous grant from the John Simon Guggenheim Memorial Foundation, which enabled me to make extended visits to the British Museum (Natural History) and the University of Leiden (The Netherlands). I am extremely grateful to the Guggenheim Foundation for financial support, continuous encouragement and flexibility.

I am greatly indebted to many people whose active cooperation has made this work possible. A very special word of thanks goes to Dr. P. H. Greenwood (British Museum) and Prof. Dr. J. W. M. Osse (Agricultural University, Wageningen, The Netherlands, formerly at the University of Leiden) for their special personal interest, extraordinary hospitality, kindness, numerous extremely fruitful discussions and for the free use of their research collections, technical facilities and equipment, often at the expense of their own research. This study is an outgrowth of one year of association with them.

I have greatly benefited from the special skills of B. van Schie (Leiden), who produced the many special electronic accessories and played a key role in the experimental design, James Chambers (British Museum) and J. L. Williams (Field Museum of Natural History) who prepared numerous excellent skeletal preparations, Patricia Chaudhury (Harvard University) and Richard Roesener (Field Museum of Natural History) who prepared the illustrations, William M. Winn (University of Illinois) who produced the photographs and made valuable suggestions, and Gordon Howes (British Museum) who assisted me with many taxonomic questions and rendered numerous personal favours. I am also indebted to G. Blokzijl (University of Groningen, The Netherlands) for the generous gift of live cichlids, to David Eccles (Fisheries Research Unit, Malawi) for collecting, identifying and preparing the Lake Malawi cichlids and to Dr. G. Alan Solem (Field Museum of Natural History) for the production and assistance in the interpretation of the Scanning Electron Micrographs, which have been made at the American Dental Association in Chicago. I would also like to express my deep appreciation to Prof. Dr. P. Dullemeijer (University of Leiden) who has continuously and unselfishly supported this project and has provided inspiring leadership to the entire staff during my stay in his department. The William F. Milton Fund of Harvard University provided funds for the preparation of the illustrations. The manuscript was read and improved by Drs. P. H. Greenwood and Stephen Jay Gould.

REFERENCES

Bock, W. J. 1959. Preadaptation and multiple evolutionary pathways. Evolution 13:194–211.

Bock, W. J. 1965. The role of adaptive mechanism in the origin of higher levels of organization. Syst. Zool. 14:272–287.

Chardon, M., and P. Vandewalle. 1971. Comparaison de la région céphalique chez cinq espèces du genre Tilapia, dont trois incubateurs buccaux. Ann. soc. roy. zool. Belge 101:3–24.

DuBrul, E. L., and D. M. Laskin. 1961. Preadaptive potentialities of the mammalian skull: an experiment in growth and form. Amer. J. Anat. 109:117–132.

DAVIS, D. D. 1949. Comparative anatomy and the evolution of vertebrates. In Genetics, Paleontology and Evolution. Ed. G. L. Jepsen, G. G. Simpson and E. Mayr. pp. 64–89. Princeton.

DAVIS, D. D. 1964. The Giant Panda: a morphological study of evolutionary mechanisms. Fieldiana: Zool. Mem. 3:1–339.

EDGEWORTH, F. H. 1935. The cranial muscles of vertebrates. Cambridge, England. 493 pp.

FRAZZETTA, T. H. 1970. From hopeful monsters to Bolyerine snakes? Amer. Nat. 104:55–72.

FRYER, G., AND T. D. ILES. 1972. The cichlid fishes of the great lakes of Africa. Oliver and Boyd, Edinburgh. 641 pp.

GOLDSCHMIDT, R. 1940. The material basis of evolution. Yale Univ. Press, New Haven. 436 pp.

GREENWOOD, P. H. 1964. Explosive speciation in African lakes. Proc. R. Inst. Gt. Br. 40:256–269.

GREENWOOD, P. H. 1965. Environmental effects on the pharyngeal mill of a cichlid fish, Astatoreochromis alluaudi, and their taxonomic implications. Proc. Linn. Soc. Lond. 176:1–10.

GREENWOOD, P. H. 1973. Morphology, endemism and speciation in African cichlid fishes. Verh. Deutsch. Zool. Gesellsch. 1973:115–124.

HAMPÉ, A. 1959. Contribution à l'étude du développement et de la régulation des déficiences et des excédents dans la pâtte de l'embryon de poulet. Arch. Anat. Microsc. Morphol. Exp. 48:347–478.

KLATT, B., AND H. OBOUSSIER. 1951. Weitere Untersuchungen zur Frage der quantitativen Verschiedenheiten gegensatzlichen Wuchsformtypen beim Hund. Zool. Anz. 146:223–240.

LIEM, K. F. 1970. Comparative functional anatomy of the Nandidae (Pisces: Teleostei). Fieldiana: Zool. 56:1–166.

MAYR, E. 1960. The emergence of evolutionary novelties. In The Evolution of Life. Ed. S. Tax. pp. 349–380. Univ. Chicago Press, Chicago.

MAYR, E. 1963. Animal species and evolution. Harvard Univ. Press, Cambridge. 797 pp.

MILLER, A. H. 1949. Some ecological and morphological considerations in the evolution of higher taxonomic categories. In Ornithologie als biologische Wissenschaft. Ed. E. Mayr and E. Schuz. pp. 84–88. Carl Winter, Heidelberg.

MOSS, M. L., AND R. W. YOUNG. 1960. A functional approach to craniology. Am. J. Phys. Anthrop. 18:281–292.

MURRAY, P. D. F. 1937. Bones. Cambridge, England. 203 pp.

NEWSOME, Y. L. 1971. Comparative osteology and relationships of neotropical cichlid fishes. Ph. D. Thesis, University of Illinois, Dept. Anatomy, Chicago, Ill.

OSSE, J. W. M. 1969. Functional morphology of the head of the perch (Perca fluviatilis L.): An electromyographic study. Netherlands J. Zool. 19:289–392.

OSSE, J. W. M., M. OLDENHAVE, AND B. VAN SCHIE. 1972. A new method for insertion of wire electrodes in electromyography. Electromyography 12:59–62.

ROSEN, D. E., AND C. PATTERSON. 1969. The structure and relationships of the paracanthopterygian fishes. Bull. Am. Mus. Nat. Hist. 141:359–474.

SCHAEFFER, B. 1965. The role of experimentation in the origin of higher levels of organization. Syst. Zool. 14:318–336.

SIMPSON, G. G. 1953. The major features of evolution. Columbia University Press, New York. 434 pp.

TREWAVAS, E., J. GREEN, AND S. A. CORBET. 1972. Ecological studies on crater lakes in West Cameroon Fishes of Barombi Mbo. J. Zool. Lond. 167:41–95.

WADDINGTON, C. H. 1962. New patterns in genetics and development. Columbia University Press, New York. 271 pp.

VANDEN BERGHE, L. 1928. Recherches sur la déglutition chez les poissons téléostéens. Bull. Acad. Roy. Belgique, Cl. Sci. 14:322–332.

VANDEWALLE, P. 1971. Comparaison ostéologique et myologique de cinq Cichlidae Africains et Sud-Américains. Ann. soc. roy. zool. Belge 101:259–292.

VANDEWALLE, P. 1972. Ostéologie et myologie de la tête de Tilapia guineensis Bleeker (Pisces, Cichlidae). Ann. Mus. Roy. Afr. Centr., Sc. Zool. 196:1–50.

AN INVERSE CORRELATION BETWEEN MERISTIC CHARACTERS
AND FOOD SUPPLY IN MID-WATER FISHES:
EVIDENCE AND POSSIBLE EXPLANATIONS

Robert Karl Johnson[1] and Michael A. Barnett[2]

ABSTRACT

In five species of mid-water fishes, *Chauliodus sloani*, *Diplophos taenia*, *Pollichthys mauli*, *Vinciguerria lucetia*, and *V. nimbaria*, the central values of meristic counts (anal fin rays, vertebrae, longitudinal photophore rows) and three measures of biological productivity (phosphate-phosphorus concentration, net primary production, zooplankton standing stocks) are correlated negatively. For the species and areas studied the meristic variation observed cannot be related to temperature, salinity, dissolved oxygen, or any other physical or chemical factor known to affect meristic variation in fishes. It is hypothesized that this relationship between meristic counts and measures of food availability involves differences in egg size, fecundity, size at hatching, and size at comparable stages of larval development between populations in different areas, and that these differences in turn reflect adaptations to low food densities in areas of low productivity and higher predator densities in areas of higher productivity.

Meristic characters have been widely used in studies of fish populations and species. Unlike body proportions or coloration, meristic characters are fixed usually at or before metamorphosis and remain constant throughout the life of an individual. Variation in meristic characters stems from both genetic variation between populations and species, and from environmental variation, which, within genetically controlled limits, can directly affect the number of parts formed in developing embryos and larvae. Recent reviews of factors known to affect meristic characters in fishes include Barlow (1961), Blaxter (1969), Garside (1966), and Fowler (1970).

An inverse relationship between vertebral and/or other meristic counts and water temperature at the time of early development has been demonstrated in numerous studies (see above review articles). Experimental studies have shown that in many cases the effect of temperature upon meristic characters occurs within a restricted period of time, the so-called sensitive period, and that variations in temperature before and after this period have no effect (Hempel and Blaxter 1961). The sensitive period may vary with different structures with the result that the timing, magnitude, and in some cases the direction of response of different structures to temperature variation differs among different species (Fowler 1970).

Hubbs (1926), Barlow (1961), and others, have suggested that the relationship between meristic counts and temperature involves differential effects of temperature on rate of growth versus rate of differentiation, with the result that accelerated growth is associated with a shortening of the sensitive period, resulting in the laying down of fewer parts. The conclusion is that conditions retarding growth rates are associated with elevated meristic counts, conditions accelerating growth rates are associated with lowered meristic counts. This explanation has been extended to factors other than temperature known to affect meristic characters in fishes: dissolved oxygen concentration (Alderice et al. 1958), salinity (Forrester and Alderdice 1966; Blackburn 1967), carbon dioxide concentration, light intensity, exposure to X-rays, etc. (see Fowler 1970).

In 1972, we reported a significant negative correlation between certain meristic counts in *Diplophos taenia* and three measures of food supply: net primary production, phosphate-phosphorus concentration, and zooplankton standing stocks (Johnson and Barnett 1972). To our knowledge, this was the first suggestion of a possible relationship between meristic counts and measures of food supply. We did not offer any explanation for this relationship in the earlier report. In the present paper we extend our information on *D. taenia* to the Atlantic Ocean, present corroborative evidence for the relationship between meristic counts and food supply based on four other species of mid-water fishes, and attempt to show that the relationship for the species and areas studied is with food supply and not temperature, salinity, or dissolved oxygen. We hypothesize that this relationship between meristic counts and food supply reflects differences in egg size, fecundity, size at hatching, and size at comparable stages of larval development between populations in different areas, and that these differences represent adaptations to low food densities in areas of low productivity and higher predator densities in areas of higher productivity.

[1]Division of Fishes, Field Museum of Natural History, Roosevelt Road at Lake Shore Drive, Chicago, IL 60605.
[2]Scripps Institution of Oceanography, University of California, San Diego, La Jolla, CA 92037.

From *Fish. Bull., U.S.* 73(2):284–298. Reprinted by permission.

METHODS

Collection and Analysis of Data

Methods of taking counts follow those of Grey (1964), Morrow (1964), and Johnson (1970). Photophore rows in a generalized stomiatoid fish are illustrated in Morrow (1964: Figure 73), but our nomenclature for segments of photophore rows follows that of Johnson (1970). All vertebral centra were counted including the compound element supporting the parhypural and hypurals (Weitzman 1967). Standard statistical texts have been used as reference material (especially Tate and Clelland 1957; Sokal and Rohlf 1969). Agreement between sets of ranks is assessed via the tau coefficient of correlation or Kendall's coefficient of concordance, W (see Tate and Clelland 1957).

Localities Studied

We have studied specimens from eight areas (Figure 1): 1) the eastern tropical Pacific (ETP) off Mexico; 2) the central North Pacific (CNP) off the Hawaiian Islands; 3) the central equatorial Pacific (CEP) at long. 145° to 150°W; 4) the western equatorial Pacific (WEP) around long. 170°E; 5) the Philippine Sea (PS); 6) the South China Sea (SCS); 7) the Gulf of Guinea (GG); and 8) the central North Atlantic (CNA) including the Sargasso Sea. All of these areas are tropical oceanic habitats and represent a wide range of physical and biological features.

Measures of Biological Productivity

The measures used to assess relative richness of food supply are phosphate-phosphorus concentration, net primary production, and zooplankton standing stocks. These three variables are highly intercorrelated (Cushing 1971). These measures were chosen because there are published attempts at contouring values of these variables on an oceanwide basis and because values for them are commonly reported in more regionally oriented studies.

Despite many problems in both sampling and interpretation associated with attempts to contour values of biological variables on an oceanwide basis and to integrate values based on a limited number of measurements over a full year, we were forced to accept such attempts as the principal basis for ranking our eight study areas with respect to the three measures of food supply. Where possible we relied on synoptic studies presenting contours on an oceanwide basis: net primary production (as mg-C/m² per day, Koblentz-Mishke et al. 1970; as g-C/m² per year, Ebeling 1962 based on Fleming and Laevastu 1956), zooplankton concentration (as parts/10⁹ by volume in the upper 150 m of the Pacific Ocean, Reid 1962), and phosphate-phosphorus concentration (as μg-

TABLE 1.—Computation of rank-sum index of productivity. This table was produced by reproducing the contours or values presented by each of the authors cited in the text for each of the three measures of productivity—net primary production (NET), zooplankton concentration (ZOO), and phosphate phosphorus concentration (PO_4-P)—within the geographic limits of each of the eight areas and then ranking the eight areas with respect to one another for each measure.

Area	NET rank	ZOO rank	PO_4-P rank	Sum of ranks	Rank-sum
ETP	1	1	1	3	1
GG	2.5	3.5	2	8	2
SCS	2.5	¹3.5	4.5	10.5	3
CEP	4	5	3	12	4
WEP	7	2	4.5	13.5	5
PS	5	6	7.5	18.5	6
CNA	6	7	6	19	7
CNP	8	8	7.5	23.5	8
		$W_{3,8} = 0.85$, $P < 0.01$			

¹Data from Brinton (pers. commun.)

at/liter contoured at 100 m in the Pacific Ocean, Reid 1962). Where these studies did not cover several of our study areas, we used regional studies (SCS: Angot, Steemann Nielsen in Wyrtki 1961; Sorokin 1973; GG: Raymont 1963, Corcoran and Mahnken 1969, Kinzer 1969, Zeitschel 1969, Riley 1972; CNA: Menzel and Ryther 1961, Raymont 1963, Corcoran and Mahnken 1969, Zeitschel 1969, Riley 1972).

We compared the contours or values for each of the three measures of productivity over all eight study areas and then ranked the eight areas with respect to each other for each measure (Table 1). As expected (Cushing 1971), the ranks for the three measures over the eight areas are highly concordant ($W_{3,8} = 0.85$, $P < 0.01$, concordance coefficient corrected for ties, see Tate and Clelland 1957). This highly significant concordance increases our confidence in this approach to ranking the eight areas with respect to productivity and allows summation of the ranks of the three measures of food supply over each area, yielding a rank-sum. We then ranked this rank-sum and obtained the following rank-index order of productivity, from highest to lowest: 1) eastern tropical Pacific, 2) Gulf of Guinea, 3) South China Sea, 4) central equatorial Pacific, 5) western equatorial Pacific, 6) Philippine Sea, 7) central North Atlantic, and 8) central North Pacific. In establishing the relationship between meristic counts and productivity we have compared central values of meristic counts with this rank-index value for productivity.

RESULTS

Diplophos taenia Günther

Diplophos taenia, a circumtropical mesopelagic gonostomatid, is the only species included in this study to occur in all eight study areas. Results for counts of anal fin rays, LLP photophores, and IPVALA photophores are illustrated in Figure 2.

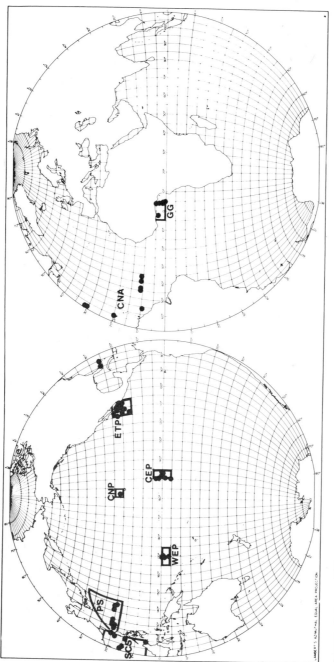

FIGURE 1.—Study areas: ETP = eastern tropical Pacific; CEP = central equatorial Pacific; CNP = central North Pacific; WEP = western equatorial Pacific; PS = Philippine Sea; SCS = South China Sea; GG = Gulf of Guinea; CNA = central North Atlantic. Localities for *Diplophos taenia* indicated by closed circles. Localities for other species were within boundaries of study areas as indicated except that all specimens of *Vinciguerria nimbaria* from the central North Atlantic were from the Ocean Acre area near lat. 32° to 33°N, long. 64°W.

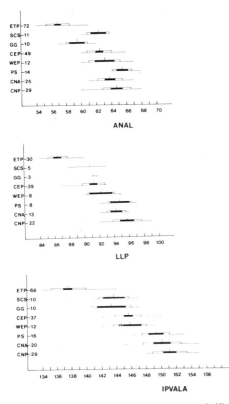

FIGURE 2.–*Diplophos taenia*. Comparison of mean (vertical line), 95% confidence limits for the mean (closed bar), one standard deviation on either side of the mean (open bar plus closed bar), and range (horizontal line) for anal fin rays (top), LLP photophores (middle), and IPVALA photophores (bottom) for specimens from eight study areas (Figure 1). Numbers on ordinate are number of specimens examined.

TABLE 2.–Agreement between segments of IC row of photophores in *Diplophos taenia*. Values are given as mean)rank. Number of specimens (*n*) is given for counts of IP and represent the minimum number of specimens counted for each character for each area.

Area	*n*	IP	PV	VAV	AC	Sum of ranks
ETP	74	15.7)8	24.9)8	15.1)8	42.0)8	32
GG	10	16.6)6	27.1)2.5	15.9)5	42.9)7	20.5
SCS	10	16.4)7	25.6)7	16.0)4	44.7)6	24
CEP	50	16.9)5	26.2)6	15.8)6	45.18)4	21
WEP	12	17.0)4	26.4)5	15.7)7	45.17)5	21
PS	18	17.1)3	26.9)4	16.3)2	46.67)3	12
CNA	25	17.4)1	27.5)1	16.2)3	46.72)2	7
CNP	29	17.3)2	27.1)2.5	16.6)1	47.5)1	6.5

$$W_{4,8} = 0.812, P < 0.01$$

In nearly all cases counts are highest in areas of lowest productivity, lowest in areas of highest productivity, and intermediate in areas of intermediate productivity. Agreement between mean

TABLE 3.–*Diplophos taenia*, computation of rank-sum index of meristic counts and comparison with rank-sum index of productivity (from Table 1). Values are given as mean (number of specimens).

	Anal fin		LLP		IPVALA		Sum of	Rank-	Productivity
Area	Mean	Rank	Mean	Rank	Mean	Rank	ranks	sum	rank-sum
ETP	57.0	8	86.5	8	137.5	8	24	8	1
	(72)		(30)		(68)				
GG	59.5	7	91.3	5	143.3	7	19	6.5	2
	(10)		(5)		(10)				
SCS	62.3	6	90.8	7	143.6	6	19	6.5	3
	(11)		(3)		(10)				
CEP	62.4	5	91.2	6	145.54	5	16	5	4
	(49)		(39)		(37)				
WEP	63.2	4	92.2	4	145.75	4	12	4	5
	(12)		(8)		(12)				
PS	65.4	1	94.8	2	149.2	3	6	2	6
	(14)		(8)		(16)				
CNA	63.8	3	94.2	3	150.2	2	8	3	7
	(25)		(13)		(20)				
CNP	64.7	2	95.7	1	151.7	1	4	1	8
	(29)		(22)		(29)				

$$W_{3,8} = 0.942, P < 0.01 \qquad Tau_8 = -0.893, P < 0.01$$

TABLE 4.–*Diplophos taenia*. Comparison of rank-sum index of meristic counts (from Table 3) with temperature at 100 m ranked over the six Pacific areas. Temperature data taken from Brinton (1962).

	Rank	
Area	Counts	Temperature
CNP	1	5
PS	2	3.5
WEP	3	1
CEP	4	2
SCS	5	3.5
ETP	6	6

$$Tau_6 = +0.13, P > 0.20$$

values for photophore row segments in terms of rank order by area, e.g. all four segments in the IC row, is highly significant ($W_{4,8} = 0.81$, $P < 0.01$, Table 2), as is the agreement between mean values for anal fin rays, LLP photophores, and IPVALA photophores ($W_{3,8} = 0.94$, $P < 0.01$, Table 3). This concordance allows computation of a rank-sum index of mean values of meristic counts (Table 3).

There exists no significant correlation between the observed meristic variation and temperature over the six Pacific areas ($tau_6 = 0.13$, $P > 0.20$, Table 4). Temperature data was taken from a chart of temperature at 100 m in the Pacific Ocean given by Brinton (1962). The 100-m depth was chosen arbitrarily, but the conclusion holds if surface temperatures, whether summer or winter, are chosen. Meristic counts for *D. taenia* are lowest in specimens from the eastern tropical Pacific where temperature values are also the lowest. This is exactly opposite to the result expected if temperature were involved in determining the meristic variation observed over the six areas. In fact the data show no relationship between meristic counts and temperature for these areas. Values of salinity in the open ocean are far too conservative to be involved in determining the observed variation (Hubbs 1925; Sverdrup et al. 1942; Barlow 1961; Blackburn 1967). Although the eastern tropical Pacific is well known for a marked oxygen minimum layer (Brandhorst 1959), and oxygen concentration variation may affect the development of meristic characters (Alderdice et al. 1958; Garside 1959, 1966), in all eight areas oxygen is essentially saturated in the wind-mixed surface layer where the larvae and probably the eggs of *D. taenia* occur. The low counts (relative to other areas) of specimens of *D. taenia* from the eastern tropical Pacific run counter to what might be expected if dissolved oxygen concentrations were involved in determining the observed meristic variation.

The rank-sum indices of meristic counts and productivity are significantly and negatively correlated (tau_8 = -0.893, $P < 0.01$, Table 3).

Pollichthys mauli (Poll)

Pollichthys mauli ranges from the western North Atlantic to the Philippine Sea. We have examined specimens of this species from the Gulf of Guinea, and the Philippine and South China seas. Results for IPVALA photophore counts (Table 5) parallel the results for *Diplophos taenia;* the counts from Philippine Sea specimens are significantly higher than counts from specimens from the South China Sea and Gulf of Guinea.

TABLE 5.—*Pollichthys mauli*, IPVALA photophores.

Area	68	69	70	71	72	73	74	75	76	77	78	n	Mean ± 95% limits
GG	1	7	5	6	1	4	—	—	—	—	—	24	70.46 ± 0.635
SCS	—	—	1	7	2	1	—	—	—	—	—	11	71.27 ± 0.528
PS	—	—	—	—	—	1	1	3	2	1	2	10	75.70 ± 1.170

Vinciguerria lucetia Garman

Vinciguerria lucetia is endemic to the eastern Pacific (Ahlstrom and Counts 1958; Craddock and Mead 1970; Gorbunova 1972). The work of Ahlstrom and Counts (1958) has made the early life history of *V. lucetia* the best known of any of the species included in this report. We have not examined any specimens of *V. lucetia* in connection with this work, but the following results of the study of this species by Ahlstrom and Counts (1958) seem to be particularly relevant to this paper: 1) In *V. lucetia* the total number of myotomes is formed in late-stage eggs, prior to hatching. 2) Metamorphosis in *V. lucetia* is marked by a period of rapid change in body proportions without a marked change in standard length. The completion of metamorphosis is signaled by the complete development of all photophores, including the late-forming photophores of the posterior VAV and mid-AC segments. 3) Metamorphosis occurs at a smaller size south of

lat. 25°N than north of lat. 27.5°N, with metamorphosis at an intermediate size in specimens from lat. 25° to 27.5°N. Mean values of vertebral and IPVALA counts are lowest in specimens taken from areas where metamorphosis occurs at a smaller size. A delay in vertebral ossification is found in specimens from areas where metamorphosis occurs at a larger size. 4) Ahlstrom and Counts (1958) report a north to south cline in mean values for IPVALA photophore counts and relate this to temperature. An east to west cline is also suggested by their data (Figure 3), with mean IPVALA counts lowest near the American continent and increasing with distance offshore. Values for productivity measures in the eastern tropical Pacific tend to fall off with increasing distance from land (Reid 1962; Koblentz-Mishke et al. 1970). If variation in photophore numbers in *V. lucetia* is related to variation in productivity, we would expect mean IPVALA counts at a given latitude to be lower near the continent and higher with increasing distance from land. Data from Ahlstrom and Counts (1958) confirm this expectation (Figure 3) for all but two latitudinal transects. Along these two transects, one just to the north of the equator, the second centered at about lat. 12°N, mean values obtained for IPVALA counts do not change or actually decrease to the westward, an apparent contradiction of our hypothesis. However, these two zonal transects fall along zonal areas of high or elevated productivity far to the westward of the American continent, and this is true for net primary production, zooplankton standing stocks, or, as illustrated (Figure 3), phosphate-phosphorus concentration. Williams (1972) relates these zonal belts of elevated productivity to the divergence systems at the equator and at the North Equatorial Countercurrent-North Equatorial Current boundary. Williams (1972) states that the zonal band at lat. 10° to 12°N is best shown by data for zooplankton stocks, but we note that this band is quite apparent for phosphate-phosphorus concentration (Reid 1962). Thus the apparently discrepant values of mean IPVALA counts from specimens of *V. lucetia* taken along these two zonal transects in fact tend to further corroborate the hypothesized inverse relationship between meristic counts and productivity.

Vinciguerria nimbaria (Jordan and Williams)

Vinciguerria nimbaria is nearly circumtropical in distribution but does not occur in the Mediterranean Sea nor in the eastern tropical Pacific (Ahlstrom and Counts 1958; Craddock and Mead 1970; Gorbunova 1972). The development of larvae of *V. nimbaria* is apparently quite similar to the development of larvae of *V. lucetia* (Ahlstrom and Counts 1958; Silas and George 1971). We have

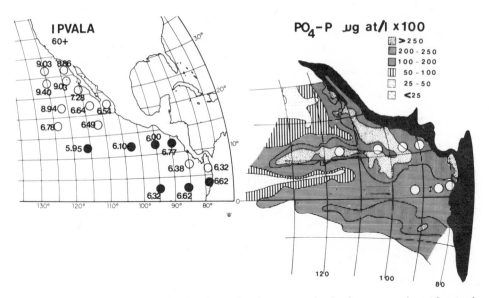

FIGURE 3.—*Vinciguerria lucetia.* Left: IPVALA photophores; values given are means based on five or more specimens taken at each locality (see text for additional explanation, data from Ahlstrom and Counts 1958). Right: phosphate phosphorus data simplified from Reid (1962).

examined specimens of *V. nimbaria* from all of our study areas except the eastern tropical Pacific (where *V.nimbaria* is replaced by *V. lucetia*) and the western equatorial Pacific (no material available).

Counts of IPVALA photophores for specimens of *V. nimbaria* are given in Table 6. Mean values for specimens from the South China Sea, central equatorial Pacific, Philippine Sea, central North Atlantic, and central North Pacific agree in perfect rank-order with the rank-sum index of meristic counts for specimens of *Diplophos taenia* from these five areas (Table 3). The mean value of counts of IPVALA photophores of Gulf of Guinea specimens does not fit this trend, it is too high. All of our material of *V. nimbaria* from the Gulf of Guinea came from a single collection at the University of Miami (UMML 21902, lat. 0°54' to 1°05'N, long. 4°53' to 4°51'E, 23-24 May 1965). We have neither additional material of nor information on *V. nimbaria* from the Gulf of Guinea, and, for the present, we are unable to explain these anomalous results.

The values obtained for specimens of *V. nimbaria* from other study areas support our hypothesis of an inverse relationship between meristic counts and productivity. This is true for both IPVALA photophore (Table 6) and vertebral (Table 7) counts.

Counts for Arabian Sea (AS, Table 6) specimens of *V. nimbaria* are taken from Silas and George (1971). They studied specimens taken off the Malabar Coast of India and found larvae of *V. nimbaria* to be most abundant along the edge of the continental shelf from Mangalore to south of Cochin. Cushing (1971) discusses the strong upwelling system occurring along this coast during the period of the Northeast Monsoon, and notes that high values of productivity occur in this area over at least half of the year and are associated with the upwelling system. Silas and George (1971) found *V. nimbaria* larvae to be most abundant during the upwelling season. Values for productivity measures in this area given by Cushing (1971) approach values for the eastern tropical Pacific, are certainly larger than values for the

TABLE 6.—*Vinciguerria nimbaria.* IPVALA photophore counts. AS = study area of Silas and George (1971) along Malabar Coast of India in the Arabian Sea, data taken from their study. Counts presented as the average between right and left sizes of each specimen.

Area	64	64.5	65	65.5	66	66.5	67	67.5	68	68.5	69	69.5	70	70.5	71	71.5	72	72.5	73	n	Mean ± 95% limits
AS	2	1	1	1	2	—	1	—	1	—	—	—	—	—	—	—	—	—	—	9	65.56 ± 1.023
GG	—	—	—	—	—	—	—	—	—	—	2	2	5	2	7	1	1	—	—	20	70.43 ± 0.380
SCS	—	—	2	1	10	4	2	1	4	—	—	—	—	—	—	—	—	—	—	24	66.46 ± 0.378
CEP	—	—	—	—	2	2	1	2	14	6	4	1	—	—	—	—	—	—	—	32	67.98 ± 0.302
PS	—	—	—	—	1	2	1	4	24	26	20	37	83	36	16	4	2	1	—	257	69.60 ± 0.126
CNA	—	—	—	—	—	—	1	—	1	2	1	4	2	1	—	—	—	—	—	12	69.12 ± 0.623
CNP	—	—	—	—	—	—	—	—	—	—	—	3	18	15	5	1	1	—	—	43	70.34 ± 0.157

TABLE 7.—*Vinciguerria nimbaria*, vertebrae.

Area	39	40	41	42	n	Mean ± 95% limits
SCS	6	5	—	—	11	39.45 ± 0.351
CEP	1	23	7	—	31	40.19 ± 0.175
PS	—	3	12	8	23	41.22 ± 0.290
CNP	—	—	6	21	27	41.78 ± 0.168

Philippine Sea, central North Atlantic, and central North Pacific, and probably significantly larger than values for the central equatorial Pacific and South China Sea. We therefore expected values for meristic counts of specimens of *V. nimbaria* from off the Mangalore Coast to be the lowest of any of these six areas. They are (Table 6).

Chauliodus sloani Bloch and Schneider

Chauliodus sloani occurs in tropical and temperate waters from the North Atlantic to the eastern Pacific, although throughout large oceanic areas it is replaced by other species of *Chauliodus*. The remaining six species of *Chauliodus*, including the recently described *C. vasnetzovi* Novikova, are limited to smaller areas, each entirely within one ocean basin (Morrow 1961; Gibbs and Hurwitz 1967; Novikova 1972).

We have examined specimens of *C. sloani* only from our Philippine Sea and central North Pacific study areas, but data from other sources (Ege 1948; Blache 1964; Gibbs and Hurwitz 1967) have made it possible to compare our results for *C. sloani* with counts for this species from other areas, and with counts for the closely related species *C. pammelas* Alcock and *C. schmidti* Ege (Table 8). IC photophore counts of *C. sloani* from central gyral areas (CNP, CNA, PS) are higher than counts from specimens taken in the South China Sea. This agrees with results for other species discussed in this paper.

The only character diagnostically separating *C. schmidti* from *C. sloani* is the lower number of serial photophores in *C. schmidti* (Morrow 1961; Blache 1964). Similarly Gibbs and Hurwitz (1967) concluded that the only characters separating *C. pammelas* from *C. sloani* were lower meristic counts (IC, VAV, vertebrae) in *C. pammelas* and greater development of the gill filaments in *C. pammelas*, with filaments both longer and with a

greater number of lamellae per side. Gibbs and Hurwitz (1967) noted that the greater gill filament development of *C. pammelas* is correlated with a well-marked oxygen minimum layer in the northern Indian Ocean habitat of this species. Gill filament length may vary intraspecifically in some wide-ranging mid-water fish species (Johnson 1974).

Both *C. schmidti*, inhabiting the eastern tropical Atlantic, and *C. pammelas*, inhabiting the northern Indian Ocean, are limited to areas of high biological productivity (Ryther and Menzel 1965; Gibbs and Hurwitz 1967; Cushing 1971). Both are distinguished from *C. sloani* by lower counts of serial photophores (and vertebrae in *C. pammelas*), and essentially only by these lower counts. In both cases the lower counts apparently agree with our hypothesized relationship between meristic counts and productivity. The counts for *C. schmidti* are from specimens taken in two areas: TAA, along the west African coast from lat. 03°56′ to 18°22′N, to the west and north of our Gulf of Guinea study area; and TAB, along the west African coast from lat. 01°20′ to 17°53′S, to the south of our Gulf of Guinea study area (Ege 1948; Blache 1964). The counts for *C. pammelas* are from specimens taken between lat. 08° and 14°N, long. 58° to 66°E, in the Arabian Sea (Gibbs and Hurwitz 1967).

In view of other results presented in this paper, particularly those for *Diplophos taenia*, we suggest that a reexamination of the status of both *C. pammelas* and *C. schmidti*, with additional study of meristic variation in *C. sloani* throughout the range of this species, are in order.

Results of the Antipodes Transect

An essentially experimental opportunity to test the hypothesized relationship between meristic counts and productivity was afforded by fishes taken by the Antipodes Expedition of the Scripps Institution of Oceanography in 1970. On this expedition 22 mid-water trawl collections were taken in the Philippine Sea and six mid-water trawl collections were taken in the South China Sea (Figure 4). Because of the 2,000 m or more sill depth separating these geographically contiguous areas, the upper water mass in both areas is the

TABLE 8.—IC photophore variation in three species of *Chauliodus*. (NIO, northern Indian Ocean, TAA, TAB, areas of eastern tropical Atlantic discussed in text).

Species	Area	58	59	60	61	62	63	64	65	66	67	68	69	n	Mean ± 95% limits
C. pammelas[1]	NIO	1	4	12	4	—	—	—	—	—	—	—	—	21	59.90 ± 0.350
C. schmidti[1]	TAA	—	—	1	7	32	14	—	—	—	—	—	—	54	62.09 ± 0.186
C. schmidti[2]	TAB	—	—	3	16	14	7	5	—	—	—	—	—	45	62.89 ± 0.335
C. sloani[3]	SCS	—	—	—	—	1	16	69	91	25	2	—	—	204	64.32 ± 0.117
C. sloani	PS	—	—	—	—	—	—	—	3	2	4	4	—	13	66.69 ± 0.714
C. sloani[3]	CNA	—	—	—	—	—	—	—	—	3	6	3	1	13	67.15 ± 0.543
C. sloani	CNP	—	—	—	—	—	—	—	2	9	7	2	—	20	66.45 ± 0.386

[1]Gibbs and Hurwitz 1967.
[2]Blache 1964.
[3]Ege 1948.

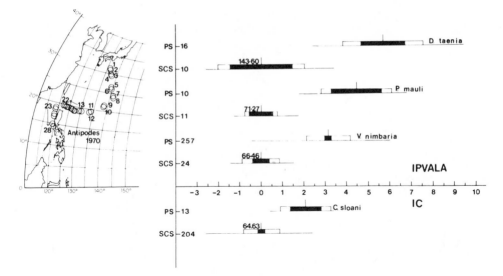

FIGURE 4.—Left: Antipodes Expedition station positions. Right: Comparison of IPVALA and IC photophore counts between specimens from South China Sea (SCS) and Philippine Sea (PS). Data presented as in Figure 2 except that mean values for South China Sea material of all four species have been set equal to zero and all other statistics are plotted as deviations from this zero point. Data for *Chauliodus sloani* from SCS are from Ege (1948); the rest is original data.

same and differences in physical parameters are minimal. Although the South China Sea is poorly known, there is little doubt that at least nearshore areas or areas over shelves of the South China Sea are substantially more productive than offshore areas in the Philippine Sea (Wyrtki, 1961; Sorokin 1973).

We predicted: 1) that values of meristic counts for species occurring in both the South China Sea and Philippine Sea would be lower in specimens from the South China Sea, and 2) that values of meristic counts for species occurring in the Philippine Sea would be lower in specimens taken near land and increase with increasing distance from shore.

In all four cases thus far examined (Figure 4) where differences exist in values of meristic counts from the two areas, the counts are significantly lower in specimens from the South China Sea. This supports our first prediction.

Vinciguerria nimbaria was the only species taken in sufficient abundance to allow a test of our second prediction. In Table 9 mean IPVALA counts for Philippine Sea specimens of *V. nimbaria* are tested for relationship with distance of site of collection from land (Japan, Ryukyu Islands, Luzon, but not Bonin or Volcano islands). While the highest mean counts were found in specimens from the 4 stations most distant from land, the data show no relationship between mean counts and distance from land (tau$_{11}$ = -0.273, $P > 0.20$). Mean IPVALA values for specimens from each of the 11 pairs of Philippine Sea stations are significantly higher than the mean IPVALA values for specimens from the South China Sea.

DISCUSSION

One fact and two assumptions are prerequisite to our discussion of the possible explanations for the relationship between meristic counts and measures of food supply. The fact: in *Diplophos taenia*, *Vinciguerria lucetia*, and *V. nimbaria*, the values of the meristic characters we have studied are fixed at or before metamorphosis (Ahlstrom, pers. commun., Ahlstrom and Counts 1958, Silas and George 1971). This is probably also true for *Pollichthys mauli* and *Chauliodus sloani*. This means that any explanation involves factors operating on eggs and/or larvae. The assumptions: 1) that the meristic variation observed is not the result of selection for certain absolute values of the meristic counts, and 2) that the same basic mechanism underlies the variation in counts for all five species in the area studied (in this discussion we ignore results for specimens of *V. nimbaria* from the Gulf of Guinea).

There are four possibilities: 1) that the observed variation is ecophenotypic, i.e. nongenetic modification of the phenotype resulting from the effects of differing food availability conditions upon early growth and development of meristic characters; 2) that the observed variation is a by-product and indicative of genetic differences between populations in these eight areas, and that these differences reflect differing selective pressures resulting from differing conditions for early growth; 3) that the observed variation is a combination of ecophenotypy and genetic differences; and 4) that the real explanation is none of these, that a causal relationship between meristic

TABLE 9.–IPVALA photophore counts of *Vinciguerria nimbaria* from the Philippine and South China seas. Antipodes station positions given in Figure 4. Distance from shore (Philippine Sea stations only) given in rank order from nearest to land to most distant offshore. R_m = rank of mean, R_d = rank of distance offshore.

Antipodes stations	65	65.5	66	66.5	67	67.5	68	68.5	69	69.5	70	70.5	71	71.5	72	72.5	n	Mean ± 95% limits	R_m	R_d
1, 2	—	—	—	—	—	—	2	—	1	1	3	1	1	—	1	—	10	69.80 ± 0.895	4	4
3, 4	—	—	—	—	—	—	3	4	3	2	4	3	3	—	—	—	22	69.47 ± 0.456	8	5
5, 6	—	—	—	—	—	—	2	2	2	1	12	8	1	—	—	—	28	69.84 ± 0.308	3	8
7, 8	—	—	—	—	—	—	1	—	2	4	10	3	1	—	—	1	22	69.95 ± 0.374	2	11
9, 10	—	—	—	—	—	—	—	—	—	2	3	2	3	—	—	—	10	70.30 ± 0.420	1	10
11, 12	—	—	—	—	—	—	1	1	2	—	1	1	—	—	—	—	6	69.17 ± 0.930	10	9
13, 14	—	—	—	—	—	1	1	1	2	3	4	1	—	—	—	—	13	69.31 ± 0.531	9	7
15, 16	—	—	—	—	—	—	1	—	1	—	1	2	1	—	—	—	6	69.83 ± 1.124	5	6
17, 18	—	—	—	—	1	1	5	6	2	1	6	3	1	—	—	—	26	69.06 ± 0.440	*11'	3
19, 20	—	—	—	—	—	—	1	4	—	3	3	1	1	1	—	—	14	69.54 ± 0.604	7	2
21, 22	—	—	1	2	—	2	7	8	5	20	36	11	4	3	1	—	100	69.59 ± 0.209	6	1

Philippine Sea, mean = 69.60 ± 0.126 Tau_{11} = −0.273 P > 0.20

	65	65.5	66	66.5	67	67.5	68										n	Mean ± 95% limits		
23, 24	1	1	5	1	—	1	—										9	66.06 ± 0.524		
25, 26	1	—	1	1	—	—	3										6	66.92 ± 1.345		
27, 28	—	—	4	2	2	—	1										9	66.56 ± 0.524		

South China Sea, mean = 66.46 ± 0.378

characters and productivity does not exist, and that we have overlooked the real meaning of our results. We are unable to deal with the third possibility and ignore the fourth possibility in our subsequent discussion.

We believe that the observed meristic variation is the result of genetic differences between populations and not the result of an ecophenotypic effect of food availability conditions on development of meristic characters. We present evidence available to support this belief, but we note that this evidence is not conclusive.

A statement of the ecophenotypic explanation is easily made. The meristic variation observed could result if the effect of low food densities upon the development of meristic characters parallels the effect of low temperature, retarding growth rates more than differentiation rates, and lengthening the period of determination of meristic characters. Because the effect of low food availability upon egg maturation appears to be a reduction of egg number and not egg size (Anokhina 1960; Blaxter 1969), any ecophenotypic effect of low food density upon meristic characters would have to operate between the onset of feeding and metamorphosis. Riley (1966) and Blaxter (1969), among others, have found for the species they have studied that the time to reach metamorphosis may be significantly increased by decreasing the density of food. Therefore an indispensable condition of the ecophenotypic explanation is that for the species studied, the final values of meristic counts are determined after the onset of feeding. If so, the meristic variation observed might result from a concordant increase in the length of the period of determination of meristic characters with a delay in time to reach metamorphosis in larvae from areas of lower productivity.

Three facts resulting from the study of the development of the eggs and larvae of *Vinciguerria lucetia* by Ahlstrom and Counts (1958) appear to support the ecophenotypic explanation: 1) Ahlstrom and Counts did find a direct rela-

tionship between size at metamorphosis (no developmental time scale is available for any of the species studied) and numbers of longitudinal photophores and vertebrae; 2) vertebral ossification and photophore formation in *V. lucetia* occur in larvae 11 mm SL or more in size, well after yolk-sac absorption and presumably after the onset of feeding; and 3) the distances between samples of *V. lucetia* utilized in construction of Figure 3 are small, much less in most cases than the distances between the eight study areas for the other species discussed in this paper. Yet the results for *V. lucetia* along the east to west transect lines apparently agree with results for the other mid-water species. We find it difficult to believe that the results for *V. lucetia* are explainable in terms of genetically distinct populations distributed along these inshore to offshore transects.

Three lines of evidence appear to contradict the ecophenotypic explanation in favor of the explanation hypothesizing that the observed meristic variation is the result of genetic differences between populations. (1) in *Vinciguerria lucetia* the total number of myomeres are formed in late stage eggs (Ahlstrom and Counts 1958). Since the number of myomeres, vertebral counts, and longitudinal photophore row counts are usually highly intercorrelated, the ecophenotypic explanation appears to be invalid in this case. (2) The data for *Vinciguerria nimbaria* may indicate the existance of separable populations in our different study areas. This is suggested by the results for the Antipodes transect (Table 9) in which is found no clear evidence for an onshore to offshore trend toward higher IPVALA counts, despite the fact that the productivity measures are higher inshore and decrease (rapidly) to seaward (Reid 1962; Koblentz-Mishke et al. 1970). Mean values of IPVALA photophore counts for specimens from each of the 11 pairs of Philippine Sea stations are significantly higher than the mean value for South China Sea specimens. This may suggest that genetically distinct, separable populations of *V. nimbaria* are found in each area. Gill raker counts for *V. nimbaria* (Table 10) apparently support this suggestion in that counts of gill rakers are discordant with counts of IPVALA photophores (Table 6) and vertebrae (Table 7). For the four Pacific areas the counts of vertebrae and IPVALA photophores for *V. nimbaria* agree in perfect rank-order with the IPVALA photophore counts for *D. taenia* (Table 10). That this is not true for gill raker counts may indicate the existence of separable populations of *V. nimbaria* in the South China Sea, central equatorial Pacific, and the North Pacific central gyral areas (Philippine Sea, central North Pacific). (3) The ecophenotypic explanation implies that in areas of low productivity elevated meristic counts result from retardation of growth and that this retardation is the result of the average survivor being underfed compared to larvae in areas of higher productivity. As year class strength in pelagic fish populations is probably largely determined in early stages of larval life and not by the total number of eggs produced or mortality during

TABLE 10.—*Vinciguerria nimbaria*, comparison of gill raker counts with vertebral and longitudinal photophore row counts.

V. nimbaria, total gill rakers on first gill arch.											
Area	17	18	19	20	21	22	23	24	25	26	*n*	Mean±95% limits
GG	—	—	—	—	—	—	3	6	10	1	20	24.45 ± 0.386
SCS	4	7	3	1	—	—	—	—	—	—	15	18.07 ± 0.489
CEP	—	—	—	4	13	13	1	—	—	—	31	21.35 ± 0.277
PS	—	2	26	54	31	2	—	—	—	—	115	20.04 ± 0.147
CNA	—	4	8	—	—	—	—	—	—	—	12	18.67 ± 0.313
CNP	—	—	3	6	3	—	—	—	—	—	12	20.00 ± 0.469

V. nimbaria and *Diplophos taenia*, comparison of counts, given as mean (rank.

	Vinciguerria nimbaria			Diplophos taenia
Area	Gill rakers	IPVALA	Vertebrae	IPVALA
SCS	18.1 (1	66.5 (1	39.4 (1	143.6 (1
CEP	21.4 (4	68.0 (2	40.2 (2	145.5 (2
PS	20.0 (2.5	69.6 (3	41.2 (3	149.2 (3
CNP	20.0 (2.5	70.3 (4	41.8 (4	151.7 (4

advanced prerecruit stages (Hempel 1965), it seems likely that selection would strongly favor any mechanisms that tended to protect the larvae of mid-water fishes occurring in areas of low productivity against starvation. The possible materials on which this selection might operate and the possible consequences on meristic characters form the basis for a second explanation of the observed meristic variation, that it is the by-product of genetic differences between separable populations in areas of low and high productivity.

Hempel (1965), Blaxter (1965), and others, concerned mainly with pelagic clupeoid fishes, have developed strong evidence that under normal circumstances the main restriction on the success of a year class occurs within a short period of larval life, the critical period of Hjort (1914, 1926) and others (e.g. Marr 1956; Schumann 1965). Selection has apparently resulted in adaptive mechanisms

tending to balance the two main dangers to larval survival: the danger of starvation and the danger of predation (Blaxter and Hempel 1963; Hempel 1965).

Blaxter (1965), Hunter (1972), and others, have shown that at the onset of feeding, just before or at the time of yolk-sac absorption, surprisingly small differences in size can significantly affect the probability of larval survival. Hunter (1972) has shown for northern anchovy *Engraulis mordax* Girard, larvae that slight increments in size are associated with highly increased searching abilities, highly increased success of attempted feeding acts, and vastly diminished minimum prey density requirements for survival. Blaxter (1965) discusses the significance of the greater spectrum of particle sizes available to larger larvae in terms of increased diversity of available prey organisms. Similar findings have been reported for other fish larvae (e.g. Arthur 1956; Einsele 1965). Size at hatching, at least for Atlantic herring, *Clupea harengus* Linnaeus, is a direct function of egg size; larger larvae hatch from larger eggs. Fecundity is inversely proportional to average egg size (Baxter 1959; Blaxter and Hempel 1963; Blaxter 1969).

We believe that the meristic variation between populations occurring in areas differing in productivity values is the result of adaptations involving the adjustment of egg and larval size to the productivity regime. We believe that these adaptations reflect differences between areas of low and high productivity in the relative importance of two principal dangers to larval survival: starvation versus predation.

We hypothesize that selection on mid-water fish populations inhabiting areas of low productivity has favored mechanisms tending to offset the danger of larval starvation, and that these populations will exhibit: 1) larger average egg size, 2) lower fecundity, and 3) larger average larval size at hatching and at comparable stages of development than populations living in areas of higher productivity. Advantages that might accrue to larger larvae in areas of lower productivity include increased mobility, a wider possible search volume, increased diversity of potential prey organisms, and a longer period of survivorship solely on yolk reserves.

The danger of starvation is presumably lower in areas of higher productivity but the danger of predation, resulting from presumed higher densities of potential predators on fish larvae, may be greater. Here selection may have favored increased fecundity tending to offset the danger of increased predation on larvae. We believe that in areas of higher productivity populations of mid-water fishes will exhibit: 1) smaller average egg size, 2) increased fecundity, and 3) smaller average larval size at hatching and at comparable stages of development than populations living in areas of lower productivity.

In developing this hypothesis we have largely followed Hempel's (1965) explanation for variations in egg size and fecundity between populations of herring in the eastern North Atlantic and North Sea. We note that there exists no evidence for increased predation pressure on larval populations of mid-water fishes in areas of higher productivity. It is possible to retain the main features of our hypothesis without including predation pressure by relating variation in fecundity and egg size solely to food density requirements. By definition, selection will favor maximizing reproductive output, thereby favoring fewer larger larvae in areas of low productivity where the danger of larval starvation is greater, and favoring higher fecundity (with the concomitant of smaller eggs and larvae) in areas where the danger of starvation is lessened.

There exists limited available evidence to support these predictions. Ahlstrom and Counts (1958) showed that egg size and size at hatching in *Vinciguerria lucetia* are directly related, the smallest larvae (at a defined stage of development) are found in areas where average egg diameters are least. They also showed that mean values of vertebral and IPVALA photophore counts are lowest in those areas where egg and larval size is least and where metamorphosis occurs earliest (i.e. at smallest size). Although no small larvae were available for this study, we were able to compare development in prejuvenile specimens of *V. nimbaria* from the central North Pacific with specimens from the central equatorial Pacific. In *V. nimbaria* the last four VAL photophores are late-forming, are laid down serially from anterior to posterior, usually the left member of a pair of VAL photophores develops just before the right, and the number yet to develop can be determined uniquely from the one to one correspondence with the posterior photophores in the VAV segment. In Figure 5 standard lengths of all available prejuvenile specimens of *V. nimbaria* from the central North Pacific and central equatorial Pacific are plotted against the number of VAL photophores left to appear. If this character can be used as an index to comparable stages of development, then at comparable stages of development the larvae from the area of lower productivity are the larger, as predicted.

We believe that the correlation between meristics and productivity results from a correlation between meristics and egg size, and that egg size and, hence, size at hatching is genetically determined features reflecting adaptation to productivity conditions. A number of authors have stated or suggested that such a correlation exists (Ahlstrom and Counts 1958; Lindsey 1958, 1961; Garside and Fry 1959). Lindsey and Ali (1971) have recently argued against this suggested relationship, despite the fact that their data showed a direct relationship between the number of anal fin rays and egg size in the medaka, *Oryzias latipes*.

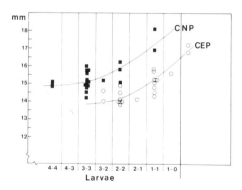

FIGURE 5.—Size of larvae of *Vinciguerria nimbaria* from the central North Pacific (CNP) and the central equatorial Pacific (CEP) at comparable stages of development. Ordinate: standard length in millimeters. Abscissa: number of VAL photophores yet to form (determined from VAV count) on each side of each specimen. Lines fitted by eye.

Blaxter and Hempel (1963) found no relationship between incubation time and egg size in herring, but did find a positive correlation between time to yolk sac absorption and egg size. If this correlation is true for the mid-water fishes considered in this report, if the correlation continues beyond the point of yolk sac absorption, and if the meristic characters in question are determined after hatching, it might result in a longer period of determination of these characters in larvae from larger eggs.

We lack essential developmental and ecological information to complete our hypothesis. We know little or nothing for most mid-water species about age and size at first spawning, number of spawnings per female, fecundity, seasonality of reproduction, course of larval development, or factors actually determining survivorship of larvae. The answer to the question of mechanism awaits the comparison of these population parameters between populations in areas of high and low productivity.

ACKNOWLEDGMENTS

We thank the following individuals and institutions for the loan of valuable specimens: R. Lavenberg, Natural History Museum of Los Angeles County (LACM), Los Angeles; E. Ahlstrom, National Marine Fisheries Service (NMFS-LJ), La Jolla, Calif.; P. Struhsaker, National Marine Fisheries Service (NMFS-H), Honolulu; P. Fourmanoir, Office de la Recherche Scientifique et Technique Outre-Mer (ORSTOM), Noumea, New Caledonia; R. Rosenblatt, D. Dockins, J. Copp, Scripps Institution of Oceanography (SIO), La Jolla; T. Clarke, Hawaii Institute of Marine Biology, University of Hawaii (UH), Kaneohe, Hawaii; C. R. Robins, University of Miami (UMML), Miami; B. Nafpaktitis and R. McGinnis,

University of Southern California (USC), Los Angeles; R. H. Gibbs, Jr., Division of Fishes, National Museum of Natural History (USNM), Washington, D.C.; R. Backus, J. Craddock, R. Haedrich, Woods Hole Oceanographic Institution (WHOI), Woods Hole, Mass.

We thank the following individuals for information from their own research and for aiding the completion of this project: E. Ahlstrom, B. Collette, D. Cohen, C. L. Hubbs, J. Kethley, G. Krefft, H. Marx, R. Rosenblatt. We thank the Division of Photography, Field Museum of Natural History, for aid in preparing the figures. This paper is based in part on the results of the Antipodes and Styx Expeditions of the Scripps Institution of Oceanography. This work was supported, in part, by NSF Grant GB 7596 to R. H. Rosenblatt and W. Newman. We are grateful to T. Poulson for critically reading the manuscript and offering valuable suggestions for its improvement. We are particarly indebted to E. H. Ahlstrom and R. H. Rosenblatt for their advice, criticism, and encouragement throughout the development of this research.

MATERIAL EXAMINED

Diplophos taenia. The material examined of this species is listed in Johnson and Barnett 1972. Supplementary station list of materials examined for a study of meristic variation in *Diplophos taenia* Guenther. Ref. Ser. Scripps Inst. Oceanogr. 72-4, 1-8 (unpublished manuscript available from the Library, Scripps Institution of Oceanography, La Jolla, Calif).

Pollichthys mauli. GG: 24 (28.5-46.9), UMML 22881 (1), UMML 24132 (1), UMML 24237 (1), UMML 24266 (3), UMML 24658 (6), UMML 27884 (6), UMML 27929 (5), UMML 28159 (1). SCS: 11 (21.1-31.1); SIO 61-744 (1), SIO 69-20, (10); PS: 10 (33.8-49.9); SIO 70-308 (1), SIO 70-309 (1), SIO 70-334 (2), SIO 70-337 (2), SIO 70-340 (4).

Vinciguerria attenuata. SCS: 71 (13.0-37.8); SIO 70-341 (5), SIO 70-343 (5), SIO 70-344 (52), SIO 70-345 (5), SIO 70-346 (3), SIO 70-347 (1). PS: 71 (13.0-28.1); SIO 70-308 (12), SIO 70-309, (10), SIO 70-310 (6), SIO 70-311 (12), SIO 70-314 (11), SIO 70-318 (1), SIO 70-333 (15), SIO 70-334, (1), SIO 70-337 (2).

Vinciguerria nimbaria. GG: 20 (21.0-37.5); UMML 21902 (20). SCS: 35 (11.7-32.0); SIO 70-341 (4), SIO 70-343 (5), SIO 70-344 (10), SIO 70-345 (5), SIO 70-346 (5), SIO 70-347 (6). PS: 729 (11.6-39.9); SIO 70-306 (63), SIO 70-308 (6), SIO 70-309 (18), SIO 70-310 (23), SIO 70-311 (29), SIO 70-314 (45), SIO 70-318 (52), SIO 70-326 (7), SIO 70-327 (3), SIO 70-328 (12), SIO 70-329 (22), SIO 70-331 (2), SIO 70-332 (11), SIO 70-333 (173), SIO 70-334 (15), SIO 70-336 (6), SIO 70-337 (14), SIO 70-339 (2), SIO 70-340 (226). CEP: FMNH (Field Museum of Natural History) 77100 32 (16.9-36.0). CNA: USNM, Ocean Acre Stations, all material from ca. lat. 32-

32.5°N., long 64°W. 12(19.1-35.8); 12-17C (1), 12-18A (2), 12-18B (2), 12-28B (1), 12-34C (1), 12-35C (1), 12-62 (1), 12-80 (1), 12-81 (1), 12-86 (1). CNP: 49 (14.1-21.0); UH 69-11-5 (49).

Chauliodus sloani. PS: 14 (42.2-214.5); SIO 70-306 (3), SIO 70-311 (2), SIO 70-326 (1), SIO 70-334 (8). CNP: 20, SIO 71-301 (1), SIO 71-307 (1), SIO 71-309 (5), SIO 71-373 (1), SIO 72-11 (2), SIO 72-16 (1), SIO 72-22 (1), SIO 72-25 (2), SIO 73-142 (1), SIO 73-149 (1), SIO 73-155 (1), SIO 73-158 (2), SIO 73-159 (1).

LITERATURED CITED

AHLSTROM, E. H., AND R. C. COUNTS.
1958. Development and distribution of *Vinciguerria lucetia* and related species in the Eastern Pacific. U.S. Fish Wildl. Serv., Fish. Bull. 58:363-416.

ALDERDICE, D. F., W. P. WICKETT, AND J. R. BRETT.
1958. Some effects of temporary exposure to low dissolved oxygen levels on Pacific salmon eggs. J. Fish. Res. Board Can. 15:229-250.

ANOKHINA, L. E.
1960. Interrelations between fecundity, variability of size of the eggs, and fatness of mother fish in Onega herring. Dokl. Akad. Nauk SSSR 133(4):960-963.

ARTHUR, D. K.
1956. The particulate food and the food resources of the larvae of three pelagic fishes, especially the Pacific sardine, *Sardinops caerulea* (Girard). Ph.D. Thesis, Univ. California, 231 p.

BARLOW, G. W.
1961. Causes and significance of morphological variation in fishes. Syst. Zool. 10:105-117.

BAXTER, I. G.
1959. Fecundities of winter-spring and summer-autumn herring spawners. J. Cons. 25:73-80.

BLACHE, J.
1964. Sur la validite de *Chauliodus schmidti* Ege 1948 (*Pisces, Teleostei, Clupeiformi, Stomiatoidei, Chauliodidae*) espece characteristique de l'Atlantique oriental. Cah. O.R.S.T.O.M. (Off. Rech. Sci. Tech. Outre-Mer) Ser Oceanogr. II(1):33-44.

BLACKBURN, M.
1967. Synopsis of biological information on the Australian anchovy *Engraulis australis* (White). Calif. Coop. Oceanic Fish. Invest. Rep. 11:34-43.

BLAXTER, J. H. S.
1965. The feeding of herring larvae and their ecology in relation to feeding. Calif. Coop. Oceanic Fish. Invest. Rep. 10:79-88.

1969. Development: Eggs and larvae. *In* W. S. Hoar and D. J. Randall (editors), Fish physiology 3:177-252. Academic Press, N.Y.

BLAXTER, J. H. S., AND G. HEMPEL.
1963. The influence of egg size on herring larvae (*Clupea harengus* L.). J. Cons. 28:211-240.

BRANDHORST, W.
1959. Nitrification and denitrification in the Eastern Tropical North Pacific. J. Cons. 25:3-20.

BRINTON, E.
1962. The distribution of Pacific euphausiids. Bull. Scripps Inst. Oceanogr., Univ. Calif. 8:51-269.

CORCORAN, E. F., AND C. V. W. MAHNKEN.
1969. Productivity of the tropical Atlantic Ocean. Proc. Symp. Oceanogr. Fish. Resour. Trop. Atl., Rev. Pap. Contrib. (UNESCO), Abidjan 1966, p. 57-68.

CRADDOCK, J. E., AND G. W. MEAD.
1970. Midwater fishes from the eastern South Pacific Ocean. Scientific Results of the SE Pacific. Exped. Anton Bruun, Rep. 3, 46 p.

CUSHING, D. H.
1971. Upwelling and the production of fish. Adv. Mar. Biol. 9:255-334.

EBELING, A. W.
1962. Melamphaidae. I. Systematics and zoogeography of the species in the bathypelagic fish genus *Melamphaes* Günther. Dana Rep., Carlsberg Found. 58, 164 p.

EGE, V.
1948. *Chauliodus* Schn., bathypelagic genus of fishes. A systematic, phylogenetic and geographical study. Dana Rep., Carlsberg Found. 31, 148 p.

EINSELE, W.
1965. Problems of fish-larvae survival in nature and the rearing of economically important middle European freshwater fishes. Calif. Coop. Oceanic Fish. Invest. Rep. 10:24-30.

FLEMING, R. H., AND T. LAEVASTU.
1956. The influence of hydrographic conditions on the behavior of fish. (A preliminary literature survey.) FAO (Food Agric. Organ. U.N.) Fish. Bull. 9:181-196.

FORRESTER, C. R., AND D. F. ALDERDICE.
1966. Effects of salinity and temperature on embryonic development of the Pacific cod (*Gadus macrocephalus*). J. Fish. Res. Board Can. 23:319-340.

FOWLER, J. A.
1970. Control of vertebral number in teleosts—an embryological problem. Q. Rev. Biol. 45:148-167.

GARSIDE, E. T.
1959. Some effects of oxygen in relation to temperature on the development of lake trout embryos. Can. J. Zool. 37:689-698.
1966. Developmental rate and vertebral number in salmonids. J. Fish. Res. Board Can. 23:1537-1551.

GARSIDE, E. T., AND F. E. J. FRY.
1959. A possible relationship between yolk size and differentiation in trout embryos. Can. J. Zool. 37:383-386.

GIBBS, R. H., JR., AND B. A. HURWITZ.
1967. Systematics and zoogeography of the stomiatoid fishes, *Chauliodus pammelas* and *C. sloani*, of the Indian Ocean. Copeia 1967:798-805.

GORBUNOVA, N. N.
1972. Systematics, distribution and biology of the fishes of the genus Vinciguerria (Pisces, Gonostomatidae). (In Russ., Engl. summ.) Akad. Nauk SSSR, Tr. Inst. Okeanol. 93:70-109.

GREY, M.
1964. Family Gonostomatidae. *In* Y. H. Olsen (editor), Fishes of the western North Atlantic, Part 4, p. 78-240. Sears Found. Mar. Res., Mem. I.

HEMPEL, G.
1965. On the importance of larval survival for the population dynamics of marine food fish. Calif. Coop. Oceanic Fish. Invest. Rep. 10:13-23.

HEMPEL, G., AND J. H. S. BLAXTER.
1961. The experimental modification of meristic characters in herring (*Clupea harengus* L.). J. Cons. 26:336-346.

HJORT, J.
1914. Fluctuations in the great fisheries of northern Europe viewed in the light of biological research. Cons. Perm. Int. Explor. Mer., Rapp. P.-V. Réum. 20:1-228.
1926. Fluctuations in the year classes of important food fishes. J. Cons. 1:5-38.

HUBBS, C. L.
1925. Racial and seasonal variation in the Pacific herring, California sardine and California anchovy. Calif. Dep. Fish Game, Fish. Bull. 8, 22 p.
1926. The structural consequences of modifications of the developmental rate in fishes considered in reference to certain problems of evolution. Am. Nat. 60:57-81.

HUNTER, J. R.
1972. Swimming and feeding behavior of larval anchovy, *Engraulis mordax*. Fish. Bull., U.S. 70:821-838.

JOHNSON, R. K.
1970. A new species of *Diplophos* (Salmoniformes: Gonostomatidae) from the western Pacific. Copeia 1970:437-443.

1974. A revision of the alepisauroid family Scopelarchidae (Pisces, Myctophiformes). Fieldiana: Zool. 66, 249 p.

JOHNSON, R. K., AND M. A. BARNETT.
1972. Geographic meristic variation in *Diplophos taenia* Günther (Salmoniformes: Gonostomatidae). Deep-Sea Res. 19:813-821.

KINZER, J.
1969. Quantitative distribution of zooplankton in surface waters of the Gulf of Guinea during August and September 1963. Proc. Symp. Oceanogr. Fish. Resour. Trop. Atl., Rev. Pap. Contrib. (UNESCO), Abidjan 1966, p. 231-240.

KOBLENTZ-MISHKE, O. J., V. V. VOLKOVINSKY, AND J. G. KABANOVA.
1970. Plankton primary production of the world ocean. *In* W. S. Wooster (editor), Scientific exploration of the South Pacific, p. 183-193. Natl. Acad. Sci., Wash., D.C.

LINDSEY, C. C.
1958. Modification of meristic characters by light duration in kokanee, *Oncorhynchus nerka*. Copeia 1958:134-136.
1961. The bearing of experimental meristic studies on racial analyses of fish populations. Proc. IX Pac. Sci. Congr. 10:54-58.

LINDSEY, C. C., AND M. Y. ALI.
1971. An experiment with medaka, *Oryzias latipes*, and a critique of the hypothesis that teleost egg size controls vertebral count. J. Fish. Res. Board Can. 28:1235-1240.

MARR, J. C.
1956. The "critical period" in the early life history of marine fishes. J. Cons. 21:160-170.

MENZEL, D. W., AND J. H. RYTHER.
1961. Zooplankton in the Sargasso Sea off Bermuda and its relation to organic production. J. Cons. 26:250-258.

MORROW, J. E.
1961. Taxonomy of the deep sea fishes of the genus *Chauliodus*. Bull. Mus. Comp. Zool. (Harvard Univ.) 125:249-294.
1964. Family Chauliodontidae. *In* Y. H. Olsen (editor), Fishes of the western North Atlantic, Part 4, p. 290-310. Sears Found. Mar. Res., Mem. I.

NOVIKOVA, N. S.
1972. A new species of the genus *Chauliodus* (Pisces, Chauliodontidae) from the Southeastern Pacific. J. Ichthyol. 12:34-41.

RAYMONT, J. E. G.
1963. Plankton and productivity in the oceans. Pergamon Press, Oxford, 660 p.

REID, J. L., JR.
1962. On circulation, phosphate-phosphorus content, and zooplankton volumes in the upper part of the Pacific Ocean. Limnol. Oceanogr. 7:287-306.

RILEY, G. A.
1972. Patterns of production in marine ecosystems. *In* J. A. Wiens (editor), Ecosystem structure and function, p. 91-110. Oregon State Univ., Corvallis.

RILEY, J. D.
1966. Marine fish culture in Britain. VII. Plaice (*Pleuronectes platessa* L.) post-larval feeding on *Artemia salina* L. nauplii and the effects of varying feeding levels. J. Cons. 30:204-221.

RYTHER, J. H., AND D. W. MENZEL.
1965. On the production, composition, and distribution of organic matter in the Western Arabian Sea. Deep-Sea Res. 12:199-209.

SCHUMANN, G. O.
1965. Some aspects of behavior in clupeid larvae. Calif. Coop. Oceanic Fish. Invest. Rep. 10:71-78.

SILAS, E. G., AND K. C. GEORGE.
1971. On larval and postlarval development and distribution of the mesopelagic fish Vinciguerria nimbaria (Jordan and Williams) off the western coast of India and the Laccadive Sea. J. Mar. Biol. Assoc. India 11:218-250.

SOKAL, R. R., AND F. J. ROHLF.
1969. Biometry, the principles and practice of statistics in biological research. W. H. Freeman & Co., San Francisco, 776 p.

SOROKIN, Y. I.
   1973. Data on biological productivity of the Western tropical Pacific Ocean. Mar. Biol. (Berl.) 20:177-196.
SVERDRUP, H. U., M. W. JOHNSON, AND R. H. FLEMING.
   1942. The oceans, their physics, chemistry, and general biology. Prentice-Hall, N.Y., 1087 p.
TATE, M. W., AND R. C. CLELLAND.
   1957. Nonparametric and shortcut statistics in the social, biological, and medical sciences. Interstate Printers and Publishers, Inc., Danville, Ill., 171 p.
WEITZMAN, S. H.
   1967. The origin of the stomiatoid fishes with comments on the classification of salmoniform fishes. Copeia 1967:507-540.

WILLIAMS, F.
   1972. Consideration of three proposed models of the migration of young skipjack tuna (*Katsuwonus pelamis*) into the eastern Pacific Ocean. Fish. Bull., U.S. 70:741-762.
WYRTKI, K.
   1961. Physical oceanography of the Southeast Asian waters. NAGA Rep. 2, 195 p.
ZEITSCHEL, B.
   1969. Productivity and microbiomass in the tropical Atlantic in relation to the hydrographical conditions (with emphasis on the eastern area). Proc. Symp. Oceanogr. Fish. Resour. Trop. Atl., Rev. Pap. Contrib. (UNESCO), Abidjan 1966, p. 69-83.

Additional Readings

CHAPTER 3

ALEEV, YU. G. 1969. *Function and gross morphology in fish.* Israel Program for Scientific Translations, Jerusalem. U.S. Department of Commerce, Washington, D.C.

BARLOW, G. W. 1961. Causes and significance of morphological variation in fishes. *Syst. Zool.* 10(3):105-117.

GANS, C. and PARSONS, T. S. 1964. *A photographic atlas of shark anatomy.* New York: Academic Press.

GOSLINE, W. A. 1961. The perciform caudal skeleton. *Copeia* 1961(3):265-270.

GOSLINE, W. A. 1971. *Functional morphology and classification of teleostean fishes.* Honolulu: University Press of Hawaii.

GREGORY, W. K. 1933. Fish skulls, a study of the evolution of natural mechanisms. *Am. Philos. Soc.* 23(2):75-481. Reprint. Laurel, Florida: Eric Lundberg, 1959.

HARDER, W. 1975. *Anatomy of fishes.* Part I: Text; Part II: Figures and Plates. Stuttgart: E. Schweizerbart'sche Verlagsbuchhandlung (Nagele U. Obermiller).

HUBBS, C. L. and HUBBS, L. C. 1945. Bilateral asymmetry and bilateral variation in fishes. *Pap. Mich. Acad. Sci., Arts and Letters* 30:299-310.

LINDSEY, C. C. 1975. Pleomerism, the widespread tendency among related species for vertebral number to be correlated with maximum body length. *J. Fish. Res. Bd. Canada* 32(12):2453-2469.

MORGENROTH, P. A. and MORGENROTH, A. M. 1969. Skeletal anatomy of the rockfish, a laboratory atlas of the skeletal anatomy of a generalized member of the genus *Sebastodes.* Humboldt State College, Department of Fisheries.

VALENTINE, D. W.; SOULE, M. E.; and SAMOLLOW, P. 1973. Asymmetry analysis in fishes: a possible statistical indicator of environmental stress. *Fish. Bull., U.S.* 71(2):357-370.

WINTERBOTTOM, R. 1974. A descriptive synonymy of the striated muscles of the teleostei. *Acad. Nat. Sci. Phil.* 125(12):225-317.

4

Phylogeny of
Teleostean Fishes

Teleostean Phylogeny

William A. Gosline

That the old Chondrostei–Holostei–Teleostei categories merely divide the actinopterygian fishes into 3 levels of structural organization is generally held. Also, it is widely agreed that the Chondrostei and Holostei each represent several separately developed lineages. Here, it is suggested, and data are presented supporting the suggestion, that the Teleostei is a monophyletic group; furthermore, that for purposes of classification the Teleostei may be considered a superorder in parallel with other lineages within the Actinopterygii, i.e., within the old chondrostean–holostean category.

Data on the circumorbital bones are presented, and the modern clupeoid and elopoid groups of fishes are further defined.

Introduction

THE objective of the present paper is to put together some of the data bearing on the phylogeny of, and to present a viewpoint concerning, the Teleostei. Whether the teleostean fishes are monophyletic or polyphyletic has been a matter of some difference of opinion. Although the basic assumption behind the recognition of the group is that it is monophyletic, a number of authors in recent years have questioned this. Thus, Gardiner (1960:351; Fig. 79, p. 369) has hypothesized an independent origin among the holostean Pholidophoridae for the leptolepid–clupeoid group on the one hand and the elopid–characinid–salmonid lineage on the other. Ørvig (1957:488) has been impressed by the preteleostean nature of siluroid bone tissue. Bertmar (1962:291) suggested that the arterial system of the characin *Hepsetus* "has not developed from any other living teleosts" but "has evolved from some fossil sub-holostean, or perhaps even from some palaeoniscoids." My own work (1960, 1961), while seemingly indicating a monophyletic teleostean origin, would suggest that if any teleostean group evolved independently, it is the hiodontid–osteoglossoid–mormyroid lineage; Greenwood (1963) has emphasized this same separation by raising the osteoglossoid fishes to ordinal rank. The paper at hand will deal primarily with the fish groups mentioned above. Before a discussion of previously published results, further data apparently bearing on the relationships of these and certain holostean groups will be added.

Most of the observations reported in this paper were made at the Museum of Zoology, University of Michigan, while on sabbatic leave. I wish to thank the authorities of that institution, and particularly Dr. R. M. Bailey, for providing me with space and facilities. I also wish to thank Dr. C. Lavett Smith of the American Museum of Natural History and Dr. Stanley Weitzman of the U. S. National Museum for their comments on portions of this paper read in draft form.

The Circumorbital Bones

A series of small ossifications more or less completely surrounds the orbit in most bony fishes. Among modern teleosts, the specializations of the individual circumorbital bones, e.g., the lacrimal, have drawn attention away from the series as a whole. In fossil fish remains, the small bones that make up the circumorbital complex are among the first to become lost or dislocated; consequently, considerable difficulty is encountered in working with this series (and probably no great reliance should be placed on circumorbital configurations shown in most reconstructions). As a result of these factors, the circumorbital bones have received little attention as a series, the closest approach to a general treatment being that in the introductory pages of Smith and Bailey (1962).

Aside perhaps from *Latimeria*, some of the sturgeons and certain osteoglossoids (see below), *Lepisosteus* is the only modern fish with a complete circumorbital ring of bony ossicles. The same thing appears to be true of the whole semionotoid group to which *Lepisosteus* belongs. In the shorter-snouted fossil genera *Tetragonolepis*, *Acentrophorus*, and *Dapedium*, judging from reconstructions (cf. Gardiner 1960:306, Fig. 42; 354, Fig. 70; and Woodward 1895:129, Fig. 25), the circumorbitals form a complete and continuous circle with the antorbital bone outside of and anteroventral to it. In the longer-snouted forms, such as *Semionotus*, *Lepidotes*, and *Lepisosteus*, the ring is still closed, but the anterior infraorbitals, along with the antor-

From *Copeia* 1965(2):186–194. Reprinted by permission.

bital, extend forward on the snout ahead of the rest of the ring. Aside from the presence of the lateral line in some of the bones and its absence in others, there seems to be little differentiation in the members of the semionotoid circumorbital series (cf. Allis 1904); nor does it appear that the upper members of the series have been derived from canal-bearing bones.

In *Amia* and the Teleostei (except certain osteoglossoids), the circumorbital series is not only incomplete, but the members of the series have become considerably differentiated. A major distinction may be made between the canal-bearing infraorbital[1] group and, where they occur at all, the canal-less (anamestic) supraorbital bones.

In *Amia*, there are no supraorbital bones. However, in the reconstruction of the fossil *Sinamia* (Stensiö 1935, according to Berg 1940:203, 204, Figs. 94, 95) a number of small supraorbital ossicles are shown. These seem to bear no resemblance to the canal-bearing infraorbital series.

In the modern teleosts, there are at most 2, anamestic supraorbital bones. Thus, contrary to my own earlier statement (Gosline 1961: 26), 2 occur in certain of the clupeiform fishes (*Phractolaemus*, Thys van den Audenaerde 1961) and characins (Allis 1904, showed 2 in his figure of *Alestes nurse*, and Weitzman 1962:65, Fig. 9, recorded 2 in a small, but not in several large, specimens of *Brycon meeki*). The great majority of modern teleosts have only 1, if any, supraorbital bone and even this disappears in all advanced members of the series (Gosline 1961). Among the extinct leptolepid–pholidophorid group, generally considered to be at the base of the teleosts, 1 to 3 supraorbital bones are usually shown in reconstructions (e.g., Nybelin 1962, Fig. 1).

The derivation of the teleostean supraorbital ossifications is unclear. They may have been of independent origin from the infraorbital series, but several bits of evidence suggest that they have evolved from parts of the canal-bearing infraorbital series which have secondarily broken off, or lost their canals or both. Thus, among the basal modern teleosts, *Arapaima* does have canal-bearing members of the infraorbital series completely closing the ring above the orbit.

Again, in a large skeleton of *Albula*, R. M. Bailey (pers. comm.) has pointed out that a small extension of the infraorbital canal does run up and back from the top of the antorbital into the supraorbital bone. In *Elops*, the bone configuration (see Nybelin 1956, Fig. 2) suggests that a similar extension of the infraorbital canal once occurred. Finally, that a member of the infraorbital series may lose its canal before the bone itself disappears has been demonstrated for the teleostean antorbital by Gosline (1961:25–31) and for the lacrimal by Makushok (1961:236–237).

Unlike the supraorbital bones, the infraorbital series is represented, at least in part, throughout the holostean and teleostean fishes. In the lower teleosts, this series extends from an antorbital bone in front through the dermosphenotic posterodorsally. The teleostean specializations of the anterior (Gosline 1961) and of the central portions of the infraorbital series (Smith and Bailey 1962) have been recently discussed. Here, only certain variations in the dermosphenotic region will be dealt with.

The first point has to do with the lateral line canals. In the actinopterygians in general, the infraorbital sensory canal runs up through the dermosphenotic and then extends back through the pterotic. Originally there appears to have been no connection between the infraorbital and supraorbital canals. However, among the holosteans and the lower teleosteans such a junction frequently, though by no means always, occurs (see, e.g., Westoll 1944:67–71; Lekander 1949:113–115; Gardiner 1960:334). Thus, among "holostean" semionotoids, a connection between the supraorbital and infraorbital canals is lacking from Gardiner's (1960:356, Fig. 71) reconstruction of *Semionotus*, but is shown in *Tetragonolepis* (1960:306, Fig. 42) and *Acentrophorus* (1960:353–354, Figs. 69–70). In *Amia*, there is no connection in the larval stage (Allis 1888) but one develops in the adult. Among teleosts, the clupeiform genus *Phractolaemus* (Thys van den Audenaerde 1961, Fig. 13) and at least the half-grown of *Hiodon* (Fig. 1A) and *Chanos* (Fig. 1B) lack an infraorbital–supraorbital junction, though the majority of the Clupeiformes have one. In Cypriniformes, such a union is lacking in most cyprinoids, but present in at least most of the other members investigated (Lekander 1949:113–114; Weitzman 1962:28).

In the great majority of teleosts with a

---

[1] In the use of the name *infraorbital* bones, Weitzman (1962:28, footnote 7) is here followed. Smith and Bailey's (1962) term *suborbital* for these bones leads to confusion with the use of the same name for a quite different series by paleontologists (see, e.g., Gardiner 1960:338–341).

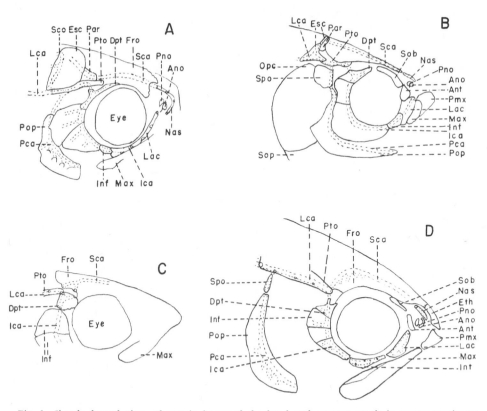

Fig. 1. Sketch, lateral view, of certain bones of the head and sensory canals in young specimens of A, *Hiodon tergisus*; B, *Chanos chanos*; C, *Coregonus clupeaformis*; and D, *Salmo gairdnerii*.

Ano, anterior nostril; Ant, antorbital; Dpt, dermosphenotic; Esc, extrascapular; Eth, ethmoid; Fro, frontal; Ica, infraorbital canal; Inf, infraorbital bone; Lac, lacrimal; Lca, lateral line canal; Max, maxillary; Nas, nasal; Opc, opercle; Par, parietal; Pca, preopercular canal; Pmx, premaxillary; Pno, posterior nostril; Pop, preopercle; Pto, pterotic; Sca, supraorbital canal; Sco, supratemporal commissure; Sob, supraorbital bone; Sop, subopercle; Spo, suprapreopercle.

supraorbital–infraorbital connection, this occurs in the interspace between the top of the dermosphenotic, the posterolateral edge of the frontal, and the front of the pterotic (approximately as in Fig. 1D); in such instances, there is no Y-shaped junction within any one bone. Sometimes, the union of the supraorbital and infraorbital canals takes place well back in the pterotic, as apparently in semionotoids, e.g., *Tetragonolepis* (Gardiner 1960: 306, Fig. 42), and sometimes within the dermosphenotic, as in *Amia*, *Thymallus*, and coregonine salmonids (Norden 1961:752–753). This same type of canal junction is almost but not quite complete in Nybelin's illustration (1962, Fig. 1B) of *Leptolepis normandica* and in the half-grown specimen of *Coregonus* illustrated in Fig. 1C.

In addition to a shifting in supraorbital–infraorbital canal connection, there have

been at least 2 major variants in dermosphenotic position (which casts doubt on the homology of the various types of "dermosphenotics," cf. Norden 1961). Generally, in the modern lower teleosts, the dermosphenotic forms part of the circumorbital series, and the hinge for movement between this series and the cranium lies between the dermosphenotic and the frontal above it. However, in the amioids (most closely approached among teleosts by the erythrinine characins), the dermosphenotic forms one of the roofing bones of the skull, and the hinge line for circumorbital series movement lies below it.

Among the teleosts, the clupeoid fishes have developed a different dermosphenotic variation. Here, the dermosphenotic does not border the orbit but seems to have been deflected backward by the upper section of the levator arcus palatini muscle, which fills the posterolateral border of the orbit; the similarly dislocated junction between the infraorbital canal and the supraorbital canal is carried back to just ahead of that with the preopercular canal. Judging from Clausen's illustration (1959, Fig. 1), the recently described Denticipitidae has the clupeoid dermosphenotic position.

ACTINOPTERYGIAN PHYLOGENIES

In the recent past, the Actinopterygii has most frequently been divided into Chondrostei, Holostei, and Teleostei. However, intensive work on each of these groups has indicated that it represents a level of structural development containing several phylogenetic lineages. This has been clearly brought out by, amongst others, Aldinger (1937) for the Chrondrostei and Gardiner (1960) for the Holostei. As to the Teleostei, all of the modern lower teleostean orders extend back separately in the fossil record as far as they can be traced, as can the principal divisions of such major orders as the Cypriniformes and Clupeiformes. Among members of the latter group, Nybelin (1961) attempted to distinguish between several lineages extending back into the Jurassic.

Nor can the chondrostean–holostean or holostean–teleostean borders be clearly defined. Thus Berg (1940:392) stated: "However, the remarkable researches of Stensiö (1932) have shown that the Chondrostei gradually pass into the Holostei and that they can be separated from the remaining orders only artificially." As to the Teleostei, Nybelin (1956:456) said of a family which everybody agrees is teleostean: "Les Elopidae m'apparaissent être des Holostéens récents aussi bien qu'*Amia* ou *Lepidosteus*."

Here, the Teleostei will not be contrasted with the Holostei as such, and the question of whether *Elops* is a holostean or a teleostean loses all meaning. The alternative suggested here is that the Teleostei be viewed as a phylogenetic lineage (rather than as a stage of structural development). Then, it can usefully be compared with other actinopterygian lineages; e.g., the Amioidea (*Amia*) and Semionotoidea (*Lepisosteus*). The data concerning the circumorbital bones presented earlier support a differentiation along such lines: the semionotoids have a complete ring of similar ossicles surrounding the eye; the amioids have the dermosphenotic forming a part of the skull roof; and, with

a very few possible exceptions, the teleosts have neither.

If this change in viewpoint regarding the Teleostei is to be accepted, it must be demonstrated that the group is not polyphyletic, i.e., that some teleosts have not evolved from the Amioidea, others from the Semionotoidea, etc. Evidence for a monophyletic teleostean origin may be drawn from 3 rather complex specializations which, so far as known, occur in the Teleostei alone and presumably developed in the group. (Such characters presumably have greater significance than the usual "loss" characters used in the past to differentiate the Teleostei from the Holostei.)

First, there is the peculiar pumping system which causes an incurrent flow of water over the nasal epithelia when the mouth is opened (Derschied 1924, Kirkhoff 1958, Gosline 1961). This rather complicated mechanism, involving diverticuli from the nasal sac, a supraorbital–antorbital strut, etc., seems to be present in all of the modern "primitive" teleosts except for the *Hiodon*-osteoglossoid–mormyroid lineage. Whether the last group never developed the nasal pump or secondarily lost it (as did, presumably, the erythrinine characins, the eels, beloniform fishes, etc.) is not known. Such a pumping system is lacking in *Amia*, *Lepisosteus*. etc., and has not been recorded in fossil "holostean" forms.

A second character, recorded from such various fishes as osteoglossoids, clupeoids, *Chanos*, and characins (cf. Thys van den Audenaerde 1961:146), is the so-called suprabranchial organ. This complex structure of unknown function seems to be considered homologous in the different fishes mentioned above.

Unlike the last 2 features, which are practically undeterminable in fossils, the caudal skeleton can often be (with proper preparation) and has recently been used in such material to excellent advantage (Nybelin 1963). To my knowledge, it provides the single best indicator for the teleosts as compared, for example, to the amioids and semionotoids.

The holostean stage of evolution was one in which each fin ray became attached to its own pterygiophore (instead of having several rays attached to a single pterygiophore as in most chondrosteans). In *Amia* and *Lepisosteus*, at least, this is as true of the major caudal rays as for the other vertical fins. The pterygiophores of the major caudal rays have apparently fused with the hemal spines of the last several vertebrae to form, at least in part, the hypurals. Thus it works out, in *Amia* and *Lepisosteus*, that there is one major caudal ray per hypural per vertebral centrum. In *Lepisosteus*, the centra in the caudal region are undivided, and the hypurals and caudal rays are few; in *Amia*, the centra in the caudal region are divided into 2, each half with a hypural, which thus, with the caudal rays, are rather numerous. In the teleosts, by contrast, there tend to be 2 to several principal caudal rays articulating with each hypural. Anterior to the hypurals, there are a number of hemal spines that also support caudal rays, but each articulates with its own centrum via a hemal arch. The hypurals, by contrast, lack hemal arches basally, and 2 to several of them usually articulate with a single centrum element (one of the lower hypurals of many clupeoid fishes forms an exception in this regard, see below).

The other principal character in the caudal skeleton differentiating teleosts from the amioids and semionotoids is that which Nybelin (1963) emphasized: namely, the presence of uroneural elements. Among fossil fishes, Nybelin has traced uroneurals back through *Leptolepis*, *Thrissops*, and *Eurycormus*. On the other hand, he was unable to find uroneurals in the amiids investigated, and they appear to be lacking in *Lepisosteus*.

If the Teleostei, as viewed here, is a monophyletic group, then the polyphyletic interpretations of Gardiner, Ørvig, and Bertmar cited in the first paragraph of this paper must be accounted for. Though a perusal of papers on the aortic arches of air-breathing fishes gives me the impression of considerable arterial variation, I have insufficient knowledge of the subject to comment intelligently on Bertmar's (1962) separate derivation of the characin arterial system. Ørvig (1957) based his postulate of a primitive type of bone tissue in catfishes on the armored forms of *Callichthys* and *Plecostomus*. Whatever the bone type, the armature of these specialized catfishes has almost certainly been secondarily evolved (cf. Gosline 1947). Gardiner's (1960) derivation of 2 teleostean lineages from the "holostean" Pholidophoridae raises 2 questions.

The first concerns the particular lineages Gardiner postulates. In one of these (1960: Fig. 79, p. 369), he placed the Leptolepidae

and the main clupeoid stock; in the other, the Elopidae, Characinidae, and Salmonidae. Nybelin (1961) postulated the same *Leptolepis*–clupeoid lineage. However, Nybelin's own data suggest at least some caution with regard to this interpretation, for the caudal skeleton of *Leptolepis* (Nybelin 1963: Figs. 8, 9, and 10) resembles the basal teleostean type found in *Elops* rather than the specialization that characterizes the clupeoids (Gosline 1960, 1961). Nor is the dermosphenotic configuration of *Leptolepis* clupeoid (see above).

If, as Gardiner (1960) and others agree, the Teleostei evolved from the Pholidophoridae, the question arises of where the Pholidophoridae ends and the Teleostei starts. Several comments but no solution to this problem will be offered. In the first place, attempts to distinguish the Pholidophoridae from the Teleostei along the old Holostei–Teleostei dividing line would seem to be futile. If teleostean specializations, such as those discussed above, rather than "holostean" losses, are to be used for characterizing the group, the Teleostei must be extended fairly deeply into the fossil record. Thus the characteristic caudal skeleton of the modern *Hiodon*, *Elops*, *Salmo*, and *Esox* (Gosline 1960) extends back at least as far as the lower Jurassic (*Leptolepis*: Nybelin 1963, Figs. 9 and 10). Indeed, it may prove that a logical phylogenetic interpretation of the Teleostei will eventually include most or all of the Pholidophoroidea (Gardiner 1960:370; Halecostomi of Arambourg and Bertin 1958).

As Nybelin (1961) pointed out, any sound interpretation of teleostean origins must be based on a thorough knowledge of prototeleostean fossil forms, and such a knowledge is not now available. The present author can only contribute comments and an extended (cf. Whitehead 1963) characterization of the modern forms of 2 groups—the elopoids and the clupeoids—that may prove of value in working out the fossil material. These characterizations will doubtless have to be modified as knowledge of fossil material accumulates, and should not be construed as hard and fast bases for including or excluding specimens from the Elopoidei and Clupeoidei. For this reason, the characters of these groups will not be dealt with in contrasting form.

CLUPEOIDEI

A synopsis of the clupeoid fishes has recently been provided by Whitehead (1963), whose classification differs from that of Gosline (1960) chiefly in excluding the alepocephaloid fishes. Probably, the alepocephaloids and clupeoids are not closely related; in any event, with the very poorly known alepocephaloids out of the way, the clupeoids are much more easily defined. (To the argument that this leaves the alepocephaloids in a limbo area of clupeiform classification, 2 replies may be made: one is that there are already a number of other peripheral groups out there with it, see Gosline 1960:368; the other is that it is high time that somebody familiar with alepocephaloids worked on their anatomy and relationships.) With the alepocephaloids excluded, the Clupeoidei becomes a relatively small, compact group. All of the following specializations would seem to characterize these fishes and to be present rarely if ever elsewhere.

1. A temporal foramen present on the side of the skull, bounded by the parietal and the frontal bones (Ridewood 1905).

2. Paired posterior frontal fontanelles present in juveniles, sometimes retained in adults (Whitehead 1963).

3. Dermosphenotic not bordering orbit (see above).

4. Swimbladder with tubular extensions entering the hind part of the skull and forming vesicles (Marshall 1962), often with a posterior exit on the abdomen (de Beaufort 1909).

5. Uroneurals fused with preural[2] centrum 1 (the terminal vertebra of my previous papers); hypural 2 (3 of my earlier publications) fused basally with ural centrum 1 (postterminal centrum 1 of Gosline); hypural 1 (2 of Gosline) not in contact with centra (Gosline 1961:6).

6. Pelvic scute present (Whitehead 1963).

7. Intermuscular bones extending down along at least the first few hypaxial intermus-

cular septa, external to the pleural ribs. Many fishes have hypaxial intermuscular bones in the caudal region, but the clupeoids appear to be the only modern forms in which these are also found in the abdominal area (personal observation amplifying Emelianov 1935).

8. Scales with both the annuli and circuli oriented nearly transversely (personal observation amplifying Lagler 1947).

The clupeoid peculiarities listed above are certainly impressive. It seems most probable, however, that they will be considerably diminished as other groups are shown to belong with the clupeoids. One modern group that may well deserve addition is the Denticipitidae (Clausen 1959; Greenwood 1960, 1963; Marshall 1962:264). Another possible candidate is the Bathylaconidae (Parr 1948). Without doubt a whole series of fossil forms will eventually be added to the clupeoids, and some of these at least should prove transitional between the modern clupeoids and less specialized forms.

ELOPOIDEI

The modern elopoids are represented by 2 quite different groups, the Elopoidae and Albuloidae (Gosline 1960). Ridewood (1904: 54), speaking of the head skeleton, said: "Such resemblances as exist between them are explicable by the fact that neither has departed to any great extent from the ancestral group from which all Teleostean fishes sprang."

The diagnostic features held in common by most or all modern elopoids are:

1. All have parasphenoid teeth. Among modern teleosts parasphenoid teeth are found elsewhere in the osteoglossoids and among certain perciform groups: pristolepids, nandids, luciocephalids, ophiocephalids (channids), and anabantids. Whether the perciform parasphenoid teeth are homologous with those of elopoids would seem dubious on a priori grounds.

2. The supraorbital sensory canal passes forward over at least one separate prenasal ossicle in *Albula, Pterothrissus* (Gosline 1961: 24, Fig. 7B), and *Elops*. That of *Elops* is shown as fused to the anterior lateral rostral by Nybelin (1956:456, Fig. 2); this may be the normal situation in the adult *Elops*, but in the half-grown specimen examined by me, the prenasal canal-bearing ossicle and the

---

[2] Nybelin (1963) has proposed a somewhat different terminology for the caudal skeleton than that used by previous authors. Whereas earlier designations have been based primarily on function, that of Nybelin is founded on structures which in my experience at least are more stable. Nybelin's names are also an improvement over those proposed by me. They will therefore be used throughout this paper. The changes, compared with my previous terminology, involve the designations for centra and the numbering of hypurals.

anterior lateral rostral are separate. Separate, canal-bearing prenasal ossicles essentially similar to those of *Pterothrissus* occur in *Halosauropsis* among the Halosauriformes. In two "long-beaked" groups, the Scomberesocidae (Beloniformes) and *Sphyraena* (Mugiliformes), what appears to be a broken-off anterior piece of the nasal bone becomes more or less closely associated with the dorsal surface of the premaxillaries; a separate prenasal ossicle also occurs in a juvenile *Caranx* (personal observations).

3. In most, perhaps all, of the modern elopoids, the dermopalatine and autopalatine are closely associated but do not completely fuse (personal observation). In all other teleosts examined, these 2 bones are completely ankylosed in the half-grown and adults.

4. Projecting laterally from the pterygoid in *Albula, Pterothrissus,* and *Tarpon* is a flange which runs out below the eyeball practically to the circumorbital bones. Such a flange is present but reduced in *Megalops* and absent in *Elops*. Elsewhere among the teleosts it occurs in the clupeoid *Dussumieria* (Ridewood 1905:472).

5. There is a median gular plate in *Elops, Megalops,* and in a reduced state in *Albula* (Nybelin 1960). Elsewhere among teleosts, a much better-developed gular plate than that of *Albula* was observed on a University of Michigan skeleton of *Osteoglossum* (UMMZ 177342-5).

6. At the base of the upper half of the anterior pectoral ray in at least *Elops, Megalops, Albula,* and *Pterothrissus,* there is a separate triangular splint (personal observation). Such a splint seems to be unknown elsewhere among teleosts.

7. *Elops, Tarpon,* and *Albula,* but not *Megalops* and *Pterothrissus,* have enlarged fulcral scales in front of the caudal fin above and below. A similar pair of fulcral scales occurs in the scopeliform fish *Aulopus* and in a modified form in the clupeiform *Chanos* (personal observations).

8. Among teleosts, *Megalops, Albula,* and *Pterothrissus* are the only known genera with 2 rows of valves in the conus arteriosus of the heart (Senior 1907).

9. The elopoids all appear to have a leptocephalous larval stage. Leptocephalous larvae seem to occur elsewhere in the Anguilliformes, Saccopharyngiformes, and possibly in Halosauriformes.

Of the features listed above, all but 2 have doubtless been carried over from a "holostean" ancestor, and even those may or may not represent teleostean specializations. The first of these is the lateral pterygoid flange (4, above); the character is unknown but also probably uninvestigated in "holosteans." The other is the leptocephalous larval stage (9); there are no data on whether or not this is a teleostean development. As for the splint at the base of the upper half of the outer pectoral ray (6), this is found in the "holostean" *Amia*.

Ridewood's statement, quoted above, that the albulid–elopid resemblances are simply primitive teleostean features is, in short, not completely invalidated. It seems most probable that concepts concerning elopoid classification will have to be revised when fossil teleosts become better known.

In the above paragraphs, emphasis has been placed on the elopoids and the clupeoids merely because additional data on them were observed. Such emphasis should not be construed as meaning that a clupeoid–elopoid cleavage is the deepest in the Teleostei. It remains my personal belief, based on anatomical and not on the more crucial fossil evidence (see also Greenwood 1963), that the *Hiodon*–osteoglossoid–mormyroid group split off from the main teleostean stem at least as early as the clupeoids, and the same may be true of the Cypriniformes.

CONCLUSIONS AND SUMMARY

The Teleostei, as a terminal member of the three-level stage-of-structural-development series Chondrostei–Holostei–Teleostei, would seem to have little phylogenetic significance. However, it seems alternatively possible to view the Teleostei as a broadly expanded lineage of interrelated fishes, i.e., as a monophyletic group. As Parsons and Williams (1963:27) have nicely stated, monophyly "must be demonstrated, as monophyly is always demonstrated, by proving, first that the differences between the groups under analysis are not so great that an immediate common ancestor is at once ruled out; and, secondly, that the similarity in several systems is detailed enough and complex enough to make convergence in all these similarities very improbable." Both aspects of such a demonstration have been dealt with above. Recent suggestions that the teleosts are polyphyletic (see INTRODUCTION) have been discussed. To me they do not seem to have a very broad or firm basis; this of course is a matter of opinion. On the other hand, all or most of the modern lower teleostean groups (and all for which an independent origin has been suggested) have representatives with the following intricate attributes: (1) a suprabranchial organ, (2) a system for pumping water over the olfactory epithelium, composed in part of a hinged supraorbital–antorbital strut, and (3) a highly complex caudal skeleton including uroneural elements, as well as hypurals which are in part, at least, more numerous than the centra they articulate with and less numerous than the caudal rays. These features have never or rarely (uroneurals in *Eurycormus*) been found elsewhere than in the Teleostei; they would, in short, appear to be teleostean developments. Among supplementary features that would seem to aid in defining the Teleostei is the circumorbital configuration treated in some detail in this paper.

If the *Teleostei* is accepted as a monophyletic lineage, rather than as a level of structural organization, the question arises of what other lineages to place parallel with it for purposes of actinopterygian classification. There is no clear answer available, but if the Chondrostei and Holostei really are polyphyletic, the following groupings, representing efforts, at least, to separate out lineages, should be among those considered: the Brachiopterygii of Stensiö (1921), the Cheirolepidomorpha, Sturiomorpha, and Elonichthyomorpha of Aldinger (1937), the Semionitoidea, Pycnodontoidea, Aspidorhynchoidea, Amioidea, and Pholidophoroidea of Romer (1945) and Gardiner (1960), and the Ospiiformoidea of Gardiner (1960: 343).

LITERATURE CITED

ALDINGER, H. 1937. Permische Ganoidfische aus Ostgrönland. Medd. om Grønland 102 (3) :1–392.

ALLIS, E. P., JR. 1888. The anatomy and development of the lateral line system in *Amia calva*. J. Morph. 2:463–540.

——. 1904. The latero-sensory canals and related bones in fishes. Internat. Monats. Anat. Physiol. 21:401–502.

ARAMBOURG, C., AND L. BERTIN. 1958. Superordres des holostéens et des halécostomes (Holostei et Halecostomi). *In* Grassé "Traité de Zoologie" 13 (3) :2173–2203.

DE BEAUFORT, L. F. 1909. Die Schwimmblase der Malacopterygier. Morphol. Jahrb. 39:526–644.

BERG, L. S. 1940. Classification of fishes, both recent and fossil. Trav. Inst. Zool. Acad. Sci. U.R.S.S., Leningrad 5:87–517.

BERTMAR, G. 1962. On the ontogeny and evolution of the arterial vascular system in the head of the African characidean fish *Hepsetus odoë*. Acta Zool. 43 (2–3) :255–294.

CLAUSEN, H. S. 1959. *Denticipitidae*, a new family of primitive isospondylous teleosts from West African fresh-water. Vidensk. Medd. Dansk naturh. Foren. 121:141–151.

DERSCHIED, J. M. 1924. Structure de l'organe olfactif chez les poissons. Premiere partie. Osteichthyes, Teleostei, Malacopterygii. Ann. Soc. Roy. Zool., Bruxelles 54:76–162.

EMELIANOV, S. W. 1935. Die Morphologie der Fischrippen. Zool. Jahrb. (Anat.) 60:133–262.

GARDINER, B. G. 1960. A revision of certain actinopterygian and coelacanth fishes, chiefly from the Lower Lias. Bull. Brit. Mus. (Nat. Hist.) , Geol. 4 (7) :239–384.

GOSLINE, W. A. 1947. Contributions to the classification of the loricariid catfishes. Arq. Mus. Nac. Brasil 41:79–144.

——. 1960. Contribution toward a classification of modern isospondylous fishes. Bull. Brit. Mus. (Nat. Hist.) , Zool. 6 (6) :325–365.

——. 1961. Some osteological features of modern lower teleostean fishes. Smithsonian Misc. Coll. 143 (3) :1–42.

GREENWOOD, P. H. 1960. Fossil denticipitid fishes from East Africa. Bull. Brit. Mus. (Nat. Hist.) , Geol. 5 (1) :1–11.

——. 1963. The swimbladder in African Notopteridae (Pisces) and its bearing on the taxonomy of the family. Bull. Brit. Mus. (Nat. Hist.) , Zool. 11 (5) :377–412.

KIRKHOFF, H. 1958. Functionell-anatomische Untersuchung des Visceralapparates von *Clupea harengus* L. Zool. Jahrb. (Anat.) 76: 461–570.

LAGLER, K. F. 1947. Lepidological studies. 1.— Scale characters of the families of Great Lakes fishes. Trans. Am. Micr. Soc. 66 (2) :141–171.

LEKANDER, B. 1949. The sensory line system and the canal bones in the head of some ostariophysi. Acta Zool. 30:1–131.

MAKUSHOK, V. M. 1961. Some peculiarities in the structure of the seismosensory system of northern blenniids (Stichaeoidae, Blennioidei, Pisces). Trudy Inst. Oceanol. 43:225–269. (In Russian.)

MARSHALL, N. B. 1962. Observations on the Heteromi, an order of teleost fishes. Bull. Brit. Mus. (Nat. Hist.) , Zool. 9 (6) :249–270.

NORDEN, C. R. 1961. Comparative osteology of representative salmonid fishes, with particular reference to the grayling (*Thymallus arcticus*) and its phylogeny. J. Fish. Res. Bd. Can. 18 (5) :679–791.

NYBELIN, O. 1956. Les canaux sensoriels du museau chez *Elops saurus* (L.). Arkiv Zool. (2) 10 (9) :453–458.

——. 1960. A gular plate in *Albula vulpes* (L.). Nature 188 (4744) :78.

——. 1961. Über die Frage der Abstammung der rezenten primitiven Teleostier. Paläont. Zeitschr. 35:114–117.

——. 1962. Preliminary notes on two species previously named *Leptolepis bronni* Agassiz. Arkiv Zool. (2) 15 (18) :303–306.

————. 1963. Zur Morphologie und Terminologie des Schwanzskelettes der Actinopterygier. *Ibid.* (2) 15 (35) :485–516.

ØRVIG, T. 1957. Paleohistological notes. 1. On the structure of the bone tissue in the scales of certain Palaeonisciformes. Arkiv Zool. (2) 10 (12) :481–490.

PARR, A. E. 1948. The classification of the fishes of the genera *Bathylaco* and *Macromastax*, possible intermediates between the Isospondyli and the Iniomi. Copeia 1948 (1) :48–54.

PARSONS, T. S., AND E. E. WILLIAMS. 1963. The relationships of the modern amphibia: a reexamination. Quart. Rev. Biol. 38:26–53.

RIDEWOOD, W. G. 1904. On the cranial osteology of the fishes of the families Elopidae and Albulidae, with remarks on the morphology of the skull in the lower teleostean fishes generally. Proc. Zool. Soc. Lond. 1904 (2) :35–81.

————. 1905. On the cranial osteology of the clupeoid fishes. *Ibid.* 1904 (2) :448–493.

ROMER, A. S. 1945. Vertebrate paleontology. Second edition. Univ. Chicago Press, Chicago, Illinois.

SENIOR, H. D. 1907. Teleosts with a conus arteriosus having more than one row of valves. Anat. Rec. 1:83–84.

SMITH, C. L., AND R. M. BAILEY. 1962. The subocular shelf of fishes. J. Morph. 110:1–18.

STENSIÖ, E. A. 1921. Triassic fishes from Spitzbergen. Part 1. Adolf Holzhausen, Vienna.

————. 1932. Triassic fishes from East Greenland. Medd. om Grønland 83 (3) :1–305.

————. 1935. *Sinamia zdanskyi*, a new amiid from the Lower Cretaceous of Shantung, China. Pal. Sinica (C) 3 (1) :1–48.

THYS VAN DEN AUDENAERDE, D. F. E. 1961. L'anatomie de *Phraetolaemus ansorgei* Blgr. et la position systématique des Phraetolaemidae. Ann. Mus. Roy. Afr. Cent., ser. 8, 103:101–167.

WEITZMAN, S. H. 1962. The osteology of *Brycon meeki*, a generalized characid fish, with an osteological definition of the family. Stanford Ichthyol. Bull. 8 (1) :1–77.

WESTOLL, T. S. 1944. The Haplolepidae, a new family of late Carboniferous fishes. Bull. Am. Mus. Nat. Hist. 83 (1) :1–122.

WHITEHEAD, P. J. P. 1963. A contribution to the classification of the clupeoid fishes. Ann. Mag. Nat. Hist. (13) 5 (60) :737–750.

WOODWARD, A. S. 1895. Catalogue of the fossil fishes of the British Museum. Part III. London.

DEPARTMENT OF ZOOLOGY, UNIVERSITY OF HAWAII, HONOLULU, HAWAII.

Phyletic Studies of Teleostean Fishes, with a Provisional Classification of Living Forms

P. H. GREENWOOD, D. E. ROSEN, S. H. WEITZMAN, G. S. MYERS

Bulletin of the American Museum of Natural History

INTRODUCTION

HISTORY

THE LATEST widely accepted general classification of teleostean fishes is that of Berg (1940) * and in neither its second edition, edited by Svetovidov (Berg, 1955), nor its German translation (Berg, 1958), is the arrangement of the teleosts materially altered. Berg's teleostean groupings, like those of Jordan (1923), closely reflect the conclusions reached by Regan in a long series of brilliant papers culminating in his brief general exposition (Regan, 1929). Regan's teleostean papers, in turn, were built upon the much earlier foundations laid by Boulenger (1904) and Woodward (1901), and, in the nineteenth century, by Günther, Cope (1871), and Gill (1872, 1893). In fact, except for relatively minor revisions, shifts, and splitting, most of the major groups of living teleosts recognized by Berg do not depart in any revolutionary way from those recognized 70 to 90 years ago by Gill.

In reviewing the literature on fish classification, we were greatly impressed by an almost forgotten scheme proposed by Garstang (1931). Garstang's classification was surprisingly modern in concept and was in effect a rebellion against the rigidity of a taxonomy in which the compartments were artificially arranged and rounded off. In Garstang's own words, a classification consisting of ". . . an array of detached and isolated orders, which conveys no explicit outline of the evolutionary succession . . ." is wrong in that "Its very flatness and lack of relief is indeed a misrepresentation of nature."

More than 20 years ago, Woodward (1942) published a prophetic little paper on the beginnings of teleostean fishes, in which he advanced the view that the Teleostei, long recognized as a natural, monophyletic group, in reality had evolved as a number of distinct lineages from diverse holostean ancestors in the Mesozoic. Indeed, during the past 35 or 40 years, it has become generally recognized by paleo-ichthyologists that the holosteans themselves represent merely a stage or level of organization into or through which numerous actinopterygian lines passed during their evolution from separate stocks of Late Palaeozoic or Early Mesozoic palaeoniscoid derivatives. Woodward's paper was not widely noted by students of living teleosts, but Bertelsen and Marshall (1956), in discussing the mirapinnids, explicitly supported the view that different teleostean lineages have attained certain comparable grades of organization. The idea of teleostean polyphyletism was expressed by Bertin and Arambourg (1958, p. 2208) in their extensive account of the group. However, their treatment of the living forms appeals to us as chiefly another reshuffling of long-recognized entities, improved here and there by Arambourg's extensive knowledge of fossil teleosts, but marred by an unfortunate lack of familiarity with many Recent groups as well as by such egregious errors as acceptance of Y. Le Danois' (1961) imprecise and unacceptable work on the tetraodontiforms.

Thus we are left at the present day with no general classification of teleostean fishes that has utilized those modern concepts of phyletic classification that have become com-

*To get complete citations for references listed in this abridged version, see the original article.

From *Bulletin of the American Museum of Natural History* 131(4):345–354. Reprinted by permission.

mon in the study of mammalian evolution (e.g., Simpson, 1945). Yet the feeling has been growing among our group and others that many of the most generally recognized teleostean orders are no more than catch-alls for separate lineages which have attained a comparable stage of specialization or complexity (see particularly Gosline, 1960).

THEORY

The problems faced in attempting a "natural" taxonomic classification of a large and varied group of organisms have been widely discussed (see Rensch, 1960, and especially Simpson, 1961). The problems are greatest when the meaningful part of the fossil record is relatively scanty, as it is in in the teleosts, and relationships must be inferred largely on the basis of the morphology of living stocks. The question of "horizontal" versus "vertical" classifications in such groups becomes essentially that of typological versus phyletic taxonomy, which Simpson (1960, pp. 46–66) has adequately discussed.

Teleostean classification, up to and including not only Berg's work, but also a very large part of that of Bertin and Arambourg (1958), has been arrived at primarily by methods that are essentially typological in nature—an attempt first to define orders and other higher taxa and then to speculate upon their origin, albeit in the light of the known fossils. In the mammals, the preponderant weight of the fossil over other evidence long ago forced mammalogists to the phyletic type of classification. No such revolution in teleostean classification has occurred up to the present day.

Of the present authors, Myers has thought for a number of years that the varied "order" of "isospondylous" or "clupeiform" fishes is a polyphyletic assemblage; Greenwood (1963) has already begun the demonstration that such is true; while Rosen (1964 and other work) has begun the dismemberment of Regan's "percomorphs," and the preliminary demonstration of the affinities of certain perchlike groups with the relatives of the salmonoids. Moreover, all of us (see especially Weitzman, 1964, p. 154, and our discussion below on the gonorynchoid fishes) have more recently begun to think that the ostariophysan fishes may be far older than was previously believed and contain separate lineages running back to a generalized Mesozoic teleostean. Our prime purpose, then, has been to separate and point out what we believe to have been the main and subsidiary phyletic lineages of teleosts and the often parallel or converging trends that characterize the evolution of these lines. We have not been especially interested in the definition of living (or fossil) "groups" as such. Definitions of higher taxa, even those based on deep and extensive study of living assemblages, are rarely very full or precise and are seldom used except by those who wish to emend them.

However, unless one wishes to abandon the principle that taxonomic classification should relfect what can be determined of phylogeny (as some people do), taxa that are obviously polyphyletic must be broken up and a new classification must be adopted.

The classification that we now propose is based on an analysis of what we consider to be the predominant evolutionary trends in the teleosts. By basing the definitions of groups solely on these trends, we have tried to free teleostean classification as much as possible from the confining influences of typology.

This classification is not intended to be definitive at any level. As originally conceived, it was to be nothing more than a series of discussions outlining some new evidence bearing on fish relationships, some new thoughts stemming from the reconsideration of old evidence, and a synopsis of certain outstanding problems. As the work proceeded we realized the need to fill in those areas with which we were not primarily concerned. Indirectly this led to the gradual compilation of a list of family-group and higher taxonomic names. This list, with the subsequent addition of synonymic familial and ordinal names, is included and is intended merely as a nucleus for further search. A series of outline drawings illustrating each of the major families mentioned in the classification is appended.

The families recognized, and their placement, follow Berg's (1940) arrangement but with emendations based on works published subsequently and on unpublished information supplied by our colleagues.

TELEOSTEAN DIVERSITY AND AGE

Although the teleosteans are far from being the well-circumscribed group that Johannes Müller (1845) and his successors believed them to be, they are at the present time well separated from the living holosteans and chondrosteans. The term "teleostean" (or "teleost") has meaning, even if it represents merely the final grand stage which so many diverse lines of actinopterygian (or teleostome) fishes have attained, and within which the actinopterygians have flowered into the largest (hence, by some definitions, the most successful) of all major vertebrate groups.

Their diveristy is astounding. Estimates of the number of living species vary from somewhat under 20,000 up to 40,000. The facts that discovery of new species and genera is still commonplace, and that new forms of considerable evolutionary importance (e.g., *Denticeps* and many recently described deepsea forms) are still being discovered at a surprising rate, demonstrate that we are further from a reasonably complete knowledge of living teleosts than we are of any other large, non-piscine, vertebrate group. Bailey (1960) estimated the present total to be somewhat fewer than 17,000 species, and Myers (1958) estimated that the eventual total number of living species will approach or surpass 30,000. The most numerous additions to the total may be expected in the deep seas and in the excessively rich fresh-water fauna of tropical America.

Unlike mammals, of which most of the living orders had their origin in the Cenozoic and of which extremely few relicts of Mesozoic or early Cenozoic type persist, a considerable number of living teleosts belong to genera close to or perhaps even identical with Eocene, Paleocene, or Cretaceous forms. Also unlike mammals, the number of known living genera and species far surpasses the number of known fossils. For these reasons, a classification based principally on the Recent teleosts, as this one is, has far more validity than would a classification based on Recent mammals, or the Recent forms of other large vertebrate groups.

Fishes of teleostean type (Leptolepididae) first appear in the known fossil record in the Middle Triassic. Some of these are so advanced in the details of their structure that we can speculate that the shift from the holostean to the teleostean level began much earlier in some forms. However, the dearth of Early Mesozoic fossils of teleostean type, except in marine Triassic and Jurassic beds in the area of the Tethys Sea, may be related to a fresh-water origin of many teleostean lines in regions where fresh-water, fish-bearing deposits are rare or undiscovered. The many teleosts known from the deposits of epeiric seas laid down during the Late Cretaceous indicate that several lineages had by then attained an organization similar to that of living forms. This statement is especially true of the elopoid and berycoid lines. However, the absence in known Cretaceous deposits of several important lines of teleostean development (notably the salmonoids and ostariophysans, which give considerable evidence of an age comparable to that of the elopoids) again leads to the suspicion that much teleostean evolution was going on in Mesozoic fresh waters—evolution of which we as yet have no trace.

By the Eocene, or possible even the Paleocene, teleostean marine shore-faunas bore a striking resemblance to modern assemblages, a fact that again is wholly unlike the situation in mammals. Since that time, a number of teleostean families appear to have undergone comparatively little change.

Unfortunately, we know compartively little about Paleogene fresh-water or deepsea fishes in any part of the world. We may presume that ostariophysan types not greatly different from living forms were in residence on nearly all the continents, a presumption based on some concrete fossil evidence. The appearance of undoubted bathypelagic stomiatoid and myctophoid fishes in Early Neogene records, in which these fishes are of wholly modern type, leads also to a presumption that they, too, arose much earlier.

We have not excluded fossils from consideration, although we do not place them in our formal classification. A number of important fossils are discussed in the expository comments preceding our classification. Paleo-ichthyologists who deal extensively with teleostean fossils are quite aware that the classification of living teleosts must be understood before the fossil record can be properly interpreted.

NATURE OF MAJOR GROUPINGS ADOPTED

ENOUGH IS SAID above about the evolutionary trends exhibited by different lineages to indicate our belief that these lineages often pass through or arrive at similar levels or stages of organization. We propose, for example, that separate evolutionary routes toward the acanthopterygian grade had been traversed by relatively unrelated lines, and we also propose that the malacopterygian level probably was attained polyphyletically from holosteans of pholidophoroid type.

The following series of synopses and discussions outline the reasons for the new alignments given in the formal classification. The principal innovations in this classification are the separation of the teleostean fishes into three divisions[1] and the realignment of taxa among eight superorders (fig. 1). Various smaller groups (suborders and families) are redistributed among orders, both new and old.

In our conception, each of the three divisions represents a distinct phyletic lineage derived from the holostean level of organization. It is presumed that in Division I a primitive elopiform ancestor has produced principally the eels and eel-like fishes and perhaps also the herring-like fishes. However, we know of no evidence to rule out the possiblity that the herrings and their allies had an independent origin from among the pholidophoroids. For the present, and because elopomorphs and clupeomorphs appear more closely related to one another than to other groups, we have followed a conventional alignment of these fishes.

In Division II there have evolved only two series of unusually specialized, and predominantly fresh-water, radiations, the Osteoglossiformes and Mormyriformes. Neither of these orders could possibly have been involved in the ancestry of other teleosteans.

By contrast with the other divisions, Division III contains the bulk of the living teleostean fishes. There have evolved within this division several radiations leading to more than one organizational level and to the dominant groups of extant fresh-water and marine species, namely, the Ostariophysi and the Acanthopterygii.

In the discussions below of the major structural and developmental divisional trends, where we outline the reasons for erecting the various new orders and superorders, a separate analysis is given of the suborders Stomiatoidei and Alepocephaloidei of Division III because of their previous placement near groups here included in Division I. The ordinal and subordinal composition of the superorder Ostariophysi is also given in detail. The one superorder not discussed at length is the Atherinomorpha. It does not fall readily within the concepts of either of two adjoining groups, the Paracanthopterygii and Acanthopterygii, although it includes forms at more or less the same organizational level as the fishes of those superorders. The main structural and developmental characteristics of the Atherini-

---

[1]Parenthetically, we should mention that the possibility of utilizing the methods of numerical taxonomy to help solve many of the major questions of relationships has occurred to us. Our reluctant conclusion has been that the work of encoding (for computer techniques) the at times esoteric (and so heavily weighted) evidence that we have dealt with would not only have violated the weightless spirit of numerical taxonomy, but perhaps been postponed presentation of our results until our respective retirement ages. However, for the benefit of our "numerical" colleagues, we have numbered our major divisions (I, II, III).

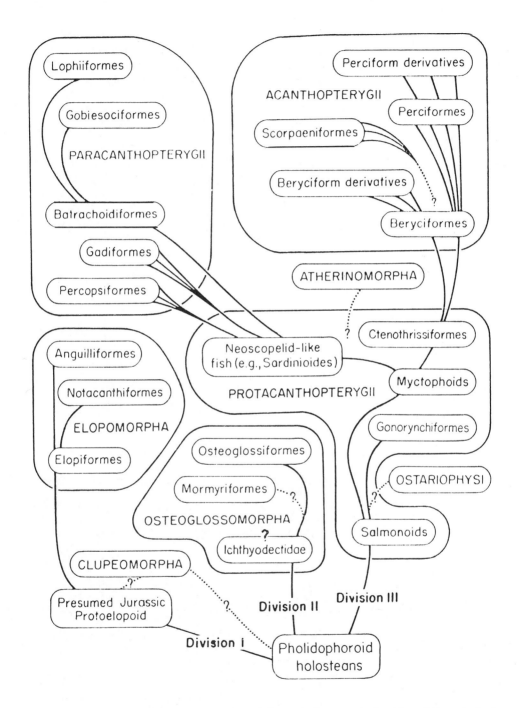

Fɪɢ. 1. Diagram showing our conception of the evolutionary relationships of the principal groups of teleostean fishes. Uncertain relationships are shown by a broken line and question mark.

formes, the only contained order of the Atherinomorpha, were described in some detail by Rosen (1964).

Among the various living primitive groups of teleosteans, only elopids (Division I) and salmonids (Division III) are sufficiently generalized to be suitable morphologically as basal types for the major teleostean radiations. Other primitive groups, for example, the clupeiforms and osteoglossiforms, are too specialized for this role. We realize that elopids, of all teleosts, possess the greatest assemblage of holostean characters. At the same time, we recognize that their larval and other specializations, and the absence of certain snout and jaw structures (see discussions below), put at least the living elopids off the main course of teleostean evolution. Salmonids, on the other hand, have none of these limitations and thus seem better to fulfill the requirements of a morphotype that may have given rise to the major radiations of Division III. A question that naturally arises from this conclusion concerns the possibilities that elopids and salmonids might have arisen polyphyletically from the holostean level or monophyletically from a single holostean or early teleostean entity. Elopids are still so close the holostean grade, however (indeed, some workers consider them to be holosteans), that a common ancestor of these two modern groups, if it existed, was itself likely to have been an advanced type of holostean fish. If this view is supported by paleontological evidence, as we think it ultimately will be, the salmonids and elopids would represent separate attainments of the teleostean grade and thus would be, *ex hypothesis*, examples of polyphyletism, at least at the teleostean level.

MAJOR TRENDS WITHIN THE DIVISIONS AND SUPERORDERS

DIVISION I

Fishes of ancestry at or near the holostean level of organization in which each contained group except for the eel-like fishes has one or more very primitive members.

Characteristic and often primitive trends include:

1. The development, particularly in the compressed, silvery, marine fishes, of a short, broad, and arcuate maxilla equipped with large movable supramaxillae in association with a high coronoid process on the dentary and articular.
2. The development of maxillary teeth that are seldom excluded from the gape, even partially.
3. The development of parasphenoid and pterygoid teeth.
4. The development in the basicranium of numerous separate intraosseous passages for the parts of the fifth and seventh cranial nerves and certain major blood vessels.
5. The development of a full complement of intermuscular bones.
6. Caudal fin, when present, with hypural supports on one to four centra.
7. The development of a functional ductus pneumaticus.
8. The development of an otophysic connection[1] not involving the intercalation of bony elements.
9. The development of an ethmoidal commissure of the cephalic lateral-line system.
10. The development of a confluence between the preopercular and infraorbital cephalic lateral-line canals, hence the formation of a recessus lateralis.
11. The development of a leptocephalous larva.

---

[1]We define "otophysic connection" as the involvement of the swim bladder with the otic region, usually effected through bilateral prolongations of the swim bladder which either come into superficial contact with the cranium in the region of the inner ear or penetrate the cranial wall and form an intimate association with the inner ear intracranially. Exceptionally the swim bladder-ear connection may be effected through a chain of ossicles linking the perilymphatic cavity with the swim-bladder wall.

ELOPOMORPHA

1. Principally marine fishes of diverse form, most of the modern species eel-like.
2. Gular plate in non-eel-like representatives.
3. Branchiostegals usually very numerous.
4. Mesocoracoid arch present only in the non-eel-like forms.
5. Hypurals, when present, on three or more centra.
6. Ethmoidal commissure present or in modified state in many groups.
7. Opercular series often reduced or even absent.
8. Larva, when known, a leptocephalus.

CLUPEOMORPHA

1. Silvery compressed fishes, usually marine, with caducous scales.
2. Branchiostegals numbering as high as 15, but usually fewer.
3. Intracranial diverticula of swim bladder forming bullae within the ear capsule.
4. Mesocorocoid arch invariably present.
5. Hypurals on one to three centra.
6. Cephalic lateral-line canals extending over operculum; usually no lateral-line pores on trunk.
7. Recessus lateralis present.

DIVISION II

Fishes of ancestry at or near the holostean level of organization in which all contained members have retained numerous primitive characteristics of the jaw suspension and shoulder girdle, and have developed complexly ornamented scales.

Characteristically primitive trends, and some of the divisional specializations, include:

1. The fusion of the premaxillae into a single bone.
2. The development of a simple, well-toothed maxilla (edentulous in the Mormyriformes), generally contributing to the gape but partially excluded in a few genera.
3. The development of parasphenoid, glossohyal, and pterygoid teeth.
4. The fusion of various elements in the palatopterygoid arch, the palatine and vomer fused in Mormyriformes.
5. The development of paired tendon bones (uncalcified in *Hiodon*) on the second hypobranchial or second hypobranchial and basibranchial, in all genera.
6. The loss, in many species, of multiple intraosseous passages in the prootic bone for the fifth and seventh cranial nerves and certain major blood vessels.
7. A reduction, in two phyletic lines, of the caudal fin and its confluence with the dorsal and anal fins.
8. The development, in those genera with a distinct caudal fin, of a supporting skeleton of which the elements are not readily homologized with similar elements in fishes of other divisions. There is a reduction in the number of hypural elements which are apparently supported by two and a half centra in all except one genus (*Hiodon*), in which three centra are involved and there is a full complement of hypurals.
9. A reduction in size, or loss, of the suboperculum.
10. The development of upper intermuscular bones only.
11. The development of a functional ductus pneumaticus.
12. The development of an otophysic connection not involving the intercalation of bony elements in the young or adults of all groups except the Osteoglossoidei in which no connection exists.
13. The development of distinctly separated preopercular and infraorbital canals and the occurrence in a single genus (*Pantodon*) of a suprapreopercular bone.
14. The development of somatic electric organs in one order.

OSTEOGLOSSOMORPHA

1. Fresh-water and predominantly tropical fishes of extraordinarily diverse body form and size, and including one form in which the pectorals are greatly expanded so as

to give the impression of a flying fish. Most species are insectivorous or piscivorous.

2. Premaxillae ankylosed to form a single median bone in one order (Mormyriformes) and in one genus of the Osteoglossoidei (*Pantodon*); the premaxillae firmly bound to the ethmovomerine region in all genera.

3. Primary bite of mouth between parasphenoid and glossohyal and basihyals.

4. Head of palatine without maxillary process.

5. Branchiostegals three to five, in two cases 11 and 13.

6. Subtemporal fossae present in only a few genera.

7. Expansive suprascapulars in all except the Osteoglossoidei.

8. A lateral cranial foramen in most species (Osteoglossoidei excepted).

9. Hypurals, in fishes with distinct caudal fins, reduced in number by fusion of the upper elements and, apparently, supported on at least two and a half centra in all.

DIVISION III

Fishes mostly of distinctively teleostean level ancestry, only a single basal group having obviously holostean affinities.

Characteristic trends include:

1. The lowering of the center of gravity and the approximation of the center of buoyancy with the center of mass.

2. The development of a large, frequently mobile premaxilla that completely or partially excludes the maxilla from the gape.

3. The loss of maxillary teeth and functional supramaxillae.

4. The loss of parasphenoid and pterygoid teeth.

5. The development of an os pharyngeus inferior and an os pharyngeus superior and the development of mm. retractores arcua branchialia attached to the third to sixth vertebrae.

6. The development in the basicranium of a common passage (trigeminofacialis chamber) for the fifth and seventh nerves and orbital artery and head vein.

7. Loss of the supraorbital bone.

8. The reduction in size of the infraorbital bones.

9. The reduction in the number of scale bones in the dorsicranium.

10. The loss or reduction of certain temporal fossae but the enlargement of the post-temporal fossa and the loss of its roof.

11. The covering of the posterior part of the dorsicranium by epaxial body muscles.

12. The elevation of the pectoral fin base on the side.

13. The forward migration of the pelvic girdle and its linkage with the pectoral girdle.

14. The reduction in the number of pectoral radials.

15. The reduction in the number of vertebrae and of pelvic and caudal fin rays.

16. Reduction of intermuscular bones.

17. Reduction of the hypural bones to a single unit on a terminal half-centrum.

18. The varied specialization of caudal fin shape.

19. The development of an adipose fin in several primitive lines.

20. The development of fin spines and ctenoid scales.

21. The development of an otophysic connection involving the intercalation of bony elements.

22. The disappearance of the ductus pneumaticus.

23. The development of distinctly separated preopercular and infraorbital canals, hence, the frequent occurrence of a suprapreopercular bone.

24. The development along the trunk of a ramus lateralis accessorius of the seventh nerve.

PROTACANTHOPTERYGH

1. Predominantly slender, predatory fishes; many generalized and some specialized forms in fresh water.

2. Photophores in oceanic representatives.

3. Widespread trend toward exclusion by premaxillae of the maxillae from the gape.

4. Widespread trend toward the development of premaxillary processes.

5. Palatopremaxillary and ethmomaxillary ligaments present in numerous representatives.

6. Upper jaw slightly protrusile in a few cases.

7. Glossohyal teeth usually prominent.

8. Branchiostegals very numerous in many instances, reduced to two or three in some cases.

9. Hyoid and branchiostegal skeleton approaching paracanthopterygian and acanthopterygian form.

10. Paired proethmoids present in many cases, often simulating ascending premaxillary processes.

11. Few species with opercular spines or serrations.

12. Mesocoracoid present in generalized lines only.

13. Baudelot's ligament to first vertebra.

14. Occasional trends for the pelvic fins to advance; pelvics commonly of more than six rays.

15. Occational trends toward elevation of the pectoral fin base on flank.

16. Vertebrae commonly more than 24, precaudal elements commonly 15 or more.

17. Hypurals on one to three centra, but a basic acanthopterygian caudal skeleton developed in some representatives and a paracanthopterygian type in others; caudal fin commonly with more than 15 branched rays.

18. Adipose fin present in most species.

19. Suprapreopercular (canal-bearing ossicle above uppermost part of preopercular canal) present in generalized representatives.

OSTARIOPHYSI

1. Predominantly fresh-water fishes of worldwide distribution on the continents and adjoining archipelagoes, of extraordinarily diverse form and habits, encompassing numerous well-toothed predatory and vegetarian types and toothless detritus and microphagous types, many of both categories with well-developed circumoral barbels.

2. Upper jaw protrusile in numerous species.

3. Major trends toward reduction in number (or absence) of jaw teeth.

4. Lower pharyngeal bones usually well developed.

5. Branchiostegals generally few in number but as many as 15 in some species.

6. Pelvic fins abdominal.

7. Hypurals on one centrum.

8. Fin spines present in numerous instances.

9. Scales present or absent, when present cycloid in most instances, ctenoid in a few, and in certain forms replaced by dense, bony plates.

10. Adipose fin in many groups.

11. Otophysic connections involving the intercalation of bony elements in all.

12. Swim bladder primitively subdivided, reduced in many species.

13. Suprapreopercular (ossicle above uppermost part of preopercular canal) in numerous species.

PARACANTHOPTERYGII

1. Mostly marine, stout, soft-bodied fishes inhabiting deep waters or when in shallow water being nocturnal or occurring in cryptic habitats.

2. Virtual loss of photophores.

3. Feeding mechanism adapted for carnivorous diet in all species.

4. Ascending process of premaxilla often joined to premaxilla by flexible cartilage, or absent; premaxilla with an articular process in all cases, and with a lateral (maxillary) process in most cases.

5. Ethmomaxillary and palatopremaxillary ligaments well developed.

6. Upper jaw not protractile.

7. Mm. levator maxillae superioris well developed, or modified and consolidated with part of m. adductor mandibulae.

8. Superficial division of m. adductor mandibulae reduced or absent.

9. M. adductor arcus palatini covering floor of orbit.

10. Ceratohyal and epihyal ankylosed.

11. Branchiostegals not exceeding six in number, the bladelike elements with an anteroproximal prong in most species; the four bladelike elements on the outer face of elevated part of hyoid bar, the anterior hairlike elements on the inner side of the depressed anterior section of ceratohyal.

12. Upper and lower pharyngeal bones well developed and toothed.

13. No subocular shelf on infraorbital bones.

14. Extrascapular bones present, often forming solid roof for posttemporal fossae.

15. Parietals meeting in midline or closely approaching one another in most species and frequently housing a posttemporal commissure of the cephalic lateral-line system.

16. Intercalar very extensive in numerous species.

17. Mucous canals prominent on head of most species.

18. Baudelot's ligament to first vertebra, or to basicranium where first vertebra is fused to basioccipital.

19. Modified epipleural ribs ("endocleithra") from exoccipitals to cleithrum in several species.

20. Mesocoracoid absent; pectoral radials two to 13, often hourglass-shaped, very long, and extending well beyond the scapulocoracoid margin.

21. Pelvic fins thoracic, jugular, or mental in all but one species, with occasionally as many as 17 rays.

22. Pleural ribs often reduced, frequently absent.

23. Caudal skeleton, when present, with two large hypurals on separate vertebrae in most, or the two fused together into a single unicentral unit.

24. Fin spines developed or not.

25. Ctenoid scales developed in some species.

26. Swim bladder frequently subdivided and connected by diverticulae to parapophyses of precaudal vertebrae, in some instances an otophysic connection involving the intercalation of bony elements.

27. Numerous species viviparous.

ATHERINOMORPHA

1. Generally small surface-feeding fishes, principally in fresh and brackish water, some marine, most fresh-water species with pronounced secondary sexual dimorphism in size, in color, and in fin shape and function; many species with bony external male genitalia developed from anal, pelvic, or pectoral fin, or some combination of these.

2. Upper jaw protractile in many species, without true ascending processes, and supported by a foundation of loose connective tissue and a complex maxillary process, without palatopremaxillary or ethmomaxillary ligaments.

3. Mm. levator maxillae superioris absent.

4. Superficial division of m. adductor mandibulae present and well developed, with a tendon to the lower maxillary shaft.

5. Upper and lower pharyngeal bones well developed, dentigerous, the upper bones consisting of a large plate made up of pharyngobranchials 3 and 4 and smaller modified pharyngobranchial 2; pharyngobranchial 1 present but obsolescent in only a few instances.

6. Ceratohyal and epihyal joined together by dorsal lamella.

7. Branchiostegals four to 15 in number.

8. Mesethmoid usually bilaminar, invariably discoidal or scalelike.

9. Infraorbital series reduced to two, rarely three, elements.

10. Opercular bones unarmed.

11. Pectoral radials four in number, cuboidal, recessed within excavation in scapulocoracoid margin.

12. Supracleithrum, when present, discoidal, confined within dorsal tip of cleithrum.

13. Baudelot's ligament to basicranium.

14. Pelvic girdle abdominal, subabdominal, or thoracic.

15. Vertebral number high in most species, precaudal number modally 20.

16. Caudal skeleton with two large hypural plates of opposite symmetry on terminal half-centrum, with in no instance more than four hypurals, of which two are invariably broad and fan-shaped.

17. Fin spines present or not.

18. Ctenoid scales in relatively few species.

19. Numerous viviparous species, some with unique encapsuled or unencapsuled spermatophores.

20. In oviparous species, egg large, demersal, with adhesive filaments, and without oil globule.

21. Embryo with heart displaced forward anterior to head.

ACANTHOPTERYGII

1. Fishes of extremely variable form and habits, principally in salt water and principally benthic and littoral.

2. Photophores very uncommon.

3. Feeding mechanisms extremely varied, permitting the utilization of numerous food sources.

4. Upper jaw protractile in many species, with a premaxilla having ascending, articular, and lateral (maxillary) processes.

5. Palatopremaxillary and ethmomaxillary ligaments present, but in some cases modified.

6. Mm. levator maxillae superioris muscle absent in all but one genus (*Polymixia*).

7. Superficial division of the m. adductor mandibulae well developed.

8. M. adductor arcus palatini usually confined to posterior wall of orbit.

9. Upper and lower pharyngeals well developed and toothed.

10. Hyoid bar with ankylosed ceratohyal and epihyal; distal, depressed section of ceratohyal with large foramen in many cases; elevated proximal part of ceratohyal and epihyal with four bladelike branchiostegals, the hairlike anterior branchiostegals, when present, or inner surface of depressed distal section of ceratohyal.

11. A subocular shelf present on the infraorbital series in numerous species.

12. Infraorbital bones frequently in contact with preoperculum.

13. Bones of head commonly with numerous pungent spines.

14. Opercular apparatus armed in many species.

15. Baudelot's ligament usually attached to basicranium, rarely (Polymixiidae and some Scorpaenidae) to first vertebra.

16. Supracleithrum strutlike, extending above cleithral tip in most members of the group.

17. Mesocoracoid absent; pectoral radials not exceeding four in number, often hourglass-shaped.

18. Pelvic fins, if present, thoracic or jugular in position, pectorals inserted high on the sides.

19. Pelvic fin typically consisting of a spine and five articulated rays except in berycoids and a few other forms.

20. Pleural ribs usually well developed.

21. Vertebrae commonly numbering 24, with usually equal numbers of caudal and precaudal elements, except in some elongate and in most fresh-water forms.

22. Hypural bones virtually always emanating from a single centrum; when on two centra, the hypurals no fewer than six in number, in no case formed as two hypural plates as in the Paracanthopterygii.

23. Caudal branched rays in most species 15, 17 in more primitive members of the group.

24. Fin spines present in most species.

25. Ctenoid scales common.

26. Presumably uniformly physoclistic.

27. Otophysic connections rare, in no case involving the intercalation of bony elements.

28. Viviparity uncommon.

29. Egg shape and buoyancy highly variable.

PROVISIONAL OUTLINE CLASSIFICATION
OF THE TELEOSTEAN FISHES[1]

DIVISION I

SUPERORDER ELOPOMORPHA
  Order Elopiformes (Isospondyli in part, Clupeiformes in part)
    Suborder Elopoidei
      Elopidae (Elopsidae in part)
      Megalopidae (Elopsidae in part)
    Suborder Albuloidei
      Albulidae (including Pterothrissidae, Bathythrissidae)
  Order Anguilliformes (Apodes, Lyomeri, Saccopharyngiformes, Monognathiformes, Anguillomorphi)
    Suborder Anguilloidei
      Anguillidae
      Moringuidae (including Stilbiscidae, Anguillichthyidae, Ratabouridae)
      Myrocongridae
      Xenocongridae (including Chlopsidae, Echelidae in part, Myridae in part, Muraenichthyidae, Chilorhinidae)
      Muraenidae (including Echidnidae, Heteromyridae)
      Heterenchelyidae (Heterenchelidae)
      Dysomminidae (Dysominidae)
      Muraenesocidae (including Sauromuraenesocidae)
      Neenchelyidae
      Nettastomatidae (Nettastomidae)
      Nessorhamphidae
      Congridae (Congeridae, Leptocephalidae, including Heterocongridae, Colocongridae)
      Ophichthidae (Ophichthyidae, including Myrophidae, Echelidae in part, Myridae in part)
      Todaridae
      Synaphobranchidae (including Ilyophidae)
      Simenchelyidae (Simenchelidae)
      Dysommidae
      Derichthyidae
      Macrocephenchelyidae (Macrocephenchelidae)
      Serrivomeridae (including Gavialicipitidae)
      Nemichthyidae (including Avocettinidae, Avocettinopsidae)
      Cyemidae
      Aoteidae (Aoteridae)
    Suborder Saccopharyngoidei
      Saccopharyngidae

---

[1] Our attention has been called to a recent purportedly complete list of the generic and familial names of fishes (Golvan, 1962). Its author does not admit to familiarity with Jordan's "Classification" (1923), and the errors in it are exceedingly numerous. In addition, a curious and little-known classification was published by E. Le Danois in 1943. Although this author's three major groups (orders) of teleosts are manifestly polyphyletic, his alignment of their contained suborders departs from those of Regan and Berg (Berg's classification was, apparently, not seen by Le Danois). We can find little to support the reasoning behind the construction of most of the proposed groups. The principal weakness of this classification lies in the author's failure to consider more than a few, generally superficial and insufficiently studied characters, combined with rather naive views on the interpretation of palaeontological evidence. Two other recent classifications, both in Japanese, which depart radically from each other and from our own, were proposed by Matsubara (1955, 1963). In these, the author follows the Stenzel system of ordinal suffixes, but his ordinal names are not incorporated in our present classification. Finally, we must mention a classification proposed by Tretiakov (1944), which is the outline of an arrangement of the orders and suborders based largely on the pattern of cephalic lateral-line canals. A number of new ordinal names were proposed which are accorded a place in our lists of synonyms.

Eurypharyngidae
Monognathidae
Order Notacanthiformes (Lyopomi, Heteromi, Halosauriformes)
Halosauridae
Lipogenyidae (Lipogenidae)
Notacanthidae
SUPERORDER CLUPEOMORPHA
Order Clupeiformes (Isospondyli in part)
Suborder Denticipitoidei
Denticipitidae (Igborichthyidae)
Suborder Clupeoidei
Clupeidae (Clupidae, including Dorosomatidae, Dorosomidae, Clupanodontidae, Dussumieridae, Dussumieriidae, Dussumeriidae, Congothrissidae, Pristigasteridae)
Engraulidae (Engraulididae, including Stolephoridae)
Chirocentridae

DIVISION II

SUPERORDER OSTEOGLOSSOMORPHA
Order Osteoglossiformes (Isospondyli in part, Clupeiformes in part)
Suborder Osteoglossoidei
Osteoglossidae (including Arapaimidae, Clupisudidae, Heterotidae)
Pantodontidae
Suborder Notopteroidei
Hiodontidae (Hyodontidae)
Notopteridae
Order Mormyriformes (Isospondyli in part, Clupeiformes in part, Scyphophori)
Mormyridae
Gymnarchidae

DIVISION III

SUPERORDER PROTACANTHOPTERYGII
Order Salmoniformes (Isospondyli in part, Clupeiformes in part, Galaxiiformes, Haplomi, Xenomi, Iniomi, Scopeliformes, Myctophiformes)
Suborder Salmonoidei
Salmonidae (including Coregonidae, Thymallidae)
Plecoglossidae
Osmeridae
Suborder Argentinoidei
Argentinidae (including Xenophthalmichthyidae)
Opisthoproctidae (including Dolichopterygidae, Macropinnidae, Winteridae, Winteriidae)
Suborder Galaxioidei
Salangidae
Retropinnidae
Galaxiidae (Galaxidae, including Paragalaxiidae)
Aplochitonidae (Haplochitonidae, including Prototroctidae)
Suborder Esocoidei
Esocidae (Luciidae)
Umbridae (including Dalliidae, Novumbridae)
Suborder Stomiatoidei
Gonostomatidae (Gonostomidae, including Maurolicidae)
Sternoptychidae (Sternoptychiidae)
Astronesthidae
Melanostomiatidae
Malacosteidae
Chauliodontidae (Chauliodidae)

Stomiatidae
Idiacanthidae (including Stylophthalmidae, Stylophthalmoidae)
Suborder Alepocephaloidei
Alepocephalidae (including Platytroctidae, Platyproctidae, Searsiidae, Searsidae)
Suborder Bathylaconoidei
Bathylaconidae
Suborder Myctophoidei
Aulopodidae (Aulopidae)
Synodontidae (Sauridae, Synodidae, Bathysauridae)
Harpadontidae (Harpodontidae)
Chlorophthalmidae
Bathypteroidae (Bathypteridae, Benthosauridae)
Ipnopidae
Paralepididae (Paralepidae, including Sudidae)
Omosudidae
Alepisauridae (Alepidosauridae, Plagyodontidae)
Anotopteridae
Evermannellidae (Odontostomidae)
Scopelarchidae
Scopelosauridae (Notosudidae)
Myctophidae (Scopelidae)
Neoscopelidae
Order Cetomimiformes (Isospondyli in part, Clupeiformes in part, Stephanoberyci-
formes in part, Scopeliformes in part, Ateleopiformes, Chondrobrachii,
Giganturiformes)
Suborder Cetomimoidei
Cetomimidae
Barbourisiidae (Barbourisidae)
Rondeletiidae
Suborder Ateleopodoidei
Ateleopodidae (Ateleopidae, Podatelidae)
Suborder Mirapinnatoidei
Kasidoridae (Kasidoroidae)
Mirapinnidae (Mirapinnatidae)
Eutaeniophoridae (Taeniophoridae)
Suborder Giganturoidei
Giganturidae
Rosauridae (based on young of giganturid)
Order Ctenothrissiformes
Macristiidae
Order Gonorynchiformes (Isospondyli in part, Clupeiformes in part, Chanoiformes)
Suborder Gonorynchoidei
Gonorynchidae (Gonorhynchidae)
Suborder Chanoidei
Chanidae (Chanoidae)
Kneriidae (including Cromeriidae, Grasseichthyidae)
Phractolaemidae
SUPERORDER OSTARIOPHYSI
Order Cypriniformes (Plectospondyli in part, Heterognathi, Gymnonoti, Glanencheli,
Eventognathi)
Suborder Characoidei
Characidae (Characinidae, including Crenuchidae, Acestrorhynchidae, Serrasal-
midae, Tetragonopteridae, Creagrutidae, Glandulocaudidae)
Erythrinidae
Ctenoluciidae (Xiphostomidae, Xiphostomatidae, including Hepsetidae in part)
Hepsetidae
Cynodontidae
Lebiasinidae (including Nannostomidae)

Parodontidae
Gasteropelecidae (Gastropelecidae)
Prochilodontidae
Curimatidae (including Anodontidae)
Anostomidae
Hemiodontidae (Hemiodidae, including Bivibranchiidae)
Chilodontidae
Distichodontidae
Citharinidae
Ichthyboridae (Icthyoboridae)
Suborder Gymnotoidei
Gymnotidae
Electrophoridae
Apteronotidae (including Sternarchidae, Sternopygidae)
Rhamphichthyidae
Suborder Cyprinoidei
Cyprinidae (including Gobiobotidae, Medidae)
Gyrinocheilidae
Psilorhynchidae
Catostomidae
Homalopteridae (including Gastromyzonidae, Gastromyzontidae, Lepidoglanidae)
Cobitidae (Acanthopsidae, including Adiposiidae)
Order Siluriformes (Plectospondyli in part, Cypriniformes in part, Nematognathi, Siluroidiformes)
Diplomystidae
Ictaluridae (Amiuridae, Ameiuridae)
Bagridae (including Porcidae, Mystidae)
Cranoglanididae
Siluridae
Schilbeidae
Pangasiidae
Amblycipitidae (Amblycepidae)
Amphiliidae
Akysidae
Sisoridae (Bagariidae)
Clariidae
Heteropneustidae (Saccobranchidae)
Chacidae
Olyridae
Malaptururidae (Malopteruridae, Torpedinidae, not an electric ray)
Mochokidae (Synodidae, Mochockidae, Mochochidae, Mochocidae)
Ariidae (Tachysuridae, Bagreidae, including Doiichthyidae)
Doradidae
Auchenipteridae (including Trachycorystidae)
Aspredinidae (Bunocephalidae)
Plotosidae
Pimelodidae (including Pseudopimelodidae, Callophysidae)
Ageneiosidae
Hypophthalmidae
Helogeneidae (Hologenidae)
Cetopsidae
Trichomycteridae (Pygidiidae)
Callichthyidae
Loricariidae (including Hypostomidae)
Astroblepidae (Argidae, Cyclopiidae, Cyclopidae)
SUPERORDER PARACANTHOPTERYGII
Order Percopsiformes (Microcyprini in part, Cyprinodontes in part, Cyprinodontiformes in part, Amblyopsiformes, Salmopercae, Xenarchi, Percopsomorphi)

Suborder Amblyopsoidei
  Amblyopsidae (Hypsocidae, Hypsaeidae)
Suborder Aphredoderoidei
  Aphredoderidae
Suborder Percopsoidei
  Percopsidae
Order Batrachoidiformes (Jugulares in part, Haplodoci, Perciformes in part, Pediculati in part)
  Batrachoididae (Batrachidae)
Order Gobiesociformes (Xenopterygii, Gobiesocomorphi, Perciformes in part)
  Gobiesocidae (including Diademichthyidae)
Order Lophiiformes (Pediculati in part)
  Suborder Lophioidei
    Lophiidae
  Suborder Antennarioidei
    Brachionichthyidae
    Antennariidae
    Chaunacidae
    Ogcocephalidae (Oncocephalidae, Onchocephalidae, Malthidae, Maltheidae)
  Suborder Ceratioidei
    Melanocetidae
    Diceratiidae (including Laevoceratiidae, Aeschynichthyidae)
    Himantolophidae
    Oneirodidae
    Gigantactinidae
    Neoceratiidae
    Centrophrynidae
    Ceratiidae
    Caulophrynidae
    Linophrynidae (including Photocorynidae, Aceratiidae)
Order Gadiformes (Anacanthini, Macruriformes, Gadomorphi, Perciformes in part)
  Suborder Muraenolepoidei
    Muraenolepididae (Muraenolepidae)
  Suborder Gadoidei
    Moridae (including Eretmophoridae, Tripterophycidae)
    Bregmacerotidae
    Gadidae (including Gaidropsaridae, Ranicipitidae)
    Merlucciidae
  Suborder Ophidioidei
    Ophidiidae (including Brotulidae, Brotulophidae, Aphyonidae)
    Carapidae (Fierasferidae, Disparichthyidae)
    Pyramodontidae
  Suborder Zoarcoidei
    Zoarcidae (including Lycodidae, Lycodapodidae, Derepodichthyidae)
  Suborder Macrouroidei
    Macrouridae (Macruridae, Macrouroididae, Coryphaenoididae, including Lyconidae)
SUPERORDER ATHERINOMORPHA
Order Atheriniformes (Synentognathi, Beloniformes, Gambusiformes, Microcyprini in part, Cyprinodontiformes in part, Percesoces in part, Mugiliformes in part, Mugilomorphi in part, Phallostethiformes, Perciformes in part)
  Suborder Exocoetoidei
    Exocoetidae (including Hemiramphidae, Hemirhamphidae, Oxyporhamphidae, Evolantiidae)
    Belonidae (Esocidae, Esocesidae as of Rafinesque, including Tylosuridae, Petalichthyidae)
    Scomberesocidae (Scombresocidae)

Suborder Cyprinodontoidei
  Oryziatidae
  Adrianichthyidae
  Horaichthyidae
  Cyprinodontidae (including Fundulidae, Orestiidae, Empetrichthyidae)
  Goodeidae (including Characodontidae)
  Anablepidae (Anablepsidae)
  Jenynsiidae (Fitzroyiidae, Fitzroyidae)
  Poeciliidae (including Tomeuridae)
Suborder Atherinoidei
  Melanotaeniidae (including Zanteclidae, Neoatherinidae)
  Atherinidae (including Bedotiidae, Pseudomugilidae)
  Isonidae
  Neostethidae
  Phallostethidae
SUPERORDER ACANTHOPTERYGII
Order Beryciformes (Xenoberyces, Berycomorphi, Berycoidei in part, Stephanoberyci-
  formes in part)
Suborder Stephanoberycoidei
  Stephanoberycidae
  Melamphaeidae (Melamphaidae, Melamphasidae)
  Gibberichthyidae
Suborder Polymixioidei
  Polymixiidae
Suborder Berycoidei
  Diretmidae
  Trachichthyidae (including Hoplopterygidae, Sorosichthyidae)
  Korsogasteridae
  Anoplogasteridae (Caulolepidae)
  Berycidae
  Monocentridae
  Anomalopidae
  Holocentridae (Holocentridae)
Order Zeiformes (Zeomorphi, Zeoidei)
  Parazenidae
  Macrurocyttidae (Zeniontidae)
  Zeidae (including Cyttidae, Cyttopsidae, Zenidae)
  Grammicolepididae (Grammicolepidae)
  Orcosomatidae
  Caproidae (Caprophonidae, including Antigoniidae)
Order Lampridiformes (Selenichthyes, Allotriognathi)
Suborder Lampridoidei
  Lampridae (Lamprididae)
Suborder Veliferoidei
  Veliferidae
Suborder Trachipteroidei
  Lophotidae
  Trachipteridae (Trachypteridae)
  Regalecidae
Suborder Stylephoroidei
  Stylephoridae (Stylophoridae)
Order Gasterosteiformes (Lophobranchii, Thoracostei, Aulostomi, Solenichthyes,
  Scleroparei in part, Syngnathiformes, Aulostomiformes, Rhamphosiformes)
Suborder Gasterosteoidei
  Gasterosteidae (Sclerogenidae in part)
  Aulorhynchidae
  Indostomidae

Suborder Aulostomoidei
  Aulostomidae
  Fistulariidae (Fistularidae)
  Macrorhamphosidae (Macroramphosidae, Rhamphosidae)
  Centriscidae (Amphisilidae)
Suborder Syngnathoidei
  Solenostomidae (Solenostomatidae, Solenostomatichthyidae, including Solenich-
    thyidae)
  Syngnathidae (including Hippocampidae, Siphostomidae)
Order Channiformes (Labyrinthiei in part, Ophiocephaliformes)
  Channidae (Ophicephalidae, Ophiocephalidae, including Paraphiocephalidae)
Order Synbranchiformes (Symbranchia, Symbranchii, Symbranchiformes, Alabiformes)
  Suborder Alabetoidei
    Alabetidae (Alabidae, including Cheilobranchidae, Chilobranchidae)
  Suborder Synbranchoidei
    Synbranchidae (Symbranchidae, including Flutidae, Monopteridae)
    Amphipnoidae
Order Scorpaeniformes (Cataphracti in part Scleroparei in part, Pareioplitae, Loricati,
    Sclerogeni, Cottomorphi, Perciformes in part)
  Suborder Scorpaenoidei
    Scorpaenidae (Sclerogenidae in part, including Tetrarogidae)
    Triglidae (Sclerogenidae in part, including Peristediidae, Peristediontidae)
    Caracanthidae
    Aploactinidae (Aploactidae, including Bathyaploactidae)
    Synancejidae (Synanceidae)
    Pataecidae (including Gnathanacanthidae)
  Suborder Hexagrammoidei
    Hexagrammidae (including Ophiodontidae, Oxylebiidae, Chiridae)
    Anoplopomatidae (Anoplopomidae, including Erilepidae)
    Zaniolepididae (Zaniolepidae)
  Suborder Platycephaloidei
    Platycephalidae (including Bembradidae, Bembridae, Parabembridae)
  Suborder Hoplichthyoidei
    Hoplichthyidae (Oplichthyidae)
  Suborder Congiopodoidei
    Congiopdidae (Agriopidae)
  Suborder Cottoidei
    Icelidae (including Ereuniidae, Marukawachthyidae)
    Cottidae (Sclerogenidae in part, including Jordaniidae, Blepsiidae, Blepisiidae,
      Scorpaenichthyidae, Ascelichthyidae, Synchiridae, Rhamphocottidae, Hemi-
      tripteridae, Neophrynichthyidae)
    Cottocomephoridae (including Abyssocottidae)
    Comephoridae
    Normanichthyidae
    Cottunculidae
    Psychrolutidae
    Agonidae (including Aspidophoroididae, Aspidophoridae)
    Cyclopteridae (including Liparopidae, Liparidae, Lipariidae, Eutelichthyidae,
      Rhodichthyidae, Cyclogasteridae)
Order Dactylopteriformes (in part Craniomi, Scleroparei, Cataphracti, and Perciformes)
  Dactylopteridae (Cephalacanthidae)
Order Pegasiformes (Hypostomides, Perciformes in part)
  Pegasidae
Order Perciformes (Percomorphi in part, Holconoti, Labyrinthici in part, Chromides,
  Pharyngognathi, Gobioidea, Jugulares in part, Malacichthyes, Icosteiformes,
  Percesoces in part, Mugiliformes in part, Polynemiformes, Rhegnopteri, Bathy-
  clupeiformes, Xenoberyces in part, Berycoidei in part, Beryciformes in part,
  Thunniformes, Plecostei, Scombriformes, Echeneiformes, Discocephali, Masta-
  cembeliformes, Opisthomi, Chaudhuriiformes, Anabantiformes, Blenniiformes,

Trachiniformes, Gobiiformes, Carangiformes, Acanthuriformes, Squamipenes, Embiotocomorphi, Gadopseiformes, Coryphaeniformes, Amphiprioniformes)
Suborder Percoidei
    Centropomidae (Oxylabracidae, including Latidae, Chandidae, Ambassidae, Ambassiidae)
    Serranidae (including Percichthyidae, Chromileptidae, Perciliidae, Moronidae, Oligoridae, Maccullochellidae, Macquariidae, Niphonidae, Plectroplitidae, Epinephelidae, Cephalopholidae, Bostockiidae, Diploprionidae, Rainfordiidae, Hypoplectrodidae, Plectropomidae, Anthiidae, Ostracoberycidae, Paracentropristidae)
    Grammistidae (including Rypticidae)
    Pseudochromidae
    Pseudogrammidae (including Rhegmatidae)
    Grammidae (including Stigmatonotidae)
    Plesiopidae (including Pharopterycidae)
    Pseudoplesiopidae
    Anisochromidae
    Acanthoclinidae
    Glaucosomidae
    Theraponidae (Teraponidae, Terapontidae, Tesapontidae)
    Banjosidae
    Kuhliidae (Duleidae, including Nannatherinidae, Nannopercidae)
    Gregoryinidae (?based on young of cheilodactylid)
    Centrarchidae (including Elassomatidae, Elassomidae, Christidae, Grystidae, Micropteridae, Eucentrarchidae)
    Priacanthidae
    Apogonidae (including Ostorhinchidae, Gymnapogonidae, Apogonichthyidae, Henicichthyidae, Henichthyidae, Dinolestidae, Cheilodipteridae, "Amiidae," Epigonidae)
    Acropomatidae (Acropomidae)
    Percidae (including Etheostomatidae, Etheostomidae)
    Sillaginidae
    Branchiostegidae (Latilidae, including Malacanthidae)
    Labracoglossidae
    Lactariidae
    Pomatomidae (including Scombropidae, Scombropsidae)
    Rachycentridae (Rhachycentridae, Elacatidae)
    Echeneidae (Echeneididae)
    Carangidae (including Seriolidae, Nematistiidae, Juvenellidae)
    Coryphaenidae
    Formionidae (Formiidae, Apolectidae)
    Menidae
    Leiognathidae (Liognathidae, including Equulidae)
    Bramidae (including Steinegeriidae, Trachyberycidae, Pteraclididae, Pteraclidae, Lepidotidae, Lepodidae)
    Caristiidae (Elephenoridae)
    Arripidae (Arripididae)
    Emmelichthyidae (including Erythrichthyidae, Erythroclidae, Dipterygonotidae, Inermiidae, Maenidae, Spicaridae, Merolepidae, Centracanthidae, Centracantidae)
    Lutjanidae (Lutianidae, Luthianidae, including Hoplopagridae, Etelidae, Verilidae, Aphareidae, Caesionidae, Caesiodidae)
    Nemipteridae (including Scolopsidae)
    Lobotidae
    Gerridae (including Eucinostomidae, Xystaemidae)
    Pomadasyidae (Pomadasidae, Haemulidae, Haemulonidae, including Gaterinidae, Pristipomidae, Pristipomatidae, Plectorhynchidae, Xenichthyidae)
    Lethrinidae (including Monotaxidae, Neolethrinidae)
    Pentapodidae

Sparidae (including Denticidae, Pimelepteridae, Paradicichthyidae, Paradichthyidae)
Sciaenidae (including Otolithidae)
Mullidae
Monodactylidae (Psettidae)
Pempheridae (including Leptobramidae)
Bathyclupeidae
Toxotidae
Coracinidae (Dichistiidae)
Kyphosidae (Cyphosidae, including Scorpididae, Scorpidae, Parascorpidae, Girellidae)
Ephippidae (including Chaetodipteridae, Platacidae, Ilarchidae, Drepanidae, Drepanichthyidae)
Scatophagidae (including Prenidae)
Rhinoprenidae
Chaetodontidae (including Pomacanthidae)
Enoplosidae
Pentacerotidae (Ilistiopteridae)
Nandidae (including Polycentridae, Pristolepidae)
Oplegnathidae (Hoplegnathidae)
Embiotocidae (Ambiotocidae, including Ditremidae, Hysterocarpidae, Holconotidae)
Cichlidae (Chromidae, not a pomacentrid)
Pomacentridae (Abudefdulfidae, Glyphiodontidae, Ctenolabridae, including Amphiprionidae, Chromidae, Premnidae)
Gadopsidae
Cirrhitidae
Chironemidae
Aplodactylidae (Haplodactylidae)
Cheilodactylidae
Latridae (Latrididae)
Owstoniidae
Cepolidae
Suborder Mugiloidei
Mugilidae
Suborder Sphyraenoidei
Sphyraenidae
Suborder Polynemoidei
Polynemidae
Suborder Labroidei
Labridae (Cyclolabridae, including Coridae, Neolabridae, Bodianidae, Harpidae)
Odacidae (including Siphonognathidae, Neodaciidae, Neoodacidae)
Scaridae (Callyodontidae, including Sparisomidae, Scarichthyidae)
Suborder Trachinoidei
Trichodontidae
Opisthognathidae
Bathymasteridae
Mugiloididae (including Pinguipedidae, Parapercidae, Parapercichthyidae)
Cheimarrhichthyidae (Chimarrichthyidae, not a catfish)
Trachinidae (including Callipterygidae)
Percophididae (Percophidae, including Bembropsidae, Bembropidae, Pteropsaridae, Hemerocoetidae)
Trichonotidae
Creediidae
Limnichthyidae (Limnichthidae)
Oxudercidae
Leptoscopidae
Dactyloscopidae

Uranoscopidae (including Astroscopidae, Pleuroscopidae)
Champsodontidae
Chiasmodontidae
Suborder Notothenioidei
Bovichthyidae (Bovichtidae, Bovictidae, Pseudaphritidae)
Nototheniidae (including Harpagiferidae, Gelidiidae)
Bathydraconidae
Channicthyidae (Channichthyidae, Chaenichthyidae)
Suborder Blennioidei
Blenniidae (including Runulidae, Salariidae, Atopoclinidae, Xiphasiidae, Nemophididae)
Anarhichadidae (Anarrhichadidae, including Anarrhichthyidae)
Xenocephalidae
Congrogadidae (including Halidesmidae, Haliophidae)
Notograptidae (including Stichariidae)
Peronedysidae (Peronedyidae)
Ophiclinidae (Ophioclinidae)
Tripterygiidae (Tripterygiontidae)
Clinidae (including Paraclinidae, Xenopoclinidae)
Chaenopsidae (including Emblemariidae)
Stichaeidae (including Lumpenidae, Xiphisteridae, Xiphidiontidae, Chirolophidae, Cebedichthyidae, Cryptacanthodidae, Cryptacanthidae)
Ptilichthyidae
Pholididae (Pholidae, including Opisthocentridae)
Scytalinidae (Scytaliscidae)
Zaproridae
Suborder Icosteoidei
Icosteidae (Acrotidae)
Suborder Schindlerioidei
Schindleriidae
Suborder Ammodytoidei
Ammodytidae (including Bleekeridae, Bleekeriidae)
Hypoptychidae
Suborder Callionymoidei
Callionymidae (including Draconettidae)
Suborder Gobioidei
Gobiidae (including Eleotridae, Milyeringidae, Doliichthyidae, Benthophilidae, Gobiomoridae, Sicydiaphiidae, Apocrypteidae, Periophthalmidae)
Rhyacichthyidae (Platypteridae)
Kraemeriidae (Psammichthyidae)
Gobioididae (including Amblyopidae, Taenioidae, Taenioididae)
Trypauchenidae
Microdesmidae (Cerdalidae, including Pholidichthyidae, Gunnellichthyidae, Paragobioididae)
Suborder Kurtoidei
Kurtidae
Suborder Acanthuroidei
Acanthuridae (Hepatidae, Acronuridae, Harpuridae, Teuthidae, Teuthididac in part, including Zanclidae, Nasidae)
Siganidae (Theutyidae, Teuthididae in part, Amphacanthidae)
Suborder Scombroidei
Gempylidae (Acinaceidae, including Lemnisomidae, Ruvettidae)
Trichiuridae (including Lepidopidae)
Scombridae (Scomberidae, including Cybiidae, Cibiidae, Thunnidae, Katsuwonidae, Scomberomoridae, Sardidae, Acanthocybiidae, Gasterochismidae)
Xiphiidae
Luvaridae (Dianidae)
Istiophoridae (Histiophoridae, including Tetrapturidae, Makairidae)

Suborder Stromateoidei
   Centrolophidae (including Icichthyidae)
   Nomeidae (Psenidae)
   Stromateidae (Pampidae)
   Tetragonuridae
Suborder Anabantoidei
   Anabantidae
   Belontiidae (Belontidae, Polyacanthidae)
   Helostomatidae (Helostomidae)
   Osphronemidae (Osphromenidae, Labyrinthicidae)
Suborder Luciocephaloidei
   Luciocephalidae
Suborder Mastacembeloidei
   Mastacembelidae (Rhynchobdellidae)
   Chaudhuriidae
Order Pleuronectiformes (Heterosomata)
Suborder Psettodoidei
   Psettodidae
Suborder Pleuronectoidei
   Citharidae
   Scophthalmidae
   Bothidae (including Paralichthyidae)
   Pleuronectidae (Planidae, including Hippoglossidae, Samaridae, Paralichthodidae,
      Rhombosoleidae)
Suborder Soleoidei
   Soleidae (including Achiridae, Trinectidae, Synapturidae)
   Cynoglossidae
Order Tetraodontiformes (Plectognathi, Diodontomorphi)
Suborder Balistoidei
   Triacanthidae (including Triacanthodidae)
   Balistidae (including Monacanthidae, Aluteridae, Aleuteridae, Psilocephalidae,
      Anacanthidae, not a sting ray)
   Ostraciontidae (Ostraciidae, including Aracanidae)
Suborder Tetraodontoidei
   Tetraodontidae (Tetrodontidae, Gymnodontidae, including Lagocephalidae,
      Chonarhinidae, Xenopteridae, Canthigasteridae, Tropidichthyidae, Ovoididae,
      Colomesidae, Sphoeroididae)
   Triodontidae
   Diodontidae
   Molidae (Orthagoriscidae, Triuridae)

MAJOR ADAPTIVE LEVELS IN THE EVOLUTION OF THE ACTINOPTERYGIAN FEEDING MECHANISM

BOBB SCHAEFFER AND DONN ERIC ROSEN

The American Museum of Natural History

INTRODUCTION

In the higher bony fishes or Osteichthyes, feeding and gill ventilation are accomplished by movements of the visceral skeleton, the shoulder girdle, and frequently also the neurocranium. The mechanism of gill ventilation has remained relatively constant throughout the history of these fishes. Most of the modifications in the splanchnocranium have been related to the dynamics of feeding.

Of the three major groups of osteichthyans (the crossopterygians, dipnoans, and actinopterygians), the primitive actinopterygian showed by far the greatest potential for adaptive change in the feeding mechanism. Except for the skull modifications in the rhipidistian-tetrapod transition, there was but one major shift in the crossopterygians—from primitive rhipidistian to coelacanth. This involved changes somewhat comparable to the first important transformation in the actinopterygian feeding mechanism (see Jarvik, 1954, Figs. 23B and 15). The characteristic architecture of the dipnoan skull, with the palatoquadrate fused to the braincase, was established in the early Devonian, and the feeding mechanism has remained essentially unchanged since that time.

In the main stream of actinopterygian evolution from palaeoniscoid to acanthopterygian, there has been a progressive improvement in a fundamentally predaceous feeding mechanism (Fig. 1). Food was probably first obtained by biting and was swallowed whole with the aid of simple, conical pharyngeal teeth. As this biting mechanism was modified and perfected through time, the potentiality for adaptive radiation in the entire feeding mechanism increased. At the lowest or palaeoniscoid level the radiation was conservative and re-stricted. The changes leading to the next or holostean level improved the basically predaceous feeding mechanism and gave rise to a number of specialized types. The rise of the teleosts from one group of holosteans involved at least two different sorts of feeding mechanisms, the clupeid and elopid. Although the phylogeny of the teleosts is poorly understood, it seems evident that the specialized clupeid type was off the main line. A conservative, predaceous elopid-like stock may well represent the base for the explosive teleost radiation that began sometime in the Jurassic (Gardiner, 1960).

THE PALAEONISCOID LEVEL AND THE BASIC ACTINOPTERYGIAN FEEDING MECHANISM

In the earliest actinopterygians, the angle of the jaw suspensorium varies from very oblique to nearly vertical. The maxillary bone, which is firmly fixed to the preopercular and infraorbital bones, forms the outer wall of a narrow chamber that contained the major portion of the adductor mandibulae muscle (Stensiö, 1921; Watson, 1925; Nielsen, 1942). The median, posterior, and ventral walls of this chamber are formed mostly by the palatoquadrate. The chamber may be open dorsally, suggesting the situation in the higher actinopterygians, or it may be closed by a median lamina of the preopercular (Fig. 4A). The palatoquadrate was movably attached to the braincase in the ethmoid region, at the basipterygoid process, and posteriorly through the hyomandibular, with which it presumably had an extensive ligamentous attachment. The mandible, which varies in length according to the angle of the suspensorium, has a nearly horizontal dorsal border and a large Meckelian fossa for the insertion of the adductor mandibulae muscle.

From *American Zoologist* 1:187–204. Reprinted by permission.

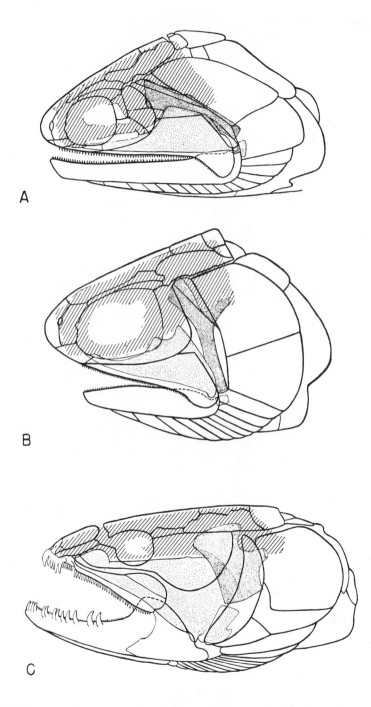

FIG. 1. Series of actinopterygian skulls from palaeoniscoid to acanthopterygian, showing changes in the angle of the jaw suspension and modifications in the palate and jaws. Each example illustrates a structural grade or level; a real evolutionary sequence is not implied. A. Palaeoniscoid (*Pteronisculus*, based on Nielsen, 1942); B. Subholostean (*Boreosomus*, after Nielsen, 1942); C. Holostean (*Amia*);

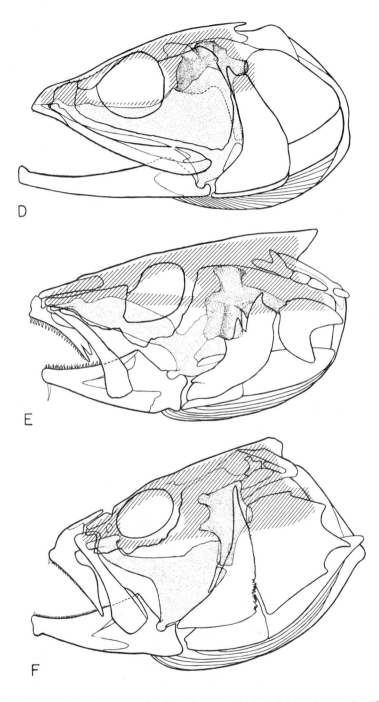

FIG. 1 cont. D. Early teleost (composite of *Notelops* and *Elops*); E. Subacanthopterygian (*Gadus*); F. Acanthopterygian (*Epinephelus*). *Gadus* is representative of a rather specialized group of teleosts sometimes aligned with the acanthopterygians. Its jaw mechanism is structurally and functionally transitional between D and F. Braincase: diagonal shading; palate and symplectic: open stippling; hyomandibular: close stippling.

The partly cartilaginous ceratohyal is flattened laterally as in higher actinopterygians. The nature of the connection between the ceratohyal and the hyomandibular is poorly documented, but in a few forms, at least, the (?) interhyal and the symplectic were apparently arranged in series, with only the symplectic in contact with the hyomandibular. Aside from the presence of separate suprapharyngobranchial elements in the first two branchial arches, the palaeoniscoid branchial skeleton, including the copula, is very similar to that of higher actinopterygians. The oral surface of the gill arches was frequently covered with small toothed dermal plates.

The disposition of the skull elements in palaeoniscoid specimens preserved with the mouth widely opened (Nielsen, 1942, Pl. 13) indicates that the jaws were abducted and visceral skeleton expanded essentially as in most living actinopterygians (Fig. 2) (Tchernavin, 1953). First, the ventral part of the shoulder girdle was pulled backward and downward by contraction of the ventrolateral body musculature that inserted on the cleithrum. Next, the anterior part of the copula and with it the front end of the hyoid bar were also pulled backward and downward by the sternohyoid muscles which extended from the cleithrum to the hyoid bar. In this way the branchial basket was expanded dorsoventrally. The mandible was then depressed by the geniohyoid muscles situated between the hyoid bar and the mandible.

The front end of the palaeoniscoid neurocranium could be elevated, as in many recent fishes, to increase the size of the mouth opening (Fig. 2A). The elevation was probably brought about by a forward and upward force acting on the palate initiated by depression of the mandible and by the contraction of the anterior myotomes of the dorsolateral muscles. The backward motion of the hyoid bar was thus limited by attachment to the fixed symplectic and by the forward movement of the palate.

These conflicting forces caused the posterior end of the hyoid bar to swing laterally. As a result, the mandibular rami, the palate, and the hyomandibular were pushed outward and the branchial basket consequently was expanded. The principal function of the hyoid bar is, therefore, to act as a lever that expands the orobranchial chamber. The importance and uniqueness of this function (see Tchernavin, 1953) may explain the essentially constant form of the hyoid bar throughout the Osteichthyes.

The lateral expansion of the orobranchial chamber in palaeoniscoids with an oblique suspensorium was limited in two ways. First, the vertical articulation of the hyomandibular with the braincase would permit it to swing only anteriorly, thereby limiting the lateral movement of the palate. Second, the lateral excursion of the posterior end of the ceratohyal was probably shorter than in the holosteans and teleosts because the ceratohyal was tied to the mandibular arch rather than separately to, the hyomandibular.

The closing of the mouth and the contraction of the orobranchial chamber involved essentially a reversal of the movements described above. When the anterior segments of the ventral body muscles and the sternohyoids relaxed, the tension on the shoulder girdle, copula, and mandibles was removed. With the mouth closed and fixed by the adductor mandibulae, contraction of the geniohyoids would pull the copula and, through the sternohyoids, the shoulder girdle forward. At the same time, adduction of the mandible and relaxation of the anterior segments of the dorsolateral muscles would permit the neurocranium to return to the resting position. These combined movements eliminated the forces acting on the ceratohyal. The forward and upward movement of the copula and the down swing of the neurocranium compressed the branchial basket dorsoventrally, whereas the constriction of the adductor hyomandibularis and the intermandibularis did the same laterally.

The structure of the jaws and the frequent presence of sharply pointed teeth suggest that most palaeoniscoids were principally predators. The deep gape and the shallowness of the orobranchial chamber with the mouth widely opened further suggest that food was usually obtained by biting rather than by filtering or by engulfing through current action. Biting is simply seizing food with the jaws or teeth. A small piece may be cut from a larger mass, or small prey may be seized and gulped whole. Larger, entire prey may also be obtained by seizing, releasing, swimming forward and seizing again—a sequence repeated until the entire prey is within the orobranchial chamber (Breder, 1925). Any of these ways may have been employed by the palaeoniscoids, depending in part on the length of the jaws and perhaps on the obliquity of the suspensorium.

The force of the bite is directly related to the mass and disposition of the adductor mandibulae muscle. In the palaeoniscoids the adductor was confined to the narrow palatoquadrate-maxillary chamber (Figs. 3 and 4A), from which it passed into the Meckelian fossa immediately anterior to the jaw articulation. Functionally, the mandible is a straight lever with a very short effort arm. Obviously the palaeoniscoid biting mechanism was efficient enough for these fishes to survive for roughly 200 million years. Compared with the holostean condition, however, the palaeoniscoid adductor was less powerful and the torque about the jaw articulation far below that in forms with a coronoid process on the mandible. Also, the expansion of the orobranchial chamber and even the depression of the mandible were less effectively accomplished at this level than at the holostean.

THE PALAEONISCOID–HOLOSTEAN TRANSITION

Throughout the history of the palaeoniscoids there was some experimentation in the feeding mechanism, mostly related to the obliquity of the suspensorium.

In a few groups of palaeoniscoids (Westoll, 1937, 1944), and in a heterogeneous assemblage of advanced chrondrosteans called subholosteans (Fig. 1B), the suspensorium is nearly vertical. The dorsal border of the maxillary-palatoquadrate chamber is open, and in the subholosteans, at least, the origin of the adductor mandibulae may have extended, in part, to the braincase. Assuming some increase in the mass of the adductor, the power of adduction was correspondingly increased. With the hyomandibular now swinging in a nearly vertical plane, the mechanism for lateral expansion of the orobranchial chamber was improved. In this connection, it should be emphasized that the palaeoniscoids and particularly the subholosteans approached the holostean level in various characters of the skull and postcranial skeleton (Schaeffer, 1956). There is now substantial evidence that this level was attained by at least three separately evolving palaeoniscoid-subholostean lines.

The final shift to the holostean grade occurred during the late Permian and the early Triassic. It involved a number of inter-related changes in the jaw mechanism that followed acquisition of a vertical suspensorium. The most important of these was the elimination of the maxillary–palatoquadrate chamber. This was brought about by separation of the maxillary from the preopercular and the infraorbital bones, by a reduction in the width of the preopercular and separation of it from the dermal elements behind the orbit, and by modifications in the shape, size, and curvature of the dermal components of the palatoquadrate (Figs. 3B and 4B). The hyomandibular became relatively shorter and broader and more closely associated with the palate, and the upper border of the mandible was elevated posteriorly as the coronoid process.

The opening of the cheek region and the changes in the palate permitted further expansion of the adductor mandibulae muscle (Fig. 3). In the evolutionary line that gave rise to the amioids and independently to the pholidophoroids (which, in turn, produced the teleosts), the adductor muscle, as in *Amia,* must have extended its origin to include the postorbital part of the braincase, the adjacent ventral surface of the skull roof, the posterior part of the palate and the hyomandibular, and the entire anterior border of the preopercular. With this expansion, the muscle increased in mass (volume and number of fibers) and became distinctly subdivided. Although the major portion of the muscle still inserted within the Meckelian fossa as in the palaeoniscoids (and as in *Amia* and most teleosts), one subdivision became attached to the posterior border of the coronoid process (Fig. 4).

The resulting increase in the absolute power of the adductor mandibulae obviously augmented the strength of the bite. The disposition of the muscle in *Amia* further indicates that its subdivision and extensive origin permits at least one part to exert maximum pull on the mandible throughout the adduction cycle. Regarding the mandible as a lever, it is apparent that the force is applied immediately in front of the fulcrum, and that the effort arm is very short compared with the resistance arm regardless of whether the coronoid process is present or absent. Assuming the resistance arm (dentigerous portion) to be of the same length in a palaeoniscoid and a holostean, the torque about the articulation will be greater in the latter simply because the mag-

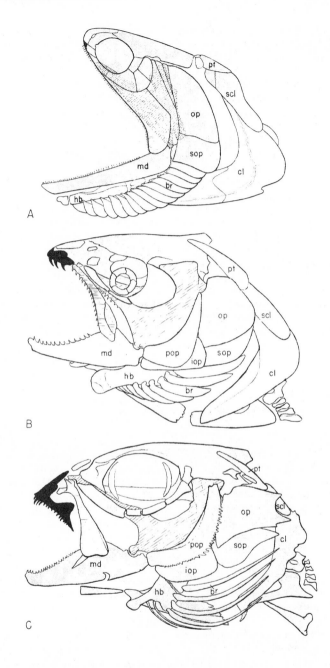

FIG. 2. The actinopterygian skull with the mouth widely opened In A. (*Pteronisculus*), the palaeoniscoid maxilla is fixed to the cheek, the braincase elevated, and the shoulder girdle moved backwards. In B. (holostean and sub–acanthopterygian condition represented by *Salmo*), the maxilla is swung forward as the mandible is depressed, the braincase frequently elevated, and the shoulder girdle moved backward and downward. In C. (the acanthopterygian *Centropristes*), the same motions occur, but in addition the premaxilla is projected forward. Note reduction in length of hyoid bar and number of branchiostegals (see footnote 1). Palate and hyomandibular: obliquely lined; maxilla: horizontally lined; premaxilla: solid black. Palaeoniscoid palate and hyomandibular as seen through cheek: oblique broken lines. Abbreviations: br, branchiostegals; cl, cleithrum; hb, hyoid bar; iop, interopercular; md, mandible; op, opercular; pop, preopercular; pt, posttemporal (suprascapular); scl, supracleithrum; sop, subopercular.

nitude of the force acting on the mandible is greater. But more than that, the elevation of the coronoid process transforms, in part, the straight lever of palaeoniscoid type into a bent lever. The straight-lever analogy still applies in the holosteans and teleosts to that portion of the mandibular ramus anterior to the coronoid, with the effort applied by the subdivisions of the adductor entering the Meckelian fossa. The bent lever refers to the coronoid process, with the effort applied by the adductor subdivision inserting along its posterior slope.

The adaptive significance of the coronoid process, which is slightly developed even in a few palaeoniscoids and is variously elevated in most of the higher actinopterygians, is perhaps best explained in terms of torque. For purposes of analysis, it may be assumed that the force is applied only at the apex of the process and at right angles to its posterior border. If the torque value is regarded as unity in the palaeoniscoids where the coronoid process is usually absent, progressive increase in the height of this process, other things being equal, results in a geometric increase in torque.

The probable modification of the uppermost palaeoniscoid branchiostegal ray into the holostean interopercular bone was associated with a new way of depressing the mandible. As van Dobben (1937) has demonstrated, contraction of the levator operculae muscle will elevate the entire opercular series and through the interopercular–mandibular ligament (which is attached to the mandible below and behind the jaw articulation), depress the lower jaw. The interopercular serves to converge the opercular series on the ligament (Fig. 2).

Aldinger (1937, p. 332) and Nielsen (1942, p. 187 and p. 350) have pointed out that the location of the hyomandibular articulation on the median face of the opercular bone would affect the ability of the dilator operculi muscle to abduct the opercular and subopercular. When this articulation is situated near the mid-point on the anterior border of the opercular, as in *Pteronisculus* and probably most other palaeoniscoids with an oblique suspensorium, the action of the dilator operculi is more limited than when the articulation is close to the anterodorsal corner of the opercular bone, as in *Amia* and most teleosts. The firm connection of the hyomandibular with

the palate and the overlying opercular elements, including the subopercular, suggests that wide abduction of the gill cover occurred only during expansion of the orobranchial chamber.

In palaeoniscoids and subholosteans with a vertical suspensorium, the relationship of the hyomandibular to the palate was clearly less binding. With a more dorsal position for the hyomandibular-opercular articulation, contraction of the dilator operculi could presumably abduct the opercular series as in the holosteans and teleosts. Closing of the gill cover must have been accomplished by an adductor operculae.

The levator operculi, representing a third dorsal subdivision of the original hyoid constrictor, may not have been fully differentiated from the adductor below the holostean level. There may have been ligamentous connections between the upper few branchiostegal rays and the mandible (*Amia* still has a ligament between the branchiostegal below the interopercular and the mandible) to tie these elements together at the point where the branchiostegal series "turns the corner" to the throat region. The branchiostegals provide an elastic cover for the opercular chamber where the latter is associated with the hyoid bar and the mandible (Woskoboinikoff, 1932).[1] With the subopercular tied to the hyomandibular as in *Pteronisculus,* elevation of the opercular series would be nearly impossible. In forms with a vertical suspensorium, this connection was certainly no more than ligamentous (as in *Amia*) and some vertical movement was perhaps possible. Until differentiation of the interopercular bone, however, this movement could not be focused on the mandible.

It is probable that the symplectic and the (?)interhyal were arranged in series in the palaeoniscoids and subholosteans. This appears to be the situation in the palaeoniscoid *Acrorhabdus* (Stensiö, 1921) and in *Polyodon*. In the holosteans and teleosts the interhyal is attached directly to the hyomandibular behind the symplectic. With the broadened and shortened hyomandibular firmly fixed to the metapterygoid, and

---

[1] At the paleoniscoid level, the number of branchiostegal rays and the length of the hyoid bar are related, in part, to the length of the mandible and obliquity of the suspensorium.

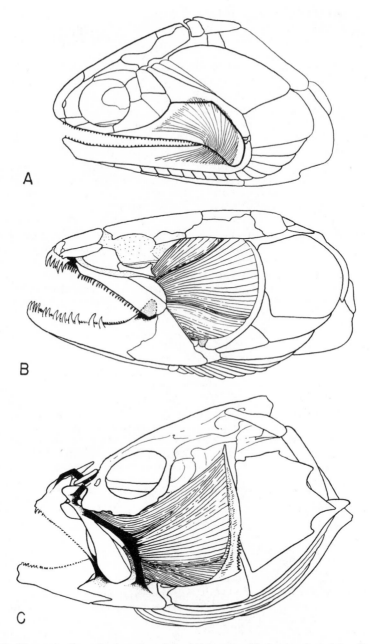

FIG. 3. Changes in size and orientation of the adductor mandibulae muscle and jaw ligaments in forms representing three major adaptive levels of the actinopterygian feeding mechanism. A. Palaeoniscoid (*Pteronisculus*), showing the probable extent of the adductor mandibulae in the maxillary–palatoquadrate chamber, as seen through the dermal bones of the cheek. The maxilla, heavily outlined, was probably without a specific ligament to the mandible. B. Holostean (*Amia*), with the postorbital bones removed to show the superficial division of the muscle, with its three components. Areas occupied by ligaments solid black, except where the maxillary-mandibular ligament extends underneath the maxilla toward the coronoid process of the mandible (darkly stippled). C. Acanthopterygian (*Epinephelus*) where the superficial division of the adductor mandibulae has been reduced to two components, both of which primarily influence the behavior of the maxilla. The now protrusile premaxilla is extensively ·braced by rostral ligaments.

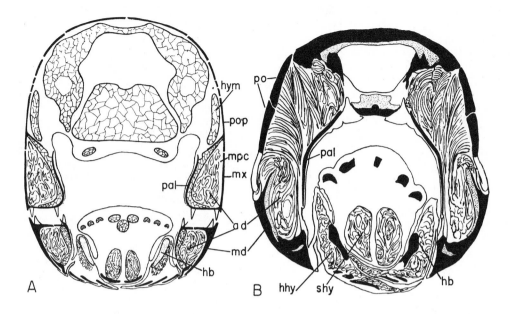

FIG. 4. Diagrammatic transverse sections of the palaeoniscoid and holostean head. A. *Pteronisculus* (partly after Nielsen, 1942). B. *Amia*. Note that the upper portion of the adductor mandibulae muscle is confined to the maxillary-palatoquadrate chamber in A, and that the absence of the chamber in B is correlated with the greater mass of this muscle. Section A is anterior to the passage of the adductor into the Meckelian fossa; section B is behind the apex of the coronoid process. Abbreviations: ad, adductor mandibulae muscle; hb, hyoid bar; hhy, hyohyoideus muscle; hym, hyomandibular; md, mandible; mpc, maxillary-palatoquadrate chamber; mx, maxilla; pal, palate; po, postorbitals; pop, preopercular; shy, sternohyoideus muscle.

the symplectic to the quadrate, the interhyal functions as a mobile pivot on which the hyoid bar can rotate laterally and swing backward. This modification probably permitted greater expansion of the orobranchial chamber than was possible with the palaeoniscoid arrangement.

In the palaeoniscoids, the labial fold presumably fitted snugly around the corner of the mouth. When the maxilla was freed from the cheek, the fold in this area broadened and became more flexible. A new ligamentous attachment developed within the fold between the posterior end of the maxilla and the coronoid process (Fig. 3A, B). Thus when the mandible was depressed, the maxilla was pulled anteriorly, pivoting at the ethmopalatine articulation. In this way the maxillary dentition was carried forward to increase the number of teeth immediately available for grasping prey, while the stretching of the labial fold behind the maxilla extended the orobranchial chamber forward.

THE HOLOSTEAN LEVEL

All these modifications leading to the holostean level greatly increased the opportunity for adaptive radiation in the feeding mechanism. Within this level, the independently derived semionotids developed short, powerful jaws and in many genera a crushing dentition. The long-snouted lepisosteids, or gars, presumably evolved from the semionotids, represent a radical departure from the ancestral skull pattern. The Mesozoic pycnodonts, which arose from equally deep-bodied palaeoniscoids and subholosteans, lost the maxilla and had the skull otherwise altered in conjunction with an extremely specialized crushing dentition.

The conservative, early Triassic parasemionotids probably represent the ancestral stock for both the amioids and the pholidophoroids (Gardiner, 1960). The amioids, represented today only by the genus *Amia,* mostly retained a more or less generalized, predaceous feeding mechanism.

One family, the Macrosemiidae, developed short, strong jaws like the semionotids, but had long, sharply pointed teeth. Another family, the Pachycormidae, questionably retained in the Amioidea, developed a heavily ossified rostrum which in one genus became elongated, as in the swordfishes.

THE HOLOSTEAN-TELEOSTEAN TRANSITION

Among the pholidophoroids there are several families with specialized jaw structure. The central stock, represented by a form like *Pholidophorus similis* (Saint-Seine, 1949, Fig. 94), shows only slight modification of the basic predaceous pattern. One character of importance is the reduction of the dorsal process of the premaxilla. The premaxilla in the palaeoniscoids and subholosteans is a small element with no indication of a dorsal process. Apparently it is frequently fused with other rostral bones, and its origin in the holosteans is obscure (see Nielsen, 1942, p. 137-140). In the semionotids and the amioids, the dorsal process is large and firmly fixed to the ethmoid part of the neurocranium. This was presumably the situation in the Parasemionotidae. The reduction of the dorsal process in the pholidophoroids and particularly in the Pholidophoridae which gave rise to the teleosts, suggests that the premaxilla may have been slightly mobile as in the isospondylous teleosts.

Although detailed studies of the pholidophoroid visceral skeleton have not yet been made, available evidence (Rayner, 1948; Saint-Seine, 1949) supports the conclusion that the holostean feeding mechanism, as described above, remained essentially unchanged during the transition to the teleost level. The significant advances here were probably related to improvement in locomotion. Coupled with the particular design of the pholidophoroid skull, the stage was set for the explosive teleost radiation.

THE EARLIEST AND SUB-ACANTHOPTERYGIAN TELEOSTS

By the late Triassic, the leptolepids, usually regarded as the first teleosts, had arisen. Their small gape and short, deep mandible suggests that they gave rise only to the clupeids and closely related groups. The main line of teleost evolution, which preserved the basic predaceous feeding mechanism, probably extended independently and through unknown Jurassic forms from the pholidophoroids to the elopids. Aside from the leptolepids (and the related lycopterids), the elopids are among the few known early Cretaceous teleost groups. There was thus a lag in the teleost radiation throughout the Jurassic, perhaps related to holostean competition. The great teleost diversification, stemming mostly from elopid-like stock, began early in the Cretaceous or perhaps in the late Jurassic. It is possible that many of the *families* of modern teleosts, including the acanthopterygian, were in existence by the close of the Cretaceous.

The major modifications in the teleost feeding mechanism during and after the Cretaceous were mostly confined to the palate and jaws.

In Cretaceous elopids such as *Notelops* (Dunkle, 1940), perhaps the earliest known predaceous teleosts,[2] and in the Recent genus *Elops* (ten pounders), many primitive characters such as a gular plate, vertical jaw suspension, postorbital lower jaw articulation, maxillary teeth, and extrascapular bones were retained (Fig. 1D). In other characters there was a marked advance. The palate probably became less well ossified as did many of the dermal bones, and the upper jaw clearly underwent specialization. The premaxilla and maxilla, which in *Amia* are arranged essentially in series, in elopids are overlapped. The overlapping or tandem arrangement of these bones, beginning in the pholidophoroids, resulted from the extension of the premaxilla posteriorly along the inferior edge of the maxilla, and from the extension of the upper end of the maxilla inward toward the premaxillary symphysis.

In elopids, apparently for the first time, the maxilla and palatine are joined by a ball and socket hinge, in contrast to the simple connective tissue hinge of the holosteans. In *Elops* the maxilla has a small bony nubbin on its inner dorsal aspect that is seated within a corresponding palatine excavation; the expanded club-shaped tip

---

[2] See above, regarding our views on the relationships of the leptolepids.

of the maxilla is joined by connective tissue to the ethmovomer block. The dorsal process of the premaxilla, well developed in most holosteans, is represented in elopids by a small, pointed elevation that articulates with the ethmoidal cartilage but which is no longer locked in position as in *Amia*. All of these modifications foreshadowed a new mobility for the upper jaw, although the symphyseal portion of the premaxilla was still held firmly to the rostrum by inelastic connective tissue.

Because of its anterior position, the premaxilla is the principal biting component of the upper jaw and the first to contact the prey. Its toothed ramus was gradually extended as a narrow strut below and parallel with the maxilla, excluding the latter from the gape of the mouth and functionally replacing it.

The adaptive modification of the premaxilla created a mechanical problem for the movable maxilla. As the maxilla rotated forward it must have pressed against the toothed ramus of the premaxilla even in the first stages of premaxillary enlargement. The original accommodation of the premaxilla to maxillary motion probably necessitated complex changes. In holosteans (except possibly in the pholidophoroids) the premaxilla is locked in position by the dorsal process, and presumably this process had to be lost before premaxillary movement was possible. The original bony contact of the premaxilla with the rostrum may have been replaced by a more flexible one of cartilage and connective tissue even in the earliest teleosts.

Growth backward of the toothed ramus of the premaxilla into the gape of the mouth and increase in the flexibility of the rostral premaxillary connection are mutually re-enforcing changes. The longer the toothed ramus of the premaxilla, the more maxillary movement is translated to it, and the greater is the need for a flexible dorsal connection in which the premaxilla can rock back and forth. Conversely, more premaxillary movement is possible as the bed of rostral connective tissue becomes more extensive, and thus more opportunity is afforded to increase the length of the premaxillary ramus. Some of the argentinids, close relatives of the smelts, provide excellent examples of these interrelated changes carried to their fullest extent.

THE ACANTHOPTERYGIAN LEVEL

The evolution of the highly kinetic acanthopterygian jaw mechanism from a relatively immobile isospondylous type apparently involved (i) a progressive shift forward of the palatoquadrate arch and the resultant forward movement of the lower jaw articulation, (ii) freeing and further enlargement of the premaxilla and exclusion of the maxilla from the gape of the open mouth, (iii) consolidation and simplification of the subdivisions of the mandibular muscles, (iv) insertions of one or more divisions of the mandibular muscles (usually the external one) on a tendon to the maxilla,[3] and (v) the origin of new ligaments from the maxilla to the ethmoid and/or palatine bone, and from the upper end of the premaxilla to the palatine (Fig. 3C). The key to all of these changes appears to have been the initial freeing of the maxilla so that it could be pulled downward and forward by the lower jaw as the mouth was opened.

The movable suspension of the maxilla from an ethmopalatine articulation is an important feature of early teleost predaceous jaw mechanisms. Later, the movement of the maxilla was to encourage indirectly the development of a system of ligaments controlling the premaxilla, as in the predaceous acanthopterygian jaw. The acanthopterygian type, which incorporates a protrusile *premaxilla,* enables the fish to project its upper jaw toward food (Fig. 2C) with great rapidity while extending the orobranchial chamber further forward than was possible by maxillary movement alone.

The predaceous mouth usually requires a solid footing for the upper jaw: the premaxilla not only must be able to resist the impact of hitting prey with force but must also provide a solid foundation for the lower jaw to snap closed against. Thus, in

---

[3] In *Amia* a component of the external division of the adductor mandibulae inserts partly on a ligament that extends from the upper third of the maxilla to the coronoid process of the mandible. Possibly this component with its ligamentous attachment to the maxilla and coronoid represents the muscle primarily involved in maxillary movement in the acanthopterygian teleosts. In serranids, at least, this ligament has a connection with the maxilla and mandible, although the mandibular section is much reduced and is absent in other percoids.

some of the more generalized acanthopterygian predators such as serranids (sea basses) and carangids (jacks), the premaxilla is held rather firmly to the rostrum and is only slightly protrusile. In such highly predaceous forms as the barracuda (*Sphyraena*) and pike killifish (*Belonesox*), both specialized descendents of fishes with strongly protrusible mouths, the premaxilla has secondarily lost its mobility to modifications that increase the strength and rigidity of the upper jaw. Hence, even the predaceous acanthopterygian mouth, like that of base-line palaeoniscoids, holosteans, and early teleosts, remains primarily a biting or snapping mouth, although the seizing mechanism has been improved significantly.

Even though the protrusile premaxilla only slightly increases the overall effectiveness of the predaceous mechanism, it greatly increases the evolutionary potential of the mouth parts. It is primarily the acanthopterygian mouth that has given rise to the enormous variety of specialized predaceous *and* non-predaceous feeding mechanisms for which the teleosts are so well known. Presumably the evolution of the acanthopterygian jaw mechanism promoted the successful exploitation of food sources that previously were largely unavailable to actinopterygian fishes. In a group of Marshallese coral reefs recently analyzed (Hiatt and Strasburg, 1960), more than 75 per cent of the resident vertebrate consumers, including such diverse feeders as primary and secondary carnivores and coral polyp, algae, and detritus eaters, belong or are related to the acanthopterygian order Perciformes. The protrusile mouth of the perciform fishes and their derivatives probably was and continues to be a major factor in their success. These dominant fishes, numbering more than 8,000 species, constitute about half of today's fresh- and saltwater ichthyofauna.

In a generalized type of protrusile upper jaw, the premaxilla is a strut-like toothed bone that extends backward and downward from the rostrum. The upper, anterior end is held loosely to the ethmoid by connective tissue. The posterior end, which stops short of the lower jaw, is joined by a ligamentous fold to the inferior edge of the maxilla. The maxilla is usually fairly long, and bowed inward at its upper end or head. On its posterior surface the head of the maxilla has a firm ligamentous connection with the palatine, and medial to this connection the maxilla has a much looser, anterior, connective tissue association with the premaxilla. The longer, posterior section of the maxilla, or arm, is joined by a ligament to the lower jaw near the coronoid process.

When the lower jaw moves downward, the arm of the maxilla is pulled downward and forward, swinging on the palatine hinge. The posterior end of the premaxilla, which is held by ligaments to the inferior edge of the maxilla, also moves forward, as does the upper end of the premaxilla, which is only gently restrained by the loose connective tissue network of the rostrum. In this manner the premaxilla slides forward until the rostral connective tissue becomes taut. This mechanism contrasts with that of the elopid, and most other sub-acanthopterygian types, in which the posterior or lower end of the premaxilla swings forward with the maxilla, but the upper end remains in place on the rostrum (Figs. 1E, 2B, and 6).

In the extended position, the protrusile premaxilla moves away from its solid footing on the rostrum (Fig. 2C). Two distinct mechanisms have arisen to brace the protruded upper jaw. One involves a modification of the head of the maxilla, and the other, the organization of the rostral connective tissues into specific ligaments.

Probably the original means of ensuring proper and continuous premaxillary support was the development of an interlocking arrangement between the premaxilla and the head of the maxilla. In many clupeids (herrings), and argentinids, the premaxilla has acquired an ascending bony process (not the holostean dorsal process), that rises upward and backward from the symphysis. The head of the maxilla has developed an anteriorly directed flange dorsally and a similar though usually smaller one ventrally. Together the two flanges form a groove into which the posterior edge of the premaxilla fits snugly when the mouth is closed. When the mouth opens, the maxillae in moving forward push the premaxillae ahead of them. The ascending premaxillary processes slide forward in a connective tissue track over the ethmoid cartilage as the maxillae rotate forward so that their grooved heads maintain contact

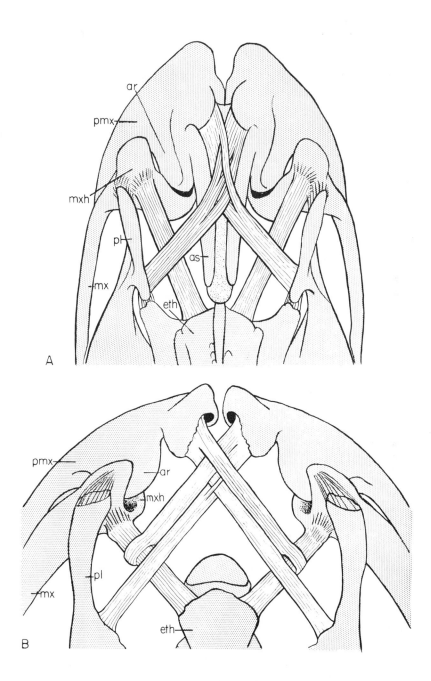

FIG. 5. Semidiagrammatic representation of the upper jaw ligaments in a sea bass (A), in which the premaxilla is protrusible, and in a cod (B), in which the premaxilla is not protrusible. Note that although both fishes have essentially similar ligaments the protrusible premaxilla has an ascending process, and the non-protrusile premaxilla does not. In the sea bass the maxilla is activated by the external division of the adductor mandibulae muscle, as is usual in fishes with protrusile premaxillae. In the cod this division of the muscle is reduced or absent and the maxilla, instead, receives an internal slip of the adductor that originates on the palato-quadrate. Abbreviations: ar, articular process of premaxilla; as, ascending process of premaxilla; eth, ethmoid region; pl, palatine; pmx, premaxilla; mx, maxilla; mxh, head of maxilla.

with the premaxillae. Thus are the premaxillae braced by the maxillae during forward movement.

In the cyprinodontiforms (killifishes) and mugiliforms (mullet, silversides, barracuda), the maxilla has become further specialized to brace the protruded premaxilla. This has been accomplished by an increase in the length of the maxillary head and the bony flanges that form the maxillary groove; hence, contact between maxilla and premaxilla is maintained throughout more of the protrusion cycle. Protrusibility of the upper jaw has been enhanced, as in many acanthopterygians, by the development of a direct ligamentous connection of the posterior end of the premaxilla with the lower jaw. Movement of the premaxilla forward is thus accomplished without the intervention of the maxilla. The maxilla in these fishes exercises principally a restraining and bracing function for the premaxilla.

In the generalized acanthopterygian fishes the protruded upper jaw is braced against the various stresses entailed in grasping food both by the maxillary head and by a series of rostral ligaments (Fig. 5A). The ligaments, that presumably arose through consolidation of less organized connective tissue along stress lines, form a system of cross-braces that provide strength in many directions. In general, the paired upper jaw ligaments in acanthopterygians and in certain soft-rayed teleosts with protrusile mouths when present are either crossed, that is, extending from the right to the left side of the jaw mechanism, or at least obliquely situated. The simplest and apparently fundamental arrangement of these ligaments to be found in the predaceous jaw is a pair running obliquely from ethmoid to maxilla crossed above by a pair connecting left and right premaxillary heads with, respectively, the right and left palatines. When an upper jaw so equipped is protruded, the forces pulling one premaxilla toward the other (and thus maintaining the symphysis in the median plane) increase with protrusion. Thus, the system of crossed ligaments combines multidirectional strength with a flexibility sufficient for protrusion, and represents an overall improvement of the jaw mechanism, predaceous and otherwise.

Protrusibility is not a necessary concomi-

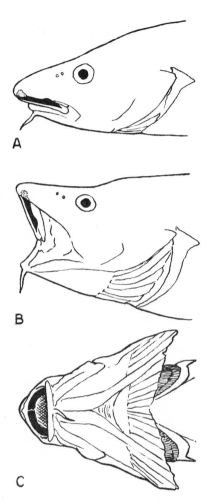

FIG. 6. Outline of head of cod (*Gadus*) showing opening of mouth, movement of the premaxilla (solid black), and expansion of orobranchial chamber. A. Side view with mouth closed. Premaxilla lies almost horizontally. B. Side view with mouth widely opened. The posterior portion of the premaxilla has been pulled forward, but the upper, anterior end has remained in place on the rostrum and this premaxilla is therefore non-protrusile. Note increase in depth of throat over the condition in A and elevation of neurocranium. C. Ventral view, showing lateral expansion of the jaws and orobranchial chamber when the mouth is widely opened. Modified from Tchernavin (1953).

tant of developing upper jaw ligaments for such ligaments occur in cods and pirate-perch which have essentially non-protrusile premaxillae (Figs. 5B and 6). Protrusibility requires also the development of elaborate premaxillary processes (ascending, articular, and lateral), special maxillary-premaxillary and maxillary-palatine associations, and particularly appropriate muscle insertions (see Gregory, 1933, and Eaton, 1935). But the appearance of ligaments controlling premaxillary motion means that the maxilla is no longer solely responsible for regulating the forward excursion of the premaxilla—a function now also assumed by the rostral ligaments. This division of responsibility may have made it possible for the head of the maxilla to become modified for new roles with a minimized risk to the protrusile mechanism of the premaxilla.

The gerrids (mojarras), specialized percoids that graze on small organisms, provide an example of the maxilla in a specialized functional association with the upper jaw. The very small mouth of the mojarra is astonishingly protrusile (Fig. 7), and is thrust rapidly out and back repeatedly during feeding. The ascending processes of the premaxillae are greatly elongated so that when the mouth is closed they extend back over the ethmoid region and over the anterior portion of the frontals. The premaxillary–palatine ligaments have lost contact with the premaxillae and have become joined together as a broad band connecting right and left palatines. Under this straplike ligament the long ascending premaxillary processes slide back and forth. The maxillae no longer act as levers to protrude the premaxillae, which now have their own independent ligamentous attachment to the lower jaw.

Abduction of the lower jaw and contraction of the external division of the adductor mandibulae muscle in the mojarra causes the maxillae to rotate *inward* approximately 90° so that their grooved heads face each other, giving the appearance of opposing parenthesis marks, thus ( ). In coming together to form this transitory, ring-like configuration, the grooved maxillary heads close around the ascending premaxillary processes in advance of the strap-like cross-palatine ligament. As the premaxillae are drawn out by the downward movement of the lower jaw, the ascending processes slide forward under the posteriorly situated cross-palatine ligament and within the roughly circular enclosure formed more anteriorly by the apposed grooves of the maxillary head. The long ascending proc-

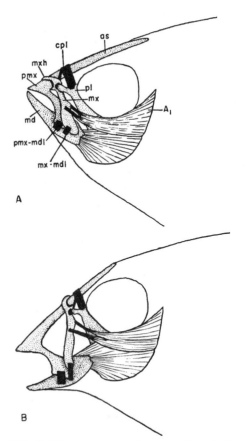

FIG. 7. Diagram representing protrusion of the upper jaw in a gerrid (mojarra). A. Mouth closed. B. Mouth protruded. See text for discussion of mechanism. Abbreviations: A_1, external division of adductor mandibulae muscle; as, ascending process of premaxilla; cpl, cross-palatine ligament; md, mandible; mx, maxilla; mxh, head of maxilla; mx-mdl, maxillary-mandibular ligament; pl, palatine; pmx, premaxilla; pmx-mdl, premaxillary-mandibular ligament.

esses of the premaxillae are supported by the maxillary track and cross-palatine ligament at all times during the forward excursion of the upper jaw, and are thus doubly supported and braced against forces that would drive them out of alignment. In summary, the maxilla of the mojarra has assumed a new role in an effective grazing mechanism as a result of having been (i) freed from its function of protruding the premaxilla by the origin of a direct ligamentous premaxillary-mandibular association, and (ii) aided in its control of premaxillary alignment by the rostral ligaments.

Paradoxically, there are teleosts in which the upper jaw is highly protrusile but lacks most or all of the typical acanthopterygian upper jaw ligaments (cypriniforms, cyprinodontiforms, mugiliforms, for example). There is a variety of reasons for thinking that such fishes may have arisen from subacanthopterygian ancestors before patterns of ligaments were stabilized. If so, each represents an early and independently successful experiment in protrusibility. But these teleost groups are exceptions that prove the rule. Combined, they produced only a limited array of specialized feeding mechanisms. The basic predaceous acanthopterygian mechanism, however, has given rise to a seemingly boundless variety. This great increase in the adaptive potential of the acanthopterygian jaw, as compared with that of predecessor types, may be attributable in some measure to the presence in the acanthopterygian mouth of a complex system of upper jaw ligaments that partially frees the maxilla for new functions.

CONCLUSIONS

1. There is excellent presumptive evidence for the existence of at least three major adaptive levels in the history of the actinopterygian feeding mechanism. These levels involved a continuum of fundamentally predaceous types extending from the Devonian to the Recent—an interval of nearly 400 million years.

2. The lowest level, represented by the palaeoniscoid fishes, had a limited capacity for adaptive change related to the rigidity of the upper jaw and palate. The basic functional pattern of the actinopterygian feeding mechanism was well established at this level.

3. The modifications that occurred during the palaeoniscoid-holostean transition represented the first radical improvement in the history of the actinopterygian feeding mechanism. They included the freeing of the maxilla from the cheek, an increase in the mass and complexity of the adductor mandibulae muscle, the development of the coronoid process on the mandible, and an increase in torque around the jaw articulation.

A change in the position of the interhyal bone permitted more efficient expansion of the orobranchial chamber.

4. The above modifications, which occurred several times independently, permitted considerable adaptive radiation in the feeding mechanism at the holostean level. The basically predaceous pattern persisted, however, in the holosteans ancestral to the teleosts.

5. The holostean–teleostean transition involved no major changes in the predaceous jaw mechanism.

6. The major modifications at the early teleostean level were confined to the palate and jaws. The earliest known predaceous teleosts had already acquired a ball and socket joint between the maxilla and palatine, in contrast to the simple connective tissue joint of the holosteans. In later but still sub-acanthopterygian teleosts, the toothed ramus of the premaxilla was extended posteriorly as a narrow strut below and parallel with the maxilla, excluding the latter from the gape of the mouth and functionally replacing it. These modifications foreshadowed a new mobility for the upper jaw that led to an intensive adaptive radiation of the later teleost feeding mechanism.

7. The origin of the protrusible upper jaw, which characterizes the acanthopterygian level, was the second major refinement in the feeding mechanism. It involved (i) the forward shift of the palatoquadrate and the lower jaw articulation, (ii) secondary simplification of the adductor mandibulae muscles, (iii) differentiation of an adductor component with a tendon to the maxilla, (iv) freeing of the premaxilla from the rostrum, and (v) the development of upper jaw ligaments that, with the maxilla, help to control the forward excursion of the now movable premaxilla.

8. The appearance of a protrusile mechanism incorporating all of the above changes was associated with a hitherto unparalleled increase in adaptive potential of the actinopterygian feeding mechanism. From this basic improvement in jaw mechanics arose the seemingly boundless diversity of feeding specializations for which the acanthopterygian teleosts are so well known.

ACKNOWLEDGMENTS

We are indebted to Dr. Eigil Nielsen for the opportunity to study the anatomy of the palaeoniscoid and subholostean skull at his laboratory in Copenhagen, to Dr. Donald P. Squires for aid in the analysis of jaw mechanics, and to Dr. C. M. Breder, Jr., for information on teleost feeding habits. Michael Insinna prepared Figures 1 and 4 and aided in the preparation of the other illustrations.

REFERENCES

Aldinger, H. 1937. Permische Ganoidfische aus Ostgrönland. Meddel. Groenland 102:1-392.

Breder, C. M., Jr. 1925. On the feeding behavior of fishes with terminal mouths. Copeia 149:89-96.

van Dobben, W. H. 1937. Ueber den Kiefermechanismus der Knochenfische. Arch. Neerlandaises Zool. 2:1-72.

Dunkle, D. H. 1940. The cranial osteology of *Notelops brama* (Agassiz), an elopid fish from the Cretaceous of Brazil. Lloydia 3:157-190.

Eaton, T. H., Jr. 1935. Evolution of the upper jaw mechanism in teleost fishes. J. Morphol. 58:157-172.

Gardiner, B. G. 1960. A revision of certain actinopterygian and coelacanth fishes, chiefly from the Lower Lias. Bull. Brit. Mus. (Nat. Hist.) 4:242-384.

Gregory, W. K. 1933. Fish skulls. A study of the evolution of natural mechanisms. Trans. Amer. Phil. Soc. 23:75-481.

Hiatt, R. W., and D. W. Strasburg. 1960. Ecological relationships of the fish fauna on coral reefs of the Marshall Islands. Ecol. Monog. 30 (1):65-127.

Jarvik, E. 1954. On the visceral skeleton in *Eusthenopteron* with a discussion of the parasphenoid and palatoquadrate in fishes. Kungl. Svenska Vetensk. Handlingar. 5:3-104.

Nielsen, E. 1942. Studies on Triassic fishes from East Greenland. I. *Glaucolepis* and *Boreosomus*. Palaeozool. Groenlandica 1:1-403.

Rayner, D. H. 1948. The structure of certain Jurassic holostean fishes with special reference to their neurocrania. Phil. Trans. Roy. Soc. London 233:287-345.

Saint-Seine, M. P. 1949. Les poissons des Calcaires Lithographiques de Cerin. Nouv. Arch. Mus. d'Hist. Nat. Lyon 2:1-351.

Schaeffer, B. 1956. Evolution in the subholostean fishes. Evolution 10:201-212.

Stensiö, E. 1921. Triassic fishes from Spitzbergen. Holzhausen Vienna 1:1-307.

Tchernavin, V. V. 1953. The feeding mechanisms of a deep sea fish. *Chauliodus sloani* Schneider. Brit. Mus. (Nat. Hist.) p. 1-101.

Watson, D. M. S. 1925. The structure of certain palaeoniscids and the relationships of that group with other bony fishes. Zool. Soc. London 54:815-870.

Westoll, T. S. 1937. On a remarkable fish from the Lower Permian of Autun, France. Ann. Mag. Nat. Hist. 19:553-578.

———. 1944. The Haplolepidae, a new family of late Carboniferous bony fishes. Bull. Amer. Mus. Nat. Hist. 83:1-120.

Woskoboinikoff, M. M. 1932. Der Apparat der Kiemenatmung bei den Fischen. Zool. Jahrb. Abt. für Anat. und Ontogenie der Tiere 55:21-488.

CELLULAR DNA CONTENT AND THE EVOLUTION OF TELEOSTEAN FISHES

RALPH HINEGARDNER* AND DONN ERIC ROSEN

Division of Natural Sciences, University of California, Santa Cruz, California 95060;
and Department of Ichthyology, American Museum of Natural History,
New York, New York 10024

The assessment of evolutionary relationships among organisms has primarily involved morphological criteria. Recently, biochemical techniques have also come to play an important role. Several of these techniques have been applied to the fishes, such as studies of protein similarities (Markert and Faulhaber 1965; Bailey et al. 1970; Wolf et al. 1969) and the measurement of cellular DNA content (Mirsky and Ris 1951; Ohno, Wolf, and Atkin 1968; Hinegardner 1968). In general, this work confirms the phylogenetic relationships that were determined by older methods. But more important, the biochemical techniques provide new insights into the nature of the evolutionary process.

It has been shown in a previous paper (Hinegardner 1968) that highly specialized fishes tend to have less DNA per cell than the more generalized, or less evolved, fishes of the same phyletic grouping. The present paper further amplifies this correlation and presents other aspects of fish evolution that correlate with cellular DNA content. This work is based on data gathered from assays of 275 different species of fishes and is part of an overall survey of cellular DNA content in the animal kingdom.

METHODS

Blood cells or sperm were assayed. These were obtained from freshly killed specimens or, for a few sperm samples, from fish that had been kept on ice for no more than 1 day. Comparison between assays of fresh and iced sperm from the same species showed no significant difference in DNA content. The cells (blood or sperm) were fixed in a solution containing 1% NaCl, 10% formalin, and 0.1 M borate buffer, pH 8.0–8.5. Samples could be stored in this solution for about 1 month with no effect on DNA content. Cells were prepared for assay using the method of Hinegardner (1971).

All cells were counted with a Coulter Counter. A known number of cells were assayed for DNA content using a modification of the fluorometric method of Kissane and Robins (1958) (Hinegardner 1971). Each preparation was assayed at least three times at each of three different concentrations.

---

* Address correspondence to Ralph Hinegardner.

Reprinted by permission from *The American Naturalist*, Vol. 106, No. 951, September–October 1972, pp. 621–644. Copyright © 1972 by the University of Chicago. All rights reserved. Printed in the U.S.A.

The sperm of the sea urchin *Strongylocentrotus purpuratus* was used as a standard. One sperm contains 0 89 $\times$ 10^{-12} g, or 0.89 picograms of DNA, or 0.98×10^9 nucleotide pairs. Two assays of this sperm at each of three different concentrations were run with each set of unknowns. Least-squares regression lines were fitted separately to assays of the unknown and the standard. Over the range of concentrations used, fluorescence is linearly related to the amount of DNA. DNA content can therefore be calculated as the ratio of the regression coefficient for the sea urchin standard over the coefficient for the cells being assayed. The error of the least-squares fit for the unknown was usually less than 5% of DNA content, and in cases where it was greater the sample was assayed again twice at each of three concentrations. The coefficient of variation (standard deviation divided by the mean) for the differences in DNA content determined by repeated assays of the same species was 5%. The average standard error for a species with 1 picogram was $\pm.017$ picograms.

Chromosome counts were made using the method described by Ohno and Atkin (1966).

DEFINITIONS

There are two terms that will be used frequently in this paper to characterize one fish relative to another. These are "generalized" and "specialized." Both terms refer primarily to morphological features. By generalized, we mean a fish that shares numerous features with other members of the taxon to which it has been assigned; in contrast, a specialized fish will share fewer characteristics with other members of its taxon and will differ from them by presence as well as absence of certain features. Generalized fishes tend to be fusiform in shape and to resemble fish such as the trout or bass. Specialized fishes may also be fusiform, but they often look very different. The sea horse is an extreme example of a specialized fish.

TELEOSTEAN CLASSIFICATION

The probable relationships by branching sequence of the major groups of living fishes are shown schematically in figure 1. We have determined the DNA content for at least some members of each group. The following is a brief summary of the basic characteristics of this classification.

The living teleosts can be divided into two major divisions: the Osteoglossomorpha and all other teleosts. The living Osteoglossomorpha are all freshwater fishes and are believed to be a separate and distinct group, not closely related to any other group of teleosts. The group includes some generalized and many specialized forms (Greenwood 1967; Nelson 1968).

Of the remaining teleosts, the Elopomorpha constitute a divergent group. The more generalized members are the tarpons (*Megalops*), tenpounders (*Elops*), and bonefishes (*Albula* and *Pterothrissus*). The eels, though more

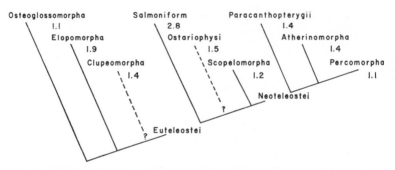

FIG. 1.—Diagram of the cladistic relationships for the major fish groups. The average DNA content for each group is given under the name.

specialized, have a number of characteristics in common with some of their more generalized elopomorph relatives. Along with certain anatomical similarities, each elopomorph whose life cycle is known has a leptocephalus larva.

The Clupeomorpha are one of the most closely defined aggregates of living teleosts. However, their relationship to other fishes is not clear. Traditionally they have been considered to be related either to the elopomorphs or to the Salmoniformes. Neither relationship has been substantiated. The Clupeomorpha have a number of unique anatomical features that set them off from both groups (Greenwood, personal communication) and they do not have a leptocephalus larva.

For various reasons, the rest of the living fishes can best be placed in a fourth major group: the Euteleostei. This is further subdivided into Protacanthopterygii (Salmoniformes), Ostariophysi, and the Neoteleostei (Rosen and Patterson 1969). "The Salmoniformes as a group contain, in mosaic occurrence, all the necessary basic specializations to have provided the evolutionary raw materials for all the more advanced groups" (Greenwood et al. 1966). In various ways the living Salmoniformes resemble the hypothetical ancestors to the more advanced groups of euteleosteans.

The Ostariophysi is a large group that is distributed worldwide and contains 5,000–6,000 known species. Most of these live in fresh water. They include the carps, minnows, loaches, and barbs, the characins, electric eels, and the catfishes. Members of the Ostariophysi have a Weberian apparatus, a structure that is unique to this group. The relationship of the Ostariophysi with the Euteleostei is problematic.

The fishes constituting the neoteleosts are most of the marine teleosts of the world, as well as many of the freshwater species. The Acanthopterygii contain more than half of all fish families, most of these being in the series Percomophora. It is the latter group that includes the bulk of the world's most specialized types of fishes.

The classification we are using is based on work of Greenwood et al. (1966), Rosen and Patterson (1969), Greenwood (personal communication), and Rosen and Greenwood (1970).

RESULTS

The first column of the Appendix contains the haploid DNA content for the fishes we have assayed. The second column gives the haploid chromosome number where it is known. The families are positioned in the table according to the phylogenetic sequence we are using.

Figure 2 shows the distribution of DNA content for all the teleosts we have assayed. The two most apparent features of this figure are the peak at 1.0 picograms and the strong skewing.

There are a number of other ways the data can be viewed. Figure 3 is a plot of the average DNA content for the members of a given family versus the position of that family in the classification scheme of the Appendix. The order in which the families are arranged, developed independently of the DNA data, is intended to go from generalized to specialized within each phyletic assemblage. Since a cladogram cannot be linearly ordered, at some points along the abscissa of figure 3 a generalized fish must necessarily follow after a specialized fish of a different taxon. However, the order of the higher taxa is also in the general direction from generalized to specialized. It is apparent in figure 3 that fishes with a high amount of DNA are almost all in the first third of the graph and that there are only a few families that average more than 1.2 picograms in the last two thirds. In general, the more specialized fishes have less DNA than generalized fishes.

Not only is there a decline in DNA content across the whole of the teleosts, but there is also a decline within groups. This usually follows the trend from generalized to specialized. For example, the DNA content of the Osteoglossomorpha goes from 1.3 picograms for a notopteroid to 0.77 for the specialized osteoglossoid, *Pantadon*. Within the Clupidae, the generalized armored herrings have more DNA than the specialized round herring, *Clupea pallasi*. In the Ostariophysi, the specialized, eel-like Gymnotidae,

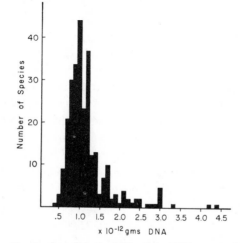

Fig. 2.–Distribution of the haploid cellular DNA content for all assayed species of fish.

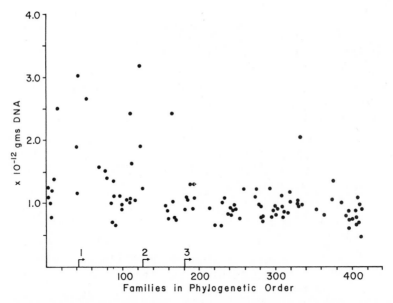

Fig. 3.—Average DNA content for families in which one or more members have been assayed. These are arranged in linear order following the sequence of the branches of fig. 1 and the order of the Appendix. The numbers on the abscissa refer to the numerical position of the families, slightly rearranged from Greenwood et al. (1966). Families to the right of arrow 1 are Euteleosts; those to the right of arrow 2 are Neoteleosts; and those beyond arrow 3 are Acanthopterygians.

which are most closely related to the Characidae, average 0.94 picograms, whereas the characids average 1.6. The cyprinids show the same trend. The more generalized *Danio* and *Brachydanio* have more DNA than the more specialized barbs. All cyprinids have more DNA than the related, and very specialized, Gyrinocheilidae with 0.65 picograms. Within the batrachoidiform lineage of the Paracanthopterygii, the generalized Batrachoididae have 2.4 picograms compared with the smaller amounts in the specialized Antennariidae (0.78 picograms) and Ogocephalidae (0.74 picograms). Among the scorpaenoids, the highest DNA values are in the generalized Scorpaenidae. The highest values in the Cottidae are found in the more generalized members. Within the Percoidei the same trend is apparent (see Appendix). The Serranidae, Percidae, Lutjanidae, Pomadaysidae, Cichlidae, and Pomacentridae are all percoids of more or less generalized body form, and they average 1.1 picograms. A somewhat more specialized group including the Pomatomidae, Rachycentridae, Echeneidae, Carangidae, Gerridae, Monodactylidae, Ephippidae, Scatophagidae, Chaetodontidae, and Embiotocidae averages 0.83 picograms. All the fish families in the Appendix beyond the Pomacentridae are specialized in various ways and, with two exceptions, all average 1 picogram or less. Within the Atherinomorpha, low DNA is associated with a particular form of specialization—viviparity. This series has a large number of viviparous species. In the family Exocoetidae, *Dermogenys pusillus* has less DNA than the oviparous *Hyporhamphus uni-*

fasciatus. The Poeciliidae, which are viviparous, have less DNA than the closely related Cyprinodontidae.

The relation between DNA and degree of specialization can also be seen in the comparison of larger groups. The Scopelomorpha, Paracanthopterygii, and Atherinomorpha are three groups of neoteleosts retaining the largest number of primitive structural characteristics and average more DNA (1.2 picograms) than the more specialized Percomorpha (0.95 picograms).

Clearly, specialization is associated with low amounts of DNA. Furthermore, generalized fishes almost always have more than 1 picogram.

There are several exceptions to this general rule that should not be overlooked. In the catfishes, most families average about 1.2 picograms. The generalized Ariidae have twice this amount, though the generalized Bagridae have only 1.1 picograms. But the specialized Callichthyidae (primarily members of the genus *Corydoras*) average almost three times as much. The Loricariidae average 1.9 picograms which is also high for a specialized fish. Both families are very speciose. The callichthyids are of particular interest in this respect. In 1960 there were about 50 recognized species of the genus *Corydorus* alone (Weitzman 1960). Today there are probably close to 100 species, and more continue to be described.

Two other specialized families that average more DNA than would be expected are the Scaridae (2.0 picograms) and the Gobiidae (1.4 picograms). These are the only Percomorpha out of 49 families examined to average significantly above 1.2 picograms. Like the two catfish families, the gobies are speciose. This is not true of the scarids, which are only moderately so.

Our data can be broken down in other ways. It is apparent from figure 3 that we have taken samples fairly uniformly throughout the Teleostei. Most of our data (78% of the families examined) and most of the world's fish families (87%) are in two major groups, the Ostariophysi and the Neoteleostei, most of the latter being in the superorder Acanthopterygii. The Ostariophysi and Neoteleostei show a number of important differences. Figure 4 uses the same coordinates as figure 2. The DNA distribution in these two groups is very different. The Ostariophysi show a broad distribution in DNA content, with a peak at about 1.2 picograms. In contrast, the neoteleostean distribution is much narrower and more symmetrical with a peak at 1.0 picograms.

A comparison of the distribution in chromosome number is even more striking. Figure 5 is a plot of *haploid* chromosome number for species in the two groups versus the number of species having a given chromosome number. Data for this figure are from the Appendix and from the literature (primarily the compilation by Chen 1967). Most Ostariophysi have either 24 or 25 chromosomes, though there are a significant number of species having more or less. The neoteleosteans are different; here there is a very sharp cutoff at 24 chromosomes. In fact, out of 119 species studied only four have more than 24 chromosomes. In one of those with 25, *Melamphaes*

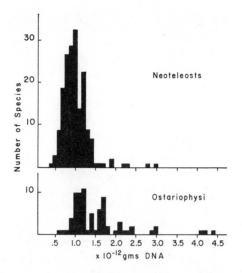

F̲ɪ̲ɢ̲. 4.—Distribution of haploid DNA content among the assayed Neoteleosts and Ostariophysian fishes.

parvus, the twenty-fifth chromosome appears to be a sex chromosome (Chen 1969). *Symphysodon aequifasciata* has 30 chromosomes (Ohno and Atkin 1966); however, of these six are microchromosomes, and there are thus 24 major chromosomes. The overall conclusion is that a chromosome number greater than 24 is exceedingly rare in the Neoteleostei. It is not clear what this means. Possibly the narrow distribution in DNA content among the neoteleosteans is a consequence of an inability to increase their chromosome number beyond that of their ancestor, thus eliminating an important route for increasing DNA content.

If changes in chromosome number have been associated with changes in DNA content, one might expect that there would be a correlation between chromosome number and DNA content, and there does seem to be one. Wolf et al. (1969) demonstrated this for the extremes in DNA content among eight related cyprinid fishes. They found that species with 50 or more chromosomes had large amounts of DNA. All the fishes we have examined with 50 or so chromosomes also have high amounts of DNA. Furthermore, there is a tendency for the inverse to be true but with some noticeable exceptions. As the Appendix shows, *Umbra limi* has 2.7 picograms of DNA but only 11 chromosomes. The general correlation between chromosome number and DNA content is illustrated in figure 6. Obviously there is scatter here, and superficially it would appear that there is no correlation. However, DNA content and chromosome number show a significant correlation ($r = .45$; $N = 72$; $P < .01$). Spearman's rank correlation coefficient, which requires no assumptions about the nature of the distribution of either parameter, is also significant at the .01 level ($r_s = .36$). The three species with 50 or more chromosomes do not significantly affect either calculation. Clearly DNA content and chromosome number are correlated.

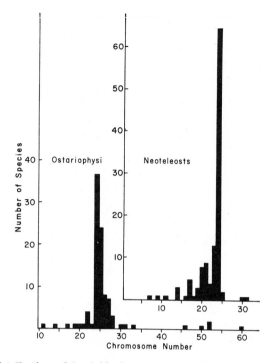

FIG. 5.—Distribution of haploid chromosome number in the Neoteleosts and Ostariophysian fishes. Data are primarily from the compilation by Chen (1967) and from the Appendix.

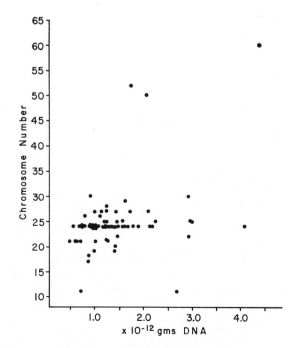

FIG. 6.—Chromosome number plotted against DNA content. The data are from the Appendix and are analyzed in the text.

DISCUSSION

The results reported in this paper and in the previous one (Hinegardner 1968) point to the same conclusion: within most taxa of fishes, generalized members have more DNA than most of those that are specialized. The question is. What does this say about fish evolution?

If specialization is the direction of evolution then there are a number of necessary consequences. The group containing the generalized fishes has almost certainly gone through less evolutionary change in reaching its present form than the group containing the specialized fishes. On the average, fishes having a generalized form have been on earth longer than those with a specialized form. A specialized fish would be expected to have fewer parts, since the derivative condition of specialization is the adaptation to a restricted mode of life not requiring the use of all structures present in the generalized form. Though it would be possible to quantitate fish parts, it is hardly necessary; even the gross picture one gets from examining fish anatomy shows that the generalized fishes have more parts. They tend to have more separate elements in the hyoid apparatus and gill arches, more vertebrae, intermuscular bones, skull bones, and fin rays. Certainly the trend is not in the opposite direction.

Rensch (1959) has described a general pattern that may be typical of the evolutionary history of most animals. First there is rapid evolutionary radiation. This is followed by extinction of some of the early forms and a gradual specialization of the remaining lines. The total number of species may increase during this phase. Accompanying this there is a loss of parts and the specialization of the remaining parts, often leading to some very unusual looking species. Gradually, most species become quite specialized and ultimately the entire lineage may become extinct.

Along with this loss of parts associated with specialization, we have shown that there is also a loss of DNA. Since the role of most of the DNA in higher organisms is not understood, we cannot say that such a loss represents the DNA associated with the lost parts. However, it would be surprising if this were not at least partly true. If a fish requires a minimum of close to 0.4 picograms of DNA per haploid cell as figure 2 indicates, then it is reasonable to postulate that individual parts of the fish also require a certain amount of DNA. It seems unlikely that all portions of the DNA encode for or control the formation of fractions of all parts of the fish. Almost certainly some of the DNA is specific for individual parts or for assemblages of related parts, and numerous genetic studies on animals and plants show this to be true. If this DNA is lost, the part cannot be formed. Loss of DNA has probably a biochemical counterpart; it should lead to a loss of enzymes and their control mechanisms representing biochemical specialization.

In contrast to the loss of DNA during fish evolution, the evolution of living organisms in general has resulted in an overall increase in DNA content. The so-called higher organisms have more than the lower ones such as the bacteria, molds, and fungi. The higher multicellular organisms have more DNA than the sponges and coelenterates (Mirsky and Ris 1951). Most of the more advanced chordates have more DNA than primitive chordates such as *Branchiostoma* (Amphioxus), and there are a few specialized fishes with unusually large amounts of DNA. What this means is that in the overall evolutionary history leading to the fishes, and probably within the fishes, there have been times when DNA content increased. These increases were then followed by gradual decreases such as suggested in figure 3.

The widespread presence of polyploidy in many plants and in the few animals, such as parthenogenetic species, where it would be expected to cause no genetic problems (Grant 1963), demonstrates that abrupt increases in DNA content are not only tolerated in many different organisms, but apparently selected for. There are a number of ways DNA content could increase by means other than polyploidy, and Ohno (1970) has summarized most of the mechanisms that have been postulated. Wolf et al. (1969) and Uyeno and Smith (1972) have good evidence for polyploidy in some cyprinids, and figure 6 suggests that polyploidy may be widespread in fishes. However, most fishes do not show the neat multiple chromosome number series often found in plants (Grant 1963), suggesting that some of the chromosomes may have fused or were lost soon after formation. The scatter in figure 6 may also indicate that mechanisms other than polyploidy have contributed to increases in DNA content, though our data do not indicate what these might be.

There is abundant evidence from isozyme studies in both fishes and in other vertebrates that gene duplication has occurred (Klose et al. 1969; Shaw 1969; Bailey et al. 1970). It would be difficult to interpret many amino acid sequence studies in any other way. In a number of animal species there are several different hemoglobins with somewhat different amino acid sequences present in the same individual. The enzymes trypsin, chymotrypsin, and elastase have similar amino acid sequences (Shotton and Hartley 1970). Dayhoff (1969) gives many more examples. All of these slightly different but related amino acid sequences are likely to have arisen as the result of some form of prior gene duplication. Of course, the DNA involved in this type of duplication may represent only a small fraction of the total.

It has been pointed out numerous times that higher organisms seem to have too much DNA. Even 1% of what they have would be enough to account for all the Mendelian genes an animal or plant would reasonably be expected to have (King and Jukes 1969). Britten and Kohne (1968) have shown that a large fraction of the DNA is redundant to various degrees. The rest is unaccounted for. In short, most of the DNA in fishes and other animals and plants has a role that cannot be clearly defined at the present time. Britten and Davidson (1969) have theorized that much of it is involved in genetic control.

Our results do not say what the DNA is doing, but they do at least tend to eliminate one possibility. It could be postulated that most of the DNA in any organism is excess and does nothing. Figure 2 indicates this is almost certainly not true. The curve cuts off very steeply on the low side and there are few fishes with very low amounts of DNA. None have less than 0.4 pico-grams. All those fishes with very low amounts of DNA are also very special-ized. It is clear that below about 0.6 picograms DNA is not discarded easily.

This conclusion can be shown another way. If a certain minimum amount of the DNA is vital, then related fishes with low amounts of DNA should have closer to the same amount (on a percentage basis) than another group of related fishes with large amounts of DNA. That is, as the minimum amount of DNA is approached, the amount that is essential becomes a larger portion of the total. Families contain related fishes, and the coefficient of variation (standard deviation divided by the mean) gives a measure of spread in DNA content within a family. Since this is a percentage, it is independent of absolute DNA content. We have computed the coefficients of variation for all families with four or more assayed members. These are plotted against DNA content in figure 7. There is some scatter here, but DNA content and coefficient of variation are strongly correlated. This cor-relation can be shown by the product-moment correlation coefficient ($r =$ .61) or by Kendall's τ ($= .37$) or Spearman's rank correlation coefficient ($r_s = .48$). All methods give a coefficient that is significant at the .025 level or less, again suggesting that most of the DNA in low DNA fishes is neces-sary.

There is another possible interpretation of our data. It could be that the large amount of DNA in surviving representatives of generalized teleosts resulted from a gradual increase in DNA with time in slowly evolving and persistent lines. In the geneological diagram in figure 1, mean DNA values

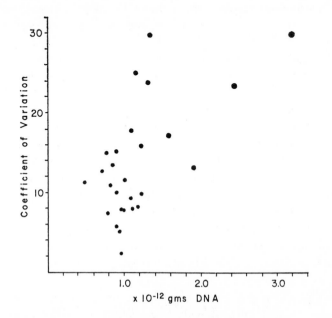

FIG. 7.—The relative spread in DNA content among species in a family (ex-pressed as a coefficient of variation) plotted against average DNA content per fish family with four or more assayed members.

are given for each major group of teleosts. The value of 2.8 picograms for the Salmoniformes includes a value of 0.7 picograms in the surf smelt (Ohno 1970). Salmoniformes, having a mean of 2.8 picograms, probably share a most recent common ancestor with the ostariophysons which have a mean of 1.5 picograms and the neoteleosts with 1.2. The living Salmoniformes, although of generalized form and having many primitive teleostean attributes, are of recent origin. The exceptionally high DNA values in this group appear therefore to represent a derived condition, possibly as a result of polyploidy. This agrees with biochemical (Bailey et al. 1970) and genetic data (Pedersen 1971) as well as with the large chromosome number. By the same token the lower mean values of the Atherinomorpha and Percomorpha (1.1 picograms) appears to represent a secondary decrease in DNA as compared with the relatively less recent sister-group lineages. The Osteoglossomorpha, which are certainly an old lineage, average no more DNA than the neoteleosts. Thus, there is no indication that DNA content within the teleosts has gradually increased with time alone.

Because most high DNA values are found in the more generalized representatives of major groups, and because such generalized species are few in number as compared with teleosts as a whole, it might be argued that high DNA content inhibits evolution or leads to extinction. Bier and Müller (1969) have postulated this for insects. In the sense that generalized teleosts with much DNA are less abundant today than related forms of more specialized aspects and lower DNA content, that argument would appear to be superficially valid. However, it is not necessarily high DNA content that leads to extinction or to the relative paucity of primitive generalized organisms in large and diversified groups, but the process of natural selection itself that favors new adaptations and, by definition, the relatively more specialized forms. A distribution in DNA content similar to figure 2 is a reasonable expectation. This reasoning may or may not apply to groups such as some amphibians or the lungfishes which have exceptionally large amounts of DNA.

CONCLUSIONS

We propose the following combination of events to explain the known distribution of DNA in the Teleostei. There are three possible changes that could be associated with DNA during evolution. (1) The amount of DNA could remain constant and be modified by mutation or recombination, (2) it could increase by duplication, or (3) it could decrease. All these changes have occurred, both alone and in combination. The first can be produced routinely in the laboratory and it is constantly occurring in nature. A combination of mutation, recombination, and natural selection is probably the basis for speciation.

DNA Increase

Instances of DNA increase associated with evolution, though not as common as simple change, have certainly occurred both in plants (Stebbins

1966) and animals (Grant 1963; Wolf et al. 1969; Uyeno and Smith 1972). Our data give further examples of DNA increases. The implications of this increase have been covered most recently by Ohno (1970) and Britten and Davidson (1971).

Some of these increases appear to have occurred recently. Probably the *Corydoras* catfishes, the gobies, and the parrotfishes (Scaridae) are not direct descendants of fishes with as much DNA as they have; all close relatives that we have assayed have less. Hence, these fishes might have evolved from a recent ancestor in which the DNA content was suddenly increased. Furthermore, the wide variation in DNA content among the assayed species of *Corydoras* is not accompanied by much anatomical change, indicating that not all of this DNA is necessary. Apparently an appreciable amount of it can be lost or added with no important change in the appearance of the fish.

Populations such as these would be ideally suited as a genetic storehouse that could provide the raw material for new groups of fishes; any nucleotide changes that were advantageous would be selected for. Many of those changes that would normally be deleterious, for example classical recessives, would tend to be harmless, since there would be at least one other segment within the duplicated set that is still operational. Furthermore, in this situation a new gene complex could appear without the total loss of the old. The overall outcome of this process should be a population of organisms with an increased amount of DNA and an increased number of components. Lines of reasoning similar to this have been presented for various groups of organisms by Watts and Watts (1968), Dayhoff (1969), and Ohno (1970).

Along with high DNA content, the *Corydoras* catfish, scarids, and to a lesser degree, the gobies, have another feature in common: their taxonomy is confusing. This confusion is not for lack of effort on the part of the taxonomist, but rather because in all three it is difficult to distinguish species boundaries. Particularly in the catfishes, small differences in color pattern are sometimes all the taxonomist has to go on. This condition would be expected in a group undergoing a rapid evolutionary radiation.

DNA Decrease

Though DNA increase is important and almost certainly yields the raw material from which new gene complexes can be made, it is only part of evolutionary history. As our data shows, most of the fishes with high DNA values have been evolutionary conservatives. Bier and Müller (1969) found a similar correlation in the insects. It is DNA loss that most closely correlates with evolutionary change in fishes. The fact that loss of components and specialization, both of which have long been recognized as important features in the evolution of practically all organisms, is almost always accompanied by DNA loss suggests more than coincidence. Since DNA plays such a central role in determining the phenotype of an organism, it would be surprising if the lost DNA were not associated with the lost parts. But which is cause and which effect? It could be that DNA loss led to a phenotypic change or that a gene complex became inactive producing the change, and because that complex no longer played a role in natural selection the DNA was deleted by some chance event. Our data do not allow us to differentiate between these two possibilities.

The important point is that a piece of DNA is lost, and with this loss a part of the genome is gone forever. This, coupled with evolution in the absence of compensatory DNA increases, would continually drive a group of organisms toward specialization by the following mechanism: When lineages evolve and acquire new adaptations, they probably cannot utilize all their former anatomical and biochemical components. Some components simply do not integrate into the new form, or at least not in their original configuration. Examples are the appendix in man, the loss of the second pair of wings in the dipteran insects, or the loss of bones associated with the jaw in the advanced fishes. Such examples are common, and many more could be given. In many cases it is even to the organism's advantage not to have some of the old components—for example, gills in adult reptiles or mammals. Since these portions of the DNA have no selective advantage and can even be disadvantageous, this DNA is always subject to deletion. Thus in the absence of DNA increase, the act of forming a new species carries with it the chance of losing DNA, and given time that will happen. This loss may be small at each step, but with enough steps it could become appreciable. Fishes have certainly gone through many steps, and they are now probably more diverse than any other major group of vertebrates.

The correlation between DNA loss and evolution is most striking in groups of fishes that show little tendency to gain DNA but have been actively evolving. The percomorphs are a particularly interesting group. Few of the large number of families examined have high amounts of DNA. Furthermore, as figure 5 suggests, they have little ability to gain DNA by polyploidization, a route used by other fishes. This group is diverse both in terms of anatomy and habitat and its evolution is characterized by loss of parts, modification of the remaining parts, specialization, and low DNA content.

The opposite situation to this is one in which little evolution has occurred. Such groups almost always have a large amount of DNA (Hinegardner 1968). In the light of our previous argument, it would be surprising if these fishes had retained an appreciable amount of useless DNA; but rather we would expect that most of the DNA is essential, whatever its role.

In the absence of DNA increase, evolution appears to drive a group of organisms toward lower and lower amounts of DNA. The loss of DNA causes or is caused by more and more specialization. Finally, the species may have so little DNA that can be modified without affecting essential components, that it becomes extinct with almost any environmental change. This is not the only path leading to extinction, but it may be an important one.

Our overall picture of evolution has these basic features: at some time the DNA content of a fish or fish ancestor increased, probably by duplication.

This organism ultimately gave rise to a group of species with an increased number of components derived from some of the duplicated DNA. Then, as members of the groups continued to evolve, they lost DNA by the mechanism we have outlined. Ultimately, some became extinct, others survived to the present. Of course, this process of DNA increase followed by decrease can occur more than once, and among the fishes there are examples of both increases and decreases. However, decreases are more common and have probably contributed most to the events that have given rise to the majority of teleosts existing today. The role of DNA change in evolution that we have proposed, gives a molecular basis for the overall process of evolution described by Rensch (1959).

SUMMARY

The haploid DNA content has been determined for 275 species of teleostean fishes. Chromosome numbers are known for 73 of these. DNA content ranges from 4.4 picograms down to a minimum of 0.4. The more specialized or evolutionarily advanced fishes usually have less DNA than the more generalized forms. There are, however, several exceptions which may represent fish groups that are now in the process of evolutionary radiation. Chromosome number and DNA content are correlated, indicating that increases in DNA may have occurred by some form of polyploidy. An increase in DNA, followed by a gradual decrease, which is associated with specialization, appears to have accompanied fish evolution.

ACKNOWLEDGMENTS

This work was supported by NSF grant GB 5371. We would like to thank Mrs. Saundra Parra for her invaluable assistance in carrying out the assays and Dr. Marshall Sylvan for his advice on statistical analysis and Dr. Elena Citkowitz for her critical reading of the manuscript. Many of the blood samples were supplied by Dr. Rimmon Fay, Pacific Bio-Marine Supply Company, and Mr. Jack Rudloe, Gulf Specimen Company. Their help is greatly appreciated. We also thank Drs. Ernest Feleppa, P. H. Greenwood, and Raymond Simon for supplying us with samples that otherwise would not have been obtainable.

APPENDIX

<small>HAPLOID DNA CONTENT AND THE HAPLOID CHROMOSOME NUMBER FOR ASSAYED FISHES</small>

Classification	Haploid DNA Content (Picograms)	Haploid Chromosome Number
Osteoglossomorpha		
Osteoglossiformes		
Notopteroidei		
Notopteridae		
Xenomystus nigri	1.3	21 (1)
Osteoglossoidei		
Osteoglossidae (Aruanas, Arapaimas)		
Osteoglossum bicirrhosum	1.0	27 (1)
Arapaima gigas	0.98	...
Pantodontidae (fresh water butterflyfish)		
Pantodon buchholzi	0.77	...
Mormyriformes		
Mormyridae (elephant fishes)		
Marcusenius longianalis	1.2	...
Marcusenius nigricans	1.0	...
Gnathonemus petersi	1.2	...
Mormyrus kannume	1.0	...
Elopomorpha		
Elopiformes		
Elopoidei		
Elopidae (ladyfish)		
Elops saurus	1.2	...
Anguilliformes		
Anguilloidei		
Anguillidae (freshwater eels)		
Anguilla rostrata	1.4	19 (4)
Muraenidae (Moray eels)		
Gymnothorax nigromarginatus	2.5	...
Gymnothorax moringa	2.4	...
Clupeomorpha		
Clupeiformes		
Clupeoidei		
Engraulidae (anchovies)		
Anchovia delicatissma	1.9	...
Engraulis mordax	1.9	24 (3)
Clupeidae (herrings)		
Pomolobus pseudoharengus	1.4	...
Alosa sapidissima	1.3	...
Alosa chrysochloris	1.1	...
Clupea harengus pallasi	0.77	26 (3)
Protacanthopterygii		
Salmoniformes		
Salmonoidei		
Salmonidae (salmon, trout)		
Oncorhynchus kisutch	3.0	30 (9)
Oncorhynchus tshawytscha	3.3	34 (9)
Esocoidei		
Umbridae (mudminnows)		
Umbra limi	2.7	11 (1,2)
Ostariophysi		
Cypriniformes		
Characoidei		
Characidae (tetras, characins)		
Gymnocorymbus ternetzi	2.1	24 (2)
Exodon paradoxus	1.7	...

Classification	Haploid DNA Content (Picograms)	Haploid Chromosome Number
Hemigrammus caudovittatus	1.7	...
Hemigrammus ocellifer	1.7	24 (2)
Leporinus striatus	1.7	27 (1)
Aphyocharax rubropinnis	1.7	...
Metynnis hypsauchen	1.7	...
Metynnis roosevelti	1.7	...
Serrasalmo sp.	1.6	31 (1)
Moenkhausia oligolepis	1.6	...
Hoplias malabaricus	1.4	20 (1)
Arnoldichthys spilopterus	1.2	28 (1)
Pyrrhulina rachoviana	1.2	21 (1)
Chalceus macrolepidotus	1.1	27 (7)
Anostomidae (headstanders)		
Chilodus punctatus	1.6	...
Anostomus anostomus	1.4	27 (1)
Gasteropelecidae (freshwater hatchet fishes)		
Carnegiella strigata	1.4	25–26 (1)
Gasteropelecus levis	1.4	...
Gymnotidae (electric eels)		
Sternopygus macrurus	0.99	24 (1)
Gymnotus carapo	0.99	19 (1)
Eigenmannia sp.	1.0	17 (1)
Apteronotidae		
Apteronotus albifrons	0.71	11 (1)
Cyprinoidei		
Cyprinidae (carps, barbs, minnows)		
Danio malabricus	2.2	25 (1)
Brachydanio rerio	1.8	24 (2)
Corassius auratus	2.0	50 (1), 52 (8), 47 (4)
Cyprinus carpio	1.7	52 (1,2) 54 (4)
Chela mouhoti	1.6	24 (1)
Leuciscus idus	1.5	25 (1)
Labeo bicolor	1.3	...
Morulius chrysophekadion	1.2	25 (7)
Garra taeniata	1.1	26 (1)
Pinephales notatus	1.2	...
Barbus titteya	1.2	24 (2)
Barbus schwanenfeldi	1.1	...
Barbus sachsi	1.0	24 (2)
Barbus everetti	0.99	...
Barbus conchonius	0.97	24 (2)
Barbus tetrazona	0.96	24 (2), 25 (3)
Balantiocheilus melanopterus	0.98	...
Cobitidae (loaches)		
Misgurnus anguillicaudatus	1.4	24 (2), 26 (4)
Acanthophthalmus kuhlii	1.2	25 (7)
Botia sp.	0.84	...
Gyrinocheilidae (hillstream fishes)		
Gyrinocheilus aymonieri	0.65	24 (1)
Siluriformes		
Ictaluridae (North American freshwater catfishes)		
Ictalurus nebulosus	1.2	...
Bagridae		
Auchenoglanis sp.	1.1	...
Bagrus dolmac	1.1	...
Parauchenoglanis guttatus	1.1	...
Leiocassis poecilopterus	0.93	...
Siluridae (glass catfishes)		
Kryptopterus bicirrhis	0.91	30 (1)
Schilbeidae		
Eutropius grenfelli	0.98	...
Schilbe marmoratus	0.98	...

Classification	Haploid DNA Content (Picograms)	Haploid Chromosome Number
Clariidae (walking catfishes)		
Clarias mossambicus	1.2	...
Clarias batrachus	1.2	27 (1)
Clarias lazera	1.2	...
Malapteruridae (electric catfishes)		
Malapterurus electricus	1.0	...
Mochokidae (up-side-down catfishes)		
Synodontis nigriventris	1.1	...
Synodontis sp.	1.2	...
Synodontis schall	1.1	...
Ariidae (sea catfishes)		
Galeichthys felis	2.5	...
Bagre marinus	2.4	...
Doradidae (dorados, talking catfishes)		
Acanthodoras spinosissimus	1.6	...
Pimelodidae		
Pimelodus clarias	1.2	...
Pimelodella gracilis	0.88	...
Callichthyidae (armoured catfishes)		
Corydoras aeneus	4.4	60 (1)
Corydoras julii	4.2	...
Corydoras melanistius	3.0	24 (1)
Corydoras undulatus	3.0	25 (1)
Corydoras punctatus	2.9	22–23 (1)
Corydoras elegans	3.0	25 (1)
Corydoras myersi	2.3	...
Callichthys callichthys	1.7	...
Loricariidae (suckermouth catfishes)		
Otocinclus affinis	2.1	...
Hypostomus plecostomus	2.1	27 (7)
Xenocara dolichoptera	1.8	...
Loricaria parva	1.6	24 (2)
Scopelomorpha		
Myctopiformes		
Synodontidae (lizardfishes)		
Synodus lucioceps	1.2	...
Synodus foetens	1.2	...
Paracanthopterygii		
Gadiformes		
Gadoidei		
Merlucciidae (hakes)		
Merluccius productus	0.98	...
Merluccius bilinearis	0.93	...
Gadidae (codfishes)		
Phycis tenuis	...	...
Microgadus proximus	0.90	...
Ophidioidei		
Ophidiidae (cusk-eels)		
Otophidium welshi	0.84	...
Otophidium scrippsi	0.68	...
Batrachoidiformes		
Batrachoididae (toadfishes)		
Opsanus beta	3.0	...
Opsanus tau	2.8	...
Porichthys notatus	2.2	24 (4)
Porichthys porosissimus	1.7	...
Lophiiformes		
Lophioidei		
Lophiidae (goosefishes)		
Lophius americanus	1.0	...

Classification	Haploid DNA Content (Picograms)	Haploid Chromosome Number
Antennaroididei		
Antennariidae (frogfishes)		
Antennarius ocellatus	0.78	...
Ogcocephalidae (batfishes)		
Ogcocephalus nasutus	0.74	...
Acanthopterygii		
Atherinomorpha		
Exocoetoidei		
Exocoetidae (flyingfishes, halfbeaks)		
Hyporhamphus unifasciatus	1.1	...
Dermogenys pusillus	0.74	24 (1, 2)
Belonidae (needlefishes)		
Strongylura exilis	1.1	...
Strongylura marinus	1.2	...
Potamorrhaphis guianensis	1.2	24 (1)
Cyprinodontoidei		
Oryziatidae (medakas)		
Oryzias latipes	1.1	24 (1, 4)
Cyprinodontidae (killifishes)		
Cyprinodon variegatus	1.6	...
Fundulus heteroclitus	1.5	24 (2)
Fundulus majalis	1.4	...
Rivulus urophthalmus	1.5	22 (1)
Aphyosemion coeruleum	1.2	...
Aplocheilus panchax	0.72	...
Poeciliidae (livebearers)		
Poecilia latipinna	0.96	24 (2)
Xiphophorus maculatus	0.95	24 (1, 4)
Xiphophorus helleri	0.95	24 (2, 6)
Gambusia affinis holbrooki	0.86	18 (1, 2), 24 (4)
Atherinoidei		
Melanotaeniidae (rainbowfishes)		
Melanotaenia nigrans	1.3	24 (1)
Melanotaenia fluviatilis	1.3	24 (1)
Atherinidae (silversides)		
Atherinops affinis	1.1	...
Percomorpha		
Beryciformes		
Berycoidei		
Holocentridae (squirrelfishes)		
Holocentrus ascensionis	0.92	...
Gasterosteiformes		
Gasterosteoidei		
Gasterosteidae (sticklebacks)		
Gasterosteus aculeatus	0.70	21 (2)
Eucalia inconstans	0.67	...
Apeltes quadracus	0.58	...
Syngnathoidei		
Syngnathidae (seahorses, pipefish)		
Hippocampus erectus	0.66	...
Syngnathus fuscus	0.66	...
Syngnathus floridae	0.64	...
Channiformes		
Channidae (snakeheads)		
Ophiocephalus obscurus	1.0	21 (1)
Scorpaeniformes		
Scorpaenoidei		
Scorpaenidae (scorpionfishes, rockfishes)		
Scorpaena braziliensis	1.4	...
Sebastodes dalli	1.1	...

Classification	Haploid DNA Content (Picograms)	Haploid Chromosome Number
Sebastodes penniger	0.97	. . .
Sebastodes paucispinis	0.96	. . .
Hexagrammoidei		
Hexagrammidae (greenlings)		
Hexagrammus decagrammus	0.84	. . .
Anoplopomatidae (sablefishes)		
Anoplopoma fimbria	0.84	
Zaniolepididae (combfishes)		
Zaniolepis latipinnis	0.93	. . .
Triglidae (searobins)		
Prionotus carolinus	0.99	. . .
Prionotus scitulus	0.79	. . .
Cottoidei		
Cottidae (sculpins)		
Rhamphocottus richardsoni	1.1	. . .
Hemitripterus americanus	0.94	. . .
Myoxocephalus octodecimspinosus	0.94	. . .
Clinocottus analis	0.93	24 (4)
Icelidae		
Icelinus filamentosus	0.90	. . .
Agonidae (poachers)		
Unidentified	0.76	. . .
Perciformes		
Percoidei		
Serranidae (sea basses)		
Epinephelus striatus	1.3	. . .
Epinephelus morio	1.3	. . .
Epinephelus guttatus	1.2	. . .
Mycteroperca tigris	1.3	. . .
Mycteroperca interstitialis	1.2	. . .
Paralabrax nebulifer	1.3	. . .
Petrometopon cruentatus	1.2	. . .
Centropristes striatus	1.2	. . .
Cephalopholis fulvus	1.2	. . .
Dermatolepis inermis	1.2	. . .
Perchichthyidae (stripped bass)		
Morone saxatilis	0.89	. . .
Priacanthidae (bigeyes)		
Priacanthus arenatus	1.1	. . .
Percidae (perches)		
Perca flavescens	1.2	. . .
Branchiostegidae (tilefishes)		
Caulolatilus princeps	0.98	. . .
Pomatomidae (bluefishes)		
Pomatomus saltatrix	0.96	. . .
Rachycentridae (cobias)		
Rachycentron canadum	0.77	. . .
Echeneidae (remoras)		
Echeneis naucrates	0.72	. . .
Carangidae (jacks, pompanos)		
Trachinotus falcatus	0.86	. . .
Chloroscombrus chrysurus	0.78	. . .
Caranx hippos	0.72	. . .
Lutjanidae (snappers)		
Lutjanus campechanus	1.4	. . .
Lutjanus griseus	1.3	. . .
Ocyurus chrysurus	1.3	. . .
Etelis oculatus	0.95	. . .
Gerridae (mojarras)		
Eucinostomus gula	0.78	. . .
Pomadasyidae (grunts)		
Haemulon plumieri	0.98	. . .
Haemulon flavolineatum	0.88	. . .
Haemulon sciurus	0.87	. . .

Classification	Haploid DNA Content (Picograms)	Haploid Chromosome Number
Haemulon melanurum	0.86	...
Orthopristis chrysoptera	0.86	...
Sparidae (porgies)		
Stenotomus chrysops	0.98	...
Diplodus argenteus	0.96	...
Diplodus holbrooki	0.94	...
Calamus calamus	0.93	...
Sciaenidae (drums, croakers)		
Pogonias cromis	0.98	...
Micropogon undulatus	0.80	...
Menticirrhus americanus	0.80	...
Cheilotrema saturnum	0.78	...
Bairdiella chrysura	0.76	...
Monodactylidae (silverdollars)		
Monodactylus argenteus	0.90	24 (2)
Kyphosidae (seachubs)		
Girella nigricans	1.1	...
Medialuna californiensis	0.81	...
Ephippidae (spadefishes)		
Chaetodipterus faber	0.93	...
Scatophagidae (scats)		
Scatophagus argus	0.77	...
Chaetodontidae (butterflyfishes)		
Chaetodon ocellatus	0.87	...
Embiotocidae (surfperches)		
Embiotoca jacksoni	1.0	24 (4)
Phanerodon furcatus	0.85	...
Zalembius rosaceus	0.82	...
Rhacochilus vacca	0.80	...
Cymatogaster aggregata	0.74	...
Cichlidae (cichlids)		
Cichlasoma meeki	1.4	24 (1)
Cichlasoma biocellatum	1.3	...
Tilapia leucosticta	1.2	...
Tilapia nilotica	1.2	...
Tilapia zillii	1.2	...
Aequidens portalegrensis	1.2	...
Geophagus jurupari	1.2	...
Pterophyllum eimekei	1.2	24 (2)
Haplochromis parvidens	1.2	...
Haplochromis squamulatus	1.2	...
Haplochromis longirostris	1.1	...
Haplochromis squamipinnus	1.1	...
Haplochromis quiarti	1.0	...
Crenicichla saxatilis	1.1	...
Apistogramma sp.	1.0	...
Pelmatochromis kribensis	1.0	24 (2)
Pomacentridae (damselfishes)		
Chromis sp.	1.1	...
Abudefduf saxatilis	1.0	...
Mugiloidei		
Mugilidae (mullets)		
Mugil cephalus	0.99	...
Sphyraenoidei		
Sphyraenidae (barracudas)		
Sphyraena borealis	1.2	...
Sphyraena argentia	0.83	...
Labroidei		
Labridae (wrasses)		
Thalassoma bifasciatum	0.98	...
Tautoga onitis	0.93	...
Tautogolabrus adspersus	0.91	...
Scaridae (parrotfishes)		

Classification	Haploid DNA Content (Picograms)	Haploid Chromosome Number
Sparisoma viride	2.1	...
Scarus vetula	1.9	...
Trachinoidei		
Bathymasteridae (ronquils)		
Rathbunella sp.	0.96	...
Blennioidei		
Blenniidae (blennies)		
Unidentified	1.0	...
Hysoblennius sp.	0.95	...
Hysoblennius hentz	0.86	...
Unidentified	0.81	...
Clinidae (clinids)		
Paraclinus sp.	1.0	...
Stichaediae (pricklebacks)		
Cebedichthys violaceus	0.81	...
Gobioidei		
Gobiidae (gobies)		
Gobius sadanundio	1.4	24 (1)
Unidentified	1.4	...
Tyhplogobius californiensis	1.2	...
Scombroidei		
Scombridae (mackerels, tunas)		
Scomberomorus regalis	1.1	...
Scomberomorus cavalla	0.95	...
Euthynnus pelamis	1.0	...
Scomber scombrus	0.97	...
Sarda sarda	0.92	...
Sarda velox	0.92	...
Xiphiidae (swordfishes)		
Xiphias gladius	0.88	...
Stromateoidei		
Stromateidae (butterfishes)		
Peprilus simillimus	0.81	...
Poronotus triacanthus	0.80	...
Anabantoidei		
Belontiidae (bettas)		
Betta splendens	0.64	21 (2)
Macropodus cupanus dayi	0.61	...
Macropodus opercularis	0.59	21 (2)
Helostomatidae (kissing gouramies)		
Helostoma rudolfi	0.88	...
Osphronemidae (gouramies)		
Trichogaster leeri	0.82	...
Trichogaster trichopterus	0.78	24 (2)
Trichogaster trichopterus (opaline)	0.68	24 ('1, 2)
Colisa lalia	0.62	...
Mastacembeloidei		
Mastacembelidae (spiney eels)		
Macrognathus sp.	0.74	...
Pleuronectiformes		
Pleuronectoidei		
Bothidae (lefteyed flounders)		
Etropus crossotus	1.0	...
Citharichthys sordidus	0.96	...
Paralichthys californicus	0.80	...
Xystreurys liolepis	0.74	24 (6)
Pleuronectidae (righteyed flounders)		
Microstomus pacificus	0.97	...
Glyptocephalus zachirus	0.84	...
Eopsetta jordani	0.75	...
Lyopsetts exilis	0.73	...
Pseudopleuronectes americanus	0.70	...
Parophrys vetulus	0.65	...

Classification	Haploid DNA Content (Picograms)	Haploid Chromosome Number
Soleoidei		
Soleidae (soles)		
Trinectes maculatus	0.65	...
Cynoglossidae (tonguefishes)		
Symphurus atricauda	1.1	...
Tetraodontiformes		
Balistoidei		
Balistidae (triggerfishes)		
Balistes sp.	0.72	...
Stephanolepis hispidus	0.68	...
Aleutera schoepfii	0.64	...
Ostraciontidae (trunkfishes)		
Lactrophrys triqueter	1.1	...
Lactrophrys trigonis	0.85	...
Tetraodontiformes		
Tetraodontoidei		
Tetraodontidae (puffers)		
Spheroides maculatus	0.50	...
Spheroides nephelus	0.50	
Tetraodon palembangensis	0.48	21 (1)
Tetraodon fluviatilis	0.39	...
Diodontidae (porcupine fishes)		
Chilomycterus schoepfii	0.90	...

NOTE.—The number in parentheses following the chromosome number indicates the reference: (1) ours; (2) Post (1965); (3) Ohno et al. (1968); (4) Chen (1967); (5) Nogusa (1960); (6) Ohno and Atkin (1966); (7) Muramota and Ohno (1968); (8) Wolf et al. (1969); (9) Simon (1963).

LITERATURE CITED

Bailey, G. S., A. C. Wilson, J. E. Halver, and C. L. Johnson. 1970. Multiple forms of supernatant malate dehydrogenase in Salmonid fishes: biochemical, immunological, and genetic studies. J. Biol. Chem. 245:5927–5940.

Bier, V. K., and W. Müller. 1969. DNS-Messungen bei Insekten und eine Hypothese über retardierte Evolution und besonderen DNS-Reichtum im Tierreich. Biol. Zentralbl. 88:425–449.

Britten, R. J., and E. H. Davidson. 1969. Gene regulation for higher cells: a theory. Science 165:349–357.

———. 1971. Repetitive and non-repetitive DNA sequences and a speculation on the origins of evolutionary novelty. Quart. Rev. Biol. 46:111–138.

Britten, R. J., and D. Kohne. 1968. Repeated sequences in DNA. Science 161:529–540.

Chen, T-R. 1967. Comparative karyology of selected deep-sea and shallow water Teleost fishes. Ph.D. thesis, Yale Univ.

———. 1969. Karyological heterogamety of deep-sea fishes. Postilla (Peabody Museum) 130:1–29.

Dayhoff, M. O. 1969. Atlas of protein sequence and structure. National Biomedical Research Foundation, Silver Springs, Maryland.

Grant, V. 1963. The origin of adaptation. Columbia Univ. Press, New York.

Greenwood, P. H. 1967. The caudal fin skeleton in osteoglossoid fishes. Ann. Mag. Natur. Hist. (13)9:581–597.

Greenwood, P. H., D. E. Rosen, S. H. Weitzmann, and G. S. Myers. 1966. Phyletic studies of Teleostean fishes, with a provisional classification of living forms. Amer. Mus. Natur. Hist. Bull. 131:341–455.

Hinegardner, R. T. 1968. Evolution of cellular DNA content in Teleost fishes. Amer. Natur. 102:517–523.

————. 1971. An improved fluorometric assay for DNA. Anal. Biochem. 39:197–201.

King, J. L., and T. H. Jukes. 1969. Non-Darwinian evolution. Science 164:788–798.

Kissane, J. M., and E. Robins. 1958. The fluorometric measurement of deoxyribonucleic acid in animal tissues with special reference to the central nervous system. J. Biol. Chem. 233:184–188.

Klose, J., U. Wolf, H. Hitzeroth, and H. Ritter. 1969. Polyploidization in the fish family Cyprinidae order Cypriniformes. Humangenetik 7:245–250.

Markert, C. L., and I. Faulhaber. 1965. Lactate dehydrogenase isozyme patterns of fish. J. Exp. Zool. 159:319–332.

Mirsky, A. E., and H. Ris. 1951. The deoxyribonucleic acid content of animal cells and its evolutionary significance. J. Gen. Physiol. 34:451–462.

Muramota, J., and S. Ohno. 1968. On the diploid state of the fish order Ostariophysi. Chromosoma 24:59–66.

Nelson G. J. 1968. Gill arches of teleostean fishes of the division Osteoglossomorpha. Linnaean Soc. New York, J. Zool. 47:261–277.

Nogusa, S. 1960. A comparative study of the chromosomes in fishes with particular considerations on taxonomy and evolution. Mem. Hyogo Univ. Agr. 3:1–62.

Ohno, S. 1970. Evolution by gene duplication. Springer-Verlag, New York.

Ohno, S., and N. B. Atkin. 1966. Comparative DNA values and chromosome complements of eight species of fishes. Chromosoma 18:455–466.

Ohno, S., U. Wolf, and N. B. Atkin. 1968. Evolution from fish to mammals by gene duplication. Hereditas 59:169–187.

Pedersen, R. A. 1971. DNA content, ribosomal gene multiplicity, and cell size in fish. J. Exp. Zool. 177:65–78.

Post, A. 1965. Vergleichende Untersuchungen der Chromosomenzahlen bei Süsswasser-Teleosteern. Z. Zool. Syst. Evolut. Forsch. 3:47–93.

Rensch, B. 1959. Evolution above the species level. Columbia Univ. Press, New York.

Rosen, D. E., and P. H. Greenwood. 1970. Origin of the weberian apparatus and the relationships of the Ostariophysan and Gonorynchiform fishes. Amer. Mus. Novitates Pub. 2428:1–25.

Rosen, D. E., and C. Patterson. 1969. The structure and relationships of the Paracanthopterygian fishes. Amer. Mus. Natur. Hist. Bull. 141:359–474.

Shaw, C. R. 1969. Isozymes: Classification, frequency, and significance. Int. Rev. Cytol. 25:297–332.

Shotton, D. M., and B. S. Hartley. 1970. Amino-acid sequence of porcine elastase and its homologies with other serine proteinases. Nature 227:802–806.

Simon, R. C. 1963. Chromosome morphology and species evolution in the five North American species of Pacific salmon (*Oncorhynchus*). J. Morphol. 112:77–97.

Stebbins, G. L. 1966. Chromosomal variation and evolution. Science 152:1463–1469.

Uyeno, T., and G. R. Smith. 1972. Tetraploid origin of the karyotype of catostomid fishes. Science 175:644–646.

Watts, R. L., and D. C. Watts. 1968. Gene duplication and the evolution of enzymes. Nature 217:1125–1130.

Weitzman, S. H. 1960. Figures and descriptions of four South American catfishes of the genus *Corydoras*, including two new species. Stanford Ichthyol. Bull. 7:140–154.

Wolf, V., H. Ritter, N. B. Atkin, and S. Ohno. 1969. Polyploidization in the fish family Cyprinidae, order Cypriniformes. Humangenetik 7:240–244.

Additional Readings
CHAPTER 4

BLACKWELDER, R. E. 1972. *Guide to the taxonomic literature of vertebrates.* Ames, Iowa: Iowa State University Press.

FREIHOFER, W. C. 1963. Patterns of the ramus lateralus accessorius and their systematic significance in teleostean fishes. *Stanford Ichthyological Bull.* 8(2):80–189.

FREIHOFER, W. C. 1970. Some nerve patterns and their systematic significance in paracanthopterygian, salmoniform, gobioid, and apogonid fishes. *Proc. Calif. Acad. Sci.,* 4th Ser., 38(12):215–264.

GOSLINE, W. A. 1959. Mode of the functional morphology and classification of teleostean fishes. *Syst. Zool.* 8:160–164.

GOSLINE, W. A. 1960. Contribution toward a classification of modern isospondylous fishes. *Bull. Brit. Mus. (Nat. Hist.), Zool.* 6(6):325–365.

GOSLINE, W. A. 1971. *Functional morphology and classification of teleostean fishes.* Honolulu: University Press of Hawaii.

GREENWOOD, P. H.; MILES, R. S.; and PATTERSON, C. eds. 1973. Interrelationships of fishes. *J. Linn. Soc. (Zool.)* 53, Suppl. 1. New York: Academic Press.

HENNIG, W. 1966. *Phylogenetic systematics.* Urbana: University of Illinois Press.

McALLISTER, D. E. 1968. Evolution of branchiostegals and classification of teleostome fishes. *Nat. Mus. Canada, Bull.* (221), Biol. Ser. 77.

NELSON, G. J. 1969. Gill arches and the phylogeny of fishes, with notes on the classification of vertebrates. *Bull. Amer. Mus. Nat. Hist.* 141(4):477–552.

NELSON, G. J. 1972. Comments on Hennig's "Phylogenetic Systematics" and its influence on ichthyology. *Syst. Zool.* 21:364–374.

PATTERSON, C. 1967. Are teleosts a polyphyletic group? *Colloques Internationaux du Centre National de la Recherche Scientifique* (163):93–109.

ROSEN, D. E., and PATTERSON, C. 1969. The structure and relationships of the paracanthopterygian fishes. *Bull. Amer. Mus. Nat. Hist.* 141:357–474.

SHAKLEE, J. B.; KEPES, K. L.; and WHITT, G. S. 1973. Specialized lactate dehydrogenase isozymes: the molecular and genetic basis for the unique eye and liver LDHs of teleost fishes. *J. Exp. Zool.* 185:217–240.

STAHL, B. J. 1974. *Vertebrate history: Problems in evolution.* New York: McGraw-Hill.

THOMSON, K. S. 1971. The adaptation and evolution of early fishes. *Quart. Rev. Biol.* 46(2):139–166.

WILLIAMS, G. C.; KOEHN, R. K.; and MITTON, J. B. 1973. Genetic differentiation without isolation in the American eel, *Anguilla rostrata. Evolution* 27:192–204.

5

Swimming and
Body Form

SWIMMING AND THE ORIGIN OF PAIRED APPENDAGES

J. R. NURSALL
University of Alberta

INTRODUCTION

Aristotle (De Incessu Animalium; De Partibus Animalium), in discussing the swimming of fish, attributed the chief propulsive power to the paired fins, reserving the caudal fin for steering, and flexion of the body for locomotion in long fish such as eels, which lack pelvic fins. Leonardo's sketches of fish suggest that he assumed that there is an analogy between swimming and flying. These observers, however, devoted most attention to locomotion of aerial and terrestrial animals.

Alphonsi Borelli (1734) provided the first comprehensive account of the swimming of fish. In his chapter XXIII, De Natatu, in a series of propositions, Borelli outlined the expansion and contraction of the air bladder to control specific gravity and position in the water (Proposition 210); dispelled the popular opinion that fins are the chief locomotory organs, for in swimming they are held at the sides (Proposition 212); and described the vibration of the tail as the direct cause of movement (Proposition 214). He noted that the caudal peduncle was laterally flexed from a point at about the level of the anal fin. The caudal fin, likened to the foot of a frog, was contracted and flexed on the outward sweep so as not to impinge on the water, then, at the greatest extent of the lateral movement it was fully extended and with the greatest speed brought back to the midline in an elliptical arc, to impel the fish forward. The sequence would then be repeated on the other side. In Proposition 215 Borelli pointed out how the body muscles are proportionately large to provide power for the tail strokes, while fins are weakly muscled.

This remained the point of view until the nineteenth century, when it was challenged by Pettigrew (1873) in England, and by the remarkable French experimenter E. J. Marey (1895). From their work it became apparent that the whole body of a fish is thrown into a sinuous curve of some dimension; propulsion is not due merely to a vibratile tail.

These studies, particularly Marey's, led to the development of analytical and experimental studies in France especially by Houssay (1912) and Magnan (1930; Magnan and Sainte-Laguë, 1929). During this period, the muscular morphology of fish was examined intensively (Langelaan, 1904; Schmalhausen, 1912; Grenholm, 1923); types of swimming were described and categorized (Breder, 1926); and in 1933, Gray described how fish exert thrust to propel themselves through the water.

THE NATURE OF FISH PROPULSION

The basic propulsive mechanism of fish was delineated by Gray (1933a, b, c, d). Gray began with the eel *(Anguilla vulgaris)* in which the body is thrown into waves of large amplitude. Comparison with other fish showed that the body waves of the eels are merely exaggerated forms of the body waves common to fish. The exaggeration of the waves made the eel particularly suitable to study.

The important characteristics of swimming are as follows:
1) Contralateral, metachronal waves are initiated anteriorly to pass caudad with increasing amplitude. These waves are engendered by serial muscular contraction.
2) It is the *transverse* movement of the body during the passage caudad of waves that provides thrust. Any short section of the body forms an angle a with its own direction of transverse movement. The angle varies from its greatest value at the top of

From *American Zoologist* 2:127–141. Reprinted by permission.

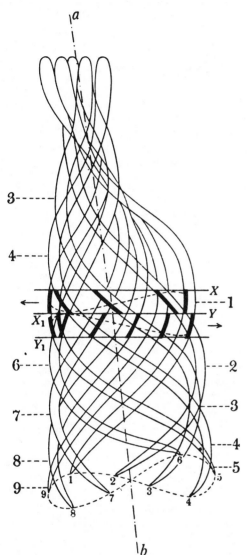

FIG. 1. Drawings of a young eel arranged to show the transverse movement of short sections of the body during the passage caudad of a body wave. Section XY is moving to the left; section $X_1 Y_1$ is moving to the right. The angle a lies between the heavy line on the fish's body and the oblique dotted line marking the path of transverse movement. (From Gray, 1933a, J. Exptl. Biol.)

the wave (where the body is maximally displaced from the midline) to a minimum as it crosses the axis of progression (Fig. 1). Moreover, the speed at which the section of the body moves from side to side across the axis of progression varies, being minimal at extreme positions and maximal as the sec-

tion of body crosses the axis of progression. In part, the magnitude of the thrust developed depends upon the value of a and the velocity at which the section of the body involved crosses the axis of progression. Thrust is maximal for any section of the body as it crosses the axis of progression.

Corollary to these characteristics is the fact that propulsion is dependent on the metachronal waves passing backward at a speed greater than the forward progression of the fish. If the form of the body wave corresponds exactly to the sinuous path travelled by the fish, no angle a is formed and thrust is not produced. Breder (op. cit.) first pointed this out and Gray (1933a, b) analyzed it geometrically, showing that with increased speed, a decreases, and the sinuous path of progression and the wave form of the body of the fish tend to approximate each other. Lighthill (1960), on theoretical grounds, suggested that wave passage should be about 5/4 of the speed of progression. In fact, as will be shown, the relative speed of wave passage varies greatly.

Further analyses by Gray (1933c) showed the same phenomena to be applicable to such fish as the whiting (*Gadus merlangus*), which is shorter in body than the eel and more typically fish-like in form. Here it was shown that a well-developed caudal fin serves mainly to preserve phase differences in the waves passing caudad along the body. By virtue of its resistance to transverse movement, the caudal fin effectively damps the lateral displacement of the body and reduces the sinuosity of the path of progression. The caudal fin does contribute significantly to thrust, but even without it many fish can proceed at almost normal speed, although their mode of swimming is markedly affected, chiefly owing to the increasing amplitude of the body wave.

Gray (1933d) extended his analysis to turning movements in fish, again to show that the basic movement is similar among all fish. What occurs is that by means of a unilateral wave of large amplitude the head of a fish is turned in a new direction and the anterior part of the body follows it, using the posterior part as a fulcrum against which to turn. At about the half-way point along the body the relationship switches, so that the posterior body swings into position on the new course, utilizing the anterior body as its fulcrum. In short-bodied fishes, the caudal fin has an essential role in providing the resistance to transverse displacement required for the posterior part of the body to act as a fulcrum. Fish with the caudal fin amputated cannot easily turn sharply.

A somewhat divergent analysis of swimming is that of Oehmichen (1958) wherein propulsion is related to the thrusting posteriorly of water entrapped in the undulations of the body in a manner analogous to the passage of water by an Archimedean screw. The argument of Oehmichen is subtle, but it lacks the clarity and experimental proof provided by Gray for his description.

THE BODY MUSCULATURE

Given the mode of swimming one must then examine the morphological mechanism behind it. It is obvious that, in most cases, body musculature and caudal fin are the effectors which are to be studied. Exceptions are those forms in which the paired fins, in a variety of ways, provide propulsion. It is beyond the scope of this paper to deal with the many ways in which the fins of fish can be used in locomotion; many of them are adaptations to highly specific modes of life (Harris, 1953; Bertin, 1958).

To some degree all fish possess a common structural heritage which reflects their aquatic environment and their need to progress through it. The body is generally more or less streamlined; it is flexible and the flesh is made up of serial muscle segments, intricately interfolded and arranged in bilateral symmetry. This pattern is seen in amphioxus and persists throughout the aquatic chordates. Nursall (1956) has dis-

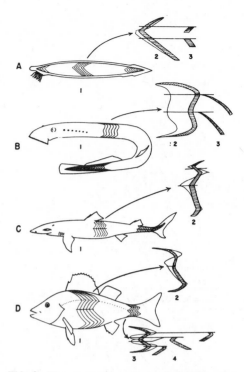

FIG. 2. The myomere pattern of fish-like chordates. All drawings are semi-diagrammatic.
A. Amphioxine; 1, lateral view of *Amphioxus*; 2, lateral view of an individual myomere; 3, horizontal sections through myomere.
B. Cyclostomine; 1, lateral view of *Petromyzon*; 2, lateral view of an individual myomere; 3, horizontal sections through myomere.
C. Piscine; 1, lateral view of *Squalus*; 2, lateral view of an individual myomere from body region.
D. Piscine; 1, lateral view of *Perca*; 2, lateral view of an individual myomere from body region; 3, lateral view of a myomere from caudal peduncle; 4, horizontal sections through myomere of caudal peduncle.
(From Nursall, 1956, Proc. Zool. Soc. London).

tinguished amphioxine, cyclostomine and two types of piscine myomere architecture (Fig. 2). While there are certain ontogenetic differences in the mode of formation of the horizontal septum (Emelianov, 1935) in chondrichthine and osteichthine myomeres, and noticeable differences in the forms of the adult myomeres, the term piscine is useful to encompass all the gnathostomatous fish, for all possess trunk and caudal peduncle myomeres which exhibit a w-shape externally. This shape reflects an in-

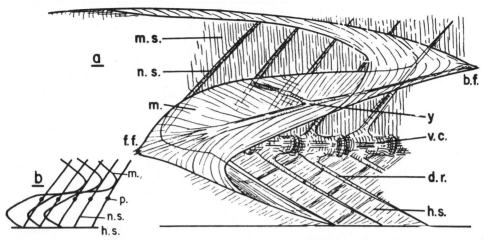

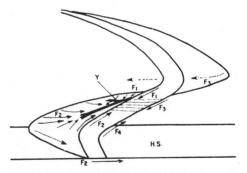

FIG. 3. a. An epaxial myoseptum, based on a dissection of *Megastomatobus*, showing the antero-posterior extent of the septum resulting from its complex deep folding.
b. diagrammatic representation of the attachment of several septa to the dorsal median septum. b.f., backward flexure of myomere; d.r., dorsal rib; f.f., forward flexure of myomere; h.s., horizontal septum; m., myoseptum; m.s., dorsal median septum; n.s., neural spine; p., point of attachment of intermuscular bone; v.c., vertebral centrum; y, intermuscular bone. (From Nursall, 1956, Proc. Zool. Soc. London).

ternal folding which serves several purposes as follows:

1) Any given myomere is extended craniad and caudad over a distance equal to several body segments. This arrangement allows the multitude of short, parallel muscle fibers to exert their effect over a relatively great distance (Fig. 3, 4). It is a remarkably effective arrangement; the large number of short fibers can exert a rapid, powerful pull; the obliquity of the myosepta extends the pull over several vertebral joints. The combination of rapidity, power, and distance of action is not commonly met with elsewhere.

2) The bending and interfolding of the myomeres permits tendinous attachments of various sorts to be developed, which improve the efficiency of the muscular action. Chondrichthyans in particular have utilized this to develop deep-lying tendons where neighboring myosepta come into apposition. In this way, several septum-like tendons are formed, against which the muscles can pull. Another way of utilizing the myomeric folding is exemplified in the tunas, in which prolongations from the

apices of the interfolded cones extend as tendons, particularly through the narrow caudal peduncle to the caudal fin. These tendons are also joined by fibers originating in superficial fasciae, which form covering aponeurotic sheets.

3) Pantin (1956) has pointed out the mechanical advantage of having muscles set

FIG. 4. Forces developed by epaxial myomeres. F_1, forces applied by the backward flexure of the myomere preceding the myomere shown. F_2, forces applied by the forward flexure of the myomere shown. F_3, forces applied by the backward flexure of the myomere shown. F_4, forces applied by the forward flexure of the myomere succeeding the myomere shown. h.s., horizontal septum; y, intermuscular bone. (From Nursall, 1956, Proc. Zool. Soc. London).

obliquely on their tendons, as in chordate myomeres. Contraction deformation is accommodated by the fibers coming to stand more upright in relation to the septa, analogously to an oblique parallelogram shortening by being converted to a rectangle, while retaining the same area. This is not to say that there is not some deformation; it can be seen through the skin of some fish, e.g., the bullhead *(Ictalurus).* An opportunity was taken to observe this in an albino specimen, where it showed particularly clearly. Bulges, owing to muscle fiber contraction and swelling, were particularly apparent at the levels of the interfolded cones. Simultaneously hollows, denoting tension, developed along the myosepta, especially those of the dorsalmost and ventralmost wings of the muscle segments.

4) As a result of any one myomere extending over several segments and overlapping several neighboring myomeres, any given vertebral joint is acted upon by several myomeres at once. Such overlapping in structure, and so in phases of myomere contraction, smoothes and reinforces the body movements. No myomere acts alone and all body reactions are graded. A consistent and equalized production of power is possible all along the body.

The part which histological structure might play in muscular activity in fish has recently been examined by Boddeke et al., (1959). They distinguished two major types of fibers: (1) broad, white fibers with short sarcomeres; (2) narrow, red fibers with long sarcomeres and much fat. The size of the sarcomere is related to speed of contraction, fibers with short sarcomeres contracting more rapidly. White fibers make up the greatest proportion of fish flesh. Red fibers, found chiefly along the horizontal septum or deep to it (see also Greene, 1913; Kafuku, 1950), are rich in myohemoglobin. The red fibers occur much more abundantly in fish with great staying power for continuous swimming (e.g., salmon, scombroids). Often the stayers have a mosaic type of musculature in which white and red

fibers are intermingled. Takeuchi (1959) has examined the neuromuscular transmission of white and red fibers in a freshwater teleost. Fish white muscle was found to correspond to frog twitch muscle, while fish red muscle corresponded to frog red muscle in reaction characteristics.

THE CAUDAL FIN

The caudal fin contributes importantly to the swimming of many fish, particularly to those which are pelagic and relatively short-bodied. The evolution, morphology, and functional significance of the caudal fin have been carefully examined by Graham-Smith (1936), Grove and Newell (1939) and Affleck (1950), among others. It is now generally recognized that a heterocercal (epibatic) caudal fin tends to raise the tail and depress the nose, as in sharks. This tendency is counteracted by the use of pectoral fins and the flattened rostrum, with secondary assistance from pelvic fins (Harris, 1936, 1938). Conversely, a hypocercal (hypobatic) caudal fin raises the front end of the body (Kermack, 1943). The presence of an air bladder in osteichthyan fish with its consequent diminution of the animal's specific gravity (Jones and Marshall, 1953) has allowed the development of homocercal (isobatic) caudal fins among this group, or specialized diphycercy or gephyrocercy in certain groups. In all cases the form of the fin, the form of the body, and the mode of life of the animal are closely related (Harris, 1934; Nursall, 1958a; E. Kramer, 1960). Because of this relationship, the spectacular convergence of animals such as the shark *(Lamna),* the tuna *(Thunnus),* ichthyosaurs, and dolphins has come about.

The caudal fin serves to increase the thrust at the posterior end of the body, to reduce the amplitude of the locomotor body wave, and reduce the yawing moment of the animal. In rapid-swimming, pelagic fish (e.g., scombroids) the tail fin is relatively rigid and has a large aspect ratio (AR = ratio of span to chord). Among the pelagic fish which swim neither as constantly nor as rapidly as scombroids, the caudal fin is flexible and, because of its intricate musculature, highly mobile. A study of the behavior of such fish at rest shows that the caudal fin is generally in motion. The motion differs from species to species as does the movement of other fins. Presumably the various combinations of fin movements serve to keep the fish at rest or in slow movement, as it wishes. The behavioral studies of cichlid fish by Baerends and Baerends-van Roon (1950) illustrate the usefulness of knowledge of specialized anatomy to ethologists. If the same intensive approach to behavioral studies is taken by other investigators, soon we shall have a large body of anatomical information which will be of wide general interest and use. Although at rest there is complex, often metachronal motion of the caudal fin, in fast movement, as in the sudden spurt forward from rest, the caudal fin is expanded and made as rigid as possible. The body of a fish appears to vibrate, so rapid is the passage of locomotor waves along it. The flexible tail fin is held most rigid at its dorsal and ventral margins. There the marginal rays are stiffer and are supported by short, stout, incomplete rays bound together relatively firmly. The center of the caudal fin, which may or may not be notched, has more flexible rays suspended in a broad, double membrane. From the central region water is spilled as the fin sweeps back and forth.

CONTROL OF SWIMMING

Experimental work with lampreys, trout, and frog tadpoles suggests that a constant rate of speed of swimming by means of metachronal body waves is not possible. Cinematographs are taken of the animal swimming across a background grid. Sequences of successful photographic records are magnified and examined frame by frame. Individual body waves are followed from initiation to end; the distance the animal travelled during the passage of the wave along the body is measured and the

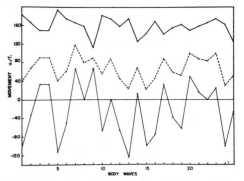

FIG. 5. The forward progression of a fish and the associated posterior displacement of the body wave. Heavy line = rate of progression in arbitrary units per frame (u./f.) of movie film; fine line = relative rate of the body wave; dashed line = mean (a qualitative measure of thrust). (From Nursall, 1958b, Copeia.)

position of the body wave relative to the ground over which the animal is passing is also noted. Positive thrust is encountered when the wave moves backward relative to the background (i.e., faster than the animal is moving forward—see above). Records of this sort show that progression is uneven and that the passage back of the body wave is also irregular (Fig. 5; Nursall, 1958b).

The irregularities in progression are minute and will not be apparent to the unaided eye or by gross measurements, i.e., timed, measured runs. They need not be important to measurements of speed of swimming, but they do suggest two things: (1) that the body waves of fish tend to coincide with the sinuous path that the fish takes through water, at which time no thrust is developed (see above), and (2) that the fish is undertaking a constant assessment of and adjustment to the conditions in the environment. Bainbridge (1958) has shown clearly how speed is related to frequency and amplitude of tail beat (Figs. 6 and 7). These body movements come about in response to immediate needs and take their effect directly on the ambient medium. Their control will depend upon the exteroception of conditions immediately affecting swimming. It must be kept in mind that the commencement of swimming alters the environment and the new conditions must then be accounted for in subsequent control of swimming.

A fish is embedded in a relatively small part of its environment in a way rather foreign to us. Its sensory perception is largely tactile and chemical. It lives in a dense medium which it disturbs each time it moves. These disturbances affect markedly the characteristics of successive moves. Particularly, the fish attempts to relate itself to its

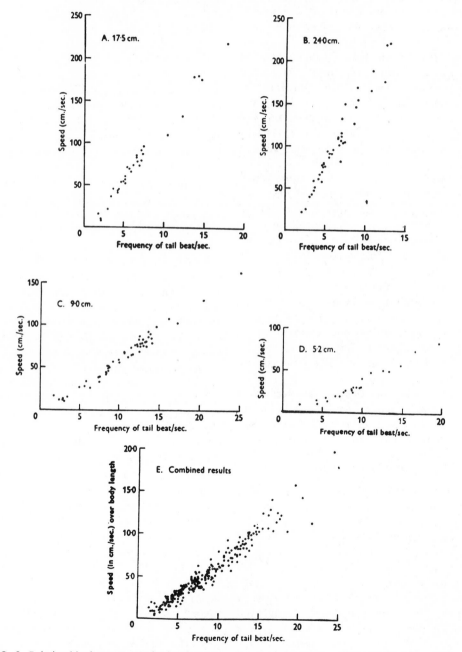

FIG. 6. Relationship between speed of swimming and frequency of tail beat in specimens of the dace, *Leuciscus leuciscus.* (From Bainbridge, 1958, Exptl. Biol.)

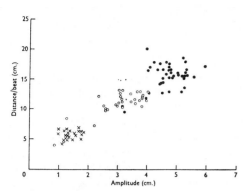

FIG. 7. Relationship between distance travelled per tail beat and amplitude of beat for three dace measuring 24.0 cm. (black dots), 17.5 cm. (circles) and 9.0 cm. (crosses). (From Bainbridge, 1958, J. Exptl. Biol.)

environment by the special sensory apparatus called the lateral line system. Work now going forward on the structure and function of the lateral line will be of immense value in interpreting the reactions of swimming fish. The experiments introduced by Jones (1956) seem to implicate the labyrinth, too, as a site of information-gathering for swimming. Undoubtedly other tactile receptors play a role as well. It should be noted that the caudal musculature of teleost fish is served by a plexus of four to six spinal nerves. Among these is a prominent trunk which passes to the caudal fin to run dorsally and ventrally between the pairs of fin rays (lepidotrichia) at their bases. It is suspected that this is a sensory trunk, gathering fibers from tactile or stretch receptors in the membranes and ligaments of the caudal fin. From this source would come information concerning hydrodynamic conditions at the caudal fin which could have an important bearing on the thrust to be developed by that part of the body. The restless tails of hovering fish may also be providing information. A search for caudal fin receptors of the sort suggested needs to be made.

Gray (1936a, b; 1939), Gray and Sand (1936a, b) and LeMare (1936) have demonstrated that the basic locomotory rhythm of the eel *(Anguilla vulgaris)* and the dogfish *(Scyllium canicula)* is inherent in the spinal cord, but also that external stimuli modify the rhythm to elicit a variety of locomotory, resistance, escape, and other patterns. It seems likely that the next productive phase of research into this aspect of fish locomotion will be into the mechanism whereby environmental information is received, distributed, and acted upon by the organism. This will be done profitably in terms of information channels and feedback.

THE ORIGIN OF PAIRED APPENDAGES

The earliest vertebrates were aquatic organisms, one of whose major specializations was an ability to swim by means of metachronal lateral undulations of the body. Immediately, they faced problems of stability in all three axes. Pitch, yaw, and roll had to be overcome before the animals could undertake more or less continuous swimming. The use of fins in stabilized swimming has been examined in detail by Harris (1934, 1936, 1937, 1938, 1953).

The widespread occurrence and functional importance of paired and median fins has led morphologists to seek archetypal origins for these structures. In the nineteenth century Gegenbaur suggested girdles and paired fins had developed from gill arches and gills. A contrary idea was put forth by Balfour and others, to the effect that paired fins and median fins were the remnants of primordial fin folds. Goodrich (1930) outlines the history of the rival concepts and the morphological and developmental considerations for each. The gill arch theory had little vogue; the fin-fold concept has been longer-lived.

The fossil record is of little help in determining a primordial pattern for the origin of vertebrate paired appendages. As Heintz (1934) has pointed out, the earliest vertebrates were probably clumsy, sluggish, bottom-dwelling forms. The earliest fossils known to us were specialized towards the possession of protective armor. These types comprised the varieties of ostracoderm agnathans. Within the ostracoderm assemblage are found a number of structural modifications suggesting attempts at the development of stabilizing structures. The cephalaspids (Osteostraci) generally possessed flat cephalothoraces with flexible postcranial bodies. There were, in some lines, tendencies to extend the carapace laterally. The flat, ventral surface of the cephalothorax would tend to stabilize the animal as it swam by undulating its body. Pitch and roll would be reduced. Some forms evolved pectoral fins, which extended back from indentations in the posterior margin of the cephalothorax on each side of the body (Westoll, 1945a, 1958). Of not much use for sculling, they probably served as elevators or pitch stabilizers. Dorsal and ventral lateral flanges along the length of the body might have lessened rolling.

The pteraspids (Heterostraci), another armored group of ostracoderms, must have been still less successful as swimmers. In many forms, e.g., *Anglaspis,* the armor was so extensive that body flexibility must have been much reduced. Here, too, the carapace was sometimes useful in providing gliding surfaces as in flattened benthic forms such as *Drepanaspis* or with extravagant lateral spinous processes as in *Dyreaspis,* but, by and large, the progression of these forms must have been wobbly, at best.

The anaspids, less heavily armored, might have become more active forms had they developed paired appendages. Post-cephalic rods in *Lasanius* are suggestive of the beginnings of the basis of pectoral fins, but reconstruction shows them to be buried in the body wall, with only a ridge to mark their presence externally (Parrington, 1958).

However, with White (1946) we must remember the possibility of a concomitant evolution of unarmored agnathans, to which *Jamoytius* may be a clue. It is entirely conceivable that both unarmored adult and larval agnathans existed. In some line, as yet undiscovered, primordial fins may occur. The evidence of *Jamoytius* is suggestive but not conclusive. Modern agnathans (lampreys and hags) lack paired fins. Unless paired fins have been second-

arily discarded by these animals, it would appear that they have managed quite well without them.

Westoll (1945b), in discussing the paired fins of placoderms, suggested the independent derivation of paired fins in Acanthodii and separately at least twice among the remainder of the placoderm fishes. None of these can be easily related to higher or lower groups of fishes. Westoll (loc. cit.; 1958) has noted that a reduction of body armor among placoderms goes with increased mobility and hydrodynamically improved paired fins.

Westoll has also criticized the impression left by Gregory and Raven (1941) that the evolution of paired appendages was essentially straightforward, in relatively strict phylogenetic sequence from agnathan beginnings. Westoll (1958) suggested, in pleasantly ephemeral terms, that "A paired line of potential skin-folding, from which keel-like structures could develop, is entirely probable." Much earlier Howell (1933) put forth the idea that, "Paired appendages are probably possible in any situation along the branchiocloacal line, developed evidently from rows of such dermal elements as scutes, on the order of those now occurring in a hypertrophied state in the sturgeon." Howell was led to this conclusion by a study of position, innervation, and phylogenetic occurrence of fins, primarily on teleosts. Perhaps it is also significant that investigations of myotypic specificity have led Sperry (1950) to consider that early in vertebrate phylogeny nerve distribution and function depended primarily on the nature of the effectors innervated, following which control has increasingly come to depend upon central self-differentiation, as vertebrates evolved. This carries the strong implication that neural distribution followed functional distinction in the matter of appendages, with which we are concerned, and that the potentiality for appendage formation could be widespread over the body.

Eaton (1945) and Lindsey (1955) discussed paired appendages in terms of fin ray structure and ontogenetic developments. Both conclude that the oft-cited occurrence of a median fin-fold in many teleost embryos is not recapitulatory evidence of a fin-fold, but a larval adaptation to beginning locomotion in the individual. Nor can they find evidence for the nature of primordial development in the structure and relationships of basals, radials, and muscles.

Shelbourne (1956) has made the interesting observation that the size of the teleost larval fin-fold is related to the osmotic requirements of the animal, ranging from the large, inflated, marginal fins of pelagic marine embryos to the ill-developed fin of demersal freshwater embryos. In this view, physiological factors might have weighed heavily in the evolution and development of the larval fin structure.

The problem of the origin of paired appendages is a vexed one, in that we are faced with a concept of primordial origin, viz., the fin-fold theory, which we cannot disprove, which is attractive as a unifying idea, yet seems to be unlikely. Paired fins, or fin-like structures, seem to have arisen independently several times. There is no clear path of evolution for these structures from the earliest vertebrates to modern cartilaginous or bony fishes. There appears to be an indefinable potentiality for the lateral development of fins, inasmuch as fins, among pelagic fish, are a necessity for stability, steering and the fine control of hovering. The paired appendages of Chondrichthyes and Osteichthyes are in all likelihood serially and broadly homologous. If we take this to suggest a common ancestry we cannot yet surely identify the ancestral taxon. Therefore, we conclude that paired appendages developed several times in response to specific requirements (primarily stability) of different forms of vertebrates. Once adopted, the fins in descendant forms could be highly modified for a variety of special functions.

THE SWIMMING OF MAMMALS

Aquatic mammals utilize a number of different swimming mechanisms. Gambarjan and Karapetjan (1961) have recently published an account of the modes and mechanisms of swimming of sea lions, seals, and sea otters. They include references to important literature. Howell (1930) gives general descriptions of the anatomy of aquatic mammals.

Our interest here resides in Cetacea. These attractive and important mammals are among the speediest of swimmers. As described by Parry (1949b, 1949c) the swimming of cetaceans provides the same sorts of thrust forces as does the swimming of fish, with certain differences in application being apparent. These are: (1) the body movement is vertical instead of horizontal; (2) the anterior body is held relatively rigid, movement being restricted to the caudal one-third of the body or thereabouts; (3) the flexion of the tail and flukes is concentrated at two points, one at the junction of the lumbar and caudal vertebrae, the other at the base of the flukes.

The muscles of propulsion are relatively simple. They are derivatives of mammalian axial musculature. Epaxial muscles insert deeply on the vertebral column and superficially to tough fasciae. A special derivative of the group flexes the flukes dorsally. Hypaxial muscles insert on the vertebrae; an incompletely differentiated muscle of this group flexes the flukes ventrally. Lateral and ventral caudal muscles assist the main groups in tail movement. The flukes lie parallel to the direction of progression at the top and bottom of the stroke and lie obliquely to the line of progression at midstroke. This is the relationship of the body and tail fin of a fish to its line of progress during swimming (see above). The schematic representation of swimming movements of a dolphin recently published by Backhouse (1960) did not show this fin posture and so appears to be misleading.

Recently, a spirited and enjoyable controversy has been flowering over the nature of wave-riding in porpoises with observational, analytical, and experimental attempts being made to solve the problem. In this paper nothing more will be done than to draw the discussion to the attention of the reader and to comment that the observations of Yuen (1961) on the postural reflexes of dolphins in the bow wave of a ship confirm chiefly that swimming organisms sensitively and rapidly adapt to changes in the forces impinging on them from their ambient medium. As Scholander (1959) commented during the course of the controversy, "We ourselves can beautifully handle unstable conditions, like standing upright and no doubt the porpoise is equally proficient in similar control functions." It is to the analysis of such control functions that reference was made above in the discussion of profitable areas into which research in the swimming of fish can proceed.

THE DEVELOPMENT OF POWER IN SWIMMING

Considerations of development of power and efficiency of swimming have been bedevilled since Gray (1936c) introduced what Parry (1949c) called Gray's Paradox, which was that, unless laminar flow of water past the body of a dolphin be assumed, the power demand might exceed the supply by about sevenfold. Many sets of experiments by many people over many years with models and inert fish provide much data on drag forces developed about fish forms, but it is doubtful if these figures are properly applicable to an actively swimming fish-like vertebrate. There always remains the probability of some unconsidered hydrodynamic effect modifying the reaction between fish and water. For example, the proportion of laminar to turbulent flow over the surface of a swimming fish is not established, yet in this resides the solution to the problem of the influence of frictional drag on progression. Gray speculated that caudal fin or fluke movements might keep boundary layer flow laminar. Richardson (1936) while showing that the presence of mucus had no appreciable effect on drag, suggested further examination of the Katzmayr effect, which is that an aerofoil may meet with

lessened resistance if it is oscillated through a small angle rather than being maintained at a constant angle of attack. Osborne (1961) considered the possibility of fish utilizing the Katzmayr effect in swimming upstream through turbulent water. Backhouse (op. cit.) also mentions the Katzmayr effect. Today there is an increasing quantity of analytic work on hydrodynamic problems directly related to the locomotion of aquatic vertebrates, e.g., Lighthill (1960), Benjamin (1960). It is not yet easy to relate the results of these mathematical treatments to fish, but one can confidently expect closer relationships between fluid mechanics and the activities of fish to be made in the near future. [See also Walters, 1962.]

Some interest has recently been shown in the idea of boundary layer control by means of a flexible surface, as suggested by M. O. Kramer, (1960a, b) and related to the structure of the skin of cetaceans. If laminar flow can be maintained or separation inhibited over their surfaces, then cetaceans would indeed benefit. It is known that flexible porpoise skin can be thrown into large folds by high speed swimming (Essapian, 1955). What relationship these folds bear to the onset of turbulence is not certain. Parry (1949a) details the microscopic structure of whale skin, which is interesting to compare to the model of Kramer.

Bainbridge (1961) has recently discussed current problems of fish locomotion. He listed seven major problems, all concerned with different interactions of body movement, water flow, and resultant drag. As a result of his own experimental work and the collation of other data, Bainbridge was able to arrive at equations from which to compute the velocity of fish-like vertebrates in turbulent or laminar flow:

$$V_{lam.} = (P\ W_m/0.085\ L^{3/2})^{2/5} \qquad (1)$$

$$V_{turb.} = (P\ W_m/0.01885\ L^{9/5})^{5/14} \qquad (2)$$

Where W_m is the weight of the propulsive musculature of the fish, L is the length of the fish and P is a Power Factor. P was

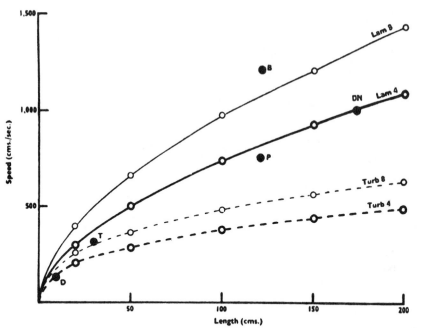

FIG. 8. Speed-length relationships calculated for laminar and turbulent flow using $P = 4 \times 10^5$ (Lam 4 and Turb 4) and $P = 8 \times 10^5$ (Lam 8 and Turb 8). The points equal measured values for various animals: D, dace; T, trout; B, barracuda: P, porpoise; DN, dolphin. (From Bainbridge, 1961, Symp. Zool. Soc. London.)

arrived at by a consideration of data from several sources relating to the power output of muscles. Information from studies of insects, amphibians, and mammals gave results for all of the same order of magnitude. Bainbridge decided that reasonable power outputs would be 8 to 17×10^5 ergs/sec/g of muscle for bursts of speed and 2 to 4×10^5 ergs/sec/g of muscle for sustained swimming. The lower figure in each pair is applicable to cold water, the higher to tropical. Relating weight to length as follows:

$$W_m = 0.005\ L^{2.9} \qquad (3)$$

Bainbridge plotted curves for laminar and turbulent flow, using $P = 4 \times 10^5$ and $P = 8 \times 10^5$ (Fig. 8). On the graph are plotted measured velocity values for dace, trout, barracuda, porpoise, and dolphin. Other similar graphs on different scales show further values including those for goldfish and whales. All the fish, with one exception, and the cetaceans fall within the region of

wholly or partly turbulent flow. It is expected that flow over the body of a swimming vertebrate will be at least partly turbulent. Thus, by the mathematical means of changing assumptions, Gray's Paradox is disposed of, but another anomalous result appears, namely the speed attributed to barracuda (*Sphyraena barracuda*) by Gero (1952). This is unexplainable in terms of Bainbridge's calculations. Also suspect then are unconfirmed figures for salmon (45 Km/hr = 28 mph), tuna (90 Km/hr = 56 mph) and marlin and swordfish (130 Km/hr = 81 mph) reported by Barsukov (1960), and for tuna (80 Km/hr = 50 mph) and sailfish (120 Km/hr = 74 mph) reported by E. Kramer (1960). Table 1 gives some speeds of swimming reported for fish under more or less controlled conditions.

Fish continue to surprise us. Osborne (1960) in a stimulating attempt to describe the hydrodynamical performance of salmon moving upstream to spawn, found a remarkably efficient performance in terms of

TABLE 1. *Some recorded fish speeds*

Common name	Scientific name	Length (L) (cm)	Speed L/sec	Speed mph	Reference
Sea lamprey	*Petromyzon marinus*	37.5	3.2	2.7	Nursall (unpublished)
Bull shark	*Carcharinus leucas*	152.4	3.4	11.8	Gero, 1952
Lemon shark	*Negaprion brevirostris*	184.2	1.3	5.4	'' ·'
Great barracuda	*Sphyraena barracuda*	129.5	9.4	27.6	'' ''
Blenny	*Zoarces viviparus*	6.4	3.3	0.5	Blaxter and Dickson, 1959
Butterfish	*Pholis gunnellus*	10.0	3.0	0.7	'' '' '' ''
Eel	*Anguilla vulgaris*	60.0	1.9	2.6	'' '' '' ''
Dab	*Pleuronectes limanda*	9.0	3.3	0.7	'' '' '' ''
Flounder	*Pleuronectes flesus*	27.5	3.8	2.4	'' '' '' ''
Lemon sole	*Pleuronectes microcephalus*	8.0	1.9	0.3	'' '' '' ''
Plaice	*Pleuronectes platessa*	8.0	3.75	0.7	'' '' '' ''
Stickleback	*Gasterosteus spinachia*	10.0	7.2	1.6	'' '' '' ''
Goby	*Gobius minutus*	7.0	3.9	0.6	'' '' '' ''
Cod	*Gadus callarius*	56.0	3.75	4.8	'' '' '' ''
Haddock	*Gadus aeglefinus*	42.0	4.3	4.1	'' '' '' ''
Whiting	*Gadus merlangus*	20.0	8.0	3.6	'' '' '' ''
Saithe	*Gadus virens*	21.0	9.5	4.5	'' '' '' ''
Herring	*Clupea harengus*	25.0	6.8	3.9	'' '' '' ''
Sprat	*Clupea sprattus*	12.0	5.0	1.4	'' '' '' ''
Mackerel	*Scomber scombrus*	38.0	7.9	6.8	'' '' '' ''
Brown trout	*Salmo trutta*	24.0	9.75	5.3	'' '' '' ''
Sea trout	*Salmo trutta*	38.0	8.4	7.3	'' '' '' ''
Goldfish	*Carassius auratus*	12.5	12.7	3.6	'' '' '' ''
Rainbow trout	*Salmo irideus*	20.0	8.5	3.8	Gray, 1953 and 1957
Goldfish	*Carassius auratus*	13.0	13.0	3.8	'' '' '' ''
Carp	*Cyprinus carpio*	13.5	12.6	3.8	'' '' '' ''
Dace	*Leuciscus leuciscus*	18.5	9.0	3.8	'' '' '' ''
Rudd	*Scardinius erythrophthalmus*	22.0	5.9	2.9	'' '' '' ''
Pike	*Esox lucius*	16.5	12.7	4.8	'' '' '' ''
Rudd	*Scardinius erythrophthalmus*	24.0	3.9	2.1	Ohlmer and Schwartzkopff, 1959
Pike	*Esox lucius*	44.0	6.4	6.4	'' '' '' ''
Perch	*Perca fluviatilis*	24.0	5.25	2.9	'' '' '' ''
Zander	*Lucioperca sandra*	44.0	4.3	4.3	'' '' '' ''
Bream	*Abramis brama*	24.0	4.0	2.2	'' '' '' ''
Roach	*Leuciscus rutilus*	24.0	5.1	2.8	'' '' '' ''
Frog tadpole	*Rana sylvatica*	3.2	3.0	0.2	Nursall (unpublished)
Common dolphin	*Delphinus delphis*	ca. 7 ft.	4.8	22.8	Steven, 1950
Fin whale	*Balaenoptera physalus*	69 ft.	0.3	16.1	Kermack, 1948
Blue whale	*Balaenoptera musculus*	85 ft.	0.4	23.0	'' ''

fuel conversion to propulsive energy, suggesting that salmon can pick their way carefully upstream, deliberately seeking low velocity water, or that they can maintain laminar boundary flow, or extract energy from river turbulence. The first of these seems to be the most likely. Probably physiological and behavioral studies of the type of Black (1958), Miller et al., (1959) and the series represented by Jonas and MacLeod (1960) will eventually provide answers to the problems defined by Osborne.

REFERENCES

Affleck, R. J. 1950. Some points in the function, development and evolution of the tail in fishes. Proc. Zool. Soc. London 120:349-368.

Backhouse, K. 1960. Locomotion and direction-finding in whales and dolphins. The New Scientist 7:26-28.

Baerends, G. P., and J. M. Baerends-van Roon 1950. An introduction to the study of the ethology of cichlid fishes. Behaviour. Supp. 1:1-243.

Bainbridge, R. 1958. The speed of swimming of fish as related to size and to the frequency and amplitude of the tail beat. J. Exptl. Biol. 35:109-133.

————. 1961. Problems of fish locomotion. Symp. Zool. Soc. London 5:13-32.

Barsukov, V. V. 1960. The speed of movement of fishes. [In Russian]; Priroda 3:103-104.

Benjamin, T. B. 1960. Effects of a flexible boundary on hydrodynamic stability. J. Fluid Mech. 9:513-532.

Bertin, L. 1958. Modifications des nageoires, p. 748-782. In P.-P. Grassé, [ed.], Traité de zoologie 13, Agnathes et Poissons, Masson et Cie, Paris.

Black, E. C. 1958. Energy stores and metabolism in relation to muscular activity in fishes, p. 51-67. In P. A. Larkin, [ed.], The investigation of fish-power problems. H. R. MacMillan lectures in fisheries, Univ. British Columbia, Vancouver.

Blaxter, J. H. S., and W. Dickson. 1959. Observations on the swimming speeds of fish. J. Cons. Intern. Exptl. Mer. 24:472-479.

Boddeke, R., E. J. Slijper, and A. van der Stelt. 1959. Histological characteristics of the body-musculature of fishes in connection with their mode of life. Proc. Konink. Nederl. Akad. Wetensch. (Amsterdam), C, 62:576-588.

Borelli, J. A. 1734. De Motu Animalium. B. Gessari, Naples. 452 p. (late edition; original published in Rome, 1680).

Breder, C. M., Jr. 1926. The locomotion of fishes. Zoologica 4:159-297.

Eaton, T. H., Jr. 1945. Skeletal supports of the median fins of fishes. J. Morph. 76:193-212.

Emelianov, S. W. 1935. Die Morphologie der Fischrippen. Zool. Jb. (Anat.) 60:133-262.

Essapian, F. S. 1955. Speed-induced skin folds in the bottle-nosed porpoise, *Tursiops truncatus*. Breviora 43:1-4.

Gambarjan, P. P., and W. S. Karapetjan. 1961. Besonderheiten im Bau des Seelöwen *(Eumetopias californianus)*, der Baikalrobbe *(Phoca sibirica)* und des Seeotters *(Enhydra lutris)* in Anpassung an die Fortbewegung im Wasser. Zool. Jb. (Anat.) 79:123-148.

Gero, D. R. 1952. The hydrodynamic aspects of fish propulsion. Amer. Mus. Nov. No. 1601. 32 p.

Goodrich, E. S. 1930. Studies on the structure and development of vertebrates. Macmillan, London (Dover Publications, Inc., N. Y. 2 vols., reprinted) 837 p.

Graham-Smith, W. 1936. The tail of fishes. Proc. Zool. Soc. London 1936:595-608.

Gray, J. 1933a. Studies in animal locomotion. I. The movement of fish with special reference to the eel. J. Exptl. Biol. 10:88-104.

———. 1933b. Studies in animal locomotion. II. The relationship between waves of muscular contraction and the propulsive mechanism of the eel. J. Exptl. Biol. 10:386-390.

———. 1933c. Studies in animal locomotion. III. The propulsive mechanism of the whiting *(Gadus merlangus)*. J. Exptl. Biol. 10:391-400.

———. 1933d. Directional control of fish movement. Proc. Roy. Soc. (London), B, 113:115-125.

———. 1936a. Studies in animal locomotion. IV. The neuromuscular mechanism of swimming in the eel. J. Exptl. Biol. 13:170-180.

———. 1936b. Studies in animal locomotion. V. Resistance reflexes in the eel. J. Exptl. Biol. 13:181-191.

——— 1936c. Studies in animal locomotion. VI. The propulsive powers of the dolphin. J. Exptl. Biol. 13:192-199.

———. 1939. Croonian Lecture. Aspects of animal locomotion. Proc. Roy. Soc. (London), B, 128:28-62.

———. 1953. The locomotion of fishes, p. 1-16. *In* S. M. Marshall and A. P. Orr, [ed.], Essays in marine biology, Oliver and Boyd, Edinburgh and London.

———. 1957. How fishes swim. Sci. Amer. 197:48-54.

Gray, J., and A. Sand. 1936a. The locomotory rhythm of the dogfish *(Scyllium canicula)*. J. Exptl. Biol. 13:200-209.

———. 1936b. Spinal reflexes of the dogfish, *Scyllium canicula*. J. Exptl. Biol. 13:210-218.

Greene, C. W. 1913. An undescribed longitudinal differentiation of the great lateral muscle of the king salmon. Anat. Record 7:99-101.

Gregory, W. K., and H. C. Raven. 1941. Studies on the origin and early evolution of paired fins and limbs. Ann. N. Y. Acad. Sci. 42:273-360.

Grenholm, A. 1923. Studien über die Flossenmuskulatur der Teleostier. Uppsala Univ. Arsskrift. Mat. Naturvet. 2:1-296.

Grove, A. J., and G. E. Newell. 1939. The relation of the tail-form in cyclostomes and fishes to specific gravity. Ann. Mag. Nat. Hist. (11) 4:401-430.

Harris, J. E. 1934. The swimming movements of fishes. Ann. Rept. Tortugas Lab., Carnegie Inst. Wash., 1933-34:251-253.

———. 1936. The role of the fins in the equilibrium of the swimming fish. I. Wind-tunnel tests on a model of *Mustelus canis* (Mitchell). J. Exptl. Biol. 13:476-493.

———. 1937. The role of fin movements in the equilibrium of the fish. Ann. Rept. Tortugas Lab., Carnegie Inst., Wash., 1936-37:91-93.

———. 1938. The role of the fins in the equilibrium of the swimming fish. II. The role of the pelvic fins. J. Exptl. Biol. 15:32-47.

———. 1953. Fin patterns and mode of life in fishes, p. 17-28. *In* S. M. Marshall and A. P. Orr, [ed.], Essays in marine biology. Oliver and Boyd, Edinburgh and London.

Heintz, A. 1934. How the fishes learned to swim. Ann. Rept. Smithsonian Inst. 1934:223-245.

Houssay, F. 1912. Forme, Puissance et Stabilité des Poissons. A. Hermann et Fils, Paris. 372 p.

Howell, A. B. 1930. Aquatic Mammals. Charles C Thomas, Springfield, Ill. 338 p.

———. 1933. Homology of the paired fins in fishes. J. Morph. 54:451-457.

Jonas, R. E. E., and R. A. MacLeod. 1960. Biochemical studies on sockeye salmon during spawning migration. X. Glucose, total protein, non-protein nitrogen and amino acid nitrogen in plasma. J. Fish. Res. Bd. Canada 17:125-126.

Jones, F. R. H. 1956. An apparent reaction of fish to linear accelerations. Nature 178:642-643.

Jones, F. R. H., and N. B. Marshall. 1953. The structure and functions of the teleostean swimbladder. Biol. Rev. 28:16-83.

Kafuku, T. 1950. "Red muscles" in fishes. I. Comparative anatomy of the scombroid fishes of Japan. [in Japanese with English summary]; Jap. J. Ichthy. 1:89-100.

Kermack, K. A. 1943. The functional significance of the hypocercal tail in *Pteraspis rostrata*. J. Exptl. Biol. 20:23-27.

———. 1948. The propulsive powers of blue and fin whales. J. Exptl. Biol. 25:237-240.

Kramer, E. 1960. Zur Form und Funktion des Lokomotionsapparates der Fische. Z. wiss. Zool. 163: 1-36.

Kramer, M. O. 1960a. Boundary layer stabilization by distributed damping. J. Aero/Space Sci. 27:69.

———. 1960b. The dolphin's secret. New Scientist 7:1118-1120.

Langelaan, J. W. 1904. On the form of the trunk-myotome. Proc. Roy. Acad. Amsterdam 7:34-40.

LeMare, D. W. 1936. Reflex and rhythmical movements in the dogfish. J. Exptl. Biol. 13:429-442.

Lighthill, M. J. 1960. Note on the swimming of slender fish. J. Fluid. Mech. 9:305-317.

Lindsey, C. C. 1955. Evolution of meristic relations in the dorsal and anal fins of teleost fishes. Trans. Roy. Soc. Canada 49, Series III, Sec. 5:35-49.

Magnan, A. 1930. Les charactéristiques géométriques et physiques des poissons, avec contribution à l'étude de leur equilibre statique et dynamique. Ann. Sci. Nat. 10me Sér.-Zool. 13:355-490.

Magnan, A., and A. Sainte-Lague. 1929. Essai de theorie du poisson. Serv. Tech. Aeronaut., Bull. Tech. No. 58:1-180.

Marey, E. J. 1895. Movement. Wm. Heinemann, London. 323 p.

Miller, R. B., A. C. Sinclair, and P. W. Hochachka. 1959. Diet, glycogen reserves and resistance to fatigue in hatchery rainbow trout. J. Fish. Res. Bd. Canada 16:321-328.

Nursall, J. R. 1956. The lateral musculature and the swimming of fish. Proc. Zool. Soc. London 126:127-143.

———. 1958a. The caudal fin as a hydrofoil. Evolution 12:116-120.

———. 1958b. A method of analysis of the swimming of fish. Copeia 2:136-141.

Oehmichen, É. 1958. Locomotion des poissons, p. 818-853. In P.-P. Grassé, [ed.], Traité de zoologie 13, Agnathes et Poissons. Masson et Cie, Paris.

Ohlmer, W., and J. Schwartzkopff. 1959. Schwimmgeschwindigkeiten von Fischen aus stehenden Binnengewässern. Naturwiss. 46:362-363.

Osborne, M. F. M. 1961. The hydrodynamical performance of migratory salmon. J. Exptl. Biol. 38:365-390.

Pantin, C. F. A. 1956. Comparative physiology of muscle. Brit. Med. Bull. 12:199-202.

Parrington, F. R. 1958. On the nature of the Anaspida, p. 108-128. In T. S. Westoll, [ed.], Studies on fossil vertebrates. The Athlone Press, London.

Parry, D. A. 1949a. The structure of whale blubber, and a discussion of its properties. Quart. J. Microscop. Sci. 90:13-25.

———. 1949b. The anatomical basis of swimming in whales. Proc. Zool. Soc. London 119:49-60.

———. 1949c. The swimming of whales and a discussion of Gray's Paradox. J. Exptl. Biol. 26:24-34.

Pettigrew, J. B. 1873. Animal Locomotion. H. S. King and Co., London. 264 p.

Richardson, E. G. 1936. The physical aspects of fish locomotion. J. Exptl. Biol. 13:63-74.

Schmalhausen, J. J. 1912. Zur Morphologie der unpaaren Flossen. II. Bau und Phylogenese der unpaaren Flossen und inbesonders der Schwanzflosse der Fische. Z. wiss. Zool. 104:1-80.

Scholander, P. F. 1959. Comment on letter by W. D. Hayes. Science 130:1685.

Shelbourne, J. E. 1956. The effect of water conservation on the structure of marine fish embryos and larvae. J. Mar. Biol. Ass. U. K. 35:275-286.

Sperry, R. W. 1950. Myotypic specificity in teleost motoneurons. J. Comp. Neur. 93:277-288.

Steven, G. A. 1950. Swimming of dolphins. Sci. Prog. 38:524-525.

Takeuchi, A. 1959. Neuromuscular transmission of fish skeletal muscles investigated with intracellular microelectrode. J. Cell. Comp. Physiol. 54:211-220.

Walters, V. 1962. Body form and swimming performance in the scombroid fishes. Am. Zoologist (this issue).

Westoll, T. S. 1945a. A new cephalaspid fish from the Downtonian of Scotland, with notes on the structure and classification of ostracoderms. Trans. Roy. Soc. Edin. 61, Part II:341-357.

———. 1945b. The paired fins of placoderms. Trans. Roy. Soc. Edin. 61, Part II:381-398.

———. 1958. The lateral fin-fold theory and the pectoral fins of ostracoderms and early fishes, p. 180-211. In T. S. Westoll, [ed.], Studies on fossil vertebrates. The Athlone Press, London.

White, E. I. 1946. Jamoytius kerwoodi, a new chordate from the Silurian of Lanarkshire. Geol. Mag. 83:89-97.

Yuen, H. S. H. 1961. Bow wave riding of dolphins. Science 134:1011-1012.

Warm-Bodied Fish

Francis G. Carey, John M. Teal, John W. Kanwisher,
and Kenneth D. Lawson

Woods Hole Oceanographic Institution, Woods Hole, Massachusetts 02543

and James S. Beckett

*Fisheries Research Board of Canada Biological Station,
St. Andrews, New Brunswick, Canada*

synopsis. Two groups of fishes, the tuna and the lamnid sharks, have evolved counter-current heat-exchange mechanisms for conserving metabolic heat and raising their body temperatures. Warm muscle can produce more power, and considering the other adaptations for fast swimming in these fish, it seems likely that the selective advantages of greater speed made possible by the warm muscle were important in the evolution of this system. Some tunas such as the yellowfin and skipjack are at a fixed temperature difference above the water, but bluefin tuna can thermoregulate. Telemetry experiments show that the bluefin tuna can maintain a constant deep body temperature during marked changes in the temperature of its environment.

The ability to swim fast has been an important development in the evolution of the large predatory fish of the open ocean. There is an abundance of food in such fast swimming prey as squid, mackerel, and herring, which is available only to swift predators. Looking at these pelagic fish, one is struck by a marked similarity in their forms. The caudal fin, which works with short rapid strokes, is a hard, crescent-shaped hydrofoil. High-speed swimming requires ample power and the fish are heavy bodied with a large bulk of muscle. They are streamlined with fins folding back into slots or depressions, and with eyes and gill covers faired-in to present a smooth unbroken surface. Of these fish, tuna have the largest bulk of muscle and appear the most streamlined. Tuna are also very fast; yellow fin (*Thunnus albacares*) and wahoo (*Acanthocybium solanderi*) can swim 70 km/hr for 10 to 20 second sprints (Walters and Fierstine, 1964).

In addition to their streamlined shape and bulky muscle, tuna have high body temperatures and we believe that this development is also associated with the evolution of high-speed swimming. The power available from muscle increases markedly with temperature. In frog muscle the

contraction-relaxation cycle speeds up some three times with a 10°C rise in temperature (Hartree and Hill, 1921). Since there is no loss in contractile force, three times the power is available from the same muscle. The bluefin tuna (*Thunnus thynnus*) found off our coasts are commonly 10°C warmer than the water and can use the additional power this would make available for high speed. The lamnid or mackerel sharks, *Isurus oxyrinchus* (mako) and *Lamna nasus* (porbeagle), also are warm-bodied, and considering their streamlined form and active way of life, it is likely that their high body temperature is also a result of evolution for speed.

Despite the advantages of an elevated muscle temperature in gaining the extra power needed for speed, few fish have warm bodies. Our measurements of body temperature for a number of species show (Table 1) that most fish are at or within a degree or so of water temperature. Blood passing through the gills remains there long enough to saturate the hemoglobin with oxygen from the water. Since thermal diffusion is more than ten times as rapid as molecular diffusion, the blood temperature attains that of the water. As the blood returns to the tissues, the oxygen it contains is used in generating metabolic heat,

Contribution No. 2638 from the Woods Hole Oceanographic Institution.

From *American Zoologist* 11:137–145. Reprinted by permission.

and the blood and tissues are warmed. On the next passage through the gills, this heat is lost to the water; thus, body temperature is determined by the amount of heat which can be generated by oxygen removed from the blood during one pass

TABLE 1. *Measured body temperatures of a number of species of fishes.**

Species	No.	Muscle Temp. °C	Surface Water Temp. °C	Difference °C
Lampris regius, Opah	1	22.6	21.6	1.0
Scieana regina (?), Corvina (from Spain)	1	19.0	19.2	—.2
Caranx pusus, Blue runner	1	31.5	30.5	1.0
Elagatis bipinnulata, Rainbow runner	1	33.6	32.1	1.5
Seriola sp. Amberjack	1	29.8	28.4	1.4
Coryphaena hippurus, Dolphin	4	27.8	26.8	1.0
Epinephelus sp. Grouper	1	28.3	28.0	0.3
Lepidocybium flavobrunneum, Escolar	1	23.0	23.2	—.2
Scomber scombrus, Mackerel	40	23.8	22.5	1.3
Scomberomorus regalis, Cero	7	30.4	29.8	0.6
Sarda sarda, Bonito	3	21.0, 20.5, 20.5	19.2	1.8, 1.3, 1.3
Auxis thazard, Frigate mackerel	6	29.5	19.2	10.3
Katsuwonus pelamis, Skipjack	3	30.2, 37.8, 37.3	18.5, 30.0, 29.0	11.7, 7.8, 8.3
Euthynnus alletteratus, Little tuna	1	31.2	19.9	11.3
Thunnus alalunga, Albacore	2	31.0, 32.0	17.8, 20.0	13.2, 12.0
Thunnus obesus, Bigeye tuna	13	28.9	21.0	7.9
Thunnus thynnus, Bluefin tuna	200	29.5	19.0	10.5
Thunnus albacares, Yellowfin tuna	23	27.5	22.5	5.0
Thunnus atlanticus, Blackfin tuna	1	30.3	28.4	1.9
Tetrapterus albida, White marlin	4	22.2	20.4	1.8
Tetrapterus audax, Striped marlin	2	24.4, 28.4	22.2, 27.2	2.2, 1.2
Makaira nigricans, Blue marlin	2	22.2, 28.8	22.2, 26.1	0, 2.7
Xiphias gladius, Swordfish	5	20.1	19.2	0.9
Sphyraena barracuda, Great barracuda	4	28.8	27.9	0.9
Remora sp.	1	28.3	28.0	0.3
Lamna nasus, Porbeagle	7	19.3	11.5	7.8
Isurus oxyrinchus, Mako	26	24.9	20.4	4.5
Cetorhinus maximus, Basking shark	5	19.1	18.0	1.1
Alopias superciliosus, Bigeye thresher shark	2	20.3, 23.0	(16.0), (21.2)	4.3, 1.8
Galeocerdo cuvieri, Tiger shark	1	24.6	24.0	0.6
Prionace glauca, Blue shark	6	21.9	21.9	0
Carcharhinus limbatus, Black tip shark	51	28.2	26.8	1.4
Carcharhinus leucas, Bull shark	1	26.3	26.7	—.4
Carcharhinus floridanus, Silky shark	4	24.9	24.3	0.6
Carcharhinus milberti, Sandbar shark	1	22.6	22.3	0.3
Carcharhinus obscurus, Dusky shark	6	22.3	22.5	—.2
Sphyrna lewini, Scalloped hammerhead	4	24.3	23.5	0.8
Sphyrna mokarran, Great hammerhead	1	23.0	23.0	0
Manta birostris, Manta ray	1	24.0	24.5	—.5

* Muscle temperature measurements were made by probing around in the fish with a long thermistor needle and recording the maximum value. Determination of water temperature was complicated by the fact that good fishing areas typically have an intricate thermal structure of thermocline and thermal inversions and it was often difficult to tell what temperature the fish had been at before being brought on deck. As a result we have listed few bottom fish which are almost always in a colder environment than the surface water. This is responsible for the few negative temperature differentials listed. The bigeye thresher sharks were caught in an area with a surface temperature of 12.7°C and 22.0°C at 30 meters. We do not know where the sharks had been swimming and the "water temperature" listed in the table is actually that of the heart and coldest muscle. Bigeye thresher sharks have a simple system of *retia* in their muscle and may well be warm.

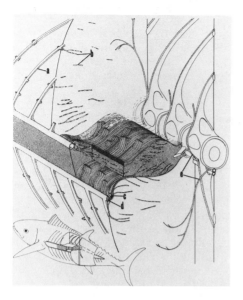

FIG. 1. Circulation in the muscles of a bigeye tuna. a, segmental artery and vein; b, vascular bands; c, cutaneous artery; d, cutaneous vein; e, arterial branches from dorsal aorta. (From Carey and Teal, 1966).

through the tissues. The heating process, metabolism, is locked to the cooling that occurs when the blood passes through the gills; therefore, the fish cannot accumulate heat to raise its body temperature. A high rate of metabolism, such as occurs during exercise, demands more oxygen, and thus more cooling, and does not cause an increase in body temperature.

From Table 1, however, it is clear that tuna and lamnid sharks do have high body temperatures. These fish conserve metabolic heat by a system of counter-current heat-exchangers located in the circulation between the gills and the tissues. The heat-exchangers act as a thermal barrier, blocking the flow of heat but permitting blood to pass and carry out its function of molecular transport.

ANATOMY OF THE HEAT EXCHANGE SYSTEM

The presence of vascular heat-exchangers changes the plan of the circulatory system.

Normally, fish have a central distribution system with the dorsal aorta and post cardinal vein running just beneath the vertebrae as the main supply and with segmental arteries and veins leading out to the periphery. In the tuna and lamnid sharks, the sytem is reversed; the main blood supply is found just beneath the skin, and small branches from it are directed inward toward the vertebrae. In Figure 1, the circulation to the muscle of a bigeye tuna (*Thunnus obesus*) is diagrammed showing the main features peculiar to warm-bodied fish. The main blood supply is through a double set of cutaneous arteries and veins running along the side of the fish and segmental vessels which run dorsally and ventrally between the skin and the muscle (Cuvier and Valenciennes, 1831). The entire system is composed of parallel arteries and veins in close contact. When swimming at cruising speed, the fish is propelled mainly by the contractions of a broad band of dark muscle located in the horizontal mid-plane (Bone, 1966; Rayner and Keenan, 1967). The blood supply to the dark muscle is the second remarkable feature of the tuna circulatory system. This vascular tissue is composed of small (0.1 mm diameter) arteries and veins which arise at right angles to the cutaneous vessels and are directed inward along the surface of the dark muscle. It is a *rete mirabile* serving as an efficient, large-capacity counter-current heat-exchanger (Carey and Teal, 1966). The mass of the *rete* is thickest and the vessels finest near its origin from the cutaneous vessels, where in a large bluefin it may be 1 cm thick. The *rete* gives off broad branches into the dark muscle as it passes inward and the numerous small vessels anastomose into a few large ones, some of which connect with the small centrally located dorsal aorta.

The blood supply to the light muscle is also unusual. The light-colored muscle is apparently used intermittently for fast swimming and may become anoxic during intense activity. The blood supply to this tissue, while ample, does not have the large capacity of that found in the dark muscle. Blood for the light muscle is supplied through segmental vessels which run over the surface of the muscle and which send numerous branches down into it. These branches are in the form of vascular

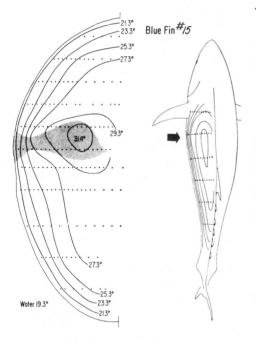

FIG. 2. Temperature distribution in a bluefin tuna, *Thunnus thynnus*. Shortly after death, temperatures were measured with long thermistor needles at points indicated by dots. Isotherms are drawn on 2.0°C contours. (From Carey and Teal, 1969*b*).

bands that appear as ribbons of alternating arteries and veins containing few or many vessels. The vascular bands form a two-dimensional heat-exchanger, and although this arrangement allows less thermal contact between the vessels than in the thick dark-muscle *rete*, the blood flow to this usually inactive tissue is probably slow and metabolic heat is retained efficiently.

The distribution of body temperatures follow the arrangement of the vascular heat-exchangers. The thermal distribution in a 500 lb bluefin tuna is shown in Figure 2. The isotherms are generally perpendicular to the course of the dark muscle *retia* and the vascular bands; the steepest thermal gradients occur along the finely divided region of the dark muscle *retia*. The highest temperatures are located in a relatively small region of dark muscle, but a large volume of dark and light muscle is also considerably warmer than the water.

The deepest muscle is not the warmest; tissues near the vertebral column are partially supplied by cold blood from the dorsal aorta, and usually have a somewhat lower temperature than the more lateral muscle.

This description of the muscle circulation applies to the bluefin, bigeye, albacore (*Thunnus alalunga*), and partially to the yellowfin. In addition, the yellowfin and particularly the skipjack (*Katsuwonus pelamis*) have another important heat exchanger for the muscle. The hemal canal of the yellowfin is large, and that of the skipjack may be even larger than the diameter of the centra of the vertebrae. A large dorsal aorta and a post cardinal vein run along floor of this space and give rise to numerous small parallel vessels which pass vertically and intermingle to form a massive *rete* filling the canal (Kishinouye, 1923). Dorsally, the small vessels in the hemal canal of each vertebra anastomose to form segmental arteries and veins which run out along the vertebral spines. We have plotted the distribution of temperature in one skipjack. These are small fish and the surface temperatures may change rapidly, so our map is not exact. However, the results are consistent with the importance of the central heat-exchanger; the warmest temperatures are found deep in the fish, near the vertebrae.

Lamnid or mackerel sharks, very different animals from the tunas, have a strikingly similar system of vascular heat-exchangers (Carey and Teal, 1969*a*). These sharks have the same reduced dorsal aorta and large cutaneous vessels to supply blood to the muscles. There is one main set of cutaneous vessels on each side, rather than two sets as found in tuna, and these give rise to a single massive *rete* serving the dark muscle. In *Isurus* (mako) this *rete* is a slab of vascular tissue as it is in the tuna, but in *Lamna* (porbeagle) and *Carcharodon* (white shark), the *rete* is diffuse, having many groups of small vessels running between the muscle fibers to the centrally located dark muscle. The segmental vessels of these sharks, as those of tuna, run over the surface of the muscle and send vascular bands down into it.

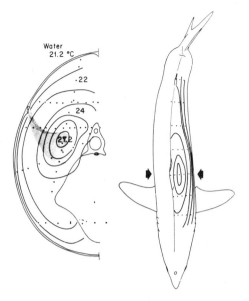

Water
21.2 °C

.22

24

27.2

FIG. 3. Temperature distribution in a mako shark,
Isurus oxyrinchus. 1.0°C isotherms. (From Carey
and Teal, 1969*a*).

These bands are generally in groups of
three vessels, vein—artery—vein, rather
than many vessels arranged artery—vein—
artery, as in the tuna. The circulatory
system of *Lamna* was described by Burne
(1923) in a paper aptly titled, "Some
peculiarities in the blood vascular system of the porbeagle shark." The distribution of temperature in the muscle of
these sharks is similar to that of the tuna,
with the highest temperatures confined to
a small region of dark muscle, rather lower
temperatures near the center line region
served by the dorsal aorta, and a sharp
thermal gradient near the surface (Fig.
3).

The viscera of some of these fishes are
also served by a heat exchange system. In
the albacore, bluefin, and bigeye tuna, *retia*
are conspicuously located on the dorsal
surface of the liver. Branches of the coelio-
mesenteric artery break up into masses of
small arteries which mingle with small
veins to form discrete organs of tightly
packed parallel vessels. In a large bluefin
some of these bundles are five cm in diameter. On the distal side of the *rete*, the

small vessels coalesce into a few large ones
which connect to the organs they serve.
This system was described by Eschricht
and Müller (1835). An illustration from
this paper is shown in Figure 4. They also
mentioned an analogous organ in *Lamna*
which is well described in Burne's (1923)
paper. Among lamnid sharks, the coelio-
mesenteric artery is absent from *Isurus,* is
very small in *Lamna,* and is small in *Carcharodon.* The main arterial supply to the
viscera is through the pericardial arteries,
normally insignificant vessels which are
greatly enlarged in these sharks. These arteries penetrate the hepatic sinuses just before the latter empty into the sinus veno-
sus. Within the hepatic sinus the artery
breaks up into a mass of anastomosing vessels of increasingly smaller dimensions until the lumen is filled by a sponge-like mass.
On the distal side, the arteries coalesce
and form single, large collecting trunks
which supply the various visceral organs.
This arterial "sponge" in the venous sinus
forms the hepatic *rete.* It is clearly a counter-current heat-exchanger, but one of different structure from the usual mass of parallel arteries and veins.

We have many measurements of visceral
temperatures from tuna and lamnid
sharks. There is large variation; temperatures range from as warm as the warmest
muscle to slightly above that of the ambient water. Apparently the visceral temperatures vary with time and circumstance,
perhaps correlating with the activity of the
digestive system. The visceral heat-
exchangers probably act to speed digestion
and absorbtion. These warm fish, particularly the tuna, have a remarkably small
mass of visceral organs. Higher temperatures may make up for the small sized
viscera by aiding the rapid processing of
food (Magnuson, 1969).

We feel that the advantages of high-
speed swimming provide an explanation
for the similarities between tuna and the
lamnid sharks. Their bulky, muscular
bodies with highly streamlined shapes, the
detailed streamlining of fins and body
openings, and the hard, narrow crescent-
shaped tails are remarkably similar and
seem well adapted for the speed needed in

the pursuit of their small, swift prey. The high body temperatures which would make additional power available from the muscle could be viewed as further evolution in this direction. The counter-current heat-exchangers which make this possible have evolved on two separate occasions to produce remarkably similar forms. Multiple, parallel arteries and veins in close contact rather than single, separate vessels are found in all organs. Cutaneous vessels of small size in most fish have enlarged to

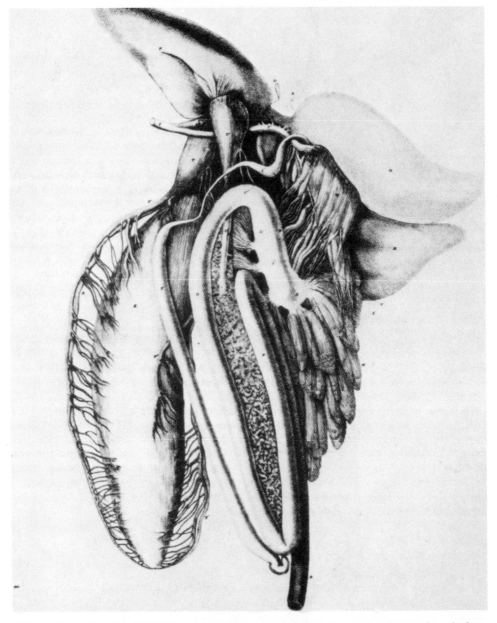

FIG. 4. Illustration from Eschricht and Müller (1835) showing the location of the visceral *retia* in a bluefin tuna. This is a ventral view of the viscera with the liver lobes raised to show the large, fusiform retia on their dorsal surface, T, U, and V.

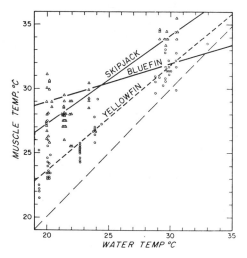

FIG. 5. Barrett and Hester's (1964) data showing the variation of muscle temperature with water temperature for skipjack and yellowfin tuna. These fish maintain fixed elevation above the water temperature. A line for bluefin, which thermoregulates, is included for comparison. (From Carey and Teal, 1966).

provide the major blood supply to the muscle, while the central dorsal aorta has been greatly reduced. The resulting pattern of circulation, with the blood supplied from the surface rather than from the center, locates the cool end of the counter-current heat-exchangers at the surface and the warm end deep in the muscle, thus reducing heat loss through the skin. Even those tuna, such as the yellowfin and skipjack, which have also evolved a major, central heat-exchanger, retain the peripheral system in a somewhat reduced form. It probably functions to reduce surface heat losses in these fishes also.

REGULATION OF BODY TEMPERATURE

If it is possible for a fish to attain an elevated body temperature, it would seem a simple matter to maintain it at a constant value. Any way of decreasing the efficiency of the heat exchangers with increasing water temperature would accomplish this. The possibility of thermoregulation has been studied in three species: skipjack, yellowfin, and bluefin. Barrett and Hester (1964) measured the muscle

temperatures of a large number of skipjack and yellowfin caught in the Pacific. It is quite clear from Figure 5 that these fish maintain a fixed temperature difference above the water. Our measurements of yellowfin temperatures from the Atlantic (Table 1) average somewhat higher than Barrett and Hester's, but show the same trend. Apparently, skipjack and yellowfin work at a constant efficiency to maintain the highest possible muscle temperature. (One skipjack we measured had a temperature as high as many mammals—37.8°C.) These fish do not occur in cold water, and are mainly found in water warmer than 20°C. The giant bluefin, on the other hand, may be found in water of 6° to 30°C. The muscle temperatures of giant bluefin from areas of different water temperature along the east coast show that these big fish control their temperatures quite well (Fig. 6, Carey and Teal, 1969b). The relationship of muscle temperature (T_m) to water temperature (T_w) for the bluefin is:

$$T_m = 0.25 T_w + 25°C$$

In 7°C water some of the fish were more than 20°C warmer than their environment and must have been conserving metabolic heat very efficiently.

It seemed possible that the apparent thermoregulation in the bluefin was the

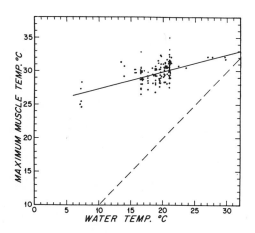

FIG. 6. Muscle temperature of bluefin tuna taken from areas of different water temperature. The muscle temperature changes only 5°C over a 20°C range. (From Carey and Teal, 1969b).

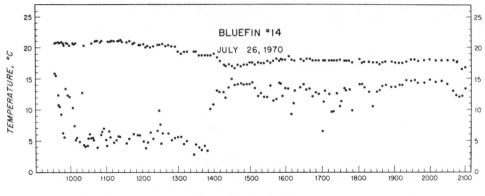

FIG. 7. Telemetry experiment on a free-swimming bluefin tuna showing the first 10 hours of a 56 hour record. The upper set of points are stomach temperature and the lower, water. Stomach temperature remained constant during an 11°C drop in water temperature which lasted for 4 hours.

result of long term adaptation to local water conditions and involved tissue and cellular changes. This is in contrast to the rapid thermoregulation of which mammals are capable. We continued our investigations with a series of telemetry experiments on free-swimming fish to see if they could maintain a constant temperature when the water temperature changed rapidly. To do this we used an acoustic telemetry system which broadcast as a series of 21 KHz sound pulses, tissue and water temperatures for alternating one minute periods. The signal was received by a directional hydrophone and it proved to be a simple matter to follow the fish by steering our ship in the direction of the strongest signal. We hoped that the fish would pass through the thermocline so that we could follow his body temperature as the water temperature changed. As commercial seiners had told us, tuna do not like to change their water temperature and most of the fish we followed maintained a remarkably constant water temperature, usually staying near the surface or on the upper side of the thermocline. Some fish would dive through the thermocline, but only spent a few minutes in the cold water before coming up again. Toward the end of last summer's experiments, however, we were lucky enough to get a most satisfactory result. This fish was a 600 lb bluefin with a transmitter in his stomach.* Water temperatures were sensed by a thermistor on a wire running up the esophagus and out the last gill slit. This particular fish had been handled quite roughly during the struggle to install the transmitter, and, possibly because of this, when released from the trap at 0930 hours he immediately went from the 16°C surface water down into deeper 5°C water and stayed there for four hours (Fig. 7). At 1400 hours he returned to 13 to 14°C water on the upper side of the thermocline and remained there for the rest of the day. While in the cold water, the stomach temperature gradually decreased from 21° to about 19°C, but remained at about 18°C after the fish returned to the warm water. Clearly this fish was maintaining a remarkably constant deep-body temperature despite an 11°C drop in water temperature for an extended period of time. Thus, large bluefin tuna can thermoregulate during rapid changes in ambient temperature.

In other experiments we followed muscle temperature and found that this is also

---

* The transmitter in the stomach may have sensed the temperature of the stomach and its contents or of the caecal mass which rests against the stomach and is quite warm. The stomach is separated from the muscle mass which extends deep below the vertebrae by the gas bladder and should not be directly influenced by muscle temperature.

well controlled during changes in water temperature. These experiments are less dramatic and less convincing, however, as we were not fortunate enough to get the marked and prolonged change in water temperature illustrated in Figure 7.

In the tuna there are no obvious shunts such as those that the surface veins provide for the brachial artery-venae comitantes heat-exchanger in the human arm. Presumably, control is achieved by degrading the efficiency of the heat-exchangers in warmer water, but though it is easy to speculate on mechanisms, we have no evidence as to how this is done.

The Atlantic bluefin tuna range from the tropics to the Arctic. They are the largest and most powerful of the tuna and undertake long seasonal migrations. They can travel over great distances rapidly, as indicated by tags returned from fish released in the Bahamas and caught less than 50 days later and 4200 miles away near Bergen, Norway (Mather, 1962). The movements of these fish do not appear to be restricted by water temperature, for their travels may take them from the near 30°C waters of the Bahamas to 6°C northern waters. The bluefin can maintain its body at a relatively constant value despite marked and rapid changes in the water temperature. We believe that this independence of water temperature gives the tuna its unsurpassed mobility. Unbounded by water temperature, it can seek favorable areas in the north for feeding and in the tropics for spawning.

REFERENCES

Barrett, I., and F. Hester. 1964. Body temperatures of yellowfin and skipjack tuna in relation to sea surface temperature. Nature 203:96-97.

Bone, Q. 1966. On the function of the two types of myotomal muscle fibres in elasmobranch fish. J. Marine Biol. Assoc. U.K. 46:321-349.

Burne, R. H. 1923. Some peculiarities of the blood vascular system of the porbeagle shark, *Lamna cornubica*. Phil. Trans. Roy. Soc. London 212B:209-257.

Carey, F. G., and J. M. Teal. 1966. Heat conservation in tuna fish muscle. Proc. Nat. Acad. Sci. U.S. 56:1461-1469.

Carey, F. G., and J. M. Teal. 1969a. Mako and porbeagle: Warm-bodied sharks. Comp. Biochem. Physiol. 28:199-204.

Carey, F. G., and J. M. Teal. 1969b. Regulation of body temperature by the bluefin tuna. Comp. Biochem. Physiol. 28:205-213.

Cuvier, G., and A. Valenciennes. 1831. Histoire naturelle des poissons. VIII. F. G. Levrault, Paris.

Eschricht, D. F., and J. Müller. 1835. Über die arteriösen und venösen Wundernetz an der leber und einen merkwürdigen bau dieses Organes beim thunfische, *Thynnus vulgaris*. Abhandl. Deut. Akad. Wiss. Berlin. p. 1-30.

Hartree, W., and A. V. Hill. 1921. The nature of the isometric twitch. J. Physiol. 55:389-411.

Kishinouye, K. 1923. Contributions to the study of the so-called scombroid fishes. J. Coll. Agric. Imperial University Tokyo 8:293-475.

Magnuson, J. J. 1969. Digestion and food consumption by skipjack tuna (*Katsuwonus pelamis*). Trans. Amer. Fisheries Soc. 98-379-392.

Mather, F. 1962. Transatlantic migration of two large bluefin tuna. J. Conseil Perm. Intern. Exploration Mer. 27:325-327.

Rayner, M. D., and M. J. Keenan. 1967. Role of red and white muscles in the swimming of the skipjack tuna. Nature 214:392-393.

Walters, V., and H. L. Fierstine. 1964. Measurement of the swimming speeds of yellowfin tuna and wahoo. Nature 202:208-209.

The Relation of Size to Rate of Oxygen Consumption and Sustained Swimming Speed of Sockeye Salmon (*Oncorhynchus nerka*)[1,2]

By J. R. Brett

Fisheries Research Board of Canada
Biological Station, Nanaimo, B. C.

ABSTRACT

The relation of size (log weight, g) to metabolic rate (log O_2-uptake, mg O_2/hr) of sockeye salmon was found to have a continuous change in slope (0.78–0.97) with increasing activity at 15 C.

The slope of the equation relating the 60-min sustained swimming speed (log speed, cm/sec) to length (cm) had a value of 0.50, demonstrating a rapid decrease in relative performance with increasing size.

INTRODUCTION

THE RELATION of weight to metabolic rate of fish has received considerable attention, particularly for resting or standard rates of metabolism (Winberg, 1956, 1961; Fry, 1957). Relatively few experiments have dealt with the influence of weight on active metabolism (Job, 1955; Basu, 1959). Intermediate levels of metabolic rate, generally designated as routine metabolism, have been investigated in a number of cases (Job, 1957; Beamish and Mookherjii, 1964; Beamish, 1964) but the level of activity is hard to standardize or relate to any discrete behaviour pattern.

It has been the aim of current studies on the metabolic rate of sockeye salmon (*Oncorhynchus nerka*) to determine the energy required to swim at any fixed speed, and to assess the separate effects of temperature and size (Brett, 1962). Experiments on 50-g yearling sockeye at acclimation temperatures ranging from 5 to 24 C have been conducted (Brett, 1964). Further experiments are reported herewith on the metabolic rates of sockeye salmon ranging in weight from approximately 3 to 1400 g, performed at 15 C in fresh water.

MATERIALS AND METHODS

A description of the tunnel-respirometer and the method of operation has been presented (Brett, 1964).

In brief, fish are forced to swim in front of an electrically charged screen (3–5 v a-c) in a plexiglass tube 11.4 cm ($4\frac{1}{2}$ inches) in diameter. The tube is expansible to any desired length by the addition of new sections (Fig. 1). A centrifugal pump recirculates the water past the fish at velocities up to 113

---

[1]Received for publication April 23, 1965.
[2]Paper No. 14 concerning the physiology and behaviour of salmonid fishes, from the Fisheries Research Board of Canada Biological Station, Nanaimo, B. C.

From *Journal of the Fisheries Research Board of Canada* 22:1491–1501. Reprinted by permission.

FIG. 1. Tunnel-respirometer with expanded plexiglass chamber providing a volume of 23.41 (7.0 gal).

cm/sec (3.7 ft/sec). New water can be exchanged at will without altering the internal flow pattern.

Each fish, or group of fish, is put through a set procedure including 36 hr of fasting and 14 hr of conditioning in the respirometer prior to the start of a test. Commencing at a low velocity, oxygen consumption rates are determined (unmodified Winkler) for two 30-min periods, followed by flushing to re-establish the oxygen level. The velocity is then increased by 9.1 cm/sec (0.3 ft/sec) and determinations repeated. This step-type procedure is continued until a fatigue velocity is reached.

Active metabolism is determined directly for the maximum sustained speed; standard metabolic rate is obtained by extrapolating the O_2-*consumption* versus *velocity* curve back to zero velocity.

With the exception of the adult salmon all samples were from cultured stocks (Table I). The adults were obtained by trapping early-run sockeye a few days after entering Stamp River, Vancouver Island, B. C. They were held in fresh water for 3 weeks prior to testing. Although fish heavier than 1400 g were available these could not swim readily in the relatively small diameter of the fish chamber.

When swimming in a closed system the cross-sectional displacement of water by the fish naturally influences the velocity over the body. Since the

TABLE I.   Metabolic rates and corresponding swimming speeds of sockeye salmon tested at 15 C.

Class		Age (yr)	Sex	Total length (cm)	Wet weight (g)	Oxygen consumption (mg O₂/kg/hr) Min observ	Max observ	Standard	¼ Active	½ Active	¾ Active	Full Active	Swimming speeds (60-min duration) ¼ Active (cm/s)	(L/s)	½ Active (cm/s)	(L/s)	¾ Active (cm/s)	(L/s)	Fatigue speed (cm/s)	(L/s)
Underyearling	(No.)			(10)[a]	(10)	..	(1)[b]	(1)	..	..	..	(1)	..	..	..	..	..	..	(1)	(1)
	Mean	0.3	Imm.	7.74	3.38	..	635	230	330	460	660	920	12.8	1.66	25.7	3.32	38.5	4.98	51.5	6.65
	S.E.			.06	.10															
Underyearling	(No.)			(9)	(9)	..	(2)	(2)	..	..	..	(2)	..	..	..	..	..	..	(9)	(9)
	Mean	0.7	Imm.	10.03	8.47	..	860	110	185	300	515	830	15.0	1.50	30.0	3.00	45.0	4.50	59.8	5.94
	S.E.			0.17	0.46															0.17
Underyearling	(No.)			(42)	(42)	..	(7)	(7)	..	..	..	(7)	..	..	..	..	..	..	(7)	(7)
	Mean	0.9	Imm.	12.78	19.1	..	655	127	..	..	..	700	..	..	..	..	..	..	53.2	4.16[c]
	S.E.			0.21	1.6															0.23
Yearling	(No.)			(10)	(10)	(7)	(8)	(10)	..	..	..	(8)	..	..	..	..	..	..	(8)	(8)
	Mean	1.4	Imm.	18.8	55.2	121	988	71	132	250	480	895	19.4	1.03	38.7	2.06	58.1	3.09	77.4	4.12
	S.E.			0.8	9.5			4.0											3.6	0.19
Adult (jacks)	(No.)			(4)	(4)	(4)	(4)	(4)	..	..	..	(4)	..	..	..	..	..	..	(4)	(4)
	Mean	3.4	♂	41.8	746	93	708	71	126	226	410	730	31.7	0.75	62.7	1.5	94.1	2.25	125	3.0[d]
	S.E.			1.13	8.9			3.9				45								
Adult	(No.)			(14)	(15)	(9)	(12)	(5)	..	..	..	(9)	..	..	..	..	..	..	..	..
	Mean	4.4	♀[e]	53.9	1432	150	658	44	88	176	350	717	35.5	0.66	71.5	1.33	107	1.99	143	2.65[f]
	S.E.			0.67	40.6			5.6				25								

[a],[b] Total number of fish tested; number of groups within total.
[c] This performance significantly low from lack of pre-exercise and tested in fall (see Fig. 3).
[d] Determined by interpolation, Fig. 3.
[e] These adults were 80% 4_2 and 93% females.
[f] Determined in an 11-inch diameter tunnel at 17 C.

displacement was less than 10% at the greatest body cross-section of the yearling fish no correction was applied. Adult fish, however, with relatively large mid-section, and consequently impeded by the increased surface drag, could not obtain more than half their normal swimming speed. That they were working hard was revealed by the observation that a tail-beat frequency of about 180–200 beats/min characterized the threshold level of sustained effort. This frequency was also the maximum sustained rate when tested in an 11-inch diameter tunnel at nearly twice the velocity.

It was therefore possible to use tail-beat frequency instead of velocity for the larger fish in order to determine the relation of oxygen consumption to intermediate levels of activity. It also made it possible to impose fatigue velocities on large fish to establish the maximum rate of oxygen uptake, despite the limitations of the small respirometer.

RESULTS

The results for each weight "class" are compiled in Table I, with metabolic rates expressed in terms of unit wet weight (1 kg). Minimum and maximum observed rates are included wherever appropriate; few cases were studied at sufficiently low velocities to warrant including many "resting" rates. Under-yearling fish were tested in groups of 4–10 fish at a time, as signified in the "Numbers" column.

The smallest fish (3.38 g) had standard and active metabolic rates of 230 and 920 mg O_2/kg/hr, whereas the largest (1432 g) had rates of 44 and 717 mg O_2/kg/hr, respectively.

The values for intermediate levels of activity corresponding to $\frac{1}{4}$, $\frac{1}{2}$, and $\frac{3}{4}$ of the 60-min sustained swimming speed, were obtained by interpolation from the O_2-consumption vs velocity curves (Fig. 2).

The maximum 60-min sustained swimming speeds (Table I) ranged from 51.5 cm/sec (1.7 ft/sec) for the shortest fish (7.74 cm total length) to 143 cm/sec (4.7 ft/sec) for the longest (53.9 cm). When expressed in terms of length/sec these speeds become 6.65 and 2.65 L/sec, indicating the reduction in relative speed which characterizes the larger fish (Fig. 3).

The sustained speed of the 12.8-cm underyearling fish has not been used in defining the speed–length relation. These fish were not pre-exercised. They were relatively fat, and were tested in the fall. These factors are sufficient to cause significant differences in performance (Wohlschlag and Juliano, 1959).

DISCUSSION

The use of groups of small fish rather than individuals was two-fold. Single, small fish in the 23-liter volume of the respirometer had too small an influence on the oxygen concentration to make $\frac{1}{2}$-hr readings feasible. In addition, the time to test individual fish (1 day) was too long for amassing comparative data.

The question arises whether grouped fish give different metabolic rates than single fish. While this forms the basis of another study it can be reported that no difference is as yet apparent under the conditions of conducting experiments with swimming fish. Variability is reduced indicating the averaging effect of a group response but also, possibly, of a reduction in restless behaviour and

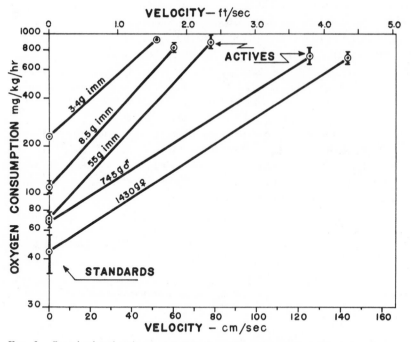

Fig. 2. Standard and active metabolic rates with corresponding 60-min maximum sustained swimming speeds for five weight "classes."

general excitement. For the present, the data on weight influence have been considered to be unaffected by any group factor.

The general equation relating metabolic rate (Y, mg O$_2$/hr) to weight (X, g) has been expressed in the form $Y = aX^b$, or $\log Y = \log a + b \log X$. Applying this transformation to the data of Table I and using the method of least squares[3] to determine the equations for standard and active metabolic rates, the slope values for b, the rate of change of metabolic rate with size can be computed (Table II, Fig. 4). A moderately fan-shaped set of lines is obtained.

STANDARD METABOLIC RATE

If all the data for standard metabolism are treated together a b-value of 0.775 ± 0.145 results (Table II). This serves to link all the observations and would appear to be best for purposes of extrapolating to weights greater than 1400 g. However, between the yearling and adult stages in fresh water a period of rapid growth characterizes sea life. A change in metabolic slope may well accompany this phase. If the early freshwater period is treated separately a b-value of 0.624 results, a significant reduction in this parameter. Just as stanzas are found in growth rate it is not unlikely that similar sorts of stanzas may characterize the rate of change of metabolic rate.

There is also a sex factor entering into the mature stage. Here, too,

---

[3]Individual points for all fish could not be used since some determinations were for groups. The means have been treated therefore as points of equal statistical weight.

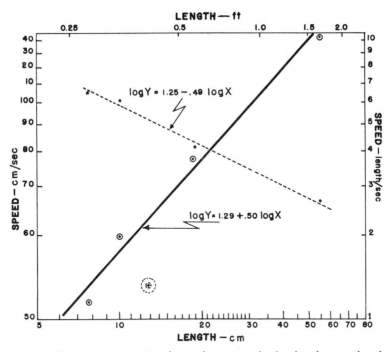

FIG. 3. Relation between 60-min maximum sustained swimming speed and total length. Speed expressed as cm/sec for solid line, and as length/sec (L/sec) for broken line. Circled point is for mean speed of the underyearling fish (12.8 cm) which were not pre-exercised and were tested in October (see text).

differences may exist as suggested by the dotted lines in Fig. 4. During maturation the gonad of the female has from two to five times the relative weight of that of the male (Idler and Clemens, 1959).

Attention is drawn to these points in order to show the potential limitations of pooled treatment of the data, at least where standard metabolism is concerned. So much has been written on the significance and interpretation of b-values since the "surface law" propounded for homeotherms over a century ago, which requires a value of $\frac{2}{3}$ or 0.67 (Bertalanffy, 1957, 1964; Kleiber, 1961) that it is not hard to make interpretive comparisons which, with closer study, may turn out to be unjustified. Although Winberg (1956) examined 266 cases for freshwater fish and was able to provide an average value of $b = 0.81$ (20 C), Heusner *et al.* (1963) in a critical study of three species (*Lebistes reticulatus, Xiphophorus helleri,* and *Aequidens latifrons*) at 25 C obtained mean slope values of 0.70, 0.78, and 0.70 (overall mean = 0.73). By contrast Beamish (1964) and Beamish and Mookherjii (1964) report b-values of 0.88 for *Salmo trutta,* 1.05 for *Salvelinus fontinalis,* 0.86 for *Catostomus commersonii,* 0.93 for *Ictalurus nebulosus,* 0.89 for *Cyprinus carpio,* and 0.85 for *Carassius auratus* (overall mean = 0.91). With such a range of difference, varying all the way from near surface proportionality (0.67) to direct weight proportionality (1.00) the value of applying a generalized relation is questionable.

Since standard metabolism relates to the maintenance costs of a nonfeeding, nondigesting, nongrowing, nonactive fish there is reason for Winberg's

TABLE II. Equations for relation between metabolic rate (Y, mg O₂/hr) and weight (X, g) at different levels of activity expressed as fractions of the maximum 60-min sustained swimming speeds. Confidence limits of slopes given for $p = 05$.

Activity level	Equation	Limits
O = Standard (total)	$\log Y = -0.632 + 0.775 \log X$	± 0.145
O = Standard (immature)	$\log Y = -0.491 + 0.624 \log X$	..
$\frac{1}{4}$ Max	$\log Y = -0.523 + 0.846 \log X$	..
$\frac{1}{2}$ Max	$\log Y = -0.357 + 0.890 \log X$	..
$\frac{3}{4}$ Max	$\log Y = -0.223 + 0.926 \log X$	..
Max = Active ($n = 6$)	$\log Y = -0.050 + 0.970 \log X$	± 0.053
Active ($n = 5$)[a]	$\log Y = -0.064 + 0.963 \log X$	± 0.012

[a]If the active metabolic rate of the 12.8-g fish tested in the fall is eliminated, a slightly reduced slope and reduced error result.

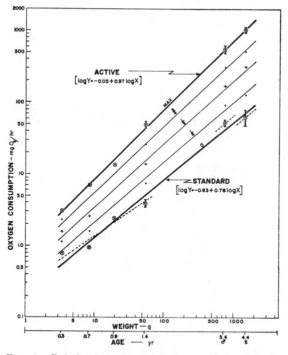

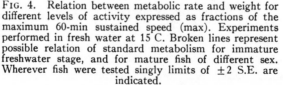

FIG. 4.   Relation between metabolic rate and weight for different levels of activity expressed as fractions of the maximum 60-min sustained speed (max). Experiments performed in fresh water at 15 C. Broken lines represent possible relation of standard metabolism for immature freshwater stage, and for mature fish of different sex. Wherever fish were tested singly limits of ±2 S.E. are indicated.

(1956) appeal for increased studies on active metabolism — ". . . there is no need for additional accumulation of data on metabolic rate of fish under conditions of weak activity or nearly resting, because not one of the basic problems of theoretical or practical interest can be solved in that manner." In medical research Drabkin (1959) makes a similar plea — "Recognition of the large variations in overall metabolic rate encountered in the customary non-basal states of the normal living body has made it necessary to refer measurements in the metabolic clinic to a more reproducible base line [than basal metabolic rate]; the BMR values . . . have tended to steer us away from the factor of performance capacity, which should be of major interest to the biologist and clinician." Drabkin further proposes an *index of metabolic expansibility*, defined as the ratio of metabolic capacity (in prolonged muscular work or at peak effort) to basal metabolism (Drabkin, 1950, 1959). This index, proposed for mammalian studies, is similar in concept to Fry's derived *metabolic scope* for fish (Fry, 1947).

ACTIVE METABOLIC RATE

The determination of active metabolic rates is not subject to certain of the factors contributing to the variability of standard metabolic rates. The effect of excitability and spontaneous movements are virtually eliminated for active metabolic rate. What is more, the latter has a magnitude which is not affected proportionally as much by small changes. The closeness of fit of the data for active metabolism supports this contention (Fig. 4). The animal must, however, be pressed to maximum performance, otherwise behavioural problems may occur which limit full metabolic expression.

Of considerable interest is the progressive increase in slope with increasing activity (Table II). Starting at 0.78 for resting state the slope rises to 0.97 for maximum sustained performance. Since a large proportion of the body of a fish is muscle the almost direct weight relation for active metabolism might be anticipated. The increase between 0 and $\frac{1}{4}$ activity is 0.07. This small increment probably accounts for the similarity of slopes (within one species) for standard and routine rates.

In contrast to the phenomenon of increasing slope values in the salmon, a decreasing slope relation characterized the relation of metabolic rate to weight for increasing work load in mice (Bertalanffy, 1964). The great difference in the problem of dissipating heat between a water-breathing poikilotherm and an air-breathing homeotherm undoubtedly accounts for major differences in slope relations for active metabolic rates.

Turning to temperature relations Job (1955) found for *Salvelinus fontinalis* that the slope value b at 5 C for active metabolic rate (0.94) was higher than for standard (0.86). At 15 C, however, the slopes were the same; whereas at 20 C the relation was reversed, the standards having a slope of 0.80 and the actives 0.75.

In the interests of accurate prediction of metabolic rate the need to establish the particular weight relation for the species concerned at the temperature and level of activity anticipated appears to be inescapable.

ACTIVE/STANDARD RATIO

If the *metabolic expansibility* index is determined it can be seen that a great difference exists between the lowest value of 4.0 for the smallest fish and 16.3 for the largest (Fig. 5). Although considerable variability exists, affected by such factors as pre-exercise, maturity, and sex, the basic influence of size can best be displayed by obtaining the Active/Standard ratios from the lines-of-best-fit relating metabolic rate and weight (Fig. 4). The progressive decrease

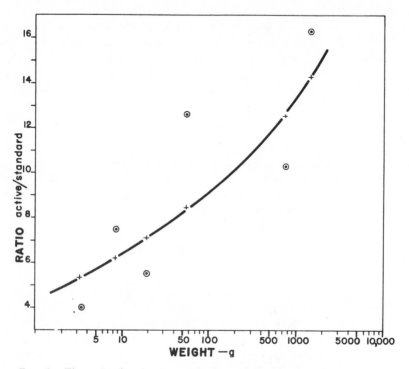

FIG. 5. The ratio of active to standard metabolic rate (metabolic expansibility) in relation to weight. Circled points are from observed mean metabolic rates; small crosses are derived from the lines of best fit, Fig. 4.

in standard metabolism with size, when related to a fairly sustained active metabolic rate, provides an increased metabolic scope.

PERFORMANCE RELATIONS

At the highest sustained level of performance the muscular demand for oxygen is met by the maximum rate of oxygen uptake. Burst speeds invoke oxygen-debt and fatigue.

The 60-min maximum sustained speed is considered here, determined as the final step in a performance sequence lasting 5–7 hr. This has been shown to approximate threshold levels of performance in tests where fixed velocities were imposed for up to 10 hr (Brett, 1964). Much of the work on swimming speed reported in the literature has been on measures of burst speeds (Bainbridge, 1960, 1962; Boyar, 1961).

The relation between body length and swimming speed (Fig. 3) follows the general equation $Y = aX^b$ where Y is swimming speed (cm/sec) and X is total length (cm). Alternatively speed has been expressed in total fish lengths/sec (L/sec). In either case the slope b approximates 0.5 indicating a rapid decay in the *relative ability* to maintain a sustained speed as size increases.

This decay occurs despite a relative increase in body musculature (45% for 30 g; 60% for 1500 g) and a progressive increase in metabolic scope. Even with these assets it is apparent that the increased hydrodynamic drag which accompanies increased size is only partially met. The metabolic process is not a match for the great energy cost of sustained high speed for large fish.

ACKNOWLEDGMENTS

Throughout the study the technical assistance of Mr D. B. Sutherland has contributed greatly to expediting the research. In addition it is a pleasure to acknowledge the assistance of Dr L. S. Smith in the determination of metabolic rates of adult salmon.

REFERENCES

BAINBRIDGE, R. 1960. Speed and stamina in three fish. *J. Exp. Biol.*, **37**(1): 129–153.
1962. Training, speed and stamina in trout. *Ibid.*, **39**(4): 537–556.

BOYAR, H. C. 1961. Swimming speed of immature Atlantic herring with reference to the Passamoquoddy Tidal Project. *Trans. Amer. Fisheries Soc.*, **90**(1): 21–26.

BASU, S. P. 1959. Active respiration of fish in relation to ambient concentrations of oxygen and carbon dioxide. *J. Fish. Res. Bd. Canada*, **16**(2): 175–212.

BEAMISH, F. W. H. 1964. Respiration of fishes with special emphasis on standard oxygen consumption. II. Influence of weight and temperature on respiration of several species. *Canadian J. Zool.*, **42**: 177–188.

BEAMISH, F. W. H., AND P. S. MOOKHERJII. 1964. Respiration of fishes with special emphasis on standard oxygen consumption. I. Influence of weight and temperature on respiration of goldfish, *Carassius auratus* L. *Ibid.*, **42**: 161–194.

BERTALANFFY, L. V. 1957. Quantitative laws in metabolism and growth. *Quart. Rev. Biol.*, **32**(3): 217–231.
1964. Basic concepts in quantitative biology of metabolism. *Helgolaender Wiss. Meeresuntersuch.*, **9**(1–4): 5–37.

BRETT, J. R. 1962. Some considerations in the study of respiratory metabolism in fish, particularly salmon. *J. Fish. Res. Bd. Canada*, **19**(6): 1025–1038.
1964. The respiratory metabolism and swimming performance of young sockeye salmon. *Ibid.*, **21**(5): 1183–1226.

DRABKIN, D. L. 1950. The distribution of the chromoproteins, hemoglobin, myoglobin, and cytochrome c, in the tissues of different species, and the relationship of the total content of each chromoprotein to body mass. *J. Biol. Chem.*, **182**(1): 317–349.
1959. Imperfection: Biochemical phobias and metabolic ambivalence. *Perspectives Biol. Med.*, **2**(4): 473–517.

FRY, F. E. J. 1947. Effects of the environment on animal activity. *Publ. Ontario Fish. Res. Lab.*, No. 55, 62 p.
1957. The aquatic respiration of fish, p. 1–63. *In* M. E. Brown [ed.] Physiology of Fishes. Vol. I. Academic Press Inc., New York.

HEUSNER, A., C. KAYSER, C. MARX, T. STUSSI, ET M. L. HARMELIN. 1963. Relation entre le poids et la consommation d'oxygène. II. Étude intraspécifique chez le poisson. *Comptes rendus des séances de la Société de Biologie*, **157**(3): 654. (C. R. Soc. Biol., Vol. 157, p. 654.)

IDLER, D. R., AND W. A. CLEMENS. 1959. The energy expenditures of Fraser River sockeye salmon during the spawning migration to Chilko and Stuart Lakes. *Int. Pac. Sal. Fisheries Comm.*, *Prog. Rept.*, 80 p.

JOB, S. V.   1955.   The oxygen consumption of *Salvelinus fontinalis*.   *Publ. Ontario Fish. Res. Lab., No.* LXXIII, 39 p.
    1957.   The routine-active oxygen consumption of the milk fish.   *Proc. Indian Acad. Sci.*, **45**: 302–313.

KLEIBER, MAX.   1961.   The fire of life.   John Wiley & Sons, N. Y., 454 p.

WINBERG, G. G.   1956.   [Rate of metabolism and food requirements of fishes].   Belorussian State University, Minsk. 251 p. [Transl. Fish. Res. Bd. Canada, No. 194.]
    1961.   New information on metabolic rate in fishes. From Voprosy Ikhtiologii, Vol. 1, No. 1(18), p. 157–165, 1961.   [Transl. Fish. Res. Bd. Canada, No. 362.]

WOHLSCHLAG, D. E., AND R. O. JULIANO.   1959.   Seasonal changes in bluegill metabolism.   *Limnol. Oceanog.*, **4**(2): 195–209.

THE RELATION BETWEEN EXERCISE AND BIOCHEMICAL CHANGES IN RED AND WHITE MUSCLE AND LIVER IN THE JACK MACKEREL,

Trachurus symmetricus

Austin W. Pritchard,[1] John R. Hunter,[2] and Reuben Lasker[2]

ABSTRACT

Glycogen, lactic acid, and fat concentration in red and white muscle and glycogen in the liver of jack mackerel, *Trachurus symmetricus*, were measured after periods of forced swimming by *Trachurus* at speeds above, below, and at the sustained speed threshold. Failure to swim at any speed was associated with an almost complete depletion of glycogen in the white muscle only. The trend of glycogen use in the red muscle closely followed that of the liver and was not correlated with failure to swim. Reduction of glycogen levels in red muscle and liver were associated with extended periods of swimming. High lipid content was characteristic of red muscle and was insignificant in white muscle. Lipid use was slow and not correlated with fatigue. A decline in lipid concentration after exercise occurred only in the red muscle and only after a swimming period of 6 hr at a subthreshold speed. High lactate levels were characteristic of both muscle types and did not appear to be related to fatigue at any swimming speed.

The high lactate levels in white muscle, the almost complete depletion of glycogen in the white muscle of exhausted fish, and the parallel pattern of glycogen depletion in red muscle and liver suggested that white muscle was the primary locomotor organ near and above the threshold for sustained speed. At these speeds red muscle like the liver may provide nutrients to the white muscle, provided time for mobilization is sufficient. At speeds below the sustained speed threshold our analysis indicated that both the red and white muscle systems were used but the relative significance of the locomotory role played by each system could not be evaluated.

The lateral musculature of many fishes may be readily segregated by color into red and white portions. Typically in active fishes the red muscle makes up from 10 to 20% of the total musculature and is arranged in a thin lateral sheet just beneath the skin whereas the white muscle makes up the underlying mass of the myotome. The two muscle types also differ in the diameter of their muscle fibers, speed of contraction, blood supply, mitochondrial content, patterns of innervation, and glycogen and fat content (Bone, 1966).

The accepted view of the function of red and white muscle tissues in fishes was outlined by Bone (1966). He concluded from his own work on dogfish and from an extensive literature review that the two muscle fibers represent two separate motor systems which operate

independently, utilize different metabolites, and serve different locomotory functions, viz., the red muscle is used for slow cruising speeds and functions by aerobic metabolism of fat whereas the white muscle is used for rapid bursts of swimming and is driven by anaerobic glycolysis. Bone's conclusions have subsequently been supported by measurements of oxygen uptake in red and white muscle by Gordon (1968) and by electrophysiological studies on oceanic skipjack, *Katsuwonus pelamis*, by Rayner and Keenan (1967). On the other hand, Braekkan (1956) and Wittenberger (1967) believe the red muscle has no independent locomotor role and functions as a metabolic organ for the white muscle. Electrode recordings from the red muscle (Bone, 1966; Rayner and Keenan, 1967) have provided irrefutable evidence for an independent locomotor function of red muscle at certain slow speeds, but the metabolic independence of the two muscle systems and their metabolic and locomotor function at higher speeds is still open

[1] Zoology Department, Oregon State University, Corvallis, Oreg. 97331.
[2] National Marine Fisheries Service Fishery-Oceanography Center, La Jolla, Calif. 92037.

From *Fish. Bull.*, U.S. 69(2): 379–386. Reprinted by permission.

to question. Although the roles assigned to the two muscle systems are dependent on swimming speed, no studies have been made on the function of the muscle systems using normally swimming intact animals at known speeds. The objective of this study was to re-examine the metabolic and locomotor roles of red and white muscle by measurement of glycogen, lactate, and fat levels in the muscle and glycogen levels in the liver in fish exposed to various velocity treatments of known strength and duration. Juvenile jack mackerel, *Trachurus symmetricus,* were used in this study because the maximum sustained speed threshold for 6 hr of continuous swimming had already been established for this species (Hunter, 1971), and consequently we were able to relate all of our chemical measurements to known levels of swimming performance.

METHODS AND PROCEDURES

SWIMMING TESTS

Jack mackerel were maintained at a regulated seawater temperature of 18.5° C in a plastic swimming pool 4.57 m diameter and fed an abundant ration of brine shrimp, *Artemia,* and chopped fish and squid each day. The fish were not fed for 20 hr prior to testing. Jack mackerel were tested in an activity chamber patterned after that of Beamish (1968) and described in detail by Hunter and Zweifel (1971). The swimming compartment of the apparatus consisted of a tube 230 cm long and 41 cm in diameter through which seawater could be moved at speeds ranging from 12 to 212 cm/sec. Fish were placed in the tube and forced to swim at a water speed for certain periods varying from 8 min to 6 hr. At the end of the swimming period they were removed and dropped immediately into liquid nitrogen and the frozen fish were stored at —30° C until used for chemical analysis. The time required for removal and freezing did not exceed 1 min.

Speed treatments for the experiments were chosen relative to the 50% endurance threshold for jack mackerel at 22 $L^{0.6}$/sec for 6 hr of swimming where L is total length (Hunter, 1971). Five jack mackerel, mean length 14.6 cm, were tested at the subthreshold speed of 19.6 $L^{0.6}$/sec (98 cm/sec); 14 jack mackerel, mean length 16.3 cm, were tested at the near threshold speed of 21.1 $L^{0.6}$/sec (113 cm/sec); and 10 jack mackerel, mean length 14.7 cm, were tested at the superthreshold speed of 27.7 $L^{0.6}$/sec (139 cm/sec). Fish tested at the subthreshold speed swam continuously for 6 hr and were sampled at the end of that period. Fish tested at the threshold speed were divided into two groups: seven fish that were sampled after

6 hr of continuous swimming; and seven fish that fell from exhaustion at some time during the 6-hr period. The latter group of seven fish were quickly removed from the apparatus and frozen as soon as they fell against the rear screen. Fish tested at the superthreshold speed were also divided into two groups: those that swam successfully for 8 min; and those that failed after 8 or less minutes of swimming.

Ten jack mackerel, mean length 14.5 cm, were used as controls. Five of the control animals were removed from the holding tank, placed in the apparatus, allowed to swim for 30 min at the slow speed of 6.2 $L^{0.6}$/sec (30 cm/sec), removed, and frozen. The other five control fish were removed from the holding tank and immediately frozen. The data from these two control groups were later combined because no difference between them was detected.

CHEMICAL ANALYSES

White and red muscle were dissected from the frozen fish while still frozen. One lateral strip of red muscle was used for fat analysis and the other divided into two equal portions for lactate and glycogen analysis respectively. About 1 g of white muscle from the dorsal portion of the myotome was used for glycogen determinations, 0.5 g for lactate, and 0.5 g for fat measurements. Fish were returned to the freezer and liver samples (0.1-0.2 g) were analyzed for glycogen about a month after the muscle determinations.

For lactate measurements muscle was quickly cut into small pieces, weighed, and homogenized in 10% trichloroacetic acid in prechilled tubes. Proteins and cellular debris were spun down in a clinical centrifuge. Aliquots of the protein-free supernatant fluid were analyzed for lactate enzymatically using the test reagents supplied by SIGMA Chemical Company.[a] The test is based on the conversion of nicotine adenine nucleotide (NAD) to the reduced form (NADH) as lactate is converted to pyruvate by lactate dehydrogenase. All readings were made at 340 mμ on a Beckman DU spectrophotometer. Results are expressed as mg of lactic acid per 100 g wet weight muscle tissue.

Muscle and liver samples for glycogen determinations were dropped into preweighed graduated centrifuge tubes containing 3 ml of 30% potassium hydroxide. Glycogen was precipitated with alcohol and determined according

---

[a] **P.O. Box 14508,** St. Louis, Mo. 63178. Reference to commercial products does not imply endorsement.

TABLE 1.—Glycogen in red and white muscle, and liver of jack mackerel following various forced swimming conditions. Red and white muscle glycogen in mg per 100 g wet weight; liver glycogen is percent of wet weight. -- indicates measurement was lost during analysis.

	Controls			19 $L^{0.6}$ Subthreshold speed			21 $L^{0.6}$ Threshold speed successes		
	Red	White	Liver	Red	White	Liver	Red	White	Liver
	76.6	85.9	6.42	15.23	53.90	0.125	26.71	204.3	0.043
	102.8	--	9.49	52.80	143.2	4.36	33.33	159.4	1.63
	176.3	--	22.74	192.5	76.69	.317	37.59	80.74	1.85
	277.8	276.8	8.75	145.2	316.2	8.31	95.93	492.8	.125
	562.0	142.6	18.59	147.6	102.6	3.16	152.4	223.2	3.42
	706.0	157.9	18.17				191.7	638.0	3.19
	1075	267.8	10.26				475.1	216.3	1.38
	1394	72.9	17.00						
	1417	71.1	11.82						
	1706	216.5	24.24						
Mean	749.4	161.4	14.75	¹110.7	138.5	¹3.25	¹144.7	287.8	¹1.66

	21 $L^{0.6}$ Threshold speed fatigued			28 $L^{0.6}$ Superthreshold speed-individually fatigued			28 $L^{0.6}$ Superthreshold speed, 8-min test		
	Red	White	Liver	Red	White	Liver	Red	White	Liver
	11.5	26.50	.078	--	--	0.546	--	39.93	10.00
	16.00	4.51	.034	149.6	8.02	4.73	298.6	141.9	10.00
	17.10	20.63	3.30	215.0	19.56	3.83	473.3	25.44	3.16
	40.55	27.77	5.04	490.4	6.76	13.23	533.1	141.0	10.94
	104.8	--	11.96	654.5	18.49	5.81	553.9	57.22	11.31
	151.8	11.15	.820						
	241.5	50.2	12.50						
Mean	¹83.27	¹23.46	¹4.82	377.4	¹13.21	¹5.63	464.7	¹81.1	9.08

¹ Differed from the controls, $P \leqslant 0.05$, Mann Whitney U test (Siegel, 1956).

to the method of Montgomery (1957). All readings were made at 490 mμ on a Beckman DU spectrophotometer. Results are expressed as mg glycogen (as glucose) per 100 g wet weight in the case of muscle, and as percent glycogen in the case of liver.

Muscle tissue was dried in an oven at 60° C to constant weight for fat analysis. Fat was removed by a soxhlet extraction with chloroform-methanol (2:1, v:v). After the extraction the solvent in the tissue was evaporated and the difference in weight of the tissue recorded (Krvarić and Mužinić, 1950).

RESULTS

Fish that swam continuously for 6 hr at the subthreshold speed of 98 cm/sec and at the threshold speed showed no difference in the glycogen content of the white muscle from the controls (Table 1). On the other hand, in fish that failed to swim the full 6 hr at the same speed the glycogen levels in the white muscle were lower and were different from the controls ($P = 0.001$ Mann Whitney U test, Siegel, 1956). Glycogen levels in white muscle of all fish tested at the superthreshold velocity were also much lower and statistically different from the controls ($P = 0.05$). The lowest glycogen levels of all were in fish that failed from exhaustion at superthreshold speeds. The values in these exhausted fish were statistically different from those of fish that swam at the same speed but

which were removed after 8 min of swimming before they could fall from exhaustion. In sum, strenuous exercise and exhaustion regardless of speed were associated with a marked depletion of glycogen reserves in the white muscle, whereas successful swimming for 6 hr at subthreshold or threshold speed produced no. significant change in white muscle glycogen.

The glycogen content of the liver and red muscle were lower and different from the controls in fish tested at threshold and subthreshold speeds ($P = 0.05$). At superthreshold speed, on the other hand, the glycogen content of the red muscle was not different from the controls and that of the liver was different only in fish that failed from exhaustion ($P = 0.02$).

Thus, the trends in the levels of red muscle and liver glycogen in relation to swimming speed were nearly the reverse of that for white muscle glycogen. Low levels of glycogen in red muscle and liver were associated with slow speeds that could be sustained for extended periods. These results suggest that glycogen from red muscle and liver provide energy to the white muscle at nearly all swimming speeds. We believe that no drop occurred in red muscle glycogen in fish fatigued at high speeds because the time was too short for the white muscle to mobilize significant amounts of glycogen. This view is supported by the negative correlation between the level of glycogen in the red muscle and swimming time to fatigue at threshold speed. This is illustrated in the following table:

Threshold speed $= 21\ L^{0.6}$

Time to fatigue (min)	Glycogen in red muscle (mg per 100 g wet weight)
282	11.5
110	16.0
131	17.1
79	40.6
15	104.
38	241.

$(r_s = -0.857,\ P < 0.05)$

In fish exercised at the superthreshold speed the lactic acid content of the red and white muscle was considerably above that of the controls and statistically different from them ($P = 0.05$) (Table 2). At threshold and subthreshold

TABLE 2.—Concentration of lactic acid in red and white muscle of jack mackerel following various forced swimming conditions. Values given are mg lactic acid per 100 g wet weight.

Controls		19 $L^{0.6}$ Subthreshold speed		21 $L^{0.6}$ Threshold speed successes	
Red	White	Red	White	Red	White
40.49	233.0	94.6	520.9	20.60	310.4
59.29	425.3	97.6	596.6	22.83	344.5
71.58	387.5	99.2	521.9	26.79	385.3
77.46	521.0	117.1	630.3	45.66	464.8
79.53	570.3	156.8	762.3	56.94	403.1
82.19	341.5			82.19	345.2
86.76	390.6			83.87	410.2
86.76	319.0				
86.76	553.4				
95.44	589.6				
Mean 76.63	433.1	¹113.1	606.4	¹48.41	380.5

21 $L^{0.6}$ Threshold speed fatigued		28 $L^{0.6}$ Superthreshold speed - individually fatigued		28 $L^{0.6}$ Superthreshold speed, 8-min test	
Red	White	Red	White	Red	White
26.23	564.6	101.2	422.9	124.2	724.1
39.61	545.3	108.4	538.6	132.3	668.9
56.58	404.4	120.4	723.1	189.0	799.9
66.6	499.2	151.9	745.8	202.8	807.4
86.76	489.7	230.5	800.6	237.4	733.5
122.5	486.2				
205.5	646.1				
Mean 86.25	519.4	¹142.5	¹646.2	¹177.1	¹746.8

¹ Differed from the controls, $P \leqslant 0.05$, Mann Whitney U test (Siegel, 1956).

speeds, the lactic acid concentration in red and white muscle formed no distinct pattern. At threshold speed the lactate levels of red and white muscle were about the same as the controls and did not differ from them except for one case where the values were actually lower than the controls; at this subthreshold speed lactate levels of red and white muscle were higher than the controls and differed statistically ($P = 0.02$). We have no explanation for these differences except to suggest that the high muscle lactate concentration in the control animals may have obscured changes resulting from moderate exercise. A larger sample size may be required to obtain reliable measurements of differences in lactic acid concentration caused by moderate exercise.

Muscle lactate level did not appear to be related to fatigue at any swimming speed. Lac-

tate levels in fish that fatigued at the threshold speed were not different from the controls. Fish that failed at superthreshold speeds had a higher muscle lactate level than did the controls but the level did not differ from that of fish that swam at the same speed but were removed before they became exhausted. These results suggest that high lactic acid concentration in muscle was not the principal cause of exhaustion.

Red muscle contained considerably more fat per unit weight than white muscle. Indeed, white muscle fat levels were almost undetectable in many cases (Table 3). White muscle fat levels did not differ from the control at any speed level. Red muscle fat did not differ from the controls at threshold and superthreshold speeds but at the subthreshold speed the mean level of fat in the red muscle was lower than the controls and differed statistically from them ($P = 0.02$). Thus only when the fish swam for at least 6 hr at subthreshold speed was there evidence of fat utilization in the red muscle.⁴ The reduction in fat in the red muscle suggests that the red muscle system may have been used at the subthreshold velocity. On the other hand, presence of high muscle lactate in both red and

TABLE 3.—Fat analyses in red and white muscle of jack mackerel following various forced swimming conditions. Where 0.0% is given for white muscle, only traces of fat were found with the chloroform-methanol extraction. For convenience zeros were used for averaging. Values given as percent dry weight of tissue.

Controls		19 $L^{0.6}$ Subthreshold speed		21 $L^{0.6}$ Threshold speed successes	
Red	White	Red	White	Red	White
20.16	1.98	15.07	0.230	16.91	0.0
21.00	0.0	15.69	2.12	22.45	0.0
21.78	.337	16.19	1.24	23.80	2.19
22.24	1.15	20.54	0.0	24.67	0.0
23.05	1.32	24.63	0.0	24.97	1.54
25.11	0.0			26.43	4.09
25.14	.390			29.37	4.10
25.89	.924				
27.29	2.65				
32.32	2.20				
Mean 24.40	1.10	¹18.42	.718	24.08	1.70

21 $L^{0.6}$ Threshold speed fatigued		28 $L^{0.6}$ Superthreshold speed - individually fatigued		28 $L^{0.6}$ Superthreshold speed, 8-min test	
Red	White	Red	White	Red	White
21.30	0.0	16.54	0.0	21.96	2.01
21.97	0.0	16.71	0.0	23.08	.04
22.47	0.0	26.47	1.22	24.20	.18
28.70	0.0	28.19	.732	25.57	.50
30.11	2.56	28.70	2.13	29.54	2.26
32.08	1.12				
32.90	6.46				
Mean 27.08	1.45	23.32	.816	24.87	.998

¹ Differed from the controls, $P = 0.02$, Mann Whitney U test (Siegel, 1956).

⁴ In an earlier and preliminary experiment, five smaller jack mackerel, mean length 9.2 cm, swam at the subthreshold speed of 12.7 $L^{0.6}$/sec (48 cm/sec) for 48 hr without failure and we recorded a decrease in the mean fat content of red muscle from 23.7% (range, 20.4-28.4%; $n = 5$) to 18.0% (range, 16.2-20.8%; $n = 5$) ($P < 0.05$).

white muscle and the drop in red muscle and liver glycogen at subthreshold speeds implies that the white muscle was also active.

DISCUSSION

Control levels of jack mackerel white muscle glycogen were similar to those recorded by Canadian workers for mixed red and white muscle in salmonids (Black, Robertson, and Parker, 1961; Black et al., 1962; Connor et al., 1964) and to those from a variety of marine teleosts (Beamish, 1968; Fraser et al., 1966; Wittenberger, 1968; Wittenberger et al., 1969). Red muscle glycogen has not often been separately determined. Our mean control value of 750 mg percent was somewhat higher than the mean of 420 mg percent reported by Wittenberger (1968) for *Trachurus mediterraneus ponticus*, a related species from the Black Sea. Fraser et al. (1966) gave a range of 215 to 279 mg percent for red muscle glycogen of cod, based on analysis of three fish in a relaxed (anesthetized) state. Wittenberger et al. (1969) reported 320 mg percent in a clupeid, *Harengula humeralis*. A much higher level of 1866 mg percent was given by Bone (1966) for dogfish. In most cases, the concentration of glycogen in red muscle was considerably higher than in white muscle.

Liver glycogen controls in jack mackerel were much higher than those reported previously in teleosts. Connor et al. (1964) for example, obtained values of about 1% in chinook and sockeye salmon and steelhead trout, and found that moderate exercise associated with ascending fishways had no effect on liver glycogen levels. Black et al. (1960) reported liver glycogen levels of 0.5-4% in rainbow trout, and Dean and Goodnight (1964) obtained 0.8-3% in four species of warmwater centrachid fishes. Values similar to ours were reported by Wittenberger and Diaciuc (1965) in carp (13.8%) and by Bellamy (1968) in recently fed red piranha (10.3%). Even if a high degree of gluconeogenesis were operative in jack mackerel, it seems unlikely that this could entirely explain the high levels of liver glycogen.

Control levels of glycogen in jack mackerel white muscle appeared to be similar to those in other fishes. However, in the red muscle and especially in the liver, glycogen levels were usually higher than in fishes studied earlier.

The most striking finding of this study was the virtually complete depletion of glycogen in the white muscle of fish that failed from exhaustion. The depletion of glycogen in white muscle occurred in all fish that failed regardless of the speed of swimming or how long they swam. In fish that did not fail at a near threshold speed of 21 $L^{0.6}$/sec (Hunter 1971) the glycogen in the white muscle did not differ from controls, whereas in the fish that failed, glycogen in the white muscle was at nearly the same low level as it was in fish that failed after a few minutes of exertion at a much higher speed. Red muscle glycogen was also depleted at some swimming speeds but the pattern of glycogen depletion in red muscle closely paralleled that of the liver. Red muscle had one-fifth the lactate found in white muscle on a percent basis but only about one-fiftieth on an absolute basis because the mass of white muscle exceeds the red by 10 to 1.

The high lactate levels in the white muscle, the almost complete depletion of glycogen in the white muscle of exhausted fish, and the parallel pattern of glycogen depletion in red muscle and liver all point to the same hypothesis. In jack mackerel at threshold and higher speeds the energy used for swimming was derived primarily from glycolysis in the white muscle which was the principal locomotor organ. Red muscle like the liver may serve as a storage organ whose resources could be used to drive the white muscle, given sufficient time for mobilization. Thus at threshold speeds, red muscle function appeared to be tied to that of the white and it could not be considered as acting independently. No change in red muscle glycogen was detected at the highest test speed, possibly because time was insufficient to mobilize the glycogen reserves other than in the white muscle itself. This time dependency for mobilizing red muscle glycogen under conditions of strenuous exercise could explain why Bone (1966), Wittenberger and Diacuic (1965), Wittenberger (1968), and Fraser et al. (1966) detected no change in red muscle glycogen afte⁻ strenuous exercise. It must be remembered that in all of these previous studies the strength and the duration of the exercise was unknown, except that it was considered to be extreme.

The decrease in fat content plus the high lactate levels suggest that the red muscle was used for swimming at subthreshold speeds. Bilinski (1969) showed that the rate of oxidation of fatty acids in red muscle of rainbow trout and sockeye salmon exceeded that in the white muscle by one or more orders of magnitude depending on the fatty acid substrate. On the other hand, neither the high oxidative capacity nor the decline in lipid levels in red muscle with moderate exercise are sufficient evidence for an independent locomotor role. In addition, the presence of high lactate levels in white muscle and the drop in the glycogen content of the white muscle indicated that the white muscle was also used at the subthreshold speed of 19 $L^{0.6}$/sec. The electrophysiological evidence for independent locomotor activity of the red muscle cannot be ignored. At some speed slower than any used in the present experiment jack mackerel may depend only on red muscle for propulsion and on lipids for fuel. At what velocity red muscle begins to play a major role or how significant this speed may be in the life of the animal are questions that remain to be answered. The most tenable explanation for these data is that both muscle systems were used at the sub-threshold speed but we are unable to choose which system played the more significant role.

Jack mackerel appear to be specialized in body form and swimming capabilities for high-speed continuous swimming (Hunter, 1971). Thus the physiological characteristics we have described, namely use of glycolysis in white muscle for swimming, high liver glycogen levels, and tolerance of high muscle lactate levels may represent specializations for high-speed swimming and may not be representative of the general pattern in fishes. On the other hand, *Trachurus* may share these characteristics with other fishes of similar habits, for example other carangids and the scombroid fishes. It seems possible that evolution may have favored the development of these physiological characteristics because severe velocity limits may be set by aerobic lipid metabolism.

ACKNOWLEDGMENTS

We thank Messrs. David Holts, William Rommel, and Andrew Kuljis for their technical assistance during this study.

LITERATURE CITED

BEAMISH, F. W. H.
  1968. Glycogen and lactic acid concentrations in Atlantic cod (*Gadus morhua*) in relation to exercise. J. Fish. Res. Bd. Can. 25: 837-851.
BELLAMY, D.
  1968. Metabolism of the red piranha (*Rooseveltiella nattereri*) in relation to feeding behaviour. Comp. Biochem. Physiol. 25: 343-347.
BILINSKI, E.
  1969. Lipid catabolism in fish muscle. *In* O. W. Neuhaus and J. E. Halver (editors), Fish in research, p. 135-151. Academic Press, New York.
BLACK, E. C., A. R. CONNOR, K.-C. LAM, AND W.-G. CHIU.
  1962. Changes in glycogen, pyruvate and lactate in rainbow trout (*Salmo gairdneri*) during and following muscular activity. J. Fish. Res. Bd. Can. 19: 409-436.
BLACK, E. C., A. C. ROBERTSON, A. R. HANSLIP, AND W.-G. CHIU.
  1960. Alterations in glycogen, glucose and lactate in rainbow and kamloops trout, *Salmo gairdneri*, following muscular activity. J. Fish. Res. Bd. Can. 17: 487-500.

BLACK, E. C., A. C. ROBERTSON, AND R. R. PARKER.
  1961. Some aspects of carbohydrate metabolism in fish. *In* A. W. Martin (editor), Comparative physiology of carbohydrate metabolism in hetero-thermic animals, p. 89-124. Univ. of Wash. Press, Seattle.
BONE, Q.
  1966. On the function of the two type of myotomal muscle fibre in elasmobranch fish. J. Mar. Biol. Ass. U.K. 46: 321-349.
BRAEKKAN, O. R.
  1956. Function of the red muscle in fish. Nature (London) 178: 747-748.
CONNOR, A. R., C. H. ELLING, E. C. BLACK, G. B. COLLINS, J. R. GAULEY. AND E. TREVOR-SMITH.
  1964. Changes in glycogen and lactate levels in migrating salmonid fishes ascending experimental "endless" fishways. J. Fish. Res. Bd. Can. 21: 255-290.
DEAN, J. M., AND C. J. GOODNIGHT.
  1964. A comparative study of carbohydrate metabolism in fish as affected by temperature and exercise. Physiol. Zool. 37: 280-299.
FRASER, D. I., W. J. DYER, H. M. WEINSTEIN, J. R. DINGLE, AND J. A. HINES.
  1966. Glycolytic metabolites and their distribution at death in the white and red muscle of cod following various degrees of antemortem muscular activity. Can. J. Biochem. 44: 1015-1033.
GORDON, M. S.
  1968. Oxygen consumption of red and white muscles from tuna fishes. Science (Washington) 159: 87-90.
HUNTER, J. R.
  1971. Sustained speed of jack mackerel, *Trachurus symmetricus*. Fish. Bull. 69: 267-271.
HUNTER, J. R., AND J. R. ZWEIFEL.
  1971. Swimming speed, tail beat frequency, tail beat amplitude, and size in jack mackerel, *Trachurus symmetricus*, and other fishes. Fish. Bull. 69: 253-266.
KRVARIĆ, M., AND R. MUŽINIĆ.
  1950. Investigation into the fat content in the sardine tissues (*Clupea pilchardus* Walb). Acta Adriat. 4: 289-314.
MONTGOMERY, R.
  1957. Determination of glycogen. Arch. Biochem. Biophys. 67: 378-386.
RAYNER, M. D., AND M. J. KEENAN.
  1967. Role of red and white muscles in the swimming of the skipjack tuna. Nature (London) 214: 392-393.
SIEGEL, S.
  1956. Nonparametric statistics: for the behavioral sciences. McGraw, New York, 312 p.
WITTENBERGER, C.
  1967. On the function of the lateral red muscle of teleost fishes. Rev. Roum. Biol., Ser. Zool. 12: 139-144.
  1968. Biologie du chinchard de la Mer Noire (*Trachurus mediterraneus ponticus*). XV. Recherches sur le métabolisme d'effort chez *Trachurus* et *Gobius*. Mar. Biol. 2: 1-4.
WITTENBERGER, C., A. CORO, G. SUÁREZ, AND N. PORTILLA.
  1969. Composition and bioelectrical activity of the lateral muscles in *Harengula humeralis*. Mar. Biol. 3: 24-27.
WITTENBERGER, C., AND I. V. DIACIUC.
  1965. Effort metabolism of lateral muscles in carp. J. Fish. Res. Bd. Can. 22: 1397-1406.

Additional Readings
CHAPTER 5

AFFLECK, R. J. 1950. Some points in the function, development and evolution of the tail in fishes. *Proc. Zool. Soc. London* 120:349–368.

ALEXANDER, R. McN. 1965. The lift produced by the heterocercal tails of selachii. *J. Exp. Biol.* 36:131–137.

ARITA, G. 1971. A reexamination of the functional morphology of the finrays in teleosts. *Copeia* 1971(4):691–697.

BLIGHT, A. R. 1977. The muscular control of vertebrate swimming movements. *Biol. Rev.* 52:181–218.

BONE, Q. 1966. On the function of the two types of myotomal muscle fibre in elasmobranch fish. *J. mar. biol. Ass. U.K.* 46(2):321–349.

BREDER, C. M. 1926. The locomotion of fishes. *Zoologica (N.Y.)* 4:159–256.

BREDER, C. M., and EDGERTON, H. E. 1943. An analysis of the locomotion of the seahorse, *Hippocampus*, by means of high speed cinematography. *Ann. N.Y. Acad. Sci.* 43:145–172.

BRETT, J. R. 1965. The swimming energetics of salmon. *Sci. Amer.* 213:80–85.

CAREY, F. G. 1973. Fishes with warm bodies. *Sci. Amer.* 228(2):36–49.

CAREY, F. G., and LAWSON, K. D. 1973. Temperature regulation in free-swimming bluefin tuna. *Comp. Biochem. Physiol.* 44A:367–374.

CAREY, F. G., and TEAL, J. M. 1969a. Mako and porbeagle: warm-bodied sharks. *Comp. Biochem. Physiol.* 28:199–204.

CAREY, F. G., and TEAL, J. M. 1969b. Regulation of body temperature by the bluefin tuna. *Comp. Biochem. Physiol.* 28:205–213.

FIERSTINE, H. L., and WALTERS, V. 1968. Studies in locomotion and anatomy of scombroid fishes. *Mem. South. Calif. Acad. Sci.* 6:1–29.

GERO, D. R. 1952. The hydrodynamic aspects of fish propulsion. *Amer. Mus. Novitates* (1601):1–32.

GORDON, M. S. 1968. Oxygen consumption of red and white muscles from tuna fishes. *Science* 159:87–90.

GORDON, M. S. 1972a. Comparative studies on the metabolism of shallow-water and deep-sea marine fishes. I. White-muscle metabolism in shallow-water fishes. *Marine Biology* 13:222–237.

GORDON, M. S. 1972b. Comparative studies on the metabolism of shallow-water and deep-sea marine fishes. II. Red-muscle metabolism in shallow-water fishes. *Marine Biology* 15:246–250.

GRAHAM, J. B. 1975. Heat exchange in the yellowfin tuna *Thunnus albacares*, and skipjack tuna, *Katsuwonus pelamis*, and the adaptive significance of elevated body temperatures in scombrid fishes. *Fish. Bull., U.S.* 73(2):219–229.

GRAY, J. 1957. How fishes swim. *Sci. Amer.* 197:48–54.

GREER-WALKER, M., and PULL, G. A. 1975. A survey of red and white muscle in marine fish. *J. Fish Biol.* 7:295–300.

HARRIS, J. E. 1953. Fin patterns and mode of life in fishes. In *Essays in Marine Biology, Elmhirst Memorial Lectures*, S. M. Marshall and A. P. Orr, eds., pp. 17–28. Edinburgh: Oliver and Boyd.

HUNTER, J. R. 1971. Sustained speed of jack mackerel, *Trachurus symmetricus. Fish. Bull., U.S.* 69(2):267–273.

HUNTER, J. R., and ZWEIFEL, J. R. 1971. Swimming speed, tail-beat frequency, tail-beat amplitude, and size in jack mackerel, *Trachurus symmetricus. Fish. Bull., U.S.* 69(2):253–267.

MAGNUSON, J. J. 1973. Comparative study of adaptations for continuous swimming and hydrostatic equilibrium of scombroid and xiphoid fishes. *Fish. Bull., U.S.* 71(2):337–356.

NURSALL, J. R. 1956. The lateral musculature and the swimming of fish. *Proc. Zool. Soc. London* 126(1):127–143.

NURSALL, J. R. 1958. The caudal fin as a hydrofoil. *Evolution* 12(1):116–120.

ROBERTS, B. L. 1969. The coordination of the rhythmical fin movement of dogfish. *J. mar. biol. Ass. U.K.* 49:357–425.

ROSENBLATT, R. H., and JOHNSON, G. D. 1976. Anatomical considerations of pectoral swimming in the opah, *Lampris guttatus. Copeia* 1976(2):367–370.

WALTERS, V. 1962. Body form and swimming performance in the scombroid fishes. *Am. Zoologist* 2:143–149.

WARE, D. M. 1975. Growth, metabolism and optimal swimming speed of a pelagic fish. *J. Fish. Res. Bd. Canada* 32:33–41.

WEBB, P. W. 1975 Hydrodynamics and energetics of fish propulsion. *Bull. Fish. Res. Bd. Canada* (190):1–158.

6

Buoyancy
Regulation

THE EFFECTS OF DIFFERENT ACCLIMATION TEMPERATURES ON GAS SECRETION IN THE SWIMBLADDER OF THE BLUEGILL SUNFISH, *LEPOMIS MACROCHIRUS*

ROGER A. MCNABB and JOHN A. MECHAM

Department of Biology, Virginia Polytechnic Institute and State University, Blacksburg, Virginia 24061

(*Received* 8 *April* 1971)

Abstract—1. After acclimation to 12, 22 or 32°C, the swimbladders of bluegill sunfish (*Lepomis macrochirus*) were partially deflated. Rates of gas secretion into the bladder were measured.

2. Total gas secretion, measured as the rate of reinflation, was temperature independent.

3. The rates of oxygen secretion into the swimbladder increased with increasing acclimation temperature; simultaneously, the rate of carbon dioxide secretion decreased.

INTRODUCTION

GASES and lipids are two components of animals that have specific gravities less than that of water. Accordingly, these materials play a central role in buoyancy adjustments of both teleosts (for gases, see Alexander, 1966; for lipids, see Brawn, 1969) and elasmobranchs (lipids, see Malins & Barone, 1970).

Most groups of teleost fish have evolved the use of a gas-filled swimbladder as a means of adjusting the specific gravity of their bodies to match that of the water in which they live. However, the use of a gas-bladder as a flotation device has several limitations. Because gases are compressible, vertical migration changes the buoyancy provided by any given swimbladder (see Alexander, 1966, for an excellent review). Another undesirable property of a gas-bladder is its temperature sensitivity. Little work has been done on the effects of temperature on swimbladder function, but several temperature-dependent variables can be expected to occur. First, temperature markedly affects gas volume and density, the very properties that make gases such good flotation media. Second, temperature affects the solubility of gases in the body fluids. In addition, temperature can alter the affinity of haemoglobin for oxygen (Florey, 1966, p. 187; Prosser & Brown, 1961, p. 216), and alter the activity of lactate dehydrogenase, two factors important in the operation of the counter-current multiplication system present in the rete mirabile–gas gland complex.

During swimbladder inflation, oxygen is secreted abundantly in most fish studied (see Fange, 1966, for a review). The bluegill Sunfish shows increased metabolism with increasing environmental temperatures (O'Hara, 1968; Spitzer *et al.*, 1969). Thus, at high environmental temperatures a competition exists,

From *Comp. Biochem. Physiol.* 40A:609–616. Reprinted by permission of Pergamon Press Ltd., Oxford, England.

between metabolism and the swimbladder inflation mechanisms, for the oxygen present in the blood of the bluegill.

We hypothesized that at high temperatures the contribution of oxygen to swimbladder inflation would be reduced, in favor of those gases not used for metabolism (i.e. nitrogen and carbon dioxide). Such a reduction could be brought about by increased affinity of haemoglobin for oxygen at high temperatures or by changes in the activity of lactate dehydrogenase in the gas-gland (either directly by temperature or by the use of an isoenzyme system, such as defined in other fish tissues (Hochachka, 1966, 1967)).

In order to determine if oxygen is used extensively in swimbladder inflation at high temperatures, we undertook a study of the effects of acclimation temperature on the gases present, and on the rates at which these gases are secreted, in the swimbladder of the bluegill sunfish.

MATERIALS AND METHODS

Experiments were performed on bluegill sunfish (*Lepomis macrochirus*) weighing from 120 to 220 g. Fish were held in epoxy-lined plywood tanks, filled to a depth of 40 cm with flowing dechlorinated tap water. The water was aerated continuously by means of airstones

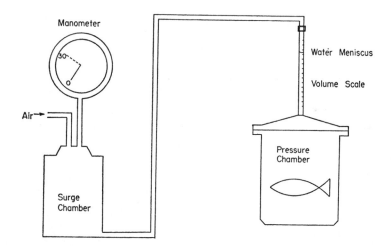

Fig. 1. Apparatus for the determination of swimbladder volume in live fish (modified from Alexander, 1959).

suspended near the bottom. All fish were acclimated for at least 3 weeks to temperatures of 12, 22 or 32°C, with a photoperiod of about 12 hr.

The apparatus used to measure swimbladder volume in live fish (Fig. 1) is similar to that described by Alexander (1959). If one measures the decrease in the volume of a fish subjected to a known increase in pressure, the volume of gas initially present in the swimbladder can be calculated, according to the formula:

$$V_0(\text{ml}) = \frac{P_1(V_0 - V_1)}{P_1 - P_0},$$

where V_0 is the swimbladder volume and $(V_0 - V_1)$, the decrease in volume due to the increase in pressure from P_0 to P_1. Swimbladder gases were analyzed for oxygen, carbon dioxide and nitrogen, using Krogh's gas microanalyzer (Hoar & Hickman, 1967). All gas volumes were corrected to STP.

Values are given as mean ± standard error (based on six to ten measurements), and statistical comparisons were made using the Student's *t*-test. Means were considered statistically significantly different at $P < 0.05$. All means tested showed homogeneity of variance by the F_{max}-test.

Fish were anaesthetized lightly in MS 222 to immobilize them and then placed in the chamber (P_0). All air bubbles were removed, and the chamber was pressurized to 30 mm Hg (P_1). The decrease in volume (V_0-V_1) was used to calculate swimbladder volume, then 50 per cent of the gas was removed from the bladder with a hypodermic syringe and a fine needle. This long-term equilibrium gas was analyzed for oxygen, carbon dioxide and nitrogen. Total swimbladder volume was redetermined 8, 16 and 24 hr later. After the 24-hr measurement, a second gas sample was taken for analysis. These procedures allowed the calculation of the rate of reinflation (total gas secretion) over the time periods 0–8, 8–16 and 16–24 hr, and the rates of oxygen, carbon dioxide and nitrogen secretion over the time interval 0–24 hr.

RESULTS

The average swimbladder volume for forty-two fish at all temperatures was 8·17 ml/100 g body weight (range 6·65–9·50). Mean volumes for 12, 22, and 32°C respectively, were 8·13, 8·13 and 8·28 ml/100 g body weight. Internal pressure in the bladder did not exceed external pressure.

The rate of total gas secretion (0–24 hr) was significantly slower at 12°C than at the higher temperatures (Fig. 2). Since partial pressures increase as filling progresses, only the early rates of gas secretion can be expected to be maximal; this is apparent in Fig. 3. Filling usually was complete before 24 hr. Consequently, 24 hr rates in Fig. 2 are less than maximal. Early maximal rates of secretion (0–8 hr, Fig. 3) are completely independent of acclimation temperature.

Rates of secretion of the individual gases present in the swimbladder were established only over the time interval of 0–24 hr (Fig. 4). In all cases, the rates of gas secretion at 12°C are significantly different from rates of secretion at 32°C.

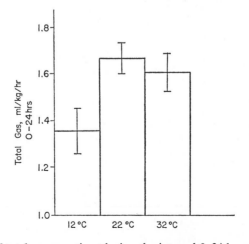

FIG. 2. Rates of total gas secretion, during the interval 0–24 hr, after 50 per cent deflation of the swimbladder. Bars show mean ± standard error.

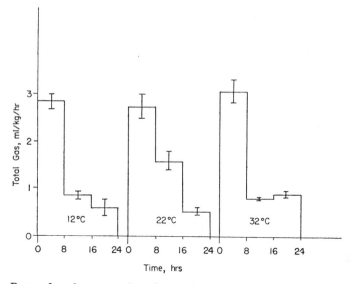

FIG. 3. Rates of total gas secretion, during the time intervals 0–8, 8–16 and 16–24
hr, after 50 per cent deflation of the swimbladder.

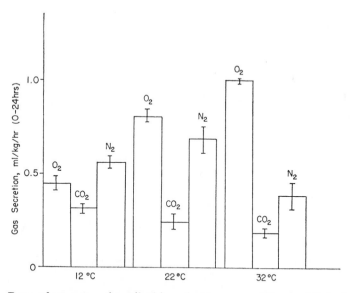

FIG. 4. Rates of oxygen, carbon dioxide and nitrogen secretion during the interval
0–24 hr, after 50 per cent deflation of the swimbladder.

Secretion rates of oxygen and carbon dioxide at 22°C are intermediate between the
rates at higher and lower temperatures, and may differ statistically from rates at
one temperature extreme or the other, but never from both 12 and 32°C simultaneously. The rate of oxygen secretion increases with increasing acclimation
temperature and the rate of carbon dioxide secretion decreases.

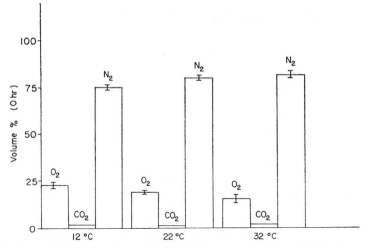

FIG. 5. Percentage composition of swimbladder gas in the bluegill, after long-term equilibration.

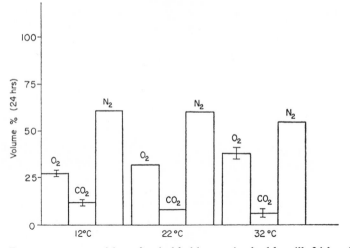

FIG. 6. Percentage composition of swimbladder gas in the bluegill, 24 hr after 50 per cent deflation.

The composition of long-term equilibrium gases (0 time) is shown in Fig. 5. Relatively little carbon dioxide is present, and although the concentrations of nitrogen and oxygen differ statistically between the 12 and 32°C fish, the gas mixtures are similar to air. Composition of gases removed from the swimbladders at 24 hr are given in Fig. 6. These gases represent mixtures of 50 per cent long-term equilibrium gases, plus 50 per cent newly secreted gases. Statistically significant differences exist between the concentrations of oxygen and carbon dioxide at 12 and 32°C, and the mixtures no longer resemble atmospheric air.

Secretion rates of oxygen, carbon dioxide and nitrogen (0–24 hr) were used to calculate the composition of gases secreted into the swimbladder (Table 1). Oxygen concentration is maximum, and carbon dioxide concentration minimum, at the highest temperature. None of the gas mixtures bear any resemblance to air.

TABLE 1—PERCENTAGE COMPOSITION OF NEWLY SECRETED GASES IN THE SWIMBLADDER OF
L. macrochirus*

Acclimation temperature (°C)	O_2	CO_2	N_2
12	33	24	43
22	46	14	40
32	64	12	24
(Air	21	—	79)

*Concentrations are calculated from secretion rates shown in Fig. 4.

As a result of deflation, all fish remained on or near the bottom, and exhibited extreme darkening of the skin. The fish returned to normal swimming, and to normal coloration, when gasbladder inflation was complete.

DISCUSSION

Contrary to our initial hypothesis, the rate of oxygen secretion into the swimbladder increases with increasing temperature. In addition, the secretory rates for nitrogen and carbon dioxide are reduced by increased temperatures.

Several things can be derived from these experiments. Most significant is the temperature independence of maximal secretory rates for total gas, over the range 12–32°C. Such temperature independence would be advantageous to a eurythermal fish such as the bluegill. Variability at later time intervals (8–16 and 16–24 hr) exists only between 22 and 32°C, and may be attributed to the differences in time at which various fish completed reinflation. This temperature independence displayed by the rate of total gas secretion is the result of a balance between reciprocal changes in the rates of oxygen and carbon dioxide secretion. Nitrogen secretion rates change in irregular ways at different acclimation temperatures. This may reflect the passive nature of nitrogen secretion (Wittenberg, 1958).

We suggest the following explanation for the changes found in oxygen and carbon dioxide secretion rates:

(1) Increased oxygen secretion at high temperatures reflects a decrease in the oxygen affinity of haemoglobin. This is a common phenomenon, both in endo- and ecto-therms, and does not represent a change due to differences in acclimation temperature (Prosser & Brown, 1961, p. 216). Increased haemoglobin levels are found in the blood of warm-acclimated trout (DeWilde & Houston, 1967). This increases the oxygen transport capacity of the blood at high temperatures and may contribute to increased oxygen secretion in warm-acclimated bluegills.

(2) Decreased carbon dioxide secretion at high temperatures reflects a decrease in plasma bicarbonate concentration. Plasma bicarbonate concentrations in frogs, toads and turtles decrease as the temperature rises (Howell et al., 1970). Since the work of D'Aoust (1970) suggests that lactic acid, in excess of buffering capacity of plasma bicarbonate, is required to permit oxygen secretion (via the Bohr and Root effects) bicarbonate concentration seems to be the factor limiting carbon dioxide secretion in these experiments.

The heart rate of bluegills acclimated to 25°C has been shown to be about three times faster than the rate at 13°C (Spitzer *et al.*, 1969). If blood flow to the rete mirabile–gas gland complex is increased accordingly, it is to be expected that gas secretion would be facilitated. Our data show only a twofold increase in oxygen secretion, and a reduction in carbon dioxide secretion of 50 per cent. In a closely related species, *L. gibbosus*, taken from these latitudes, Roberts (1967) has shown that the cardiac rate exhibits a marked maximum near 23°C. Heart rates at higher and lower acclimation temperatures are much lower. This may mean that nitrogen secretion rates vary more in relation to blood flow, than do the rates of oxygen and carbon dioxide secretion.

During inflation, all fish showed darkening of the skin. A cholinergic inflation reflex has been proposed for the swimbladder (Fänge, 1966). Inflation may result in a generalized parasympathetic activation, and parasympathetic innervation is known to disperse pigment in the melanocytes of many fishes (Florey, 1966, p. 360). This hypothesis is consistent with the inability of a sympathetic hormone (adrenalin) to alter lactate production in the isolated gas gland of the bluegill (Deck, 1970).

Acknowledgements—Part of this study was carried out as a class project in comparative physiology, conducted by R. A. McNabb. We wish to thank the other class members, Donald E. Spiers, Donley Hill and Michael Horrell, for some of the early measurements, We are indebted especially to Mr. W. T. Waller for his assistance with computer techniques.

REFERENCES

ALEXANDER R. McN, (1959) The physical properties of the swimbladder in intact Cypriniformes. *J. exp. Biol.* **36**, 315–332.

ALEXANDER R. McN. (1966) Physical aspects of swimbladder function. *Biol. Rev.* **41**, 141–176.

BRAWN V. M. (1969) Buoyancy of Atlantic and Pacific herring. *J. Fish. Res. Bd Can.* **26**, 2077–2091.

D'AOUST B. G. (1970) The role of lactic acid in gas secretion in the teleost swimbladder. *Comp. Biochem. Physiol.* **32**, 637–668.

DECK J. E. (1970) Lactic acid production by the swimbladder gas gland *in vitro* as influenced by glucagon and epinephrine. *Comp. Biochem. Physiol.* **34**, 317–324.

DEWILDE M. A. & HOUSTON A. H. (1967) Hematological aspects of the thermo-acclimatory process in the rainbow trout. *J. Fish. Res. Bd Can.* **24**, 2267–2281.

FÄNGE R. (1966) Physiology of the swimbladder. *Physiol. Rev.* **41**, 141–176.

FLOREY E. (1966) *An Introduction to General and Comparative Animal Physiology.* W. B. Saunders. Philadelphia.

HOAR W. S. & HICKMAN C. P., JR. (1967) *A Laboratory Companion for General and Comparative Physiology.* Prentice-Hall, Englewood Cliffs, N.J.

HOCHACHKA P. W. (1967) Organization of metabolism during temperature compensation. In *Molecular Mechanisms of Temperature Adaptation* (Edited by PROSSER C. L.). Publication No. 84, A.A.A.S., Washington, D.C.

HOWELL B. J., BAUMGARDNER F. W., BONDI K. & RAHN H. (1970) Acid–base balance in cold-blooded vertebrates as a function of body temperature. *Am. J. Physiol.* **218**, 600–606.

MALINS D. C. & BARONE A. (1970) Glyceryl ether metabolism: regulation of buoyancy in dogfish, *Squalus acanthias. Science, N.Y.* **167**, 79–80.

O'HARA J. (1968) The influence of weight and temperature on the metabolic rate of sunfish. *Ecology* **49**, 159–161.

PROSSER C. L. & BROWN F. A., JR. (1961) *Comparative Animal Physiology.* W. B. Saunders, Philadelphia.

ROBERTS J. L. (1967) Metabolic compensations for temperature in sunfish. In *Molecular Mechanisms of Temperature Adaptation* (Edited by PROSSER C. L.). Publication No. 84, A.A.A.S., Washington, D.C.

SPITZER K. W., MARVIN D. E., JR. & HEATH A. G. (1969) The effect of temperature on the respiratory and cardiac response of the bluegill sunfish to hypoxia. *Comp. Biochem. Physiol.* **30**, 83–90.

WITTENBERG J. B. (1958) The secretion of inert gas into the swim-bladder of fish. *J. gen. Physiol.* **41**, 783–804.

Key Word Index—Temperature; gas secretion; swimbladder; fish; bluegill sunfish; *Lepomis macrochirus.*

BLOOD pH EFFECTS IN EIGHT FISHES FROM THE TELEOSTEAN FAMILY SCORPAENIDAE*

GEORGE WHITNEY BAINES

Marine Science Institute, Department of Biological Sciences, University of California, Santa Barbara, CA 93106, U.S.A.

(Received 3 June 1974)

Abstract—1. The effects of changes in pH on the oxygen equilibria of erythrocytes of *Scorpaena guttata* and seven species of *Sebastes* (Teleostei: Scorpaenidae) from the coast of California were investigated.

2. Erythrocyte suspensions were equilibrated with various concentrations of oxygen in a flowing gas tonometer and the per cent saturation was measured photometrically in the Soret band.

3. Results show that the magnitude of the Root effect varies consistently with the requirements of the swimbladder filling mechanism. Sedentary fish that live in shallow water have smaller pH effects whereas active forms from deeper water have greater pH effects. *Scorpaena guttata*, which lacks a swimbladder, has the smallest pH effect.

INTRODUCTION

THE BUOYANCY of most teleostean fishes is maintained by swimbladders that are inflated with gases that come from the blood. Oxygen is the principal gas transferred from the blood into the bladder. Therefore, the blood and the oxygen it contains play a major role in hydrostatic maintenance, especially in deep-living fishes, which must maintain swimbladder volume at high ambient pressure, and in vertically migrating fishes, which must adjust volume to varying pressure (Scholander & van Dam, 1953).

The depth at which a given species lives and its patterns of activity are related to interspecific differences in oxygen affinity of the blood (Manwell, 1957). For example, a deep-water fish with a swimbladder needs a mechanism for releasing oxygen from the blood at relatively high partial pressure to fill its swimbladder. But a co-occurring species without a swimbladder needs only to release oxygen at low partial pressure to supply tissue respiration.

The affinity of blood for oxygen and other ligands is altered substantially by variables of blood chemistry, such as pH, salt concentration and temperature, all of which affect the three-dimensional conformation of the hemoglobin molecule (Antonini, 1967). Of major importance to the animal is the so-called "Bohr effect", originally described as the effect of CO_2 on blood–oxygen affinity (Bohr *et al.*, 1904), but later attributed to changes in pH (Barcroft, 1928). However, CO_2 does have some effect aside from pH changes (Riggs, 1960). In the normal or "alkaline" Bohr effect, decreasing pH lowers the affinity of hemoglobin for oxygen, so that the oxygen dissociation curve (per cent oxygenated hemoglobin plotted as a function of tissue pO_2) shifts to the right. This assures a steady and sufficient supply of oxygen to active tissues, which generate large amounts of CO_2 and lower the ambient pH (Riggs, 1959).

In fishes, therefore, the Bohr effect may be a basis for releasing oxygen from the blood to inflate the swimbladder. Early studies indicated that a relatively high pCO_2 not only produced a larger Bohr effect in fish than in mammals (Krogh & Leitch, 1919), but also seemed to depress the oxygen-binding capacity absolutely (Root, 1931). This latter apparent property of fish blood to remain unsaturated in the presence of relatively high oxygen tensions is called the "Root effect". It is distinguished from the Bohr effect, under which the blood can always ultimately be saturated. Further studies with more fishes showed that the Root effect: (1) occurs at ambient pO_2's exceeding that of air (0·2 atm) up to at least 1 atm (Green & Root, 1933) and sometimes in excess of 140 atm (Scholander & van Dam, 1954); (2) occurs in hemoglobin as well as whole blood (Root & Irving, 1941); (3) results primarily from lowered pH rather than from increasing pCO_2 (Root & Irving, 1943); (4) varies in magnitude among species with different modes of life (Hall & McCutcheon, 1938; Root & Irving, 1940, 1941, 1943); and (5) is associated with the presence of a swimbladder (Manwell, 1960; Fauge, 1966).

Even so, the Root effect disappears in some cases at very high oxygen tensions (up to 140 atm have been used), such as those in the swimbladders of fish that live at great depths (Scholander & van Dam, 1954). Therefore, it should probably be considered as an extension of the Bohr effect, rather than an independent process (Riggs, 1965). But such fish have swimbladders filled with 80–90% oxygen (Scholander & van Dam, 1953; Kanwisher & Ebeling, 1957), so the question remains as to just how very deep-water fish fill their swimbladders.

In any event, the Root effect probably releases oxygen in the rete mirabile (a counter current multiplier) at sufficient pressure to fill the swimbladder of fish living in shallow to moderate depths (Kuhn *et al.*, 1963; Alexander, 1966; Steen, 1970). If so, it should vary predictably in magnitude among related species having different depth regimes.

* This research was supported by the following grants: NSF Sea Grant Program GH 43, NSF GH 95 and USDC 2-35208-6.

From *Comp. Biochem. Physiol.* 51A:833–843. Reprinted by permission of Pergamon Press Ltd., Oxford, England.

Most previous comparative studies of the Root effect in fishes involved more or less unrelated species. Therefore, to further substantiate the swimbladder-filling function of the Root effect, I tried to find out if it does indeed vary in a logical way within a relatively homogeneous taxonomic group of fishes. Specifically, I tested the hypothesis that the Root effect should (1) increase with the characteristic depth of habitat and/or bathymetric activity of selected species of congeneric rockfishes that occur off Santa Barbara, and (2) that it is least developed in the sympatric California scorpionfish which is in the same family (Scorpaenidae) as the rockfishes, but which lacks a swimbladder.

The rockfishes comprise a large assemblage of morphologically similar fishes, which are mostly restricted to the Pacific coast of North America. Why so many similar species can live together in the same general area has been the subject of much speculation (Chen, 1971). Although adjacent species may resemble each other anatomically, however, they may differ substantially in their physiological responses to, for example, different depth and temperature regimes. This study compares such a response in blood–gas chemistry among rockfishes living at different depths.

MATERIALS AND METHODS

Fish were obtained by hook and line from off the coast of Santa Barbara, California, either (1) from a boat by fishing in areas with large concentrations of rockfish such as oil platforms, reefs and kelp beds, or (2) underwater by a Scuba diver holding a short pole with a baited hook in front of certain desired fish. The latter method was especially effective for catching *Scorpaena guttata* and other bottom forms. All fish were brought back alive in aerated tanks and maintained in flowing sea water tanks at the marine laboratory at the University of California, Santa Barbara. The fishes were observed underwater at the time of capture and in aquaria at the marine laboratory. Most fish were maintained for about 1 week before they were used for experimentation, so that they could recover from being hooked and captured. For a few fishes which were tested on the same day as capture, the results were the same as with the fish held for a while. Once the fish start feeding, usually within the first week, they can be kept for extended periods of time (over 2 months for most). Repeated samples can be drawn from the same fish, allowing 1 week or longer intervals between samples, if the fish is fairly large (over 6 in.).

Eight species of fish from the family Scorpaenidae were used in this study: *Scorpaena guttata*, and seven species of *Sebastes* (*S. rastrelliger*, *S. carnatus*, *S. chrysomelas*, *S. vexillaris*, *S. mystinus*, *S. serranoides* and *S. entomelas*).

In these experiments, erythrocyte suspension instead of hemoglobin solutions were used to investigate the relation between oxygen affinity and pH. Erythrocytes are more representative of whole blood because: (1) the erythrocyte cell membrane alters the properties and arrangement of fish hemoglobin (Black & Irving, 1938; Steen & Turitzin, 1968; Thomas, 1971); (2) the Root effect begins about one pH unit higher in whole blood or erythrocytes than in hemoglobin solutions (Root & Irving, 1943); (3) phosphorylated organic compounds normally present within the erythrocyte cause changes in the oxygen affinity, increase the Bohr effect and modify the heme–heme interactions (Benesch & Benesch, 1967; Gillen & Riggs, 1971); and (4) certain other chemicals modify the equilibrium curve differently in whole blood

than in hemoglobin solutions (Agostoni *et al.*, 1973).

The blood sample was taken from the heart of the fish immediately before the experiment. Blood was drawn into a syringe with heparinized culture medium, then diluted with additional medium and centrifuged lightly (500–750 rev/min for 2 min at 5°C). After the first centrifugation the cells were washed or resuspended gently in fresh unheparinized medium, then centrifuged again. After the supernatant was drawn off, the cells were resuspended and transferred to a tonometer flask with a photometer cuvette attached where the pH was measured on a Beckman Zeromatic or Metrohm E300 glass electrode meter and adjusted to the desired value with diluted HCl or NaOH.

Considerable effort went into the selection and preparation of media. The "Ringer's" solution suggested for marine teleosts in Young (1933) and Pantin (1948) proved insufficient. The cells would not last the 3–4 hr necessary for an experiment to be completed. In most cases hemolysis would occur very slowly but constantly. A full balanced salt solution adapted for marine teleosts was used (modified Hank's BSS from Wolf & Quimbly, 1970). Even this medium had to be modified by leaving out the carbonate ion and rebalancing for sodium, then adding 0·01 molar Bis–Tris buffer to stabilize the pH (see Table 1 for formulation of the medium).

The samples were equilibrated with various gas mixtures that were allowed to flow through the flasks containing the samples. This system of flowing gas mixtures (as compared with non-flowing systems of gas mixtures that sit over the sample) is more accurate for this type of experiment because it eliminates some critical problems. Sources of error in the non-flowing systems are: (1) vessel volume is quite critical and can be very difficult to control if the vessel contains rubber parts or sliding parts; (2) the usual method of changing the pO_2 of the gas mixture by injecting small increments of pure oxygen into the vessel after it has been flushed with pure nitrogen is difficult to do accurately, especially at

Table 1. Hank's BSS medium modified for preserving blood of marine teleostean fishes

Constituent	Amount
NaCl	12.309 grams
KCl	0.40
Glucose	1.00
Na_2HPO_4	0.0322
KH_2PO_4	0.06
$MgSO_4 \cdot 7H_2O$	0.10
$MgSO_4 \cdot 6H_2O$	0.10
$CaCl_2 \cdot 2H_2O$	0.19
Bis–Tris	2.092
(bis(2-hydroxyethyl)imine-tris(hydroxy-methyl)methane)	
H_2O	1.0 liter

Note: 1 mg of sodium heparin USP (148,000 units activity per gram from porcine intestinal mucosa) was added per ml. of medium when first drawing the blood sample.

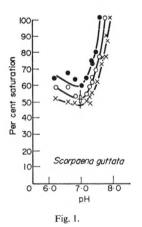

Fig. 1.

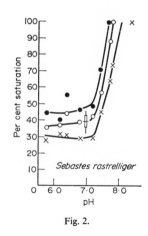

Fig. 2.

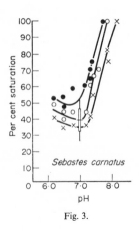

Fig. 3.

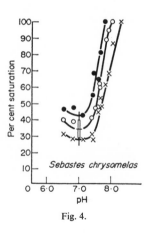

Fig. 4.

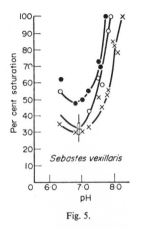

Fig. 5.

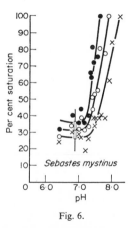

Fig. 6.

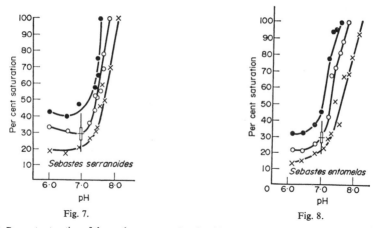

Fig. 7.　　　　　　　　　　　　　　　　Fig. 8.

Figs. 1–8. Per cent saturation of the erythrocytes as a function of pH. A separate figure is presented for each species of rockfish in the study. Each line represents the per cent saturation of the erythrocytes when exposed to constant pO_2 at various pH's. ●, 21% O_2 (air) (~ 156 mm Hg) balance N_2; ○, 10% O_2 (~ 75 mm Hg) balance N_2; ×, 5% O_2 (~ 37.5 mm Hg) balance N_2. (Lines fitted by hand.)

low pO_2's; and (3) the hemoglobin binding the oxygen changes the pO_2, so that to compensate for this, either a systematic error must be derived and added or the vessel must be made large so that the error is minimal. The "flow-through" method has the disadvantages that the gases must be humidified and equilibrated for temperature and that flowing gases will interact with media and cause pH changes unless adequate buffering is provided.

The erythrocytes were equilibrated in three-necked flasks (50 cm³), which served as tonometer vessels. The flasks had a spectrophotometer cuvette attached to a ground glass fitting in one neck and the other two necks sealed with rubber syringe caps. Gas mixtures were injected through one rubber cap and exhausted through a needle in the other, so that the gases passed over the suspended erythrocytes as the flasks were gently shaken back and forth in the water-bath. The water-bath was maintained at 10°C and could hold three flasks at a time. The gases were humidified by bubbling through distilled water in tubes that were also in the water-bath, thus bringing the gases to the same temperature as the samples.

Thirty min were found to be more than adequate for all except the initial equilibration with pure nitrogen, for which 1 hr was allowed. Varying the order in which the gas mixtures were presented had no noticeable effect on the results, so that a normal order of presentation was conveniently established from lowest to highest per cent oxygen.

Various gas mixtures were used to produce the changes in pO_2. These were made in gas cylinders and measured on a Varian Aerograph gas chromatograph with two columns, one of silica gel and the other of Molecular Sieve 5A. This machine was able to measure the concentration of all physiological gases (O_2, N_2, CO_2, CO, etc.) very accurately ($\pm 0.01\%$). Mixtures varied from as little as 1% O_2 mixed with nitrogen to pure oxygen. Seven mixtures were commonly used: pure N_2 and 1, 2, 5, 10, 21 and 100% O_2.

The absorbance of the erythrocyte suspension was determined with a Beckman Ratio Recording Spectrophotometer DK-2A. This instrument has a refrigerated cuvette holder that was connected to the water-bath. All measurements were made at 10°C. This instrument was used to plot out spectral absorption at wave lengths varying from 700 to 350 nm. From this plot, per cent saturation and baselines were determined for the sample

in the Soret band at 435 nm (cf. Manwell, 1957a). Justifications and criticisms of these methods are found in Riggs (1951, 1965, 1970), Manwell (1957a, 1958), Enoki & Tyuma (1964) and Anderson & Antonini (1968).

At the end of most experimental runs the erythrocyte suspension was (1) re-equilibrated with pure nitrogen to check for the presence of methemoglobin, which if present would disqualify the run, and (2) recentrifuged to check for cellular breakage, by scanning the supernatant fluid; if no breakage had occurred then no hemoglobin spectra would appear. At the end of every run, the pH of the sample was checked, and a variation of no more than 0.05 pH units was allowed. Approximately 2000 determinations were made on just over 300 samples of blood.

Blood smears were taken for all species, stained in Wright's stain and compared. No significant interspecific differences in cell morphology or counts were observed.

RESULTS

The findings of this study indicate that: (1) all of the species of *Sebastes* tested have strong Bohr and Root effects, (2) *Scorpaena guttata*, which lacks a swimbladder, has greatly reduced Bohr and Root effects and (3) within the genus *Sebastes* the magnitude of the pH effects correlate with depth of normal habitat of the fish and with increased activity of the fish. *Sebastes* that live at greater depths have larger pH effects on the oxygen affinity of the erythrocytes than other *Sebastes* that live normally in shallower water. Normally sluggish species tend to have lesser pH effects on their erythrocytes than fish which normally lead more active lives.

In order to make interspecific comparisons more obvious, the data supporting these findings are plotted in curves showing the per cent saturation of the erythrocytes as a function of pH (Figs. 1–8). From these curves it can be seen that the group of *Sebastes* is quite distinct from *Scorpaena guttata*. These curves clearly show the range of pH effects and the critical values for each of the pO_2's used, and show the pH effect on the hemoglobin within the erthrocytes like a typical enzyme equilibrium system. For each of the species, curves are plotted for constant pO_2 levels of 5% (~ 37.5 mm Hg), 10% (~ 75 mm Hg) and 21% (air or ~ 156 mm Hg) oxygen. With greater pH effect, the curve is depressed more in its horizontal segment, meaning that the per cent saturation of the erythrocyte is lower at pH's of 7.1 or less. Further lowering of the pH below 6.0 causes changes due to cellular breakage and methemoglobin formation. At the pH 7.0 level of the 10% oxygen curve, the mean, its 95 per cent confidence interval and range of ten or more experimental runs are graphed. These are collected and compared in Fig. 9.

Per cent saturation of erythrocytes equilibrated with 10% oxygen at a pH of 7.0.

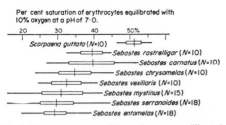

Fig. 9. Per cent saturation of the erythrocytes equilibrated with 10% oxygen at a pH of 7.0 for all species in the study. (The middle horizontal line represents the mean value, the box shows the extent of the 95 per cent confidence interval of the mean and the vertical lines represent the total range of the samples.)

From these results, the species of *Sebastes* can be ranked in order of increasing erythrocyte pH effects. This can most clearly be seen by examining Fig. 9 which shows the per cent saturation of the erythrocytes equilibrated with 10% oxygen at a pH of 7.0 (these are the distribution figures from Figs. 1 to 8). The pH of 7.0 was chosen because it represents a point where the pH depression of the oxygen affinity is complete for the erythrocytes. The use of the 10% oxygen level was chosen for convenience and because it represents a reasonable mode among the values of pO_2's that the blood in these fish presumably encounters. Five, 21 or 100% oxygen levels could have been presented as well but show the same relationship, and 10% pO_2 seem to give the most consistent results. By choosing one value such as 10% oxygen, it is much easier to quantify the interspecific differences in a way that can be easily compared.

Of all the samples represented in Fig. 9 the means differed significantly among all species (ANOV, $P = 0.001$), and among the seven species of *Sebastes* without *S. guttata* ($P = 0.005$) (Table 2).

Since these methods of graphically presenting the results are not standard, a more common form is presented in Fig. 10 in order that the results may be compared to others in the literature. This presents the results by graphing the function, log $p50$ (the pO_2 at which the erythrocytes are 50% saturated with oxygen) vs. the pH. Interspecific differences between these closely related species are not as apparent here because the functions are all straight lines within the ranges of variables investigated (pH 6.0–8.5 and pO_2's from 15 to 750 mm Hg). In this function, rather large changes in the pH

effects are represented in small displacements of the lines to the right. In Fig. 10 *S. rastrelliger* shows greater pH effects on its erythrocytes than does *S. guttata*. Other *Sebastes* species have lines resembling that of *S. rastrelliger* but shifted slightly further to the right.

Table 2. Analysis of variance—all subjects from Fig. 9

	df	SS	MS	F_s
Variation among species	7	4405.4	629.3	11.7
Variation within species	94	5052.8	53.8	
Total variation	101	9458.1		

$$F_{.001\ (7,60)} = 4.09$$

Analysis of Variance – <u>Sebastes</u> species only from Fig. 9

	df	SS	MS	F_s
Variation among species	6	1364.0	227.3	3.8
Variation within species	85	4987.9	58.7	
Total variation	91	6351.9		

$$F_{.005\ (6,60)} = 3.49$$

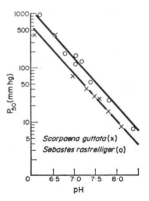

Fig. 10. $p50$ as a function of pH for the California scorpionfish *S. guttata* and the Grass rockfish *S. rastrelliger*. ($p50$ is the pO_2 at which the erythrocytes are 50% saturated with oxygen.) ×, *S. guttata*; ○, *S. rastrelliger*. (Lines fitted by hand.)

DISCUSSION

The results of this study show a clear relationship between the magnitude of the pH effects seen in the erythrocytes and the expected activity of the gas-secreting apparatus of the swimbladder. This has been shown before in rather diverse groups of fish with greatly differing ancestry and anatomy, but here it can be seen that differences in magnitude exist even among very closely related fish with similar anatomy. This indicated that changes in some of these fundamental blood properties have occurred to adapt closely related fishes to characteristically different regimes of activity and habitat.

To reach this conclusion an understanding of the possible uses of the pH effects in the blood is necessary. The most frequently mentioned function of the Root effect is filling of the swimbladder. The fact that a small change in pH can cause dissociation of large amounts of oxygen indicates that the Root effect is involved with secretion of oxygen into the gas bladder. Also fishes that show a marked Root effect generally have well-developed gas bladders, where rapid filling requires a greater release of oxygen from the blood (Root, 1931; Root *et al.*, 1938). Manwell (1960) concluded that the Root effect is part of the gas bladder filling mechanism.

The swimbladder and associated structures seem to be the primary site of action for the Root effect. There are other possibilities, however, that are only rarely mentioned in the literature. Some of these should be discussed along with the reasons why they are not considered as being of major importance.

Perhaps the Root effect is involved in tissue metabolism, but its magnitude and variability seem too large to serve any such general metabolic purpose. Why would some species need it for general use and others not? Other possibilities include its use by some other specialized organ that requires greater concentrations of oxygen than most tissues. Such an organ might be recognized by the presence of intensive vascularization specialized to increase blood flow and concentrate oxygen (retia). In addition to the universal association of retia mirabilia with the gas bladder, such vascular counter-current exchange mechanisms are found in the red muscles of certain fishes, notably the tuna and some sharks, and in the choroid coat of the eye. The retia of the red muscle is probably involved in heat rather than oxygen exchange (Carey & Teal, 1969) and occur in non-teleosts without gas bladders, such as the Mako shark where the Root effect is unknown. Also the thickness of the capillary walls is probably too great to allow efficient oxygen transfer (Carey, 1973). The choroidal rete is a logical site of action for the Root effect. High oxygen tensions occur in the retinal areas of some fish that have these structures (Wittenberg & Wittenberg, 1962) and these are necessary for the normal function of the retina for at least some teleosts (Fonner *et al.*, 1973). However, the tautog (*Tautoga onitis*), the toadfish (*Opsanus tau*) and the goosefish (*Lophius americus*), which show marked Root effects (Green & Root, 1933), have relatively low oxygen tensions in their eyes (Wittenberg & Wittenberg, 1962). All things considered, therefore, the gas bladder seems to be the major site of action.

Current knowledge of the filling mechanism of the swimbladder has recently been reviewed by Steen (1970) and by Satchell (1971). The process of gas secretion involves the rete mirabile and chemical phenomena in the blood. The rete mirabile, which is closely associated with the gas gland of the swimbladder, produces a constant diffusion gradient. The rete works as a counter-current multiplier of gas partial pressures (primarily O_2, N_2 and CO_2) that creates large increases in gas pressure in the distal "hairpin" end of the system at the swimbladder. A mathematical model of how the rete works was suggested by Kuhn *et al.* (1963) and revised by Alexander (1966). Scholander (1954) described the anatomy of the system. The second part of the filling mechanism is the chemical system

of gas release, which most importantly decreases the affinity of blood for oxygen at lower pH's (Root and Bohr effects). Release of oxygen into the efferent ends of the juxtaposed loops of the rete creates the efferent–afferent pO_2 gradient that effects the counter-current multiplier. Blood in the distal loop of the rete is acidified, as carbon dioxide and lactic acid enters from the actively metabolizing cells of the surrounding gas gland (Ball *et al.*, 1955). The increasing concentration of hydrogen ions, coming mainly from the lactic acid source, causes the blood to release oxygen, mainly via the Root effect. Also, the increasing concentration of lactate reduces the solubility of all gases dissolved in the blood so that they are "salted out".

Scholander & van Dam (1954) questioned the overriding role of the Root effect in maintaining the counter-current multiplier when they showed that, at very high pO_2's, as would occur in the gas bladder of deep-sea fish, the Root effect seems to disappear in some species. But these results and others do not deny the importance of the Root effect because they represent an equilibrium state rather than a dynamic state as would be found in the blood flowing within the rete. That is, equilibrium is probably never really reached under natural conditions. The importance of this concept was demonstrated by Berg & Steen (1968), who showed that the rate of release of oxygen at lowered pH (Root off-shift) is greatly increased, whereas the rate of uptake of O_2 by the hemoglobin (Root on-shift) is greatly decreased. This rate differential means that blood releases oxygen very rapidly at first encounter with low pH, but takes up oxygen much more slowly as the pH rises in the blood leaving the rete. In the eel, the Root off-shift has a half time of 0.05 sec, whereas the on-shift has a half time of 10–20 sec (Berg & Steen, 1968).

From published studies (Steen, 1963, 1970) then, the filling mechanism is summarized as follows. The arterial blood entering the rete mirabile is well oxygenated at normal pH. As it flows into the afferent loops at the rete it receives oxygen, carbon dioxide and acid from the juxtaposed efferent vessels of the rete. As it nears the hairpin end it is enriched with oxygen as its pH decreases, causing the Root off-shift to rapidly dissociate oxygen from the hemoglobin. The resulting multiplied increase in pO_2 causes oxygen to diffuse into the gas bladder, probably taking along with it other inert gases as well. The increase in lactate "salts out" all gases, whose tensions are multiplied in the distal rete. In this way, nitrogen, for example, may also diffuse into the bladder. As the blood returns via the efferent portion of the rete, it has a very high oxygen tension, but most of the oxygen is in solution outside of the erythrocytes and returns to the hemoglobin very slowly during the Root on-shift. The oxygen and the acid diffuse back into the afferent portions of the rete and continue the process. Because of the longer duration of the Root on-shift there is little chance of the hemoglobin recombining with the oxygen until a blood cell has been swept out of the rete system. Thus oxygen and other gases are left behind to recirculate through the rete mirabile or diffuse into the bladder. It was demonstrated by Berg & Steen (1968) that the pO_2 of the efferent blood in an actively secreting system decreases away from the rete. This shows that the Root on-shift was slowly allowing the small portion of dissolved oxygen remaining in the plasma to recombine with the hemoglobin but not until after it had left the rete.

There are a number of ways that fishes could change the ability to inflate the swimbladder or increase the pressure of the contained gases. All of these approaches seem to be on a species-wide basis, and there seems to be no indication in the literature or in the present experiments that an individual fish can change these blood properties over a period of time. Manwell (1957b, 1958) showed that some fish do have ontogenetic changes in their blood properties but this is also a species-wide phenomenon and not the adaptation of an individual fish to external conditions. One way that the rate of filling can be altered is by evolution of changes in the anatomy of dimensions of the rete system. Changes in the length or number of capillaries would modify the filling capacity. A number of these variations can be seen in any of the anatomical discussions of the rete system (Jones & Marshall, 1953; Marshall, 1966; Satchell, 1971). Another alternative is to change the capacity of the blood to release oxygen under the conditions present in the rete. Fishes show great variation in this capacity, i.e. in their Root effect (Root, 1931; Green & Root, 1933; Willmer, 1935; Hall & McCutcheon, 1938; Fish, 1956).

There are two variations in the way in which evolution of differences in the magnitude of the Root effect might come about. The first would involve changes in amino acid sequences or chemical groups, which have been recently identified as accounting for at least 75 per cent of the Bohr effect of mammalian hemoglobin (Kilmartin & Rossi-Bernardi, 1969; Perutz et al., 1969). Presumably the same sites are responsible for the Root effect. Changes in these or other sites that alter the pH-sensitive parts of the protein moiety of the hemoglobin molecule would affect the magnitude and rate of the Root effect. But direct evidence for this from fish is still lacking. The second way, which really includes the former, would involve the differential action of multiple hemoglobins. The blood of most fish contains more than one kind of hemoglobin (Buhler & Shanks, 1959; Buhler, 1963; Giovenco et al., 1970; Anderson et al., 1973) and at least most of the members of the family Scorpaenidae have more than one hemoglobin normally present in their blood (Tsuyuki et al., 1968). For many fresh water fishes, it has been shown that one hemoglobin type shows neither Root nor Bohr effect, whereas another shows large Root and Bohr effects (Binotti et al., 1971; Powers, 1972; Gillen & Riggs, 1973). In these fish changes in the magnitude of the overall Root effect could have evolved by changing the proportions of these hemoglobin types. Forms requiring a greater Root effect could alter the proportions in favour of the Root-active types.

The Root effect is probably disadvantageous to fish that do not need it. Indeed, blood that so suddenly releases its oxygen is probably non-adaptive for normal tissues, where a more gradual release of oxygen would better serve tissue metabolism. Each species of fish probably acquires the level of Root effect needed to release oxygen to its swimbladder, depending on its particular lifestyle and buoyancy requirements.

The determination of the magnitude of the Root effect from erythrocytes rather than hemolysates or extracted hemoglobin represents an important step toward the understanding of the system of gas release as it exists in the whole organism. As the effects of the various chemical components within the erythrocyte upon the hemoglobin molecule are discovered, it is becoming more and more evident that the behavior of the hemoglobin is highly modified when it is within the erythrocyte. Indeed, when the Root effect was first studied it was thought only to occur in the whole blood but not in hemolysates of some fish (Root & Irving, 1940, 1941). It was later found that there was indeed a Root effect in hemolysates but that it occurred up to one full pH unit lower than in erythrocytes (Root & Irving, 1943). This property of the erythrocyte bringing the Root effect up to within the normal physiological pH range of the blood was used as evidence by Manwell (1957a) of the importance of the effect on the blood physiology of fish.

Phosphorylated organic compounds that are normally present in the erythrocyte have been demonstrated to greatly modify the oxygen affinity. Benesch & Benesch (1967) demonstrated a depression in the oxygen affinity caused by 2,3 diphosphoglycerate in human erythrocytes and Gillen & Riggs (1971) showed that ATP had a similar effect within the erythrocytes of a cichlid fish, as well as causing an increase in the Bohr effect and modifying the heme–heme interactions of the hemoglobin molecules. Further discussion of some of the properties of the erythrocyte that affect oxygen equilibria can be found in Riggs (1965).

A word of caution should be injected here. Just as studies from hemoglobin solutions are not completely comparable with studies from erythrocytes, extrapolation from erythrocyte studies to whole blood and especially whole blood within capillaries of the animal should not be made carelessly. It has been shown that the oxygen affinities of human erythrocytes, at least, are changed when they are within small capillaries. Distortions of the cell membrane seem responsible (Drake et al., 1963). From this work and the work of Krogh (1929) which showed that considerable distortion of erythrocytes was necessary for passage through the smaller capillaries, it should be realized that some modifications of the properties of erythrocytes and hemoglobin are expected within the animal.

Within the group of seven species of *Sebastes* in the present study, there seem to be two factors that influence the degree of the Root effect: (1) bathymetric distribution and (2) activity regime. Generally the data show that within this group, the deeper-living species have the greater Root effect. This is best demonstrated by comparing the shallower species *S. rastrelliger* and *S. carnatus* with the deeper species *S. vexillaris* (Table 3). All three species are fairly sedentary but differ in vertical distribution with the depth of the bottom on which they live (Limbaugh, 1955; Phillips, 1957; Quast, 1968; Larson, 1972). The shallowest-living species, *S. rastrelliger*, has the smallest Root effect, while the

Table 3. Summary of activity, depth regime and pH effects of the species studied

	gas bladder	active swimmer	depth*	mean % saturation with 10% O_2 at pH 7.0
Scorpaena guttata	no	no	25	51.21
Sebastes rastrelliger	yes	no	25	39.42
" carnatus	yes	no	30	39.49
" chrysomelas	yes	no	20	34.77
" vexillaris	yes	no	50	32.32
" mystinus	yes	yes	50	31.05
" serranoides	yes	yes	80	29.77
" entomelas	yes	yes	120	29.26

* Greatest depth taken according to Phillips (1957).

deepest-living species, *S. vexillaris*, has the largest effect. This is expected because the greater the depth at which the fish lives, the greater the ambient pressure against which its bladder must be inflated and, therefore, the greater the partial pressure that must be generated by its filling mechanism. Also, the data show that more active fish, which swim up and down in the water column, have a greater Root effect. The body form of these active swimmers is much more streamlined and laterally compressed than the other fishes that sit on the bottom (Limbaugh, 1955; Phillips, 1957). *S. mystinus*, which often commutes between the surface and bottom at 30–40 ft depths, has a greater Root effect than *S. vexillaris*, which is restricted to the bottom in the same locality. This is expected because the greater the regular vertical excursion of a fish, the more it must regulate its swimbladder volume by deflating through the "oval" in the bladder wall, then inflating through the rete and gas gland.

From Scuba observations, as well as observations in aquaria, it is easy to see why the "bottom-sitting" species can make do with a smaller filling mechanism. They tend to remain almost motionless on the bottom and move only when disturbed. They apparently wait for their prey or slowly forage about the bottom within a limited area at a more or less constant depth (Ralph Larson, personal communication). While doing this, they probably adjust their buoyancy so that it is slightly on the negative side. Occasionally, they become neutrally buoyant and "hang" next to kelp or rocks, but when doing this they remain as though suspended and do not move rapidly upward. Having this activity pattern, the "bottom-sitters" need not make rapid or drastic adjustments in swimbladder volume.

Groups of active "midwater" rockfishes (*S. mystinus*, *S. serranoides* and *S. entomelas*) can be seen constantly swimming and foraging (Limbaugh, 1955; Hobson, 1965; Quast, 1968). They pursue discrete prey (bite at fishing lures) and often change their foraging depth during the day (Cannon, 1956). Obviously, they must often adjust their swimbladder volume if they are to remain nearly neutrally buoyant and so minimize the energy cost of foraging. The activity regimes, depth of habitats and pH effects of all the experimental fishes are summarized in Table 3.

S. guttata is an obligatory "bottom-sitter" because it lacks a swimbladder. Cryptically colored, it is beset with small fleshy flaps (cirri) so that it blends in almost perfectly with the vari-colored tufted mat of algae and sedentary animals covering much of the bottom within its normal habitat. Even the water exhaled out its gill slits is directed upward so as not to disturb the algae or move the fish (Ebeling, personal communication). It has the smallest pH effects among all species tested. This is expected because it has no swimbladder to fill. That is, the lack of a substantial effect of pH on its blood oxygen affinity is consistent with the hypothesis that the primary function of the Root effect is to release oxygen for swimbladder inflation.

REFERENCES

AGOSTONI A., BERFASCONI C., GERLI G. C., LUZZANA M. & ROSSI-BERNARDI L. (1973) Oxygen affinity and electrolyte distribution of human blood: changes induced by propranolol. *Science, Wash.* **183,** 300–301.

ALEXANDER R. McN. (1966) Physical aspects of swimbladder function. *Biol. Rev.* **41,** 141–176.

ANDERSON M. E., OLSON J. S., GIBSON Q. E. & CAREY F. G. (1973) Studies on ligand binding to hemoglobins from teleosts and elasmobranchs. *J. biol. Chem.* **248,** 331–341.

ANDERSON S. R. & ANTONINI E. (1968) The binding of carbon monoxide and human hemoglobin. *J. Biochem.* **243,** 2918–2920.

ANTONINI E. (1967) Hemoglobin and its reaction with ligands. *Science, Wash.* **158,** 1417–1425.

BALL E., STUTTMATTER F. & COOPER O. (1955) Metabolic studies on the gas gland of the swimbladder. *Biol. Bull. mar. biol. Lab., Woods Hole* **108,** 1–17.

BARCROFT J. (1928) *The Respiratory Function of the Blood. Part II. Hemoglobin.* Cambridge University Press, Cambridge.

BENESCH R. & BENESCH R. E. (1967) The effect of organic phosphates from the human erythrocyte on the allosteric properties of hemoglobin. *Biochem. biophys. res. Commun.* **26,** 162–167.

BERG T. & STEEN J. B. (1968) The mechanism of oxygen concentration in the swimbladder of the eel. *J. Physiol., Lond.* **195,** 631–638.

BINOTTI I., GIOVENCO S., GIARDINA B., ANTONINI E., BRUMORI M. & WYMAN J. (1971) Studies on the functional properties of fish hemoglobins—II. The oxygen equilibrium of the isolated hemoglobin components from trout blood. *Archs Biochem. Biophys.* **142,** 274–280.

BLACK E. C. & IRVING L. (1938) The effect of hemolysis upon the affinity of fish blood for oxygen. *J. cell. comp. Physiol.* **12,** 255–262.

BOHR C., HASSELBALCH K. & KROGH A. (1904) Über einen in biologischer Beziehung wichtigen Einfluss, den die Kohlensaurespannung des Blates auf dessen Sauerstoffbindung übt. *Skand. Arch. Physiol.* **16,** 402.

BUHLER D. R. (1963) Studies on fish hemoglobins. *J. biol. Chem.* **238,** 1665–1674.

BUHLER D. R. & SHANKS W. E. (1959) Multiple hemoglobins in fishes. *Science, Wash.* **129,** 899–900.

CANNON R. (1956) *How to Fish the Pacific Coast.* Lane, Menlo Park.

CAREY F. G. (1973) Fishes with warm bodies. *Sci. Am.* **228**, 36–44.

CAREY F. G. & TEAL J. M. (1969) Regulation of body temperature by the blue fin tuna. *Comp. Biochem. Physiol.* **28**, 205–213.

CHEN LO-CHAI (1971) Systematics, variation, distribution and biology of rockfishes of the subgenus *Sebastomas. Bull. Scripps Institution of Oceanography* No. 18, pp. 1–115. University of California Press, Berkeley.

DRAKE E. M. S., GILL S. J., DOWNING M. & MALONE C. P. (1963) Environmental dependency of the reaction of oxygen with hemoglobin. *Archs Biochem. Biophys.* **100**, 26–31.

ENOKI Y. & TYUMA J. (1964) Further studies of hemoglobin-oxygen equilibrium. *Jap. J. Physiol.* **14**, 280–298.

FANGE R. (1966) Physiology of the swimbladder. *Physiol. Rev.* **46**, 299–322.

FISH G. R. (1956) Some aspects of the respiration of six species of fish from Uganda. *J. exp. Biol.* **33**, 186–195.

FONNER D. P., HOFFERT J. R. & FROMM P. O. (1973) The importance of the counter current oxygen multiplier mechanism in maintaining retinal function in the teleost. *Comp. Biochem. Physiol.* **46A**, 559–567.

GILLEN R. G. & RIGGS A. (1971) The hemoglobins of a freshwater teleost *Cichlasoma cyanoguttatum*—I. The effects of phosphorylated organic compounds upon the oxygen equilibrium. *Comp. Biochem. Physiol.* **38B**, 585–595.

GILLEN R. G. & RIGGS A. (1973) Hemoglobins of a fresh-water teleost, *Cichlasoma cyanoguttatum* (Baird and Girard)—II. Subunit structure and oxygen equilibria of the isolated components. *Archs Biochem. Biophys* **154**, 348–359.

GIOVENCO S., BINOTTI I., BRUMORI M. & ANTONINI E. (1970) Studies of the functional properties of fish hemoglobins—I. The oxygen equilibrium of trout hemoglobin. *Int. J. Biochem.* **1**, 57–61.

GREEN A. A. & ROOT R. W. (1933) The equilibrium between hemoglobin and oxygen in the blood of certain fishes. *Biol. Bull. mar. biol. Lab., Woods Hole* **64**, 383.

HALL F. G. & MCCUTCHEON F. H. (1938) Affinity of hemoglobin for oxygen in marine fishes. *J. cell. comp. Physiol.* **11**, 205–212.

HARDIN JONES F. R. & MARSHALL N. B. (1953) The structure and functions of the teleostean swimbladder. *Biol. Rev.* **28**, 16–83.

HOBSON E. S. (1965) Forests beneath the sea. *Animals* **7**, 506–511.

KANWISHER J. & EBELING A. (1957) Composition of the swimbladder gas in bathypelagic fishes. *Deep Sea Res.* **1957**, 211–217.

KILMARTIN J. V. & ROSSI-BERNARDI L. (1969) Inhibition of carbon dioxide combination and reduction of the Bohr effect in haemoglobin chemically modified at its α-amino groups. *Nature, Lond.* **222**, 1243.

KROGH A. (1929) *Anatomy and Physiology of Capillaries.* Yale University Press, New Haven.

KROGH A. & LEITCH I. (1919) The respiratory function of the blood in fishes. *J. Physiol., Lond.* **52**, 288–300.

KUHN W., RAMEL A., KUHN H. J. & MARTI E. (1963) The filling mechanism of the swimbladder: generation of high gas pressures through hairpin counter-current multiplication. *Experientia* **19**, 497–511.

LARSON R. (1972) The food habits of four Rockfishes (*Scorpaenidae, Sebastes*) off Santa Barbara, Calif. Master's thesis, University of California, Santa Barbara.

LIMBARGH C. (1955) Fish life in the kelp beds and the effects of kelp harvesting. University of California Institute of Marine Resources, La Jolla, IMR Ref. 55–9.

MANWELL C. P. (1957a) The respiratory pigments. Doctoral thesis, Stanford University, Stanford, California.

MANWELL C. P. (1957b) Alkaline denaturation of hemoglobin of postlarval and adult *Scorpaenichthys marmoratus. Science, Wash.* **126**, 1175–1176.

MANWELL C. P. (1958) Fetal–maternal shift in the ovoviviparous spring dogfish *Squalus suckleyi. Physiol. Zoöl.* **31**, 93–100.

MANWELL C. P. (1960) Comparative physiology: blood pigments. *Ann. Rev. Physiol.* **22**, 191–231.

MARSHALL N. B. (1966) *The Life of Fishes.* World Publishing, Cleveland, Ohio.

PANTIN C. F. A. (1948) *Notes on Microscopical Technique for Zoologists.* Cambridge University Press, London.

PERUTZ M. F., MUIRHEAD H., MAZZARELLA L., CROWTHER R. A., GREER J. & KILMARTIN J. V. (1969) Identification of residues responsible for the alkaline Bohr effect in haemoglobin. *Nature, Lond.* **222**, 1240.

PHILLIPS J. B. (1957) A review of the rockfishes of California (family Scorpaenidae). *Calif. Dept. Fish Game Fish Bull.* **104**, 1–158.

POWERS D. A. (1972) Hemoglobin adaptation for fast and slow water habitats in sympatric catostomid fishes. *Science, Wash.* **177**, 360–362.

QUAST J. C. (1968) Fish fauna of the rocky inshore zone. In *Utilization of Kelp-bed Resources in Southern California* (Edited by NORTH W. J. & HUBBS Q. L.). (*Calif. Dept. Fish Game Fish Bull.* **139**, 35–55.)

RIGGS A. F. (1951) Properties of tadpole and frog hemoglobin. *J. gen. Physiol.* **35**, 23–40.

RIGGS A. F. (1959) Molecular adaptation in hemoglobins. *Nature, Lond.* **183**, 1037–1038.

RIGGS A. F. (1960) Nature of Bohr effect. *J. gen. Physiol.* **43**, 737–752.

RIGGS A. F. (1965) Functional properties of hemoglobins. *Physiol. Rev.* **45**, 619–673.

RIGGS A. F. (1970) Properties of fish hemoglobins. In *Fish Physiology* (Edited by HOAR W. S. & RANDALL D. J.). Academic Press, New York.

ROOT R. W. (1931) Respiratory function of the blood of marine fishes. *Biol. Bull. mar. biol. Lab., Woods Hole* **61**, 427–456.

ROOT R. W., BLACK E. C. & IRVING L. (1938) Effect of carbon dioxide on the oxygen-combining power of whole and hemolyzed marine fish blood. *Anat. Rec. Philad.* **72**, Suppl. 1938, 46.

ROOT R. W. & IRVING L. (1940) The influence of oxygenation upon the transport of carbon dioxide by the blood of the marine fish—*Tautoga onitis. J. cell. comp. Physiol.* **16**, 85–96.

ROOT R. W. & IRVING L. (1941) The equilibrium between hemoglobin and oxygen in whole and hemolyzed blood of the tautog, with a theory of the Holdane effect. *Biol. Bull. mar. biol. Lab., Woods Hole* **81**, 307.

ROOT R. W. & IRVING L. (1943) The effect of carbon dioxide and lactic acid on the oxygen-combining power of whole and hemolyzed blood of the marine fish *Tautoga onitis* (Linn.). *Biol. Bull. mar. biol. Lab., Woods Hole* **84**, 207.

SATCHELL G. H. (1971) *Circulation in Fishes.* Cambridge University Press.

SCHOLANDER P. F. & VAN DAM L. (1953) Composition of the swimbladder gas in deep sea fishes. *Biol. Bull. mar. biol. Lab., Woods Hole* **104**, 75–86.

SCHOLANDER P. F. & VAN DAM L. (1954) Role of hemoglobin in secretion of gases into swimbladders of deep sea fishes. *Biol. Bull. mar. biol. Lab., Woods Hole* **107**, 247–249.

STEEN J. B. (1963) Physiology of the swimbladder in the eel *Anguilla vulgaris*—III. Mechanism of gas secretion. *Acta physiol. scand.* **59**, 221–241.

STEEN J. B. (1970) The swimbladder as a hydrostatic organ. In *Fish Physiology* (Edited by HOAR W. S. & RANDALL D. J.), Vol. 4. Academic Press, New York.

STEEN J. B. & TURITZIN S. (1968) Nature and biological significance of the pH difference across red cell membranes. *Resp. Physiol.* **5**, 234.

THOMAS N. W. (1971) The form of hemoglobin in the erythrocytes of the cod, *Gadus callarias. J. Cell Sci.* **8**, 407–412.

TSUYUKI H., ROBERTS E., LOWES R. H. & HADAWAY W. (1968) Contribution of protein electrophoresis to rockfish (Scorpaenidae) systematics. *J. Fish. Res. Bd Can* **25**, 2477–2501.

WILLMER M. H. (1935) Some observations on the respiration of certain tropical fresh water fishes. *J. exp. Biol.* **11**, 283–306.

WITTENBERG J. B. & WITTENBERG B. A. (1962) Active secretion of oxygen into the eye of fish. *Nature, Lond.* **194**, 106–107.

WOLF K. & QUIMBLY M. C. (1970) Fish cell and tissue culture. In *Fish Physiology* (Edited by HOAR W. S. & RANDALL D. J.). Academic Press, New York.

YOUNG J. Z. (1933) The preparation of isotonic solution for use in experiments with fish. *Publ. Staz. zool. Napoli* **12**, 425–431.

Key Word Index—Root effect; Bohr effect; erythrocytes; oxygen affinity; swimbladder; teleosts.

THE MECHANISM OF SECRETION OF INERT GASES INTO THE FISH SWIMBLADDER

by J. D. ABERNETHY[*]

(From the Department of Physiology and the Center for Theoretical Biology, State University of New York at Buffalo.)

(*Received December 6, 1971. Accepted for publication April 28, 1972.*)

Summary. Gases which are customarily viewed as biologically inert may nevertheless be secreted into the swimbladder at high pressure just like their biologically active counterparts, O_2 and CO_2. The late Werner Kuhn proposed that the mechanism for all gases was countercurrent multiplication of small changes in partial pressure initiated by secretions of the gas gland situated near the bend of the multiplier loop. Hitherto this hypothesis has been confirmed only for O_2 and CO_2: an analysis of swimbladder data on argon/nitrogen ratios presented here gives the required confirmation in the inert gas case. A second part of this paper deals with the nature of the secretory agent relevant to inert gas. Kuhn postulated the secretion of an electrolyte to salt out dissolved gas in addition to lactic acid secretion known to be operative in the release of O_2 and CO_2. This postulate may be redundant: lactic acid is shown to release N_2 from fish red cells perhaps by a pH-related change in haemoglobin polar groups. Countercurrent multiplication of all gases would thus be under the control of a single agent. Interspecies variations in swimbladder gas content would not be inconsistent with this unitary theory since these may merely reflect interspecies variations in the development of the multiplier apparatus and probable variations in the pH-effect also.

INTRODUCTION.

The late Werner Kuhn showed the power of the interdisciplinary approach when he introduced the concept of countercurrent exchange into biology from the field of physical chemistry in order to explain the generation of high sodium concentrations in the hairpin loops of Henle in the renal medulla (Kuhn and Ryffel, 1942). The concept was subsequently applied in several areas of biology and, in particular, enabled Scholander (1954) to end the speculations of six generations of biologists by providing the first satisfactory explanation for the generation of high gas pressures in the fish swimbladder. Scholander (1954) described the exquisite design of the countercurrent apparatus, the *rete mirabile*, which consists of an array of densely-packed thin-walled capillaries arranged in parallel to give maximal contact area between venous and arterial streams. The theoretical analysis of countercurrent multiplication of swimbladder gases was then taken up by Kuhn and Kuhn (1961) who postulated that the essential step in the process, the creation of a chemical potential gradient from venous to arterial streams, was effected through the secretion of an agent into the venous

---

[*] Present address: Department of Physical Biochemistry, The John Curtin School of Medical Research, The Australian National University, Canberra, A.C.T., Australia.

From *Aust. J. Exp. Biol. Med. Sci.* 50:365–374. Reprinted by permission.

stream by the gas gland situated at the hairpin bend of the capillary loops. For oxygen and carbon dioxide this agent was shown to be lactic acid which acts on haemoglobin through the Bohr and Root effects to increase the partial pressure of dissolved O_2 and, by lowering pH, achieves a similar increase in dissolved CO_2 (Kuhn, Ramel, Kuhn and Marti, 1963; Steen, 1963). For the biologically inert gases nitrogen and argon it is likely that they, too, undergo countercurrent multiplication, since they are also at a higher partial pressure than the surrounding medium. In fact, the partial pressure of N_2 may be increased as much as tenfold without, necessarily, any increase in the partial pressure of O_2 (Sundnes, Enns and Scholander, 1958). This led Kuhn and Kuhn (1961) to postulate that, in the case of the inert gases, the gas gland secreted a second agent, an electrolyte such as NaCl, into the venous stream of the *rete*, thus raising the partial pressure of dissolved gas, relative to the arterial stream, by the well-known salting-out effect (Battino and Clever, 1966).

In this paper we obtain confirmation for the hypothesis that inert gases are also secreted by countercurrent multiplication through an analysis of argon/nitrogen ratios in swimbladder gas. However, we also show that the yet unfounded assumption of Kuhn and Kuhn (1961) that the gas gland secretes an electrolyte in order to initiate countercurrent multiplication of inert gas may, in fact, be unnecessary. Working on the eel, Steen (1963) affirmed the presence of excess lactic acid in the venous stream of the *rete mirabile* during active filling of the swimbladder, and also made the surprising discovery that lactic acid releases not only O_2 and CO_2 from eel blood, but also argon and nitrogen. Steen's results pointed to some pH-related solubility change in the red cell fraction of fish blood, but not in mammalian blood, and which operated only at temperatures below 20°.

It seemed important to confirm or deny Steen's findings (1963) not only because of implications for swimbladder theory but also because physiologists have accepted as axiomatic that inert gases are passive agents free of the complexities of O_2 and CO_2 and pH-sensitive interactions with haemoglobin (van Slyke, Dillon and Margaria, 1934). The findings reported below confirm those of Steen (1963), in this case on a fish with a characteristically high inert gas content in the swimbladder. Before proceeding, however, some discussion of the salting-out effect is warranted since it is central to swimbladder theory and has some bearing on the experimental technique.

Salting-out of gases in solution.

The change in solubility, a, of a given gas due to added electrolyte is obtained from the empirical salting-out equation derived by Setschenow (Randall and Failey, 1927), namely,

$$a = a_0.\exp{(-K.\triangle M)} \qquad\qquad 1a$$

where a_0 is the initial solubility, K a constant specific for a particular gas-electrolyte pair, and $\triangle M$ is the concentration of added electrolyte in moles/litre. Using the Henry's Law property of inert gases in solution, i.e., that for a given concentration partial pressure, P, and solubility are in inverse proportion, equation 1a has the equivalent form,

$$P = P_o.\exp\ (K.\triangle M) \qquad\qquad 1b$$

It follows that δ, the fractional change in partial pressure due to added electrolyte, can be written to the first approximation as

$$\delta = \triangle P/P \simeq K.\triangle M \qquad\qquad 1c$$

for sufficiently small $\triangle M$. The mechanism underlying equation 1a is ill understood although it is known that the salting-out constant K tends to increase with both the molecular size and polarisability of the gas concerned, and decreases with temperature (Battino and Clever, 1966). The powerful effect of ionic valency on the salting-out capabilities of different electrolytes is shown by the fact that, with some exceptions, K increases roughly in proportion to the ionic strength of equimolar solutions, indicating that K increases with the square of the ionic charge (Randall and Failey, 1927). Likewise, weak electrolytes have but a small salting-out effect. Equation 1a is a valid approximation in the physiological range for the effect of NaCl on nitrogen and argon. In preliminary experiments these gases were found to have nearly identical K values (K_{N_2} = 0·327, K_{Ar} = 0·309 at 37·2°) in agreement with published data (Morrison and Johnstone, 1955) and presumably because the larger size of the argon molecule is offset by its smaller polarisability. For the purposes of this paper a common value of K has been assumed.

MATERIALS AND METHODS.

Estimation of inert gas concentration was done by gas chromatography (Farhi, Edwards and Homma, 1963) in contrast to the indirect method of Steen (1963) (residual volume of gas after extraction of O_2 and CO_2). The blood was collected from a number of Great Lakes whitefish, a freshwater physostome *coregonus clupeaformis*, which almost always has a high fraction (99%) of N_2 in the swimbladder. A small number of swimbladder gas samples were also taken [immediately after fish had been netted and hauled to the surface], stored underwater, and analysed next day for argon and nitrogen. Red cell suspensions were made necessary because of obstinate *in vitro* clotting of whole blood. From the stored citrated blood (11-27 days old, haematocrit 42%) washed red cells were prepared and suspended in an equal volume of Tris buffer (0·05M) at 10°. In each of four experiments a number of samples were equilibrated with air in a tonometer in which pH was lowered by the addition of small quantities of concentrated lactic or 1·5N hydrochloric acid. Nitrogen content was compared to that of air-equilibrated distilled water. Moderate to severe *in vitro* haemolysis occurred during the tonometer stage (30-60 min).

A number of similar experiments were performed on heparinised whole blood 1-5 days old collected from whitefish and two other freshwater species, yellow pike and catfish.

RESULTS.

For 5 whitefish caught at a depth equivalent to 4 atmospheres the mean Ar/N_2 ratio was 93% relative to that of air and the mean fractional N_2 content was 0·968 (air = 0·7808). Nitrogen solubility of whitefish red cell suspensions, relative to distilled water at 10°, shows a decrease with decreasing pH, the line fitted by linear regression analysis having a slope of 4% per unit of pH (Fig. 1). Reversing the pH change with 1·5N NaOH in one experiment reversed the change in solubility. Whole whitefish blood showed a trend of similar magnitude but the clotting problem impaired the reproducibility of the result. No change in solubility was detected in whole blood from yellow pike and catfish at 10°. The mean nitrogen content of swimbladder gas samples from 7 whitefish was 97·5%, from 3 yellow pike 68·5% and from 1 catfish 80·9%.

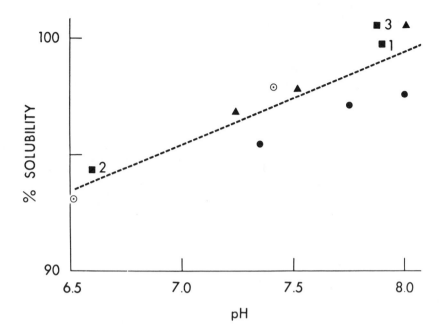

Fig. 1. Solubility of N_2 at 10° (relative to water) in whitefish red cell suspension. pH lowered by concentrated lactic acid (dotted circles, squares) or 1·5N HCl (closed circles, triangles). pH restored by 1·5N NaOH in one sequence (squares). Linear regression analysis of the 3-5 duplicate y-values (N_2 content analyses) for each of 11 x-values (pH measurements) yields a slope of 4% per unit of pH with 95% confidence intervals $4 \pm 1·3\%$. The probability that N_2 solubility is independent of pH is $P \ll 0·005$. This change in solubility is small but nevertheless sufficient to initiate countercurrent multiplication.

DISCUSSION.

Differential behaviour of argon and nitrogen in the swimbladder:
confirmation of countercurrent hypothesis.

Despite modification in detail, as discussed below, the theory of Kuhn and Kuhn (1961) can be used to explain deviations in the relative proportions of inert gases with respect to that obtaining in the environment.

From consideration of the steady state in the countercurrent loop, Kuhn and Kuhn (1961) set up a first-order differential equation with constant coefficients expressing change in partial pressure, P, with distance, x, along the afferent limb of the loop, i.e.

$$dP(x)/dx = \frac{\varGamma.\delta}{u.a.a} .P(x), \; P(o) = P_o \qquad \text{2a}$$

which has the solution at distance L, corresponding to the hairpin bend of the loop,

$$P_L = P_o.\exp\frac{(\varGamma.\delta.L)}{u.a.a} \qquad \text{2b}$$

where $\varGamma$ = permeability of the membrane separating the afferent and efferent streams to the gas, a = gas solubility in blood, δ = fractional change in partial pressure across the loop due to the transverse chemical potential gradient secondary in the model of Kuhn and Kuhn (1961) to a transverse electrolyte gradient (equation 1c), u = linear velocity of blood, and a = diameter of capillary perpendicular to plane of separation. The equation could also represent the situation of a non-constant transverse gradient by suitably redefining δ as a mean value. This equation is valid only in an ideal steady state in which no gas is lost by diffusion along the *rete*. Kuhn and Kuhn (1961) showed that back diffusion can be ignored since *rete* blood flow exceeds a critical value and renders such diffusion insignificant.

In order to compare two gases such as argon and nitrogen, it is convenient to combine those system parameters not involving physical properties of the gases. This is facilitated by the fact that permeability of biological membranes to inert gases, Γ, may be taken to be proportional to the product $d.a_m$, d being the diffusivity of the gas, and a_m the solubility in the membrane (Jones, 1950). Assuming further that a_m is proportional to a, equation 2b can be rewritten

$$P = P_o.\exp(A.d.\delta) \qquad\qquad 2c$$

where A represents the combined system parameters. For a given δ, the relative degree of multiplication of two gases depends critically on their relative diffusivities: in respect of argon and nitrogen the relative diffusivity calculated from Graham's law is $d_{Ar}/d_{N_2} = 0\cdot84$. Assuming $\delta_{Ar}/\delta_{N_2} \leqslant 1$ (this is justified in the case of the salting-out model of Kuhn and Kuhn (1961) and is also true of Steen's data (1963) on lactic acid) gives the result that the ratio of partial pressures in swimbladder gas under the above hypothesis should be less than air and water.

Analysis of present and published data does indeed show a significant lowering of the Ar/N_2 ratio. (Mean Ar/N_2 ratio = $91\cdot7\% \pm 3\cdot0$ S.E. (n = 27) relative to that of air). Moreover, increasing the degree of multiplication by increasing A or δ in the exponent of equation 2c should lead to a progressive decrease in this ratio. The prediction is, in general, satisfied by the data, as shown in Fig. 2, using the partial pressure of nitrogen as an approximate index of the degree of multiplication. This index would be exact if gas transport in either direction was zero. The theoretical line represents the ideal steady state using $d_{Ar}/d_{N_2} = 0\cdot84$ and $\delta_{Ar}/\delta_{N_2} = 1$. This line partitions the graph into two mutually exclusive zones and, theoretically, the data should fall into one or other, depending on the presence or absence of active secretion. During active secretion the Ar/N_2 ratio rises essentially because the greater solubility of argon $(a_{Ar}/a_{N_2} = 2\cdot2)$ allows for a correspondingly greater flux through the *rete*. For example, freshly secreted gas may have a ratio twice that of air (Wittenberg, 1958). Conversely, a decrease in Ar/N_2 ratio would be expected from absorption through the swimbladder wall, again because of the difference in physical solubility (Piiper, Humphrey and Rahn, 1962). In the steady state the balance between secretion and absorption is struck in favour of a higher Ar/N_2 ratio relative to the ideal steady state ratio essentially because the active countercurrent multiplication process dominates the passive absorptive process (this assertion can be made quite rigorous). The data values, except where indicated, represent swimbladders that were in a steady state according to the available information and are consistent with the predicted elevation of the Ar/N_2 ratio with respect to the ideal steady-state values. The broken symbols in Fig. 2 refer to data of Sundnes *et al.* (1958); Sundnes (1959) on fish taken during their annual seasonal

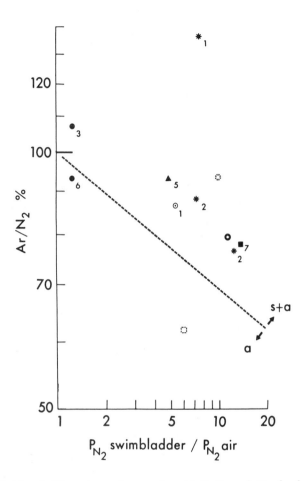

Fig. 2. Swimbladder Ar/N$_2$ ratio v. degree of multiplication of N$_2$; log-log plot. Present whitefish data represented by closed triangle. Remaining points for various species have been extracted from the literature (mean with sample size appended if known, otherwise mid point of range). Broken symbols refer to swimbladders that were probably either filling (circle), or emptying (square). Theoretical line represents ideal steady state (assuming $\delta_{Ar} = \delta_{N_2}$) and arrows indicate directions in which data would be expected to deviate as a result of absorption with or without ongoing secretion (s+a, a). Reference key: closed circle, Wittenberg (1958); star, Scholander and van Dam (1953); closed square, Scholander, van Dam and Enns (1956); dotted circle, Tait (1956); open circle; Sundnes (1963); broken circle, Sundnes (1959); broken square, Sundnes, Enns and Scholander (1958).

vertical migrations for spawning and, judging from depth of catch and O$_2$ content, were undergoing filling (broken circle) and emptying (broken square) to maintain neutral buoyancy. There is thus qualitative agreement with theory providing the reasonable assumption $\delta_{Ar} \leqslant \delta_{N_2}$ is correct. Despite evidence to the contrary, if δ_{Ar}/δ_{N_2} was shown in fact to be greater than $1/(d_{Ar}/d_{N_2})$ then it is clear from equation 2c that the Ar/N$_2$ ratio ought to increase with degree of multiplication. The above demonstration of low Ar/N$_2$ ratios would then amount to a contradiction of the countercurrent multiplication theory as applied to inert gases.

Nitrogen solubility and pH.

The number and scope of these experiments was limited by the technical difficulties encountered and by a source of blood restricted through depletion of the local whitefish population (by the lamprey and other ecological disturbances). Nevertheless, the above results are consistent with Steen's (1963) findings as to the direction of the change in solubility with pH. In both cases the reversibility of the response excludes a salting-out effect from the added electrolyte. In any case, to have achieved a comparable salting-out effect with HCl would have required a 50-fold increase in the quantities actually added (calculation based on data for effect of HCl on gas solubilities (Randall and Failey, 1927)). A salting-out effect due to change in ionic strength of the buffer is ruled out because, for a weak monoacidic base such as Tris, the ionic strength is determined essentially by the ionic strength of the added electrolyte, in this case lactic acid, HCl and NaOH. One important difference, however, between the two sets of results is that Steen (1963) found not a linear relationship but a fairly abrupt change of about 9% between pH $7\cdot7$ and $7\cdot5$ in whole eel blood at $6\cdot5°$. Such a step change carries implications as to mechanism so that further experimentation on the discrepancy between the two results is desirable.

Further work by Berg and Steen (1968) has shown that, contrary to theory, rapid pH equilibration takes place across the loop and obliterates the pH gradient, but in spite of this a diffusion gradient for O_2 persists because of dynamic lags in the Root effect. A similar modification would be needed for complete acceptance of lactic acid as the effective agent for the release of the inert gases.

Mechanism of pH-effect.

The cause of such a pH-related solubility change might be related to the theory of Pauling (1961) on the formation of microcrystals of hydrates between water molecules and non hydrogen-binding anaesthetic agents including nitrogen and argon. Hydrate stability is increased as temperatures approach $0°$ and by protein side chains whose influence might conceivably vary with their degree of dissociation. Secondly, direct binding of inert gases in aqueous solutions of haemoglobin on other proteins is known to occur (Yeh and Peterson, 1965), although no specific sites have been assigned except for xenon and myoglobin (Schoenborn, Watson and Kendrew, 1965). Binding is pH dependent in the case of bovine serum albumen (Wetlaufer and Lovrien, 1964). Thirdly, haemoglobin is amphoteric and the change in solubility may be simply a salting-out effect due to the influence of pH on the polar groups. According to the work of Gary-Bobo and Solomon (1968), the net charge (positive or negative) on a haemoglobin molecule increases by 10 per unit of pH on either side of the isoelectric point, so the calculated increase in ionic strength would bring about a salting-out effect of 9% assuming [Hb] = $3\cdot7$ mmol/1 (20%) and an initial K_{Hb} equal to that of NaCl at $10°$. Because of the assumptions involved, no great weight can be put on this calculation, but it does indicate that haemoglobin could act as a salting-out agent under the influence of pH and would, in some sense, redeem the original postulate of Kuhn and Kuhn (1961). The temperature effects noted by Steen (1963) could be explained simply by a decrease in K_{Hb} with increase in temperature. For example, K_{NaCl} (w.r.t. N_2) decreases about

30% over the range 10-37°. Interspecies differences in the pH-effect would require explanation under this hypothesis.

Can a single agent occount for interspecies variation in gas composition?

The hypothesis that all swimbladder gases are under the control of a single powerful secretory agent has the appeal of simplicity but does not account for the marked interspecies differences in gas proportions without further explanation. The data indicate that there may be interspecies differences in the inert gas pH-effect which parallel variations in swimbladder N_2 content. But the mere existence of a measurable pH-effect would not, in itself, account for the virtual exclusion of O_2 from the whitefish and others of the coregonid and cyprinid families: other things being equal, N_2 secretion must inevitably be overwhelmed by oxygen secretion because of the O_2 binding capacities of haemoglobin. The explanation developed below turns on the fact that secretion is opposed by absorption and that both factors determine whether the balance is struck in favour of one gas or another.

In general a high N_2 fraction (99%) is seen only in freshwater fish living at pressures of 15 atmospheres or less and in whom the *rete* is poorly developed. In fact, in the case of the coregonid species, a *rete* was thought to be absent until Fahlen (1959) showed otherwise. On the other hand, the *rete* is very well developed indeed in terms of both length and number of vessels in abyssal marine fish living at pressures up to 400 atmospheres (Marshall, 1960) and in fish which undergo extensive vertical migrations (Wittenberg, Schwend and Wittenberg, 1964). In these types the N_2 fraction is low, being replaced by O_2 and even CO_2. There thus appears to be correlation between *rete* development and fractional gas concentration, positive for O_2 and negative for N_2.

Swimbladder gas composition is the result of a dynamic balance between ongoing secretion and absorption of each of the constituents represented for purposes of discussion by N_2 and O_2. The need for continual transport of gas into the bladder by the *rete* severely interferes with its function as a pressure multiplier: in the case of O_2 pressure, attenuation is especially marked near the upper limit of gas flow (Kuhn and Marti, 1966) but can be partially compensated by quite small increases in the length or number of vessels. It is not difficult to show that a similar inverse relationship between pressure and gas flow would hold for N_2 but without the distinctive high flow cut-off. Likewise, pressure-flow curves for absorption of N_2 and O_2 from gas pockets are distinctly different. For N_2 a rising transmural partial pressure results in a proportional increase in efflux, whereas with O_2 the efflux curve initially rises steeply until saturation of blood draining the gas pocket wall occurs, leaving only O_2 in physical solution available for further transport (van Liew, Schoenfisch and Olszowka, 1968). It is clear that in fish with a limited *rete* structure these two non-linearities in secretion and absorption might well combine to favour retention of N_2 at the expense of O_2. This explanation would require a knowledge of the parameters of secretion and absorption for complete validation but is consistent with the finding that a freshwater fish with a high N_2 fraction failed to fill its swimbladder when O_2 replaced the N_2 in the environment, even though some potential to secrete O_2 had been demonstrated (Krohn and Piiper, 1962).

These results illustrate the basic soundness of the analysis of Kuhn and

Kuhn (1961) of countercurrent multiplication of inert gases and also serve as a foundation for extrapolation to the kidney where the renal countercurrent mechanisms and high salt concentrations might likewise result in behaviour distinct from that expected of truly inert agents (Abernethy, 1972).

Acknowledgements. The author acknowledges the guidance and provision of facilities by Professor Hermann Rahn and is grateful to Dr. Walter Garey and the Ontario Fisheries Research Board for help in collection of specimens.

REFERENCES.

ABERNETHY, J. D. (1972): 'Inert gases in the kidney: influence of the countercurrent multiplication of sodium.' *Aust. J. exp. Biol. med. Sci.*, **50**, 375.

BATTINO, R., and CLEVER, H. L. (1966): 'The solubility of gases in liquids.' *Chem. Rev.*, **66**, 395.

BERG, T., and STEEN, J. B. (1968): 'The mechanism of oxygen concentration in the swimbladder of the eel.' *J. Physiol.*, **195**, 631.

FAHLEN, G. (1959): '*Rete mirabile* in the gas bladder of coregonus lavaretus.' *Nature*, **184**, 1001.

FARHI, L. E., EDWARDS, A. W. T., and HOMMA, T. (1963): 'Determination of dissolved N_2 in blood by gas chromatography and (a-A)N_2 difference.' *J. appl. Physiol.*, **18**, 97.

GARY-BOBO, C. M., and SOLOMON, A. K. (1968): 'Properties of hemoglobin solutions in red cells.' *J. gen. Physiol.*, **52**, 825.

JONES, H. B. (1950): 'Nitrogen elimination.' In "Medical Physics", O. Glasser (ed.), Year Book Publishers, Chicago, vol. II, p. 855.

KROHN, H., and PIIPER, J. (1962): 'Gassekretion in die Schwimmblase der Schleie [Tinca tinca (L.)] in Wasser mit erniedrigtem N_2-Druck.' *Naturwissenschaften*, **49**, 428.

KUHN, W., and KUHN, H. J. (1961): 'Multiplikation von Aussalzund anderen Einzeleffekten fur die Bereitung hoher Gasdrucke in der Schwimmblase.' *Z. Electrochem. angew. phys. Chem.*, **65**, 426.

KUHN, H. J., and MARTI, E. (1966): 'The active transport of oxygen and carbon dioxide into the swimbladder of fish.' *J. gen. Physiol.*, **49**, 1209.

KUHN, W., and RYFFEL, K. (1942): 'Herstellung konzentrierter Lösungen aus verdünnten durch blosse Membranwirkung. Ein Modellversuch zur Funktion der Niere.' *Hoppe-Selyer's Z. Physiol. Chem.*, **276**, 145.

KUHN, W., RAMEL, A., KUHN, H. J., and MARTI, E. (1963): 'The filling mechanism of the swimbladder. Generation of high gas pressures through hairpin countercurrent multiplication.' *Experientia*, **19**, 497.

MARSHALL, N. B. (1960): 'Swimbladder structure of deep-sea fishes in relation to their systematics and biology.' *"Discovery" Rep.*, **31**, 1.

MORRISON, T. J., and JOHNSTONE, N. B. (1955): 'The salting-out of non-electrolytes. III. The inert gases and sulphur hexafluoride.' *J. chem. Soc.*, 3655.

PAULING, L. (1961): 'A molecular theory of general anesthesia.' *Science*, **134**, 15.

PIIPER, J., HUMPHREY, T., and RAHN, H. (1962): 'Gas composition of pressurized perfused gas pockets and the fish swimbladder.' *J. appl. Physiol.*, **17**, 275.

RANDALL, M., and FAILEY, C. W. (1927): 'The activity coefficient of gases in aqueous salt solutions.' *Chem. Rev.*, **4**, 271.

SCHOENBORN, B. P., WATSON, H. C., and KENDREW, J. C. (1965): 'Binding of xenon to sperm whale myoglobin.' *Nature*, **207**, 28.

SCHOLANDER, P. F. (1954): 'Secretion of gases against high pressures in the swimbladder of deep sea fishes. II. The *Rete Mirabile*.' *Biol. Bull.*, **107**, 260.

SCHOLANDER, P. F., and VAN DAM, L. (1953): 'Composition of the swimbladder gas in deep sea fishes.' *Biol. Bull.*, **104**, 75.

Scholander, P. F., van Dam, L., and Enns, T. (1956): 'Nitrogen secretion in the swimbladder of whitefish.' *Science*, **123**, 59.

Steen, J. B. (1963): 'The physiology of the swimbladder of the eel *anguilla vulgaris*. I. The solubility of gases and the buffer capacity of the blood.' *Acta physiol. scand.*, **58**, 124.

Sundnes, G. (1959): 'Gas secretion in coregonids.' *Nature*, **183**, 986.

Sundnes, G. (1963): 'Studies on the high nitrogen content in the physostome swimbladder.' *Rep. Norw. Fishery mar. Invest.*, **13** (5), 1.

Sundnes, G., Enns, T., and Scholander, P. F. (1958): 'Gas secretion in fishes lacking *rete mirabile*.' *J. exp. Biol.*, **35**, 671.

Tait, J. S. (1956): 'Nitrogen and argon in salmonid swimbladders.' *Can. J. Zool.*, **34**, 58.

van Liew, H. D., Schoenfisch, W. H., and Olszowka, A. J. (1968): 'Exchanges of N_2 between a gas pocket and tissue in a hyperbaric environment.' *Resp. Physiol.*, **6**, 23.

van Slyke, D. D., Dillon, R. T., and Margaria, R. (1934): 'Studies of gas and electrolyte equilibria in blood.' *J. biol. Chem.*, **105**, 571.

Wetlaufer, D. B., and Lovrien, R. (1964): 'Induction of reversible changes in proteins by nonpolar substances.' *J. biol. Chem.*, **239**, 596.

Wittenberg, J. (1958): 'The secretion of inert gas into the swim-bladder of fish.' *J. gen. Physiol.*, **41**, 783.

Wittenberg, J. B., Schwend, M. J., and Wittenberg, B. A. (1964): 'The secretion of oxygen into the swim-bladder of fish. 3. The role of carbon dioxide.' *J. gen. Physiol.*, **48**, 337.

Yeh, S., and Peterson, R. E. (1965): 'Solubility of krypton and xenon in blood, protein solutions, and tissue homogenates.' *J. appl. Physiol.*, **20**, 1041.

THE BUOYANCY OF BATHYPELAGIC FISHES WITHOUT A GAS-FILLED SWIMBLADDER

By E. J. DENTON

The Plymouth Laboratory

and N. B. MARSHALL

British Museum (Natural History)

(Plates I and II, and Text-figs. 1–3)

INTRODUCTION

The upper reaches of the deep ocean contain many bathypelagic fishes with a capacious, gas-filled swimbladder. But living within and below this region are also numerous species in which this hydrostatic organ is absent or markedly regressed (Marshall, in preparation). In the neritic province nearly all the fishes that swim freely at the various water levels (and can stay poised at a particular level without undue effort) have a well-developed swimbladder, the capacity of which is about equal to 5 % of the body volume (Jones & Marshall, 1953). Having this amount of gas, these fishes are able to keep their weight in water close to the vanishing point. If such a fish were deprived of its swimbladder, it could keep at a constant level only by exerting a downward force equivalent to 5 % of its weight in air. The swimbladder thus saves the fish the energy needed for such effort, which is quite appreciable.

The advantage to a fish of being in neutral buoyancy can be illustrated by the following simple calculations. A fish deprived of the gas in its swimbladder would have a reduced weight in water of 5–8 % of its weight in air (depending on whether it were a a marine or freshwater fish). To stay at constant level it would have to exert a downward force equal to its reduced weight (and unlike terrestrial animals, pelagic creatures only exert forces on the surrounding medium by making movements). When it is remembered that even an active pelagic fish seldom exerts a force of more than 25–50 % of its weight in air for more than a very brief period (Gray, 1953), the force necessary for a fish to maintain its level appears to be considerable.

How considerable an economy the swimbladder allows can be further evaluated by realizing that the drag of the water opposing a fish's movement is proportional to (velocity)[1] for laminar flow and approximately (velocity)^2 for turbulent flow (Kermack, 1948; Hill, 1950). Thus for some active pelagic fish a force of 7 % of the body weight would enable a fish to *sustain continuously* a horizontal velocity of 43 % or 53 % (depending on whether the flow is laminar or turbulent) of that velocity which it would have if it exerted *continuously* a force of 25 % of its body weight, a force fishes *seldom* exert. (If we take our reference velocity as that given by a fish exerting 50 % of its body weight then 7 % would give a sustained velocity of 27 % or 37 % of this velocity). The above calculations were made by E. J. Denton and T. I. Shaw.

Denton, E. J. & Marshall, N. B., "The buoyancy of bathypelagic fishes without a gas-filled swimbladder." *J. Mar. Biol. Ass. U.K.* 37:753–767. Reprinted by permission of Cambridge University Press.

The mackerel (*Scomber scombrus*) is one of the few freely swimming fishes from the neritic region without a swimbladder, and it is noticeable that it can only maintain its level in the water by restless and vigorous activity. This unceasing motion is perhaps the price paid for a facility of moving up and down quickly in the top layers of the sea; for to come quickly to the surface from 20 m would increase the volume of a swimbladder threefold, and, apart from the danger of internal damage, the fish would have to exert an upward force equal to about 10% of its weight in order to go down again.[1].

The 5% relation between the swimbladder and body volume is also found in bathypelagic teleosts (Kanwisher & Ebeling, 1957). This might suggest that the species without a swimbladder were faced with the same problems as the mackerel. But many of these fishes have fragile, lightly ossified skeletons, the scales are reduced or absent, and the muscle layers of the trunk and tail are thin. This must lead to some reduction of their weight in water and it has been suggested (Marshall, 1954, 1955) that they are not much heavier than their surroundings. Measurements by one of us (E.J.D) have shown this is certainly true of two fairly common bathypelagic fishes without a swimbladder, *Gonostoma elongatum* (order Isospondyli, suborder Stomiatoidea) and *Xenodermichthys copei* (order Isospondyli, suborder Clupeoidea). Analysis of their chemical composition has revealed how this reduction of specific gravity is achieved. However, in evading, or almost evading, the buoyancy problem, it is the muscles used in propulsion that are particularly reduced. Nevertheless, the proportion of muscle (as indicated by total protein) falls less than does the downward force which has to be exerted to keep the fish in a given horizontal plane. Because of loss of speed, this might, however, seem to be like 'jumping from the frying pan into the fire', but consideration of the biology and environment of the bathypelagic fishes without a swimbladder reveals much of how this problem seems to have been met.

MATERIAL AND METHODS

The buoyancy of the fish

These experiments were made in the Bay of Biscay aboard R.V. 'Sarsia'. The deep-sea fish were caught in an Isaacs-Kidd mid-water trawl, the live fish being put into sea water previously cooled to about 10° C. A piece of cotton was threaded through the lower jaw of a fish and the fish was weighed in air on a 100 g spring balance, and in sea water using a torsion balance of 1 g full-scale deflexion. The torsion balance was on a gimbal table and it proved possible to measure the weight of the fish in sea water to a few milligrams. Great care was taken for the weighing under sea water to have no bubbles of air on or inside the deep-sea fish and both spring balance and torsion balance were frequently checked with known weights. After checking the

---

[1] Dr G. Hughes (private communication) has noted that a considerable fraction of a fish's metabolism may be devoted to providing the flow of water across the gills. A fish like a mackerel which uses its forward motion to provide much of this flow may not be at such a disadvantage as simple calculation might suggest.

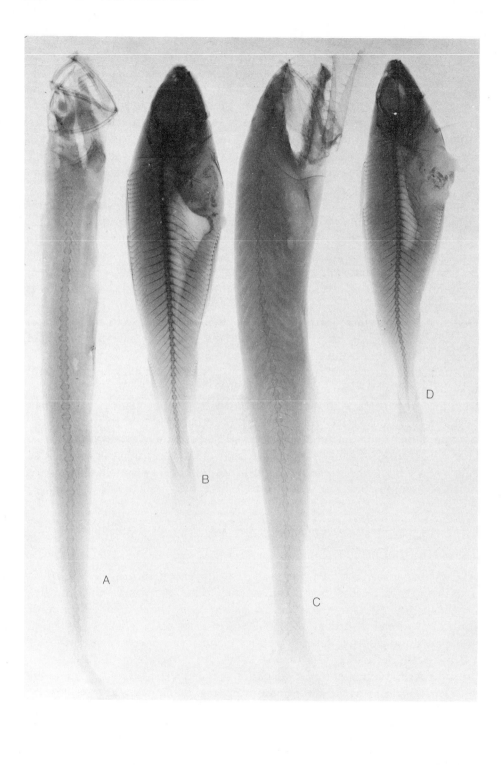

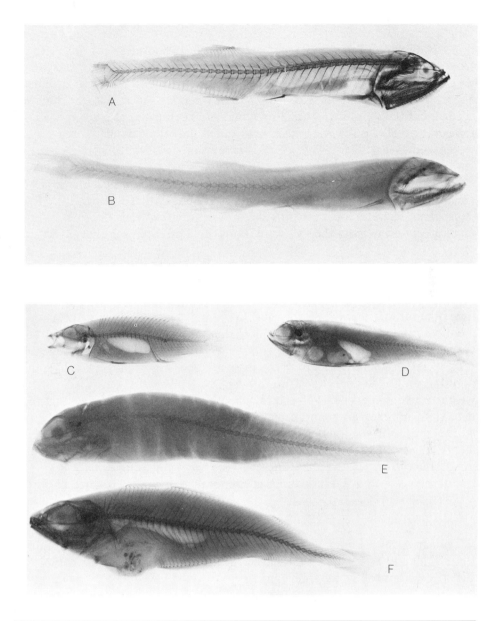

EXPLANATION OF PLATES

PLATE I

Radiographs comparing the degree of ossification of (A) *Chauliodus sloanei*, (B) *Gadus minutus*, (C) *Gonostoma elongatum*, and (D) *Gadus minutus*. Of the two specimens of *G. minutus* the second (D) is much smaller than either of the bathypelagic fish. The swimbladders of *G. minutus* appear as light areas in the body. Magnification × ⅘.

PLATE II

Radiographs (above) showing the difference in ossification between (A) *Gonostoma bathyphilum* and (B) *G. elongatum*; and (below) comparing the degree of ossification of (C) *Ctenolabrus rupestris*, (D) *Diaphus rafinesquei*, (E) *Xenodermichthys copei*, and (F) *Gadus minutus*. Magnification × ⅘.

weight in sea water several times the fish was taken out of sea water, gently dried and placed in a dry honey jar or Kilner jar and stored in a deep-freeze. Before using the fish for chemical analysis the jar and fish were weighed and after removing the fish and drying the jar this was weighed alone. The difference between these two weights gave a check on the accuracy of the weighing of the fish which had been made at sea. At sea the temperature of the sea water used was noted and samples of the sea water were taken in sealed jars. The specific gravities of the samples were measured with a hydrometer on returning to Plymouth.

The common bathypelagic fish *Chauliodus sloanei* has a thick transparent gelatinous envelope around its body. It was thought that this might be less dense than sea water and thus provide some positive buoyancy. Pieces of this material cut away from the fish were, however, found to be heavier than sea water.

Direct measurements were made of the contribution of the swimbladder gases to the buoyancy of the coastal fish *Ctenolabrus rupestris*. Specimens of this fish, freshly killed, were weighed in air and in sea water after opening the fish, puncturing the swimbladder and squeezing out its gas. These measurements showed that such a fish without the gas in its swimbladder would have a weight in sea water of about $5 \cdot 4\%$ of its weight in air. This weight must in very large part be attributed to the muscles (the largest single tissue component), for isolated pieces of muscle had in sea water about 5% of their weight in air. Experiments on coastal fish of different species showed that the density of muscle varies appreciably; the weight of hake (*Merluccius merluccius*) muscle in sea water was only $3 \cdot 2\%$ of its weight in air. These experiments suggested that a variation in the proportion of protein might be an important variable in the 'buoyancy balance sheet' of fishes. That this is so was borne out by the determinations of chemical composition described below.

Chemical analysis

The chemical analyses were made with the advice and help of Mr E. I. Butler. Not all fishes were analysed in the same way but the most complete analyses were made in the following way:

The fish were ground with sand and anhydrous calcium sulphate and Soxhlet extracted with 40°–60° petroleum ether. The residue was reground and dried in an oven for several hours when further extracts were made until no further material could be extracted. The residue, insoluble in petroleum ether, was extracted in a Soxhlet apparatus with 96% alcohol to constant weight of extract. The nitrogen in the final residue was estimated, and the alcohol extract refluxed with 40°–60° petroleum ether and filtered. The filtrate contained only that fraction of the animal's fat which was extractable by alcohol but not petroleum ether and this was estimated by drying the filtrate to constant weight. The alcohol-soluble ether-insoluble nitrogen was estimated using the method of Kjeldahl.

As a check on this method the procedure was varied. On occasions total nitrogen was estimated using whole fish, whilst on other occasions the fat was extracted after grinding with sand fish which had been oven dried (105° C) to constant weight. The various methods used gave results which were in good agreement with one another.

The dry weights given in this paper are those of fish cut into very small pieces and dried in an oven at 105° C to constant weight.

RESULTS

The buoyancy of Gonostoma and Xenodermichthys

All the fishes used were caught alive and in very good condition. The values for the (weight in sea water/weight in air) × 100 were for, 6 *Gonostoma* 0·54, 0·68, 0·90, 0·34, 0·40, 0·90 (average 0·63) and for 6 *Xenodermichthys* 1·4, 1·1, 1·4, 1·1, 1·2, 1·3 (average 1·25).

The sea water used for these buoyancy measurements was found to have a salinity close to that in which the fish live, i.e. about 35·5 g of salt in 1000 g of sea water. These fish are usually found down to 1000 m and, in the water of the Atlantic from which they were taken, there is little change in salinity between the surface and 1000 m (Cooper, 1952). The maximum error in the above figure for (weight in sea water/weight in air) which might be attributed to differences in salinity was 0·05 and this is disregarded.

Radiographs

The radiographs (Pls. I and II) show that the skeletons of *Chauliodus*, *Gonostoma* and *Xenodermichthys* are very poorly ossified in comparison with specimens of coastal fish *Gadus minutus* of comparable weight. The deep sea myctophid *Diaphus rafinesquei* which *has* a swimbladder is seen to have a skeleton as well ossified as that of a *Ctenolabrus rupestris* of about the same weight. Pl. II shows the remarkable difference in ossification between *Gonostoma elongatum* and *Gonostoma denudatum* both bathypelagic fish, the former without, and the latter with, a gas-filled swimbladder.

The otoliths of the bathypelagic fish without swimbladders are very small when compared with those of the fish with swimbladders. Particularly striking is the contrast between the large otoliths of the small fish *Diaphus rafinesquei* with the tiny otoliths of *Chauliodus sloanei*.

Chemical analyses

The principal results of the chemical analyses are given in Table I. Components are given as percentage of wet weight. The protein is taken as being 6·025 × the total nitrogen (see Love, 1957).

Part of the lipid material in fish is bound in such a way as not to be extractable in petroleum ether. This is a small fraction of the total lipid in fish which have a good deal of fat but an important fraction when there is little fat (Lovern, 1955). After extracting with petroleum ether some fish were therefore further extracted with 96% alcohol to constant weight of extract. This alcohol was shaken with petroleum ether and the residue from the ether, after evaporation, was taken as the ether inextractable fat. Part of the total nitrogen of the fishes was non-protein nitrogen and this was estimated on the alcohol extract after shaking it with petroleum ether. For one *Gonostoma* the extra fat corresponded to 0·5% of the wet weight and for two *Gonostoma* the non-protein nitrogen to 0·05 and 0·04% of the wet weight. For *Xeno-*

TABLE 1. CHEMICAL ANALYSES

Fish	Fat extractable in 40°–60° petroleum ether	Total N$_2$	Protein	Dry weight	$\dfrac{\text{Wt. in sea water}}{\text{Wt. in air}} \times 100$
Gonostoma elongatum	2·6	—	—	—	0·68
,,	5·3	—	—	—	—
,, *	3·4	0·71	4·3	12·6	0·34, 0·4
,,	—	1·01	6·0	—	0·54
,,	—	0·87	5·2	—	—
Xenodermichthys copei	0·51	—	—	—	—
,,	0·55	—	—	—	—
,,	—	1·2	7·2	—	—
,,	—	—	—	9·8	—
,, *	—	1·2	7·2	11	1·1, 1·2
Ctenolabrus rupestris	—	2·76	16·6	—	—
,,	—	—	—	28	—
,,	—	—	—	26	—
,,	0·5	—	—	—	—
Labrus bergylta†	—	2·72	16·4	—	—

* Two fish taken together.   † These fish have a gas-filled swimbladder.

dermichthys the extra fat corresponded to 0·7% of the wet weight and the non-protein nitrogen to 0·04% of the wet weight. These are figures which would give only very small corrections and they are not taken into account in the Discussion below.

DISCUSSION

Buoyancy properties

The buoyancy measurements were made at around 10° C which is close to the normal environmental temperature for these fishes. They were left for some time in sea water at this temperature before the measurements were made.

The measurements were made in the laboratory on R.V. 'Sarsia' with the fish under sea water at atmospheric pressure, but the fish are often caught at depths around 500 m where they are subject to pressures of around 50 atmospheres. This change in pressure can, however, make very little difference to the buoyancy of the fish, for the change in volume of water when the pressure is raised from 1 to 50 atmospheres is only one of about 0·2% and the volume of the fish will change in much the same way as does the sea water, leaving a residual change in buoyancy which is only a small fraction of 0·2%. We can therefore accept the surprising fact that *Gonostoma* is often within ½% and *Xenodermichthys* within 1·2% of neutral buoyancy despite the fact that neither fish has a gas-filled swimbladder.

The chemical analyses show quite clearly how this is achieved. These are extremely watery fishes with poorly ossified skeletons. The dry weight of

Gonostoma and *Xenodermichthys* are only 12·5 and 10% respectively of their weights, whereas the *Ctenolabrus rupestris*, used as a control, had a dry weight of about 28% of its wet weight. The fat content of the deep-sea fishes is not particularly high, averaging about 3%, but the protein content of about 5% of their dry weight is very low indeed when compared with the corresponding 16% for the typical coastal fishes, *Ctenolabrus rupestris* and *Labrus bergylta*.

Most of the data in the literature is for edible portions of fish (see Vinogradov, 1953, pp. 463–566). Shewan (1951) gives total nitrogen figures varying from 2·42 to 3·78% for skeletal muscles of many teleosts. These values may be compared with the 2·76–2·74 given here for whole wrasse used for control experiments. The protein content of the principal organs of higher vertebrates is shown in the *Handbook of Biological Data* (1956) as varying from about 10% for brain and spinal cord through about 20% for skeletal muscle to 30% for skin.

Marine fishes normally derive a considerable degree of buoyancy from the fact that their body fluids are considerably more dilute than sea water. The figures given by Krogh (1939) for the extracellular fluids of marine teleosts suggest that these have an approximate osmotic pressure of about 40% that of sea water. The intracellular fluids will be in osmotic equilibrium with the extracellular fluids, although the components will be different. The principal intracellular cation is probably potassium rather than sodium (this in itself will affect the density little), and most of the anions will be organic compounds such as the organic phosphates of muscle and the haemoglobin of red blood cells whose contribution to density has to some extent been included in the organic analysis. The intracellular concentration of chloride will almost certainly be very much lower than the extracellular concentration. We will, however, in the absence of good analyses, make the assumption that both the deep-sea fish and the wrasse have body fluids whose density lies half way between that of distilled water and sea water. [Preliminary analyses indicate that this cannot (in terms of density) be very seriously in error.] It is now possible to draw up balance sheets to explain the buoyancy properties of a deep-sea fish and a wrasse (Text-fig. 1, Tables 2 and 3). The negative weights imply that the component has a positive buoyancy in sea water.

Some idea of the contribution of the mineral components of bone is given by ashing the fish. Ashings in a platinum crucible of whole deep-sea fish (*Xenodermichthys copei*) gave for a high temperature (around 1000° C) an ash of 1·2% and for a low temperature (around 450° C) an ash of 1·9%. The corresponding figures for ash from wrasse (*Ctenolabrus rupestris*) were both 4·5%. The ash from wrasse contains large recognizable fragments; skull, vertebrae, etc., whilst that of the deep-sea fish is very much less in amount and much more powdery (Text-fig. 2). Some of the ash is sodium, potassium and chloride. Estimates made of these components on water extracts from the ashes indicate that the remaining mineral components account for 1·2% and 0·7% of the two deep-sea fish ashed. The densities of salts found in bone, e.g. apatite, (Harrow, 1954) are close to 3 (*International Critical Tables*, 1928) so that the contribution of this material to the buoyancy of the

TABLE 2. BALANCE SHEET FOR *GONOSTOMA ELONGATUM*

Component	% wet weight	Specific gravity	Weight in sea water/100 g of fish
Fat	3·7	0·91*	−0·5
Protein	5·0	1·33†	+1·1
Body fluids (water + dissolved salts)	87·6	1·013	−1·2
Other components including bone	3·2‡		+1·1‡

Buoyancy. These fish had no gas-filled swimbladder and their average weight in sea water was approximately +0·5 % of their weight in air. (Wet weight)

* *Handbook of Biological Data* (1956).
† Höber, (1954). Specific gravity taken as the reciprocal of the partial specific volume.
‡ These values are given by difference.

TABLE 3. BALANCE SHEET FOR *CTENOLABRUS RUPESTRIS*

Component	% wet weight	Weight in sea water/100 g of fish
Fat	0·5	−0·1
Protein	16·6	+3·8
Body fluids	73·3	−0·9
Other components including bone	9·2*	+2·6*

Buoyancy. This fish without its swimbladder has a weight in sea water of +5·4 % of its weight in air

* These values are given by difference.

fish will be about +0·6 g/100 g of fish for *Xenodermichthys,* which is a value rather smaller than that given in the above table on *Gonostoma* for 'other components including bone'.

General biological considerations

While these findings are striking in themselves, they may be seen in better perspective against a more general biological background.

Bathypelagic fishes without a gas-filled swimbladder are quite diverse. The main groups in the order Isospondyli are Melanostomiatidae, Stomiatidae, Chauliodontidae, Idiacanthidae, Malacosteidae (stomiatoids), Alepocephalidae (clupeoids) and Bathylogidae (salmonoids). Of the order Iniomi, the entire suborder Alepisauroidea consists of fishes without any known trace of a gas-filled swimbladder at any stage of their life history (Marshall, 1955), and the same is true of the ceratioid angler-fishes (Bertelsen, 1951). Finally, there are the fishes of the small orders, Giganturoidea, Lyomeri, Cetunculi and Miripinnati, the last having a functional gas-filled swimbladder during the larval phase (Bertelsen & Marshall, 1956). These groups and a few not mentioned, make up nearly half of the bathypelagic fish fauna.

In these fishes the nature and extent of the tissues appear to be very similar to the two species we have analysed in detail. The stomiatoid species certainly

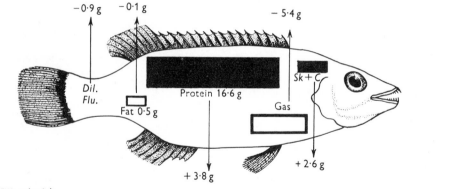

Ctenolabrus rupestris

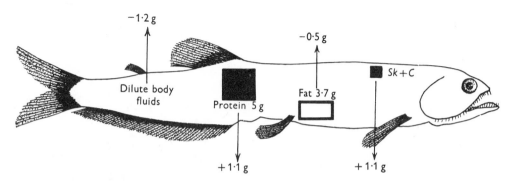

Gonostoma elongatum

Text-fig. 1. Diagram of the 'buoyancy balance sheet' for a bathypelagic fish *Gonostoma elongatum* without a swimbladder (below) and a coastal fish *Ctenolabrus rupestris* with a swimbladder (above). Positive values are given for those components of the fish which are heavier than the sea water which they displace and thus tend to 'sink' the fish, whilst negative values are given for those components which displace more sea water than their own weight and thus tend to 'float' the fish. Weights given per 100 g of fish. *Dil. Flu.*, dilute body fluids; *Sk + C*, skeleton and other components.

have lightly ossified skeletons (the scales are absent or poorly developed) and a correspondingly reduced musculature. Concerning the melanostomiatids and *Idiacanthus*, Beebe & Crane (1939) remark that '...as usual in deep-sea fish, the jaws are the only really strongly ossified parts of the body, the gill arches usually come next, then the tip of the caudal penduncle, while the skull proper, the rest of the vertebral column and the supports of the vertical fins are ossified very late, and then usually weakly.'

These observations also apply to the alepisauroid fishes (Marshall, 1955) and particularly to the Lyomeri, which have a persistent notochord and a very reduced skeleton (Tchernavin, 1947). The weak lateral muscles in one species (*Eurypharynx pelecanoides*) is well shown in transverse sections figured by Nusbaum-Hilarowicz (1923). The vertebral column is not immediately surrounded by the myotomes, but by extensive fluid-filled cavities, which

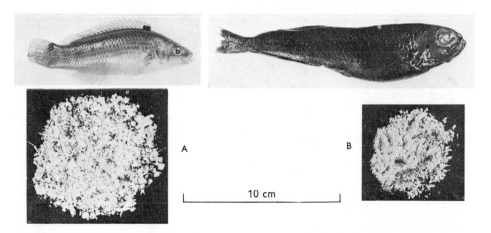

Text-fig. 2. A, a coastal fish with a swimbladder, *Ctenolabrus rupestris*, wet weight 16·7 g; with ash obtained from it shown below, weight 0·76 g. B, a deep-sea fish without swim-bladder, *Xenodermichthys copei*, wet weight 31·2 g; with ash obtained from it shown below, weight 0·33 g.

appear to be lymphatic in nature (Text-fig. 3). The ceratioid angler-fishes also have weakly developed lateral muscles and lightly ossified skeleton (Bertelsen, 1951).

But, as we have already seen, such weakness of the skeletal and muscular systems is not true of bathypelagic fishes with capacious gas-filled swim-bladders (for instance, the Myctophidae). Here we need only draw attention to the radiograph (Pl. II) of *Gonostoma elongatum* and *G. denudatum*. Earlier reference has been made to this (Marshall, 1954), but the plate gives more striking proof than words of the difference in ossification between these two related deep-sea fishes. The skeleton of *G. denudatum* (the outline of the swim-bladder can also be seen) stands out sharply beside that of *G. elongatum*, in which the swimbladder is regressed and invested with fat. (It should be stressed that both fish are of adult size and that this difference between them can also be readily appreciated when they are handled).

While the bathypelagic fishes with a well developed, gas-filled swimbladder tend to be concentrated at depths above 1000 m, those lacking this organ are found at all mid-water levels known to contain fish. Of the groups listed above, most of the stomiatoids, bathylagids, alepisauroids, giganturoids and Miripinnati tend to occur above the 1000 m level, while the Lyomeri and ceratioid angler-fishes are mostly fished below this depth (for a review of the vertical distribution and references, see Marshall, (1954)). The latter seems to be also true of many alepocephalids,[1] but not of such forms as *Searsia* (Grey, 1956).

Turning now to the physical nature of their environment, most species of

---

[1] Judging from trawl catches, a number of species appear to live close to the deep sea floor.

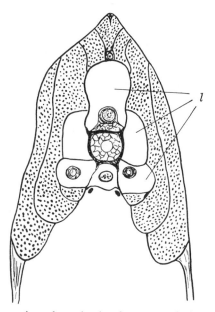

Text-fig. 3. Transverse section through the fore-part of the trunk of the gulper-eel, *Eurypharynx pelecanoides*, showing the extent of the muscle (dotted) and the lymphatic spaces (*l*). (After Nusbaum-Hilarowicz, 1923).

bathypelagic fishes are found in the tropical and temperate regions of the ocean between depths of about 250 m down to at least 3000 m. Owing to the rapid fall of temperature below the thermocline there is a corresponding increase in viscosity (between the above levels the laminar viscosity will be increased by a maximum factor of about 1·66). At the cooler, lower levels, a fish will thus gain more support from the surrounding water. If heavier than water it will sink more slowly, but it will find movements more difficult to make. At all events, it is interesting that the ceratioid angler-fishes, which appear to be little more than floating traps, make up most of the fish fauna at these lower levels.

Except for the Cetunculi and Miripinnati, which take small prey, particularly copepods (Bertelsen & Marshall, 1956), most of the bathypelagic fishes without a swimbladder consume a wide range of food organisms. Considering only their larger prey, the stomiatioid groups, the alepisauroids (excluding the paralepidids), the giganturoids, the Lyomeri and the ceratioid angler fishes are able to capture and master relatively large fishes, which may even be longer than themselves.

It is thus perfectly clear that these deep-sea predators are not handicapped by their relatively feeble muscular system. And, as we have seen, the main structures for holding and swallowing the prey, the jaws and gill arches, are supported by the most firmly ossified parts of the skeleton. Sections through the lower jaws of *Gonostoma elongatum* and *Diaphus rafinesquei* (a lantern fish with a capacious swimbladder) showed that the degree of ossification was much the same, but that the bone was thinner in the former. (This fish has a standard length of 205 mm and a lower jaw length of 36 mm, the bone of the latter having a maximum thickness of 0·03 mm. The corresponding measurements in the lantern fish are, 74, 16 and 0·12 mm). However, just beneath the tooth-bearing surface of the lower jaw and continuing to the angle, the bone in the gonostomatid has a honeycomb-like structure, which must give extra strength along the biting edge.

But while the jaws and associated structures have a relatively robust framework, the fish (or squid) has first to be caught. Observations on the capture of large prey have yet to be made, although both Mackintosh and Gunther (Clarke, 1950) watched a silvery stomiatoid fish attacking a swarm of krill at the surface. Gunther wrote: 'In its manner of lurking and snapping prey it resembled the freshwater pike.' Beebe & Crane (1939) observed that melanostomiatid fishes brought up alive '...swam about and snapped with all the accuracy of balance and swiftness of surface fish'.

However, fishes with thin lateral myotomes are hardly fitted to be tireless hunters, and this is borne out by their body forms and fin patterns. Like the pike, or better still the garfishes (Belonidae), the melanostomiatids, stomiatids and malacosteids have slim, elongated bodies and the dorsal and anal fins are opposed and set well back, close to the caudal fin. As in the species that Gunther saw, they are fishes which hover and dart after their prey. The combined dorsal, anal and caudal fins must form a powerful swimming organ (Beebe & Crane, 1939). Even more important, this fin arrangement will not only enable the fish to get away quickly from a hovering position but also confer stability during the dart (see Harris, 1952).

Dr S. Smith has noted from the radiographs that the myotomes are of relatively constant width along the length of the fish. We may compare the rapidly diminishing width of myotome on moving close to the tail of *Gadus minutus* with the almost constant width of myotome of the deep sea fish. The deep sea fish have not therefore flexible tails adapted for delicate movements.

The alepisauroids also tend to have an elongated pike-like form (the paralepidids are known as barracudinas), but only the anal fin has a posterior setting. One species, *Paralepis rissoi*, was observed from a bathyscaphe by Furnestin (1955), who describes it as hovering in a vertical position with the head or tail uppermost, apparently keeping its level by the flickering of the small dorsal fin. Then, from this position, the fish would suddenly 'jack-knife' and dart off. At least some of the other paralepidids may be expected to behave in a similar way, while a hovering-darting habit is likely to be common to all alepisauroids.[1]

The ceratioid angler-fishes achieve even greater economy of effort by luring their prey to within striking distance (Bertelsen, 1951). They are clearly floating traps *par excellence*. Brauer (1908) thought that the luminous chin barbels of stomiatoid fishes might also be used as lures, while in *Chauliodus* the long

---

[1] The scopelarchids and evermannellids have upwardly directed, tubular eyes and thus might be expected to adopt a horizontal position when hovering.

second ray of the dorsal fin, which is tipped with luminous tissue, also appears to be an angling device (Tchernavin, 1953). Some of the stomiatoids even have light organs within the mouth. It is also conceivable that the spongy luminous tissue on the tail of the gulper-eel, *Saccopharynx*, may also act as a lure.

Lastly, it should be emphasized that these fishes live in the quieter parts of the ocean under the thermocline, which has an average depth of about 75 m. Above the thermocline the currents are relatively fast and wind-driven; below this level the (density) currents are more sluggish and the water is much less turbulent. In these deeper reaches a fish with relatively reduced propulsive powers can use these to greater effect (during a sudden dart) than under more boisterous conditions.

To summarize, bathypelagic fishes without a swimbladder often radically reduce their weight in water by developing lightly ossified skeletons, which are associated with reduced muscular systems, particularly along the trunk and tail.[1] In spite of this many of them are able to capture and swallow large prey. However we must add that this tendency is not invariable among such predacious fishes. Certain of the Astronesthidae and *Chiasmodon* (the great swallower) have well developed swimbladders (together with firm skeletons and fairly thick lateral myotomes). A closer comparison between these bathypelagic fishes and those without a swimbaldder would clearly be interesting.

We should like to thank Mr G. Parish for advice and help with the radiography, and Captain C. A. Hoodless and the crew of R.V. 'Sarsia' for their co-operation. We are grateful to Mr R. G. Maddock for excellent technical assistance.

SUMMARY

Gonostoma elongatum is often within 0·5%, and *Xenodermichthys copei* within 1·2%, of neutral buoyancy despite the fact that neither of these fish has a gas-filled swimbladder.

The dry weights of *Gonostoma elongatum* and *Xenodermichthys copei* are only about 12·6 and 10% of their wet weights compared with 28% for a typical coastal marine fish *Ctenolabrus rupestris*.

The fat content of *Gonostoma elongatum* and *Xenodermichthys copei* is not particularly high, averaging about 3% of their wet weight, but their protein content which is only about 4–7% of their wet weight is very low indeed when compared with the corresponding 16% for a typical coastal marine fish.

Radiographs of *Gonostoma elongatum*, *Xenodermichthys copei* and *Chauliodus sloanei* show that their skeletons are poorly ossified when compared with that of *Gadus minutus* a typical coastal marine fish of the same size, whereas

---

[1] It is difficult to imagine a much weaker skeleton without much weaker muscles for, as A. V. Hill (1950) writes: 'Athletic animals in fact, have rather a small factor of safety...if a man's muscles could be altered without altering his general design, so as to allow him to run 25% faster or jump 50% higher, athletics would become a highly dangerous pastime; pulled tendons, torn muscles, even damaged bones, would be so frequent as to make it prohibitive.'

the skeleton of *Diaphus rafinesquii* is ossified as well as that of *Ctenolabrus rupestris* a coastal marine fish of similar size. The skeleton of *Gonostoma denudatum*, a bathypelagic fish with a swimbladder, is shown to be very well ossified in contrast with that of the related species *Gonostoma elongatum*.

The ash of *Xenodermichthys* was found to be about 1·5% of the wet body weight, whilst that of *Ctenolabrus rupestris* was about 4·5%.

The 'design' of these fish in relation to the life they lead is discussed. The muscular system is particularly reduced along the trunk and tail; whilst the jaws and gill arches, the main structures for holding and swallowing their prey, are supported by the most firmly ossified parts of the skeleton. These fish are almost certainly not tireless hunters, but rely on quick darts, often using luminous lures to attract their prey. Many of them could be simply described as floating traps.

REFERENCES

BEEBE, W. & CRANE, J., 1939. Deep sea fishes of the Bermuda Oceanographic Expeditions. Family Melanostomiatidae. *Zoologica, N.Y.*, Vol. 24, pp. 65–238.

BERTELSEN, E., 1951. The Ceratioid fishes. *Dana Rep.* (Vol. 7), No. 39, 184 pp.

BERTELSEN, E. & MARSHALL, N. B., 1956. The Miripinnati, a new order of teleost fishes. *Dana Rep.* (Vol. 8), No. 42, 34 pp. Copenhagen.

BRAUER, A. (1908). Die Tiefsee-fische. II. Anatomischer Teil. *Wiss. Ergebn. Valdivia*, Bd. 15, Lf. 2, 266 pp.

CLARKE, R. 1950. The bathypelagic angler fish *Ceratias holbölli* Kröyer. *Discovery Rep.*, Vol. 26, pp. 1–32.

COOPER, L. H. N., 1952. The physical and chemical oceanography of the waters bathing the Continental Slope of the Celtic Sea. *J. mar. biol. Ass. U.K.*, Vol. 30, pp. 465–510.

FURNESTIN, J. 1955. Une plongée en bathyscaphe. *Rev. Trav. Pêches marit.*, T. 19, No. 4, pp. 435–42.

GRAY, J., 1953. The locomotion of fishes. *Essays in Marine Biology*, pp. 1–16. Edinburgh: Oliver and Boyd.

GREY, M., 1956. The distribution of fishes found below a depth of 2000 metres. *Fieldiana, Zool.*, Vol. 36, (No. 2), pp. 75–337.

Handbook of Biological Data (1956). Editor: W. S. Spector. Ohio, U.S.A.: Wright Air Development Centre.

HARRIS, J. E., 1952. Fin patterns and mode of life in fishes. *Essays in Marine Biology*, pp. 17–28. Edinburgh: Oliver and Boyd.

HARROW, B., 1945. *Text-book of Biochemistry*. Philadelphia: W. Saunders.

HILL, A. V., 1950. The dimensions of animals and their muscular dynamics. *Sci. Progr. Twent. Cent.*, Vol. 38, No. 150, pp. 209–30.

HÖBER, R., 1945. *Physical Chemistry of Cells and Tissues*. London: Churchill.

International Critical Tables of Numerical Data Physics, Chemistry and Technology, 1928. Vol. 3, New York: McGraw Hill.

JONES, F. R. H. & MARSHALL, N. B., 1953. The structure and functions of the teleostean swimbladder. *Biol. Rev.*, Vol. 28, pp. 16–83.

KANWISHER, J. & EBELING, A., 1957. Composition of the swimbladder gas in bathypelagic fishes. *Deep-Sea Res.*, Vol. 4, pp. 211–17.

KERMACK, K. A., 1948. The propulsive powers of blue and fin whales. *J. exp. Biol.*, Vol. 25, pp. 237–40.

KROGH, A., 1939. *Osmotic Regulation in Aquatic Animals*. Cambridge University Press.

LOVE, R. M., 1957. The Biochemical Composition of Fish. In *The Physiology of Fishes*, Vol. 1, edited by Margaret E. Brown, pp. 401–18. New York: Academic Press.

LOVERN, J. A., 1955. *The Chemistry of Lipids of Biochemical Significance*. London: Methuen.

MARSHALL, N. B., 1954. *Aspects of Deep Sea Biology*. London: Hutchinsons.

—— 1955. Alepisauroid fishes. '*Discovery*' *Rep.*, Vol. 27, pp. 303–36.

—— (in preparation). The swimbladders of deep sea fishes.

NUSBAUM-HILAROWICZ, J., 1923. Études d'anatomie comparée sur les poissons provenant des compagnes scientifiques de S.A.S. le Prince de Monaco. *Résult. Camp. sci. Monaco*, Fasc. 65, pp. 1–100.

SHEWAN, J. M., 1951. The chemistry and metabolism of the nitrogenous extractives in fish. *Symp. biochem. Soc.*, No. 6, pp. 28–48. Cambridge University Press.

TCHERNAVIN, V. V., 1947. Six specimens of Lyomeri in the British Museum (with notes on the skeleton of Lyomeri). *J. Linn. Soc. (Zool.)*, Vol. 41, pp. 287–350.

—— 1953. *The Feeding Mechanisms of a Deep Sea Fish* Chauliodus sloanei *Schneider*, viii + 101 pp. London: British Museum (Nat. Hist).

VINOGRADOV, A. P., 1953. *The Elementary Composition of Marine Organisms*. (Efron and Stlow, translators). New Haven: Yale University Press.

Additional Readings

CHAPTER 6

ALEXANDER, R. McN. 1966. Physical aspects of swimbladder function. *Biol. Rev.* 41:141–176.

BONE, Q. 1973. A note on the buoyancy of some lanternfishes (Myctophoidei). *J. mar. biol. Ass. U.K.* 53(3):619–633.

BROWN, D. Scott, and COPELAND, D. E. 1977. Overlapping platelets: a diffusion barrier in a teleost swimbladder. *Science* 197:383–384.

D'AOUST, B. G. 1970. The role of lactic acid in gas secretion in the teleost swimbladder. *Comp. Biochem. Physiol.* 32:637–668.

DENTON, E. 1960. The buoyancy ot marine animals. *Sci. Amer.* 203(1):118–128.

DENTON, E. J. 1961. The buoyancy of fish and cephalopods. *Prog. Biophysics and Biophysical Chem.* 11:177–234.

FANGE, R. 1966. Physiology of the swimbladder. *Physiol. Rev.* 46:299–322.

GORDON, M. S. 1970. Hydrostatic pressure. Chapter 11, pp. 445–464 in W. S. Hoar, and D. J. Randall, eds., *Fish Physiology*, Vol. 4. New York: Academic Press.

JONES, F. R. H. 1952. The swimbladder and the vertical movements of teleostean fishes. II. The restriction to rapid and slow movements. *J. Exp. Biol.* 24:94–109.

JONES, F. R. H., and MARSHALL, N. B. 1953. The structure and functions of the teleostean swimbladder. *Biol. Rev.* 28:16–83.

KANWISHER, J., and EBELING, A. W. 1957. Composition of the swimbladder gas in bathypelagic fishes. *Deep-Sea Res.* 4(3):211–217.

KUHN, W.; RAMEL, A.; KUHN, H. J.; and MARTI, E. 1963. The filling mechanism of the swimbladder. Generation of high gas pressures through hairpin countercurrent multiplication. *Experientia* 19:497–512.

LEE, R. F.; PHLEGER, C. F.; and HORN, M. H. 1975. Composition of oil in fish bones: possible function in neutral buoyancy. *Comp. Biochem. Physiol.* 50B:13–16.

MAGNUSON, J. J. 1970. Hydrostatic equilibrium of *Euthynnus affinis*, a pelagic teleost without a gasbladder. *Copeia* 1970(1):56–85.

MARSHALL, N. B. 1960. Swimbladder structure of deep-sea fishes in relation to their systematics. Discovery Reports 31:1–121.

MARSHALL, N. B. 1970. Swimbladder development and the life of deep-sea fishes. *Proc. Inter. Symp. Biol.* Sound Scattering Ocean, G. B. Farquhar, ed. U.S. Navy: Maury Center for Ocean Science, Wash. D.C.: 69–73.

O'CONNELL, C. P. 1955. The gasbladder and its relation to the inner ear in *Sardinops caerulea* and *Engraulis mordax*. *Fish. Bull., U.S.* (104), 56:505–533.

PHLEGER, C. F. 1971. Pressure effects on cholesterol and lipid synthesis by the swimbladder of an abyssal *Coryphaenoides sp. Am. Zool.* 11:559–570.

PHLEGER, C. F., and BENSON, A. A. 1971. Cholesterol and hyperbaric oxygen in swimbladders of deep-sea fishes. *Nature* 230:122.

ROBERTS, B. L. 1969. The buoyancy and swimming movements of electric rays. *J. mar. biol. Ass. U.K.* 49:621–640.

SCHOLANDER, P. F. 1954. Secretion of gases against high pressures in swimbladders of deep sea fishes II. The rete mirabile. *Biol. Bull.* 107:260–277.

SCHOLANDER, P. F., and VAN DAM, L. 1953. Composition of the swimbladder gas in deep sea fishes. *Biol. Bull.* 104:75–86.

SCHOLANDER, P. F., and VAN DAM, L. 1954. Secretion of gases against high pressures in the swimbladder of deep sea fishes. I. Oxygen dissociation in blood. *Biol. Bull.* 107:247–259.

STEEN, J. B. 1963. The physiology of the swimbladder of the eel *Anguilla* I. The solubility of gases and the buffer capacity of the blood. *Acta Physiol. Scan.* 58:124–137.

STEEN, J. B. 1963. The physiology of the swimbladder of the eel *Anguilla* II. The reabsorption of gases. *Acta Physiol. Scan.* 58:138–149.

STEEN, J. B. 1970. The swimbladder as a hydrostatic organ. Chapter 10, pp. 413–443, in W. S. Hoar, and D. J. Randall, eds. *Fish Physiology*, Vol. 4. New York: Academic Press.

TODD, E. S., and EBELING, A. W. 1966. Aerial respiration in the longjaw mudsucker *Gillichthys mirabilis* (Teleostei: Gobiidae). *Biol. Bull.* 130(2):265–288.

7

Respiration

How a Fish Extracts Oxygen from Water

By DR. GEORGE M. HUGHES
Magdalene College, Cambridge

The folded surfaces of the gills may far exceed the external body in area. In its respiratory process the fish uses the "counter-current" technique well known to engineers, together with a remarkable two-pump mechanism providing a continuous flow of water through the gills.

Fishes soon die for lack of oxygen when they are removed from water; this is so well known that we speak of "a fish out of water" to describe an inability to cope with a new environment. Yet in water there is only one-thirtieth the volume of oxygen contained in the same volume of air. In this article I shall discuss the mechanisms which, although they cannot make use of the rich supply of oxygen in the air, enable the fish to solve the not inconsiderable problem of extracting oxygen from water.

A 100-gram river fish needs about 5 cubic centimetres of oxygen per hour when at rest, and up to three or four times this amount when normally active. Even if it were 100 per cent efficient at removing this oxygen, the fish would have to pass at least 15 to 30 cubic centimetres of water across its respiratory surfaces each minute. To handle that volume of air would not be difficult, but with water far more work is required because the density of the medium is nearly 1,000 times greater and 100 times more viscous. One or 2 per cent of the oxygen intake of a man at rest is spent in work done by the respiratory muscles. The figure for a fish is likely to be many times greater. In addition, the rate of diffusion of oxygen is 300,000 times slower in water than it is in air.

How, then, does a fish overcome problems which appear so much greater than those facing terrestrial vertebrates; and why should it die under conditions which appear more favourable?

Part of the answer to these questions lies in the structure of the respiratory surfaces of the fish and in the nature of the flow across them. The gills are a very finely divided series of plates, presenting an enormous surface of contact to the water, which passes across them in a single direction, unlike the tidal flow of the mammalian lung. When the fish is removed into air, the loss of support from the water, together with surface tension, render the effective surface area of the gills extremely small: the result in most cases is oxygen deficiency and death.

The total surface exposed to the respiratory current of water varies between fishes according to their activity. In very active fish such as mackerel it may be over 1,000 square millimetres per gram of body weight, which is equivalent to more than ten times the external body surface. A measure of the efficiency of the extraction mechanism is its ability to utilize up to 80 per cent of the oxygen contained in the water passing over the gills. The highest figure determined in man is about 25 per cent. Such efficient extraction by the fish can be explained by the so-called "counter-current" relationship between the flow of the blood and of the water, and by the remarkable pumping mechanism which affords a continuous flow of water across the gills throughout the whole respiratory cycle.

Counter-current between the blood and water.—The counter-current principle operates in many places in animals where efficient exchange of dissolved materials or of heat is required between two fluids. Such systems have long been used by engineers in heat

This article first appeared in *New Scientist London*, the weekly review of Science and Technology, 11:346–348.

exchange mechanisms. One of the first to appreciate its importance in animal physiology was van Dam, who in 1938 described its operation in fish gills. Here it ensures that blood which is about to leave the gills almost fully saturated with oxygen meets water entering with its full oxygen content, while blood deficient in oxygen entering the gills meets water from which most of the oxygen has already been removed. In this way there is always a greater tension of oxygen in the water than in the adjacent blood, so that oxygen continues to pass into the blood throughout its passage across the gill.

The effectiveness of this arrangement is shown by the sharp decrease in uptake of oxygen (from 51 per cent to 9 per cent) when the direction of the flow of water through the gills is reversed experimentally.

For maximal effectiveness of exchange it is also important that the two fluids come into close contact and that their rates of flow are adjusted to one another. The distance over which the oxygen has to diffuse from the water to the blood corpuscles is small, because the corpuscles are nearly as wide as the thin folds of the gill in which they circulate, and outside the folds the water passes on both sides (see Figure 1*c*). There is, as yet, little information concerning the volume of blood flowing through the gills in a given interval of time, but there are certainly reflex mechanisms which ensure that some relationship exists between the heart beat and respiratory frequency. The heart beat is usually slower than the respiratory frequency and in some instances it is synchronized with a particular phase of the respiratory cycle, but this is by no means always true. In a trout for example, these frequencies are almost the same; they slip gradually out of step, although the heart tends to beat when the mouth is closing. In other cases the heart beat is slower than that of the breathing in a simple ratio.

Such mechanisms ensure that there is always a good supply of water from which the blood can obtain its oxygen. This is important, because the blood can carry 10-15 times as much oxygen as the same volume of water.

Continuous flow across the gills.—When breathing, a fish opens its mouth and water is drawn into the buccal cavity; and after passing over the gills it leaves the opercular cavities through slits which appear when the gill covers (opercula) expand and come away from the side of the fish. This discontinuous flow into and out of the system gives a false impression of the flow across the gills themselves. Evidence for a truer description has recently been obtained by recording pressure changes on both sides of the gills by means of sensitive gauges—condenser manometers. These experiments on three freshwater species, which I have done in collaboration with Dr. G. Shelton, showed that with the exception of a brief period there is a pressure gradient (i.e., the pressure of water in the buccal cavity exceeds that in the opercular cavities) throughout the whole breathing cycle. It is almost certain, therefore, that as a result water will pass continuously across the gills and so greatly increase the uptake of oxygen.

The mechanism which makes it possible involves the operation of two pumps slightly out of phase with one another, as illustrated diagrammatically in Figure 2. In the fish the pumping actions are due to changes in volume of the cavities, produced by muscular action. As we shall see later, the gill resistance is more complicated than the simple sieve depicted in the diagrams. During the inspiratory phase the buccal cavity expands and water enters through the mouth. At the same time the opercular cavities expand, but water cannot enter through their external openings because a thin membrane around the outer rim functions as a valve. During expansion of the opercular cavity the hydrostatic pressure becomes less than that in the buccal cavity and water is drawn across the gills: the opercular cavity acts as a *suction pump*. During the phase of decrease in volume, which also starts in the

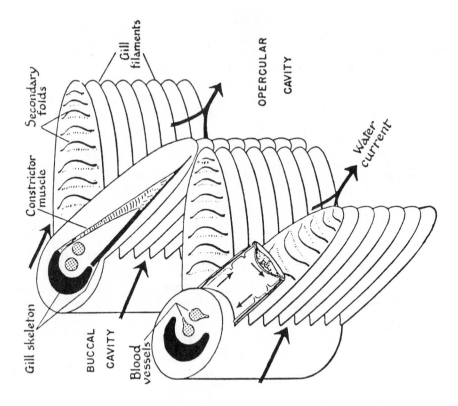

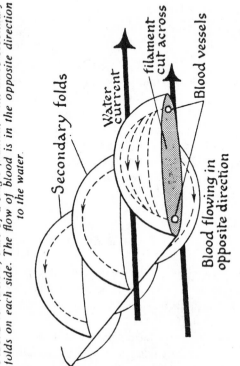

FIGURE 1a. (Above) Diagram to show the position of the four gill arches beneath the operculum on the left side of a fish.
FIGURE 1b. (Right) Part of two of these gill arches are shown with the filaments of adjacent rows touching at their tips. The blood vessels which carry the blood before and after its passage over the gills are shown.

FIGURE 1c. (Below) Part of a single filament with three secondary folds on each side. The flow of blood is in the opposite direction to the water.

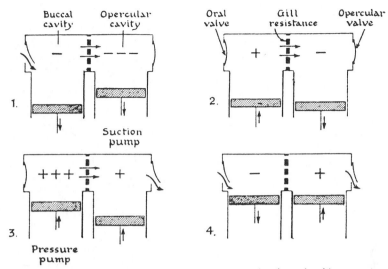

FIGURE 2. *Diagrammatic representation of the double-pumping mechanism which maintains an almost continuous flow of water across the gills. The two major phases of the cycle are (1) in which the opercular suction pumps are active and (3) when the buccal pressure pump forces water across the gills. The two transition phases (2) and (4) each takes up only 1/10th of the whole cycle. The pressures in the cavities are given with respect to that of the water outside.*

buccal cavity, the pressure becomes greater than the external water as the mouth begins to close. It is functionally closed even in those fishes which do not close their mouths completely because of the presence of two thin membranous valves which project from just behind the upper and lower lips. During this phase, the increase in pressure within the buccal cavity is greater than that in the opercular cavities and water continues to pass across the gills: the buccal cavity acts as a *pressure pump.*

The pressure difference curves (Figure 3) show that during nearly the whole of the cycle there is an excess pressure tending to force water across the gills from buccal to opercular cavity. There is a brief period, however, during which this pressure difference is reversed and there will be a tendency for the flow to go in the opposite direction, but, as it is so brief and the pressure difference so low, the inertia of the water makes any actual reversal unlikely. In this way, then, a continuous flow of water is maintained over the gills in a direction opposite to that of the blood and a very high percentage of the oxygen in the inspired water is removed from it.

There are many interesting variations on this basic plan which have been revealed using similar techniques on marine species, for example, the relative contribution of the two pumps, buccal and opercular, in fishes occupying different habitats. Fish which are predominantly swimmers have the buccal pump better developed, although in some cases neither pump operates during the swimming movements of the fish. A notable example of this is the mackerel, which is obliged to swim continuously in order to maintain the flow of water through its gills. In other cases, such as leopard sharks which I observed in the Marineland Aquarium, California, pumping movements are not present during swimming, but appear as soon as the fish comes to rest.

Fish which spend most or all of their time on the sea bottom have enlarged opercular cavities supported by additional skeletal rays and the suction pump is better developed.

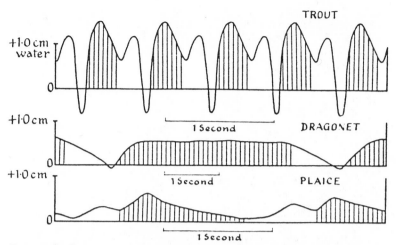

FIGURE 3. *Curves to show the pressure difference between the buccal and opercular cavity in three fishes. Positive values indicate a greater pressure in the buccal cavity. The opercular suction phase (4) is shaded and forms a greater part of the cycle in the dragonet and plaice. The absence of any negative phase in the latter is probably because it can actively close the opercular opening.*

Such fish as the bullhead, gurnard, dragonet, plaice and other flat-fishes are of this type. In the dragonet, for instance, gradual opercular expansion maintains a fairly constant differential pressure across the gills; then, during a relatively brief contraction phase, water is expelled from both cavities out of the narrow opercular openings.

In flat-fishes which lie permanently on one side and are almost buried when resting on the sea bottom, other problems arise. The gills are equally developed on both sides of plaice and sole, and it seems certain that the water is pumped through both opercular cavities. The danger of sand entering the cavities and damaging the gills is a very real one. No reversal occurs in the differential pressure of these fish, and this is probably due to the active control of the opercular valves which will, therefore, prevent the entry of even the slightest current.

Just as the working of the two pumps is related to the habitat of the fish, so there are corresponding variations in the structure of their gills. Bottom-living fish generally have smaller gill areas and coarser sieves. The sieves are made up of many thousands of pores which are found between the gill filaments—the double rows of thin plates which are stacked all the way round each side of the four bony arches on both sides of the fish (Figure 1a). They form a continuous meshwork extending across the whole of the side walls of the pharynx. As the tips of the filaments are splayed out by the elastic properties of the supporting skeleton they remain in contact with one another at their tips, and water passes between the slits provided by the plates of adjacent filaments. These are not simple slits, however; the upper and lower surfaces of each filament have thin projections which form the actual respiratory surfaces. It is the collapse of these secondary folds and the consequent reduction in effective area for gaseous exchange that leads to asphyxiation when most fish are brought on to the land. The closer these folds, (horse mackerel 39 per millimetre, herring 33), the more readily they occlude one another. In those fishes of the sea-shore that are exposed by the tide, such as some gobies, the secondary folds are widely spaced (15 per millimetre), and different species have supporting structures which are greater the longer their exposure on the sea-shore.

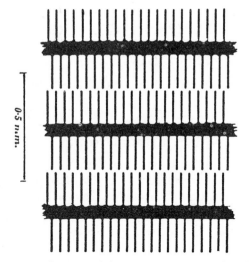

FIGURE 4. *Diagram of a part of the sieve provided by the filaments and their secondary folds in a tench. The section passes through three filaments and shows secondary folds projecting alternately above and below the surface of each filament. The water flows at right angles to the paper.*

The sieve provided by the gills is a very fine one and is shown in Figure 4. At first sight the dimensions appear too small to allow sufficient flow of water with pressure differences of only one three-thousandth of an atmosphere which have been found in many species. The number of pores is so large, however (for example, a quarter of a million in a 130-gram tench), that calculations based on an equation similar to Poiseuille's for the flow through each of them give figures for the total flow which are at least as great as the rates of flow which have been measured in fish at rest. But at higher rates it is likely that an increasing fraction of the water escapes between the tips of the filaments. Such "short-circuiting" may account for the lower utilization of oxygen and the apparent fall in gill resistance which we have observed at these rates of flow. The gill resistance is certainly not constant during the respiratory cycle. Ciné-films of small transparent gobies and young conger eels have shown that there is a definite phase in the respiratory cycle when the tips of the filaments separate and allow an increase in the short-circuited flow. During very active pumping, the process will be accentuated by the yielding of the gills to the increased pressure difference. Contact between the filament tips is maintained entirely by the elasticity of the gill rays, there being no active muscles which can keep them spread out. The constrictor muscles shown in Figure 1*b* function when the fish makes "coughing" movements, whereby the pressure gradient is reversed and a rapid reversal of flow cleans the gills.

These are but a few of the features found in the respiratory mechanisms of fishes during investigations of the past few years. A great deal remains to be learned about the detailed relationships between the flow of water and blood across the gills and the uptake of oxygen, to say nothing of the wide variety of adaptations which await investigation in the fish living under different conditions. Like so many problems investigated by present-day zoologists, the physical and physiological aspects have here illuminated our extensive knowledge of the animal's natural history and structure.

THE MUSCULAR BASIS OF THE RESPIRATORY PUMPS IN THE TROUT

By C. M. BALLINTIJN* and G. M. HUGHES†

Department of Zoology, Cambridge

(*Received* 1 *March* 1965)

INTRODUCTION

The respiratory pumps of a teleost consist of a buccal cavity and two opercular cavities, separated by the gills (Hughes, 1960; Hughes & Shelton, 1958, 1962; Woskoboinikoff, 1932). Volume changes of the cavities, caused by movements of bone arches and the operculi, result in the pumping action of the system.

In these pumps a fairly large number of muscles are working on a complex mechanism of bones, ligaments and articulations. Several authors (Baglioni, 1910; v. Dobben, 1937; Henschel, 1939, 1941; Holmquist, 1910; Hughes & Shelton, 1962; Kirchhoff, 1958; Willem, 1931, 1940, 1947; Willem & de Bersaques-Willem, 1927; Woskoboinikoff, 1932) have described this system and made an attempt to understand its working principles. Many theories have been developed to indicate which muscles take part in respiration and the role they play. In most papers the evidence for the theory is purely anatomical: the position and insertion of a muscle are used to explain its role. As, however, the moving parts of the teleost head skeleton articulate with one another in a complex way and are also coupled by means of ligaments, a great deal of interaction takes place and consequently contraction of one of several muscles can give rise to the same, or almost the same movement. Experiments in which muscles or ligaments are cut (Henschel, 1939, 1941; Holmquist, 1910) give more direct evidence. The possibility exists, however, that the function of one muscle is taken over by another that is inactive during normal respiration, so that from experiments of this kind the only valid conclusion is whether a given muscle can or cannot be missed.

The contraction of a muscle is associated with electric potential changes which can be led off with a pair of fine electrodes put into the muscle. The recording of this electromyogram makes it possible to be more certain if, and precisely when, a muscle is active.

With this technique an analysis has been made of the activity pattern in the head muscles of the trout in relation to the movements and pressures recorded simultaneously from the buccal and opercular cavities.

MATERIALS AND METHODS

The trout used were obtained from a hatchery (Nailsworth, Gloucestershire). They were kept in stock tanks with running tap-water in the basement of the laboratory. The temperature was about 13° C.

* On leave from the Zoological Laboratory of the University, Groningen, The Netherlands. Supported by a grant of the Netherlands Organization for the Advancement of Pure Research (Z.W.O.).
† Present address: Department of Zoology, University of Bristol.

From *J. Exp. Biol.* 43:349–362. Reprinted by permission.

During the experiments the animals were put in a glass trough containing 10 l. M.S. 222 solution at 0·03–0·05 ‰, and when anaesthetized they were fixed in a clamp. At the beginning of each experiment the temperature of the solution was the same as in the stock tanks and it was not allowed to rise above about 16° C. After an experiment the fish, brought back to the stock tank, very quickly recovered and showed normal activity.

During an experiment simultaneous recordings were made of the movement of the lower jaw, the movement of the operculum, the pressure in the buccal cavity, the pressure in the opercular cavity, and the electromyograms of four muscles.

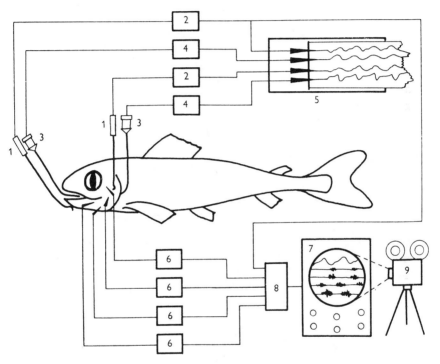

Fig. 1. Experimental set-up. For description see text.

Fig. 1 shows a block diagram of the experimental set-up. The movements were converted into an electric signal with R.C.A. 5734 mechano-electric transducers (1) and a bridge circuit (2), and the pressures converted with Hansen condenser manometers (3) and a capacity transducer circuit (4) (Hughes & Shelton, 1958). These signals were recorded on a four-channel Ediswan pen recorder with a frequency response up to 90 cvc./sec. (5).

The potentials of each muscle were led off with a pair of stainless-steel electrodes, insulated with araldite except for the tip.

After amplification with Tektronix type 122 preamplifiers (6), the myograms of four muscles were displayed on a Tektronix 532 oscilloscope (7) through a five-channel coincidence switching unit (8). On the fifth channel, the movement of either mouth or operculum was displayed. It served to correlate the pen recordings made simultaneously with the oscillograph records, filmed with a Dumont oscillograph camera (9).

RESULTS

Before considering the results of the electromyographic, movement and pressure recordings it is necessary to be clear about the morphology of the skeleton and musculature of the trout head. The account which follows is partly based upon our own observations but it is also necessary to review previous work, most of which was done with purely morphological methods.

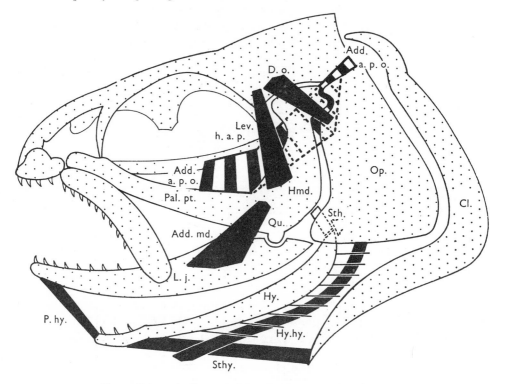

Fig. 2. Schematic diagram of the respiratory muscles of a trout.

Pal. pt.	Palato-pterygoid		Lev. h. a. p.	Levator hyomandibulae et arcus palatini
Qu.	Quadrate		Add. a. p. o.	Adductor arcus palatini et operculi
Hmd.	Hyomandibula			
Op.	Operculum			
L. j.	Lower jaw		Add. md.	Adductor mandibulae
Hy.	Hyoid		P. hy.	Protractor hyoidei
Cl.	Cleithrum		Hy.hy.	Hyohyoideus
Sth.	Stylohyal		Sthy.	Sternohyoideus
D. o.	Dilator operculi			

1. The skeleton

In Fig. 2 a schematic diagram is given of the bones and muscles of a trout head. The skeleton is composed of the following units:

(a) The *palatal complex*, the major components of which are hyomandibula, quadrate and palato-pterygoid, is suspended from the neurocranium at two points. Anteriorly it articulates with the ethmoidal region, posteriorly with the otic capsule. The connexion between metapterygoid-hyomandibula and quadrate-symplectic consists of rather flexible cartilage.

(*b*) A second functional unit is the *lower jaw*, which articulates posteriorly with the quadrate. Anteriorly its two rami have a flexible connexion, so that besides opening and closing movements it can expand laterally when the palatal complex expands.

(*c*) The third unit will be referred to as the *hyoid* and is composed of the ventral elements (ceratohyal, basihyal, copula) of the hyoid arch. These elements support the floor of the buccal cavity and are connected to the hyomandibula through an intermediate bone, the stylohyal. The stylohyal articulates with both the hyomandibula and the ventral elements of the hyoid arch and the latter articulates also with the interoperculum. The ventral junction of the two halves of the hyoid is flexible. The branchiostegal rays are implanted along the hyoid.

(*d*) The branchial arches are stretched between the most ventral element of the hyoid, the basihyal, and the neurocranium.

(*e*) The *operculum* consists of four parts: the preopercular, interopercular, subopercular and opercular bones. The latter articulates with the hyomandibula, and the interoperculum articulates with the stylohyal–hyoid junction.

(*f*) The *cleithrum* forms the posterior border of the opercular cavities.

2. *Muscles*

The muscles working this system can be divided into two groups, of which one expands the respiratory cavities and the other reduces their volume. Essentially every moving element has its own abductor and adductor muscles, but through the coupling between the elements a given muscle can affect a greater part of the system than only the bones to which it is attached.

The *levator hyomandibulae et arcus palatini* lifts and abducts the palatal complex and so gives rise in the first place to a lateral expansion of the buccal cavity, of which it forms the sides. As, however, the lower jaw, the hyoid and the operculum are connected to the hyomandibula–quadrate part of the palatal complex, expansion of the latter also results in abduction of the operculi and in lateral expansion of the jaw and hyoid.

The antagonist of the levator hyomandibulae et arcus palatini in the trout is a strip of muscle fibres, inserted on one side of the neurocranium and on the other side running along the inside of the palato-pterygoid, the hyomandibula, the operculum and the dorsal rim of the operculum. In other species this muscular sheet is divided into different muscles: the adductor arcus palatini et hyomandibulae, the adductor operculi and the levator operculi (Dietz, 1912). In the following account this sheet is referred to as *adductor arcus palatini et operculi*. Besides adducting the palatal complex it adducts and lifts the operculum.

The abductor of the operculum is the *dilator operculi* muscle. Some authors (van Dobben, 1937; Henschel, 1941; Holmquist, 1910) believed that the levator operculi lifts the operculum synchronously with its abduction by the dilator operculi. The fact, however, that in trout the adductor operculi and levator operculi are one strip of muscle suggests the contrary. Indeed, our records show that activity in the adductor and levator regions of this muscular strip is synchronous and alternates with contraction of the dilator operculi.

Movements of the operculum are transmitted to the lower jaw by the mandibulo-interopercular ligament that connects the interopercular bone with a process of the lower jaw behind the articulation with the quadrate (van Dobben, 1937; Holmquist,

1910). Consequently levation of the operculum by the levator operculi part of the strip also produces depression of the lower jaw. According to Holmquist and van Dobben, this movement is reinforced by contraction of the dilator operculi.

The *protractor hyoideus* is sometimes called geniohyoideus, but according to Edgeworth (1931) the development of this muscle in *Lepidosteus* and the Teleostei does not justify the use of this name. It is attached anteriorly on the lower jaw and posteriorly on the hyoid and has been regarded as the abductor muscle of the lower jaw (Allis, 1897; Baglioni, 1907; Vetter, 1878). Even the double function of abducting the lower jaw and adducting the hyoid arch has been ascribed to it, but Holmquist (1910)

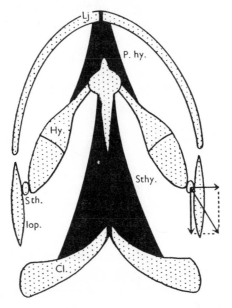

Fig. 3. Ventral view of the floor of the mouth and the hyoid.

L. j.	Lower jaw	Sth.	Stylohyal	Sthy.	Sternohyoideus
Hy.	Hyoid	Iop.	Interoperculum	P. hy.	Protractor hyoidei
Cl.	Cleithrum				

concludes from his extirpation experiments that it only adducts the hyoid arch. This view was confirmed by Hughes (Hughes & Shelton, 1962) using electromyography. The lower jaw thus has no abductor muscle of its own. It is, however, abducted through levation of the operculum and also through movements of the hyoid which will be described later.

A large muscle, the *adductor mandibulae*, connects the lower jaw with the hyomandibula bone. It shuts the mouth.

Contraction of the *sternohyoideus muscle*, which connects the basal part of the hyoid arch with the cleithra, retracts and abducts the hyoid arch and so lowers the floor of the mouth. This also produces a force along the hyoid bones (Figs. 2, 3) working against the stylohyal and interoperculum. This force can be resolved into two components: one abducting the interoperculum, stylohyal, and through the latter the palatal complex (Henschel, 1941); the second component results in a caudal movement of the interoperculum. This caudal movement is transferred to the lower jaw by the mandibulo-interopercular ligament and lowers the mandible. Besides this there are the following direct connexions between the hyoid arch and the lower jaw: the hyoideo-mandibular ligament, the protractor hyoidei, and the skin. These elements are stretched during more extensive abductions and exert a direct traction on the lower jaw (van Dobben, 1937; Holmquist, 1910; Kirchhoff, 1958).

As mentioned above, the protractor hyoideus adducts the hyoid arch. According to Holmquist (1910) the lower jaw is fixed by the adductor mandibulae when the protractor hyoideus contracts so that the hyoid arch is adducted and the floor of the mouth raised by this muscle.

Evidence in the literature regarding the function of the hyohyoideus muscles which interconnect the branchiostegal rays and cross ventrally to the contralateral side is not unanimous. Borcea (1906) and Henschel (1941) both divide this muscle for a flatfish into an inspiratory and an expiratory part. Holmquist (1910) thinks that expansion or contraction of the branchiostegal membrane through this muscle depends on the position of the mouth and the direction of the contraction wave in the muscle. Hughes & Shelton (1962) conclude that in some fishes, during opercular expansion, the opercular membrane is actively held close to the cleithral girdle, dorsally through contraction of the levator operculi and ventrally through contraction of the hyohyoideus.

Skeletal couplings

The units which make up the teleost skull are connected with one another in a complex way. The following account is based on a study of the skeleton both in isolation and with the muscles and ligaments *in situ*. The results of the electromyographic work have also been of value in this connexion.

The couplings (Fig. 4) between skeletal units which play an important part in the trout mechanism can be summarized as follows:

1. Coupling brought into action by contraction of the *levator operculi* part of the *adductor arcus palatini et operculi*:

A. Lowering of the jaw. Levation of the operculum produces depression of the lower jaw by way of the operculum, the inter-operculum and the ligament to the angular which lies behind the articulation of the lower jaw with the quadrate, and therefore gives depression.

2. Couplings brought into action by contraction of the *sternohyoideus*:

A. Lowering of the jaw may involve three couplings: (*a*) The sternohyoideus depresses the hyoid, which is connected by the ligamentum hyoidei-mandibularis to the mandible, and this produces a lowering of the jaw. (*b*) Depression of the hyoid is also accompanied by its retraction and the force along the hyoid may be resolved into two components. One of them presses backwards on the inter-operculum, which is connected by a ligament to the angular bone, which then depresses the lower jaw (coupling 1). (*c*) The sternohyoideus action also lowers the mandible when the hyoid has been pulled a good distance back because the skin becomes stretched and the passive elastic properties of the protractor hyoidei also help in this action.

B. Expansion of the operculum results from contraction of the sternohyoideus in two ways: (*a*) Owing to the flexibility of the anterior parts of the hyoid it expands laterally when the sternohyoideus contracts. This produces expansion of the operculum through the inter-opercular bones. (*b*) There is a mechanism for expansion of the operculum as a result of movement of the hyoid because the operculum is attached to the hyomandibula and so expands with it.

C. Expansion of the palatal complex. Lateral expansion of the hyomandibula, produced above, also results in expansion of the whole palatal complex of which it forms a part.

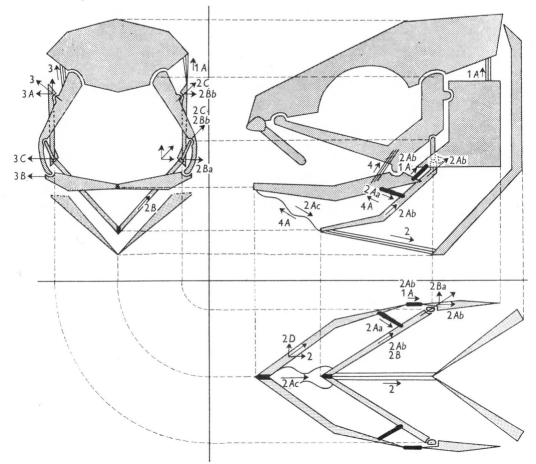

Fig. 4. Three-dimensional diagram of the couplings. The numbering refers to the description in the text. Bone is stippled, muscle striped and ligaments black.

D. Increase in the size of the mouth. The lower jaw articulates with the quadrate, which is connected to the hyomandibula, and therefore the posterior ends of the lower jaw expand laterally, and as the junction of the two rami is flexible this produces a widening of the mouth. This mechanism plays no part in respiration but is probably important in feeding as it results in an increase in the effective cross-sectional area of the mouth.

E. Expansion of the branchial arches. The branchial arches are joined ventrally to the copula, which is connected to the hyoid. Consequently, retraction of the hyoid by the action of the sternohyoideus not only affects the copula but also produces a backward movement and consequent expansion of the branchial arches. In this way further expansion of the oro-branchial cavity is produced.

3. *Couplings brought into action by the levator hyomandibulae et arcus palatini:*

A. Lateral expansion of the operculum. Expansion of the palatal complex by contraction of this muscle results in abduction of the hyomandibula, which produces opercular expansion.

B. Lateral expansion of the lower jaw because it articulates with the quadrate, which is connected to the hyomandibula and adducts with it.

C. Lateral expansion of the hyoid, which is connected to the hyomandibula through the stylohyal.

4. *Couplings brought into action by the adductor mandibulae:*

A. When this raises the lower jaw it has the effect of raising the hyoid through the action of the hyoideo-mandibular ligament and protracting it because the floor of the mouth is stretched. As a result the hyomandibula is adducted and with it the operculum.

5. *Couplings brought into action by the hyohyoideus (constrictor in origin):*

A. When this muscle contracts it effectively raises the copula and results in a folding of the branchial arches and more or less helps to adduct the operculum.

This, then, is a summary of some of the main couplings found in the trout.

It cannot be overemphasized that, although the skeletal couplings are similar in many species of fish, the muscle co-ordination is not necessarily the same. From the results obtained so far it has been found that, for the same species and even the same individual, many different patterns of muscle action are possible, each of which can be effective in producing normal ventilation. Clearly the interspecific differences may be quite marked.

3. *Electromyography*

By correlating the pressure and movement records from the pen recorder with the electromyographic records from the oscilloscope (Fig. 5), a composite picture has been obtained of the activity of several head muscles as related to the operation of the respiratory pumps.

In Fig. 6 such correlated records are reproduced for two sets of respiratory muscles. Fig. 7 gives a summary of all the muscles that were recorded from and forms a basis for the following account.

To the left of the diagram (Fig. 7) the mouth is open and the operculi are abducted, or nearly abducted. Contraction of the adductor mandibulae starts the cycle with adduction of the lower jaw. When the respiratory movements are strong, the protractor hyoideus and the hyohyoideus contract synchronously or slightly after the adductor mandibulae. As the lower jaw is fixed by the latter muscle, the protractor hyoideus moves the hyoid arch forwards and upwards and so raises the floor of the mouth. The hyohyoideus contracts the branchiostegal apparatus and also raises the hyoid arch, because its fibres cross to the opposite side. This lifting of the hyoid arch adducts the hyomandibula (Henschel, 1941) and the interoperculum, with which it articulates, and so initiates adduction of the palatal complex and operculum. Contraction of the branchiostegal membrane reinforces the adduction of the operculum.

When depth and frequency of respiration are low the protractor hyoideus and the hyohyoideus are not active. Adduction of the lower jaw, however, results in lifting of the hyoid arch through the hyoideo-mandibular ligament, so that all the above-mentioned movements can take place, but with less force.

The adductor arcus palatini et operculi often commences its activity during the last part of the adductor mandibulae contraction. Its activity, however, is low at first, but as soon as the adductor mandibulae stops firing its activity reaches a high level. It adducts and lifts the operculum, pulling it laterally and ventrally close to the body. The lifting motion pulls the interoperculum in a dorso-caudal direction and this action, because of the mandibulo-interopercular ligament, results in abduction of the lower jaw (Holmquist, 1910; van Dobben, 1937).

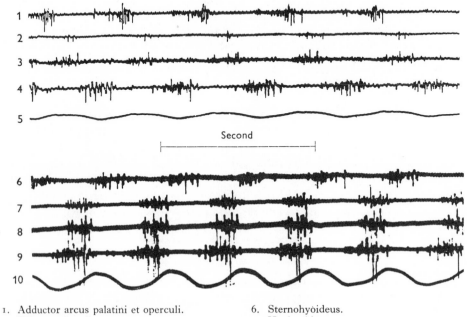

1. Adductor arcus palatini et operculi.
2. Dilator operculi.
3. Levator hyomandibulae et arcus palatini.
4. Adductor mandibulae.
5. Movement of operculum, abduction ↓.

6. Sternohyoideus.
7. Hyohyoideus.
8. Protractor hyoidei.
9. Adductor mandibulae.
10. Movement of operculum, abduction ↓.

Fig. 5. Electromyograms of the head muscles of a trout.

When the ventilation is strong the sternohyoideus becomes active at this time and supports the abduction of the lower jaw; it lowers the hyoid arch and moves it backwards; this pushes the interopercular bone in a dorso-caudal direction, resulting through mediation of the mandibulo-interopercular ligament in depression of the lower jaw. Besides that, the hyoideo-mandibular ligament, and also, as soon as it is stretched, the protractor hyoid muscle and the skin of the floor of the mouth, all exert a traction on the lower jaw, opening the mouth. The role of the protractor hyoideus is an entirely passive one; activity could never be detected during this phase of the movements.

When electrical activity in the adductor arcus palatini et operculi stops, that in the levator hyomandibulae et arcus palatini begins and produces abduction of the palatal complex and opercula. In two of our records activity in this muscle was much earlier, approximately coinciding with the activity in the adductor mandibulae. This could be due to extreme variability in the timing of the levator hyomandibulae et arcus palatini.

The possibility, however, that the electrodes were not leading-off potentials from the levator hyomandibulae et arcus palatini, but rather those of the adductor mandibulae, is supported by the following facts:

(*a*) both muscles are close together and the adductor mandibulae is a very big muscle partly overlying the other;

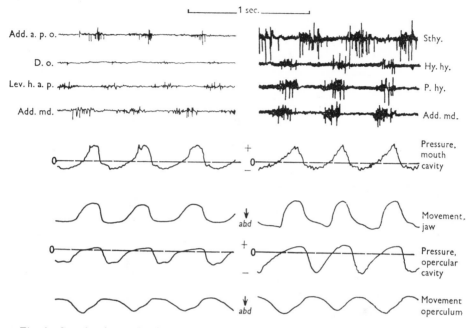

Fig. 6. Correlated records of electromyograms, respiratory movements and water pressures in buccal and opercular cavities. For abbreviations see Fig. 2.

(*b*) in the movement records no abductor component can be detected during activity in this muscle;

(*c*) one of our records of the levator hyomandibulae et arcus palatini shows double activity: one burst of high amplitude when this muscle is normally active, and another of low amplitude, synchronous with the adductor mandibulae and obviously recorded from that muscle (for instance through a leak in the electrode insulation).

With stronger respiratory movements the levator hyomandibulae et arcus palatini is also supported by contraction of the sternohyoideus; abduction of the hyoid abducts the hyomandibula as well (Henschel, 1941), as soon as it is no longer held adducted by the adductor arcus palatini et operculi. The palatal complex and the operculum are abducted because of their connexion with the hyomandibula.

Only during strong breathing movements is abduction of the operculum reinforced by contraction of the dilator operculi.

DISCUSSION

As a result of this work it appears that the muscular basis of the trout respiratory pumps is relatively simple, but this simplicity results from the intricate nature of the couplings between different parts of the skeletal system. Thus a particular movement of part of the skeleton may be produced by several different patterns of muscular co-ordination. Correspondingly, the contraction of a given muscle affects many different parts of the system. These general conclusions emphasize the value of electromyography as a technique for the elucidation of the activity of muscles during rhythmic movements. Furthermore, because of the complex interaction between

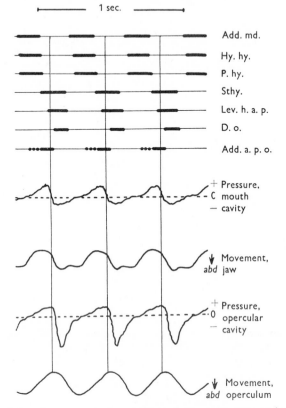

Fig. 7. Time relations between muscle activity and the movements and pressures of the respiratory pumps. For abbreviations see Fig. 2.

parts of the teleost head skeleton it is important to realize that when a given muscle is active it may prevent the action of certain couplings, as well as operating others. Clearly the total pattern of muscular activity is what is most important. By comparison of the muscle action potentials in relation to the movement records it has been possible to recognize those couplings which are most important under different circumstances (Figs. 5–7). And it is now possible to give an account of the different patterns of ventilation in fish showing different intensities of pumping. As yet no quantitative measurements have been made of the ventilation volume but a relative estimate has been made by reference to the amplitude and frequency of the respiratory movements.

The respiratory cycle

In the trout three muscles are of prime importance: the adductor mandibulae and the 'palatal complex muscles' levator hyomandibulae et arcus palatini and adductor arcus palatini et operculi. During shallow ventilation electrical activity can be recorded only in these muscles. The cycle starts with activity in the adductor mandibulae alone and this results, often after a short delay, in a closing movement of the mouth. Through coupling 4A the hyoid is protracted and the hyomandibula is adducted. The operculum although connected to the hyomandibula, does not adduct immediately and may even go on expanding because it is forced open by the passage of the exhalant water current. The pressure in both buccal and opercular cavities is positive as a result of the reduction in volume produced by the closing action of the jaws and operculum.

Following the activity of the adductor mandibulae, the adductor arcus palatini et operculi begins to contract. Its primary action is to lift and adduct the operculum, drawing it close to the body (often the movement record becomes steeper when this muscle becomes active), and it adducts the palatal complex, thereby compressing the buccal cavity laterally. Secondarily it depresses the lower jaw through coupling 1A; that is: operculum → interoperculum → mandibulo-interopercular ligament → lower jaw. The pressure in the opercular cavity reaches a maximum when the operculum is maximally adducted. The buccal pressure initially rises steeply as a result of the lateral compression by the palatal complex and then returns to zero as the mouth opens. The last part of the activity in the adductor arcus palatini et operculi normally overlaps the commencement of activity in its antagonist, the levator hyomandibulae et operculi. This ensures a gradual and smooth reversal in the direction of movement as the palatal complex expands and widens the buccal cavity. It is accompanied by expansion of the opercular cavity because the opercular bones articulate with the hyomandibula, which is a part of the palatal complex. The buccal pressure falls below zero, but the opercular pressure becomes more negative because the flap valves of the expanding opercula remain in contact with the sides of the fish, supported by the cleithral girdle. Consequently water can only enter the opercular cavities through the gill resistances. As a result of these pressure changes a current of water flows across the gills throughout the cycle (Hughes & Shelton, 1957, 1958, 1962).

During the last part of the opercular expansion there is often a complete absence of electrical activity in any of the muscles. Presumably the expanded palatal complex begins to adduct because of elastic and gravitational forces and the resulting water current may even abduct the operculum.

After this brief pause in muscular activity, during which the mouth is often not completely open, the cycle starts again with contraction of the adductor mandibulae.

During stronger ventilation more of the head muscles become active, the frequency increases and excursions of the moving parts become greater, but no consistent changes in the overall pattern of movement can be detected. This is not surprising because the effect of increased activity in any muscle would benefit a large part of the system through the numerous couplings. Three muscles that come into action with stronger ventilation are sternohyoideus, protractor hyoideus and hyohyoideus. The adductor arcus palatini et operculi now shows low amplitude activity during the latter part of the adductor mandibulae contraction.

The influence of the sternohyoideus is very widespread. It abducts the hyoid and through couplings 2A–E it lowers the jaw, expands the branchial arches and abducts the palatal complex and operculum as soon as they are no longer adducted by the adductor arcus palatini et operculi. Thus it increases the size of both the buccal and the opercular cavities.

The activity in the adductor mandibulae, protractor hyoideus and hyohyoideus is almost synchronous, with a tendency for each muscle to start its activity a little later than the one before in this order. The protractor hyoideus is clearly an antagonist of the sternohyoideus and primarily it protracts the hyoid. The hyomandibula, as a part of the hyoid arch, is also adducted as a result of its contraction and with it the rest of the palatal complex (reverse of coupling 2C). The operculum, through its articulation with the hyomandibula, also takes part in the adduction as soon as it is no longer forced open by the passing water current (reverse of coupling 2B (b)). Finally, activity of the adductor mandibulae also results in the branchial arches being contracted (reverse of coupling 2E). The volume of all the respiratory cavities is decreased by these movements.

The hyohyoideus contracts the floor of the mouth, folds up the branchiostegal apparatus and reinforces opercular adduction and thus helps decrease the volume of the buccal and opercular cavities. The dilator operculi reinforces the opercular abduction. Appreciable activity in this muscle is only found, however, during strong ventilation.

It is apparent from this account that ventilation in a bony fish involves a pumping mechanism on either side of the gill resistance but that the two pumps are coupled together to such an extent by the skeletal mechanism that the action of almost all the muscles affects both pumps. In terms of the model originally suggested (Hughes, 1960) it is clearly necessary that the two pistons should be coupled together by a spring of varying stiffness (Hughes, 1964).

Similar conclusions have also been reached as a result of a further investigation of the respiratory pumps of the dogfish (Hughes & Ballintijn, 1965). In the dogfish the presence of elastic components in the walls of the pumps also plays an important part. Such components are also involved in the teleost but do not fulfil so important a role. In the trout they are less important than in fish with a very flexible wall to the opercular cavity, such as in eels. It is of interest that for both the trout and the dogfish normal quiet respiration is produced by activity which is restricted to some lateral plate muscles. During more intense ventilation muscles in the ventral part of the head come into action. In the dogfish these are of myotomic origin and some of those in the trout are also of this type. From an evolutionary point of view this is what might be expected, as the lateral plate muscles are primarily concerned with the visceral skeleton and only later in evolution is it supposed that the hypobranchial musculature became involved in their movements.

SUMMARY

1. An account is given of the muscles and skeleton of the trout head and of the mechanisms coupling the different functional components of the skull.

2. The activity of the main respiratory muscles has been recorded electromyographically and simultaneously with pressure and movement recordings from the buccal and opercular cavities.

3. The muscles may be divided into two main groups according to whether they are active during the expansion or contraction phase of the pumps. The protractor hyoideus (geniohyoideus) was found to be active only during the contraction phase.

4. There are differences in the muscles that are active, depending upon the depth of ventilation. Shallow ventilation is maintained by the adductor mandibulae, adductor

arcus palatini et operculi, and levator hyomandibulae et arcus palatini. During deeper ventilation the sternohyoideus, protractor hyoideus and hyohyoideus muscles come into action. Only during strong ventilation does contraction of the dilator operculi play a part in opercular abduction.

5. There are variations in the pattern of muscular activity in different individuals and also in the same individual at different times. Such differences in muscular activity are not clearly reflected in the movement and pressure recordings, because of the complex couplings between different parts of the pumping mechanism.

6. As contraction of most muscles affects both the opercular and buccal cavities it is concluded that a model of teleost ventilation based upon a double pumping mechanism must incorporate the couplings between these pumps.

REFERENCES

ALLIS, E. P. (1897). The cranial muscles and cranial nerves of *Amia calva*. *J. Morph.* **12**, 487–808.

BAGLIONI, S. (1907). Der Atmungsmechanismus der Fische. *Z. allg. Physiol.* **7**, 177–282.

BAGLIONI, S. (1910). Zur vergleichende Physiologie der Atembewegungen der Wirbeltiere. I. Fische. *Ergebn. Physiol.* **9**, 90–137.

BORCEA, I. (1906). Observations sur la musculature branchiostégale des Téléostéens. *Ann. sci. Univ. Jassy*, **4**, 203–25.

DIETZ, P. A. (1912). Vergelijkende anatomie van de kaak en kieuwboogspieren der Teleostei. Dissertation, University of Leiden.

DOBBEN, W. H. VAN (1937). Über den Kiefermechanismus der Knochenfische. *Arch. néerl. Zool.* **2**, 1–72.

EDGEWORTH, F. H. (1931). On the muscles used in opening and shutting the mouth. *Proc. Zool. Soc. Lond.* **3**, 817–18.

HENSCHEL, J. (1939). Der Atmungsmechanismus der Fische. *J. Cons. int. Explor. Mer*, **14**, 249–60.

HENSCHEL, J. (1941). Neue Untersuchungen über den Atemmechanismus mariner Teleosteer. *Helgoländ. wiss. Meeresunters.* **2**, 244–78.

HOLMQUIST, O. (1910). Der Muskulus protractor hyoidei und der Senkungsmechanismus des Unterkiefers bei den Knochenfischen. *Acta Univ. lund.* N.S. 6, **21**, 1–27

HUGHES, G. M. (1960). A comparative study of gill ventilation in marine teleosts. *J. Exp. Biol.* **37**, 28–45.

HUGHES, G. M. (1964). Fish respiratory homeostasis. *Symp. Soc. Exp. Biol.* **18**, 81–107.

HUGHES, G. M. & BALLINTIJN, C. M. (1965). The muscular basis of the respiratory pumps in the dogfish (*Scyliorhinus canicula*). *J. exp. Biol.* **42**, 363–83.

HUGHES, G. M. & SHELTON, G. (1957). Pressure changes during the respiratory movements of teleostean fishes. *Nature, Lond.*, **179**, 255.

HUGHES, G. M. & SHELTON, G. (1958). The mechanism of gill ventilation in three freshwater teleosts. *J. Exp. Biol.* **35**, 807–23.

HUGHES, G. M. & SHELTON, G. (1962). Respiratory mechanisms und their nervous control in fish. *Advanc. comp. Physiol. Biochem.* **1**, 275–364.

KIRCHHOFF, J. (1958). Functionell anatomische Untersuchung des Visceralapparates von *Clupea harengus* L. *Zool. Jb.* (Abt. 2), **76**, 461–540.

VETTER, B. (1878). Untersuchungen zur vergleichende Anatomie der Kiemen- und Kiefermuskulatur der Fische. *Jena Z. Naturw.*, **12**, 431–550.

WILLEM, V. (1931). Les manœuvres respiratoires chez les poissons et les Amphibiens. *Mém. Acad. R. Belg. Cl. Sci.* **10**, 1–194.

WILLEM, V. (1940). Nouvelles observations sur les manœuvres respiratoires des Téléostéens. *Bull. Acad. R. Belg. Cl. Sci.* **26**, 211–29.

WILLEM, V. (1947). Les manœuvres respiratoires chez les poissons téléostéens. *Bull. Mus. Hist. nat. Belg.* **23**, 1–15.

WILLEM, V. & DE BERSAQUES-WILLEM, L. (1927). Les types de mouvements respiratoires chez les Téléostéens. *Mém. Acad. R. Belg. Cl. Sci.* **9**, 1–38.

WOSKOBOINIKOFF, M. M. (1932). Der Apparat des Kiemenatmung bei den Fischen. Ein Versuch der Synthese in der Morphologie. *Zool. Jb.* (Abt. 2), **55**, 315–488.

ACTIVE BRANCHIAL AND RAM GILL VENTILATION IN FISHES [1]

JOHN L. ROBERTS

*Department of Zoology, The University of Massachusetts, Amherst, Massachusetts 01002;
and Marine Biological Laboratory, Woods Hole, Massachusetts 02543*

Fish biologists have long known that adult mackerel and tunas (Scombridae) can be kept alive only in tanks of a shape and size that permit continuous swimming at speeds just over 1 km·hr⁻¹. Hall (1930) dramatically demonstrated the physiological basis for this observation in 1930. He found Atlantic mackerel, *Scomber scombrus*, slowed in swimming by towing erlenmeyer flasks could not maintain normal blood-oxygen saturation values as could unimpeded fish. These results and the absence of visible ventilation movements in adult swimming mackerel led him to conclude that open-mouth swimming (ram gill ventilation) is routine for this fish, and that the ability to effectively ventilate gills by mouth and opercular pumping had been lost.

Now it is known that other pelagic and mid-water fishes can readily suspend active breathing when on the move at velocities about 1.5 km·hr⁻¹ or higher and also resort to ram ventilation of the gills (Muir and Buckley, 1967, remora; Smith, Brett and Davis, 1967, sockeye salmon; Roberts, 1970, 1974, four marine species). Yet these other fishes, unlike scombrids, retain the ability to ventilate at rest in the water column or when maneuvering at slow speed. In other words, the mackerel-like fishes seem to have "outgrown" the capacity of their active ventilatory systems (buccal and opercular pumps) to oxygenate the blood as adults so that continuous swimming becomes a survival necessity.

Many factors tied to the life styles evolved by different lines of fishes played significant roles in the development of the ability to transfer from active to ram gill ventilation when swimming speed picks up from rest (Hughes, 1960a; Hughes and Shelton, 1962). Most crucial must have been the relatively higher metabolic cost of oxygen uptake from water compared to air; a cost largely due to the low solubility of oxygen and the work of pumping water, a respiratory medium of high viscosity and density (Hughes and Roberts, 1970; Randall, 1970b). Consequently, it seems decidedly of advantage for a good swimmer to switch from active to ram ventilation as it grows to a size at which it can routinely cruise fast enough to overcome gill flow resistance, but still ensure complete blood oxygenation. This analysis substantiates this view with detailed and updated experiments. A brief resumé of these was reported earlier (Roberts, 1970).

MATERIALS AND METHODS

Experiments were completed with the five species of fishes listed in Table I. They were obtained by trapping in Buzzards Bay by the aquarium staff, National Marine Fisheries Service, Woods Hole, Massachusetts, or by bait and lure casting off the stone jetty in Woods Hole Harbor. The blue-runners, scup, and mullet

[1] This investigation was supported by research grant, GB 8022, from the National Science Foundation, and by a NRC-NOAA Senior Research Associateship from the National Research Council.

From *Biol. Bull.* 148(1):85–105. Reprinted by permission.

248

TABLE I

*Species used to determine swimming velocities for conversion
from active to passive gill ventilation*

Species	N	Standard length, cm (range)	Weight, g (range)	Experimental temperature, °C
Atlantic mackerel *Scomber scombrus*	5	19.1 (15.8–20.0)	71.9 (43.0–83.3)	18.5–22.0
Blue runner *Caranx crysos*	7	19.2 (17.6–20.5)	153.3 (114–178)	18.5–19.5
Bluefish *Pomatomus saltatrix*	11	19.3 (17.5–22.0)	105.2 (62.9–141)	16.0–19.5
Northern scup *Stenotomus crysops*	5	17.2 (14.5–18.5)	102.4 (72.2–115)	19.5–20.0
Striped mullet *Mugil cephalus*	4	20.5 (19.3–21.4)	101.7 (90.6–110)	20.0–20.5

were young adults of smaller than average size. The mackerel and bluefish juveniles were of a size commonly called "tinker" mackerel and "snapper blues." Except for the mackerel that were used soon after capture at the capture temperature, the fish were kept in the large holding tanks of the aquarium in running sea water. To some extent, the experimental and holding temperatures were seasonally dependent. Most of the experiments were done during summer months and continued into late fall as the sea-water temperature at the laboratory intake warmed from 14 to 22° C (August) and fell again to about 12° C (December). In all cases, the experiments were done either at the intake temperature or at higher temperatures maintained by mixing of "raw" intake water and warmed sea water from the large reservoir in the recirculating system of the aquarium. During holding periods the fish were fed daily on diced herring and soft-shell clams.

Since completion of studies at Woods Hole for species listed in Table I, preliminary results to be reported elsewhere have been obtained using similar procedures. These results are included in Table III (Roberts, unpublished) and in the discussion. The report on the sand tiger shark given in Table III was based on repeated visual inspection of a single specimen swimming in the large display tank at the aquarium at Woods Hole. Remarks on non-ventilating rockfish apply to the blue rockfish, *Sebastes mystinus,* the olive rockfish, *Sebastes serranoides,* and the bocaccio, *Sebastes paucispinis* taken at Tanner Bank near San Clemente Island, California.

Activity recording during swimming

Swimming apparatus. The fish were made to swim against a pump stream in a version of the swimming chamber used by Sutterlin (1969) in order to determine critical swimming velocities for transitions from active to passive gill ventilation (Fig. 1). The centrifugal pump (neoprene body and impeller) of 1/3 hp produced flow velocities up to 90 cm·sec^{-1} in the plexiglas swimming tube (78.5 mm ID) by control of a PVC ball-valve located between the pump outlet and the pitot flow meter. Microturbulent flow and a uniform front were maintained by a ball "spreader" and three, 16-mesh stainless-steel screens at the front

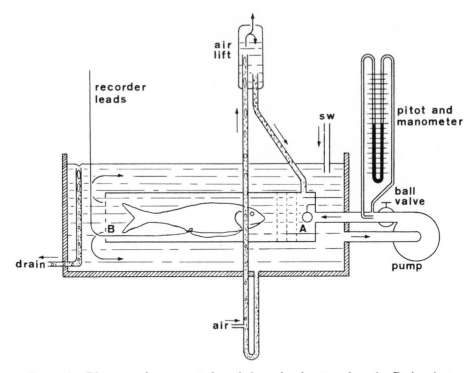

FIGURE 1. Diagrammatic representation of the swimming tunnel used. Design features are similar to those of Sutterlin (1967) with the addition of the air lift circulator for maintaining a slow velocity flow through the tunnel, and fitting around the outer chamber of a 1/4 inch-mesh galvanized Faraday cage. The symbols *A* and *B* represent respectively, the front ball spreader and flow screens, and the rear retainer screen (see text). Temperature control was obtained by use of a thermoregulator-heater located in the outer bath and operated at a set point higher than the entering sea water (*sw*).

of the swimming tube. The rear end of the tube was fitted with a coarser screen of 6-mesh to confine the fish within the tube and to permit free movement of the electrode cable trailing from the fish as it changed its position in response to changes in flow velocity.

Calibration of flow velocity. The pitot flow-meter was calibrated indirectly because the flow relationships between the inflow tube from the pump and the swimming chamber proved to be non-linear largely due to back-pressure effects of the spreader ball and the three front screens. Two methods were used that gave similar flow rates for given deflections of the mercury manometer (tubing spaces, water filled). For the first method, slugs of methylene blue dye injected into the pump intake were timed as they passed between the last flow-control screen at the front, and the rear screen of the swimming tube. The second method (Sutterlin, 1969) was used with the bath filled with fresh water and depended upon timing conductance changes in the stream flow between the electrode pairs located in the walls of the swimming tube, front and rear, as small amounts of saturated KCl, injected into the pump intake, passed the electrodes. Corrections for fish displacement were not made for the cross-sectional area of the fish seldom exceeded 1/10 of the swimming tube.

Electrode placement and activity waveforms. Each fish was anesthetized in MS 222 solution (0.1 g·l⁻¹) for insertion of electrode pairs for recording waveforms of muscle action potentials related to respiratory and cardiac cycles (Roberts,

1964; Sutterlin, 1969; Spoor, Neiheisel and Drummond, 1971). Electrode pairs were made up of lapwound, 1-m lengths of 45 gauge, insulated stainless-steel wire (Johnson, Matthey and Co., Ltd., England, annealed, epoxy coated) with bared and hooked tips threaded through 22 gauge syringe needles. These were inserted, one pair into the pericardial space, and the other into one of the ventilatory muscles, usually the *adductor mandibularis*. The needles were withdrawn after electrode placement, and the wires secured by skin ties at the insertion site and again at the anal opening. In this way, looping of the formed cable around the tail and tangling was minimized after recovery of the fish in the swimming tube. When tail-beat frequencies were to be recorded (*e.g.*, mullet), *mu*-metal bands (high magnetic permeability) were wrapped around the caudal peduncle for proximity detection of lateral tail movements. A detector coil with permanent field magnets was fitted around the outside of the swimming tube for this purpose. It was made up by winding 38 gauge enameled magnet wire around a coil form incorporating eight Alnico bar magnets (6 mm by 48 mm long, spaced 20 mm; 4 each side). The magnets were oriented parallel to the tube axis with like polarity (north to north) on each side, but opposite in polarity between the two sides, in order to maximize the horizontal magnetic flux density across the tube. The finished coil form was potted in epoxy resin to form a loose fitting, short cylinder. The lead cable incorporated a two-stage RC filter to reduce 60 cycle interference. Distortion of the field by the moving tail band of *mu*-metal generated an AC signal at the tail-beat frequency adequate for polygraph recording at a gain level of 10 to 50 $\mu V \cdot mm^{-1}$.

Usually it was possible to record waveform of both cardiac and ventilatory cycles on a single channel of the R-series Dynographs used (Beckman Instruments, Inc.). This was done by trial-and-error combination of the four electrode leads in the trailing cable, and by appropriate adjustments of the band-pass filters on the input couplers of the polygraph. When clear differentiation of the two waveforms was not possible on one channel, or when tail-beat frequencies were desired, two recording channels were used (*e.g.*, Fig. 4, mackerel and mullet). Usually, the high frequency components of the EMG (electromyogram) signals were suppressed by band-pass control so that only the slow wave part of the signal was displayed by the pen writer. This was done usually to enable differentiation of ECG (electrocardiogram) and EMG waveforms on a single record channel.

Training and experimental procedures

One to several hours allowed recovery from anesthesia once the fish were put into the swimming tube with the air-lift circulation on. Additional time was required to train fish to swim steadily in the pump stream flow as velocities were changed. The most effective training method was to just slightly open the control valve with the pump running so that the fish drifted to the rear screen. Within 5 to 10 minutes, the fish would begin slow swimming to avoid tail flexion against the screen. Flow velocity was then slowly increased until the fish again stopped or began dart swimming or thrashing. When this happened, the pump was shut off and the animal given a brief rest lasting 5 to 10 minutes before another training period. Training was considered complete when the animal would maintain a relatively fixed position between front and back screens as the control valve was turned from off to full on and the reverse.

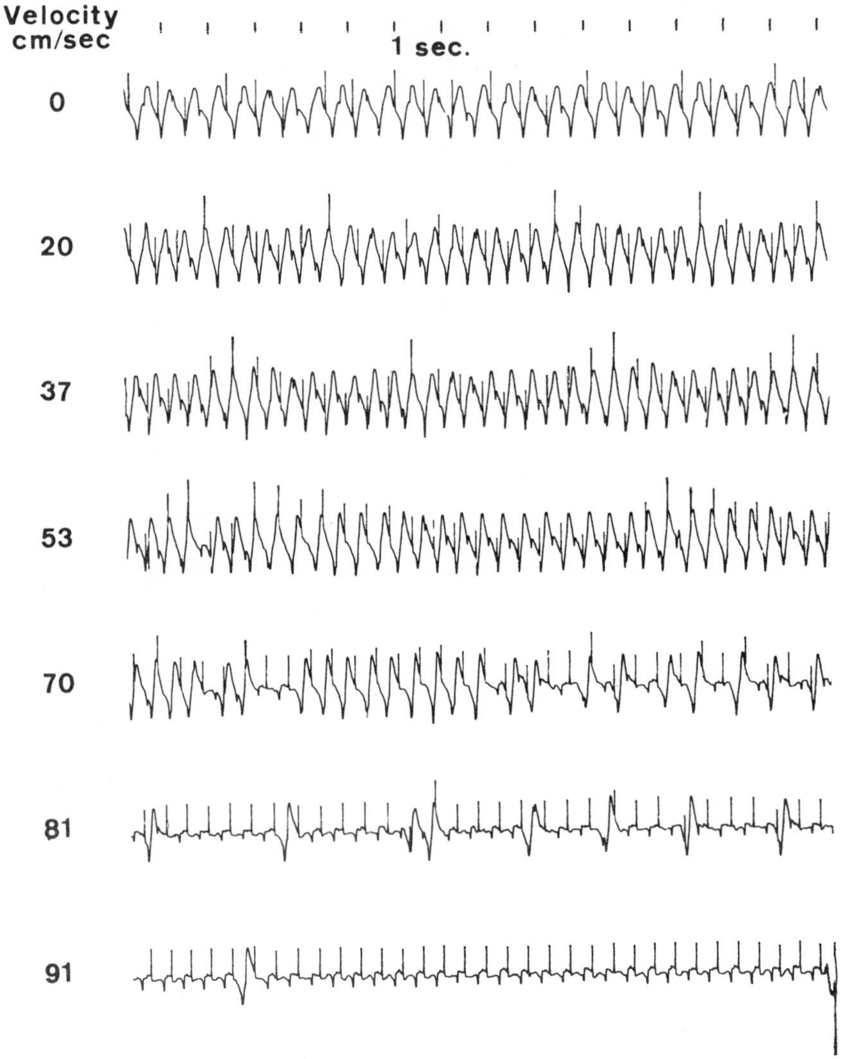

FIGURE 2. A combined sequence of EMG slow-wave components recorded from the *adductor mandibularis* muscle (left side) and the ECG of a bluefish during acceleration to and above a swimming speed sufficient to support ram gill ventilation. The time marks in this and subsequent figures denote 1-second intervals.

Once a fish was trained to sustain swimming over the complete velocity range of the apparatus, a routine procedure was followed. A rest period of about 10 minutes was allowed after each swimming bout. Transition velocities for ram ventilation were established in most cases by four swimming periods. The pump was turned on after a rest period and the control valve opened in stages to give flow velocities that approximated step increases of 5 to 10 $cm \cdot sec^{-1}$ flow velocity (manometer pressure equivalent) until the velocity maximum for the pump was reached. Sufficient time was allowed at each step to allow the manometer to stabilize and to obtain a 15 second polygraph record of cardiac and opercular cycles. The entire range of possible flow velocities with the fish swimming was covered in this way in about 10 minutes. Following the rest period, the sequence was repeated in reverse order. The reverse sequence was begun with the pump full on and then followed by step-wise reductions in pump flow until the pump was fully throttled, and the fish again at rest.   One repeat usually sufficed unless excessive electronic noise or weak muscle signals made derivation of event rates from the polygraph record difficult.

RESULTS

Ram ventilation

Critical swimming velocity.   The transition to ram gill ventilation in fish is a graded process as swimming picks up from rest.   The first indication that a critical swimming speed has been reached is signalled by the drop-out of single cycles.   The drop-out continues until only occasional ventilatory movements and "coughs" are noticed.   A graded series just following the training period for a bluefish is illustrated in Figure 2.   Return of active movements with gradual reductions in swimming velocity to below critical shows nearly the same sequence, but in reverse order.   Generally, subsequent swimming bouts with this and the other ram-ventilating species showed some decrease in the velocity critical for the transition to ram ventilation.   In fact, transition speeds of experienced fish may fall to less than half that observed in initial tests so that switch-over to ram ventilation can occur at a surprisingly slow swimming speed.   This contrast is best noted by comparison of the bluefish swimming bout given as Figure 2 and the transition range for all bluefish tested summarized in Table II.

Although patterns for conversion to ram gill ventilation of different fish are similar, there does seem to be great variation between individuals in their behavioral selection of swimming velocities for switching ventilation modes.   Figure 3 shows conversion patterns for each of the five mackerel used in the study (see also Heath, 1973).   Clearly, the transition can be gradual or abrupt, and with or without a marked increase in the frequency of active respiratory movements prior to adoption of the ram mode.

TABLE II

Mean values and ranges for opercular (O) and cardiac (C) rate changes in resting and active marine fishes

Species (N)		Aquarium display cpm	Resting rate swimming tube cpm	Active rate at transition velocity cpm	Active rate at 90 cm ·sec⁻¹	% change from rest		Swimming speed at transition cm·sec⁻¹
						At transition	At 90cm ·sec⁻¹	
Mackerel (5)	O	—	124 (110–140)	134 (125–175)	—	8	—	67 (53–75)
	C	—	100 (72–133)	121 (89–140)	126 (98–140)	21	26	
Blue runner (7)	O	—	80 (52–105)	119 (90–135)	—	49	—	48 (35–75)
	C	—	43 (26– 62)	62 (50– 92)	72 (57–105)	44	67	
Bluefish (11)	O	77 (SD, ±13)	99 (65–145)	138 (105–185)	—	39	—	69 (49–82)
	C	—	83 (52–115)	113 (92–160)	117 (98–160)	36	41	
Northern scup (5)	O	51 (SD, ±10)	148 (120–180)	196 (175–200)	—	32	—	66 (44–79)
	C	—	81 (54–105)	142 (80–150)	146 (130–160)	75	80	
Mullet (4)	O	—	148 (113–180)	—	201 (130–232)	—	36	—
	C	—	104 (88–120)	—	124 (112–132)	—	19	

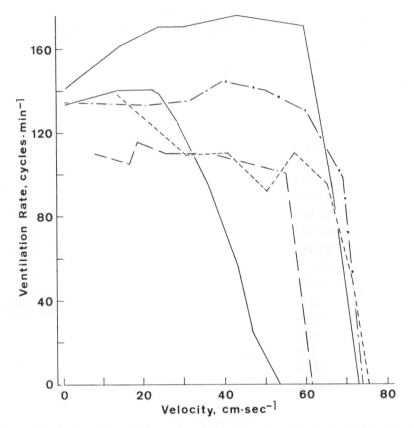

FIGURE 3. Active gill ventilation rates of five Atlantic mackerel (see Tables I and II) relative to enforced swimming speed. Rates were determined by counting all cyclic ventilatory movements that appeared on 30-second strips of polygraph record.

Conversions to ram ventilation, the mullet excepted, were completed at velocities under 90 cm·sec⁻¹ by all the fish tested. This is a swimming-speed equivalent of 2.7 to 4.7 BL·sec⁻¹ (body lengths per second) according to the size of the mackerel used (Figs. 3 and 4). This range does not substantially exceed the open-sea cruising speed expected for mackerel of this size or roughly 2 BL·sec⁻¹, as based on Magnuson's estimates for speed minimums required to maintain hydrostatic equilibrium (1970). Table II gives similar ranges and mean values for complete adoption of ram ventilation by all of the species groups studied.

Individuals of all species tested occasionally stopped swimming at flow velocities that were above critical and drifted to the rear screen of the chamber. When this happened, ventilation movements most often reappeared immediately and continued until swimming was resumed. Two of the blue runners continued ram ventilation in several swimming bouts after drifting back to the rear screen. This unusual tactic was not observed in swimming bouts with the other marine species. Note also (Table II) that the average transition velocity for blue runners seems to be lower than for the other ram ventilators. A notable exception to be considered later, is the remora which ram ventilates attached to its swimming host, but only above velocities of about 1 km (Muir and Buckley, 1967).

None of the mullet showed signs of even partial conversion to ram ventilation during enforced swimming, despite the fact that they trained readily to steady

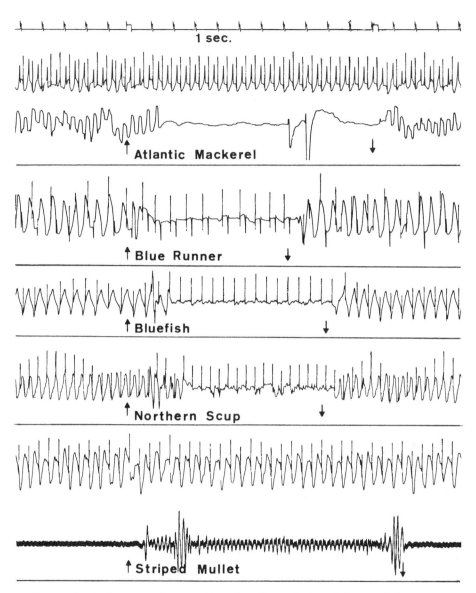

FIGURE 4. Active to passive transitions in gill ventilation of five marine species from rest to swimming just above transition velocities following turn-on (arrow up) and turn-off (arrow down) of the pump. The lower trace for the Atlantic mackerel is shown for clarity in separation of cardiac and ventilatory events. The lower record for the striped mullet represents tail-beat frequency recorded by proximity detection of the movement of *mu*-metal bands around the caudal fin peduncle. Changes in heart rates are slight due to the lack of rest periods prior to these sequences.

swimming in the apparatus. These fish appeared to be in excellent health, but had all been captured and held in the aquarium at Woods Hole about 1 month prior to their use. All survived the swimming bouts for at least a month after electrode removal in one of the holding tanks. Figure 4 includes a typical record with a simultaneous display of tail beats obtained by proximity detection as the pump flow was valved from off to full-on to induce swimming at 85 to 90 cm·sec^{-1}. The records shown for the other species were obtained in a similar way by rapid

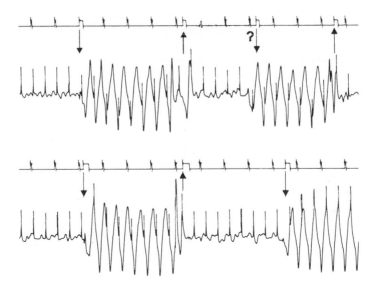

FIGURE 5. Repeated sequences of pump valving to vary swimming speeds of a bluefish from just above to just below velocities for conversion between active and passive modes of gill ventilation. Up and down arrows indicate respectively, decreasing and increasing pump flow.

valving of the pump output to produce swimming at speeds below and above the active to passive transitions in ventilation.

Transition characteristics. Figure 4 also demonstrates that timing differences are consistent between the onset of ram ventilation and return to active ventilation when swimming speeds are abruptly increased or decreased by manipulation of the pump flow. The return to active ventilation by most of the fish used generally was found to require less time than switching to the ram mode. Figure 5 contrasts in that conversions between ventilatory modes by this bluefish proved to be nearly equal in timing. The second, early return to active ventilation (Fig. 5, down arrow) most likely represents a single movement, seen to occur normally in some swimming bouts (Fig. 2, 91 cm·sec⁻¹). Allowing for the chance occurrence of single respiratory movements and possible operational errors, a great number of switching-time measurements indicate that all of the ram ventilators can initiate active ventilation in as short a period as 0.2 second following sudden drops in the speed of water flow to below critical swimming rates for ram ventilation.

Usually the transition to the ram mode was marked by completion of at least one complete ventilatory cycle before actual ram gill ventilation began. Strong "coughs" were sometimes seen, both at the onset of ram ventilation, and preceding the return of rhythmic breathing, as swimming velocities were made to change above and below critical speeds for switching between modes. In other respects, the pattern of single ventilatory movements shows little change in amplitude or timing as swimming begins and the supression of individual cycles occur with ram gill ventilation (Fig. 2).

Frequency changes—branchial and cardiac pumps

Gill ventilation rates of wired fish recorded before and after swimming bouts (30 minutes rest) all greatly exceed rates determined for inactive, undisturbed fish. For example, Table II lists rates for experimental bluefish and scup as well as rates for display fish at the aquarium at Woods Hole. The latter were recorded at 9 a.m. before public open hours (Logan and Roberts, unpublished observations; Roberts, 1974). Large differences such as these can be expected because handling fish elevates their metabolism and excitability for prolonged periods (Roberts, 1964; Muir and Buckley, 1967; Sutterlin, 1969; Spoor, Neiheisel and Drummond, 1971). The same can be said for heart-beat rates although these were not recorded along with opercular frequencies of the display bluefish and scup.

Table II also shows that heart and ventilatory rates increase proportionally with swimming velocity, although variability is large. Beyond the transition speed for conversion to ram ventilation, heart rates of all species increased with further increase in swimming speed. No obvious cardiac rate changes or alterations in ECG patterns were found associated with conversions between active and passive gill ventilation (Figs. 2, 4, and 5). Even at the higher swimming velocities, visual stimuli (shadows, movements of the operator) produced the well-known reflex bradycardia (Labat, 1966; Randall, 1970a; Roberts, 1973). Therefore, considerable reserve accommodation in cardiac function remains at moderate swimming velocities, and at speeds higher than necessary to support ram ventilation.

DISCUSSION

In a sense it is surprising that the use of ram gill ventilation is widespread among fishes other than those known to be high-speed or continuous swimmers of open-water habit. Yet, if the supposition is correct that ventilatory efficiency improves with conversion from active to passive ventilation once swimming velocity reaches 1.5 km sec^{-1} (Brown and Muir, 1970) the advantage of conversion between stops for feeding or other fish activity becomes more obvious (Roberts, 1974).

There is a proviso, however. That is, successful ram ventilation seems to require that a fish be above a certain size so its normal cruising speed exceeds the velocity minimum for support of the passive ventilation mode. For example, it was mentioned above that scombrids have outgrown the capacity of their active branchial pump system so adult survival is dependent upon continuous swimming for a variety of reasons (Hall, 1930; Brown and Muir, 1970; Magnuson, 1970, 1973). Apparently the Atlantic mackerel, and most scombrids as well, lose the ability to ventilate the gills by rhythmic breathing as an ontogenetic development. Captive juvenile Atlantic mackerel ranging in body size from 2 to 12 cm actively ventilate their gills and often "stand dead in the water" (personal observations, aquarium, Woods Hole). Most likely, fish this small simply are not able to swim continuously at speeds fast enough to sustain ram ventilation.

Table III lists species known to utilize ram ventilation. It includes only two species from among the sharks and omits many probable ram ventilators from both major classes of fish only for the reason that many reports lack reasonable substantiation. The list is based upon careful visual, physiological and cinema-photographic monitoring. Brief comments on habitats were abstracted from the monographs of Bigelow and Schroeder (1953) and Miller and Lea (1972) for the coastal marine fishes of the Atlantic northeast and California, respectively. Common names and ordering of the families and species have followed the recommendations of the Committee on Names of Fishes, American Fisheries Society (1970).

Just as important is the fact that some fish do not ram ventilate at all. The mullet is a curious exception for it is an inshore, near surface high-speed swimmer. It has an unusually small mouth and feeds mostly on plankton and algae. Per-

TABLE III

Ram ventilating fish

Species and systematic position	Habitat	Method	Source

Chondrichthyes
  Odontaspididae
    Odontaspis taurus
    (sand tiger)
	subtidal, beaches
	and bays
		visual count,
		aquarium
			Roberts (unpublished) von Wahlert (1964)

Carcharhinidae
    Triakis semifasciata
    (leopard shark)
	subtidal, beaches
	and bays
		cinema photography, aquarium	Hughes (1960)

Osteichthyes
  Salmonidae
    Onchorhynchus nerka
    (sockeye salmon)
	pelagic and mid-water, anadromous	branchial pressures	Smith *et al* (1967)

Salmo gairdneri (rainbow trout)	fresh waters and anadromous	electromyograms	Roberts (unpublished)

Percichthyidae
    Morone saxatilis
    (striped bass)
	near shore pelagic
	and fresh waters,
	anadromous
		electromyograms	Roberts (this paper)

Echeneidae
    Remora remora
    (remora)
	open ocean, surface
	to mid-water
		cinema photography, water tunnel	Muir and Buckley (1967)

Pomatomidae
    Pomatomus saltatrix
    (bluefish)
	near shore and bays,
	pelagic to mid-water
		electromyograms	Roberts (this paper)

Carangidae
    Caranx crysos
    (blue runner)
	near shore and bays,
	pelagic to mid-water
		electromyograms	Roberts (this paper)

Trachurus symmetricus (jack mackerel)	near shore to open ocean, pelagic to mid-water	electromyograms	Roberts (unpublished)

Sparidae
    Stenotomus chrysops
    (scup)
	demersal to mid-water	electromyograms	Roberts (this paper)

Kyphosidae
    Medialuna californiensis
    (halfmoon)
	mid-water, kelp beds	electromyograms	Roberts (unpublished)

Scombridae
    Katsuwonus pelamis
    (skipjack tuna)
	pelagic, open ocean	cinema photography (NMFS, Honolulu)	Brown and Muir (1970)

Scomber japonicus (Pacific mackerel)	near shore, pelagic	electromyograms	Roberts (unpublished)
Scomber scombrus (Atlantic mackerel)	near shore, pelagic	electromyograms	Roberts (this paper)

haps the mullet's active respiratory mode is somehow linked with its feeding style during swimming.

Demersal fish, notably those equipped with large branchiostegal baskets (see McAllister, 1968) probably do not convert to passive gill ventilation at any swimming velocity. Their respiratory apparatus is well designed for respiration in standing water and functionally, the opercular pump dominates. About 90% of the respiratory cycle at rest is spent in slow opercular aspiration of water through the gills with the mouth open (Hughes, 1960a; Hughes and Roberts, 1969; Roberts, 1974). Consequently, respiration rates of these fish usually are considerably lower than their cardiac rates (Hughes, personal communication; Roberts, 1974). In fact, comparison of resting ventilation and cardiac frequencies serves as a "rule of thumb" to differentiate between fish that depend primarily upon the action of the opercular pump and fish in which branchial ventilation is equally shared by the buccal and opercular pumps. For these, rate ratios of about one can be expected. The latter pattern for propelling water across the gills generally prevails among fast swimmers of mid-water and pelagic habits. The fast swimmers usually are good ram ventilators as well.

For an example, the family Scorpaenidae can be cited. The family includes two major groups, the scorpionfish and the rockfish, *Sebastes*. All have well-developed branchiostegal rays and membranes. A number of the rockfish have evolved away from a strictly demersal existence. Some closely resemble the sea basses (Serranidae) of the genus *Paralabrax* in body form, development of the branchiostegal system and habits. None of these fish types so far examined ram ventilate (*P. clathratus*; *S. mystinus, serranoides, paucispinis*). Yet, with the exception of the blue rockfish, *S. mystinus*, all trained rapidly to enforced swimming at speeds well above the requirement for sustained ram ventilation.

Another fish, the anadromous striped bass, *Morone saxatilis* (Percichthyidae), sometimes included with the Serranidae (Miller and Lea, 1972), seems ready to adopt the ram mode of gill ventilation at a swimming speed of about 50 cm·sec^{-1}. Only a single specimen was tested (total length, 46 cm). Unlike the serranids, however, the branchiostegals of the striped bass are much reduced and the cardiac-ventilatory rate ratio is about one.

Just as extensive development of the branchiostegal system facilitates respiration in quiet water, this development probably sets a limit to the speed at which fish can cruise routinely and still ensure reasonable energy expenditures for gill ventilation. Structural stability of the lightly-build branchiostegal rays and membranes, and the drag resistance they present when laterally expanded during swimming are important considerations. But as yet, no detailed hydrodynamic analyses exist to describe the array of niche compromises made during the evolution of modern fishes to meet the joint needs of respiratory gas exchange, and swimming for prey capture, migration, and reproduction.

Experimental verification that many swimming fish ram ventilate has been a relatively simple task. Providing the answers to why and how ram gill ventilation occurs has been more difficult. Of the two questions, the answer to why is the hardest to supply in satisfactory form at the present stage of investigations on fish energetics. A large part of the problem rests with assessing the efficiency of gill ventilation in swimming fish and hence, the work load of ventilation with respect to total body metabolism (see also Jones, 1971).

Estimates of energetic costs of active gill ventilation versus total metabolism in resting fish range from a low of 0.5% (Alexander, 1970) to as high as 43% (Schumann and Piiper, 1966). Jones calculations for a trout model (1971), reveal a theoretical cost as small as 1%, despite assumption of a low resting efficiency for the operation of the branchial musculature in propelling water through the gills (3 to 4% efficiency). Intermediate cost estimates of 10% (Hughes, 1973) and 5 to 15% (Cameron and Cech, 1970) also have been suggested. However, the general accuracy of these estimates as applied to rhythmic gill ventilation is doubtful due to the complex hydrodynamic integration of changing flow rates and pressure profiles that occurs during single respiratory cycles

(Hughes and Saunders, 1970; Ballintijn, 1972). The critical factors of environmental temperature and oxygen availability also must be considered for both exert strong influences upon ventilatory stroke volume, coupling of the branchial pumps, and hence upon respiratory efficiency (Hughes and Roberts, 1970; Hughes and Saunders, 1970; Heath and Hughes, 1973).

Respiratory energetics of sluggish demersal species that have elaborate branchiostegal systems scarcely are comparable with the energetics of pelagic, high-speed swimmers which have only remnants of branchiostegal rays and membranes. The energy cost of active ventilation for a bottom-living fish probably is high, but affordable. They often are opportunistic predators that swim in short darts to seize prey or swim slowly to feed on other sluggish bottom species. Midwater and pelagic fish contrast for they usually depend upon chasing down active prey or upon planktonic gathering and are more or less continuous swimmers. Their metabolic costs for gill ventilation also may be high during brief pauses in swimming, but the cost probably does not increase proportionately with total metabolism during swimming up to ram-ventilating speeds. The reason is that when a fish begins to swim, its forward motion causes pressure to rise at the mouth, partially relieving power requirements for the buccal fore-pump (Hughes, 1960a; Hughes and Shelton, 1962; Cameron and Cech, 1970). Opercular aspiration also may be facilitated by the venturi effect as water streaming along the body passes the gill-cover margins in spite of some drag losses due to cyclic abductions of the opercular doors (also see Brown and Muir, 1970).

Further acceleration to a ram speed results in a graded transfer of the metabolic cost of rhythmic ventilatory movements to the drag forces of swimming (Brown and Muir, 1970). Some lesser amount of energy must be reserved for tonic holding of the mouth gape and the opercular exit slots to sizes suitable for respiratory needs once the conversion to ram gill ventilation is complete. Thus, the switchover from active to passive gill ventilation is a tactic that probably saves considerable energy. However, not all of the savings result simply from the transfer of respiratory work from one set of muscles to another. Loss in locomotory efficiency is also a probable consequence of rhythmic gill ventilation, especially at high speeds. For example, cyclic variations occur in the cross-sectional area of the head as the opercular doors open and close. Changes in mouth gape also occur with operation of the buccal phase of branchial pumping. Such drag oscillations are likely as well to generate periodic turbulence, adding still further to the work load of swimming. Little is known about these factors and their effects on swimming. But, the available evidence shows that the events of gill ventilation and of swimming must be tightly coupled by unavoidable hydrodynamic interactions. The same should be true of their relative metabolic efficiencies.

Only a single study has been directed toward assessment of the work load during ram gill ventilation. Brown and Muir (1970) have calculated the ventilation drag-resistance of a 44-cm skipjack tuna (K. pelamis) swimming at a basal speed of 66 cm·sec^{-1} to be about 7% of the total body drag. Translation of the drag forces into metabolic expenditures for swimming and other functions, has led them to estimate the cost of ram ventilation for a tuna swimming at basal speed to range from 1 to 3% of total metabolism—a cost much lower than most prior estimates for active ventilation in non-swimming fish.

Aside from the fact that ram gill ventilation is used by most active fish that have been tested (Table III), one unusual example also attests to the efficacy of the ram mode. The small shark sucker (R. remora) normally is a sluggish swimmer that uses active ventilation. Yet when this fish attaches to a passing shark or other large swimming host, it too can adopt the ram mode when the host reaches the requisite speed. In a sense, they gain a "free ride" by transferring the work load of gill ventilation to their hosts. But, they seem to do it by using neural adaptations for ram ventilation that most likely are ancestral to the adaptations which permit their form of locomotory and feeding commensalism (Table III). Muir and Buckley (1967) have found that remoras placed in a water tunnel would attach to the wall as flow velocities through the tunnel reached 20 to 30 cm·sec⁻¹. Switch-over from active to passive gill ventilation was found to range from 50 to 80 cm·sec⁻¹. This is a range remarkably similar to the transition velocities reported here for other marine species (Table II).

The work expended by a species in ventilating its gills between a dead stop and a burst of maximal swimming must represent a compromise with costs of other activities as defined by its niche and physical factors in its habitat. Ultimately, as Brett has shown (1964) for the sockeye salmon (*O. nerka*), the maximal sustainable swimming speed of a fish will be limited by the cost of gill ventilation, and its ability to manage an oxygen debt, combined with the costs of cardiac pumping as Jones suggests (1971). This means that routine levels of activity in swimming, feeding, and ventilating the gills will represent partitioning of energy available for these functions according to a fish's life style whether it is benthic or pelagic, and whether it is a sluggish swimmer or a very active one. If Jones' (1971) and Brown and Muir's (1970) attempts to model ventilatory energetics are reasonable, the costs of gill ventilation for active fish that ram ventilate may remain as low as 1 to 3% of total metabolism over a wide range of swimming speeds.

What speed might mark an upper limit for a good swimmer is difficult to estimate, but it is probably not less than cruising velocities for most pelagic species. Very likely another factor becomes significant at still higher speeds or during burst swimming. A fall in the %-utilization of oxygen from the respiratory stream should occur as the ventilatory minute-volume increases with increasing metabolic needs (Hughes, 1966; Randall, 1970b; Hughes and Morgan, 1973). This represents a loss in respiratory efficiency that would be additive to the work load of swimming.

Much could be learned to substantiate their trout and skipjack estimates by use of water or wind tunnel models. In fact, the brancial system of fish respiring in the ram mode resembles, in an engineering sense, the design of a combined impact-reverse pitot tube with variable up- and downstream orifices. The comparison has limits. The pitot tube typically is a zero-flow pressure measuring device so the resistance between orifices is infinite. The branchial system differs in that through-flow occurs as a volume rate determined primarily by the resistivity of the gill screen. Figure 6 illustrates the pressure differential developed between impact and reverse openings of a pitot tube located in a "swimming" respirometer of the Blažka type (loaned by Dr. F. E. J. Fry, University of Toronto) relative to water flow velocities from 0 to 120 cm·sec⁻¹. The extrapolated buccal-post branchial pressure range also is shown (ordinate). This range of pressure differences corresponds to minimal and maximal swimming speeds for ram gill ventilation by the fish species listed in Table II (*i.e.,* blue runner and bluefish, respectively). Assuming that a resemblance to the combined impact-reverse pitot is reasonable, then an across-gill pressure drop as low as 0.5 cm enables some fish to swim as slowly as 35 cm·sec⁻¹ and still support ram gill ventilation.

Muir and Buckley (1967) have determined via buccal and opercular cannulas that the average pressure necessary to force water through the gills of actively breathing remoras is 0.87 cm. Yet, these investigators have estimated that the

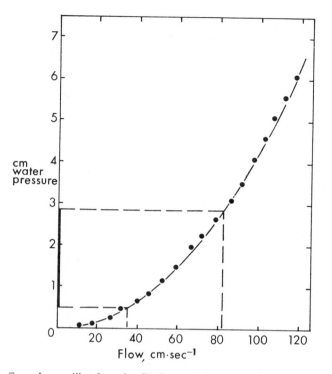

FIGURE 6. Secondary calibration of a Blažka swimming tunnel (respirometer type) with a combined impact-reverse pitot tube in the axial flow of the swimming chamber to give pressure equivalents of flow velocity in centimeters of water. The primary calibration was obtained by use of a ducted, impeller flow-meter (Marine Advisers Inc., La Jolla, California; model B-7C). Minimal and maximal estimates for across-gill differential pressures have been extrapolated on the ordinate according to the range of swimming speeds permitting ram gill ventilation for the fishes listed in Table II.

passive mode of ventilation in swimming remoras requires an across-gill pressure drop of 1.87 cm water pressure. The latter figure probably is too high for a minimal value for it was based on the use of a simple impact pitot that does not correct for static pressures generated in the positive-pressure pumping system they employed. However, if the minimal swimming speed for conversion to ram ventilation by a remora is selected (page 583, 50 cm·sec⁻¹, Muir and Buckley, 1967), and the curve in Figure 6 is used, a differential of just over 1 cm water pressure results. Therefore, when an allowance is made for inertial losses that must occur with branchial flow-rate changes during active as opposed to passive gill ventilation, the suggested minimal value of a 0.5 cm differential pressure to support ram gill ventilation seems acceptable.

The transition to ram ventilation from active gill ventilation in swimming teleosts superficially resembles breath holding in man and diving aerial-breathers among vertebrates. It is marked by cessation of rhythmic breathing and seems not to be mediated by chemoreceptive detection of changes in the concentration of respiratory gases or pH. Recent experiments to be reported elsewhere, indicate that the transition swimming velocity for ram ventilation is only slightly increased by warming (1° C per minute; bluefish, blue runners) or by dropping the pO₂ in a swimming tunnel (halfmoons, jack mackerel), and then only at extremes.

Active ventilation in resting fish is driven by the combined actions of the buccal and opercular pumps; effected by contractions in antagonistic arrangements of the branchial musculature (Ballintijn and Hughes, 1965; Ballintijn, 1972). Pressure generated by streaming flow at the mouth allows transfer of much of the ventilatory work to the swimming musculature as the transition swimming speed for ram ventilation modes is accomplished by reflex conversion of motor outputs from the medullary respiratory areas of the CNS from a cyclic to a tonic drive of the branchial muscles.

The fact that tonic control of the buccal musculature is maintained during ram gill ventilation has been verified for a mackerel by Brown and Muir (1970). They found that progressive reductions in the pO_2 of water circulating in a water-tunnel respirometer results in graded increases in mouth gape at fixed swimming speeds. Furthermore, the mouth of an anesthetized fish usually is forced fully open or fully closed in the stream flow of a swimming tunnel, depending upon the streamline shape of the head and the degree of mouth gape when the flow is started. Clearly, mouth gape opening is not a passive process in swimming fish that do ram ventilate.

Despite the large effort that has been spent on the examination of adaptive respiratory reflexes in fish, specific receptors for initiating reflex action have not been identified. However, it is known that proprioceptive elements sensitive to gill filament displacement are located in the gill arches (Sutterlin and Saunders, 1969). Pertinent to this discussion are receptors for monitoring water flow velocity, and muscular activity effecting ventilation and swimming.

Delay in the return of active gill ventilation is so short in a ram ventilating fish when swimming slows or stops, that reflex switching by way of oxygen sampling is unlikely for this event (Figs. 4, 5). Return of rhythmic breathing in bluefish and blue runners can occur within 0.3 second of flow shut-down in a swimming tunnel. Timing in the blocking of rhythmic movements as swimming begins at speeds above the transition speed for ram gill ventilation is a different case. Several seconds may elapse before a fish begins to ram ventilate, but during this time there will not have been any interruption of the branchial water flow.

Receptor systems subject only to minor influences by metabolic loading or by temperature change would seem to provide the most reliable cues for switching between ventilatory modes. Mechanoreceptors sensitive to water flow velocity such as elements of the acoustico-lateralis system, and proprioceptors in the gill arches and the swimming musculature (stretch receptors) are likely candidates for this function. Monitoring of water flow velocity over the body and through the branchial chambers, and the detection of tail-beat frequency should be influenced only by the properties of water as a flowing fluid (see Hughes and Roberts, 1970; Randall, 1970b). Consequently, the thermal error in receptor functioning should be negligible for fish swimming at set velocities over the temperature range of their usual habitats.

Although both receptor detection of water-flow rates and events in swimming may be critical for reflex conversion to ram gill ventilation as reported above, some exceptions have been noted. Two of the blue runners from the group listed in Table II were found to continue ram gill ventilation after drifting to the rear screen of the swimming apparatus during swimming bouts. No obvious signs of fatigue were observed when they quit swimming. Under the unnatural circumstances of forced holding of these fish in a stream flow, it is possible that conditioning occurred that permitted continuation of the ram mode. A similar explanation might be applied to the ram gill ventilation of remoras attached to the wall of a swimming tunnel. However, Muir and Buckley (1967, page 582) also have reported that the swimming musculature becomes relaxed when the flow reaches ram ventilating speeds so that the body ". . . often swayed with the current." Assuming that proprioceptive return is critical to reflex control of ram ventilation in the remora as well, stretch receptor systems still could be activated by passive tail oscillations at frequencies dependent upon water flow velocity.

The author is grateful to Dr. Reuben Lasker for his editorial review of the manuscript, his encouragement, and his sponsorship of that part of the study carried out at the Southwest Fisheries Center, La Jolla, California. Gratitude is also due Directors Dr. Robert L. Edwards (Center Director, Woods Hole, Mass.), and Dr. Brian J. Rothschild (Center Director, La Jolla, Calif.) of the National Marine Fisheries Service for the use of facilities. Special thanks are due Charles L. Wheeler, Aquarium Director (NMFS, Woods Hole, Mass.), his assistant, Harold Ruschky, and Roger Leong, Fisheries Biologist (NMFS, La Jolla, Calif.) for collection and care of the marine fishes used in this study. Data obtained by Sister Mary Arthur Logan during her tenure as a National Science Foundation Summer Research Participant (grant to the University of Massachusetts) also is gratefully acknowledged.

Summary

1. Characteristics of cyclic breathing movements have been examined in a number of fish species at rest and during swimming acceleration to velocities above those sufficient to induce transfers from active to passive gill ventilation (ram gill ventilation). They were trained to swim in one of several types of swimming tunnels after electrode implants to permit recording of ECG's and ventilatory muscle EMG's.

2. Transfer to the ram mode of gill breathing is marked by a drop-out of individual cyclic breathing movements as swimming increases from rest. When the swimming speed reaches about 65 cm·sec^{-1}, most fish that use ram gill ventilation complete conversion to the ram mode (35 to 82 cm·sec^{-1}, range of all fish tested). This is equivalent to an across-gill differential pressure of 2.1 cm H_2O as measured with a combined impact-reverse pitot tube as an approximate model. Generally, a fish must be swimming to ram gill ventilate, but some exceptions are noted such as the shark-riding remoras.

3. Control of the transfer between gill ventilation modes appears basically to be a reflex shut-down of rhythmic breathing initiated by mechanoreceptive detection of water flow-velocity and the detection of swimming movements. Reflex transitions between active and passive breathing seem to happen too rapidly for a sufficient change of respiratory gas concentrations to occur and allow triggering of chemoreceptors.

4. No unusual events are detectable in the ECG's of swimming fish as they reach and surpass speeds sufficient to maintain the ram mode. Cardioacceleration varies as between sluggish and active swimmers, but seems to be independent of the mode of gill ventilation used.

5. Generally, demersal fishes that depend mainly upon the opercular phase for active gill ventilation, strongly aided by a well-developed branchiostegal system, do not ram ventilate. Conversely, nearly all species in which the work share of active ventilation is about equally buccal and opercular, probably use ram gill ventilation when they reach the requisite swimming speed. These are mostly midwater to pelagic in habits so for them, transfer of the muscular work of gill ventilation from the branchial to the swimming musculature seems to serve a dual function—a reduction in the cost of breathing, and an improvement in swimming efficiency.

NOTE ADDED IN PROOF

Jones and Schwarzfeld (1974, *Resp. Physiol.*, **21**: 241–254) have revised Jones' earlier estimate (1971) for the oxygen cost of breathing to total metabolism in rainbow trout upward from one to ten per cent on the basis of measurements with hatchery fish.

LITERATURE CITED

ALEXANDER, R. McN., 1970. *Functional Design in Fishes.* Hutchinson, London, 160 pp.

BAILEY, R. M., J. E. FITCH, E. S. HERALD, E. A. LACHNER, C. C. LINDSEY, C. R. ROBINS AND W. B. SCOTT, 1970. *A List of Common and Scientific Names of Fishes from the United States and Canada.* American Fisheries Society, Special Publication No. 6.

BALLINTIJN, C. M., 1972. Efficiency, mechanics and motor control of fish respiration. *Resp. Physiol.*, **14**: 125–141.

BALLINTIJN, C. M., AND G. M. HUGHES, 1965. The muscular basis of the respiratory pumps in the trout. *J. Exp. Biol.*, **43**: 349–362.

BIGELOW, H. B., AND W. C. SCHROEDER, 1953. Fishes of the Gulf of Maine. *Fishery Bulletin of the Fish and Wildlife Service,* 53: 1–577.

BRETT, J. R., 1964. The respiratory metabolism and swimming performance of young sockeye salmon. *J. Fish. Res. Board Can.*, 21: 1183–1226.

BROWN, C. E., AND B. S. MUIR, 1970. Analysis of ram ventilation of fish gills with application to skipjack tuna (*Katsuwonus pelamis*). *J. Fish. Res. Board Can.*, 27: 1637–1652.

CAMERON, J. N., AND J. J. CECH, JR., 1970. Notes on the energy cost of gill ventilation in teleosts. *Comp. Biochem. Physiol.*, **34**: 447–455.

HALL, F. G., 1930. The ability of the common mackerel and certain other marine fishes to remove dissolved oxygen from sea water. *Amer. J. Physiol.*, **93**: 417–421.

HEATH, A. G., 1973. Ventilatory responses of teleost fish to exercise and thermal stress. *Amer. Zool.*, 13: 491–503.

HEATH, A. G., AND G. M. HUGHES, 1973. Cardiovascular and respiratory changes during heat stress in rainbow trout (*Salmo gairdneri*). *J. Exp. Biol.*, 59: 323–338.

HUGHES, G. M., 1960a. A comparative study of gill ventilation in marine teleosts. *J. Exp. Biol.*, 37: 28–45.

HUGHES, G. M., 1960b. The mechanism of gill ventilation in the dogfish and skate. *J. Exp. Biol.*, 37: 11–27.

HUGHES, G. M., 1966. The dimensions of fish gills in relation to their function. *J. Exp. Biol.*, 45: 177–195.

HUGHES, G. M., 1973. Respiratory responses to hypoxia in fish. *Amer. Zool.*, 13: 475–489.

HUGHES, G. M., AND M. MORGAN, 1973. The structure of fish gills in relation to their respiratory function. *Biol. Rev.*, 48: 419–475.

HUGHES, G. M., AND J. L. ROBERTS, 1969. Gill ventilation in the sea-robin, sculpin, scup and toadfish. *Amer. Zool.*, 9: 1101.

HUGHES, G. M., AND J. L. ROBERTS, 1970. A study of the effect of temperature change on the respiratory pumps of the rainbow trout. *J. Exp. Biol.*, 52: 177–192.

HUGHES, G. M., AND G. SHELTON, 1962. Respiratory mechanisms and their nervous control in fish. Pages 274–364 in O. Lowenstein, Ed., *Advances in Comparative Physiology and Biochemistry.* Academic Press, New York.

JONES, D. R., 1971. Theoretical analysis of factors which may limit the maximum oxygen uptake of fish: The oxygen cost of the cardiac and branchial pumps. *J. Theor. Biol.*, 32: 341–349.

LABAT, R., 1966. *Electrocardiologie chez les poissons Téléostéens: Influence de quelques facteurs écologiques. Ph.D. thesis, University of Toulouse,* 175 pages.

McALLISTER, D. E., 1968. Evolution of branchiostegals and classification of teleostome fishes. *National Museum of Canada Bull.*, 221: *Biol. Ser.* 77.

MAGNUSON, J. J., 1970. Hydrostatic equilibrium of *Euthynnus affinis*, a pelagic teleost without a gas bladder. *Copeia,* **1970** (1): 56–85.

MAGNUSON, J. J., 1973. Comparative study of adaptations for continuous swimming and hydrostatic equilibrium of scombroid and xiphoid fishes. *Fish. Bull. (U. S.)*, 71: 337–356.

MILLER, D. J., AND R. N. LEA, 1972. *Guide to the Coastal Marine Fishes of California. California Department of Fish and Game, Fish Bulletin,* 157: 1–235.

MUIR, B. S., AND R. M. BUCKLEY, 1967. Gill Ventilation in *Remora remora*. *Copeia,* 1967 (3) : 581–586.

RANDALL, D. J., 1970a. The circulatory system. Pages 133–172 in W. S. Hoar, and D. J. Randall, Eds., *Fish Physiology, Vol. IV.* Academic Press, New York.

RANDALL, D. J., 1970b. Gas exchange in fish. Pages 253–292 in W. S. Hoar, and D. J. Randall, Eds., *Fish Physiology, Vol. IV.* Academic Press, New York.

ROBERTS, J. L., 1964. Metabolic responses of sunfish to photoperiod and temperature. *Helgolaender Wiss. Meeresuntersuch.,* 9 : 459–473.

ROBERTS, J. L., 1970. Gill ventilation in swimming fish. *Amer. Zool.,* 10 : 516.

ROBERTS, J. L., 1973. Effects of thermal stress on gill ventilation and heart rate in fishes. Pages 64–86 in W. Chavin, Ed., *Responses of Fish to Environmental Changes.* Charles C Thomas, Springfield.

ROBERTS, J. L., 1974. Respiratory adaptations of aquatic animals. In press in F. J., and W. B. Vernberg, Eds., *Physiological Adaptation to the Environment.* Intext, New York.

SCHUMANN, D., AND J. PIIPER, 1966. Der Sauerstoffbedarf der Atmung bei Fischen nach Messungen an der narkotisierten Schlei (*Tinca tinca*). *Pflugers Arch. ges. Physiol.,* 288 : 15–26.

SMITH, L. S., J. R. BRETT AND J. C. DAVIS, 1967. Cardiovascular dynamics in swimming adult sockeye salmon. *J. Fish. Res. Board Can.,* 24 : 1775–1790.

SPOOR, W. A., T. W. NEIHEISEL AND R. A. DRUMMOND, 1971. An electrode chamber for recording respiratory and other movements of free-swimming animals. *Trans. Amer. Fish. Soc.,* 100 : 22–28.

SUTTERLIN, A. M., 1967. Effects of exercise on cardiac and ventilation frequency in three species of freshwater teleosts. *Physiol. Zool.,* 42 : 36–52.

SUTTERLIN, A. M., AND R. L. SAUNDERS, 1969. Proprioceptors in the gills of teleosts. *Can. J. Zool.,* 47 : 1209–1212.

VON WAHLERT, G., 1964. Passive Atmung bei Haien. *Naturwissenschaften,* 51 : 297–298.

Positive Buoyancy and Air-breathing: A New Piscine Gas Bladder Function

ERIC S. TODD

Dormitator latifrons is unique among known air-breathing fishes in that it emerges an external respiratory organ when in hypoxic water. The fish normally does so by using supports or generating positive buoyancy by inflation of the gas bladder. To inflate the gas bladder in hypoxic water fish must first emerge the external respiratory organ. The gas bladder is then inflated with oxygen and carbon dioxide. However, inflation of the gas bladder did not commonly occur in the laboratory unless fish were away from visual and auditory disturbances.

One of the most important functions ascribed to the piscine gas bladder is that of maintaining neutral buoyancy by decreasing the density differences between fish and the surrounding water. Although much is understood about the physiological processes of secretion and absorption of gases in the gas bladder, remarkably little is known about the use fish make of this ability. Most evidence indicates that several fish species which make diurnal changes in depth simply maintain a quantity of gas which provides them with neutral buoyancy at the top of their vertical range (Alexander, 1967).

In western Panama I observed that the brackish water eleotrid, *Dormitator latifrons* (Richardson), is a facultative air-breather which in hypoxic water emerges a flat, highly vascularized, epithelial surface on the top of its head. Aerial oxygen is absorbed through this external respiratory organ (Todd, 1972). However, before I observed *D. latifrons* air-breathing in the field, I discovered that two fish taken directly from the field were apparently able to survive hypoxic water (< 1 mg O_2/1) in a laboratory bucket by floating a blood reddened, respiratory surface out of water. When I tried to repeat this observation with another 28 fish taken directly from the field they were unable to emerge the respiratory surface in smooth walled buckets of hypoxic freshwater, and all died within several hours. Because the fish did not gulp and hold air in an internal respiratory chamber while air-breathing, I investigated the problem of how this fish produces sufficient buoyancy in its physoclistic gas bladder such that its external respiratory organ is raised out of hypoxic water into the air.

METHODS AND RESULTS

Gas samples from the gas bladder, usually taken by puncture with a syringe, were analyzed for percentages of oxygen and carbon dioxide using a Scholander microgasometric analyzer (Scholander et al., 1955). Dissolved oxygen was measured with a commercial galvanic type oxygen analyzer (Duxbury, 1963).

First, I investigated if the gas bladder was indeed responsible for the fish's positive buoyancy. Fish were individually dip netted from an oxygen deficient, brackish water pond near Farfan Beach, Canal Zone and immobilized by pithing. After pithing, fish were placed on the bottom of a bucket filled with the 3‰ seawater of the pond. All air that had been trapped in the buccal, pharyngeal and opercular cavities while the fish were handled in air was completely removed under water. Fish that floated to the surface and emersed a portion of their bodies were classified as being positively buoyant. Some fish floated high out of the water with non-respiratory areas of the head and back exposed. Those fish that remained on the bottom or below the water surface were considered to be negatively or neutrally buoyant. Immediately after determination of the buoyancy condi-

From *Copeia* 1973(3):461–464. Reprinted by permission.

tion, the abdomen and gas bladder were cut open under water and the gas from the gas bladder liberated. Gas was trapped in a funnel attached to a fluid filled, inverted burette. Twenty positively buoyant fish showed significantly larger volumes of gas ($\bar{x}$, 16.8 ml; ± SE,1.2) than twenty other fish that were negatively or neutrally buoyant ($\bar{x}$ 7.3 ± 1.5 ml). The average weights of the two groups were 230 ± 10.4 and 248 ± 8.0 grams, respectively. In the laboratory when gas was removed from the gas bladders of positively buoyant fish floating in smooth walled buckets of hypoxic water, the fish always sank and died. However, the positively buoyant controls always survived. The controls were stuck with a needle but no gas was withdrawn. Furthermore, with all gases removed from the digestive tract and gas bladder the average density of ten fish that had been positively buoyant in freshwater was 1.0711 g/cc ± SE 0.0027 while the average tissue density of ten fish that were previously negatively buoyant in the same freshwater was 1.0804 g/cc ± 0.0025. These tissue density differences could not account for the fact that previously one group had been positively buoyant while the other was neutrally or negatively buoyant.

Because *D. latifrons* is normally exposed to fluctuating salinities in its shallow, estuarine water habitat, I investigated if an increase in water density could increase buoyancy sufficiently to enable the fish to float the respiratory organ above the water surface. When ten fish were transferred from oxygenated freshwater to hypoxic (< 2 mg O_2/l) seawater five of the fish immediately floated and could breath air on the surface. Ten controls transferred from oxygenated freshwater to hypoxic freshwater all sank and died. Oxygen and carbon dioxide samples taken from the gas bladders of ten positively buoyant fish in oxygenated, 28‰ seawater averaged 25.7% (range, 19.7-37.2) oxygen and 0.9% (range, 0.1-1.2) carbon dioxide.

By weighing ten fish individually in both freshwater and 28‰ seawater the increase in buoyancy in seawater was determined. These fish had been kept in the laboratory in freshwater for one month. Seawater provided an average lifting force on the bodies of 4.6 grams while the average weight of the excised respiratory organs in air was 5.5 grams.

When fish with physoclistic gas bladders suddenly move upwards their gas bladder expands and they become more positively buoyant. Although the brackish water habitat of *D. latifrons* is typically shallow, I tested if the fish used such a method to increase its positive buoyany in hypoxic water. Three, freely swimming groups of five fish each were each allowed to deoxygenate a 2.5 m column, 30 cm in diameter, of 28‰ seawater after having been held in cages at a 2.5 m depth in oxygenated seawater for three days. However, fish did not rapidly rise to the surface when the water became hypoxic and so little if any expansion of gas bladder gases probably occurred. Moreover, experimental animals always died in the smooth walled columns without becoming positively buoyant. Five control fish survived in a column containing supports near the water surface on which the fish could climb and emerge the respiratory organ.

To examine the rates at which gas bladders of fish recently captured from the field are inflated with oxygen and carbon dioxide gases were measured among five groups containing 5-6 fish each. After all the gas bladders had been emptied by coelomic puncture and fish had been placed in a tank of oxygenated freshwater (6 X 8 X 0.5 m) one group was sampled at six hours and four other groups at 12, 24, 48 and 72 hours respectively. After six hours gas bladders showed high levels of oxygen and carbon dioxide (see Table 1). These fish did not become positively buoyant nor did 48 other fish kept for three months in the same oxygenated, freshwater tank. After two weeks in oxygenated freshwater the gas bladders of ten of the above 48 fish averaged 37% oxygen (range, 20.0-56.1) and 1.0% carbon dioxide (range, 0.5-2.2).

Observations in the field suggested that fish fill their gas bladders in hypoxic water after climbing onto supports, thereby emerging the air-breathing organ. In an impoundment there was an area where people constantly frightened fish away from their perches and where oxygenated, tidal seawater periodically entered. Most of the fish in this area were neutrally or negatively buoyant. When the oxygen concentration of the water

TABLE 1. Percentage of Oxygen and Carbon Dioxide (O_2/CO_2) in Refilled Gas Bladders at Different Time Intervals After Removal of the Original Gases. Twenty-nine fish sampled.

		Time after removal (hours)		
6	12	24	48	72
81.0/ 7.6		77.9/2.6	73.0/0.0	74.7/1.9
79.9/19.7	52.0/20.3	90.3/2.4	84.0/2.9	83.6/3.0
59.9/ 5.0	74.4/ 7.5	83.7/3.4	80.0/1.0	78.3/2.1
85.0/ 9.4	76.0/10.4	69.2/1.2	85.0/2.3	77.0/3.0
71.0/ 6.0	72.3/ 5.8	57.3/2.5	69.5/2.7	84.2/4.1
87.7/ 8.9	61.0/ 5.1	50.0/4.1	87.3/3.4	48.5/2.9
Mean 74.4/ 9.4	67.1/ 8.1	71.4/2.7	79.8/2.1	73.4/2.8

increased from 0.5 to 1.9 mg $O_2/1$, most of the emerged fish had left their perches and moved into the more oxygenated seawater. They returned to their perches when the surrounding water again became hypoxic hours later. Positively buoyant fish were found in a secluded area of this impoundment which could be approached only by boat. This area was also free of tidal influences. Possibly, positively buoyant fish were numerous in the latter area because inflation of the gas bladder could occur there without interruption.

Neutrally or negatively buoyant fish away from any under water supports were able to breathe air temporarily in hypoxic water by swimming at the surface. This activity only allowed portions of the respiratory organ to be emerged and eventually the exhausted fish sank and died, probably of asphyxia. I observed that if no supports were available for negatively or neutrally buoyant fish in hypoxic water they frequently jumped out of the water. For example, after jumping completely from the water two fish lay quietly on a flat terrestrial support for 3.5 hours. Five negatively buoyant fish swimming at the surface averaged only 13.2% oxygen (range, 2.5–26.3) but a high average of 3.9% carbon dioxide (2.7–6.0). After several hours in a tank of hypoxic water without supports five fish averaged only 3% oxygen (0.5–8.0) and all died in the tank within several hours. Controls in oxygenated water averaged 37% oxygen (20.0–56.1).

To examine how fish fill their gas bladders in hypoxic water I placed seven fish in a tub of hypoxic water containing chicken wire supports on which they could climb and emerge the respiratory organ. Fish quickly found and climbed onto the supports, emerging the respiratory organ. After 48 hours the supports were removed and the fish were still negatively buoyant. The gas bladders averaged 21.5% oxygen (range, 13.1–31.7) and 2.8% carbon dioxide (range, 1.5–6.5). I then placed four groups containing 10, 12, 12 and 12 neutrally or negatively buoyant fish in four separate tubs of hypoxic freshwater ($<2 O_2/1$) with supports on which the fish could climb. After a 72 hour period only eight fish in the four tubs were positively buoyant when the supports were removed, and 38 of the 46 fish died within several hours of removing the supports. None of the positively buoyant fish died when the supports were removed.

Since air-breathing fish in the field were easily frightened from their perches by noise I repeated the above experiment but in addition covered and carefully removed the tubs of fish from visual and auditory disturbances. One hundred and four neutrally or negatively buoyant fish were used in eight groups of 10 or 14 fish each. One group was left in a tub of hypoxic water with supports for six hours and then the supports were removed. None of these fish were positively buoyant, and all died within several hours after the supports were removed. However, the seven other groups of fish maintained in tubs of hypoxic water with supports for 9, 12, 24, 48, 72, 96 and 120 hour periods respectively were all seen to be positively buoyant at the end of each time period and only one fish died when the supports were removed. Fourteen of the positively buoyant fish picked at random from the tubs averaged 8.5% carbon dioxide (range, 5.5–10.2) and 42% oxygen (range, 29.5–69.1). Five other fish placed in a tub of hypoxic water averaged 2.6% carbon dioxide (range, 1.7–4.1) and 24.1% oxygen (range, 17.6–35.7) after two hours on the supports, although they were not positively buoyant. The results indicate that within nine hours, undisturbed, air-breathing fish can actively secrete sufficient oxygen and carbon dioxide into the gas bladder to produce positive buoyancy.

DISCUSSION

Positive buoyancy in *D. latifrons* is mediated behaviorally, physiologically and possibly fortuitously when fish encounter water of sufficiently increased salinity.

Although the obvious advantage of positive buoyancy is that fish are independent of supports and are not restricted to any one area, it would be disadvantageous for threatened fish to develop a positive buoyancy which could hinder escape from predators. Non-respiratory areas of the head and back may be emerged by some fish when freely floating at the surface. However, excessive inflation of the gas bladder is probably usually prevented because fish on the perches are easily frightened into the hypoxic water where absorption of gas bladder oxygen can take place. In the laboratory few fish became positively buoyant if they were exposed to auditory or visual disturbances. Other evidence shows that *D. latifrons* is very resistant to anoxia, and, therefore, if frightened it can survive long exposure to low ambient oxygen. If sufficient absorption of gas bladder oxygen occurs the fish will again become negatively buoyant. Negatively buoyant fish captured in the field while swimming at the surface to emerge the respiratory organ showed high levels of carbon dioxide but low levels of oxygen in the gas bladder. These figures indicate that oxygen was being absorbed probably as a result of the exposure to hypoxic conditions, but as indicated by the high percentages of carbon dioxide, inflation of the gas bladder had recently occurred probably while the fish were breathing air on supports.

Most physoclistic fishes initially show high percentages of carbon dioxide and oxygen when inflating the gas bladder (Kuhn et al., 1963), and many can inflate the gas bladder within 4 to 48 hours (Alexander, 1967). Not only can *D. latifrons* rapidly fill the gas bladder (within six hours), but also it maintains a high percentage of oxygen in the gas bladder for unusually long periods in oxygenated water (Todd and Ebeling, 1966). *D. latifrons* initially fills the gas bladder with carbon dioxide and oxygen. Some fishes fill the gas bladder with nitrogen (Steen, 1970). If *D. latifrons* filled the gas bladder with nitrogen, buoyancy control probably could not be achieved with the same facility gained by using oxygen. The partial pressure of nitrogen in the blood remains high in shallow water, and the diffusion of nitrogen from the gas bladder would be slow relative to that of oxygen in hypoxic water. The advantage of using oxygen is that this probably allows a behavioral control of buoyancy which would most simply satisfy the immediate requirements of the animal.

ACKNOWLEDGMENTS

I thank Alfred W. Ebeling for use of the Scholander microgasometric analyzer. The work was supported by a Postdoctoral Fellowship from the Smithsonian Institution and was carried out at the Smithsonian Tropical Research Institute, Canal Zone.

LITERATURE CITED

ALEXANDER, R. MCN. 1967. Functional Design in Fishes. London, Hutchinson and Co. LTD.
DUXBURY, A. C. 1963. Calibration and uses of a galvanic type oxygen electrode in field works. J. Limn. Ocean. 8:483–485.
KUHN, W., A. RAMEL, H. J. KUHN and E. MARTI. 1963. The filling mechanism of the swimbladder. Generation of high gas pressures through hairpin countercurrent multiplication. Experientia 19:497–512.

SCHOLANDER, P. F., L. VAN DAM, C. L. CLAFF and J. W. KANWISHER. 1955. Microgasometric determination of dissolved oxygen and nitrogen. Biol. Bull. 109:328-336.

STEEN, J. B. 1970. The swimbladder as a hydrostatic organ, p. 413-443. *In*: Fish Physiology, Editors W. S. Hoar and D. J. Randall, New York and London, Academic Press, 4.

TODD, E. S. 1972. Hemoglobin concentration in a new air-breathing fish. Comp. Biochem. Physiol. 42A:569-573.

——, and A. W. EBELING. 1966. Aerial respiration in the long jaw mudsucker *Gillichthys mirabilis* (Teleostei: Gobiidae). Biol. Bull. 130:265-288.

DEPARTMENT OF ZOOPHYSIOLOGY, UNIVERSITY OF AARHUS, DK-8000, AARHUS C DENMARK.

OXYGEN UPTAKE AND CIRCULATION BY A HEMOGLOBINLESS ANTARCTIC FISH (*CHAENOCEPHALUS ACERATUS* LONNBERG) COMPARED WITH THREE RED-BLOODED ANTARCTIC FISH

GEORGE F. HOLETON*

University of Toronto, Dept. of Zoology, Toronto M5S IAI, Ontario, Canada

Abstract—1. The respiration of a hemoglobinless Antarctic fish *Chaenocephalus aceratus* Lönnberg and three red-blooded Antarctic fish was examined.

2. The gill irrigation of *C. aceratus* requires very little energy and is similar to many benthic fishes.

3. *C. aceratus* has low blood pressure and high cardiac output. Enlarged capillaries are implicated.

4. The P_{O_2}† gradient from water to blood of *C. aceratus* is similar to other fish but the P_{O_2} gradient from blood to tissues is high.

5. The oxygen consumption of *C. aceratus* is low but comparable to other red-blooded Antarctic fish.

6. *C. aceratus* has less resistance to hypoxia than red-blooded Antarctic fish.

INTRODUCTION

SEVERAL workers have reported the lack of functionally significant levels of hemoglobin in the blood of Antartic fish of the family Chaenichthyidae (called "icefish") (Ruud, 1954, 1958, 1965; Martsinkevitch, 1958; Hureau, 1966).

It has been observed that fish from high latitudes have low levels of hemoglobin compared to tropical fish (Scholander & Van Dam, 1957; Tyler, 1960; Kooyman, 1963; Grigg, 1967; Everson & Ralph, 1968).

There are also a number of observations of individual fish and amphibians surviving with greatly reduced hemoglobin levels arising from natural and experi-

---

* The author has received financial support during the course of this study from a N.E.R.C. Grant issued to Professor G. M. Hughes of the Department of Zoology, University of Bristol. Logistical support and research facilities for this study were generously provided by the British Antarctic Survey, 30 Gillingham Street, London, S.W.1.

† Symbols—$\dot{V}_G$: volume of water passed over gills/unit time per unit weight. $\dot{V}_{O_2}$: O_2 uptake/unit time per unit weight. $\dot{Q}$: Cardiac output/unit time per unit weight. P: partial pressure of gas. α: solubility coefficient. w: water. b: blood.

Subscripts—I: referring to water in buccal cavity (inspired). E: referring to water in opercular cavity (expired). a: arterial blood leaving gills. $\bar{v}$: mixed venous blood entering gills. G: gills.

From *Comp. Biochem. Physiol.* 34A:457–471. Reprinted by permission of Pergamon Press Ltd., Oxford, England.

mental causes (Wells, 1918; Nicloux, 1923; Schlicher, 1926; DeGraaf, 1957; Ewer, 1959; Ryback, 1960; Stolk, 1960; Anthony, 1961; Steen & Berg, 1966; Flores & Frieden, 1968; Cameron & Wohlschlag, 1969). Some of the animals in these reports were obviously handicapped by the shortage of hemoglobin but others, notably the fish used by Nicloux (1923) and Anthony (1961), were not outwardly affected by the incapacitation of their hemoglobin by carbon monoxide.

Fox (1954) concluded that many fish must use their hemoglobin only in emergencies. However, active fish need the use of some of their hemoglobin even for resting respiration. Holeton (in preparation) has demonstrated that rainbow trout cannot survive exposure to 5 per cent carbon monoxide at temperatures above 5·0°C.

How have the chaenichthyids managed to do without hemoglobin? Part of the answer lies in their special environment with its low temperatures and high oxygen content. The low temperatures mean that the fish will have low oxygen-consumption levels. The high content of oxygen in water means that less water will have to be pumped over the gills in order to obtain oxygen. These points have been made repeatedly by Ruud (1954, 1958, 1965).

In most areas frequented by chaenichthyids annual temperatures rarely vary more than a few degrees from the freezing point although both Andriashev (1962) and Hureau (1966) mention temperatures reaching between 5 and 8°C. Temperatures as high as these are not widespread. In East Cumberland Bay, South Georgia, weekly water samples were taken from 12 November 1930 to 29 March 1931. These showed considerable fluctuations in surface temperatures but temperatures at 75 m ranged from $-0·88$ to $+1·55$°C (Discovery Reports, 1932). The waters around Signy Island, where the present study was carried out, are similarly cold. Two water samples drawn from near the bottom in Borge Bay, Signy Island, at sites where considerable numbers of *Chaenocephalus aceratus* were taken gave the following information:

18 December, 1968: depth 55 m, $-0·36$°C, oxygen 11·4 ppm.
11 February, 1969: depth 75 m, $+1·00$°C, oxygen 11·1 ppm.

Another environmental factor contributing to the success of the chaenichthyids is the abundance of food in the Antarctic seas. There is evidence that the chaenichthyids eat large quantities of food. *C. aceratus* were taken at South Georgia (present study) and at Signy Island (Ralph & Everson, 1968) with large fish in their gullets. Olsen (1955) reported a diet of small fish for *C. aceratus* but also stated that two pelagic chaenichthyids, *Pseudochaenichthys georgianus* and *Champsocephalus gunnari*, feed on dense shoals of krill (*Euphausia superba*). A very large haul of *C. aceratus* taken in Borge Bay, Signy Island, during the current study consisted largely of individuals with their mouths and stomachs filled with krill. Crew members of the British Antarctic Survey Vessel, R.R.S. *John Biscoe*, described fish captured in a bay of King George Island in the South Shetlands in December 1968 which had white gills and overall colour and morphology closely resembling *C. aceratus*, whose mouths and stomachs were filled with krill.

Although chaenichthyids may eat large quantities of food at times, there is a probability that they only feed sporadically. Hureau (1966) reported that *Chaenichthys rhinoceratus*, from Kerguelen Islands, was usually captured with its stomach empty. Olsen (1955) made similar observations on *C. aceratus* in South Georgia. In the present study *C. aceratus* taken near Signy Island usually had empty stomachs. Thus the balance of evidence available supports Ruud's (1965) observation that icefish probably eat large quantities of food at infrequent intervals. Such a feeding pattern would not require high levels of oxygen uptake as much of the feeding would be done by burst activity and the energy required could be obtained anaerobically.

Olsen (1955) found that the red-blooded *Notothenia rossii* and the two icefish *Pseudochaenichthys georgianus* and *Champsocephalus gunnari* had similar growth rates in waters around South Georgia. He concluded that in spite of the low oxygen capacity of their blood, the icefish do not seem handicapped in competition with other species possessing normal red blood.

Since it is well established that chaenichthyids are successful and well differentiated ecologically (Andriashev, 1962), it is interesting to consider the details of their respiration. Ruud (1965), Steen & Berg (1966), and Everson & Ralph (1970) have pointed out that there are compensations in the circulatory system of the icefish which offset the lack of hemoglobin. Certainly marked changes from the normal respiratory pattern would be expected but the exact nature of these changes has not been defined.

The purpose of this study was to examine the factors affecting the oxygen exchange of a large benthic chaenichthyid, *C. aceratus*. This examination covers the resting respiration. In order to have a basis for comparison, the resting respiration of the antarctic nototheniids, *Notothenia neglecta* (Nybelin) and *Notothenia gibberifrons* (Lönnberg), and the Antarctic bathydraconid, *Parachaenichthys charcoti* (Vaillant), were also investigated though not as intensively as *C. aceratus*.

MATERIALS AND METHODS

Fish were netted from the bottom of waters off Signy Island (60°43′ S, 45°36′ W) at depths from 8 to 220 m during the months from December 1968 to March 1969. Identification was based on descriptions by Norman (1938). Uninjured fish were removed from the net, placed in tubs of sea water and transported to the British Antarctic Survey Biological Laboratory on Signy Island within half an hour.

The fish were held in round, black polythene tubs through which was run sea water at temperatures which ranged from 0·3 to 1·4°C during the course of 4 months.

The following is a brief description of the three species of red-blooded fish.

Notothenia neglecta—a very abundant species found in shallow waters to a depth of 40 m. These fish were hardy and the most active in the holding tanks. They are blunt, heavy-bodied fish reaching weights up to 3 kg. The fish used in the experiments weighed about 1 kg and were typical of the average weight encountered.

Notothenia gibberifrons—these were taken in roughly equal numbers with *C. aceratus* at depths below 60 m. *N. gibberifrons* and *C. aceratus* constituted over 95 per cent of all fish caught at depths greater than 90 m. *N. gibberifrons* is demersal. Although more slender than *N. neglecta* they are blunt-headed and their mouths are small. The average weight of the experimental fish was 470 g although weights up to 1 kg were observed. *N. gibberifrons* was not active in captivity.

Parachaenichthys charcoti—one 557-g specimen was captured on the bottom at a depth of 75 m. A long slender fish, its head is like *C. aceratus* in configuration with a long snout, large opercula and branchiostegal complexes. The skin is free of scales like *C. aceratus*. Its behaviour in captivity indicated it was a benthic fish and although responsive to disturbance it was not spontaneously active.

Although no difficulty was experienced in keeping *N. neglecta* and *P. charcoti*, a large portion of the icefish and *N. gibberifrons* died within a few days of capture. Those surviving this period had a low mortality.

Fish were anaesthetized in a 1 : 15,000 solution of MS-222 (tricaine methanesulphonate) and placed upon an operating table similar to that described by Smith & Bell

(1964). The gills of the anaesthetized fish were irrigated continuously with water during the operation.

The ventral aorta of *C. aceratus* was cannulated by inserting into the vessel a 20-gauge hypodermic needle attached to a polythene tube (pp 90, 0·86 mm i.d.) 60 cm long. The point of entry was the floor of the mouth between the second and third gill arches. Once the cannula was in the vessel, it was secured in place by stitching it to the tongue. The cannula was passed to the exterior through a 2-mm hole punched in the tip of the tongue and floor of the mouth and then secured to the jaw externally by a stitch in the skin.

The dorsal aortae of some chaenichthyids and four *N. gibberifrons* were cannulated as described by Smith & Bell (1964) using a 20-gauge hypodermic needle tip on 60 cm of pp 90 polythene tubing.

The cannulae for the blood vessels were filled with heparinized saline (20 i.u./ml). The saline was as described by Wolf (1963) but with 14·75 g/l NaCl instead of 7·25 g/l. The additional NaCl was added to bring the ionic concentrations up to levels found in chaenich-thyid blood (R. N. Smith, personal communication).

Cannulation of the buccal cavity of all fish was carried out as described by Saunders (1961) using 60 cm or pp 90 polythene tubing.

The opercular chamber on one side was cannulated as described by Holeton & Randall (1967a) using 60 cm of pp 90 polythene tubing. The use of such a cannula for sampling expired water from the opercular cavity is justifiably subject to the criticism of Garey (1967) that sampling from a single site may not give values representative of the average expired water. This source of variability can be minimized by careful placement of the opercular cannula. In this case the cannula was placed near the mid-position of the opercular opening close to the posterior margin of the operculum but not so close to the opercular value as to interfere with its operation.

Initial measurements on *C. aceratus* with the opercular cannula opening fitted flush with the inner opercular surface produced results indicating variable expired water oxygen tensions and low percentage utilizations. It was thought that water next to the opercular surface may not have come in contact with the gills; Hughes & Knights (1968) mention such a possibility. Raising the opening of the cannula a few mm clear of the inner opercular surface resulted in considerably higher percentage utilizations and more uniform expired water oxygen tensions being measured. Only measurements made with the modified cannulae were used in this paper.

An alternative to sampling the expired water from a cannula is to collect all the water pumped over the gills in a given period of time and measure the volume and oxygen content of the collected sample. This method has been used by a number of workers (Van Dam, 1938; Hughes & Shelton, 1962; Lenfant & Johansen, 1966; Hughes, 1967; Piiper & Schu-mann, 1967; Hughes & Knights, 1968) and is best suited for use on fish with restricted opercular openings. *C. aceratus* has large, easily deformed opercula and very long opercular openings and is not suited to this direct method. Sampling expired water from a selected site with a small cannula, the method employed in this study, has the advantage that it does not impair the fish's breathing.

When necessary, ECG wires were implanted under the skin in the heart region; 42 s.w.g. diamel-coated stainless steel wire was used and anchored with a stitch in the skin. The ECG's were amplified with a Devices AC7 preamplifier and displayed on a Devices four-channel pen recorder.

On completion of the surgical procedures, the fish was removed from the operating table and placed in a respirometer filled with flowing sea water. The respirometers were Perspex boxes with lids which could be sealed. Water was passed through them at a con-trolled temperature and rate of flow. The respirometers were chosen to fit the fish with as little dead space as possible but without actually touching the fish. The water was re-circulated by means of a pump. A gas exchange column was included in the circuit for controlling the gas content of the water.

Oxygen consumption of the fishes was determined by measuring the P_{O_2} of the water entering and leaving the respirometer at known flow rates. Alternatively, the air supply to the gas-exchange column could be turned off and the rate at which the fish lowered the oxygen in the recirculating system measured. The lowest oxygen levels attainable by the fish were determined in this way.

The oxygen tension of the water and blood samples were measured with a Beckman Macro Oxygen Electrode and a Beckman Model 160 Physiological Gas Analyser. Blood measured in this manner was returned to the fish after determinations of oxygen tension.

Blood pressures and pressures generated in the buccal cavity by breathing movements were measured using Devices strain-gauge-type pressure transducers and their output was displayed on a Devices four-channel pen recorder.

The fish were given at least 8 hr to settle and recover from the operation before measurements were made. Most of the fish were in the respirometers for periods ranging from 2 to 10 days and observations were made frequently throughout this time. The "resting" respiratory parameters measured in this case are the lowest levels that the fish achieved over the period of observations. Only values which persisted for at least half an hour were included in this report. The temperature at which the observations were made ranged from 0 to $+1.2°C$ but never varied more than $0.3°C$ over a few hours.

Care was taken to disturb the fishes as little as possible.

RESULTS

1.   *The oxygen extraction system of* C. aceratus

The head of *C. aceratus* is very large in proportion to the rest of the fish. The large opercular pumps and smaller buccal pump work together at an average frequency of 13 c/min to move water over the gills with pressure fluctuations in the buccal cavity averaging 0.15 mm Hg. The average percentage of oxygen removed from the respiratory water (per cent utilization) was 18 per cent but occasionally rose to 40–60 per cent.

2.   *The oxygen-transporting system of* C. aceratus

The blood of *C. aceratus* lacks significant numbers of erythrocytes. No trace of red colour was observed in the whitish translucent whole blood. The plasma was water-clear, and the cell mass at the bottom of a spun hematocrit tube was creamy white in colour and constituted approximately 1 per cent of the blood. Careful exsanguination of five fish ranging in weight from 522 to 2240 g yielded an average of 4.2 per cent of body weight of blood. The actual blood volume of *C. aceratus* is considerably higher than the exsanguination values (E. Twelves, personal communication).

The heart rate, blood pressure and blood oxygen tensions of *C. aceratus* are listed in Table 1. The average arterial–venous P_{O_2} difference was 97 mm Hg but in some cases this difference was observed to be as small as 65 mm Hg. Generally the highest $Pa_{(O_2)}$'s were associated with the lowest $P\bar{v}_{(O_2)}$'s.

The heart of *C. aceratus* appeared very large compared to other fish.

3.   *Interactions between extracting and transporting systems of* C. aceratus

The mean oxygen partial pressure gradient from respiratory water across the gill membranes to the blood (ΔP_G) is computed as follows:

$$\Delta P_G = \frac{(P_{I(O_2)} - Pa_{(O_2)}) + (P_{E(O_2)} - P\bar{v}_{(O_2)})}{2}$$

TABLE 1—RESPIRATORY CHARACTERISTICS OF RESTING *C. aceratus*

Parameter	Average	Range	Sample size
W., males (g)	564	502–627	4
W., females (g)	1411	860–1823	17
Breathing rate (per min)	13	7–17·5	19
Buccal pressure fluctuations (mm Hg)	0·15	0·10–0·30	17
Opercular P_{O_2} (mm Hg)	120	45–139	16
Utilization per cent	18	3–59	16
Heart rate (per min)	14	7–17·5	22
Dorsal aorta/Blood pressure (mm Hg)	15/10	18/13–10/5	5
P_{O_2} (mm Hg)	120	108–134	4
Ventral aorta/Blood pressure (mm Hg)	20/12	25/17–13/8	15
P_{O_2} (mm Hg)	25	10–40·5	11
Oxygen consumption (mg O_2/kg per hr)	23·5	13·9–28·0	17

Blood Pressure figures represent systolic/diastolic pressures.

Calculations using the data from Table 1 show *C. aceratus* has a mean ΔP_G of 60 mm Hg. In two cases where all necessary values were simultaneously available from individual fish over a period of several days, it was found that ΔP_G ranged from 46 to 63 mm Hg.

$Pa_{(O_2)}$ was often observed to be higher than $P_{E(O_2)}$ indicating that *C. aceratus* uses a counter-current flow arrangement between blood and water.

The volume of water moved over the gills ($\dot{V}_G$) and the gill blood flow (cardiac output $\dot{Q}$) can be estimated from the Fick principle as follows:

$$\dot{V}_G = \frac{\dot{V}_{O_2}}{(P_{I(O_2)} - P_{E(O_2)}) \times \alpha\, w_{O_2}}$$

$$\dot{Q} = \frac{\dot{V}_{O_2}}{(Pa_{(O_2)} - P\bar{v}_{(O_2)}) \times \alpha\, b_{O_2}}$$

The value of 0·67 vol per cent for the oxygen capacity of *C. aceratus* blood reported by Ruud (1954) was used in computing $\dot{Q}$.

The resting $\dot{V}_G$ of *C. aceratus* is 197 ml/kg per min and resting $\dot{Q}$ is 61 ml/kg per min. This is a ventilation perfusion ratio ($\dot{V}_G : \dot{Q}$) of 3·2 : 1. In cases where the fish had high percentage utilizations, the calculated $\dot{V}_G$'s were much smaller and $\dot{V}_G : \dot{Q}$ approached 1 : 1.

4. *Comparison of resting respiration of* C. aceratus *with red-blooded fish from the same environment*

Respiratory characteristics of the four species of fish are summarized in Tables 2 and 3.

Table 2—Oxygen extraction system characteristics of four species of Antarctic fish

Parameter	C. aceratus		N. gibberifrons		N. neglecta		P. charcoti	
Breathing rate (c/min)	13·0	(19)	26·5	(7)	25·7	(3)	11·0	(1)
Breathing pressure (buccal—mm Hg)	0·15	(17)	0·30	(7)	0·62	(3)	0·15	(1)
Expired P_{O_2} ($P_{E(O_2)}$) (mm Hg)	120	(16)	85	(6)	100	(2)	—	
Utilization %	18	(16)	38	(6)	34	(2)	—	
Estimated $\dot{V}_G$ (ml/kg per min)	197	(16)	99	(6)	123	(2)	—	
Resting $\dot{V}_{O_2}$ (mg O_2/kg per hr)	23·5	(17)	23	(6)	28·7	(2)	24·8	(1)

Figures in brackets represent sample size. (Temperature $0·5 \pm 0·5°C$.)

Table 3—Circulatory characteristics of four species of Antarctic fish

Parameter	C. aceratus		N. gibberifrons		N. neglecta		P. charcoti	
Heart rate (beats/min)	13·8	(22)	16·0	(6)	15·0	(2)	10·5	(1)
Dorsal aortic blood pressure (mm Hg)	15/10	(5)	10/7	(2)	—		—	
Hematocrit %	Less than 1%		30·3	(6)	25·2*		39	(1)
Ventricle wt. (% of body wt.)	0·300	(73)	0·061	(47)	0·100	(19)	0·082	(1)
Av. wt. of fish used (g)	1250	(22)	438	(7)	978	(3)	557	(1)

Figures in brackets indicate sample size. (Temperature $0·5 \pm 0·5°C$.)

* From Everson & Ralph (1968).

The resting $\dot{V}_{O_2}$ of all four species is similar (Table 2).

C. aceratus and *P. charcoti* have similar breathing characteristics but differ from *N. gibberifrons* and *N. neglecta*.

The ability of *C. aceratus*, *N. gibberifrons* and *N. neglecta* to maintain oxygen uptake at low environmental P_{O_2}'s was tested by sealing off the respirometer circuit to outside sources of oxygen and allowing the fish to lower the oxygen level in the water. Five *N. gibberifrons* and one *N. neglecta* were able to lower the environmental P_{O_2} to values ranging from 14 to 20 mm Hg without the fish showing undue signs of distress. The experiments were terminated when the oxygen level of the environmental water was no longer being lowered at an appreciable rate. Similar experiments with *C. aceratus* produced very different results. Two of the fish stopped breathing at 44 and 49 mm Hg P_{O_2} and efforts to revive the fish were unsuccessful. A third *C. aceratus* showed signs of distress at an environmental P_{O_2} of 65 mm Hg and the experiment was terminated at this point. This fish quickly recovered when the oxygen level was restored.

DISCUSSION

There were no significant sex-linked differences in any of the respiratory parameters of *C. aceratus* so data for both sexes were pooled.

1. *The oxygen extraction system*

C. aceratus has large opercular pumps and the contribution of the branchiostegal complex to movement of water is considerable. Superficially at least, the oxygen-extracting system of *C. aceratus* is typical of a benthic teleost.

The gill arches of *C. aceratus* are long and support a gill array with a large area through which water can flow. The spacing of secondary lamellae on the gill filaments is wide (Hughes, 1966; Steen & Berg, 1966). This gill arrangement offers low resistance to the flow of water (Hughes, 1966).

There is physiological evidence to support the morphological evidence that movement of water over the gills of *C. aceratus* requires little energy. The calculated $\dot{V}_G$ of *C. aceratus* is lower than V_G values reported for other teleosts (Hughes, 1967; Holeton & Randall, 1967b; Stevens & Randall, 1967b; Hughes & Umezawa, 1968). The slow breathing movements generate only low pressures in the buccal cavity. As the area of the gill sieve is large and $\dot{V}_G$ is low, the velocity of water passing over the gills must be slow.

Since *C. aceratus* is benthic and has little need of a streamlined configuration, the bulkiness of its oxygen extraction system is not a great disadvantage. The oxygen extraction system of *C. aceratus* is similar to that of many benthic teleosts and the specializations for low-energy-cost gill irrigation may be characteristic of the benthic habit rather than the lack of hemoglobin.

2. *The oxygen transporting system of* C. aceratus

Oxygen transport by the circulatory system can be described by the following relationship:

$$\dot{V}_{O_2} = \dot{Q} \, (Pa_{(O_2)} \times \alpha b_{O_2}) - (P\overline{v}_{(O_2)} \times \alpha b_{O_2})$$

With icefish the factor αb_{O_2} is greatly reduced by the lack of hemoglobin. There are a number of alternatives open to the fish to offset the low blood oxygen-carrying capacity.

1. $\dot{V}_{O_2}$ can be reduced. The $\dot{V}_{O_2}$ of *C. aceratus* is low as a result of low environmental temperatures.

2. Increasing $Pa_{(O_2)}$ and decreasing $P\overline{v}_{(O_2)}$ maximizes the amount of oxygen carried by the blood. The $Pa_{(O_2)}$ of *C. aceratus* is higher than the $Pa_{(O_2)}$ of some fish (Stevens & Randall, 1967b; Garey, 1967; Piiper & Schumann, 1967). However $P\overline{v}_{(O_2)}$ of *C. aceratus* is also high compared to other fish (Garey, 1967; Piiper & Schumann, 1967), and increased blood oxygen capacity realized by *C. aceratus* from increased $Pa_{(O_2)} - P\overline{v}_{(O_2)}$ is slight.

3. An increase of the factor $\dot{Q}$ is a major circulatory compensation to offset the lack of hemoglobin. The $\dot{Q}$ of *C. aceratus* is high compared with most values of $\dot{Q}$ reported for other fish (Holeton & Randall, 1967b; Stevens & Randall, 1967b; Murdaugh *et al.*, 1965; Piiper & Schumann, 1967). Everson & Ralph (1970) also suggest that the $\dot{Q}$ of *C. aceratus* is high.

In order to deal with a high $\dot{Q}$, *C. aceratus* has a large slow-beating heart (Table 3). The large heart of *C. aceratus* has been commented upon by others (Ruud, 1965; Steen & Berg, 1966; Everson & Ralph, 1970).

The cost of circulation is proportional to the flow $\dot{Q}$ times the blood pressure. Thus a large increase in $\dot{Q}$ with no other changes in the circulatory system would be accompanied by high blood pressures and a large work load upon the heart. However, the blood pressure of *C. aceratus* is lower than the values listed for most fish (Mott, 1957; Randall *et al.*, 1965), indicating that *C. aceratus* has reduced peripheral vascular resistance. Resistance can be lowered by either increasing the number or the bore of vessels

If *C aceratus* decreases vascular resistance by increasing the number of vessels, the number of additional vessels required would be considerable. The blood velocities in the capillaries would remain unchanged but as the oxygen content of the blood is low this would present a problem, for if capillary oxygen delivery is to be maintained the velocity of the blood must increase. Circulation to the tissues of blood of low oxygen content at normal velocity would result in low $P\bar{v}_{(O_2)}$'s. However, *C. aceratus* has high $P\bar{v}_{(O_2)}$'s, a fact which does not fit this hypothesis.

The alternative way of reducing vascular resistance by increasing the bore of the vessels is more plausible. From the Poiseuille equation it is known that laminar flow in a tube at a given pressure varies as the fourth power of its radius. Thus even a slight increase in the bore of the icefish's blood vessels could produce a marked decrease in vascular resistance. There would also be higher blood velocities in the capillaries with subsequently improved oxygen delivery. This hypothesis fits with the observed high $P\bar{v}_{(O_2)}$'s. There is morphological evidence to support this second hypothesis as Steen & Berg (1966) show sections of the gills of *C. aceratus* clearly illustrating that the blood passages in the secondary lamellae are larger than those of other teleosts.

3. *Interactions between extracting and transporting systems of* C. aceratus

The means "resting" oxygen consumption of *C. aceratus* was $23 \cdot 5 \pm 2 \cdot 0$ mg O_2/kg body wt. per hr (95 per cent confidence limits). Oxygen consumption was roughly proportional to body weight. The slope (*b*) of the least-squares linear regression line fitted to the data was $0 \cdot 00246$ mg/kg per hr per g body wt. change. This latter figure is not particularly meaningful as variability of oxygen consumption was large in relation to the weight range of fish examined. The correlation coefficient (*r*) for oxygen consumption mg/kg per hr against body weight was only $0 \cdot 29$.

Body movements made by the fish were recorded by the sensitive buccal pressure-measuring equipment. Examination of these records showed that the fish would remain still for several hours at a time, once they became accustomed to the respirometer. Thus resting oxygen consumption reported in this study is probably close to standard oxygen consumption.

Ralph & Everson (1968) report an oxygen consumption of $45 \cdot 2$ mg/kg per hr for *C. aceratus*. This is nearly twice as high as the value observed in the present study even though both values were observed at similar temperatures. Some of the discrepancy can be accounted for by differences in treatment of data and by differences in experimental methods.

The figure reported by Ralph & Everson was obtained by extrapolating a regression line fitted to data from nine fish covering a small weight range. If instead, their data are averaged then a value of 35·7 mg/kg per hr for the oxygen consumption of *C. aceratus* is obtained which is closer to the value observed in the present study.

The oxygen consumption of the fish used by Ralph & Everson was determined shortly after admission of the fish into the respirometers. Fry (1957) has pointed out that the handling of fish required to put them into the experimental chamber is sufficient stimulus to cause them to consume oxygen at their maximum rate for some time afterwards. It seemed likely that the oxygen consumption values for *C. aceratus* reported by Ralph & Everson are representative of slightly disturbed fish.

The use of a counter-current flow arrangement between blood and water by *C. aceratus* was indicated by observations of dorsal aortic oxygen tensions higher than expired water oxygen tensions. Verification of use of the counter-current flow arrangement has also been obtained for the eel (Steen & Kruysse, 1964) and rainbow trout (Holeton & Randall, 1967b).

C. aceratus has a mean oxygen tension gradient from water to blood ($P\Delta_G$) of 60 mm Hg. This is comparable to ΔP_G values obtained from data published on other fish. The rainbow trout at 15°C has a ΔP_G of 44 mm Hg (Holeton & Randall, 1967b) and this rises to 75 mm Hg at 5°C (Stevens & Randall, 1967b). The carp at 10°C has a ΔP_G of 67 mm Hg (Garey, 1967) and ΔP_G of the dogfish at 17°C is 72 mm Hg (Piiper & Schumann, 1967).

The method used for computing ΔP_G assumes linearity of the oxygen tension–oxygen content relationship of the blood over the physiological range. This may be an oversimplification in all these cases except that of *C. aceratus* which has no hemoglobin.

The transfer factor (T_{O_2}) is a term describing the quantity of oxygen moved across the gills per unit P_{O_2} gradient ($\dot{V}_{O_2}/\Delta P_G$). It is useful for comparing the relative permeability of the gills of fishes to oxygen, but can be affected by temperature. T_{O_2} for the rainbow trout drops from 0·027 ml/kg per min per mm Hg at 15°C to 0·006 ml/kg per min per mm Hg at 5°C (Randall *et al.*, 1967). The icefish *C. aceratus* has a T_{O_2} of 0·0046 ml/kg per min per mm Hg at 0·5°C which is only slightly lower than the rainbow trout at 5°C. The data of Piiper & Schumann (1967) indicate a T_{O_2} for *Scyliorhinus stellaris* of approximately 0·0093 ml/kg per min per mm Hg, which is twice as high as the T_{O_2} of *C. aceratus* but was obtained at a temperature of 17°C.

The resting ventilation–perfusion ratio ($\dot{V}_G/\dot{Q}$) of *C. aceratus* is approximately 3 : 1, a value far lower than perfusion ratios reported for other fish which generally range from 10 : 1 to 20 : 1 (Robin *et al.*, 1966; Holeton & Randall, 1967b; Piiper & Schumann, 1967). A very high $\dot{V}_G/\dot{Q}$ of 95 : 1 for rainbow trout at 5°C is reported by Stevens & Randall (1967b). Rahn (1966) pointed out that the large $\dot{V}_G/\dot{Q}$ values for aquatic respiration is attributable to the low solubility of O_2 in water. By similar reasoning the lower $\dot{V}_G/\dot{Q}$ of *C. aceratus* is due to the low solubility of 0_2 in hemoglobinless blood.

4.   *Comparison of* C. aceratus *with other red-blooded fish from the same environment*

There are some striking differences in the circulatory characteristics of the blood of *C. aceratus* compared with the blood of the other three species examined.

Estimates of oxygen capacity of the blood of the four species were obtained from hematological information on Antarctic fish (Ruud, 1954; Hureau, 1966; Grigg, 1967; Everson & Ralph, 1968; and the present study). The approximate blood oxygen capacities are: *C. aceratus*, 0·67 vol per cent; *N. neglecta*, 6·25 vol per cent; *N. gibberifrons*, 6·50 vol per cent; *P. charcoti*, 6·00 vol per cent. The red-blooded species enjoy a 9·0 to 9·7–fold margin in blood oxygen-carrying capacity over *C. aceratus*.

The few values obtained for dorsal aortic blood pressure of *N. gibberifrons* indicated that its resting blood pressure was slightly lower than that of *C. aceratus*.

The heart of *C. aceratus* is larger than those of the other three species. Assuming the stroke volumes of the ventricles of these fish are nearly proportional to their weights when physiological conditions are similar, then the product of ventricle weight and resting heart rate gives a rough index of resting cardiac output: *C. aceratus*, 3·80 output units; *N. neglecta*, 1·50 o.u.'s; *N. gibberifrons*, 0·98 o.u.'s; *P. charcoti*, 0·86 o.u.'s. These figures suggest *C. aceratus* pumps three to four times as much blood as the red-blooded species.

The relative amounts of oxygen that the circulatory systems of the resting fish could transport can be estimated by multiplying the rough cardiac output estimates by the respective blood oxygen capacities:

C. aceratus	(3·80 o.u.'s × 0·67 vol per cent) =	2·5 capacity units.
N. gibberifrons	(0·98 o.u.'s × 6·50 vol per cent) =	6·4 capacity units.
N. neglecta	(1·50 o.u.'s × 6·25 vol per cent) =	9·4 capacity units.
P. charcoti	(0·86 o.u.'s × 6·00 vol per cent) =	5·2 capacity units.

While these figures are not accurate, it is apparent that *C. aceratus* has the lowest oxygen-transporting capacity when resting even though it pumps the most blood.

It is also possible to estimate what percentage of the oxygen-carrying capacity of their blood is actually used by the red-blooded species under resting conditions making use of the following information:

1.   The relative carrying capacity of the oxygen transport systems of all four fish.

2.   The oxygen consumptions.

3.   The fact that *C. aceratus* uses 63 per cent of the oxygen-carrying capacity of its blood when resting.

Calculations based upon this information suggest that *N. gibberifrons* uses only 25 per cent, *N. neglecta* only 21 per cent, and *P. charcoti* only 33 per cent of the oxygen-carrying capacity of their blood when resting. These estimates are only approximate and depend upon assumptions about stroke volume of the heart which have not as yet been verified.

The average blood to tissue oxygen tension gradient of *C. aceratus* is much higher than other Antarctic fish. Since the blood oxygen tension–oxygen content relationship is linear, the average blood to tissue gradient is equal to $\frac{1}{2}$ ($Pa_{(O_2)}$ + $P\bar{v}_{(O_2)}$) minus tissue oxygen tension. The tissues P_{O_2} must be lower than $P\bar{v}_{(O_2)}$ therefore the blood to tissue P_{O_2} gradient of *C. aceratus* must be greater than $\frac{1}{2}(120+25)-25 = 48$ mm Hg.

In contrast to the linear blood oxygen dissociation relationship of *C. aceratus*, the dissociation characteristics of the blood of Antarctic fish possessing hemoglobin are highly non-linear. Grigg (1967) lists the P_{50} values of the blood of four Antarctic nototheniids as follows: *Trematomus bernacchii*, 8·5 mm Hg; *T. centronotus*, 7·8 mm Hg; *T. hansoni*, 10·8 mm Hg; *T. borchgrevinki*, 21·5 mm Hg. The blood of these fish would still be highly saturated at a tension equivalent to the average blood-to-tissue P_{O_2} gradient of *C. aceratus* so their average blood-to-tissue gradient must be considerably lower than that of *C. aceratus*.

The presence of blood pigments enhances the rate of diffusion of oxygen even at low P_{O_2}'s (Wittenberg, 1959, 1963; Hemmingsen, 1963; Moll, 1966). Also the Bohr and Root effects of hemoglobin enhance diffusion by raising the blood-to-tissue oxygen tension gradient at sites of CO_2 production. As *C. aceratus* lacks hemoglobin and its benefits of diffusion facilitation, it may be that a high blood-to-tissue P_{O_2} gradient is a necessary compensating factor in maintaining the movement of oxygen from the blood to the tissues.

The resting oxygen consumption of all four species was similar although the oxygen consumption of *N. neglecta* was slightly higher than the others. This may be due to *N. neglecta* being a more active fish, as it was the most active species in the holding tanks. As the average weights of the species examined were of the same order of magnitude, the effect of size upon oxygen consumption/unit weight were ignored. Ralph & Everson (1968) also report little difference between the oxygen consumption of *C. aceratus* and other Antarctic species. However, their interpretation of the oxygen consumption of *C. aceratus* may be too high as has already been discussed. The oxygen consumptions they report are higher than these reported here, but all their fish were treated in a similar manner and the comparative aspect of their study is valid.

Hureau (1966) reported that *Chaenichthys rhinoceratus*, a Kerguelen chaenichthyiid, had a lower oxygen consumption than several red-blooded nototheniids, but his data were obtained at 9–11°C. These temperatures are higher than these fish would normally encounter and so the oxygen consumption measured may represent upper limits of metabolic rate rather than normal oxygen consumption.

Only easily demonstrated advantage that the red-blooded fish have over the icefish is their resistance to hypoxia. *C. aceratus* died when oxygen tensions below 50 mm Hg in the ambient water were encountered. *N. neglecta* and *N. gibberifrons* were able to consume oxygen down to 15 mm P_{O_2} and survive. How great an advantage this resistance to hypoxia confers remains a matter of conjecture. Oxygen levels in Antarctic waters are usually very high (Discovery Reports, 1932).

Acknowledgements—I wish to thank the British Antarctic Survey for providing the facilities for this work and in particular Mr. Eric Twelves of the Survey whose fishing skill ensured a generous supply of live fish.

REFERENCES

ANDRIASHEV A. P. (1962) A general review of the Antarctic fish fauna. In *Biogeography and Ecology in Antarctica* (Edited by VAN OYE P. & VAN MIEGHEM J.), pp. 491–550. Dr. W. Junk Publishers, The Hague.

ANTHONY E. H. (1961) Survival of goldfish in presence of carbon monoxide. *J. exp. Biol.* **38**, 109–129.

CAMERON J. N. & WOHLSCHLAG D. E. (1969) Respiratory response to experimentally induced anemia in the pinfish (*Lagodon rhomboides*). *J. exp. Biol.* **50**, 307–317.

DeGraaf A. R. (1957) A note on the oxygen requirements of *Xenopus laevis*. *J. exp. Biol.* **34**, 173–176.

Discovery Reports (1932) Marine biological station reports. *Discovery Reports* **4**, 222–229.

Everson I. & Ralph R. (1968) Blood analyses of some Antarctic fish. *Br. Antarct. Surv. Bull.* No. 15, 59–62.

Everson I. & Ralph R. (1970) (In press).

Ewer D. W. (1959) A toad *Xenopus laevis* without hemoglobin. *Nature, Lond.* **183**, 271.

Flores G. & Frieden E. (1968) Induction and survival of haemoglobin-less and erythrocyte-less tadpoles and young bullfrogs. *Science* **159**, 101–103.

Fox H. M. (1954) Comment on the article of Prof. J. T. Ruud. *Nature, Lond.* **173**, 850.

Fry F. E. J. (1957) The aquatic respiration of fish. In *The Physiology of Fishes*. (Edited by Brown E. Margaret) Vol. 1, pp. 1–60. Academic Press, New York.

Garey W. F. (1967) Gas exchange, cardiac output and blood pressure in free swimming carp (*Cyprinus carpio*). Ph.D. dissertation, University of New York at Buffalo.

Grigg G. C. (1967) Some respiratory properties of the blood of four species of Antarctic fishes. *Comp. Biochem. Physiol.* **23**, 139–148.

Hemmingsen E. A. (1963) Enhancement of oxygen transport by myoglobin. *Comp. Biochem. Physiol.* **10**, 239–244.

Holeton G. F. & Randall D. J. (1967a) Changes in blood pressure in the rainbow trout during hypoxia. *J. exp. Biol.* **46**, 297–305.

Holeton G. F. & Randall D. J. (1967b) The effect of hypoxia upon the partial pressure of gases in the blood and water afferent and efferent to the gill of rainbow trout. *J. exp. Biol.* **46**, 317–327.

Hughes G. M. (1966) The dimensions of fish gills in relation to their function. *J. exp. Biol.* **45**, 177–195.

Hughes G. M. (1967) Experiments on the respiration of the trigger fish (*Balistes capriscus*). (*Experientia* **23**, 1077.

Hughes G. M. & Knights B. (1968) The effect of loading the respiratory pumps on the oxygen consumption of *Callionymus lyra*. *J. exp. Biol.* **49**, 603–615.

Hughes G. M. & Shelton G. (1962) Respiratory mechanisms and their nervous control in fish. *Adv. com. Physiol. Biochem.* **1**, 275–364.

Hughes G. M. & Umezawa S.-I. (1968) Oxygen consumption and gill water flow in the dogfish *Scyliorhinus canicula* L. *J. exp. Biol.* **49**, 557–564.

Hureau J. C. (1966) Biologie de *Chaenichthys rhinoceratus* Richardson, et problème du sang incoloré des Chaenicthyidae, poissons de mers australes. *Bull. Soc. zool. fr.* **91**, No. 4, 735–751.

Kooyman G. L. (1963) Erythrocyte analysis of some Antarctic fishes. *Copeia* No. 2, 457–458.

Lenfant C. & Johansen K. (1966) Respiratory function in the elasmobranch *Squalus suckleyi* G. *Respir. Physiol.* **1**, 13–29.

Martsinkevitch L. D. (1958) Cellular make-up of the blood of white-blooded fish (Chaenicthyidae) from the Antarctic. *Soviet Antarctic Expedition Information Bulletin* **1**, 1964, 137–138. Elsevier, Amsterdam, London, New York.

Moll W. (1966) The diffusion coefficient of haemoglobin. *Respir. Physiol.* **1**, 357–365.

Mott J. C. (1957) The cardiovascular system. In *Physiology of Fishes* (Edited by Brown M. E.) pp. 81–108. Academic Press, New York.

Murdaugh H. V., Robin E. D., Millen J. E. & Drewry W. F. (1965) Cardiac output determinations by the dye-dilution method in *Squalus acanthias*. *Am. J. Physiol.* **209**, 723–726.

Nicloux M. (1923) Action de l'oxyde de carbone sur les poissons et capacité respiratoire du sang de ces animaux. *C. r. Séanc. Soc. Biol.* **89**, 1328–1331.

Norman J. R. (1938) Coast fishes. Part III. The Antarctic zone. *Discovery Reports* **XVIII**, 1–104.

Olsen S. (1955) A contribution to the systematics and biology of chaenicthyid fishes from South Georgia. *Nytt. Mag. Zool.* **3**, 79–93.

Piiper J. & Schumann D. (1967) Efficiency of O_2 exchange in the gills of the dogfish *Scyliorhinus stellaris*. *Respir. Physiol.* **2**, 135–148.

Rahn H. (1966) Aquatic gas exchange: Theory. *Respir. Physiol.* **1**, 1–12.

RALPH R. & EVERSON I. (1968) The respiratory metabolism of some Antarctic fish. *Comp. Biochem. Physiol.* **27**, 299–307.

RANDALL D. J., HOLETON G. F. & STEVENS E. D. (1967) The exchange of oxygen and CO_2 across the gills of rainbow trout. *J. exp. Biol.* **46**, 339–348.

RANDALL D. J., SMITH L. S. & BRETT J. R. (1965) Dorsal aortic blood pressures recorded from the rainbow trout. *Can. J. Zool.* **43**, 863–872.

ROBIN E. D., MURDAUGH H. V. & MILLEN J. E. (1966) Acid–base, fluid, and electrolyte metabolism in the elasmobranch. Part three. *J. cell. comp. Physiol.* **67**, 93–100.

RUUD J. T. (1954) Vertebrates without erythrocytes and blood pigment. *Nature, Lond.* **173**, 848–850.

RUUD J. T. (1958) Vertebrates without blood pigment: a study of the fish family Chaenicthyidae. *Proc. 15th Int. Congr. Zool. London* 1958, Sect. 6, paper 32, 526–528.

RUUD J. T. (1965) The ice-fish. *Scient. Am.* **213**, 108–114.

RYBACK B. (1960) A pale hag-fish. *Nature, Lond.* **185**, 777.

SAUNDERS R. L. (1961) The irrigation of the gills in fishes—I. Studies of the mechanism of branchial irrigation. *Can. J. Zool.* **39**, 637–653.

SCHLICHER J. (1926) Vergliechend physiologische Untersuchungen der Blutkörperchenzahlen bei Knockenfischen. *Zool. Jb.* **43**, 121–200.

SCHOLANDER P. R. & VAN DAM L. (1957) The concentration of hemoglobin in some cold water Arctic fishes. *J. cell. comp. Physiol.* **49**(1), 1–4.

SMITH L. S. & BELL G. R. (1964) A technique for prolonged blood sampling in free swimming salmon. *J. Fish Res. Bd. Can.* **21**(4), 711–714.

STEEN J. B. & BERG T. (1966) The gills of two species of haemoglobin-free fishes compared to those of other teleosts—with a note on severe anaemia in an eel. *Comp. Biochem. Physiol.* **18**, 517–526.

STEEN J. B. & KRUYSSE A. (1964) The respiratory function of teleostean gills. *Comp. Biochem. Physiol.* **12**, 127–142.

STEVENS E. D. & RANDALL D. J. (1967a) Changes in blood pressure heart rate and breathing rate during moderate swimming activity in rainbow trout. *J. exp. Biol.* **46**, 307–315.

STEVENS E. D. & RANDALL D. J. (1967b) Changes of gas concentrations in blood and water during moderate swimming activity in rainbow trout. *J. exp. Biol.* **46**, 329–337.

STOLK A. (1960) Lack of haemoglobin in a fish. *Nature, Lond.* **185**, 625–626.

TYLER J. C. (1960) Erythrocyte counts and haemoglobin determinations for two Antarctic nototheniid fishes. *Stanford icthyol. Bull.* **7**, 199–201.

VAN DAM L. (1938) On the utilization of oxygen and regulation of breathing in some aquatic animals. Ph.D. Thesis, University of Groningen.

WELLS M. M. (1918) The reaction and resistance of fishes to carbon dioxide and carbon monoxide. *Bull. Ill. St. Lab. Nat. Hist.* II, 557.

WITTENBURG J. (1959) Oxygen transport—a new function proposed for myoglobin. *Biol. Bull.* **117**, 402–403.

WITTENBURG J. B. (1963) Facilitated diffusion of oxygen through haemerythrin solutions. *Nature, Lond.* **199**, 816–817.

WOLF K. (1963) Physiological salines for freshwater teleosts. *Progve Fish. Cult.* **25**, 135–140.

Key Word Index—Antarctic fish; hemoglobinless fish; icefish; respiration of fish; oxygen consumption; breathing rate; gill irrigation; breathing pressures; hypoxia; ventilation perfusion ratio; circulation; blood pressure; heart rate; heart size; capillary size; cardiac output; blood oxygen tensions; transfer factor of gills; P_{O_2} gradient water to blood; P_{O_2} gradient blood to tissues.

Additional Readings

CHAPTER 7

BALLINTIJN, C. M. 1969. Functional anatomy and movement coordination of the respiratory pump of the carp (*Cyprinus carpio* L.). *J. Exp. Biol.* 50:547–567.

BERG, T., and STEEN, J. B. 1965. Physiological mechanisms for aerial respiration. *Comp. Biochem. Physiol.* 15:469–484.

DAVIS, J. C., and RANDALL, D. J. 1973. Gill irrigation and pressure relationships in rainbow trout. *J. Fish. Res. Bd. Canada* 30:99–104.

GRIGG, G. C. 1974. Respiratory function of blood in fishes, pp. 331–368, in M. Florkin and B. T. Scheer, eds., *Chemical Zoology, Deuterostomians, cyclostomes, and fishes*, Vol. 8. New York: Academic Press.

HUGHES, G. M., and MORGAN, M. 1973. The structure of fish gills in relation to their respiratory function. *Biol. Rev.* 48:419–475.

JOHANSEN, K. 1966. Airbreathing in the teleost *Symbranchus marmoratus*. *Comp. Biochem, Physiol.* 18:383–395.

JOHANSEN, K. 1968. Air-breathing fishes. *Sci. Am.* 219(4):102–111.

JOHANSEN, K. 1970. Air breathing in fishes. Chapter 9, pp. 361–411, in W. S. Hoar and D. J. Randall, eds., *Fish Physiology*, Vol. 4. New York: Academic Press.

KRAMER, D. L., and GRAHAM, J. B. 1976. Synchronous air breathing, a social component of respiration in fishes. *Copeia* 1976(4):689–697.

MEEK, R. P., and CHILDRESS, J. J. 1975. Respiration and the effect of pressure in the mesopelagic fish *Anoplogaster cornuta* (Beryciformes). *Deep-Sea Res.* 20:1111–1118.

MUIR, B. S., and KENDALL, J. I. 1968. Structural modifications in the gills of tunas and some other oceanic fishes. *Copeia* 1968(2):388–398.

POWERS, D. A. 1972. Hemoglobin adaptation for fast and slow water habitats in sympatric catostomid fishes. *Science.* 177:360–362.

POWERS, D. A. 1974. Structure, function, and molecular ecology of fish hemoglobins. *Ann. N.Y. Acad. Sci.* 241:472–490.

RANDALL, D. J. 1970. Gas exchange in fish. Chapter 7, pp. 253–292, in W. S. Hoar and D. J. Randall, eds., *Fish Physiology*, Vol. 4. New York: Academic Press.

RANDALL, D. J. 1970. The circulatory system. Chapter 4, pp. 133–172, in W. S. Hoar and D. J. Randall, eds., *Fish Physiology*, Vol. 4. New York: Academic Press.

RIGGS, A. 1970. Properties of fish hemoglobins. Chapter 6, pp. 209–252, in W. S. Hoar and D. J. Randall, eds., *Fish Physiology*, Vol. 4. New York: Academic Press.

SATCHELL, G. H. 1971. Circulation in fishes. *Cambridge Monographs in Experimental Biology*, No. 18. Cambridge: Cambridge University Press.

SHELTON, G. 1970. The regulation of breathing. Chapter 8, pp. 293–359, in W. S. Hoar and D. J. Randall, eds., *Fish Physiology*, Vol. 4. New York: Academic Press.

SMITH, K. L. Jr., and HESSLER, R. R. 1974. Respiration of benthopelagic fishes: in situ measurements at 1230 meters. *Science* 184:72–73.

YAZDANI, G. M., and ALEXANDER, R. McN. 1967. Respiratory currents of flatfish. *Nature, Lond.* 213:96–97.

8

Feeding

Mechanics of the feeding action of various teleost fishes

R. McN. ALEXANDER

Department of Zoology, University of Leeds

(*Accepted 14 April 1970*)

(With 5 figures in the text)

Pressure changes have been recorded from the buccal cavities of nine species of teleost as they sucked food into their mouths. Some of the pressures recorded are discussed in relation to the sizes of the muscles responsible. Cinematograph films have been used to estimate how much the volume of the orobranchial chamber increases as food is sucked in. Some peculiarities in the feeding movements of *Taurulus*, *Ictalurus* and *Anguilla* are described and discussed.

Introduction

Most teleosts take food into their mouths by sucking it in, by enlarging their buccal and opercular cavities (Alexander, 1967). A recent paper (Alexander, 1969) presented records of the pressure in the buccal cavity of the Golden orfe, *Idus idus* (L.) (Cyprinidae), during feeding. Pressures of -50 to -105 cm water were recorded as food was sucked in, and $+1$ to $+9$ cm water as water taken in with the food was driven out through the opercula. (Pressures are given throughout this paper relative to the pressure of the water around the fish.) It was estimated that to produce the most strongly negative pressures, all the muscles principally involved would have to exert tensions near the maximum isometric tensions which have been measured in experiments with excised vertebrate striated muscles. Cinematograph films of the fish were made at the same time as the pressure records. These and other films of the fish feeding were used to estimate the volume of water drawn in through the mouth in the feeding action.

The previous paper (Alexander, 1969) dealt only with *Idus*. This paper describes further work, using the same methods, which was undertaken to learn something of the differences between teleosts in the mechanics of their feeding actions. It deals with nine more species, chosen for their diversity.

Osse (1969) made an electromyographic study of feeding in *Perca*, which confirmed that the sequence of muscle action is, for the most part, the same as had previously been inferred from anatomical studies and by analogy with respiration. He also took cinematograph films and determined from them the area of the open mouth and the rate of expansion of the orobranchial chamber. He applied Bernoulli's theorem to these data and estimated as a rough approximation that the pressure in the buccal cavity as food is sucked in should be -20 cm water. He realized that reliance on the theorem, which applies only to conditions of steady flow (defined by Tietjens, 1957), might give rise to error. The pressure records which have now been obtained (Alexander, 1969, and this paper) show much larger negative pressures than Osse estimated for *Perca*, in all the species investigated.

From *J. Zool., Lond.* 162:145–156. Reprinted by permission of The Zoological Society of London and the author.

Material and methods

Specimens of the following species were used:

Anguilliformes	*Anguilla anguilla* (L.)
Osteoglossiformes	*Papyrocranus afer* (Günther)
Cypriniformes	*Carassius auratus* (L.)
Siluriformes	*Ictalurus melas* (Rafinesque)
Scorpaeniformes	*Taurulus bubalis* (Euphrasen)
Perciformes	*Pterophyllum scalare* (Lichtenstein)
	Tilapia mariae Boulenger
	Blennius pholis L.
	Macropodus opercularis (L.)

The *Anguilla* were almost 30 cm long but the standard lengths of the other specimens were all between 5 and 12 cm.

The methods will be given only in outline here, as they have already been described in detail (Alexander, 1969). The fish were trained to take rings of earthworm body wall off the free end of a fine nylon tube, of which the other end was connected to a pressure transducer. They had to put their mouths round the end of the tube as they sucked the food off, so the transducer was exposed to the pressure in the buccal cavity. The electrical output of the transducer was amplified and recorded on an ultraviolet recorder. The transducing system had a resonant frequency before damping of about 100 Hz and was critically damped. Cinematograph film was taken at about 60 frames/sec simultaneously with about half of the pressure records of each species. A mirror was fixed under the food at 45° to the axis of the camera so that the films showed ventral as well as lateral views of the fish. A device which was used to correlate the time scale of the pressure record with the film allowed an error of half a frame (about 8 msec) either way. The apparatus was exactly as described previously, except that a finer nylon tube was used in the experiments on *Macropodus*.

Most of the records were obtained with a single specimen of each species, but a few were obtained for a second *Anguilla*, a second *Ictalurus* and two additional *Carassius*. Three specimens of *Idus* were used in the previous investigation (Alexander, 1969). In no case were consistent differences observed between pressure records for different members of the same species.

So that the movements made by the fish in the experiments could be compared with more natural feeding movements, cinematograph films were taken of each species picking a few pieces of earthworm off a low glass platform. A mirror was fixed under the platform at 45° to the horizontal so that the films showed ventral as well as lateral views of the fish.

Rough estimates were made of the volume of water drawn in through the mouth in the feeding actions of most of the species. Films both of feeding from the transducer and of feeding from the platform were used for this purpose. The calculations were carried out in the same way as before (Alexander, 1969) except that allowance was made for the angle between the axis of the hyomandibular articulation, and the median plane. This explains the slight discrepancy in the data for *Idus* between Table II and Alexander (1969). It proved impossible to make reliable estimates of the angle through which the suspensorium swings in *Anguilla* and *Blennius*, in which thick skin conceals the positions of the underlying bones. The volume of water drawn in by *Anguilla* was estimated from measurements taken from the films of the height and width of the head in three transverse planes, before and after expansion of the orobranchial chamber. No estimate was made for *Tilapia*, in which some adduction occurs at the joint between the hyomandibular and the opercular as the orobranchial chamber is expanded, because this movement would complicate estimation.

Results

Pressure records

Some typical pressure records are shown in Fig. 1. Each record shows a pulse of negative pressure as the fish sucked or tried to suck the food off the nylon tube. The films taken at the same time as the records shown in Fig. 1(a),(b),(c),(g),(h),(i) and (j) show the food moving up the tube into the mouth of the fish during the pulse of negative pressure (at the second pulse only in the case of Fig. 1(a)). Those taken with Fig. 1(d) (*Ictalurus*) and

1(f) (*Anguilla*) show that the fish failed to suck the food off but eventually gripped it with its teeth and pulled it off. In the case of Fig. 1(e) (*Anguilla*) the fish moved its head forward over the food so as to hide it at the beginning of the second suck, and it is not possible to see whether it was sucked or pulled off the tube. In many of the records the rise in pressure after the minimum does not appear smooth, but has an irregularity at about the moment when the mouth closes. This is probably an artefact due to the jaws closing on the nylon tube. The irregularity is usually small in amplitude but is quite large in some records of *Carassius* (Fig. 1(b)). In most of the records the pulse of negative pressure is immediately followed by a small pulse of positive pressure, as the water which has been sucked in is driven out again through the opercula. This cannot be distinguished in most records of *Anguilla*, and seldom involves pressures greater than $+6$ cm water in any species. Many of the records, including Fig. 1(b),(c),(d) and (f), end with a small artefact at the moment when the fish removed its mouth from the tube.

Quantitative information about the pressure records is given in Table I. For most species, the lowest pressure which can be developed in the buccal cavity in feeding seems to lie between -80 and -140 cm water, but *Papyrocranus*, *Pterophyllum*, *Tilapia* and *Macropodus* can develop -230 to -400 cm water. These four species were the only tropical ones used, and were kept at a higher temperature than the others. It seemed possible that their ability to develop large negative pressures might be at least partly due to the effect of temperature on the properties of muscle (see Hill, 1951; Close & Hoh, 1968). This was tested with *Macropodus* by making groups of records alternately at intervals of a few days, with the aquarium water at 15–17°C and at 25–27°C. No records were made after a change of temperature until the temperature had been constant for many hours. The same fish was consistently able to develop more strongly negative pressures at the higher temperatures than at the lower ones. Records of 35 sucks at 15–17°C were obtained and the pressures attained in the four strongest ranged from -200 to -230 cm water. Records of 36 were obtained at 25–27°C and the pressures attained in the four strongest ranged from -280 to -300 cm water. The 10°C rise in temperature apparently increased the negative pressure which could be developed by about 30%. This effect is far too small to account for the difference between the pressures developed by *Pterophyllum*, *Tilapia* and *Macropodus* on the one hand, and the coldwater species on the other.

TABLE I

Data from the pressure records. The minimum (i.e. most strongly negative) pressure shown in any record, and the mean duration of the pulses of negative pressure in the records, for each species

	Temperature (°C)	Minimum pressure (cm water)	Mean duration (msec)
Anguilla	18	-140	110
Papyrocranus	25	-230	30
Idus	20	-105	70
Carassius	18	-90	70
Ictalurus	18	-80	60
Taurulus	17	-125	45
Pterophyllum	27	-400	30
Tilapia	26	-360	40
Blennius	17	-100	70
Macropodus	15–17	-230	50
	25–27	-300	40

Table I shows that the mean duration of the pulses of negative pressure varied between species from 30 msec for *Papyrocranus* and *Pterophyllum* to 110 msec for *Anguilla*. The records for *Macropodus* suggest that the pulses tend to be briefer at high temperatures than at low ones, but the apparent difference is not statistically significant.

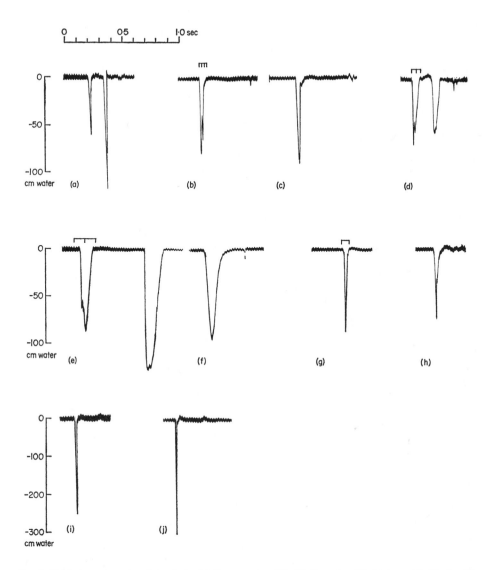

FIG. 1. Typical pressure records made by (a) *Papyrocranus*, (b), (c) *Carassius*, (d) *Ictalurus*, (e), (f) *Anguilla*, (g) *Taurulus*, (h) *Blennius*, (i) *Macropodus*, (j) *Pterophyllum*. The time scale is the same for all the records but (i) and (j) have a pressure scale different from the others. In cases where the cinematograph films are reproduced in subsequent Figures the times of the frames reproduced are indicated by marks above the pressure record.

Cinematograph films

Idus were found to open their mouths wider and keep them open longer when feeding from the platform than when feeding from the nylon tube (Alexander, 1969). It was, therefore, doubtful whether the negative pressures recorded in the experiments were typical of normal feeding. There seems to be far less doubt in the case of *Carassius*. Figure 2 shows cinematograph sequences of *Carassius* feeding from the glass platform and from the nylon tube. In each of the sequences frame 1 shows the fish approaching the food. Frame 2 shows the mouth open with the premaxillae fully protruded. Expansion of the buccal and opercular cavities has started: the head is a little wider than in frame 1 and the ventral surface has been lowered below the ventral edge of the preopercular bone. The geniohyoideus muscle has become prominent in the ventral view. The food has entered the mouth. In frame 3 the mouth is closed (Fig. 2(a)) or closing round the tube (Fig. 2(b)) in which the lower jaw is completing its movement and is blurred in the original photograph. The ventral surface of the head has been lowered further, by depression of the hyoid bars, and the head is wider. It has reached its maximum width in frame 4, but the opercular valves are not yet open. The two sequences shown in Fig. 2 are closely similar in the amplitudes and rates of movement of the various parts of the head, including the mouth. Each is typical of the sequences which were taken. It seems likely that the pressures recorded in the experiments are similar to those developed in feeding from the platform, and in normal feeding.

It is not possible from the films which have been taken to make so close a comparison, between the feeding action in taking food from the nylon tube and from the platform, for every species. In some species such as *Pterophyllum* the movements are very rapid and film taken at a higher frame speed would be necessary for a satisfactory comparison. In others such as *Blennius* thick skin hides the underlying bones and makes it difficult to judge the degree of abduction of the suspensoria. No consistent difference was observed between the action of feeding from the tube and from the platform, for any species except *Idus.*

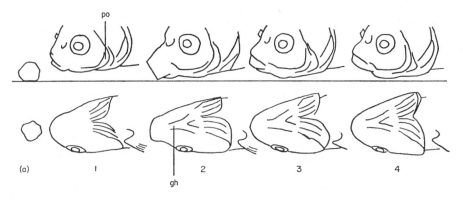

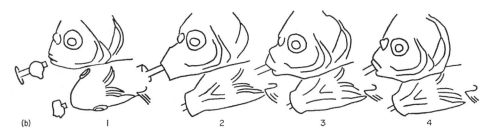

FIG. 2. Tracings of four successive frames of cinematograph films taken at 60 frames/sec of *Carassius* feeding (a) from the glass platform and (b) from the tube attached to the transducer. The pressure record corresponding to (b) is reproduced as Fig. 1(b). gh, Geniohyoideus; po, preopercular.

Estimates of the amount of expansion of the orobranchial chamber in the feeding action are given in Table II. For each species, each of the movements involved in the feeding action tended to be fairly constant in amplitude, but where marked variation was found a value in the upper part of the range has been used in the Table. The methods of estimation are so rough that only large differences between species can be considered significant. In most of the species the volume of the orobranchial chamber increases by

5–8 cm³/100 g body weight. It might be expected that the increase in volume in feeding would be equal to the maximum respiratory stroke volume. No values of stroke volume for species used in this investigation seem to have been published but Professor G. M. Hughes informs me that he has measured stroke volumes up to 4·0 cm³/100 g for *Callionymus lyra* L. and 5·0 cm³/100 g for *Salmo gairdneri* Richardson. It is estimated that *Anguilla* expands its orobranchial chamber by only 2·3 cm³/100 g, but it is too different in shape from typical teleosts for similarity in this matter to be expected.

TABLE II

Movements involved in expanding the orobranchial chamber in the feeding action, and estimates of the increase in volume. Angles are given in degrees and increases in volume in cm³/100 g body weight

	Anguilla	*Papyrocranus*	*Idus*	*Carassius*	*Ictalurus*	*Taurulus*	*Pterophyllum*	*Macropodus*
Angle through which suspensorium is abducted		12	15	8	7	17	10	6
Increase due to abduction of suspensorium		5·5	4·7	3·8	2·6	6·7	3·4	3·5
Angle moved by cranium relative to girdle		10	8	6	14	12	8	10
Increase due to movement of cranium and girdle		1·0	0·6	0·6	2·9	3·6	1·3	2·5
Increase due to depression of tongue		1·0	1·6	0·8	3·6	3·2	1·3	0·4
Total increase	2·3	7·5	6·9	5·2	9·1	13·5	6·0	6·4

Taurulus expands its head more than the other species. Figure 3(a) shows particularly how very much wider the head becomes as the orobranchial chamber expands. Even when it is fully expanded, the long spines on the preopercula do not stand out from the head as much as they do in the defensive posture of this fish, in which the preopercula are abducted relative to the rest of the suspensorium by (presumably) contraction of the very large levatores hyoidei (see Cowan, 1969, on another cottid, and Allis, 1909). *Taurulus* was also unusual in the manner of its approach to the food. Instead of approaching slowly like the other species it always settled on a solid surface rather less than its own length away from the food, and from there made a sudden dash at the food. It did this when feeding both from the tube and from the platform. The fish accelerated at the beginning of the dash by means of a backward stroke of its large pectoral fins and side-to-side movements of the tail. The specimen of total length 8·2 cm reached speeds up to 47 cm/sec in about 60 msec, involving an acceleration of 800 cm/sec². It braked as it reached the food by abducting the pectoral and pelvic fins and erecting the anterior dorsal fin (Fig. 3(a)), decelerating at up to about 1500 cm/sec². *Taurulus* feeds similarly in its natural habitat, capturing passing prawns etc. by darting suddenly from a position of concealment (Yonge, 1949).

Figure 3(b) shows three frames from the film of *Ictalurus* taken with the pressure record reproduced as Fig. 1(d). The orobranchial chamber is contracted in frame 1 and expanded (without dislodging the food) in frame 3, and the opercula are open in frame 5. This and other film sequences of *Ictalurus* feeding from the tube and from the platform show that the head gets little wider as it expands, but gets much deeper. Depression of the tongue accounts for an unusually large proportion of the increase in volume of the orobranchial chamber (Table II). An argument presented in the Discussion indicates that depressing the tongue a long way in feeding is a more or less inevitable consequence of having a wide head.

Table II gives the angle moved by the cranium relative to the pectoral girdle, but does not show how much either the cranium or the girdle moved relative to the trunk. In all species the cranium is raised relative to the trunk and in most the girdle moves little relative to the trunk. (The films show that the girdle of *Pterophyllum* moves less and the cranium more than still photographs previously led me to believe (Alexander, 1967).) However, considerable movement of the girdle occurs in *Anguilla*, When the orobranchial

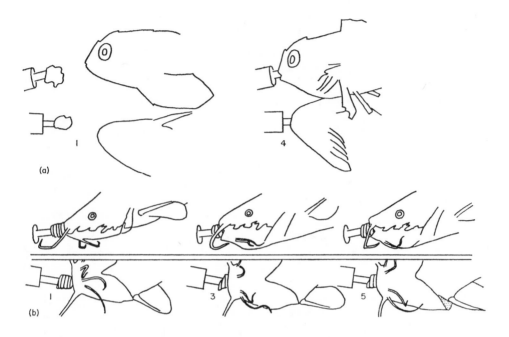

FIG. 3. Tracings of selected frames from (a) the cinematograph film of *Taurulus* corresponding to the pressure record reproduced as Fig. 1(g); and (b) the film of *Ictalurus* corresponding to Fig. 1(d). The films were taken at 60 frames/sec and the numbers give the relative positions of the frames in each sequence.

chamber is expanded, two bumps appear in the ventral profile (arrowed in Fig. 4(b), frame 5). It seems plain from Fig. 4(a) that the anterior bump is due to the usual depression of the hyoid bar and tongue, and the posterior one to rotation of the pectoral girdle about its dorsal end.

Many of the characteristics of the Anguilliformes have probably evolved as adaptations to life in crevices and burrows (Gosline, 1959; Nelson, 1966). The whole body is longer and narrower than in typical teleosts. Narrowing of the head has involved displacement of the gills from a position mainly ventral to the cranium to one mainly posterior to it. The opercular region is consequently very long and the pectoral girdle is detached from the cranium. Figure 4(a) shows the peculiar structure of the long opercular region of *Anguilla*. The opercular and subopercular bones are very small and the large part of the lateral wall of the opercular cavity which is stippled in Fig. 4(a) is stiffened only by the very long, curved branchiostegal rays. It is much more flexible than the opercula of typical teleosts, and is drawn inwards to form a concavity in the side of the head by the negative pressure developed in the orobranchial chamber in feeding (Fig. 4(b), frame 5). (The head is narrower in the region of the concavity in frame 5 than in frame 1 although the anterior part of the head is wider and the whole head is deeper than in frame 1.) The concavity appears in the films of *Anguilla* taking food from the platform as well as in the films of it feeding from the tube. It disappears at the end of the phase of negative pressure (Fig. 4(b), frame 11).

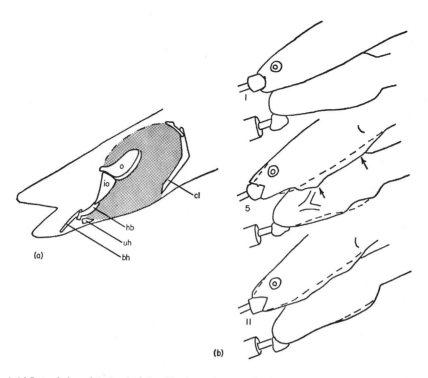

Fig. 4. (a) Lateral view of the head of *Anguilla*, drawn from an alizarin preparation, showing some of the bones, The part of the lateral wall of the opercular cavity which is stiffened only by branchiostegal rays is stippled. bh. Basihyal; cl, cleithrum; hb, hyoid bar; io, interopercular; o, opercular; uh, urohyal. (b) Tracings of selected frames from the cinematograph film of *Anguilla* corresponding to the pressure record reproduced as Fig. 1(e). The film was taken at 60 frames/sec and the numbers show the relative positions of the frames in the sequence. The outline of frame 1 is superimposed as a broken outline on frames 5 and 11. The arrows are referred to in the text.

Discussion

Forces exerted by muscles

Excised vertebrate striated muscles contracting isometrically at the resting length at temperatures of 20°C or more exert forces up to about 3×10^6 dyn/cm² cross-sectional area (Fenn & Marsh, 1935; Wells, 1965). (Rather smaller forces are developed at lower temperatures.) Muscles in intact animals may of course be able to exert larger forces. *Idus* was found able to reduce the pressure in its orobranchial chamber to -105 cm water and it was shown that this required stresses of nearly $2 \cdot 5 \times 10^6$ dyn/cm² in the muscles principally involved (Alexander, 1969). Pressures of -300 cm water or lower have now been recorded from the buccal cavities of *Macropodus*, *Tilapia* and *Pterophyllum*. Do these imply very large stresses in the muscles?

We will consider the case of *Pterophyllum*, calculating forces in the same way as for *Idus*. The measurements refer to a specimen of standard length 4·5 cm. The first moment of area of the lateral wall of the orobranchial chamber about the hyomandibular articulation was estimated from a photograph to be 0·30 cm³. The lowest pressure recorded was -400 cm water (-4×10^5 dyn/cm²) and we can estimate that this pressure would exert a moment of $4 \times 10^5 \times 0 \cdot 30 = 1 \cdot 2 \times 10^5$ dyn cm about each hyomandibular articulation. This must have been balanced by the moments due to the levatores hyoidei and to the hyoid bars pressing on the interoperculars. The levatores hyoidei are small and their tendons run very close to the hyomandibular articulations. A rough calculation indicates that they are unlikely to supply more than 5% of the moment about each hyomandibular articulation, so that at least $1 \cdot 1 \times 10^5$ dyn cm must be supplied by the action of the sterno-hyoideus and rectus abdominis on the hyoid bars. Each hyoid bar presses against the interopercular $0 \cdot 55$ cm from the axis of the hyomandibular articulation, so the lateral component of the force it exerts on the interopercular must be $1 \cdot 1 \times 10^5 / 0 \cdot 55 = 2 \cdot 0 \times 10^5$ dyn. This is $P \tan \theta / 2$, where P is the longitudinal force exerted on the urohyal by the sternohyoideus and rectus abdominis, and θ is the angle between the hyoid bar and the median plane (see Alexander, 1969). An alizarin preparation of *Pterophyllum* was arranged with the orobranchial chamber expanded, so that the ventral edges of the preoperculars were the same distance apart (relative to the length of the head) as in the frame correspond-ing to the end of the pulse of negative pressure in the cinematograph film taken with the pressure record reproduced as Fig. 1(j). θ was measured from a photograph of this prepara-tion, and found to be about 60°. Hence the force P can be estimated to be $2 \times 2 \cdot 0 \times 10^5 \cot 60° = 2 \cdot 3 \times 10^5$ dyn. The area of the sternohyoideus and rectus abdominis muscles was measured in a transverse microscope section and found to be $0 \cdot 062$ cm². The section was taken posterior to the urohyal so as to cut all the muscle fibres. Since the angle of pinna-tion is small we can estimate the tensile stress in these muscles as $2 \cdot 3 \times 10^5 / 0 \cdot 062 = 3 \cdot 7 \times 10^6$ dyn/cm². This value seems high, but it is based on very rough anatomical data and one cannot exclude the possibility of an error of as much as 25%. A similar calculation for *Tilapia* indicates that the sternohyoideus and rectus abdominis would have to exert 3×10^6 dyn/cm² to produce the observed pressure of -360 cm water. The large negative pressures developed by *Pterophyllum* and *Tilapia* seem to imply large, but not enormous, stresses in the muscles.

Depression of the tongue

It was found that depression of the tongue contributes far more to expansion of the orobranchial chamber in *Ictalurus* than in species with narrower heads. The argument which follows leads to an explanation for this.

Consider the teleost represented in Fig. 5. It will be convenient to suppose that the axes of the articulations of the hyomandibulars with the cranium are parallel to the line of action of the sternohyoideus and rectus abdominis, and to the long axis of the body. Let the area projected onto a vertical longitudinal plane of the lateral wall of the orobranchial chamber be A, with its centroid a distance a ventral to the axis of the hyomandibular articulation. Let the area projected onto a horizontal plane of the floor of the orobranchial chamber be B. Then at an instant during feeding when the pressure in the orobranchial chamber is $-\Pi$ an inward moment $\Pi A a$ about the hyomandibular articulation will act on each lateral wall of the chamber and an upward force ΠB will act on the floor of the chamber. These must be balanced by forces acting through the hyoid bars, produced by contraction of the sternohyoideus and rectus abdominis. (The levator hyoidei presumably plays a part in balancing the moment but because it is small and because its line of action

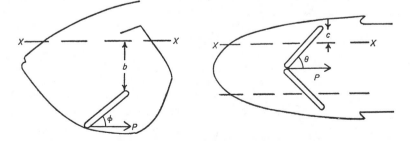

FIG. 5. Diagrammatic lateral and ventral views of the head of a teleost, showing the hyoid bars and the distances and angles which are used in the text to describe their position. P, The force exerted on the urohyal by the sterno-hyoideus and rectus abdominis; $X \ldots X$, the axis of the hyomandibular articulation.

lies close to the axis of the articulation, this part must be small in most species, and will be ignored. It was estimated that the maximum moment exerted by it is likely to be only 25 % of the maximum moment exerted by the sternohyoideus and rectus in *Idus* (Alexander, 1969) and roughly 5 % in *Pterophyllum* (this paper).) Each hyoid bar has movable joints with the urohyal and interopercular and can presumably only transmit forces along the straight line which runs through these joints. Let the angle between this line and the long axis of the body have a projection θ on a horizontal plane and a projection ϕ on a vertical longitudinal plane (Fig. 5). Then, if the sternohyoideus and rectus together exert a force P the force transmitted along each hyoid bar must have a longitudinal component $\frac{1}{2}P$, a transverse component $\frac{1}{2}P \tan \theta$ (Alexander, 1969) and a vertical component $\frac{1}{2}P \tan \phi$. The transverse and vertical components must provide the moment required to balance the moment ΠAa, so that if the bar presses on the interopercular at a distance b ventral to the hyomandibular articulation and c lateral to it.

$$\Pi Aa = \tfrac{1}{2}Pb \tan \theta + \tfrac{1}{2}Pc \tan \phi. \tag{1}$$

The vertical components of the forces in the two bars must together equal the force ΠB so that

$$\Pi B = P \tan \phi. \tag{2}$$

Hence

$$\tan \phi / \tan \theta = Bb/(2Aa - Bc)$$

and for a typical teleost for which $b \simeq 2a$

$$\frac{\tan \phi}{\tan \theta} \simeq \frac{B}{A - (Bc/2a)}. \tag{3}$$

For a fish with a narrow head $B \ll A$ and c is small even when the suspensoria are abducted, so $\phi \ll \theta$. This means that the hyoid bars cannot be swing down very far in feeding and depression of the (narrow) floor of the orobranchial chamber cannot contribute very much to enlargement of the chamber. For a fish with a wide head $B \geqslant A$ and c may be larger, so that $\phi > \theta$ and depression of the (broad) floor of the orobranchial chamber may make a substantial contribution to its enlargement.

Summary

Pressure changes have been recorded from the buccal cavities of nine species of teleost as they sucked food into their mouths. Cinematograph films were taken at the same time.

The lowest pressure recorded was about -100 cm water for most of the species, but -400 cm water for *Pterophyllum*. Some of the pressures are discussed in relation to the sizes of the muscles responsible.

It is estimated that the orobranchial chamber expands, as food is sucked in, by 5–8 cm³/100 g body weight in most of the species.

Some peculiarities in the feeding movements of *Taurulus*, *Ictalurus* and *Anguilla* are described and discussed.

The experiments described in this paper were carried out in the Department of Zoology, University College of North Wales, Bangor.

REFERENCES

Alexander, R. McN. (1967). *Functional design in fishes*. London: Hutchinson.

Alexander, R. McN. (1969). Mechanics of the feeding action of a cyprinid fish. *J. Zool., Lond.* **159**: 1–15.

Allis, E. P. (1909). The cranial anatomy of the mail-cheeked fishes. *Zoologica, Stuttg.* **22** (Heft 57): 1–219.

Close, R. & Hoh, J. F. Y. (1968). Influence of temperature on isometric contractions of rat skeletal muscles. *Nature, Lond.* **217**: 1179–1180.

Cowan, G. I. McT. (1969). The cephalic and caudal musculature of the sculpin (*Myoxocephalus polyacanthocephalus*) (Pisces: Cottidae). *Can. J. Zool.* **47**: 841–850.

Fenn, W. O. & Marsh, B. S. (1935). Muscular force at different speeds of shortening. *J. Physiol., Lond.* **85**: 277–297.

Gosline, W. A. (1959). Mode of life, functional morphology and the classification of modern teleostean fishes. *Syst. Zool.* **8**: 160–164.

Hill, A. V. (1951). The influence of temperature on the tension developed in an isometric twitch. *Proc. R. Soc.* (B) **138**: 349–354.

Nelson, G. J. (1966). Gill arches of teleostean fishes of the order Anguilliformes. *Pacif. Sci.* **20**: 391–408.

Osse, J. W. M. (1969). Functional morphology of the head of the perch (*Perca fluviatilis* L.): an electromyographic study. *Neth. J. Zool.* **19**: 289–392.

Tietjens, O. G. (1957). *Applied hydro- and aeromechanics*. New York: Dover.

Wells, J. B. (1965). Comparison of mechanical properties between slow and fast mammalian muscles. *J. Physiol., Lond.* **178**: 252–269.

Yonge, C. M. (1949). *The sea shore*. London: Collins.

DIGESTIVE SYSTEM AND SENSORIAL FACTORS IN RELATION TO THE FEEDING BEHAVIOUR OF FLATFISH (PLEURONECTIFORMES)

By

S. J. DE GROOT

Netherlands Institute for Fishery Investigations, IJmuiden, Netherlands

Flatfishes (Pleuronectiformes), belonging to the families Bothidae, Pleuronectidae and Soleidae were studied. A division could be made into fish-feeders, crustacea feeders and polychaeta-mollusca feeders. This division is based on experiments in which the behaviour of the fish was studied in relation to different sensory factors (olfaction and vision) and was confirmed by morphological study of the digestive tract and gill rakers. As a rule the Bothidae are fish feeders, the Pleuronectidae crustacea feeders, and the Soleidae polychaeta-mollusca feeders. However exceptions occur, especially in the Pleuronectidae.

INTRODUCTION

The aim of this investigation was to obtain a better insight into the feeding behaviour in connexion with the sensory faculties and comparative morphology of the digestive system in a number of species of flatfish. Several species of Bothidae, Pleuronectidae and Soleidae were studied. In an earlier publication (DE GROOT, 1967) it was stated that according to the type of food a subdivision can be made into fish feeders, crustacea feeders and polychaeta-mollusca feeders. The Bothidae feed, as a rule, on fish or on other quick moving animals, such as shrimps. The Soleidae are polychaeta-mollusca feeders. The Pleuronectidae take up an intermediate position. We find genuine fish feeders like the halibut (*Hippoglossus hippoglossus* L.) and more or less pure crustacea feeders like the dab (*Limanda limanda* L.), but also polychaeta mollusca feeders such as the lemon sole (*Microstomus kitt* Walb.).

THE ROLE OF VISUAL AND OLFACTORIAL FACTORS IN CONNEXION WITH THE FEEDING BEHAVIOUR

The following species have been investigated: sole (*Solea solea* L.), dab, plaice (*Pleuronectes platessa* L.), flounder (*P. flesus* L.), brill (*Scophthalmus rhombus* L.), turbot (*S. maximus* L.). For the experiments circular plastic tanks were used (diameter 200 cm). The animals were fully adapted to captivity and were in good condition. Visual, chemical, and mechanical sense organs were studied. Moving models were offered as visual stimuli. These models were moved slowly across the line of vision at a distance of some 20 cm. The objects used were black wooden balls of various diameters, 1, 2, 4 and 8 cm, plastic

From International Council for the Exploration of the Sea. *J. du Conseil* 32(3):385–395. Reprinted by permission.

shrimps and little wooden fishes painted with aluminium paint (length about 8 cm). The chemical stimuli, which were sometimes used in combination with visual stimuli, consisted of mussel or shrimp juice. In addition to this, with turbot and brill, juices of sole and smelt (*Osmerus eperlanus* L.) were also used. By means of a thin plastic tube (diameter 2 mm) tied to a perspex rod and on which the models could be attached, the chemical stimuli were added to the ball or plastic shrimp. For this purpose a hole was drilled through the ball or shrimp. The tube was fixed to one side of this hole, while on the other side there was a small plug of cotton-wool to prevent the juice flowing away too quickly. The juice was pressed through this tube by a hypodermic syringe.

The stimulus was presented to the fish for at most one minute, at a distance of 20 cm with a gentle motion. If the fish swam up to it making biting movements, the reaction was noted as positive. If the fish swam away from the stimulus this was called negative; if there was doubt as to the reaction, it was noted as doubtful. If at the end of the day, the fish proved unwilling to eat, the results obtained on that day with this fish were left out of consideration. The data obtained in these experiments are summarized in Table 1.

SOLE

The sole is a night feeder and has its period of greatest activity during the night (CUNNINGHAM, 1890; STEVEN, 1930; BOEREMA and STAM, 1952; KRUUK, 1963).

During the present experiments it appeared that in the daytime soles swam up to several objects as a possible prey and nibbled at them. They did this with plastic shrimps and wooden balls of 1, 2 and 4 cm diameter. On the other hand all the animals showed strong flight reactions when presented with a larger 8 cm ball. The fish which were buried in the sand jumped out of it and swam away in panic. In case of the 4 cm balls some soles showed signs of flight. When, however, the balls of 4 cm and 8 cm were presented together with a chemical stimulus, all the animals swam up to the ball of 4 cm and bit at it (positive reaction), one individual also positively approached the 8 cm ball, but the other animals reacted with flight. This phenomenon can be explained by the Law of stimulus summation (Reizsummen Regel), discovered by SEITZ (1940) (see TINBERGEN, 1951). It will therefore be clear that in their search for food soles use both vision and chemical clues. Therefore in my opinion PIPPING's (1927 b) view that the sole does not react visually to food, but finds its food exclusively by olfactory clues, needs revision.

The following observation might give us a possible explanation of the nature of the strong flight reaction. When a few cod (*Gadus morhua*), length 60 cm and about 10 cm diameter were released in a tank also containing buried soles, the latter jumped out of the sand and a strong flight reaction was observed.

PLAICE, FLOUNDER, DAB

Plaice, flounder and dab are day feeders. Their greatest bottom activity is in the daytime (DE GROOT, 1964). Unlike the sole, these fishes do not approach wooden balls of 1, 2 and 4 cm diameter as prey. To the ball of 8 cm diameter they hardly reacted with flight, and usually swam away slowly. Once or twice plastic shrimps were approached as prey and were bitten at, but only when the

TABLE 1. The reactions of different species of flatfish to different types of stimuli. Each type was offered 30 times in a random sequence. + positive response; − negative response; ? doubtful response; chem = chemical stimulus. For further explanation see text.

Stimulus type	Sole			Plaice			Flounder			Dab			Turbot			Brill		
	+	−	?	+	−	?	+	−	?	+	−	?	+	−	?	+	−	?
1 cm ball	19	11	−	−	29	1	−	30	−	2	28	−	−	30	−	−	30	−
2 cm ball	19	11	−	1	29	−	−	30	−	−	30	−	−	30	−	−	30	−
4 cm ball	18	12	−	−	30	−	−	30	−	−	30	−	−	30	−	−	30	−
8 cm ball	3	27	−	−	30	−	−	30	−	−	30	−	−	30	−	−	30	−
shrimp model	19	11	−	2	28	−	3	26	1	23	7	−	26	4	−	28	2	−
fish model	−	−	−	−	−	−	−	−	−	−	−	−	30	−	−	30	−	−
1 cm ball + chem	20	10	−	30	−	−	30	−	−	28	−	2	−	30	−	−	30	−
2 cm ball + chem	21	9	−	30	−	−	28	−	2	30	−	−	−	30	−	−	30	−
4 cm ball + chem	17	13	−	29	1	−	20	5	5	28	2	−	−	30	−	−	30	−
8 cm ball + chem	4	26	−	26	4	−	20	6	4	25	3	2	−	30	−	−	30	−
shrimp model + chem	30	−	−	30	−	−	30	−	−	30	−	−	25	5	−	24	4	2
chem. only	30	−	−	30	−	−	30	−	−	30	−	−	−	30	−	−	30	−
small jet of seawater	25	5	−	10	20	−	8	20	2	−	30	−	−	30	−	−	30	−

shrimp was moved. This was especially the case with the dab and occasionally the artificial shrimps were even swallowed. If, however, the balls were presented together with a chemical stimulus, the fish swam up to the balls and even bit at them.

We also studied the reactions of the fishes to a chemical stimulus only. For this purpose a bent glass tube was hidden under the sand with an aperture just above the sand 5 cm away from the fish. At first seawater from the tank itself was squirted through the tube. This only caused some reaction with plaice. After that a strongly diluted solution of shrimp juice in seawater was squirted slowly through the tube. All the three species reacted to this, but in slightly different ways. Plaice and flounder localized the aperture from which the solution flowed and bit at it, the plaice more often than the flounder, but the dab swam round and round the aperture making biting movements all the time, but did not localize it. When, however, a ball of 2 cm diameter was placed at a distance of 10 cm from the aperture, the dab bit it at once. This phenomenon can also be explained by the Law of stimulus summation (SEITZ, 1940). An investigation by CREUTZBERG (1946) into the food of plaice has shown that this fish has a preference for the siphons of bivalves. Possibly little currents of water play a part here. The eyes of the different species also show differences. The dab has the largest eyes, those of plaice and flounder are equally large. If now we compare what is known about the food they take, we see that there is a general resemblance, but that there are shifts of accent. The dab is the most active feeder, a good shrimp hunter. The plaice, on the other hand, feeds chiefly on animals that move slowly or hardly at all, as e.g. *Pectinaria*. The flounder takes up a position in between (FULTON, 1905; TODD, 1915; STEVEN, 1930; HARTLEY, 1940; CREUTZBERG, 1946; KÜHL, 1963). Recapitulating, we may say that the behaviour of plaice, flounder and dab respectively corresponds in broad outline, but that there are specific differences as to the degree in which they make use of chemical clues in combination with the visual system in finding their food. But it is certain that the three species possess and make use of a well developed chemical sense. However this faculty is not so pronounced as in the sole, and plaice, flounder and dab are all day feeders. Older views, such as those of BATESON (1890), PIPPING (1927 a), CREUTZBERG (1946), that the three species make no use of a chemical sense in their search for food, needs revision.

TURBOT, BRILL

Turbot and brill are very active day feeders, their food consisting mainly of fish. (FULTON, 1905; HARTLEY, 1940; RAE, 1957). The animals did not react to wooden balls of 1, 2 or 4 cm diameter, even when these were combined with a chemical stimulus, even when this chemical stimulus consisted of fish juices of sole or smelt. They showed no reaction to a chemical stimulus presented without a simultaneous visual stimulus. On the other hand the 8 cm diameter ball caused a flight reaction, the animals buried in the sand came out of it and swam away quickly. Wooden models of fish were looked upon as prey and the animals bit them when they were presented to them as swimming fishes.

Plastic shrimps were also seen as prey and bitten at, and even swallowed occasionally. Recapitulating, turbot and brill tend to be strongly visually orientated in their search for food. There is no evidence that chemical clues play any part in the capture of prey.

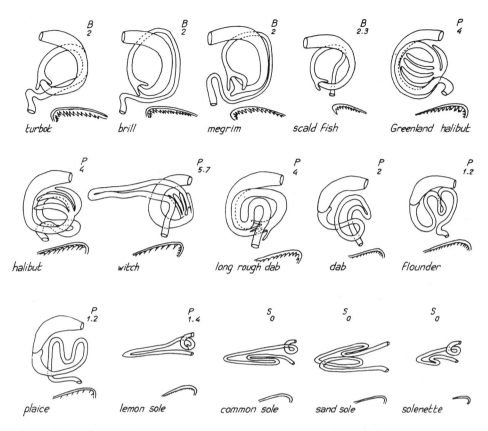

Figure 1. The form of the alimentary tract and structure of the gill rakers in different flatfish.
B: Bothidae; P: Pleuronectidae; S: Solidae.
The number of pyloric appendices are indicated.

COMPARATIVE MORPHOLOGY OF THE DIGESTIVE SYSTEM IN CONNEXION WITH THE FEEDING BEHAVIOUR

The following species have been investigated: scaldfish (*Arnoglossus laterna* Walb.), megrim (*Lepidorhombus whiffiagonis* Walb.), brill, turbot, long rough dab (*Hippoglossoides platessoides* Fabr.), halibut, Greenland halibut (*Reinhardtius hippoglossoides* Walb.), witch (*Glyptocephalus cynoglossus* L.), dab, lemon sole, flounder, plaice, solenette (*Bugglossidium luteum* Ris.), sole, sand sole (*Solea lascaris* Ris.).

Descriptive work on the morphology of the digestive system of flatfish has been carried out by DAWES (1929) and KOLTZER (1956). DAWES studied the alimentary tract of plaice and KOLTZER compared topographical features of the viscera of several species of flatfish. On morphology in connexion with feeding behaviour, work has been done by HATANAKA (1954), OCHIAI (1966) and SUYEHIRO (1934, 1941).

DUNCKER (1895) found that the number of pyloric appendices varied from 0–3 in flounder and from 2–4 in plaice. SVETOVIDOV (1934), who reviewed the literature, found a correlation between numbers of pyloric appendices and the character of the food. He found that they increased with the size of the food. However, the findings of MARTIN and SANDERCOCK (1967), who studied pyloric appendices and gill raker development in lake trout, do not agree with this rule. SVETOVIDOV also describes the correlation between the character of the food of fishes and the number of gill rakers (especially herring species). DOBBEN (1937) and FLÜCHTER (1963) studied the morphology of the jaw apparatus of several species of flatfish.

METHODS

For each individual of the species investigated a sketch was made of the gill rakers and of the viscera *in situ*. Then the following measurements were made:
1. Length of whole alimentary tract uncoiled from lips to anus.
2. Length from lips to oesophagus (buccal and pharyngeal cavity).
3. Length of oesophagus and stomach to pyloric valve.
4. Length of duodenum.
5. Length from intestino-rectal valve to anus.

Of each of the parts 2 to 5 the percentage has been calculated from the whole tract. Further it was noted how many pyloric appendices were found, if any.

RESULTS

A representative sketch of the gill rakers and viscera *in situ* of each of the species studied is given in Figure 1. If we observe the form of the viscera, we see at once that there is a uniformity between the species belonging to the Bothidae (turbot, brill, megrim and scaldfish). They have a rather simple intestinal loop and large gill rakers. The form of the viscera of halibut, Greenland halibut, and long rough dab (Pleuronectidae) follows nearly the same pattern, with the exception that there are 4 instead of 2 pyloric appendices.

In the case of the Greenland halibut and halibut, the pyloric appendices are of enormous dimensions compared with those of the Bothidae. The form of the intestine of the witch has some similarities with that of the lemon sole. However, this is not supported by the relative dimensions of different parts of the whole tract. The gill rakers are sharply pointed and there are 5–7 pyloric appendices. The similarities with the lemon sole are perhaps due to the fact that the witch is a polychaeta-mollusca feeder. In the other Pleuronectidae there is a striking uniformity between the intestinal loop of dab, flounder and plaice. The loop is more complicated and the gill rakers have fewer teeth. However, the form of the intestine of the lemon sole does not fit into this picture. This type is also observed in the Soleidae (common sole, sand sole and solenette).

The gill rakers of the lemon sole have more teeth, but they are smaller than those of the Pleuronectidae mentioned above.

The gill rakers of the common sole, sand sole, and solenette are very small if present at all. In the lemon sole and Soleidae the intestinal loop has deeply penetrated the body, and the dimensions of the oesophagus and stomach are reduced. In the sand sole the loop in the oesophagus and stomach has disappeared. This description is supported by the relative dimensions of the differeut parts of the whole tract (Fig. 2). The buccal and pharyngeal cavities,

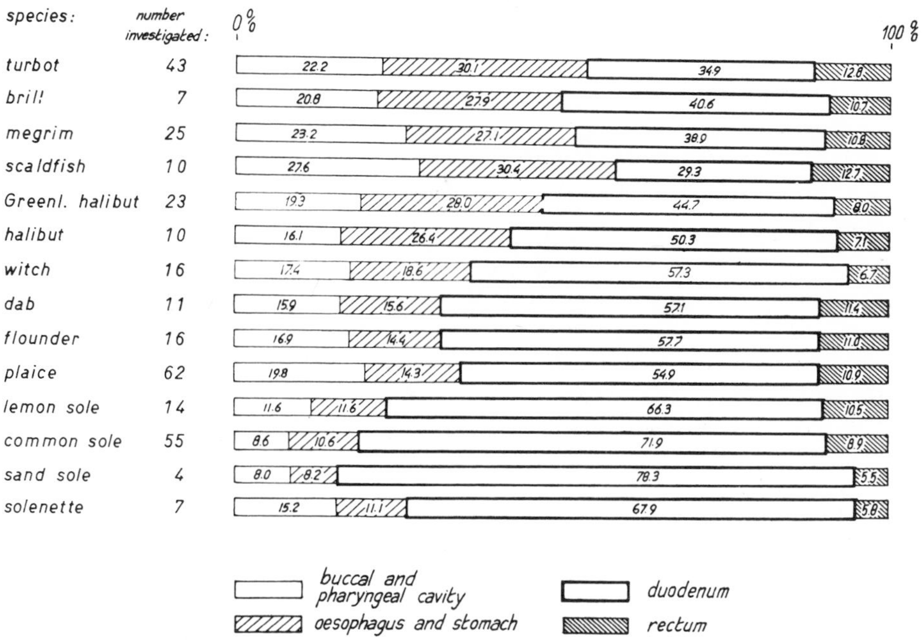

species:	number investigated:	0% 100%
turbot	43	22.2 / 30.1 / 34.9 / 12.8
bril!	7	20.8 / 27.9 / 40.6 / 10.7
megrim	25	23.2 / 27.1 / 38.9 / 10.8
scaldfish	10	27.6 / 30.4 / 29.3 / 12.7
Greenl. halibut	23	19.3 / 28.0 / 44.7 / 8.0
halibut	10	16.1 / 26.4 / 50.3 / 7.1
witch	16	17.4 / 18.6 / 57.3 / 6.7
dab	11	15.9 / 15.6 / 52.1 / 14.1
flounder	16	16.9 / 14.4 / 57.7 / 11.0
plaice	62	19.8 / 14.3 / 54.9 / 10.9
lemon sole	14	11.6 / 11.6 / 66.3 / 10.5
common sole	55	8.6 / 10.6 / 71.9 / 8.9
sand sole	4	8.0 / 8.2 / 78.3 / 5.5
solenette	7	15.2 / 11.1 / 67.9 / 5.8

☐ buccal and pharyngeal cavity   ☐ duodenum
▨ oesophagus and stomach   ▧ rectum

Figure 2. The relative lengths of different parts of the alimentary tract in certain flatfish.

oesophagus and stomach, of the Bothidae form about 50% of the whole tract.

The halibut and Greenland halibut are following more or less the same pattern. On the other hand dab, flounder, and plaice, show a different patttern. Here the part formed by the buccal and pharyngeal cavities, oesophagus and stomach, is only about 20% of the whole tract. Again we observe that the lemon sole fits better into the picture of the Soleidae, with a percentage of about 20% or less.

The importance of these differences can be clearly understood if we consider the food taken by these species. Turbot, brill, megrim, scaldfish, halibut and Greenland halibut are fish feeders, they have to take their prey at once and completely before digestion takes part. The food, however is digested relatively quickly. Lemon sole, common sole, sand sole and solenette, on the other hand, are polychaete feeders, and take small prey frequently which is often contaminated with indigestible items. Therefore a long alimentary tract is very useful.

The dab, flounder and plaice, crustacea feeders, take up a position between these two groups.

The structure of the gill raker also gives an indication of the type of food consumed. They are indispensable to the fish feeders, and prevent the prey, which is taken alive, from struggling out of the mouth. Therefore they are large and on each "raker" we find a series of small teeth. Polychaeta feeders do not need large gill rakers, for once the prey has been sucked in, it easily passes through to the stomach. Again we observe that dab, flounder and plaice take up an intermediate position. From the three species mentioned the dab feeds the most on moving prey (shrimps).

GENERAL DISCUSSION

Reviewing the experiments on the sensory faculties we are struck by the fact that the sole, a night feeder, reacts so well to visual stimuli, and that the other species, all day feeders, do this only in part. This may be explained by the assumption that the sole, as a nocturnal animal, has a much less differentiated visual prey scheme than the visual feeders – the day feeders – and that, once accustomed to tank life the sole approaches a simple visual stimulus by day in its neighbourhood as prey. The visual feeders, however, only react to much more differentiated stimuli, such as exact replicas or models of fishes; balls have no significance for them. The species investigated can be divided into three groups: (1), the non-visual feeders – the night feeders – which feed on invertebrates, a prey that moves slowly or not at all and is found in the bottom or near it; (2), the visual feeders – the day feeders – which eat prey that moves quickly, such as fish and find this prey exclusively visually; and (3), a group of day feeders, which although visual feeders, may use chemical clues in their search for food. They find their food in or near the bottom. To the first group belongs the sole, to the second belongs the turbot and brill, and to the third the plaice, flounder and dab.

This division is confirmed by EVAN's (1937) work. He studied the comparative anatomy of the brain in flatfishes, and distinguished four types: the sole type; the plaice type; the turbot type and the halibut type. The sole type is characterized by large olfactory lobes and small optic lobes (common sole). The plaice type is characterized by olfactory lobes moderate in size, but very large optic lobes (plaice, dab, lemon sole, witch (*Pleuronectes cynoglossus* L.). The turbot type is characterized by small olfactory bulbs, but well developed optic lobes (turbot, brill, megrim). The halibut type differs little from the turbot type except in size (halibut).

Recapitulating the results found by comparing the alimentary tracts and gill rakers of these flatfish, we find that the Bothidae studied have very heavily teethed gill rakers, and a simple intestinal loop. They all possess well developed pyloric appendices. The Soleidae have no toothed gill rakers and a complicated intestinal loop which penetrates deeply into the body. They do not possess pyloric appendices. The Pleuronectidae studied present a more complicated picture. The group as a whole takes up an intermediate position between the Bothidae and Soleidae. Some species like the Greenland halibut, halibut and long rough dab link up with the Bothidae, others like the lemon sole have more connexion with the Soleidae. Plaice, flounder and dab form a group inbetween; they have toothed gill rakers, although less toothed than in the Bothidae and have a complicated intestinal loop. Pyloric appendices are present.

In the flatfish studied we get a confirmation of SVETOVIDOV's results. However we also observe an increase in size of the pyloric appendices correlated with the size of the prey. A good example of this is found in halibut. The physiological function of pyloric appendices in the digestion of fishes is not yet quite clear. According to some authors the pyloric appendix is only an absorbent organ, according to others it has a secretory function as well. Pyloric appendices enlarge the surface of the alimentary tract; for a secretory surface there follows a greater quantity of digestive juices, and better assimilation of food will be the consequence of increase in the surface of the absorbent organ.

FLÜCHTER could demonstrate that plaice was functionally adapted to feed on

TABLE 2. Summary of the results

Family	Type	Way of finding food	Form of intestine	Form of gill rakers	Olfactory lobe (After EVANS, 1937)	Optic lobes (after EVANS, 1937)
Bothidae	fish-feeder	vision	simple loop	heavily toothed	small	large
Pleuronectidae	Crustacea-feeder	Mainly vision but also olfaction	complicated loop	less toothed	medium	large
Soleidae	Polychaeta-mollusca-feeder	Olfaction but vision possible	more complicated loop	few or no teeth	large	small

small food items, especially burrowed molluscs. Halibut, turbot and megrim were very well adapted to feed on larger prey. Halibut bites into its prey with its jaws. Turbot and megrim enlarge their mouth cavity enormously and suck their prey.

From an earlier investigation (DE GROOT, 1967), we know that the Pleuronecti-formes can be subdivided according to the type of food into fish feeders (Bothidae), crustacea feeders (Pleuronectidae) and polychaeta-mollusca feeders (Soleidae). Here also we observe that in the Pleuronectidae there are some exceptions, halibut and long rough dab are fish feeders and the lemon sole is a pronounced polychaeta-mollusca feeder. EVANS could distinguish four types according to the type of brain. However it should be remembered that the fourth type (the halibut type) is based on a species which taxonomically belongs to the Pleuronectidae, although feeding like the Bothidae species.

The results may be summarized as follows. Bothidae, fish feeders, feed during the day-time and find their food only by sight. They have a simple intestinal loop and the gill rakers are heavily toothed. Soleidae are polychaeta-mollusca feeders, feeding during the night, and find their food mainly by olfactory clues, but still posses the possibility of finding their food visually. The Pleuronectidae, mainly crustacea feeders, are day feeders and find their food mainly visually, but also use olfaction. This group includes species which have moved towards the feeding behaviour and anatomical features of the Bothidae on one hand or the Soleidae on the other. Table 2 summarizes the results schematically.

ACKNOWLEDGEMENTS

Very special thanks are due to Dr. N. NIKITOPOULOU, Institute of Physiology, Medical School of Athens, University, Greece and Mr. J. A. R. A. M. VAN HOOFF, Laboratory of Comparative Physiology, Utrecht University, Holland, for their interest and criticism. I also wish to thank Mr. P. KANNEWORFF, Greenland Fisheries Investigations, Denmark, for collecting specimens of the Greenland halibut.

REFERENCES

BATESON, W., 1890. "The sense-organs and perception of fishes, with remarks on the supply of bait". J. mar. biol. Ass. U.K., **1**: 225–56.

BOEREMA, L. K., and STAM, A. B., 1952. "A preliminary note on the sole in the Dutch coastal area". ICES CM 1952, 2 pp. (mimeo).

CREUTZBERG, P. H., 1946. "Waarnemingen over het voedselzoeken van schol, bot en schar". Unpubl. manuscr. in Zool. Sta., Den Helder, Netherlands.

CUNNINGHAM, J. T., 1890. *A treatise on the common sole.* Marine Biological Association, Plymouth. 147 pp.

DAWES, B., 1929. "The histology of the alimentary tract of the plaice (*Pleuronectes platessa*)". Q. Jl micros. Sci., **73**: 243–74.

DOBBEN, W. H. VAN, 1937. "Über den Kiefermechanismus der Knochenfische". Archs néerl. Zool. **2**: 1–72.

DUNCKER, G., 1895. "Variation und Verwandtschaft von *Pleuronectes flesus* L. und *Pl. platessa* L.". Wiss. Meeresunters. Abt. Helgoland, **1**: (2) 47–104.

EVANS, H. M., 1937. "A comparative study of the brains in pleuronectidae". Proc. R. Soc., B **122**: 308–42.

FLÜCHTER, J., 1963. "Funktionell-morphologische Untersuchungen über die Kieferapparate einiger Plattfische". Zool. Beitr., **8**: 23–94.

FULTON, T. W., 1905. "Report on the distribution and seasonal abundance of flatfishes (Pleuronectidae) in the North Sea 1902–1903". Rep. N. Sea Fish. Invest. Comm., **1**: 471–618.

GROOT, S. J. DE, 1964. "Diurnal activity and feeding habits of plaice". Rapp. P.-v. Réun. Cons. perm. int. Explor. Mer., **155**: 48–51.

GROOT, S. J. DE, 1967. "A review paper on the behaviour of flatfishes". FAO conference on fish behaviour in relation to fishing techniques and tactics. Bergen, Norway. FR: FB/67/R/7. 26 pp. (mimeo).

HARTLEY, P. H. T., 1940. "The Saltash tuck-net fishery and the ecology of some estuarine fishes". J. mar. biol. Ass. U.K., **24**: 1–68.

HATANAKA, M., 1954. "Inter-specific relations concerning the predacious habits among benthic fish". Tohoku. J. agric. Res. **4**: 177–89.

KOLTZER, I., 1956. "Vergleichende Untersuchungen über die Leibeshöhlen Verhältnisse der Plattfische". Z. Fisch., **4**: 595–634.

KRUUK, H., 1963. "Diurnal periodicity in the activity of the common sole *Solea vulgaris* Quensel". Neth. J. Sea Res., **2**: 1–28.

KÜHL, H., 1963. "Über die Nahrung der Scharbe (*Limanda limanda* L.)" Arch. FischWiss., **14**: 8–17.

MARTIN, N. V. and, SANDERCOCK, F. K., 1967. "Pyloric caeca and gill raker development in Lake trout, *Salvelinus namaycush*, in Algonquin Park, Ontario". J. Fish. Res. Bd Can., **24**: 965–74.

OCHIAI, A., 1966. "Studies on the comparative morphology and ecology of the Japanese soles". Spec. Rep. Misaki mar. biol. inst., (3) 97 pp.

PIPPING, M., 1927a. "Der Geruchsinn der Fische mit besonderer Berücksichtigung seiner Bedeutung für das Aufsuchen des Futters". Acta Soc. Sci. fenn. Comm. Biol., **2**: (4) 1–28.

PIPPING, M., 1927b. "Ergänzende Beobachtungen über den Geruchsinn der Fische mit besonderer Berücksichtigung seiner Bedeutung für das Aufsuchen des Futters". Acta Soc. Sci. fenn. Comm. Biol., **2**: (10) 1–10.

RAE, B. B., 1957. "A preliminary account of the turbot in Scottish waters". Scott. Fish. Bull., (8) 10–12.

SEITZ, A., 1940. "Die Paarbildung bei einigen Cichliden I." Z. Tierpsychol., **4**: 40–84.

STEVEN, G. A., 1930. "Bottom fauna and the food of fishes". J. mar. biol. Ass. U.K., **16**: 677–706.

SUYEHIRO, Y., 1934. "Studies on the digestive system and the feeding habit of the important fishes of the North Pacific II. The plaice, *Lepidopsetta mochigarei* (Snyder) and the halibut, *Hippoglossoides elassodon* (Jordan and Snyder)". Bull. Jap. Soc. scient. Fish., **3**: 65–2.

SUYEHIRO, Y., 1941. "A study of the digestive system and feeding habits of fish. (Pleuronectidae)". Jap. J. Zool., **10**: 224–33.

SVETOVIDOV, A., 1934. "On the correlation between the character of food and the number of pyloric caeca in fishes". Dokl. Akad. Nauk SSSR., **3**: (1) 70–2.

TINBERGEN, N., 1951. *The study of instinct.* Clarendon Press, Oxford. 228 pp.

TODD, R. A., 1915. "Report on the food of the plaice". Fishery Invest., Lond., Ser. 2, **2**: (3) 31 pp.

Additional Readings

CHAPTER 8

ALEXANDER, R. McN. 1967. The functions and mechanism of the protrusible upper jaws of some acanthopterygian fish. *J. Zool., Lond.* 151:43–64.

COWEY, C. B., and SARGENT, J. R. 1972. Fish nutrition. *Adv. Mar. Biol.* 10:383–492.

EBELING, A. W., and CAILLIET, G. M. 1975. Mouth size and predator strategy of midwater fishes. *Deep-Sea Res.* 21:959–968.

GROOT, S. J. de. 1971. On the interrelationships between morphology of the alimentary tract, food and feeding behavior in flatfishes (Pisces: Pleuronectiformes). *Neth. J. Sea Res.* 5:121–196.

IVLEV, V. S. 1961. Experimental ecology of the feeding of fishes. New Haven and London: Yale University Press.

KEAST, A., and WEBB, D. 1966. Mouth and body form relative to feeding ecology in the fish fauna of a small lake, Lake Opinicon, Ontario. *J. Fish. Res. Bd. Canada* 23:1845–1874.

LIEM, K., and OSSE, L. 1975. Biological versatility, evolution, and food resource exploitation in African cichlid fishes. *Am. Zool.* 15:427–454.

MONTGOMERY, W. L. 1977. Diet and gut morphology in fishes, with special reference to the monkey-face prickleback, *Cebidichthys violaceus* (Stichaeidae: Blennioidei). *Copeia* 1977(1):178–182.

OVERNALL, J. 1973. Digestive enzymes of the pyloric caeca and of their associated mesentary in the cod *(Gadus morhua). Comp. Biochem. Physiol.* 46B:519–531.

PHILLIPS, A. M. Jr., 1969. Nutrition, digestion, and energy utilization. Chapter 7, pp. 391–432, in W. S. Hoar and D. J. Randall, eds., *Fish Physiology,* Vol. 1. New York: Academic Press.

SHAEFFER, B., and ROSEN, D. E. 1961. Major adaptive levels in the evolution of the acanthopterygian feeding mechanism. *Am. Zool.* 1:187–204.

TANAKA, S. K. 1973. Suction feeding by the nurse shark. *Copeia* 1973(3):606–608.

WERNER, E. E. 1974. The fish size, prey size, handling time relation in several sunfishes and some implications. *J. Fish. Res. Bd. Canada* 31(9):1531–1536.

WERNER, E. E., and HALL, D. J. 1974. Optimal foraging and the size selection of prey by the bluegill sunfish *(Lepomis macrochirus). Ecology* 55(5):1042–1052.

⸺ 1976. Niche shifts in sunfishes: experimental evidence and significance. *Science* 191:404–406.

WINDELL, J. T. 1967. Rates of digestion in fishes, pp. 151–173, in S. Gerking, ed., *The Biological Basis of Freshwater Fish Production.* New York: John Wiley & Sons, Inc.

⸺ 1971. Food analysis and rate of digestion. Chapter 9, pp. 215–226, in W. E. Ricker, ed., *Methods for assessment of fish production in fresh waters,* IBP Handbook No. 3, Oxford and Edinburgh: Blackwell Scientific Publications.

ZARET, T. M., and RAND, A. S. 1971. Competition in tropical stream fishes: support for the competitive exclusion principle. *Ecol.* 52(2):336–342.

9

Sensory Mechanisms

THE VISUAL PIGMENTS OF EPIPELAGIC AND ROCKY-SHORE FISHES[1]

F. W. MUNZ

Department of Biology, University of Oregon, Eugene, Oregon

(*Received* 19 *June* 1964)

Abstract—Visual pigments of eleven species of marine teleost fishes have been studied in aqueous digitonin extracts of dark-adapted retinae. Five species that occur in habitats along rocky coasts have "rhodopsins" with λ_{max} near 500 mμ. In six epipelagic species the visual pigments are also "rhodopsins", but there is a trend for λ_{max} to be at shorter wavelengths. These results are correlated with the spectral transmission of sunlight by the types of sea water in which these fishes live. In addition, a second "rhodopsin", more sensitive to red light, has been characterized in several of the species.

IN recent years several investigators have studied the visual pigments of marine teleost fishes selected from restricted habitats (e.g. DENTON and WARREN, 1957; WALD *et al.*, 1957; and MUNZ, 1958a, 1958c). Their findings have been correlated with physical features of the environment, such as depth (WALD *et al.*, 1957) or light (all references cited above). These surveys are, as yet, fragmentary. In spite of this, there is a substantial spectral range in the density maxima of visual pigments from species in each habitat. The interpretations that have been put forward must, therefore, be regarded as tentative and as forming a basis for further experiments.

The present paper describes the results of experiments with the visual pigments of eleven species of marine teleost fishes from either of two fairly distinct habitats. These pigments are photosensitive, with characteristics closely resembling those of known visual pigments. They are all "rhodopsins", by which I mean only that the chromophore is retinene₁. They may or may not be derived from retinal rods (for further discussion of the troubled topic of visual-pigment nomenclature, see DARTNALL, 1962, p. 389). The visual pigments of the rocky-shore species are quite "typical" rhodopsins, i.e. with spectral density maxima (λ_{max}) very close to 500 mμ. They are similar to the rhodopsins that have been well studied in many amphibians and mammals and that were once assumed to be characteristic of marine teleosts (WALD, 1936). In the more or less truly epipelagic species, there is a trend for λ_{max} to be shifted to shorter wavelengths. This situation is analogous to that found in bathypelagic fishes[2] (DENTON and WARREN, 1957; WALD *et al.*, 1957; and MUNZ, 1958a) and suggests that similar environmental factors may have led to the selection of these visual pigments in the two groups.

---

[1] Some of the data presented here are from a Ph.D. dissertation submitted at the University of California, Los Angeles.

[2] Pelagic animals swim or drift freely in the ocean. Epipelagic forms live in the uppermost 100–200 m and bathypelagic forms in deeper water (though some may come to the surface at night).

From *Vision Research* 4:441–454. Reprinted by permission.

MATERIAL AND METHODS

The retinae of dark-adapted eyes were removed in dim red light and hardened with 4% potassium alum solution. The alum solution was removed by centrifugation and then the retinae were washed twice in distilled water and once in alkaline (pH 8·6) borate–KCl buffer, with light centrifugation each time to allow separation from the supernatant fluid. The retinal material was extracted with two successive portions of 2% aqueous digitonin solution made up in borate–KCl buffer (pH 8·3). The extracts were stored in darkness at 5–10°C until used.

After centrifugation the retinal extracts were analysed in a Beckman DU spectrophotometer with photo-multiplier attachment. 2% digitonin solution was used as a blank; the temperature was regulated at 20 ± 1°C. Optical density of the extracts (1 cm light path) was measured from 700 to 320 mμ at 20 mμ intervals, followed by an interlaced return series of measurements, also at 20 mμ intervals. A Bausch and Lomb grating monochromator with interference filters placed in the exit light path provided narrow-band colored light

TABLE 1. SPECTRAL CHARACTERISTICS OF RETINAL EXTRACTS

Species	Family	Number of eyes	Sample	D_{min}/D_{max}	Adjusted λ_{max}* (mμ)
Rocky-Shore Fishes					
Paralabrax clathratus	Serranidae	8	1A	0·34	502‡
			1B	0·38	502‡
Chromis punctipinnis	Pomacentridae	4	2A	0·93	496
Coryphopterus nicholsii	Gobiidae	30	3A	0·64	501‡
			3B	0·70	501‡
			3C	—†	—†
Scorpaena guttata	Scorpaenidae	2	4A	0·51	499
Axoclinus carminalis	Tripterygiidae	30	5A	0·72	501
Epipelagic Fishes					
Caranx hippos	Carangidae	4	6A	0·40	499
			6B	0·58	499
Trachurus symmetricus	Carangidae	11	7A	0·79	498
Sarda chiliensis	Scombridae	2	8A	—†	—†
Scomber japonicus	Scombridae	4	9A	0·66	491
			9B	0·95	494
Scomberomorus concolor	Scombridae	12	10A	0·56	493‡
			10B	0·43	491‡
Scomberomorus sierra	Scombridae	6	11A	0·72	494‡

* The measured λ_{max} of the density spectrum of the unbleached extract is corrected by means of D_{min}/D_{max}, in order to estimate the true λ_{max} of the visual pigment, if homogeneous (see CRESCITELLI and DARTNALL, 1954).

† Extract impure, ratio greater than one.

‡ Two photosensitive pigments were present in the extract.

(half band-widths between 10 and 15 mμ), which was used to bleach the extracts. Following exposure to light the extracts were returned to the spectrophotometer and the density spectrum measured as before. In this way the effects on each extract of several bleaching wavelengths were studied successively. White light from a 60W tungsten bulb was also employed as a bleaching source. This procedure of partial bleaching was devised by DARTNALL (1952) and its application to the study of visual pigments has been fully described by him (1957, 1962).

DARTNALL's (1953) nomogram is useful in the comparative study of visual pigments. This is based on the observation that all visual pigments, especially those with a retinene$_1$ chromophore, have spectra of the same shape if plotted against frequency rather than wavelength. With the nomogram one can construct the theoretical density spectrum of a "rhodopsin" with any given λ_{max}. In the species examined in the present study, the visual pigments were all "rhodopsins", based on retinene$_1$. This was shown by the spectral location of the product of bleaching (λ_{max} 366 to 368 mμ with hydroxylamine present, or 375 to 380 mμ with it absent; CRESCITELLI, 1958a).

The fishes were collected between 1955 and 1958. All of the species here called "rocky-shore" species usually occur along rocky coasts from the surface to moderate depths. The serranid *Paralabrax clathratus* (Girard), pomacentrid *Chromis punctipinnis* (Cooper), and scorpaenid *Scorpaena guttata* Girard range along the coasts of California and Baja California. The goby, *Coryphopterus nicholsii* (Bean), lives on small sandy spaces in rocky areas from just below the tidal zone down to at least 70 m, from Southern California to British Columbia. The tripterygiid *Axoclinus carminalis* (Jordan and Gilbert) is from the Gulf of California. The animals used in this study were caught at Santa Catalina Island, California, except for the single specimen of *Scorpaena*, which was brought in alive from a bait-dealer in Los Angeles, and those of *Axoclinus*, which were caught at Bahía San Carlos, near Guaymas, Sonora, Mexico.

The species here called "epipelagic" belong to two families. The carangid *Trachurus symmetricus* (Ayres) and scombrid species, *Sarda chiliensis* (Cuvier) and *Scomber japonicus* Houttuyn, all range widely in the eastern Pacific Ocean. The carangid *Caranx hippos* (Linnaeus) and scombrids, *Scomberomorus concolor* (Lockington) and *S. sierra* Jordan and Starks, are more restricted to tropical or subtropical waters in the eastern Pacific. The specimens of *Caranx* were caught at San Blas, Nayarit, Mexico. *Trachurus* was taken at Guadalupe Island, Baja California, Mexico, and *Scomber* at Santa Catalina Island. *Sarda* and *Scomberomorus* were caught at Bahía San Carlos.

TABLE 2. ROCKY-SHORE FISHES. DETAILS OF BLEACHING EXPERIMENTS

Species	Sample	Bleaching wavelength (mμ)	λ_{max} (mμ)	ΔD_{max}
Paralabrax clathratus	1A	653	518	0·069
		640	502	0·133
		605	503	0·171
		605	498	0·190
		White	496	0·049
	1B*	650	520	0·061
		605	502	0·276
		590	500	0.165
		White	—†	0·007
Chromis punctipinnis	2A	640	—†	0·005
		606	498	0·022
		580	500	0·049
Coryphopterus nicholsii	3A‡	640	515	0·018
		606	502	0·126
	3B‡	640	510	0·018
		606	502	0·101
		580	502	0·078
		White	499	0·059
	3C*§	580	500	0·078
		White	—†	0·006
Scorpaena guttata	4A	640	503	0·039
		606	504	0·107
		560	502	0·228
Axoclinus carminalis	5A	640	500	0·011
		606	503	0·050

* Hydroxylamine added to extract.
† Difference small, with no clear peak.
‡ Extract of outer segments of retinal cells.
§ Extract of retinal residues.

Rocky-Shore Fishes

Single retinal extracts of five unrelated species of teleost fishes were shown to have rhodopsins with λ_{max} near 500 mμ (Table 1). These preparations varied considerably in freedom from light-absorbing stable impurities (D_{min}/D_{max}; see CRESCITELLI and DARTNALL; 1954). After allowance was made for these impurities, however, the estimated

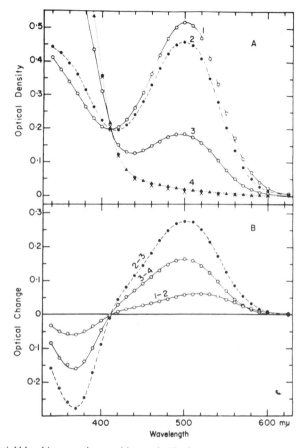

FIG. 1A. Partial bleaching experiment with sample 1B of *Paralabrax clathratus*. Curve 1, initial density spectrum; curve 2, after 60 min exposure to λ650 mμ light, curve 3, after 40 min exposure to λ605 mμ light; curve 4, ▲ after 65 min exposure to λ590 mμ light; ×, after 10 min exposure to white light.

FIG. 1B. Difference spectra; upward changes indicate loss of density, downward changes gain in density. Curve 1–2, result of λ650 mμ irradiation; 2–3, λ605 mμ irradiation; and 3–4, λ590 mμ irradiation.

wavelength of maximum density ranged only from 496 to 501 mμ (Table 1, adjusted λ_{max}). Confirmation was obtained in partial bleaching experiments designed to test the homogeneity of the extracts (Table 2). In three species the extracts were substantially homogeneous, evidently containing only a single light-sensitive component, as shown by the unchanged spectral position of successive difference spectra. The other two, *Paralabrax clathratus* and the bluespot goby, *Coryphopterus nicholsii*, contained relatively small proportions of a second visual pigment. That of *Coryphopterus* was only a trace, but the second pigment of *Paralabrax* was present in an amount great enough to be analysed (see below). It has been shown (CRESCITELLI, 1958a; MUNZ, 1956) that where hydroxylamine can be used, λ_{max} of the difference spectrum coincides with that of the density spectrum. In the absence of this retinene-trapping reagent, on the other hand, the peak of the difference spectrum is shifted about two mμ towards longer wavelengths. Study of the tabulated data has resulted in estimating λ_{max} of these rhodopsins as 500 ± 1 mμ, except in the case of the blacksmith, *Chromis punctipinnis*, which has a rhodopsin with $\lambda_{max}=498\pm2$ mμ.

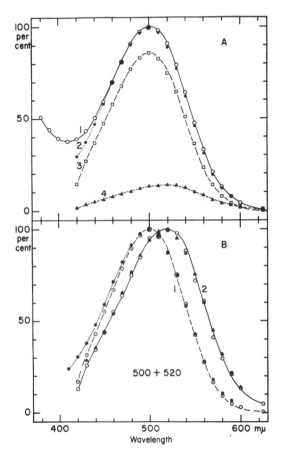

FIG. 2A. Curve 1, density spectrum of sample 1B of *Paralabrax clathratus*; curve 2, constructed from Dartnall's nomogram, assuming $\lambda_{max}=502$ mμ. Curves 1 and 2 scaled to 100% at their maximum. Curve 3, difference spectrum of red-insensitive component (sample 1B, curve 3–4); curve 4, difference spectrum of red-sensitive component (1B, curve 1–2). Curves 3 and 4 scaled so as to approximate in sum to the total difference spectrum.

FIG. 2B.   Difference spectra of visual pigments of *Paralabrax clathratus*, scaled to 100%. ○, red-insensitive component (sample 1B, curve 3–4); ○, red-sensitive component (1B, curve 1–2). ●, constructed from Dartnall's nomogram, $\lambda_{max}=500$ mμ; ▲, constructed from Dartnall's nomogram, $\lambda_{max}=518$ mμ.

The extract of the kelp bass, *Paralabrax clathratus*, proved to be more interesting, because it contained a small proportion of a second visual pigment. This was not obvious in the unbleached extract, but was shown by partial bleaching with deep red light, both in the presence and absence of hydroxylamine (Table 2; Fig. 1). The red-sensitive pigment appeared to be a second "rhodopsin" (spectral maximum of the bleaching product formed with hydroxylamine present was 367 mμ; see CRESCITELLI, 1958a) with λ_{max} near 520 mμ. Usually enough of the more abundant, though less red-sensitive, component of such a mixture is also bleached to distort the difference spectrum of the red-sensitive pigment (DARTNALL, 1956, 1957, 1962). The result is a difference curve broader than that of the pure pigment and with λ_{max} intermediate between the density maxima of the pure pigments. Comparison of such a difference spectrum with the nomogram curve most closely fitting it will show any appreciable distortion of this sort. This has been done for both photosensitive components of *Paralabrax* (Fig. 2B). The nomogram construct (λ_{max} 518 mμ) fits the difference spectrum of the red-sensitive pigment (Curve 2) nearly as well as the construct (λ_{max} 500 mμ) fits the difference spectrum of the much more abundant typical rhodopsin

TABLE 3. EPIPELAGIC FISHES. DETAILS OF BLEACHING EXPERIMENTS

Species	Sample	Bleaching wavelength (mμ)	λ_{max} (mμ)	ΔD_{max}
Caranx hippos	6A*	650	—†	0·020
		605	499	0·264
		590	496	0·100
	6B	605	502	0·143
		605	499	0·150
		580	500	0·097
Trachurus symmetricus	7A	640	—†	0·001
		White	497	0·078
Sarda chiliensis	8A	640	490	0·098
		White	490	0·091
Scomber japonicus	9A	677	—†	0·022
		631	497	0·093
		606	492	0·121
		580	493	0·075
	9B*	640	—†	0·014
		580	491	0·223
		White	—†	0·012
Scomberomorus concolor	10A	606	512	0·020
		White	487	0·056
	10B*	606	505	0·029
		482	485	0·080
Scomberomorus sierra	11A*	650	528	0·054
		620	497	0·024
		590	486	0·073
		560	485	0·057
		White	—†	0·004

* Hydroxylamine added to extract.
† Difference small, with no clear peak.

(Curve 1). There is just a trace in Curve 2 of the broadening that must be due to bleaching of the second component, indicating that λ_{max} of the red-sensitive pigment must be at a slightly longer wavelength than 518 mμ. If its λ_{max} were at 523 mμ, Curve 2 must represent a mixture of this pigment with the "chief" rhodopsin (λ_{max} 500 mμ). Curve 2 cannot be matched by any combination of these components, however, indicating that λ_{max} of the red-sensitive pigment must be less than 523 mμ. For these reasons, its λ_{max} is estimated to be 520$\pm$3 mμ.

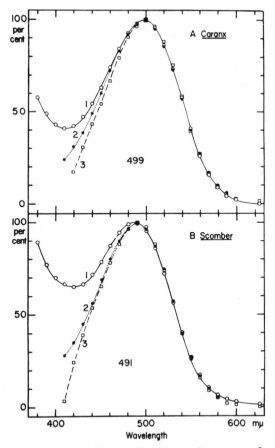

FIG. 3A. Curve 1, density spectrum of sample 6A of *Caranx hippos*; curve 2, constructed from Dartnall's nomogram, $\lambda_{max}=499$ mμ; curve 3, hydroxylamine difference spectrum (sample 6A, curve 2–3). All curves scaled to 100% at their maximum.

FIG. 3B. Curve 1, density spectrum of sample 9A of *Scomber japonicus*; curve 2, constructed from Dartnall's nomogram, $\lambda_{max}=491$ mμ; curve 3, hydroxylamine difference spectrum (sample 9B, curve 2–3). All curves scaled to 100% at their maximum.

Epipelagic Fishes

Similar experiments with retinal extracts of six epipelagic species disclosed a series of "rhodopsins" (Tables 1 and 3). The rhodopsin of the crevalle jack, *Caranx hippos*, is "typical", with λ_{max} 499$\pm$1 mμ (Fig. 3A). Partial bleaching experiments (Table 3) showed the substantial homogeneity of this visual pigment. Although the experiment with the visual pigment of the jack mackerel, *Trachurus symmetricus*, was not as thorough, it seems probable that a single photosensitive component was present, with λ_{max} estimated at 497$\pm$2 mμ. This shift in λ_{max} to shorter wavelengths was more pronounced in the Pacific mackerel, *Scomber japonicus*. The retinal extract contained a homogeneous "rhodopsin" with λ_{max} 491$\pm$1 mμ (Fig. 3B). The partial bleaching experiment with an impure retinal extract of the bonito, *Sarda chiliensis*, established the substantial homogeneity of the visual pigment and that its λ_{max} is 488$\pm$2 mμ (Table 3).

Completing this series were the two species of Spanish mackerel (*Scomberomorus*).

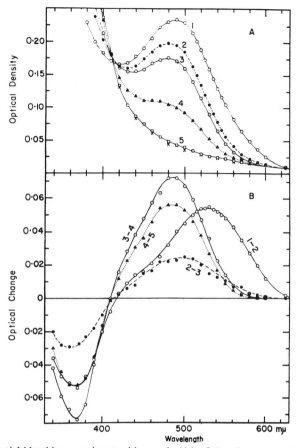

FIG. 4A. Partial bleaching experiment with sample 11A of *Scomberomorus sierra*, to which hydroxylamine had been added. Curve 1, initial density spectrum; curve 2, after 60 min exposure to λ650 mμ light; curve 3, after 60 min exposure to λ620 mμ light; curve 4, after 60 min exposure to λ590 mμ light; curve 5, □ after 30 min exposure to λ560 mμ light; ×, after 10 min exposure to white light.

FIG. 4B. Difference spectra; upward changes indicate loss of density, downward changes gain in density. Curve 1–2, result of λ650 mμ irradiation; 2–3, λ620 mμ irradiation; 3–4, λ590 mμ irradiation; and 4–5, λ560 mμ irradiation.

Partial bleaching experiments established that the "rhodopsin" present as the greater proportion of the total photosensitive pigment has λ_{max} 486±1 mμ (Table 3; Fig. 5B, Curve 1). In addition to this pigment, however, there is another, which is much more sensitive to red light. The partial bleaching experiment with the retinal extract of *S. sierra* showed that both pigments have the same product of bleaching (Fig. 4) and are both "rhodopsins". As with *Paralabrax*, a nomogram construct was fitted to the difference spectrum obtained by bleaching with red light (Fig. 5B, Curve 2). The close coincidence of the experimental data and the nomogram points establishes that this second "rhodopsin" has λ_{max}=530±3 mμ. Curve 2 cannot be matched by any combination of "rhodopsins" with λ_{max} 535 and 486 mμ, indicating that λ_{max} of the red-sensitive component must be less than 535 mμ. The visual pigments appear to be the same in both species of Spanish mackerel, but the red-sensitive component of *Scomberomorus concolor* was not as well characterized as that of *S. sierra*, in experiments done three years later.

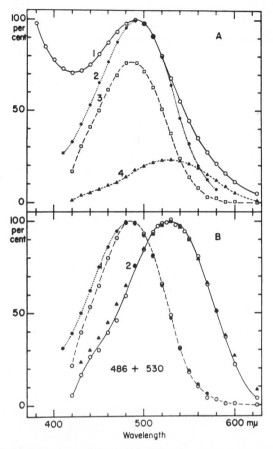

FIG 5A. Curve 1, density spectrum of sample 11A of *Scomberomorus sierra*; curve 2, constructed from Dartnall's nomogram, assuming λ_{max}=494 mμ. Curves 1 and 2 scaled to 100% at their maximum. Curve 3, difference spectrum of red-insensitive component (sample 11A, curve 3–5); curve 4, difference spectrum of red-sensitive component (11A, curve 1–2). Curves 3 and 4 scaled so as to approximate in sum to the total difference spectrum.

FIG. 5B.   Difference spectra of visual pigments of *Scomberomorus sierra*, scaled to 100%. ○, red-insensitive component (sample 11A, curve 3–5); ○, red-sensitive component (11A, curve 1–2). ●, constructed from Dartnall's nomogram, λ_{max}=486 mμ; ▲, constructed from Dartnall's nomogram, λ_{max}=530 mμ.

DISCUSSION

"Rhodopsins" and the Photic Environment

The "rhodopsins" described in this paper will increase the already well-founded impression of an astonishing diversity of visual pigments among teleost fishes (see Tables in DARTNALL, 1962, pp. 529–531). An attempt to correlate the spectral position of "rhodopsins" with the phylogenetic relationships of marine teleosts showed no evident trends except that closely related species often have very similar visual pigments (MUNZ, 1957). The spectral locations of these "rhodopsins" have been correlated much more successfully with the general habitat occupied in the case of bathypelagic (DENTON and WARREN, 1957; MUNZ, 1958a) and turbid-water marine species (MUNZ, 1958c). WALD *et al.* (1957) attempted a correlation of this sort also: with depth of habitat. To what extent need the conclusions drawn in these earlier studies be modified by results obtained with epipelagic and rocky-shore teleosts?

The five species called "rocky-shore" fishes in the present study are a conservative group, with respect to their visual pigment. The sheephead, *Pimelometopon pulchrum*, should also be included: it is a species living in rocky habitats from the surface to moderate depths. Its "chief", or more abundant, rhodopsin has $\lambda_{max} = 497$ mμ (MUNZ, 1958b). In these species the range of λ_{max} of the chief rhodopsin is only from 497 to 500 mμ. It might be possible to extend this list somewhat by including one or more of the species examined by WALD *et al.* (1957), but these authors did not state whether they tested the homogeneity of the visual pigments reported. Their results, therefore, are not included here.

In marked contrast is the situation in the "epipelagic" species, in some of which the chief "rhodopsin" has shifted its spectral position to shorter wavelengths. These fishes all live in surface waters often well away from the coast or belong, at least, to families (jacks and mackerels) with many epipelagic members. In this small sample of six species, the chief "rhodopsin" ranged in λ_{max} from 499 to 486 mμ. Further work designed to test the general validity of this trend is desirable.

The apparent correlation between depth of habitat and λ_{max} of the visual pigment (WALD *et al.*, 1957) is clearly incompatible with the experimental results presented here and should be abandoned. Marine teleosts living near the ocean surface may have "rhodopsins" ranging in λ_{max} all the way from 486 to 499 mμ (epipelagic species), 497 to 500 mμ (rocky-shore species) or 504 to 512 mμ (turbid-water species; MUNZ, 1958c). This would represent a depth range from 140 fathoms below the surface to about 80 fathoms above it, by extrapolation of the scheme of WALD *et al.* (1957, Fig. 2). Whatever may be shared by bathypelagic and some epipelagic fishes besides the spectral position of their "rhodopsins", it is not depth of habitat.

Another possible interpretation of these results is that there is a general correlation between the spectral location of "rhodopsins" and the dominant wavelengths of light in each habitat. This correlation appears to be valid in the case of bathypelagic fishes (DENTON and WARREN, 1957; WALD *et al.*, 1957; and MUNZ, 1958a) and probably also for fishes inhabiting the turbid coastal waters along sandy shores and bays (MUNZ, 1958c). It can be extended to rocky-shore and epipelagic species.

Measurements of the spectral distribution of sunlight with a submarine photometer by JERLOV and KULLENBERG (1946) and JERLOV (1951) showed that the wavelength of maximum light transmission in different types of sea water varies from 470 to 600 mμ. Thus, the clearest ocean water has a maximum at 470 mμ and average oceanic water at 475 mμ. In the clearest coastal water this maximum is at 500 mμ, but in average coastal water it is shifted to about 550 mμ. Average inshore water has a maximum at about 600 mμ. The spectral transmission curves are broad, but unlike the density spectra of different visual pigments, they are not merely translated along the wavelength scale. Rather, the shift in λ_{max} of transmission in this series of water types represents the progressive narrowing of the transmission curve of pure water by blocking off the short-wavelength end of the spectrum. This is due in part to light-scattering by suspended particles and in part to absorption by plant pigments such as chlorophyll (YENTSCH, 1960). As would be expected, therefore, the transmission is substantially reduced in coastal and inshore waters. Jerlov measured the spectral distribution of sunlight in sea water and calculated the transmission maxima by using the known spectral distribution of solar energy at the earth's surface. To illustrate the effects of these transmission differences, even in the upper water layers, the relative spectral distribution of sunlight remaining at a depth of 10 m (5 m in the two most turbid water types) has been calculated (on an energy basis). This information is presented graphically in Fig. 6. The clearest and average oceanic water are Jerlov's Types I and II (JERLOV, 1951, p. 51), and the clearest coastal, average coastal and average inshore types are Types 1, 5 and

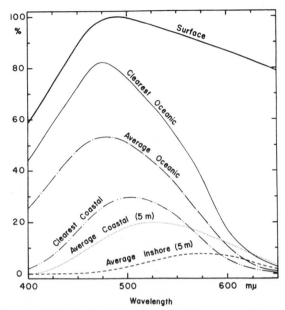

FIG. 6. Relative spectral distribution of solar energy in different types of sea water. Ordinate in relative energy units, expressed as percentage of the maximum energy incident at earth's surface. The curve for sunlight at the earth's surface is from the data of Birge and James (in CLARKE, 1939). The spectral distribution of sunlight remaining at a depth of 10 m (5 m in the two most turbid water types) was calculated from the data of JERLOV (1951) and JERLOV and KULLENBERG (1946). See text for details.

8, respectively, from JERLOV and KULLENBERG (1946). It should be emphasized that these curves are only approximate, for several factors will influence the spectral distribution in any actual experiment. Among these are solar altitude, cloud cover, spectral transmission of the water mass being studied and depth at which the measurements are made. Nevertheless, the measurements of JERLOV (1951) at many oceanic stations resemble the calculated curves. The variation among individual water samples will be much greater close to shore, but the curves still serve to illustrate the range to be expected. Thus, although a rigorous treatment is not possible, it can be said that there exists a rough series of marine environments distinguished by the λ_{max} of available light.

The spectral positions of the "rhodopsins" of marine teleosts appear to be correlated with this feature of the photic environment and adapted to it. Those fishes living in the "bluest" environments—bathypelagic and epipelagic species—are similar in having visual pigments with spectral maxima not far removed from the wavelengths at which the most energy is available. This parallelism between the two ecological assemblages of pelagic fishes is regarded as considerably strengthening the interpretations presented here. The same correlation holds true for rocky-shore fishes, which usually live in the clearest coastal waters. Species inhabiting the turbid, greenish-yellow water characteristic of sandy coasts and bays do show a tendency for their visual pigments to shift to longer wavelengths, but only by five or 10 mμ. In view of the red-sensitive, second "rhodopsins" possessed by some marine species (next section), it is not clear why this shift should be so limited. Nonetheless, comparison of the visual pigments of *Coryphopterus* and its turbid-water relatives (MUNZ, 1958c, Fig. 1) suggests that even small shifts may substantially increase the sensitivity to longer wavelengths. In other words, the visual pigments of marine bony fishes appear to have been selected to confer greater sensitivity in the spectral region that predominates in the particular aquatic environment that they inhabit. Undoubtedly there are exceptions to this statement; but, in general, it would account for the diversity of the "rhodopsins" of marine teleosts, in contrast to the more stable situation in terrestrial vertebrates (the geckos are a fascinating exception; CRESCITELLI, 1956, 1958a, 1958b, 1963). In fresh-water fishes the presence of retinene₂ pigments ("porphyropsins") complicates matters, and no comparable generalizations have yet been hazarded.

The Second "Rhodopsin"

Not infrequently in experiments of the type described, a second "rhodopsin" may be detected in retinal extracts of a particular species. The most noted example has been the "iodopsin" of the chicken (WALD *et al.*, 1955). Others have been more or less fully characterized in the pigeon (BRIDGES, 1962), certain geckos (CRESCITELLI, 1958b, 1963), a bathypelagic teleost (MUNZ, 1958a), the sheephead (MUNZ, 1958b) and several other marine fishes (WALD *et al.*, 1954). At least in the case of the chicken the second visual pigment has been claimed to be a cone pigment. The second "rhodopsins" of *Paralabrax clathratus*, *Scomberomorus concolor* and *S. sierra* may also be added to this list. The visual pigments of *Paralabrax clathratus* (λ_{max} 500 and 520 mμ) are very similar to those of the sheephead (λ_{max} 497 and 520 mμ), which lives in a similar rocky-shore habitat.

The red-sensitive "rhodopsin" of the Spanish mackerels deserves special mention as a possible visual pigment of the cones. It is present in enough concentration to be readily apparent in the density spectrum of the unbleached retinal extract, forming approximately one-fourth of the total visual pigment present. There is no interference from the light-absorbing carotenoids that complicate experiments with the chicken and pigeon. In addition, the red-sensitive pigment is not destroyed by hydroxylamine or by alkaline conditions. Experimentally, therefore, this system may have several desirable features. But is the red-sensitive pigment a cone pigment? No answer is possible yet. It is true, however, that the rapid-swimming, active scombrid fishes possess large eyes with fairly numerous large cones in the retinae. O'CONNELL (1963) has made a careful study of the retinal histology and relative abundance of visual receptors in several marine teleosts, including the jack mackerel and Pacific mackerel. Among fishes, the scombrids would seem to be an obvious group to examine for cone pigments. This argument is somewhat vitiated, however, by the frustrations experienced by a number of investigators who have attempted to extract visual pigments from the pure-cone retinae of several terrestrial vertebrates (DARTNALL, 1960). Clearly the last words on this subject remain to be written, but the eyes of the mackerels and tunas may furnish valuable material for future experiments.

Acknowledgements—The short list of species examined in this study scarcely suggests the efforts that were made during three years to obtain them. I wish to acknowledge the debt that I owe Dr. BOYD W. WALKER for his help following an automobile accident that cut short one of the expeditions to Mexico. To my fellow graduate students who had the misfortune to be with me on that trip, I continue to be grateful for the way in which they gave up their own plans and handled the emergency. I am also glad to acknowledge the help and advice of Drs. F. CRESCITELLI and C. L. HUBBS.

REFERENCES

BRIDGES, C. D. B. (1962). Visual pigments of the pigeon (*Columba livia*). *Vision Res.* **2**, 125–137.
CLARKE, G. L. (1939). The utilization of solar energy by aquatic organisms. In *Problems in Lake Biology*, *Publs. Am. Assoc. Adv. Sci.* **10**, 27–38 (Ed. MOULTON, F. R.). Science Press, Lancaster, Pa.
CRESCITELLI, F. (1956). The nature of the gecko visual pigment. *J. gen. Physiol.* **40**, 217–231.
CRESCITELLI, F. (1958a). The natural history of visual pigments. *Ann. N. Y. Acad. Sci.* **74**, 230–255.
CRESCITELLI, F. (1958b). Evidence for a blue-sensitive component in the retina of the gecko, *Oedura monilis*. *Science* **127**, 1442–1443.
CRESCITELLI, F. (1963). The photosensitive retinal pigment system of *Gekko gekko*. *J. gen. Physiol.* **47**, 33–52.
CRESCITELLI, F. and DARTNALL, H. J. A. (1954). A photosensitive pigment of the carp retina. *J. Physiol.* **125**, 607–627.

DARTNALL, H. J. A. (1952). Visual pigment 467, a photosensitive pigment present in tench retinae. *J. Physiol.* **116**, 257–289.

DARTNALL, H. J. A. (1953). The interpretation of spectral sensitivity curves. *Brit. med. Bull.* **9**, 24–30.

DARTNALL, H. J. A. (1956). Further observations on the visual pigments of the clawed toad, *Xenopus laevis. J. Physiol.* **134**, 327–337.

DARTNALL, H. J. A. (1957). *The Visual Pigments.* Methuen, London.

DARTNALL, H. J. A. (1960). Visual pigments of colour vision. In *Mechanisms of Colour Discrimination*, pp. 147–161 (Ed. GALIFRET, Y.). Pergamon Press, London.

DARTNALL, H. J. A. (1962). The photobiology of visual processes. In *The Eye*, vol. 2, pp. 323–533 (Ed. DAVSON, H.). Academic Press, New York.

DENTON, E. J. and WARREN, F. J. (1957). The photosensitive pigments in the retinae of deep-sea fish. *J. Mar. biol. Ass. U.K.* **36**, 651–662.

JERLOV, N. G. (1951). Optical studies of ocean waters. *Svenska Djuphavexpeditionen 1947–48*, Rep. **3**, 1–59.

JERLOV (JOHNSON), N. G. and KULLENBERG, B. (1946). On radiant energy measurements in the sea. *Svenska hydrogr.-biol. Komm. Skr., 3:e Ser. Hydrografi* **1**, 1–27.

MUNZ, F. W. (1956). A new photosensitive pigment of the euryhaline teleost, *Gillichthys mirabilis. J. gen. Physiol.* **40**, 233–249.

MUNZ, F. W. (1957). *The photosensitive retinal pigments of marine and euryhaline teleost fishes.* Ph.D. Thesis, University of California, Los Angeles.

MUNZ, F. W. (1958a). Photosensitive pigments from the retinae of certain deep-sea fishes. *J. Physiol.* **140**, 220–235.

MUNZ, F. W. (1958b). Retinal pigments of a labrid fish. *Nature, Lond.* **181**, 1012–1013.

MUNZ, F. W. (1958c). The photosensitive retinal pigments of fishes from relatively turbid coastal waters. *J. gen. Physiol.* **42**, 445–459.

O'CONNELL, C. P. (1963). The structure of the eye of *Sardinops caerulea, Engraulis mordax*, and four other pelagic marine teleosts. *J. Morph.* **113**, 287–329.

WALD, G. (1936). Pigments of the retina. II. Sea robin, sea bass and scup. *J. gen. Physiol.* **20**, 45–56.

WALD, G., BROWN, P. K. and BROWN. P. S. (1957). Visual pigments and depths of habitat of marine fishes. *Nature, Lond.* **180**, 969–971.

WALD, G., BROWN, P. K. and SMITH, P. H. (1954). Red-sensitive pigments of the fish retina. *Am. Soc. exp. Biol., Feder. Proc.* **13**, 316.

WALD, G., BROWN, P. K. and SMITH, P. H. (1955). Iodopsin. *J. gen. Physiol.* **38**, 623–681.

YENTSCH, C. S. (1960). The influence of phytoplankton pigments on the color of sea water. *Deep Sea Res.* **7**, 1–9.

THE EVOLUTION OF PHOTOPIC VISUAL PIGMENTS IN FISHES[1]

W. N. McFarland

Section of Ecology and Systematics, Cornell University,
Ithaca, New York 14850, U.S.A.

and

F. W. Munz

Department of Biology, University of Oregon,
Eugene, Oregon 97403, U.S.A.

(*Received* 15 *August* 1974; *in revised form* 5 *January* 1975)

Abstract—The feeding strategies of diurnal, tropical marine fishes correlate with the visual pigments extracted from their retinae and with the photic environments in which they hunt prey. Two basic feeding modes prevail: (1) silhouetting prey from below against the surface background light; and (2) contrasting prey against other fields of view, which are more monochromatic. Fishes that silhouette prey from below possess a single visual pigment matched to the spectral distribution of downwelling light. This maximizes the contrast between the brighter background and darker target. To predators that view prey in the horizontal field, their targets may appear either darker or brighter than the background. The photocontrast of a nonreflective target is maximized by a class of cones with a matching visual pigment. But the contrast of reflective ("bright") targets is enhanced by visual pigments offset from the spectral distribution of the monochromatic blue background. Thus, the evolutionary selection of multiple photopic systems, and of color vision itself, is probably related to the maximization of visual contrast against monochromatic backgrounds.

DEDICATION

As graduate students during the 1950s, both of us were privileged to know Gordon Walls. His unending curiosity into the mysteries that surround vertebrate vision has left its mark on each of us. This paper considers environmental factors and evolutionary pressures that may have molded vertebrate color vision. The data we present lend support to the suggestion made by Walls in *The Vertebrate Eye* that color vision evolved to enhance contrast between object and background. We therefore dedicate this paper to Gordon Lynn Walls, out of respect for his memory and his insight.

INTRODUCTION

Among the vertebrates, color vision is present in many diurnal fishes, some amphibians, and most lizards, turtles, and birds. In mammals it is well developed only among higher primates (Walls, 1942). How color discrimination evolved is a question of central importance to vertebrate biology and of keen interest to man. From the recent microspectrophotometric studies of Marks (1965), Brown and Wald (1964), and Liebman (1972), it seems firmly established that vertebrate color vision depends, for the most part, on different classes of photoreceptor cells, each defined by a different spectral photosensitivity. Considered as a behavior, color discrimination is a diurnal phenomenon, a fact that agrees with the presence of differ-

ent visual pigments in the cones of those vertebrates investigated (birds may provide an exception; Liebman, 1972). Clearly, in considering vertebrate color vision, one deals with photopic visual processes (although there may be occasional exceptions among deep-sea fishes).

Many suggestions have been formulated over the years to explain the evolution of vertebrate color vision. Most have dealt with possible modifications of photoreceptors and neuronal layers of the retina (see especially Edridge-Green, 1920; Ladd-Franklin, 1929; Willmer, 1949; Pickford, 1951) and have hardly considered function. Only Wallace (1891, p. 411) and Walls (1942, p. 463) appear to have seriously asked the question "Why color vision?" Each suggested that color detection originated to provide for the strongest contrast and, therefore, to enhance the visibility of objects against the background. We believe that this simple and prescient suggestion is correct.

What types of evidence are required to test their hypothesis? In our view at least four types of data are necessary: (1) histological examination of retinal structure; (2) spectrometric measurement of the cone pigments from an assemblage of vertebrates; (3) accurate description of the photic environment in which the visual behaviors of these animals are performed; and (4) knowledge of those critical behaviors which require photopic vision. Data fulfilling these requirements are available for some marine tropical fishes. It is our purpose to formulate a more detailed hypothesis on how color discrimination may have evolved in fishes and to examine the evidence relevant to this hypothesis. We feel that the arguments, although speculative, also provide a clearer picture of how photopic visual pigments serve a species.

[1] This investigation was supported by research grants (EY00323 and EY00324) from the Division of Research Grants and Fellowships, National Eye Institute, National Institutes of Health, U.S. Public Health Service.

From *Vision Research* 15: 1071–1080. Reprinted by permission.

OFFSET VISUAL PIGMENTS—A BASIS FOR COLOR DISCRIMINATION

John Lythgoe indicated that the visual pigments of several fishes do not match the spectrum of background spacelight against which objects are detected (Lythgoe, 1966, 1968). Rather, he felt that their visual pigments are displaced or "offset" to longer wavelengths. In a forceful argument, based in part on the visual contrast equations developed by Duntley (1962, 1963), Lythgoe suggested that the offsetting of visual pigments serves to enhance the contrast and, therefore, the visibility of targets seen against the underwater spacelight. Since the visual pigment data he obtained represented rod pigments (Lythgoe, 1966; Dartnall and Lythgoe, 1965), Lythgoe properly applied his argument to scotopic visual function. The absence of a spectral match between pigment and available light suggested that evolutionary forces molding scotopic vision had selected for enhanced contrast rather than for maximum photosensitivity.

At that time the twilight spectrum near the surface in clear seas was believed to be similar to the daytime underwater spectrum, although slightly red shifted (Lythgoe, 1966). We later demonstrated, however, that the underwater spectrum is subject to a blue shift during twilight and that the absorbance characteristics of the scotopic pigments of coral-reef fishes match the "bluish" twilight spectrum (Munz and McFarland, 1973). We concluded that offsetting of the rod pigments does not exist, at least in this extensive sample of fishes. Selective forces have operated to maximize photosensitivity rather than contrast, as suggested by Lythgoe.

Nevertheless, there is a compelling logic in Lythgoe's discussions of how an offset visual pigment might serve a species to enhance contrast. We wondered, for example, whether offset visual pigments might function in photopic vision. In fact, as we pondered its implications in early 1968, his entire thesis seemed to fit to what we knew of the diurnal visual behaviors of tropical marine fishes. The subsequent steady accumulation of data on the photopic visual pigments of these fishes (Part I of this series) and our increased understanding of the daytime photic environment (Part II) have convinced us that Lythgoe's argument should be applied to photopic vision. We should like to review, therefore, the concept set forth by Lythgoe (1966) of how an offset visual pigment enhances contrast, but we shall put it within the framework of photic conditions that prevail in a clear tropical sea during the day (Part II), not during twilight or at night.

As an example, consider the spectral distribution of light cast on the various parts of its retina when a fish is swimming either 1 m beneath the surface or somewhat deeper at 25 m. In general, the upward lines of sight will contain considerably more green, yellow and red light than the horizontal and downward lines of sight, especially at 1 m (Fig. 1). At 1 m, the median wavelength for the spectral distribution along the upward lines of sight will be around 525–550 nm and in the horizontal and downward directions 455–470 nm (Fig. 1 and Part II, Table 3). For 25 m, the spectral distribution is very different in the upward lines of sight, since long wavelengths are attenuated in the longer optical path (Fig. 1). In detection of an object at either depth, the degree

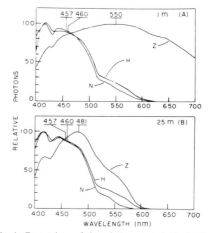

Fig. 1. Comparison of the relative spectral distributions of light in a clear, deep tropical sea along different lines of sight, with the receptor (a) at 1 m beneath the surface and (b) at 25 m beneath the surface. Z = zenith, H = horizontal, and N = nadir line of sight. Numbers above each curve are the λP_{50} spectral index values (in nanometers). Note the similarity in shape between the horizontal and nadir distributions and the difference between the zenith distributions.

of contrast produced between object and background will depend on several factors. These are: object direction, size, distance and reflectivity, and several features of the fish's eye, especially the spectral absorptive properties of the pre-retinal media and the visual pigments. If object size, distance and position are constant, then for each depth it is possible to assess the effect of matched and offset visual pigments on visual contrast for both bright and dark targets. Light from the horizontal background surrounding either a bright or dark object is very blue (λP_{50} = ca. 460–470 nm, Fig. 1). To match this background a fish would need a photopic visual pigment with a λ_{max} near 460 nm. Against this background an object will appear brighter than background only if the reflected light that lies within the absorption spectrum of the matched photopic pigment is more intense than the background. Yellow and red light, which would be reflected from the object for several meters at 1-m depth, would not be detected. A dark nonreflective object, on the contrary, would be readily distinguished from the "bright" background by lack of stimulation of the cone cells that the color shades. In a very real sense an eye with a matched visual pigment detects the presence of an object by not "seeing" it, for both contrast and sensitivity are maximized for dark objects. To represent this visual condition we shall use the symbol C^m, where C stands for cone cell and m a visual pigment spectrally matched to the background spacelight (Fig. 2).

What happens if the visual pigment has a different spectral photosensitivity than C^m? Suppose a λ_{max} at 520 nm rather than 460 nm. This condition, i.e. an offset visual pigment, we represent by the symbol C^o. The photocontrast of a reflective object viewed horizontally would be greater than for C^m since the C^o pigment would be less sensitive than the C^m pig-

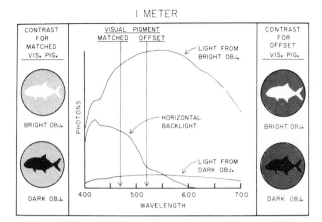

Fig. 2. Comparisons of the relative photocontrast of "bright" (reflective) and "dark" (nonreflective) objects viewed along the horizontal line of sight at 1 m beneath the surface by fishes with visual pigments matched to (P469), or offset from (P521), the backlight. Both bright and dark targets are assumed to be grey. Light reflected into the horizontal field includes direct reflections of sunlight. Close to the bright objects, reflected light will be 50 to 100 times more intense than the radiance of the horizontal background (scaling not indicated on the ordinate). The insets portray the relative photocontrasts that would be produced by each visual pigment. The matched pigment enhances the contrast of a dark object and the offset pigment results in contrast enhancement of a bright target.

ment to background light. For the same reason, a dark object would produce less contrast for C^o than for C^m. As Lythgoe (1966, 1968) pointed out, offsetting a visual pigment reduces photosensitivity to available light, but enhances contrast to reflective targets. Nonreflective targets, as demonstrated, are detected best by a matching (C^m) visual pigment.

Maximum visibility of both reflective and nonreflective objects, therefore, requires more than a mosaic of cones all containing the same visual pigment. Manifold systems are required—at the least, two classes of cones. This would require both C^m and C^o cones in the same retina. The trichromatic retina could provide for a matched cone pigment (C^m) and two offset pigments (C^o), one at longer and the second at shorter wavelengths than C^m. The evolution of high visual acuity with maximum contrast under varied photic conditions would favor the selection and maintenance of separate visual pathways for these different cones. In other words, we have described the elements necessary for color vision.

Would a multiple visual pigment system function as well at greater depths? To match the horizontal visual field at 25 m beneath the surface, a visual pigment should absorb maximally somewhere near 460 nm (Fig. 1). A λ_{max} in this region would also provide a good match to downwelling light at 25 m ($\lambda P_{50} = 481$ nm, Fig. 1b). Far less long-wavelength light penetrates this deeply (Fig. 1b). Thus, both the background and the light reflected from an object will be blue. An offset pigment with its λ_{max} at 520 nm would be less effective at 25 m than it is near the surface. For dark objects at 25-m depth, as at 1 m, the C^o pigment would be less photosensitive to the background light than the C^m pigment (Fig. 3). As the total visual field becomes more nearly monochromatic, therefore, offsetting diminishes as an effective photochemical means of enhancing contrast. One might predict, therefore, that single, matched photo-

pic visual pigments would be typical of fishes that dwell at greater depths, and that multiple photopic pigments (both matched and offset) would be common in surface fishes.

We have considered two simple cases where the background spacelight, with one exception, is spectrally narrow banded (Fig. 1). Only downwelling light at 1 m beneath the surface has a broad spectrum compared to either horizontal or upwelling light (Fig. 1). Thus, the spacelight background will be brighter and spectrally broader for a fish near the surface when it looks up than when it looks in other directions. This photic condition leads to the conclusion that both C^m and C^o cones, when directed upward, could function only by silhouetting objects against the surface light. Even highly reflective objects, although brighter than dark objects, would appear dim relative to the "bright" surface. In this line of sight, both C^m and C^o pigments would match background light since their absorbance spectra are narrower than, and contained within, the broad spectrum of downwelling light. It is only when visual tasks assume a horizontal or downward axis that the background spectrum narrows (Fig. 1). Under this condition offsetting becomes important to the enhancement of contrast. And this is only true near the surface. At greater depths, of course, the C^m pigment ($\lambda_{max} = ca.$ 460 nm) effectively matches downwelling light (Fig. 1). The spectrum reflected from objects is almost as narrow as that of the background light, diminishing the effectiveness of offsetting farther from the water surface.

Spectral narrowing of the background against which objects are viewed can be considered the essential environmental factor that allows for selection of multiple photopic pigments. Light levels must be great enough to permit a high degree of visual acuity. These conditions are typical of aquatic habitats during the day, and it is significant that color vision

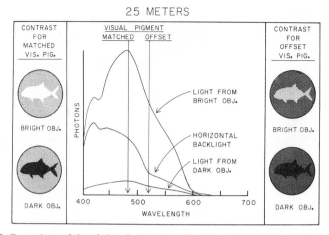

Fig. 3. Comparisons of the relative photocontrast of "bright" and "dark" objects viewed along the horizontal line of sight at 25 m beneath the surface by fishes with visual pigments matched to (P483), or offset from (P521), the backlight. Assumptions as in Fig. 2. At 25 m depth, reflections from bright objects will be from 20 to 40 times more intense than the radiance of horizontal backlight. The matched pigment produces greater photocontrast than the offset pigment for both bright and dark objects.

is widely distributed among fishes. Lythgoe's discussions of offset visual pigments indicate that contrast is most enhanced when "bright" targets, reflecting a broad spectrum, are viewed against a spectrally narrow background. Our measurements show that in the open sea this condition occurs throughout the lower visual hemisphere (see Part II). In shallow littoral depths, as typified by coral reefs, the horizontal lines of sight are most nearly monochromatic. Downward lines of sight are spectrally broad, very much like downwelling light near the surface (see Part II). To relate the different photopic visual pigments present in tropical fishes to their behaviors, one must also differentiate between pelagic and shallow-water fishes. Because the relationships are clearer, we shall consider first the behavior and visual pigments of pelagic fishes. Later we shall attempt to unravel the more complex situation presented by coral-reef fishes.

BEHAVIOR AND VISUAL PIGMENTS OF TROPICAL PELAGIC FISHES

The pelagic fishes that we have investigated are either surface limited or ascend from greater depths to feed at or near the surface. All are diurnal predators. The mahi mahi (*Coryphaena hippurus*), which is surface limited, and the skipjack tuna (*Katsuwonus pelamis*), which lives at greater depths, provide specific examples. The mahi mahi probably seldom ventures below depths of 15 m; it feeds mostly in the upper 6 m (Rose and Hassler, 1974). Both its morphology and visual system support this view. The mahi mahi chases flyingfish, sauries, carangids, and crustaceans at the surface; and its main visual axis is oriented forward along the horizontal line of sight, with well-developed binocularity (Tamura and Wisby, 1963). The skipjack swims deeper (at least to 70 m, according to Talbot and Penrith, 1963, and Blackburn, 1965) and feeds at depth or takes surface prey by rushing up from deeper water. Its visual axis is directed upward and forward (Tamura and Wisby, 1963). Thus, the skipjack must detect surface prey against

the "bright" surface light. For mahi mahi, prey must be contrasted against a "bluish" background which is less "bright" than the downwelling surface light. What are the specific differences in photic conditions for these two distinctive feeding modes? Can the demonstrated differences in the visual pigments of these two species be related to the different photic conditions associated with their dissimilar feeding modes?

In Part I we showed that the retinal extracts of skipjack never contained more than a single visual pigment (P483₁). Although we obtained a few dark-adapted specimens, most of the individuals were caught during the day and killed immediately. Therefore, the cones were included in the material that was extracted. Two other tunas (*Euthunnus yaito* and *Neothunnus macropterus*) and the related wahoo (*Acanthocybium solandri*) and marlins (*Istiompax marlina* and *Makaira ampla*) all had single visual pigments with nearly the same λ_{max} (Munz and McFarland, 1973). But these are active diurnal predators with many cones (Tamura and Wisby, 1963). Why don't they also have a visual pigment, sensitive to longer wavelengths, of the type that we have ascribed to the cones (Part I)? Of course, the tunas live in a very "blue" environment, where such a pigment might not absorb enough light to be effective. It occurred to us in Hawaii, while making light measurements, that the visual pigment that we extract probably comes from both rods and cones. Shortly after our return, we were excited by the report of Liebman and Granda (1971) that in two species of turtles the "rod pigment" also occurs in one class of cones. This corroboration of our guess by microspectrophotometry (MSP) has been extended to a frog, a salamander, and a fish (Liebman, 1972, 1973).

At the depths from which the skipjack hunts (25 m or more), available light is predominantly blue. The spectra of downwelling and horizontal light at 25-m depth and the absorbance spectrum of its visual pigment are compared in Fig. 4. (We do not know the effective concentration of this pigment in the cones

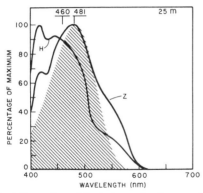

Fig. 4. Comparison of the background radiance spectra at 25 m depth (heavy lines; Z = zenith and H = horizontal line of sight) and the absorbance spectrum of visual pigment P483 of the skipjack (area covered by diagonal lines). Radiance and absorbance spectra have been scaled to the same maximum. The λP_{50} values of the horizontal (460 nm) and zenith (481 nm) radiance spectra are indicated.

and must use absorbance, rather than the appropriate absorption function, which would be slightly broader.) It is clear that P483 provides an excellent spectral match to the light available in all visual fields; it is a visual pigment of the C^m type. The lack of sufficient yellow and green light in downwelling light at these depths accounts for the absence of multiple visual pigments. To be sure, an offset pigment at 520 nm might enhance the contrast of highly reflective objects. But its advantage is questionable since most natural targets are protectively colored. Rather, we suggest that a maximum sensitivity to background spacelight is more advantageous for detecting objects viewed from below. In our experience objects viewed from below, whether reflective or nonreflective, almost invariably appear darker than the surface. For this visual task a spectrally-matched visual pigment provides both maximum sensitivity and contrast. In a discussion of feeding behavior by sea lions, Hobson (1966) pointed out that they almost always dive below their prey and strike upward. This tactic is used whether the prey are near the surface or at depth. The sea lion obtains an advantage because its attack is directed from the prey's dimmest visual field. But, significantly, the prey also are silhouetted against the brighter surface. The feeding behavior of other tunas is generally similar to that of the skipjack, but some species (e.g. *Neothunnus macropterus*) swim at depths as great as 150 m (Blackburn, 1965).

These ideas received an independent confirmation from the electrophysiological investigation of Tamura, Hanyu and Niwa (1972). The spectral sensitivity of the S-potential, retinal ganglion cell potential, and the gross electroretinogram were recorded from the skipjack and two other species of tunas. In every case only a spectral pattern of the luminosity type was obtained. They never saw a response of the chromaticity type. The authors concluded that these tunas are probably color-blind. In their apparatus, narrowband stimuli were obtained by interference filters. The filter at 497 nm produced a greater response than

the adjacent 465- and 525-nm filters. Inspection of their records indicates that the maximum sensitivity is at a wavelength near 485 nm (rather than at 497 nm itself, as stated in their paper). Our own results and interpretations are completely consistent with this work.

The retinal extracts of mahi mahi represent an opposite extreme from the simplicity of the tunas. There is almost a surfeit of visual pigments (ternary mixtures are not easy to analyze!). In Part I we have described the evidence that there are three visual pigments ($P521_1$, $P499_1$ and $P469_1$) in this species. There, we ascribed P499 to the rods and P521 and P469 to the cones. But by analogy with the cases already discussed, might not P499 also be a cone (as well as rod) pigment? We shall make this assumption although a microspectrophotometric analysis is clearly desirable. It should be pointed out, however, that our general argument does not stand or fall upon this assumption.

The photic environment of the mahi mahi is also more complex than in the case of the skipjack. Let us consider, in as much detail as the current data allow, therefore, the visual task facing the mahi mahi as it lurks a meter or two beneath the surface, seeking prey. (This description is accurate, because the species is well known for hanging about in the shade of any debris floating at the surface. Even in schools, the mahi mahi is phlegmatic, in sharp contrast to the tunas.) Reflective targets are important. For example, the downwelling light that is then reflected horizontally from the silver flank of a flyingfish should contain approximately equal numbers of photons in the blue and green regions of the spectrum (*ca.* 450–530 nm), in addition to a substantial amount of yellow light (Fig. 5, curve Z). Background spacelight is more monochromatic and blue or blue-green, depending on the depth (Fig. 5, curve H). The P521 is clearly offset from the background light and is of the C^o type. This visual pigment, which is the

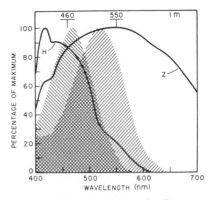

Fig. 5. Comparison of the background radiance spectra at 1 m depth (heavy lines; Z = zenith and H = horizontal line of sight) and the absorbance of two visual pigments of the mahi mahi (areas covered by diagonal lines). The blue-sensitive pigment (P469) is to the left of the more red-sensitive P521, and they overlap. The middle pigment P499 has been omitted for clarity of the figure. Radiance and absorbance spectra have been scaled to the same maximum. The λP_{50} values of the horizontal (460 nm) and zenith (550 nm) radiance spectra are indicated.

most abundant of the three in extracts of light-adapted fish (Part I, Table 6), is well suited for the detection of bright objects against the horizontal background. Each of the other visual pigments (P499 and P469) is probably used either as a matching (C^m) or as an offset (C^o) pigment, depending on the depth beneath the surface and the line of sight (Fig. 5). In water less clear than at Eniwetok, P499 may almost match the horizontal background light; P469 would, therefore, be offset to shorter wavelengths. At somewhat greater depths, or looking downward, the roles of these two pigments would be reversed. Therefore, the mahi mahi is well equipped to detect targets, whether dark or reflective, in both the horizontal and downward directions, and from the surface down to a moderate depth. Does this species have color vision? This seems likely, but we are uncertain. At any rate, almost any target except the most cleverly countershaded should be perceived with maximum contrast from the background. (A rapid dash at the prey from a considerable distance completes this behavior.) One final complication: the mahi mahi has a yellow lens. Although we have not measured the transmission spectrum of the pre-retinal media, the yellow color of the lens probably acts only as a cutoff filter for short wavelengths and, therefore, should not affect the general argument.

Two other pelagic fishes, the carangid *Elagatis bipinnulatus* and the scombrid *Scomberomorus commersoni*, possess two extractable visual pigments. *Elagatis*, interestingly, has two pigments with λ_{max} values at 520 and 500 nm. Like the mahi mahi, it tends to live near the surface, although we are less sure that it is as strictly surface limited. Certainly, very similar photic conditions would prevail for both species when feeding. The two pigments, therefore, can be interpreted to maximize the ability of this carangid to detect both reflective and nonreflective targets. We consider $P520_1$ offset and $P500_1$ more closely matched to the background radiance in the horizontal field. In *Scomberomorus*, on the other hand, the two visual pigments are separated by a wider wavelength interval (λ_{max} 520 and 485 nm). This fish strikes at surface prey from below. Like the tunas, *S. cavalla*, the Caribbean counterpart of *S. commersoni*, has its visual axis directed upward and forward (Tamura and Wisby, 1963). But we have seen small groups of *S. cavalla* moving 3–10 m beneath the surface strike at highly reflective bait drifted to these depths. Thus, *Scomberomorus* is capable of taking prey near the surface when viewed horizontally. These scombrids, therefore, appear to occupy a position intermediate to the deeper-living billfishes, tunas, and wahoos, and the surface-limited mahi mahi and *Elagatis*.

SPECIAL FEATURES OF THE PHOTIC ENVIRONMENT

(1) *Countershading*

This discussion, in general, has assumed that visual tasks are performed by various pelagic predators against a background spacelight that varies in a precise manner in its levels of radiance and spectral composition for the different visual fields (Fig. 1). To a large extent this is true, but photic conditions also vary in other ways. For example, prey are not just reflective, but invariably are intricately countershaded to minimize contrast to background radiance.

This has been demonstrated by Denton and Nicol (1966), who have provided understanding of the physical basis of countershading. Two major properties are involved: general body shape and varying dorsoventral structural coloration. In general, to minimize detection from below, many pelagic fishes are laterally compressed. In this way the shadow cast against the bright surface background, although present, is minimal. Countershading functions best when prey are viewed from other directions. In the pelagic environment, the colors of most prey fishes match photic conditions. Thus, dorsally, many fishes are extremely blue, blue–greenish, or both. This dorsal coloration fades laterally into highly reflective, silvery sides and ventral surfaces. Of course, varied body shapes and countershading conceal predators as well as prey. In the mahi mahi, for example, blue–green and blue coloration occur dorsally and the body is deep and laterally compresssd. This shape could serve two functions. First, lateral compression minimizes the shadow the body casts and reduces its visibility to deeper-dwelling predators (large tunas, billfishes). Second, it reduces the cross-sectional profile that the mahi mahi might present when approaching prey. Deeper-living predators, such as tunas, have much rounder body cross-sections to accommodate the large trunk and caudal muscles that supply the propulsive force for their high velocity attacks. Generally, their dorsal surfaces are dark blue. They are, therefore, virtually invisible against the dark blue background of the deep water from which they attack. Innumerable examples exist, but the point is that the evolutionary forces that have molded predator–prey interactions in the pelagic environment have selected for body shapes and countershaded coloration that makes visual detection, at best, very difficult.

(2) *Flicker*

Biologically-induced flicker—target motion. Another factor that must influence target detection results from flicker of a target. This can be produced by locomotion of predator or prey in such a manner that reflections of downwelling light from the body surfaces momentarily increase or decrease in intensity. For example, flashes of light are commonly observed among schools of fish as individuals turn or roll. Whether such sudden and dramatic changes in the visibility of a single fish increase the success of predators is debatable. Actually such flashes may divert the attention of a predator from other fishes in a school, which although "dimmer" are constantly visible (Hobson, 1968). But flashes of a single fish might alert a predator, if seen against a constant background (see below).

Physically-induced movement—surface disturbance. Flicker also results from disturbance of the water surface. When measuring underwater light, a flat calm surface is preferred, for even small ripples produce bothersome oscillations in the record. But calm surface conditions are seldom characteristic of the ocean. Fishes, whether predator or prey, to survive must hunt and hide in spite of disturbed optical conditions. How then might surface flicker affect the visibility of objects? It is common experience to anyone who dives that a small area of the surface when viewed from below is alternately brighter and dimmer than the average background radiance. A larger area of the surface, therefore, is seen to dance with flickers. In a like manner, downwelling rays which flicker will produce reflections from objects that also wax and wane in intensity. Viewed from below, a fish would flicker like the surface. Specifically, the silvery sides and ventral surfaces of countershaded fishes would enhance such reflections. These reflections, therefore, mimic surface flicker and should reduce the chance of detection.

A reflective object viewed horizontally or from above, however, would flicker against a non-flickering blue background. But here the darker coloration of the dorsal surfaces would reduce reflections from surface light. When viewed horizontally, it is our personal experience that well-countershaded fishes seldom flicker. Countershading, consequently, is very effective in that it minimizes the chances that a fish will be detected under both disturbed and calm surface conditions.

Countershading, however, cannot obscure all reflections, and it remains likely that prey are often initially detected by sudden unavoidable reflections produced from surface flicker or by body movements. Ultimate success in the tracking and capture of prey, nevertheless, depends on continuous visual fixation of the target. This must be accomplished whether flicker is present or not. It is our contention, since countershading is so effective under varied optical conditions, that this critical aspect of predatory behavior, i.e. closure on prey, succeeds only because contrast vision has been maximized through natural selective forces. For visual pigments it has culminated in the presence of two or three pigments in surface-feeding predators. And this is the basis of hue discrimination.

BEHAVIOR AND VISUAL PIGMENTS OF CORAL-REEF FISHES

As indicated earlier, the photic environment in shallow tropical seas is more varied than in pelagic habitats. This is especially true of coral reefs, where there are "kaleidoscopic" arrangements of colors that span the visible spectrum. And it is true of the "targets" as well as the coral backgrounds. The astonishingly varied hues and patterns of coral-reef fishes are equalled among vertebrates only by birds. Their intense coloration contrasts vividly with the cryptic countershaded color patterns of pelagic fishes. Indeed, when diving, one is astonished that most reef fishes are so conspicuous. That the varied color patterns function as identification marks, cryptic colors, warning signs, or as behavioral releasers is documented elsewhere (Cott, 1940; Lorenz, 1962; Breder, 1972). Given this array of colors, whatever their specific functions, it is hard to avoid the assumption that most species must discriminate hues. What general correlations, therefore, can be made between the varied behaviors of different reef species, their extractable visual pigments, and the photic environment?

(1) Visual acuity and predator–prey interactions

A puzzling aspect of predator–prey interactions within the coral-reef community is the conspicuousness of prey fishes during the day. Their bright, contrasting coloration readily signals their presence. But what seems even more perilous than the colors of these fishes is their position on the reef. Many species,

especially damsel fishes, can be observed feeding on particulate matter in the water column between the coral heads and the surface. Perhaps it is significant that many of these species are countershaded and not emblazoned with color, for their position should make them ready targets for predators. But many other reef fishes (butterflyfishes, wrasses, triggerfishes, surgeonfishes and parrotfishes), most of which are conspicuously colored, also enter the water column above the reef. Their excursions are shorter, but all stray sufficiently far from cover that they should be vulnerable. Surprisingly, however, they are seldom attacked. This aspect of predator–prey interaction has been amply verified and discussed by Hobson (1968, 1972). We have suggested that the ineffectiveness of predators during the day results from their relatively lower visual acuity compared to the diurnal fishes upon which they prey (Munz and McFarland, 1973). The predators have cone densities that do not exceed 40,000 cells/mm^2 of retina. In contrast, the diurnal fishes (whether carnivore, omnivore or herbivore) all have cone densities that exceed 40,000 cells/mm^2. High cone densities are present throughout most of the retina. With this potential for high acuity over most of the visual field, a diurnal reef fish must have excellent surveillance of its surroundings. One can conclude simply that the prey have a visual advantage over their predators during the day. Threatening movements by a predator are detected immediately by the prey and evasive behaviors initiated. Often this involves movement toward the reef substrate or the tightening of a fish school (Hobson, 1968). Importantly, Hobson stresses that fish predation, if it occurs during the daytime, succeeds only when the prey is wounded or sick, i.e. it strays or deviates from normal behaviors. With this tactic, predators, although they may remain in the vicinity of their prey during the day, do not exert themselves in fruitless chases.

(2) Significance of λ_{max} of multiple visual pigments

How might the visual pigments relate to predator–prey interactions? We detected multiple visual pigments in 84 of the 99 species of diurnal reef fishes that we investigated. Of the 84 species with mixtures, 32 yielded enough of the red-sensitive component for estimation of its λ_{max} (Part I, Table 3). The red-sensitive pigments all have λ_{max} values between 518 and 541 nm. We have assumed that the other, more blue-sensitive (and more concentrated) pigment in each retinal extract is a scotopic pigment of the rods (Munz and McFarland, 1973). But let us also assume here—as we have for pelagic fishes that possess multiple pigments—that the blue-sensitive pigments function as photopic (cone) pigments as well as in scotopic vision. If this is correct, most diurnal reef fishes possess at least two photopic pigments—one with its λ_{max} near 525 nm, and one other between 480 and 500 nm.

Several features of these visual pigments can be related to the behaviors of coral-reef fishes and to photic properties of the reef habitat. In each species the individual λ_{max} values and their spectral separation are like those of pelagic fishes that possess multiple pigments. We believe that these similarities result from the action of similar selective forces related to photic conditions and visual requirements. For example, at any given depth beneath the surface, the spectral distribution and total radiance in the upward and horizontal fields of view are similar for the reef and pelagic habitats (Part II, Tables 3 and 4). Only the downward visual fields differ dramatically. In the shallow coral-reef habitat, both the spectrum and radiance of upwelling light are affected by the reflective properties of the substrate and by the depth (optical path length).

Function of multiple pigments in the upward and horizontal visual fields. Most reef fishes are shallow-water forms. Although some species occur at depths greater than 100 m (Brock and Chamberlain, 1968; Strasburg, Jones and Iversen, 1968), most live above 30 m and are abundant only in the uppermost 20 m, as are living corals. The horizontal background light is blue (Part II, Fig. 3) unless nearby coral heads are in the line of sight. At these depths there is also sufficient downwelling light in the wavelength range between 500 and 600 nm to produce target reflections at intensities that exceed photopic thresholds. As a result, the visual pigments with λ_{max} near 525 nm can function as offset pigments to enhance contrast of reflective objects as they do in pelagic surface predators.

The more blue-sensitive pigments can match the background light either when dark targets are viewed horizontally or, in greater depths, when they are silhouetted against the surface. Consider the following diurnal reef fishes: *Abudefduf abdominalis*, with $P496_1$ and $P527_1$; *Naso brevirostris*, $P492_1$ and $P523_1$; and *Chromis verater*, $P480_1$ and $P518_1$ (Part I, Table 3). *Abudefduf* typically inhabits reef structures close to the surface. As a cone pigment, P496 would be ideally suited to match the background radiance in a manner analogous to that described for the 500-nm pigments of the mahi mahi and *Elagatis*. In contrast, *Chromis* is characteristic of much greater depths. It seldom occurs above 20 m and is most abundant at approx 100 m (Brock and Chamberlain, 1968). Over this depth range, P480 is positioned centrally within the spectrum of available light and is a matching pigment. It would certainly provide maximum absorption of downwelling surface light between 20 and 60 m (Part II, Table 3). In the horizontal field of vision, or at greater depths, P480 would be offset slightly to longer wavelengths. But P480 should produce a good general spectral match to the background radiance in all visual fields. *Naso brevirostris* is intermediate in depth distribution (2–30 m). P490 provides an excellent compromise match to downwelling light from about 3 to 25 m ($\lambda P_{50} = ca.$ 510–480 nm; Part II, Table 3). If used in horizontally directed vision, P490 would be matched in shallow surface waters (1–3 m), but displaced about 10–15 nm to longer wavelengths at greater depths. This offset is analogous to the situation in *Chromis verater*. We feel that P490 is an evolutionary compromise that provides a fair visual match to background light in all directions of regard.

Function of multiple pigments in the downward visual field. In shallow depths, visual and optical problems are complex since background radiance and spectral distribution depend on substrate reflectivity, total depth, and the position of the receptor system in the water column (Part II, Tables 3 and 4). The backgrounds of coral, sand, and rubble are complex, in contrast to the remarkably uniform upwelling radiance in pelagic habitats. These backgrounds complicate the visual tasks of reef fishes, making it likely that more than one photopic mechanism would be developed. This may account for the presence of an offset pigment (P518) in the deep-dwelling *Chromis verater*, unlike its pelagic counterpart, the skipjack.

Consider the photic conditions facing *Abudefduf abdominalis* as it swims in the surge zone, in very shallow water (1 m). In the horizontal visual field, λP_{50} will vary around 492 m, a wavelength suggesting that P496 represents a general match to the background light. In contrast, if the bottom is reflective, the spectral distribution of background light that is cast on the dorsal retina would be greenish ($\lambda P_{50} = $ 528 nm; Part II, Table 3) as is light cast on the ventral retina ($\lambda P_{50} = $ 515 nm). Although reasonably well matched to the "greenishness" of the upward and downward visual fields, P527 is offset some 30 nm from the horizontal field. In this instance, what we usually consider the offset visual pigment (P527) can function to enhance contrast for both bright and dark targets, depending on their direction.

Similar reasoning suggests that P496, which matches horizontal spacelight, would be offset toward shorter wavelengths in viewing the zenith and nadir. But it is not. Rather, just beneath the surface, P496 matches all visual fields. We reemphasize that the spectral distribution of downwelling light near the surface as compared to greater depths is less monochromatic and quite flat between 450 and 600 nm (Fig. 1). Therefore, visual pigments that absorb maximally at any wavelength within this spectral region trap photons equally well and are matched rather than offset from background. The significance of the λ_{max} position of P496 in *Abudefduf abdominalis* lies, however, in its match to the horizontal visual field, from which P527 is offset.

Thus, as among the pelagic fishes, there appears to be a specific correspondence between habitat depth and visual behaviors on one hand and the visual pigments on the other. We have assumed that in most reef fishes the rod pigment is also contained within one class of cones. Although the diurnal species usually have an additional, more red-sensitive pigment, there may be others that we have not extracted. *Chaetodontoplus mesoleucas* is the only reef fish from which we obtained clear evidence of three pigments. Microspectrophotometry will be needed to answer these questions.

CONCLUSIONS

Except in tunas, multiple visual pigments are generally present in retinal extracts of diurnal, tropical marine fishes. We have measured the daytime photic conditions where these fishes actually live. We believe that the photopic visual pigments have evolved so that their spectral photosensitivities are either matched to, or offset from, the spectral distribution of available light. This conclusion is based on John Lythgoe's analysis (1966, 1968) of how the spectral position of visual pigments can maximize either photocontrast or photosensitivity. In our view, whether a visual pigment is considered matched or offset depends largely upon the background radiance associated with the lines of sight for which it is used. A given pigment can probably be used in either way, depending on the background light. The evolutionary selection of matching or offset visual pigments is not fortuitous, but depends upon the importance of dark or reflective targets, respectively, in the visual tasks associated with the animal's behavior.

In general, most of the surface and subsurface diurnal fishes that we sampled possess either binary or ternary mixtures of visual pigments. Many or even all of these may be derived from classes of cones in the retina. We have argued that the primary function of multiple systems seems to be enhancement of photocontrast (for diverse targets), as suggested by Gordon Walls (1942). The essential factor in the selection of multiple systems of photopic pigments was a narrowing in the spectrum of background light against which objects were viewed (Wallace, 1891). For broad flat spectra, as represented in downwelling surface light of tropical seas, all the known visual pigments of fishes must be matched pigments, for their narrower bandwidths absorb within the broad spectrum of available light. Offset visual pigments, therefore, must have been selected for only when the background radiance approached monochromaticity. In clear seas this condition has probably always been characteristic of horizontal radiance fields. Perhaps selective pressure for offset pigments was provided when early Ordovician or Silurian vertebrates gave up their benthic existence to become free-swimming. Certainly the horizontal visual fields would take on greater importance for the location of food and, significantly, would have been monochromatic and blue. The multiple systems of visual pigments were developed for daytime use, where light intensity would favor the separate pathways required for high visual acuity. These are the elements needed for "color vision" (i.e. hue discrimination). Thus, we hypothesize that elements of color vision first evolved in a fishlike vertebrate to provide better photocontrast and that this selection was given positive thrust by a narrowing of the spectrum of background light.

Monochromatic photic conditions are typical of aquatic habitats and color vision is widely distributed among fishes. But is the hypothesis more general? We think so. For example, may color vision in terrestrial vertebrates also find its evolutionary explanation in the presence of monochromatic backgrounds? For aquatic turtles the photic situation is similar to that of fishes. But for lizards, birds, and primates different photic conditions must prevail. Is it possible that the green mantle against which and within which tropical and temperate birds feed, hide, and hunt could act in this sense? Would the diffuse blue skylight, from which hawks and other birds of prey strike, effect an evolution of matched and offset visual pigments in their diurnal prey? In fact, man's color sense may owe its existence to the arboreal behavior of his progenitors and greenness of the habitat in which they lived. High photocontrast, as well as good visual acuity and binocularity, would certainly be beneficial to the complex analyses of three-dimensional space required for brachiation. These thoughts generalize the hypothesis and invite quantitative study of the interrelationships between photopic visual pigments of varied terrestrial vertebrates, their visual behaviors, and the photic backdrop against which such behaviors are executed. Whatever the results, they would provide a fitting memorial to Gordon Lynn Walls.

Acknowledgements—With Parts I and II and also our 1973 paper, this culminates an investigation that began eight years ago in 1967. But the roots of our inquiry began to grow much earlier, when we were both graduate students at the University of California, Los Angeles. Although they have not been directly involved in these particular studies, two of our professors had an immense influence on our training and, of necessity, our motivation and views of biology. To Dr. Frederick Crescitelli we are grateful for continually insisting that we be as precise as technique would allow and, always, that we interpret data in terms of their significance in natural history. We have tried here. We thank Dr. Boyd W. Walker for imparting to us his affection for fishes and his insight that biological understanding requires the integration of information at many levels. We hope that this background is expressed in our papers, for these studies reflect their efforts as well as our own. Each deserves our lifelong gratitude and respect.

We are grateful to Mrs. Alberta Jackson for technical assistance in typing and proofing the manuscript.

REFERENCES

Blackburn M. (1965) Oceanography and the ecology of tunas. *Oceanogr. Mar. Biol. Ann. Rev.* **3**, 299–322.

Breder C. M. Jr. (1972) On the relationship of teleost scales to pigment patterns. *Contr. Mote Mar. Lab.* **1**, 1–79.

Brock V. E. and Chamberlain T. C. (1968) A geological and ecological reconnaissance off western Oahu, Hawaii, principally by means of the research submarine "Asherah". *Pacific Sci.* **22**, 373–401.

Brown P. K. and Wald G. (1964) Visual pigments in single rods and cones of human retina. *Science* **144**, 45–52.

Cott H. B. (1940) *Adaptive Coloration in Animals.* Methuen, London.

Dartnall H. J. A. and Lythgoe J. N. (1965) The spectral clustering of visual pigments. *Vision Res.* **5**, 81–100.

Denton E. J. and Nicol J. A. C. (1966) A survey of reflectivity in silvery teleosts. *J. mar. biol. Ass. U.K.* **46**, 685–722.

Duntley S. Q. (1962) Underwater visibility. In *The Sea* (Edited by Hill M. N.), pp. 452–455. Interscience, New York.

Duntley S. Q. (1963) Light in the sea. *J. opt. Soc. Am.* **53**, 214–233.

Edridge-Green F. W. (1920) *The Physiology of Vision,* 2nd edition. London.

Hobson E. S. (1966) Visual orientation and feeding in seals and sea lions. *Nature, Lond.* **210**, 326–327.

Hobson E. S. (1968) Predatory behavior of some shore fishes in the Gulf of California. *Bur. Sport Fish. and Wildlife, Res. Rep.* **73**, 1–92.

Hobson E. S. (1972) Activity of Hawaiian reef-fishes during the evening and morning transitions between daylight and darkness. *Fish. Bull. Nat. Mar. Fish. Ser.* **70**, 715–740.

Ladd-Franklin C. (1929) *Colour and Colour Theories.* Harcourt Brace, New York.

Liebman P. A. (1972) Microspectrophotometry of photoreceptors. In *Photochemistry of Vision* (Edited by Dartnall H. J. A.), *Handbook of Sensory Physiology,* Vol. VII/1, pp. 481–528. Springer-Verlag, Berlin.

Liebman P. A. (1973) Microspectrophotometry of visual receptors. In *Biochemistry and Physiology of Visual Pigments* (Edited by Langer H.), pp. 299–305. Springer, Berlin.

Liebman P. A. and Granda A. M. (1971) Microspectrophotometric measurements of visual pigments in two species of turtle, *Pseudemys scripta* and *Chelonia mydas. Vision Res.* **11**, 105–114.

Lorenz K. (1962) The function of colour in coral reef fishes. *Proc. R. Instn Gt Br.* **39**, 282–296.

Lythgoe J. N. (1966) Visual pigments and underwater vision. In *Light as an Ecological Factor* (Edited by Bainbridge R., Evans G. C. and Rackham O.), pp. 375–391. Blackwell, Oxford.

Lythgoe J. N. (1968) Visual pigments and visual range underwater. *Vision Res.* **8**, 997–1012.

Marks W. B. (1965) Visual pigments of single goldfish cones. *J. Physiol., Lond.* **178**, 14–32.

Munz F. W. and McFarland W. N. (1973) The significance of spectral position in the rhodopsins of tropical marine fishes. *Vision Res.* **13**, 1829–1874.

Pickford R. W. (1951) *Individual Differences in Colour Vision.* Routledge & Kegan Paul, London.

Rose C. D. and Hassler W. W. (1974) Food habits and sex ratios of dolphin *Coryphaena hippurus* captured in the western Atlantic Ocean off Hatteras, North Carolina. *Trans. Am. Fish. Soc.* **103**, 94–100.

Strasburg D. W., Jones E. C. and Iversen T. B. (1968) Use of a small submarine for biological and oceanographic research. *J. Cons. Perm. Int. Explor. Mer.* **31**, 410–426.

Talbot F. H. and Penrith M. J. (1963) Synopsis of biological data on species of the genus *Thunnus (sensu lato)* (South Africa). *F.A.O. Fish. Rept, No. 6* **2**, 608–646.

Tamura T., Hanyu i. and Niwa H. (1972) Spectral sensitivity and color vision in skipjack tuna and related species. *Bull. Jap. Soc. scient. Fish.* **38**, 799–802.

Tamura T. and Wisby W. J. (1963) The visual sense of pelagic fishes, especially the visual axis and accommodation. *Bull. mar. Sci. Gulf and Caribb.* **13**, 433–448.

Wallace A. R. (1891) *Natural Selection and Tropical Nature,* 2nd edition. Macmillan, London.

Walls G. L. (1942) *The Vertebrate Eye and its Adaptive Radiation.* Cranbrook Institute of Science, Bloomfield Hills, Michigan.

Willmer E. N. (1949) Some evolutionary aspects of mammalian colour vision. *Proc. Linn. Soc. Lond.* **161**, 97–108.

Orientation by Taste in Fish of the Genus Ictalurus

J. E. BARDACH, J. H. TODD, R. CRICKMER

ABSTRACT

Fish of the genus Ictalurus can find distant chemical clues by means of taste alone, and they exhibit true gradient searching in the absence of a current. Neither unilateral nor bilateral deprivation of the sense of smell impaired their searching ability, but unilateral deprivation of taste receptors which are spread over body and barbels of the animals caused pronounced circling toward the intact side. The relation of swimming paths of the fish to the chemical in the water suggested that comparisons of concentrations were made in time and space.

Olfaction has long been recognized as a primary sensory modality which aids animals to locate distant clues. Taste, in fish as in other vertebrates, has been considered as a closeup sense, used in testing the palatability of food [1]. Temporal and spatial patterns of taste stimuli have been considered relatively unimportant, because of the belief that an animal can locate a food source only by direct contact [see 2].

Some fish, however, have an extremely well-developed taste sense, with branches of cranial nerves distributed on the head, on the flanks even to the tail, and on the fins or barbels, or both [3]. *Ictalurus nebulosus* and *I. natalis*, the brown and yellow bullheads belonging to this group, have thousands of external taste buds on the body, with especially dense concentrations on the barbels [4]. Our experiments and observations have established that taste alone can guide these fish to sources of chemical stimuli at least 25 fish lengths away, the limits of our tank. Also, the fish need no current to locate such a source; that is, they perform a true gradient search by means of taste.

Bullheads of the two species between 19 and 27 cm in total length (mean 22.6 cm), trapped from local lakes, were blinded with phemerol [5]. Some also had their olfactory tracts severed or their nares cauterized, others had some or all of their barbels amputated, and still others had portions of their seventh cranial nerves severed just outside the cranium. Each fish was kept singly in a 26.6-liter aquarium; some were fed liver, others dry pellets. Among the latter, a positive feeding response to cysteine hydrochloride was established; electrophysiological tests had shown that bullheads both smell and taste this substance [6]. Moreover, untrained bullheads placed in our tanks approached a nozzle from which a solution of this substance emanated.

Searches for chemical stimuli were recorded in a large, flat tank (2 by 3 m) containing 600 liters of water. The water was 10 cm deep, and it could be made to flow at speeds up to 12 liters per minute. Fluorescent compounds helped to ascertain the constancy of flow patterns, which were similar from trial to trial at a given current velocity. On the ceiling above the tank were four ultraviolet fluorescent lights (GE No. 40BLB, 40 watts each). Also on the ceiling above the tank a remotely controlled Pentax HIA 35-mm camera was centered with a 28-mm lentar lens and a Kodak wratten gelatin filter 25A, loaded with Tri X Kodak film. The stimulus solution—either droppings from thawed slices of 1 part pork liver diluted in 10 parts water—or cysteine hydrochloride—was released, anywhere in the tank through a suspended, remotely operated 50-ml syringe with a long glass nozzle. In some tests the solution was made visible by releasing fluorescein, rhodamine B, or vegetable dyes with it.

A red plastic disk about 1 cm in diameter, sprayed with a commercial fluorescent paint, was sewn onto the skin on the head of each fish, approximately at eye level. Each

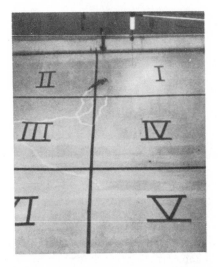

Fig. 1. Bullhead bearing a fluorescent tag approaching the release point of dilute liver extract mixed with fluorescein. [Time exposure, with final flash by P. Davis]

Fig. 2. Bullhead seeking barbel contact with a chemical in the surface film. [Flash photo by P. Davis]

fish was used only once or twice, except for those we subjected to progressive sensory deprivation by removing successive sets of barbels. In their case the point of stimulus release in the tank was varied from test to test, and the tests were spaced several weeks apart.

Most tests were done in the evening when there was little noise in the building and when bullheads are active. The fish was placed in the tank 6 to 8 hours before a test. When it had been quiet for at least 10 minutes, we released the stimulus; liver juice was used somewhat more often than cysteine hydrochloride. The photographed searching behavior was the same in either case, as was the behavior of the two species within the size ranges used. Stopwatch timing with one watch was begun at the release of the stimulus, while a second stopwatch measured the interval between arousal and the completion of the search. We began exposing the film when the animal showed that it had perceived the stimulus, and we continued the exposure until it found the source. The light trace made by the swimming fish (Fig. 1) appeared on a positive photographic copy as a white line. Its intensity was in inverse proportion to the swimming speed and could be made very clear by adjusting the photographic printing period.

Dye was used only in a few photographed trials because it masked the trace of the fish. Details of swimming behavior, when dyes were used with the stimulus, were therefore observed rather than recorded photographically. When a mixture of the dye and stimulus first reached the previously resting fish, it began its search. Fluorescein alone elicited barbel movements or yawning and sometimes swimming, but never search. Vegetable dyes, which did not permit photography in ultraviolet light but had distribution patterns like those of the fluorescent ones, were disregarded by the animals.

Typically, a blinded bullhead would show that it had perceived a chemical by what is best described as a startled response: the barbels stiffened, the body became rigid for a moment, the head began a slow to-and-fro movement, and the fish almost immediately began swimming.

This pattern of head movement was recorded in 90 out of 122 photographed tests of blinded but otherwise intact animals. In the remaining tests the fish just began to search.

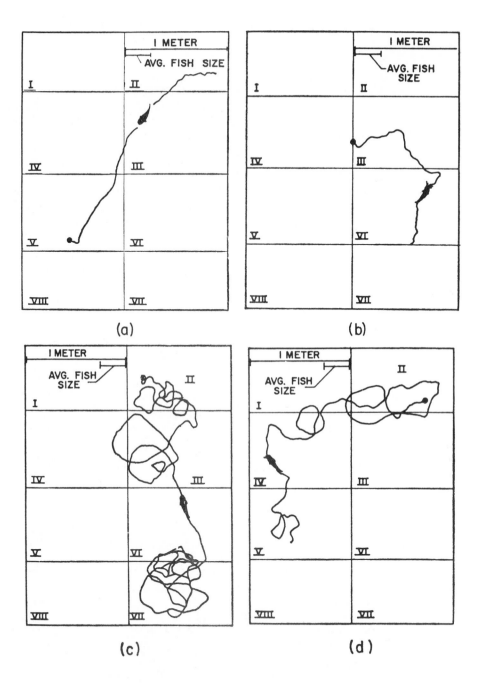

Fig. 3. Traces of fish under various experimental conditions. (a) Trace of a bullhead that started to search for the release point of 0.01M cysteine hydrochloride into slowly flowing water 3 minutes after the release of the chemical. (b) Diagram (from a photograph) of a distribution of fluorescein, 3 minutes after the dye was released from the same point as in part (a), with photographic trace of bullhead superimposed. (c) and (d) Traces of blind bullheads locating the source of diluted liver extract in water without a current, illustrating the reduction of circling in still as compared to flowing water.

When the fish began their to-and-fro movements they often sought contact with the surface film by means of their nasal and maxillary barbels (Fig. 2). At this moment, one or the other of the maxillary barbels was raised and lowered, covering an angle of almost 90°. The lateral movements, combined with the raising and lowering of the barbels, suggest that the fish often compared the chemical concentrations to the right and left of it, either simultaneously or in close succession. A typical trace of a blinded but otherwise intact animal in a current shows this initial scanning (Fig. 3a, sections III and VI).

When the fish reached the vicinity of the release of the stimulus, its momentum carried it beyond the scent cloud (Fig. 3b), but it immediately swung around and reentered the cloud. Repeated maneuvers of this kind resulted in the typical figure-eight search, early reported for many fishes [7]. Going in and out of a scent cloud in this manner implies that consecutive reactions of different receptors were compared to govern the animal's muscular response. When the bullhead finally mouthed the nozzle, at the release point we considered that it had completed the search and stopped the camera. The stimulus diffused more slowly in still water than in a current; consequently, search was begun after a longer time interval without current, up to 18 minutes in some instances, than in flowing water where search began from between 1 to 10 minutes after the stimulus was released; the latency depended on the speed of flow and where the fish was at rest in the tank.

Without a current, some fish found the release point of a diffused chemical with less circling and figure-eight movement (Fig. 3c). Others, swimming slowly, approached the nozzle in an almost straight line (Fig. 3d), a feat their experimental running mates never attained in any of the more than a hundred tests with a current. In still water a chemical gradient persists relatively undisturbed, but in flowing water eddies change the relative concentration continuously, especially at the edges of the field occupied by the chemical. Our tests suggest that in still water, gradient search by means of taste (Figs. 3, c and d; 4, a and b) might depend on the fish's ability to compare taste bud responses from the barbels with those from the flanks and the caudal peduncle; such neural processes would explain the almost straight approach under optimum conditions (Fig. 4a).

We do not yet know whether eliminating the olfactory sense impairs searching behavior. With liver juice or $0.01M$ cysteine hydrochloride released at a rate of 5 ml per minute into 600 liters of water, bullheads tested with or without a current but without sense of smell had neither a longer mean searching period nor a greater range of searching times than did the other fish that had all chemical sensors intact.

The gustatory acuity of bullheads may approach the olfactory acuity of many other fish [8]. Indeed, at the stimulus concentrations we used, the progressive removal of pairs of barbels in fish with their head and body taste buds still intact, either olfactorily capable or not, did not affect the time intervals between the alert to the stimulus and the completion of the search.

Yet the role of olfaction in orientation by bullheads remains puzzling, especially since initial head movements at slow swimming speed by fish with cauterized nares only occurred twice in 20 trials, that is, 10 percent of the times, as opposed to 74 percent in the much larger sample of fish with intact chemical senses. What is more, a fish in still water, without functional nares and barbels but with head, oral, flank, and tail taste buds intact, once alerted, could swim in 24 seconds almost directly to the release point of the stimulus while following a chemical gradient (Fig. 4a).

In contrast to Parker's classic observations of lopsided search after one naris of a shark had been similarly treated [9] —an observation not corroborated by later work [10] — one-sided elimination of smell in bullheads did not affect their searching ability (Fig. 4b). But when all barbels, or barbels and also flank taste buds, were made inoperative on one side only, creating an imbalance in taste input, the nine fish used in 27 trials always circled pronouncedly toward the intact side. The one-sided looping occurs both in a current (Fig. 4c) and in still water (Fig. 4d).

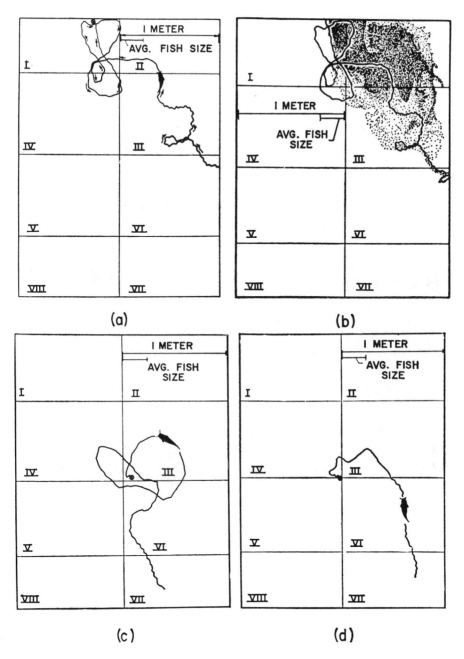

Fig. 4. Traces of blinded bullheads. (a) With cauterized nares and without nasal, maxillary and mental barbels, locating the source of dilute liver extract in still water. (b) With left naris cauterized searching, in still water, for the source of dilute liver extract. There is a high efficiency of finding the source and the left turns in spite of one-sided nasal cautery. (c) With all barbels removed and innervation to taste buds on right flank severed, circling towards the side of greater sensory input while locating the release point of dilute liver extract in a current. (d) With all right barbels removed, locating the source of dilute liver extract in still water, apparently with less circling toward the intact side than in the current (part c).

It has not yet been possible to completely eliminate the gustatory faculty of bullheads surgically in order to study the olfactory component alone, since the taste fibers are distributed at least in the widely branched seventh, ninth, and tenth cranial nerves [11], and extend to taste buds in the mouth, the pharynx, the gill cavity, and all over the head and body. This spread of taste sensors enables fish of this genus, and probably others with body taste buds, to compare the concentrations of chemical stimuli which they can then locate by taste alone over distances greater than hitherto suspected.

J. E. BARDACH**
J. H. TODD*
R. CRICKMER*

*School of Natural Resources, University of Michigan, Ann Arbor
**Hawaii Institute of Marine Biology, University of Hawaii at Manoa

REFERENCES AND NOTES

1. H. Teichmann, *Ergeb. Biol.* 25, 177 (1962); G. H. Parker, *Smell, Taste and Allied Senses in the Vertebrates* (Lippincott, Philadelphia, 1922), pp. 42–66.
2. P. Marler and W. Hamilton, III, *Mechanisms of Animal Behavior* (Wiley, New York, 1966).
3. W. Freihofer, *Stanford Ichthyolog. Bull.* 8, 81 (1963).
4. C. J. Herrick, *Bull. U.S. Fish Comm.* 22, 239 (1904).
5. T. Walker and A. Hasler, *Physiol. Zool.* 22, 45 (1945).
6. M. Fujiya and J. E. Bardach, *Bull. Japan Soc. Sci. Fisheries* 32, 45 (1966).
7. J. Uexkuell *Z. Biol.* 32, 548 (1895).
8. J. E. Bardach, in *Symposium on the Chemical Senses and the Nutritive Processes*, in press.
9. G. H. Parker, *Bull. U.S. Bur. Fisheries* 33, 61 (1914).
10. H. Teichmann and R. Teichmann, *Pubbl. Staz. Zool. Napoli* 31, 76 (1959).
11. C. Ariens Kappers, C. Huber, E. Crosby, *The Comparative Anatomy of the Nervous System of Vertebrates Including Man* (Macmillan, New York, 1936), vol. 11, pp. 343–362.
12. This work was supported by NIH grant NB 04687.
* Present address, Department of Zoology, University of Washington, Seattle.

20 December 1966

Seeing the World through a New Sense: Electroreception in Fish

*Sharks, catfish, and electric fish use low-
or high-frequency electroreceptors, actively and passively,
in object detection and social communication*

Theodore Holmes Bullock

Surely no other branch of physiology has provided more novelty than sensory physiology, if we may use as evidence the continued discovery of new organs and of functions for hitherto unexplained organs. We are inured to surprises year after year, such as the demonstration of infrared receptors, aerodynamic or wind-speed receptors, polarized light detection, and fantastic abilities in chemoreception, hydrostatic pressure, magnetic-field and sonar reception, and others.

How should we name new sense organs? This is far from a trivial question and will repay our brief consideration. Given that a stimulus has been found which elicits impulses in a sensory nerve, how should the receptor be designated? An innocent-sounding issue, it conceals pitfalls that have trapped more than a few physiologists and requires a real understanding of the biological meaning of the organ.

In general we cannot depend on the good fortune we have in the case of eyes and ears, in which the function is more or less obvious from accessory structures or exclusive sensitivity to only one mode of stimulation. Nor can we simply say that the function is determined by the stimulus to which an organ is most sensitive. How many degrees of temperature stimulus are equal to one gram of mechanical stimulus? High sensitivity to one form of stimulus may be incidental to a normal use in a less familiar modality.

Many receptors are ambiguous. They respond, for example, to a certain temperature *and* a certain mechanical event or other input. Are they ambiguous only to us or also to their possessors? How can we be satisfied that we have tried all the relevant forms of stimulation? When can we name an organ by function? An example will help and will lead us into the topic of the title.

The best case illustrating the basic issues and principles involved in this question is that of certain classical structures widespread in the skin of all sharks and rays, called ampullae of Lorenzini. These are tiny bladders, richly innervated and connected to a surface pore by a long canal. After decades of speculation centered on mechanoreceptive functions, electrophysiological techniques in 1938 revealed an unprecedented sensitivity to temperature, and for years the ampullae were the first physiologically studied thermoreceptors (Sand 1938).

From *American Scientist* 61:316–325. Reprinted by permission.

Doubts crept in, however, as to whether the ampullae really function as thermoreceptors for the shark. If so, why the long canal? New studies reactivated the old idea of mechanical sensitivity. Excitation by electric current was also noted, but neither form of energy seemed likely to be the natural "adequate stimulus." Even the eye can be stimulated by pressure and electric shock. Much more interesting was the later discovery that these organs will alter their nerve impulse traffic to the brain when slightly diluted or concentrated seawater is encountered, and we wondered whether their function is detection of variations in salinity of the environment.

Finally—and I believe that word is justified—a Dutch biophysicist named A. J. Kalmijn, in the laboratory of Sven Dijkgraaf, showed that sharks use these ampullae of Lorenzini to detect prey buried in the sand (Fig. 1). He found that the ampullae are excited by the feeble, steady electric field that leaks out of the buried flatfish prey. The shark detects and aims an attack at the flatfish even when it is covered with an agar plate that prevents mechanical, visual, and chemical cues, but is transparent to electric current. It also attacks buried electrodes that carry current equivalent to that of a flatfish. Therefore, we must call the ampullae electroreceptors, by the definitive criterion of behavior.

I have recounted this piece of scientific drama to emphasize the conceptual and tactical problem of defending the proposed function(s) of a receptor (Bullock 1973; Kalmijn and Bullock 1973). Physiological methods alone cannot establish the proper functional designation of a sense organ. There must be evidence of the normal availability and biological significance of the presumptive adequate stimulus, preferably by behavioral response appropriate to that form of information.

Natural electric stimuli

What does the world look like to a creature with the amazing sensitivity to electrical fields in water of 0.01 $\mu v/cm$ (= 1 $\mu v/m$, or 1 flashlight cell per 1,500 km)? What are the kinds and sources of voltage fields in nature? Which signals are useful and which are noise?

Surveying sixty species of animals from eight major branches of the animal kingdom, Kalmijn, now at the Scripps Institution of Oceanography, found that nearly all, including man, emit into seawater d.c. fields which even at tens of centimeters distance are well above the shark threshold. A.c. fields due to muscle and heart activity are generally much smaller. The d.c. fields are presumably incidental voltages of diverse origin, including millivolt potentials between body fluids and ocean and between different parts of the body. Although quite variable they may signal the position, orientation, type, and physiological condition of the animal. A wound, for instance, markedly increases the voltage gradient. Even a minor scratch can double the voltage gradient from a man in seawater (to one that would be detectable by a shark at more than 1 meter).

The class of electrical signals arising from living organisms can be called bioelectric signals. Very likely there are biological meanings other than the localization of prey—social signals between conspecifics, for example. This is especially true for the a.c. bioelectric fields emitted by the numerous species of electric fish, as we will see below. The field is just opening up.

Figure 1. Feeding responses of the shark, *Scylliorhinus canicula*. The agar chamber is not to scale. Solid arrows indicate movements of the shark; dashed arrows, the flow of seawater through the chamber. (From Kalmijn 1971, by permission of the *Journal of Experimental Biology*.)

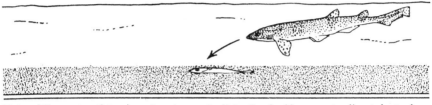

Plaice (*Pleuronectes platessa*) under the sand elicits the shark's accurate, directed attack.

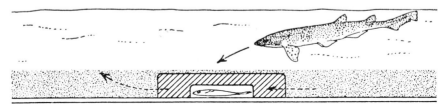

The shark also attacks accurately when the plaice is in an agar chamber, "transparent" to electric current, with a resistivity about equal to that of the medium.

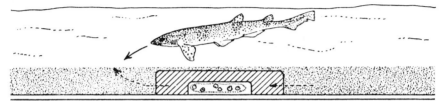

Only if the plaice has been chopped up and frozen for a long time, exaggerating the olfactory stimulus and fragmenting the d.c. field, will the shark diffusely search in the downstream area.

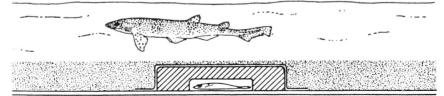

If the agar is covered by an insulating plastic film the response is lost.

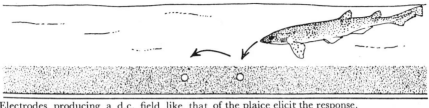

Electrodes producing a d.c. field like that of the plaice elicit the response.

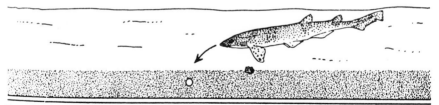

Even in the presence of a piece of food the response is still directed toward the dipole source (only one electrode shown).

Table 1. Modes and roles of receptor function

MODE	ROLE
Passive (animal detects fields from external sources)	**Electrolocation**
Animate (membrane potentials of other organism)	*Close range*
d.c. (e.g. gill potentials)	passive detection of other fish
a.c.-slow (d.c. modulated by slow movements)	active detection of objects and spaces
a.c.-fast (muscle, heart, electric organ action potentials)	*Long range*
Inanimate sources	directional navigation
motion of water mass in earth's magnetic field	**Electrocommunication**
electrochemical, atmospheric, geological processes	*Constant signals*
	related to place, kind, sex, individual
	Changing signals
	related to food, threat, attack, submission, mating
Active (animal detects fields caused by its own activity)	
Animate (membrane potentials from own body)	
d.c., a.c.-slow, a.c.-fast (same as for passive mode above)	
Inanimate sources	
induced potentials from swimming in earth's magnetic field	

In addition to the world of bioelectric signals there is a world of inanimate fields. We are now testing whether large homogeneous fields such as those induced by the motion of water masses, like the great ocean currents and rivers, through the earth's magnetic field can be used as navigational clues. The signals are known to be present; the sharks are amply sensitive to detect them. Similarly, the fields caused by waves and tides and by magnetic variations as well as by the sharks' own swimming are strong enough to be detected by sharks, though we do not know that they use them.

There may conceivably be signals from local fields straying out from ore

bodies of certain kinds, possibly useful in the way topographic features of the landscape are. There are fields caused by earthquakes and other episodic events such as eruptions and crustal movements. In shallow water complex activity results from atmospheric disturbances such as lightning and ionosphere reverberations, including what used to be called "static," and also from slow changes like day-night alternations. There are chemical potentials at sharp discontinuities like river bottoms and at gradual boundaries—perhaps less usable for that reason—like river mouths and thermoclines.

Many of the available fields may represent background noise out of which signals must be extracted. Our understanding of the uses made of inanimate fields is quite embryonic, but it is as though a door has been opened. Surprises can be expected—such as the well-documented hypersensitivity to mechanical stimuli in catfish at a certain place in Japan during and for some hours before earthquakes, behavior which is evidently dependent on changes in the electrical currents in the earth, picked up by the freshwater stream (Hatai and Abe 1932; Kokubo 1934; Kalmijn and Bullock 1973).

The world of natural waters, being a more or less good conductor, is busy with electrical currents, on a millimeter and a kilometer scale, from d.c. to hundreds of kHz, from fractions of microvolts to several millivolts per meter and locally even higher. Man is "polluting" the waters and the ground with far higher currents in return paths from power lines, leakage, and high-power broadcasting. We are beginning to learn that many fish normally detect and are influenced by feeble currents (Fig. 2).

In what follows we shall recognize two modes of detection—passive and active; two roles in the biology of the species—"electrolocation" of objects and "electrocommunication" of social signals (Table 1); and two classes of sense organs—receptors tuned to low frequency and those tuned to high frequency (Fig. 3). The three dichotomies are not equivalent, and many of the permutations are known or suspected—e.g. passive detection of objects by low-frequency receptors (the shark and flatfish case of Fig. 1), active electrolocation by low-frequency receptors (the case of navigation with the aid of currents induced by swimming in the earth's magnetic field), and passive detection of social signals from conspecifics by high-frequency receptors.

Passive electroreception

We have already seen one example of the passive mode in Figure 1 and suggested others, e.g. the navigation by electric currents induced by water masses such as the Gulf Stream moving in the earth's magnetic field (see Table 1). How does the shark sample the electric field, since he has to look at two points and complete a circuit between them? Figure 4 shows the relevant features of the animal's interior and skin in relation to a large homogeneous field in the milieu (Kalmijn and Bullock 1973).

In seawater the body fluids of vertebrates have a higher resistivity than the milieu, and the skin is only a moderately good insulator. The ampullary organs are remarkable in two ways: the jelly in the canals has a very low resistivity, whereas the resistivity of the canal walls is very high. The result is that the sense cells in the bottom of the ampullae face outward to a jelly virtually at the same potential as that in the sea at the pore, while the inner face is bathed by body fluid virtually at the same potential as that of the seawater just outside the skin at that point (see Fig. 4). The long canal therefore enables the sense cell to sample the field at two widely separated points. Sharks and rays have hundreds of these canals, radiating in various directions and reaching lengths, in rays, of up to one-third of the body length. The remarkable saltwater catfish *Plotosus* also has these organs and the electroreceptive ability.

What about freshwater species? Figure 4 shows that the situation is drastically different in electrosensitive freshwater species. The body fluids are nearly isopotential throughout because of the high skin resistance, and thus the inner side of a receptor cell is at the same potential as the external

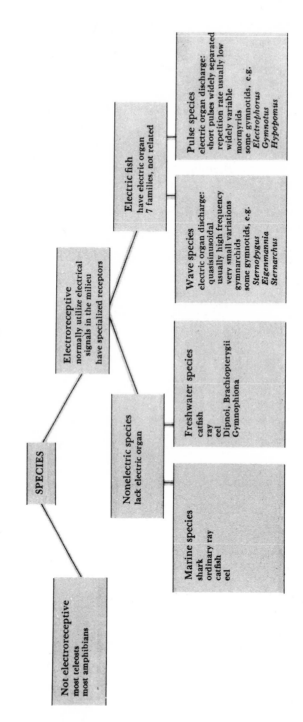

Figure 2. Relationships and characteristics of electroreceptive fish.

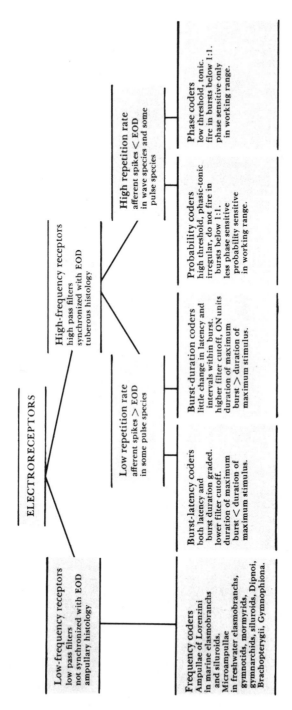

Figure 3. Present knowledge permits recognizing two broad classes and five coding types of electroreceptors, with the characteristics and distributions shown here. EOD = electric organ discharge. ON refers to responses to stimulus onset. See Fig. 7 for explanation of coders.

ELECTRORECEPTORS

Low-frequency receptors
low pass filters
not synchronized with EOD
ampullary histology

High-frequency receptors
high pass filters
synchronized with EOD
tuberous histology

Low repetition rate
afferent spikes > EOD
in some pulse species

High repetition rate
afferent spikes < EOD
in wave species and some
pulse species

Frequency coders
Ampullae of Lorenzini
in marine elasmobranchs
and siluroids.
Microampullae
in freshwater elasmobranchs,
gymnotids, mormyrids,
gymnarchids, siluroids, Dipnoi,
Brachopterygii, Gymnophiona.

Burst-latency coders
both latency and
burst duration graded.
lower filter cutoff.
duration of maximum
burst < duration of
maximum stimulus.

Burst-duration coders
little change in latency and
intervals within burst.
higher filter cutoff, ON units
duration of maximum
burst > duration of
maximum stimulus.

Probability coders
high threshold, phasic-tonic
irregular, do not fire in
bursts below 1:1.
less phase sensitive
probability sensitive
in working range.

Phase coders
low threshold, tonic.
fire in bursts below 1:1.
phase sensitive only
in working range.

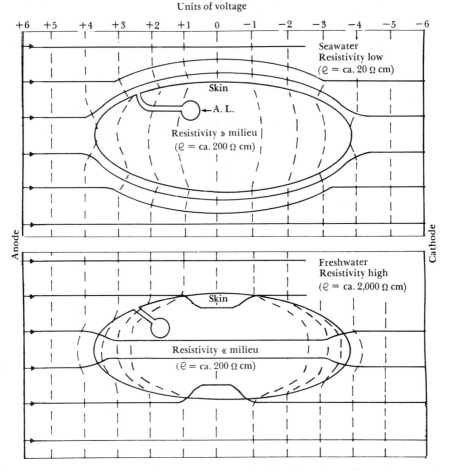

Figure 4. Schematic representation of marine elasmobranch or teleost in seawater (*above*) and elasmobranch or teleost adapted for freshwater (*below*). Note that the mural resistance of the skin in ohm/cm^2 is relatively low in the marine and high in the freshwater forms shown, which are probably typical for elasmobranchs evolutionarily adapted to the respective habitats and for electric fish. A.L. = ampulla of Lorenzini, with sensory membrane at the bottom and canal with very low resistance jelly and very high resistance walls. The interior represents mean tissue fluid resistivity (ρ). The marine elasmobranch employs a long canal to put a considerable part of the external voltage gradient across its sensory membrane; the well-adapted freshwater form (*Potamotrygon* or electric fish) needs no long canal to achieve the same result away from the electrical equator because the whole interior is virtually isopotential with the equator. The marine form does not load the external field because its tissue fluids are higher in resistivity; the freshwater form loads the external field only moderately because its skin resistance is so high.

field near the middle of the animal. Therefore there is no need for long tubes. We made a study of the unusual freshwater-adapted elasmobranch, the Amazon stingray *Potamotrygon*, and found exactly this—microscopic ampullae and tubes just reaching through the skin (Szabo et al. 1972). Virtually the same situation is true for the freshwater teleosts (gymnotids, mormyrids, gymnarchids, and silurids at least) that have ampullary sense organs and electroreception of low-frequency fields.

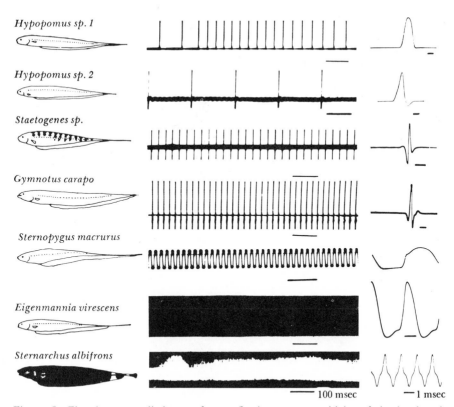

Hypopomus sp. 1

Hypopomus sp. 2

Staetogenes sp.

Gymnotus carapo

Sternopygus macrurus

Eigenmannia virescens

Sternarchus albifrons

— 100 msec   — 1 msec

Figure 5. Electric organ discharges from several species of the South American family Gymnotidae. Each discharge is shown beside the fish it comes from and on both slow (*left*) and fast (*right*) time bases. Upward deflection means positivity of the head end. The last two are wave species; all the others are pulse species. (From Hagiwara and Morita 1963, by permission of the American Physiological Society.)

One further indication of the adaptation of the ampullary receptors is the frequency range of electrical events to which they are sensitive. This is strictly confined to very slow events, between 0.1 and 10 Hz at least in the shark. Sensitivity extending down to 0.1 Hz gives the animal access to d.c. fields in the water, because of its own swimming and swerving. The fall in sensitivity above 10 Hz cuts out higher-frequency noise and corresponds with the surprising fact that the fast electrocardiographic, locomotor, and respiratory muscle action potentials of the fish upon which the shark *Scyliorhinus* preys are much weaker than the d.c. stray fields from their gills and buccal membranes.

Passive reception of low-frequency, feeble voltage gradients is now known to occur in elasmobranchs, catfish, and common eels (Anguillidae), and electric fish of the families Gymnotidae, Mormyridae, and Gymnarchidae; it can be suspected in several other groups. It is usually attributable to structures of the type called ampullary organs, but we must not be surprised if some other types turn up in addition. Passive reception by high-frequency receptors will be dealt with below under communication.

Active electroreception

Active electroreception is best known in electric fish in the object-detecting mode, using high-frequency recep-

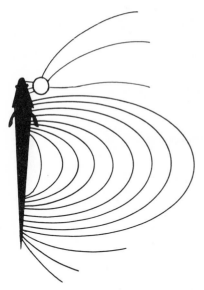 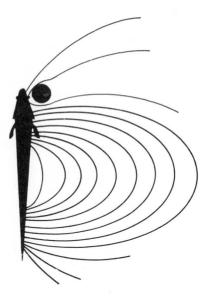

Figure 6. The electric field on one side of an electric fish, shown by current lines, and the distortions due to objects of low conductivity (*right*) and high conductivity (*left*).

(After Lissmann and Machin 1958, by permission of the *Journal of Experimental Biology*.)

tors. Even before Kalmijn's discovery of the normal role of ampullae as electroreceptors, Lissmann (1958) had reopened an old question—namely, whether the electric organs in so-called pseudoelectric fish could be functional. It had been concluded that these small electric organs were useless because they were too puny to be offensive or defensive. But Lissmann found that they were discharging in a pulsatile way all the time, night and day (Fig. 5), and he proposed an electrolocating or object-detecting function (Fig. 6).

Here, then, is a proposal for an electrosensitive system that is *active* in the same sense that a bat's echolocation is. It measures not the time of return of a signal, since that is virtually instantaneous, but the shape of the field. Receptors must be widely distributed over the body, while the brain must do a spatial computation and could, in principle, infer size, distance, shape, and quality of an object, with certain ambiguities (Ben-

nett 1970; Scheich and Bullock, forthcoming). This proposed function has now been amply confirmed by behavioral experiments.

Largely through the work of my colleagues S. Hagiwara, S. Chichibu, H. Scheich, and several others, as well as important work by M.V.L. Bennett, in New York, and A. Fessard and T. Szabo, in Paris, the required new class of receptors has been found and characterized. These were the first electroreceptors discovered and shown to satisfy the criteria of response to natural stimuli mentioned above. The excitement of discovering receptors for a new modality or view of the world was then enhanced by the finding that there are several kinds of such receptors (see Fig. 3). These differ in their mode of coding intensity, as illustrated in Figure 7.

Unraveling the codes in the sensory nerve fibers occupied several years and is not really completed yet. The fundamental problem illuminated by these exotic electric fish is: How is

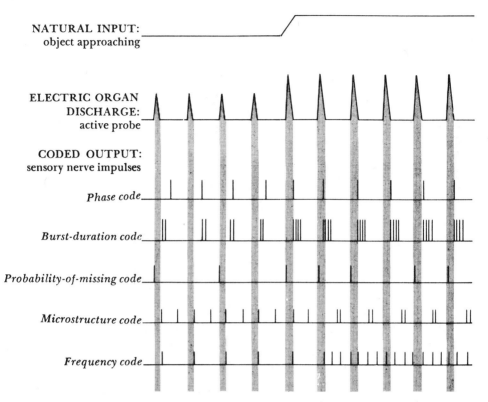

NATURAL INPUT:
object approaching

ELECTRIC ORGAN
DISCHARGE:
active probe

CODED OUTPUT:
sensory nerve impulses

Phase code

Burst-duration code

Probability-of-missing code

Microstructure code

Frequency code

Figure 7. Diagram of several hypothetical types of afferent nerve fibers from electroreceptors, each encoding in a different way the step of intensity of the electric field caused by introduction of a natural stimulating object. All types shown have been found in electric fish except the microstructure code, which is known from other animals. (After Bullock 1968, by permission of the National Academy of Sciences.)

information represented in streams of nerve impulses? Like many basic questions of neurobiology, answers or clues from lower species may help us to understand the brains of higher forms. It had been thought that mean frequency was *the* code of the nervous system, but these fish happen to be favorable for revealing several other codes (see Fig. 7) among the theoretical candidates (Perkel and Bullock 1968). One is a phase shift without frequency change, another is a burst duration, and another a probability-of-missing code.

The frequency code is also used—in ampullary receptors like those of the shark, which "listen" only to very slow potentials, mainly passively,

and do not even "hear" the electric organ discharges because they are too fast or too brief. We worked out some of the codes quantitatively (Scheich et al. 1973), and it seems reasonable to expect to see some of them turn up in respectable higher animals! The general principle we induce is that brains do not operate with just one code, waiting to be broken, but at least several, perhaps a good many, working in parallel (Perkel and Bullock 1968).

Electrolocation and electrocommunication

We have referred to some known and some suspected uses of electroreception in what may be called the electrolocating role (see Table 1), detecting objects or prey in the near field, directions relative to earth or water current in the far field, employing both the active and the passive modes. Little is known of the skill or resolution in electrolocation; however, two methods have been developed for quantitative estimation of performance by Lissmann and Machin and by Heiligenberg.

The first named authors trained *Gymnarchus* to discriminate between two porous pots 50 mm in diameter, both containing aquarium water, but one containing a 4 mm glass rod and the other a 6 mm glass rod. Heiligenberg (manuscript) measured the gain and phase of a response which might be called the electrokinetic response in *Eigenmannia*. A blinded fish, even without special training, tends to hover between vertically suspended strips of plastic just as normal fish do among water plants, roots, and rocks. When the strips are slowly moved left and right relative to the fish, it moves similarly, maintaining a position centered between the strips to an accuracy limited by the frequency of the sinusoidal strip movement and the size and distance between strips. Controls with electrically transparent agar strips show no such following.

These methods indicate that the near-field object location of good insulators is useful to some centimeters, doubtfully to decimeters, varying with water conductivity, object size, container size, and other factors. Passive electrolocation like the sharks' detection of hidden flatfish is useful to sizable fractions of a meter in seawater. These or improved methods should permit future analyses of the parameters of discrimination, the biophysical bases of discrimination, and the brain mechanisms involved in electrolocation. Another role of electroreception, which is particularly developed in the

electric fish—the families that possess electric organs in addition to electroreceptors—is the social signaling or electrocommunicating role. Even if there were no special alterations of the electric organ discharge (EOD) correlated with behavior, the presence of the EOD of the species' characteristic shape and frequency range and of the repetition rate characteristic of the individual provides information on the location, species, individual identity, and in at least one species (*Sternopygus macrurus*, Hopkins 1972) the sex, for any receiver equipped to understand this information. But by adding alterations in EOD many more signals of social significance are possible.

Before looking further at social communication it will be helpful to make still another distinction. Among the electric fish there are "wave" species and "pulse" species, the distinction being based on the form of the electric organ discharge. Wave species emit a continuous, nearly sinusoidal voltage. Different species discharge within characteristic ranges, *Sternopygus macrurus* at 50 to 150 Hz, *Eigenmannia virescens* at 250 to 600, *Sternarchus albifrons* at 750 to 1,250, and *Sternarchorhamphus sp.* at up to more than 2,000 Hz (all at 27°C). The discharge frequency of each individual is ordinarily extremely regular and does not change for long periods, or changes less than 2 percent, with state of arousal, feeding, touch, vibration, light, or conspecific fish.

The pulse species normally discharge at a few pulses per second, up to 100 per sec, usually quite irregularly. The pulses are 0.2 to 2 msec long, and the intervals between them from 10 msec to a second or more. They continually change rate by large percentages, with arousal, food, touch, vibration, light, or other fish, in a highly labile manner.

Figure 8. Schematic diagram of the system causing the JAR (jamming avoidance response) of high-frequency weakly electric fish. ΔF is the stimulus frequency minus the fish frequency. (After Bullock et al. 1972b, by permission of Springer-Verlag.)

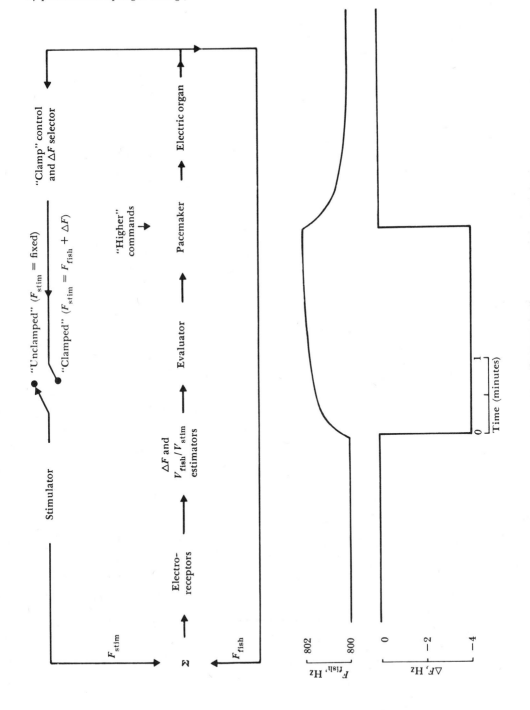

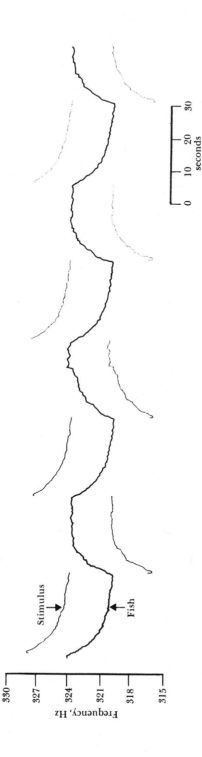

Figure 9. The JAR of *Eigenmannia* stimulated with alternately plus and minus $\Delta F = 4$ Hz, "clamped" so that the stimulator follows any changes in fish frequency to maintain the ΔF. The reversal of stimulus sign occurs automatically every 25 sec. The fish tries to escape by shifting its frequency in the correct direction to increase the ΔF. The two frequencies are continuously measured by triggering a 10 MHz precision clock with zero crossings and counting the clock cycles, without dead time. (From Bullock et al. 1972a, by permission of Springer-Verlag.)

Social signals

We are learning that both wave and pulse species make social signals of some variety by modifications of EOD, and thus a busy electrical world of electrocommunicating signals is added to the cacophony of inanimate electrical events in the microvolt range. Without detailing them and their social contexts, still quite incompletely known, we can safely list several kinds of discharge alterations as correlates of social situations, perhaps having significance as threat, warning, submission, and announcement of food or other object of special interest (Möhres 1957; Black-Cleworth 1970; Hopkins, dissertation; Moller and Bauer, in press). Alterations include frequency rises of different form, amount, and duration; brief chirps or beeps; shorter or longer silent periods (ca. one-quarter to several seconds); and in a few cases amplitude modulations and chords (two frequencies at once).

One form of response deserves special attention because of its accessibility to analysis in terms of sensory input, central evaluation, and EOD control. In species with a steady hum, like *Gymnarchus* and *Eigenmannia*, at 250 to 500 per sec, and *Sternarchus*, at 750 to 1,250 per sec, there is a small but definite frequency shift whenever another fish, or a stimulus simulating one, with a frequency within 1 or 2 percent comes into range (Figure 8). If, for example, a fish is firing along at 800 EOD's per sec and a stimulus appears at 796 per sec (a 0.5 percent difference, undetectable to the human ear if converted into sound), the EOD will glide slowly up to 801 or 802 or 803, depending on the stimulus voltage. If we flip the stimulus frequency every 30 sec from 4 Hz below to 4 Hz above the fish's frequency, the EOD will slide up or down, respectively, again and again without fatigue (see Fig. 9). I call this the

JAR, for jamming avoidance response (Bullock et al. 1972a, b). It is a dependable quantifiable, reflexlike, normal social response, inviting study as an example of behavior. We already know something of its afferent and efferent bases from previous analyses of the receptor types, the electric organ, and its control and command system in the brain (Fig. 10).

Eigenmannia and *Sternarchus* give best responses to a difference of 3 or 4 Hz (Fig. 11), respond less to 10 or 15 Hz, and ignore a 30 Hz difference. They respond definitely though weakly to a difference of 0.1 Hz but ignore a stimulus of exactly their own frequency. The fish always responds in the right direction, without hunting, even when the fraction-of-a-second latent period gives it less than a tenth of a beat cycle. It reacts to the second, third, fourth, or fifth harmonic if we add or subtract a few Hz, and the best difference frequency is still 3 Hz; therefore the stimulus is a beat frequency, not the percentage difference.

The electric organ is paced by a command unit in the brain, cycle by cycle, and thus the central nervous system has a reference against which it might measure the strange rhythm. But if the command output is interrupted and the electric organ silenced, it can be shown that the fish does not in fact use the command rhythm, which goes merrily on in the pacemaker center.

The fish, it seems, must get both rhythms through the sense organs. They can be any two rhythms, as long as they are a few Hz apart. For example, after silencing the EOD we can deliver two sine waves, such as 323 and 326, or 502 and 505, or 241 and 244, and there will be a response measured as change in pacemaker rhythm; but the response cannot have a "correct" direction

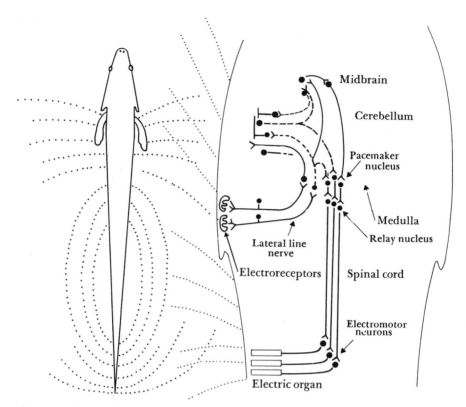

Figure 10. Diagram of the anatomy of the JAR system. Dashed lines represent hypothetical connections. Dotted lines are current lines in the fish's electric organ field. (After Bullock et al. 1972a, by permission of Springer-Verlag.)

if no clue indicates whether the difference should be regarded as plus or minus. Normally, the asymmetry of the EOD wave form, like a clipped sine wave, provides this clue, and then the fish analyzes the small frequency differences in the time domain. The range of effective stimuli can be described in terms of sidebands and can be generated by AM, FM, or phase modulation. Figure 12 shows a recent diagram of the components of the system, considered as an example of input processing and output control.

The smooth and continuously gradable control of frequency of EOD in these wave fish is correlated with a high precision of the regularity of the discharge frequency—at least 100 times better than familiar rhythmic nerve cells and biological clocks. The standard deviation of single intervals (= periods), over thousands of cycles, without averaging, is 0.01 percent or 0.1 μsec in *Sternarchus!*

This regularity allows the fish to use their object-detecting ability in the presence of neighbors with frequencies only a few Hz away and to use re· ceptors that code electric-field strength with high-precision phase shifts. These features of high temporal resolution require the stable detection of very small frequency differences both in respect to magnitude and sign. We have found higher-order neurons in the midbrain (torus semicircularis) that can do this, apparently by integrating lower-order phase and probability-coded impulses. Other units in the lobus lateralis posterior and cerebellum

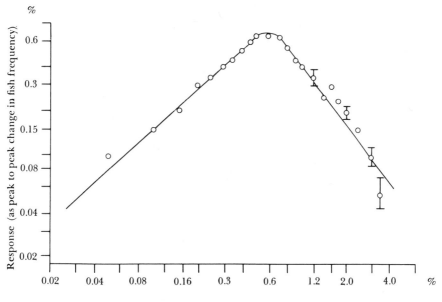

Figure 11. Response as function of ΔF (neglecting its sign). JAR elicited as in Figure 9 with different values of ΔF. Vertical bars are estimated confidence limits. (From Bullock et al. 1972b, by permission of Springer-Verlag.)

seem less specialized for microsecond temporal analysis and may be better adapted to object detection.

Wave vs pulse species

We are struggling even to speculate on the adaptive value of the two general types of species, the high-frequency, high-regularity wave species and the low-frequency, irregular pulse species. The former should be more sensitive to object detection, since they sample the world so often and can average many independent samples. They should also be able to detect each other at greater distances, if the brain can process input as the human brain does in hearing a musical tone against loud noise—that is, they should be less troubled by interference from "static" than the pulse species are. The low-frequency, variable-interval pulse species should be less bothered by coincident discharge from other fish, since simultaneous

pulses will be rare, especially a whole series in succession such as normally occurs during every beat cycle of two or more wave fish.

Either type can be expected to detect not only ohmic discontinuities in the milieu but also capacitative impedance because of the regular frequency in the wave species and the uniform, brief spikes in the pulse species. Experiment has confirmed this for single afferent fibers in *Eigenmannia* (Scheich et al. 1973). Here is yet another new look at the world. It may permit discriminating on a new dimension among objects such as other organisms. At present we know little about the capacity of natural objects. The capacity of a cubic centimeter of muscle tissue is about 0.1 to $0.01\mu F$, whereas the single electroreceptor of *Eigenmannia* can detect 0.0004 μF in a certain geometry—that is, the receptor is far more sensitive than necessary to detect such an object.

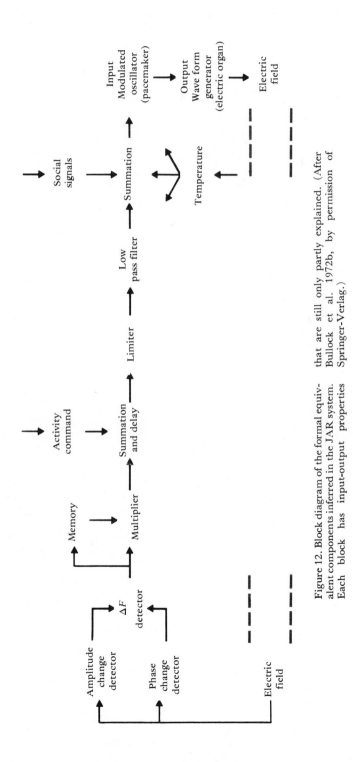

Figure 12. Block diagram of the formal equivalent components inferred in the JAR system. Each block has input-output properties that are still only partly explained. (After Bullock et al. 1972b, by permission of Springer-Verlag.)

Even for object detection by local conductance discontinuity—objects like rocks or fish—we know little about the parameters used by fish or the limits of performance in respect to discrimination of size, shape, distance, conductance, or motion. Since the electric field from the fish's discharge falls off with the cube of distance and an object distorting the field can be regarded as a dipole source whose effect also falls off with the cube of distance, we may expect object detection to be effective only at close range. However, the consequences of many factors are not yet fully assessed: the high sensitivity of receptors, especially to differences in electric field intensity, and the large number of receptors; the large size of the relevant brain regions; the special geometry of the electric field; the pattern of resistances in the fish's skin and its sense organs; to say nothing of the electrical parameters of objects normally important to these fish.

In spite of many unknowns in the evaluation of their roles in the animal's life, it has recently become clear that several families of fish have developed low- and high-frequency electroreceptors useful in active and passive electrolocation and electrocommunication, and that their sensitivities give access to a busy world of both signals and noise.

Theodore H. Bullock is a professor in the Department of Neurosciences of the School of Medicine and head of the Neurobiology Unit of the Scripps Institution of Oceanography at the University of California, San Diego. As a comparative neurologist he has studied the brain, synapses, giant fibers, and sense organs of animals from porpoises to jellyfish. With G. A. Horridge he wrote a two-volume treatise, Structure and Function in the Nervous Systems of Invertebrates *(W. H. Freeman Co., San Francisco).*
Born in China, Dr. Bullock did his graduate work in zoology at Berkeley and then worked successively at Yale, the University of Missouri, and UCLA before going to La Jolla, with summers at Woods Hole or other marine stations or on expeditions. He is a member of the National Academy of Sciences and the American Philosophical Society and served as president of the American Society of Zoologists in 1965. He began to search for electroreceptors in 1959 and has had many collaborators in that work, including S. Hagiwara, N. Suga, T. Szabo, P. S. Enger, S. Chichibu, A. J. Kalmijn, and H. Scheich, with support from the NSF, ONR, and NIH. Address: Department of Neurosciences, UCSD, La Jolla, CA 92037.

References

Bennett, M. V. L. 1970. Comparative physiology: Electric organs. *Annu. Rev. Physiol.* 32:471–528.

Black-Cleworth, P. 1970. The role of electrical discharges in the non-reproductive social behavior of *Gymnotus carapo* L. (Gymnotidae Pisces). *Anim. Behav. Monog.* 31:1–77.

Bullock, T. H. 1968. The representation of information in neurons and sites for molecular participation. *Proc. Nat. Acad. of Sci.* 60(4):1058–68.

Bullock, T. H. Forthcoming. An essay on the discovery of sensory receptors and the assignment of their functions together with an introduction to electroreceptors. In *Handbook of Sensory Physiology III*, A. Fessard, Ed. New York: Springer-Verlag.

Bullock, T. H., R. H. Hamstra, Jr., and H. Scheich. 1972a. The jamming avoidance response of high frequency electric fish. I. General features. *J. Comp. Physiol.* 77:1–22.

Bullock, T. H., R. H. Hamstra, Jr., and H. Scheich. 1972b. The jamming avoidance response of high frequency electric fish. II. Quantitative aspects. *J. Comp. Physiol.* 77:23–48.

Hagiwara, S., and H. Morita. 1963. Coding mechanisms of electroreceptor fibers in some electric fish. *J. Neurophysiol.* 26:551–67.

Hatai, S., and N. Abe. 1932. Responses of the catfish, *Parasilurus asotus*, to earthquakes. *Proc. Imp. Acad.* 8:375–78.

Heiligenberg, W. In press. The electromotor response in the electric fish *Eigenmannia*. *Nature*.

Hopkins, C. D. 1972. Sex differences in electric signalling in an electric fish. *Science* 176:1035–37.

Hopkins, C. D. Patterns of electrical communication among gymnotid fish. Ph.D. dissertation, 1972, Rockefeller University, New York.

Kalmijn, A. J. 1971. The electric sense of sharks and rays. *J. Exp. Biol.* 55:371–83.

Kalmijn, A. J., and T. H. Bullock. Forthcoming. The role of electroreceptors in the animal's life. I. The detection of electric fields from inanimate and animate sources other than electric organs. In *Handbook of Sensory Physiology III*, A. Fessard, Ed. New York: Springer-Verlag.

Kokubo, S. 1934. On the behavior of catfish in response to galvanic stimuli. *Sci. Rep. Tohoku Univ.* (D)9:87–96.

Lissmann, H. W. 1958. On the function and evolution of electric organs in fish. *J. Exp. Biol.* 35:156–91.

Lissmann, H. W., and K. E. Machin. 1958. The mechanism of object location in *Gymnarchus niloticus* and similar fish. *J. Exp. Biol.* 35:451–86.

Möhres, F. P. 1957. Elektrische Entladungen im Dienste der Revierabgrenzung bei Fischen. *Naturwissenschaften* 44:431–32.

Moller, P., and R. Bauer. In press. "Communication" in weakly electric fish, *Gnathonemus petersii* (Mormyridae). II. Interaction of electric organ discharge activities of two fish. *Anim. Behav.*

Perkel, D. H., and T. H. Bullock. 1968. Neural coding. *Neurosciences Research Program Bulletin* 6:221–348.

Sand, A. 1938. The function of the ampullae of Lorenzini with some observations on the effect of temperature on sensory rhythms. *Proc. Roy. Soc. B* 125:524–53.

Scheich, H., and T. H. Bullock. Forthcoming. The role of electroreceptors in the animal's life. II. The detection of electric fields from electric organs. In *Handbook of Sensory Physiology III*, A. Fessard, Ed. New York: Springer-Verlag.

Scheich, H., T. H. Bullock, and R. H. Hamstra, Jr. 1973. Coding properties of two classes of afferent nerve fibers: High frequency electroreceptors in the electric fish, *Eigenmannia*. *J. Neurophysiol.* 36:39–60.

Szabo, T., A. J. Kalmijn, P. S. Enger, and T. H. Bullock. 1972. Microampullary organs and a submandibular sense organ in the freshwater ray, *Potamotrygon*. *J Comp. Physiol.* 79:15–27.

Additional Readings

CHAPTER 9

ALI, M. A., ed. 1975. *Vision in fishes.* New York: Plenum Publishing Company.

BENNETT, M. V. L. 1971. Electric organs. Chapter 9, pp. 347–492, *in* W. S. Hoar and D. J. Randall, eds., *Fish Physiology*, Vol. 5. New York: Academic Press.

BENNETT, M. V. L. 1971. Electroreception. Chapter 10, pp. 493–574, *in* W. S. Hoar and D. J. Randall, eds., *Fish Physiology*, Vol. 5. New York: Academic Press.

BERNSTEIN, J. J. 1970. Anatomy and physiology of the central nervous system. Chapter 1, pp. 1–90, *in* W. S. Hoar and D. J. Randall, eds., *Fish Physiology*, Vol. 4. New York: Academic Press.

CAHN, P. H., ed. 1967. *Lateral line detectors.* Bloomington: Indiana University Press.

CAHN, P. H., ed. 1972. Sensory factors in side to side spacing and positional orientation of the tuna, *E. affinis*, during schooling. *Fish. Bull. U.S.* 70(1):197–204.

DIAMOND, J. 1971. The Mauthner cell. Chapter 9, pp. 265–346, *in* W. S. Hoar and D. J. Randall, eds., *Fish Physiology*, Vol. 5. New York: Academic Press.

DIJKGRAAF, S. 1963. The functioning and significance of the lateral line organs. *Biol. Rev., Cambridge* 38:51–105.

DISLER, N. N. 1971. Lateral line organs and their importance in fish behavior. *Israel Program for Scientific Translations, Jerusalem.* U.S. Department of Commerce, Washington, D.C.

DODSON, J. J. and LEGGETT, W. C. 1974. Role of olfaction and vision in the behavior of American shad (*Alosa sapidissima*) homing to the Connecticut River from Long Island Sound. *J. Fish. Res. Bd. Canada* 31:1607–1619.

FENWICK, J. C. 1970. The pineal organ. Chapter 2, pp. 91–108, *in* W. S. Hoar and D. J. Randall, eds., *Fish Physiology*, Vol. 4. New York: Academic Press.

FLOCK, A. 1971. The lateral line organ mechanoreceptors. Chapter 8, pp. 241–264, *in* W. S. Hoar and D. J. Randall, eds., *Fish Physiology*, Vol. 5. New York: Academic Press.

HARA, T. J. 1970. An electrophysiological basis for olfactory discrimination in homing salmon: a review. *J. Fish. Res. Bd. Canada* 27(3):565–586.

HARA, T. J. 1971. Chemoreception. Chapter 4, pp. 79–120, *in* W. S. Hoar and D. J. Randall, eds., *Fish Physiology*, Vol. 5. New York: Academic Press.

HARRIS, G. G. and VAN BERGEIJK, W. A. 1962. Evidence that the lateral-line organ responds to near-field displacements of sound sources in water. *J. Acoust. Soc. America* 34(12):1831–1841.

INGLE, D. 1971. Vision: electrophysiology of the retina. Chapter 2, pp. 59-78, *in* W. S. Hoar and D. J. Randall, eds., *Fish Physiology,* Vol. 5. New York: Academic Press.

KALMIJN, A. J. 1971. The electric sense of sharks and rays. *J. Exp. Biol.* 55(2):371-384.

KLEEREKOPER, H. 1969. *Olfaction in fishes.* Bloomington: Indiana University Press.

LAWRY, J. V., Jr. 1973. A presumed near field pressure receptor in the snout of the lanternfish, *Tarletonbeania crenularis* (Myctophidae). *Mar. Behav. Physiol.* 1:295-303.

LISSMAN, H. W. 1963. Electric location by fishes. *Sci. Amer.* 209(3):50-59.

LOWENSTEIN, O. 1971. The labyrinth. Chapter 7, pp. 207-240, *in* W. S. Hoar and D. J. Randall, eds., *Fish Physiology,* Vol. 5. New York: Academic Press.

MUNZ, F. W. 1971. Vision: visual pigments. Chapter 1, pp. 1-32, *in* W. S. Hoar and D. J. Randall, eds., *Fish Physiology,* Vol. 5. New York: Academic Press.

MURRAY, R. W. 1971. Temperature receptors. Chapter 5, pp. 121-134, *in* W. S. Hoar and D. J. Randall, eds., *Fish Physiology,* Vol. 5. New York: Academic Press.

OGURI, M. and OMURA, Y. 1973. Ultrastructure and functional significance of the pineal organ in teleosts, pp. 412-432, *in* W. Chavin, ed., *Responses of Fish to Environmental Changes.* Illinois: Charles C. Thomas.

PROTASOV, V. R. 1970. Vision and near orientation of fish. *Israel Program for Scientific Translations, Jerusalem.* U.S. Department of Commerce, Washington, D.C.

ROMMEL, S. A., Jr and McCLEAVE, J. D. 1973. Sensitivity of American eels (*Anguilla rostrata*) and Atlantic salmon (*Salmo salar*) to weak electric and magnetic fields. *J. Fish. Res. Bd. Canada* 30(5):657-663.

TAVOLGA, W. N. 1971. Sound production and detection. Chapter 6, pp. 135-206, *in* W. S. Hoar and D. J. Randall, eds., *Fish Physiology,* Vol. 5. New York: Academic Press.

TAVOLGA, W. N., ed. 1976. Sound reception in fishes. *Benchmark Papers in Animal Behavior,* No. 7. Pennsylvania: Dowden, Hutchinson & Ross.

TOMITA, T. 1971. Vision: electrophysiology of the retina. Chapter 2, pp. 33-58, *in* W. S. Hoar and D. J. Randall, eds., *Fish Physiology,* Vol. 5. New York: Academic Press.

10

Osmoregulation

Osmotic and Ionic Changes in Blood and Muscle of Migrating Salmonids

GWYNETH PARRY

Head of Biology, Central Electricity Research Laboratories, Leatherhead, Surrey.

(Received 23 December 1960)

INTRODUCTION

Osmoregulation in teleost fishes, whether they live in fresh water or in the sea, is a physiological activity very closely related to their survival. Yet in spite of the importance of osmoregulation surprisingly little is known about how fish deal with the physiological problem inherent in living in hypoosmotic and hyperosmotic environments. The ability of some fishes to regulate in both environments during migrations is of even greater interest. In his classical review of osmoregulation in aquatic animals, Krogh (1939) emphasizes the lack of direct evidence in the study of migrating diadromous fishes. He says: ' . . . A small number of teleosts are able to stand a fairly rapid transference from fresh water to sea water and vice versa, and some of these undertake regular migrations between the two media, but the peculiarities which are responsible for this power are not at all clear in spite of the considerable amount of work spent upon the problem.' Some advances can be recorded; thus Pyefinch (1955) in his review of the literature on the Atlantic salmon writes, ' . . . the physiological and biochemical studies over the last twenty years or so have shown the advances that can be made now that general knowledge of endocrine organs and hormones has made it possible to investigate their function in fishes. Studies of the internal environment will not . . . provide the complete answer to the many outstanding problems of migration and smolt development, but further advances in this field, supplemented by appropriate investigation in the external environment, could provide a much more complete picture of these phases in the life-history of the salmon.'

In the years between the publication of these two accounts many data have been accumulated in the field of the physiology of migrating fishes, but relatively little information is available about the chemistry of the internal environment, about permeability, or about renal physiology, all of which would seem to be particularly relevant to a study of migration in diadromous fishes. The present study has been undertaken to provide information about the level of some ions in blood and muscle during the life-history and migratory periods of the salmon.

Such a migratory fish as the salmon might seem to be an ideal example for a study of euryhaline behaviour. In many ways this is so, but there are disadvantages. There is a long period in the life of the Atlantic salmon which is almost unknown, and when it is not possible to obtain any physiological material, namely the sea-water period. The adult fish almost always have to be studied in field conditions since they are large for the resources of most laboratory aquarium facilities, and for the same reason difficult to move from one place to another. Also, since they are economically important, the young stages are valuable as potential adults, and the adult ones valuable in themselves, so that the numbers required for physiological work are not always easy to obtain.

METHODS

Fish of the species *Salmo salar* (L.) were used for most of the analyses; wild fish were collected from many different places in Great Britain, and some young fish were reared

From *J. Exp. Biol.* 38:411–427. Reprinted by permission.

from eggs in laboratory conditions. Comparative analyses were made also on other *Salmo* species in Britain, i e. *S. trutta* (L.) as freshwater 'brown trout' or marine 'sea trout' and *S. gairdnerii* (Richardson), the rainbow trout (hatchery reared). Blood samples were obtained by cardiac puncture, with or without anaesthesia, without harming the fish. The most convenient anaesthetic was found to be 'Metacaine'* in a concentration of 1:10,000. Some other anaesthetics, viz. metycaine, trichlorethylene, carbon dioxide and urethane were tried but found to be less successful. Pre-spawning adult fish were netted at the mouths of rivers and blood was obtained from these by cardiac puncture immediately after the fish had been stunned.

Blood samples from very small fish were collected in soda glass cannulae, and immediately transferred to liquid paraffin in polythene sample tubes in the field. In the laboratory the blood samples were transferred to 'Damarda't-lined watchglasses which induced serum and a clot to separate. For larger fish, glass or nylon hypodermic syringes were used and the blood was stored for short periods under paraffin in polythene bottles, and frozen with 'Drikold.' As soon as possible the blood was centrifuged, and the plasma separated.

The freezing-point depression of the blood (Δ, $°C.$) was measured in very small quantities (0.001 ml. or less) in silica capillaries, using Ramsay's cryoscopic apparatus (Ramsay, 1969; Ramsay & Brown, 1955). Sodium, potassium and calcium were estimated by a flame photometry (EEL photometer) using standard solutions and dilutions of a standard sea water for comparison and calibration. Carbonate was measured in freshly collected blood samples by the micro-diffusion method of Conway (Conway, 1957). Chloride was estimated either by a Conway micro-diffusion method, and/or by a potentiometric titration with silver nitrate.

Some attempts were made to estimate trimethylamine and its oxide, either after a steam distillation extraction or by a microdiffusion method. Although considerable amounts were found in muscle extracts, none could be detected in blood samples of either the freshwater or marine salmon.

BLOOD SALT CONCENTRATIONS

(a) DURING THE LIFE HISTORY

This has been measured in blood from the young salmon embryos, in hatched alevins, fry, parr, smolts before and during their migration, in marine adults returning to spawn, in spawning adults and in the spawned kelts in both fresh water and sea water. The results are shown in Table 1 and in Fig. 1.

It can be seen that Δ_{blood} is at a constant level during the freshwater juvenile life, except for a rise during the first few weeks of life from 0.49° C. at hatching to 0.56° C. in the alevins and fry. This rise in blood concentration is apparent in the yolk-sac bearing alevin before feeding is initiated, and leads one to suppose that ionic regulation has begun already at this early stage. Busnel, Drilhon & Raffy (1946) measured the blood concentration in hatching eggs and found similar low figures for Δ_{blood} (0.49° C.) and a rise as the alevin develops (to 0.59° C. after 31 days). A rather higher figure (0.61° C.) is reported for 'Vesicular alevins' by Auvergnat & Sécondat (1941). The blood concentration rises slightly during the first year of freshwater life, but thereafter remains constant through the 'parr-smolt' transformation when the seaward migration begins.

When the parr metamorphoses into the smolt there is no significant change recorded for Δ_{blood}; that is, there is no increase in total blood concentration prior to entry into sea

*M.S. 222 from Sandoz Ltd.

†'Damarda' formite resin from Bakelite Ltd.

TABLE 1   Freezing-point depression (Δ, °C) of blood of salmon, Salmo salar

Stage in life history	Sampling time	Environment	Δ, °C. ± S.E. (N)
Eggs	January	Fresh water	0·49 ± 0·03 (12)
Alevins 6 days post-hatch	February	Fresh water	0·56 ± 0·02 (4)
Fry 3 months	April	Fresh water	0·56 ± 0·03 (32)
Parr 1 year 3 months	May	Fresh water	0·61 ± 0·02 (13)
Smolts 2 years 3 months	May	Fresh water	0·58 ± 0·08 (12)
Smolts 3 years 6 months	August	Fresh water	0·65 ± 0·10 (15)
Adult pre-spawning	July	Sea water	0·64 ± 0·01 (7)
Adult spawning	December	Fresh water	0·61 ± 0·05 (17)
Adult kelts	January	Fresh water	0·63 ± 0·01 (4)
Adult kelts	February	Sea water	0·69 ± 0·04 (7)

S.E. is standard error of mean; N is number of measurements.

water, nor is there evidence for a 'demineralization' of the blood to stimulate a sea-going urge (cf. Fontaine & Callamand, 1940, 1948; Kubo, 1953). However, a greater variability in the results was found at this stage and this may represent a degree of sensitivity of the smolt (Fontaine & Callamand, 1948), or of hormone 'unbalance' in the fish at this time (Hoar, 1951). A similar variability (in sodium content of the blood) has been reported by Koch & Evans (1959) for wild migratory smolts.

If smolts were kept in fresh water beyond the time of migration, Δ_{blood} was found to be higher than in the migrating smolts. For example, fish from the River Piddle at Wareham (Dorset) kept in tanks of running hard water at Stevenage (Water Pollution Research Laboratory) for 12 months and hatchery-reared fish of similar age from the Scottish Hydro-Electric Board's hatchery at Invergarry, Inverness-shire, kept for a similar period in soft water, both showed this trend. There was no indication of a seasonal return to normal during the annual smolt migration; the rise observed could have been the result of ageing or of artificial feeding.

Very little is known of the life of the salmon in sea water and no material of this stage was obtained for the present study.

Adults from sea water, returning to the spawning grounds in the river, were captured in sea water at the mouth of the River Dee, Aberdeen. They had Δ_{blood} of the same order of that of other marine fishes, although it is about 10% lower in concentration than that of many estimates reported in the literature (Black, 1957). This lower value is probably due to the difference in techniques for measuring Δ_{blood}. There is no reason to believe that the figures obtained from these fish did not represent the level of blood concentration in sea-living salmon. When the adult salmon reached the spawning ground and had been in a freshwater environment for 3–4 months, Δ_{blood} dropped to 0.61° C., which was a little higher than the level for juvenile salmon in fresh water. Spawned fish, although starving and exhausted, are still able to regulate since the blood does not fall below this level of concentration. However ability to osmoregulate is impaired to some degree, as the spawned kelts after 5–6 months of starving freshwater life cannot survive or maintain their normal blood concentration when transferred directly to sea water. Similar values are reported in the literature for adult salmon; Benditt, Morrison & Irving (1941) give Δ_{blood} = 0.77° C. for salmon in ½ sea water (Δ = 0.87° C.), and figures reported for adult spawning salmon in fresh water are Δ_{blood} = 0.64–0.66° C. (Fontaine, 1954; Hoar, 1953).

(b) OTHER SALMONID SPECIES

Freezing-point measurements of the blood of two other *Salmo* species obtainable in Britain are shown in Table 2. No significant differences could be found between fish of the different species of similar age groups. The same general rise in blood concentration,

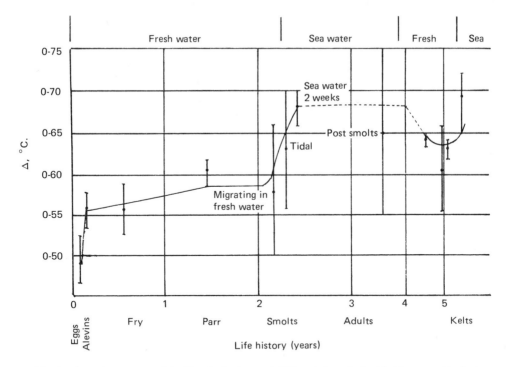

Fig. 1. Osmotic pressure of the blood of salmon at different times in its life history and in fresh
water and sea water.

observed in *S. salar* with increasing age, can be seen in *S. trutta* and *S. gairdnerii*.

Some figures for the Pacific genus *Oncorhynchus* from the literature seem to be considerably higher in range. Thus, Greene (1926) gives $\Delta_{\text{blood}} = 0.61\text{--}0.67°$ C. for adults of
O. tchawytscha in fresh water and 0.76° C. for these fish in sea water; and Kubo (1953),
for *O. masou* gives 0.60–0.69° C. for fish in fresh water and 0.75–0.90° C. for fish in sea
water. It is possible that this difference is a real one, related to the difference in species
or environment, but it seems more probable that it reflects different techniques of freezing-
point measurement. A summary of the figures reported in the literature for different species is given in Table 3.

(c) TRANSFER TO DIFFERENT SALINITIES

The osmotic changes in the blood after transfer of the fish from fresh water to sea
water is of particular interest in these migrating fish. The experimental transfer, to sea
water and its dilutions, of young parr and smolts (1 and 2 years old) of three species of
Salmo has been described in previous papers (Parry, 1958, 1960). In general, salmonids of
age group 2+ years were able to tolerate a direct transfer from fresh water to full strength
sea water. The changes in blood concentration following the transfer were measured by
determining the freezing-point depression. It was found that for fish of the 2+ year age
group 150- 300 hr. were required for the fish to be able to regulate its blood concentration
to the normal levels. except in the case of the migrating smolt of *S. salar* which regulated
its blood within a 24 hr. period.

An attempt was made to find out what happened to smolts during similar conditions
in a river. Smolts were trapped at a station (on the River Coquet, Northumberland) just
above tidal water, and were transferred a mile downstream into tidal water. The blood
concentration of these fish can be compared with that of fish living naturally in this environment and also with fish from the same population transferred to running sea water in

TABLE 2 Freezing-point depression of blood (Δ, °C.) of other salmonid species

Species	Stage in life history	Environment	Δ, C. ± S.E. (*N*)
S. trutta	Eggs 6 days	Fresh water	$0\cdot47 \pm 0\cdot03$ (24)
	Parr 8 cm.	Fresh water	$0\cdot57 \pm 0\cdot06$ (13)
	'Smolt' 14 cm.	Fresh water	$0\cdot57 \pm 0\cdot01$ (13)
	Adult 20 cm.	Fresh water	$0\cdot59 \pm 0\cdot01$ (7)
	Finnock 20 cm.	Sea water	$0\cdot69 \pm 0\cdot27$ (7)
S. gairdnerii	Parr 9 cm.	Fresh water	$0\cdot57 \pm 0\cdot03$ (7)
	'Smolt' 15 cm.	Fresh water	$0\cdot55 \pm 0\cdot07$ (23)
	Adult 25 cm.	Fresh water	$0\cdot57 \pm 0\cdot02$ (23)
	Adult 25 cm.	Sea water (6 days)	$0\ 71 \pm 0\cdot02$ (4)

S.E. is standard error of mean; *N* is number of measurements.

the laboratory. The temperature of the river water and of the running sea-water tanks was about 10° C. during these experiments (Table 4). Freezing-point measurements of the water in the tidal reach of the river gave values of Δ between 0.09 and 1.00° C. at different states of the tide. A few fish were caught (by rod and line) in the same part of the river and the blood was sampled; the experimental fish were held in a keep-box immersed in the river. It is interesting to note that the naturally occurring fish, which had been in the tidal reaches for an unknown time, had blood no more concentrated than that of fish in fresh water above the tide. Of the smolts confined in a keep-box, the ones sampled after three tides showed a higher blood concentration than those sampled after seven tides. Two explanations can be put forward for this: (1) that the abrupt transfer to a higher salinity could not be compensated by the osmoregulatory mechanisms; or (2) that diuretic loss of water consequent upon the confinement in the keep-box was preventing the reduction in urine flow which is a necessary part of the physiological adjustment of the fish to higher salinities.

Fish from the same population, transferred directly to running sea water, also showed a rise in blood concentration above the level normal for these fish in sea water, but this was controlled within 12 days.

A similar transfer of adult fish, but from fresh water to sea water, was attempted in January 1959 (Table 5). The design of this experiment was the same as the previous one, i.e., the fish were transported from the freshwater traps and confined in keep-boxes immersed in sea water. The sea water in Morecambe Bay where the experiment was made, had a freezing-point depression of $\Delta = 1.60°$ C. at the time of the experiment. The inability of the salmon kelts to osmoregulate is very much more marked than that of the salmon smolts in spite of a more favourable surface/volume ratio. Again, some of the increase in blood concentration could have been brought about by diuresis, but it is clear that whatever the cause, control had not been gained after 4 days in sea water. A contributory cause towards this inability to regulate could have been the low temperature of the water, which was at about 0° C. at this time, with ice forming on the inshore surface of the sea. A subsequent experiment in January 1960 with kelts kept in larger tanks of running water indicated a better degree of control with Δ_{blood} maintained at about 0.90–1.00° C., but in this case the sea water in Morecambe Bay was much diluted by rain water run-off, and the freezing-point of the sea water was only $\Delta = 1.20°$ C. The temperature in the 1960 experiment was similar to that of the earlier one.

A similar experiment with fresh-run adult fish moving into fresh water from sea water would be interesting, but so far is not available. The changes in the blood of a species of Pacific salmon, *Oncorhynchus nerka*, have been followed in natural conditions along the length of the Fraser River (Idler & Tsuyuki, 1958), and showed a gradual decline of blood concentration of about 5% of the marine level.

TABLE 3   Freezing-point depression of blood of salmonids (from the literature)

Species	Stage in life history	Environment	Δblood, °C.	Author
S. salar	Eggs hatching	Fresh water	0·49	Busnel et al. (1946)
	Alevins 31 days post-hatch	Fresh water	0·59	Busnel et al. (1946)
	Vesicular alevins'	Fresh water	0·61	Auvergnat & Sécondat (1941)
	Adult	½ sea water ($\Delta = 0·87°$ C.)	0·77	Benditt et al. (1941)
	Adult	Fresh water	0·64	Benditt et al. (1941)
	Adult	Fresh water	0·65	Fontaine (1954); Hoar (1953)
	Adult spawning	Fresh water	0·66	Fontaine (1954)
S. gairdnerii	Adult	Fresh water ($\Delta = 0·02°$ C.)	0·50	Busnel (1943)
O. tchawytscha	Adult	Sea water	0·76	Greene (1926)
	Adult	Fresh water	0·74	
	Adult spawning	Fresh water	0·67	
	Adult spawning	Fresh water	0·61	
O. masou	Smolt, migrating	Fresh water	0·70-0·76	Kubo (1953, 1955)
	Adult	Fresh water	0·60-0·69	
	Adult	Sea water	0·75-0·90	

TABLE 4   Transference of migrating salmon smolts to sea water and tidal water

(Temperature about 10°C.)

Conditions	Δblood, °C ± S.E. (N)
Smolts from freshwater trap	0·59 ± 0·05 (12)
Smolts naturally in tidal part of river	0·60 ± 0·02 (4)
Smolts kept in tidal reaches for 3 tides	0·67 ± 0·05 (6)
Smolts kept in tidal reaches for 7 tides	0·63 ± 0·07 (3)
Smolts in sea water 1 day	0·65 (2)
Smolts in sea water 3 days	0·73 (2)
Smolts in sea water 12 days	0·68 ± 0·02 (8)

S.E. is standard error of the mean; N is number of measurements.

TABLE 5   Transference of salmon kelts to sea water

(Temperature about 0°C.)

Conditions	Δblood, °C. ± S.E. (N)
Kelts trapped in fresh water	0·62 ± 0·07 (3)
Kelts 1 day in sea water	1·18 (2)
Kelts 2 days in sea water	1·02 (2)
Kelts 3 days in sea water	0·90 ± 0·02 (4)
Kelts 4 days in sea water	1·10 (1)

S.E. is standard error of the mean; N is the number of measurements.

LEVELS OF INORGANIC IONS IN THE BLOOD

Estimates of the total ions in the blood can be calculated from the measurement of blood from the relationship that 283 m-equiv. monovalent strong electrolyte per kg. water has $\Delta = 1°$ C. (Ramsay & Brown, 1955). The freezing-point measurements of blood discussed in the previous section thus show that the total ionic concentration rises after hatching from 148 m-equiv./kg. to about 160–170 m-equiv./kg. There is no rise in premigratory smolts, but there is a rise of about 12% to 200 m-equiv./kg. in smolts in tidal water or in sea water; this is maintained in the pre-spawning marine adult. The ionic concentration of the blood drops a little while the adult completes its spawning migration into fresh water.

Results of analyses are shown in Table 6 and summarized in Fig. 2. Sodium and chloride are numerically the most important ions of the total ionic concentration. In blood from juvenile fish in fresh water, sodium and chloride are present in sufficient concentrations to account for almost all the ions present. But in adult pre-spawning fish the chloride concentration is considerably less than the value expected from measurements of the freezing-point. This anionic deficiency is not covered by high carbonate. Analyses of carbonate show very similar levels in both sea-water and freshwater fish (within the limits of experimental error, which are quite serious with regard to this ion). It might be thought that sea-water levels of carbonate would rise with low plasma chloride, or drop with high plasma chloride (Fontaine & Boucher-Firly's hypothesis, 1934). The order of concentration of carbonate found, however, makes it unlikely that this ion can play much of a part in maintaining the total anionic concentration.

Both anionic and cationic organic constituents may be important, but analyses of plasma for trimethylamine oxide failed to indicate this substance in the plasma, although the methods employed should have been adequate (for the 1 ml. samples) if it had been present in significant quantities. No estimates of ammonia have been made. Further work is in progress to determine whether amino acids play an important part in osmoregulation during the transference from one salinity to another, as they do in some invertebrates (Shaw, 1958).

In general the levels of individual ions follow the pattern expected from the freezing-point data. There is some indication that a size-concentration effect (Houston, 1950) is present; i.e. the concentrations of sodium and chloride in the plasma drop between that of the very young fingerlings and that of the 2-year smolt stage. Freshwater and sea-water levels of plasma potassium seem to be about the same, and the range is well within that reported in the literature (Field, Elvehjem & Juday, 1943; Phillips & Brockway, 1958; Gordon, 1959a, b; Houston, 1959).

The plasma ion-levels of migrating smolts, and of smolts transferred artifically to sea-water are interesting. Pre-migratory smolts in fresh water showed relatively variable figures for both freezing-point determinations and for inorganic analyses. This is shown by the larger standard errors of the figures in Tables 6 and 4. A similar variability is reported in plasma sodium levels of Atlantic salmon smolts (Koch & Evans, 1959). This high level of variability, however, is likely to be a reflexion of the curious physiological state of the smolt, rather than of direct osmotic significance.

ION CONCENTRATIONS IN MUSCLE

The levels of inorganic ions in the muscle are of interest, from the osmotic point of view, in relation to their levels in the blood. In a migratory fish such as the salmon even greater interest hinges on the response of the muscle, as well as the blood, in conformity with the external salinity changes which the animal encounters during its migrations. There are two possible responses of muscle tissue to such changes: (1) it can follow the

TABLE 6 Ions in blood plasma of *Salmo salar*

Fish, age, etc.	Medium	Ions, mM./kg. weight ± S.E. (N)					Total ions calculated from Δ m-equiv./kg.
		Na$^+$	K$^+$	Ca^{2+}	Cl$^-$	CO$_2^-$	
Parr	Fresh water	117·0 ± 17·6 (9)	2·19 ± 0·85 (8)	2·33 (3)	129·8 ± 21·5 (9)	—	160
Smolts	Fresh water	131·2 ± 52·0 (15)	3·03 ± 0·91 (11)	2·00 ± 1·40 (4)	182·7 ± 10·5 (3)	7·3 ± 3·0 (6)	174
Post-smolts	Fresh water	155·8 ± 44·0 (20)	3·28 ± 0·51 (19)	—	132·8 ± 45·3 (11)	—	185
Smolts	Sea water 2 weeks	159·3 ± 25·3 (11)	3·62 ± 1·63 (9)	—	166·3 ± 56·7 (4)	—	194
Adults	Sea water	211·9 ± 106·2 (19)	3·15 ± 2·05 (18)	3·43 ± 1·39(13)	156·7 ± 72·2 (10)	11·0 ± 2·4 (11)	182
Adults	Fresh water (head of tide)	180·6 ± 76·9 (5)	1·86 ± 1·20 (5)	3·98 ± 1·09 (5)	—	—	—
Adults spawning	Fresh water	176·0 ± 37·0 (39)	3·03 ± 0·92 (29)	3·45 ± 0·90 (27)	172·4 ± 75·8 (12)	—	174
Adults	Fresh water	157·0 ± 62·0 (8)	3·77 ± 0·95 (7)	3·72 ± 0·98 (6)	—	—	180
Adult kelts	Fresh water + 2 – 5 weeks in $\frac{2}{3}$ sea water	211·3 ± 15·5 (4)	4·08 ± 0·86 (4)	3·38 ± 1·33 (4)	—	—	200
Adult kelts	Fresh water +2 days sea water	294·0 ± 72·5 (5)	3·44 ± 0·40 (5)	3·98 ± 1·30 (6)	—	—	—

S.E. is standard error of mean; N is number of measurements.

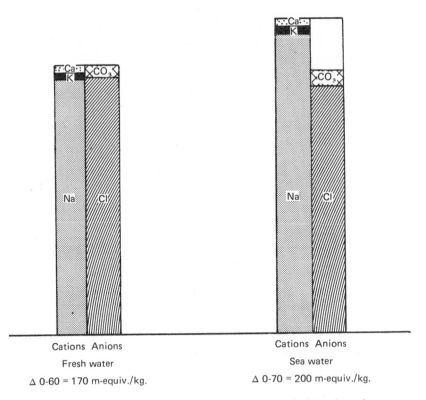

Cations Anions
Fresh water
Δ 0-60 = 170 m-equiv./kg.

Cations Anions
Sea water
Δ 0-70 = 200 m-equiv./kg.

Fig. 2. The inorganic composition of the blood plasma of adult salmon in fresh water and sea water.

osmotic and ionic changes in the blood, more or less closely, or (2) it can behave differently and thus act as a reservoir of ions or water to buffer blood changes (Drilhon & Pora, 1936).

Analyses of the water content and some of the common inorganic ions which have been studied in blood plasma have been made for muscle (Table 7), and a pictorial summary is shown in Fig. 3.

TABLE 7   Inorganic ions in salmon muscle

Fish	Conditions	‰ water	mM/kg. water			
			Na	K	Ca	Cl
Smolt	Fresh water	—	16·3*	210*	3·14*	2·60*
Smolt	2 weeks in sea water	792	33·3	185	3·55	—
Adults	Sea water	676	28·1	206	2·84	6·12
Adults	Fresh water, head of the tide	641	29·7	194	2·95	—
Adults	Fresh water, spawning	776	66·4	261	2·84	—
Adults	Fresh water, kelts	805	45·5	199	2·22	—
Adults	Two-thirds sea water, 4 weeks	778	54·7	200	2·16	—
Adults	Sea water, 3 hours	779	80·7	205	2·99	—
Adults	Sea water, 2 days	822	36·7	238	1·94	—

*Figures for mM./kg. wet weight of muscle. All the figures are the means of a number of observations.

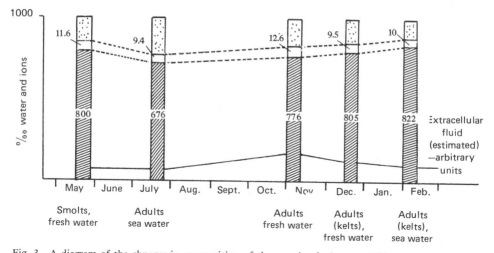

Fig. 3. A diagram of the chnages in composition of the muscle of salmon at different times in its life history and in different environments.   ⊠ , organic constituents; ☐, inorganic constituents (enlargeci); ⊠, water.

If one compares, first of all, the muscle of freshwater spawning adults and the fresh-running sea-water adults, there are some quite marked differences to be seen. The water content of the whole muscle has increased considerably, by nearly 15%, during the passage of the fish upstream in a period of about 5 months. This increased water content of the muscle, however, does not mean that the whole has become more dilute or watery, as both the sodium and the potassium content of the whole muscle has increased, the sodium by 100% and the potassium by 25%. This increase probably means that the extracellular space of the spawning fish in fresh water has increased. At the same time the calcium content. which might be expected to be inside the muscle fibres rather than in the extracellular fluid, remains the same. That these changes come after and not before entry into fresh water is shown by the analyses of muscle from a fish at the head of the tide on its way upstream. The analyses for this fish are substantially the same as those for the sea-water fish.

Analyses of muscle from migrating smolts in fresh water show an interesting contrast, in that although the water content of the muscle is high, the sodium is low. This could be interpreted in terms of a small extracellular space, but with the usual ionic content inside the muscle, because in this case the potassium (which will be mainly inside the cells) is high. A comparison of the two measurements of chloride in the muscle substantiate this point. The figure for muscle from adult sea-living fish is about twice that of the smolt. Most of the chloride will be in the extracellular space, and thus the figures would represent a small extracellular space in the smolt, but a larger one in the marine adult.

Kelts which have been in fresh water for 9–10 months show different changes. In these fish the water content of the muscle is high (800‰) and the sodium content is mid-way between that of the young freshwater fish, and the adult spawning fish in fresh water. This could indicate an enlarged extracellular space (as in the spawning fish), but also a dilution of the muscle fibre contents, a conclusion borne out by the lower potassium content and by the drop in calcium.

Next we can consider the changes which follow the transfer of fish from one salinity to another when the fish is not in equilibrium osmotically. Two weeks after the transfer of migrating smolts to sea water the water content is scarcely reduced at all, nor does the sodium increase appreciably. Potassium, however, does drop. These changes could be interpreted as a movement of both water and ions out of the muscle fibres into a slightly increased extracellular space. It must be remembered that at the same time the blood becomes concentrated to some extent, so that the water movement could be an osmotic one and the ion extrusion from the fibres could be stimulated by the subsequent concentration within them; it is known that muscle fibres have well-developed powers of ion regulation. The slight increase in extracellular space could be the result of a time lag in these processes.

When the adult spent fish are subjected to the reverse change of salinity, the results are different. Kelts acclimatized to Morecambe Bay sea water (at a salinity equivalent to about two-thirds of oceanic water) showed a slight reduction in water content of the muscle, but retained the high sodium level. Potassium was lower than in spawning fish, but the same as in marine ones, while calcium was low, as in the spent fish. Thus, following our previous interpretation, the extracellular space is still enlarged, and this is indicated also by a high sodium content. The potassium is at the level characteristic of the fresh-run sea-living adult, so that in other respects the muscle is in equilibrium with the blood and with the external salinity, after this period of acclimatization. However, the figures for fish transferred to an artificial* sea water for much shorter periods, show a pronounced disequilibrium 3 hr. after the transfer. The water content, perhaps surprisingly, had not changed very much from the $800\%_{00}$ characteristic of the kelts in fresh water, so that although there was some osmotic depletion of water from the muscle into the blood, this is not so high as one might expect from the increase in blood concentration which follows such a transfer (Δ_{blood} changes from $0.63°$ C. to about $1.00°$ C.). The potassium does not change much in this period, but the sodium content does so very sharply. Thus while the volume of extracellular space only changes to a moderate degree, its ion concentration probably does increase, possibly by the movement of sodium from the blood plasma into the extracellular space. After a longer period in the artificial sea water, the water content of the muscle increases, while the sodium declines to a more normal level and the potassium increases a little. Presumably the extracellular space increases again at this time, as osmotic control in the blood is re-established by the movement of water into the extracellular space only; some of this water may come from the muscle fibres, since their potassium content is increased. That the fish is far from achieving equilibrium conditions is shown by the marked divergences of these analyses from those for fresh-running sea fish, as well as from a study of the blood changes at this time.

Values for the extracellular space are obviously of great importance in checking the assumptions made in this interpretation. Unfortunately, while such values can be obtained for small fish in aquarium conditions, e.g. in smolts being transferred from fresh water to sea water, it is very difficult to arrange an experiment to obtain values directly for the larger adult fish.

Similar increases in extracellular space of adult *Salmo gairdnerii* recently transferred from fresh water to sea water have been reported by Houston (1959) from similar data, but Gordon (1959a), studying salinity transfers in *S. trutta*, thinks that the extracellular compartment is more or less constant. One of the most important differences between the experiments of these two authors and the ones described here is that the changes reported in this paper are those shown by the naturally migrating fish, at the relevant times of the year, so that the three sets of experiments may not be strictly comparable.

Sodium in the muscle of adult fish is reported to be subject to considerable seasonal and reproductive changes, e.g. in *S. trutta* (Gordon, 1959a) and in *Oncorbynchus nerka* (Idler & Tsuyuki, 1958). Some of the change from 66 mM./kg. in spawning fish, to 45 mM./kg. in the post-spawned fish could be due to this. It is tempting to correlate the changes during the reproductive period with changes in availability of steroid hormones;

*Made by adding the appropriate quantity of Tidman's Sea Salt to Morecambe Bay sea water.

Canadian workers have found high levels of cortisone and cortisol in adult fish just prior to spawning (17 times the normal human level), while in fish before entry into fresh water the level was only one-sixth of this (Idler, Ronald & Schmidt, 1959): Spalding (unpublished, reported in Chester Jones, 1956) showed that dosing brown trout with DCA or cortisone raised the sodium and lowered the potassium in muscle. Similar changes in the concentrations of steroids in *S. salar* have been found during the parr-smolt change (Fontaine & Hatey, 1954).

Trimethylamine oxide, while apparently absent from the blood in significant quantities was found in the muscle to a variable extent. In post-migratory smolts still in fresh water the concentration was 35 mg. %. in fresh-running marine adults it was 75 mg. %, and has risen as high as 250 mg. % in adult spawning fish in fresh water. Kelts in fresh water 3–4 months after spawning had very variable concentrations between 100 and 176 mg. % The presence of any trimethylamine at all in the juvenile freshwater fish is interesting in view of the hypothesis that this substance is a characteristic of marine fish only, although it has previously been reported for freshwater fish (Anderson & Fellers, 1952). This trimethylamine is unlikely to be derived from the diet, but could represent the final stage of a basic metabolic pathway which is relatively inoperative in the juvenile fish. The measurements of trimethylamine in the adult fish are very interesting, in that the level is so high in the spawning fish. This must argue against an osmoregulatory function for this substance (Beatty, 1939) since one would expect the opposite change. It must be remembered that the spawning fish are starving, and perhaps the high level of trimethylamine present in the muscle arises from the metabolism of its own tissues during this period. The lower and extremely variable concentrations found in spent kelts could relate to their degree of debilitation.

DISCUSSION

Some specific points arising from this investigation may be mentioned. The anionic deficiency of the blood in the marine fish is of great interest osmotically, and attempts are being made to characterize this.

Nitrogen-containing compounds are possible contributors to the ion content of the plasma. Ammonia seems seldom to have been investigated in salmonids. Its concentration is likely to be low, however (reported as 0.104 mg. % in laked *Salvelinus* blood) since both the kidney and gill epithelia of teleosts are permeable to it. In teleosts generally the blood level is low. Trimethylamine or its oxide is a possible non-protein nitrogen constituent but this was not found in any significant amounts in the plasma, even though it is present in the muscles. Betaine is another possibility which has not yet been investigated. Protein nitrogen, as amino acids, seems to be present in the blood in significant amounts. Hoar (1953) records *ca.* 70 mg./l. protein in 'mature' (?sea water) adults and a drop to 33 mg./l. in spawning fish. Recent analyses of amino acids in the blood of rainbow trout and salmon kelts indicate levels of amino acids between 30 and 60 mg./l.* How this is related to the spawning migration and to the freshwater-sea-water transfer is not yet known.

Cholesterol is another organic constituent of blood which may be important osmotically, first, in a direct concentration effect, and secondly because of its water-binding affinities. In the Pacific salmon, *Oncorhynchus nerka*, the total cholesterol in the blood is reduced from nearly 600 mg. % at the beginning of the spawning migration to 200 mg. % at the point of spawning. The pre-spawning level is singularly high in comparison with warm-blooded animals (Idler & Tsuyuki, 1958). Similar high levels have been reported for other fish (carp, 662 mg. %, Field *et al.* 1943) and for other salmonids (in a Japanese river, probably *O. keta*, 150 mg. %, Okamura 1935). The relationship between cholesterol levels and water balance would be an interesting problem.

*Determined by C. B. Cowey, N.I.R.D., Shinfield, Reading.

The possible presence of other, unspecified constituents in the plasma should not be overlooked. Recent investigations of the osmotic behaviour of some arctic fish have shown that these teleosts can raise the total osmotic concentration of the blood to equivalence with sea water. The extra blood concentration was not contributed by the common inorganic ions, nor by glucose, glycerol, proteins, urea or ammonia (Scholander, Van Dam, Kanwisher, Hammel & Gordon, 1957).

PRE-MIGRATORY CHANGES IN WATER AND ELECTROLYTE METABOLISM

Some authors, notably Kubo (1953), Pickford & Atz (1957), Fontaine & Callamand (1948) and Fontaine (1951) have reported falling plasma and tissue concentrations of chloride in pre-migratory juvenile and adult fish, and have suggested that this is a characteristic of anadromous species. Fontaine & Callamand further suggested that the electrolyte depletion plays a role in the initiation of the seaward migration by producing increased activity in the fish. Investigations by Fontaine & Baraduc (1954), Fontaine, Lachiver, Leloup & Olivereau (1948), Fontaine & Leloup (1950, 1952), Hoar (1952) and Swift (1955, 1959) of changes in the thyroid gland, and changes induced by dosing salmonid fish with thyroid hormones, indicate that the increased activity undoubtedly shown by migrating smolts is related to the activity of this gland.

On the other hand, Hoar (1953) and Nishida (1953) relate the pre-migratory decrease in chloride to the development at this stage of numbers of 'chloride-secretory cells' in the gills of the two *Oncorhynchus* species they studied, viz. *masou* and *nerka*. This hypothesis is difficult to test. In *S. salar* these cells are present in the fry as soon as the gills are functional, generally some 2 years prior to migration. Whether the number of these cells increases before the seaward migration, is difficult to establish; also one might ask if the cells are non-functional during 2 years of juvenile freshwater life. Alternatively, a suppression of the freshwater salt absorbing mechanism could occur as a pre-adaptation to marine osmoregulation, especially as certain other biochemical characteristics of the young fish change at this time to those characteristic of the adult marine fish. It seems clear from experiments described in the literature that an adjustive period is necessary after the fish has entered sea water before it can deal adequately with the different osmotic situation. Black (1957) and Houston (1959) found independently that for chum salmon fry 36 hr. is necessary for adequate regulation to be developed in sea water; Keys (1933) found a period of about 50 hr. for *Anguilla vulgaris*; Houston (1959) and I (Parry, 1958) find about 50 hr. necessary for *S. gairdnerii* in 50% sea water; and my figures for *S. trutta* of smolt size and age indicate that about 200 hr. is necessary in (50% sea water), although migrating smolts of *S. salar* were much better able to adjust to the salinity change. Following this adjustive phase, a second or regulative phase takes its place and regulation of the plasma and muscle concentrations brings the levels of individual ions to those characteristic of marine teleosts. Histological changes in the acidophil cells in the gills (Vickers, 1958) after transfer of fish to saline media, indicate a similar time for an adjustive, followed by a regulative phase. A more recent electron microscope study of these cells (Houston & Threadgold, 1961) could support this conclusion.

Thus, far from a condition of pre-adaptation to a marine life, which the falling chloraemia of the migrating smolt has been said to induce, there are indications that the young fish are unprepared, or very inadequately prepared, physiologically for this change, and require a considerable time before the regulative phase can be brought into play. Salmonids (and other euryhaline diadromous fish) differ from other teleosts in their ability to reach this regulative phase before they suffer ill-effects from the imbalance of ions in plasma and muscle in the adjustive phase, and to be able to regulate after the fashion of both marine and freshwater teleosts, according to the environment in which they find themselves.

SUMMARY

1. Osmoregulation of the Atlantic salmon in fresh water and sea water, and during transfers from one salinity to another, has been studied by measuring the freezing-point and the levels of some inorganic ions in the blood plasma, and water content and ions in whole muscle.

2. An increase in blood concentration of about 12% follows the transfer of juvenile fish (smolts) from fresh water to sea water; and a fall of concentration of about 5% follows the transfer of the adult fish from sea water to fresh water.

3. Some changes in analyses of whole muscle indicate changes in the extracellular compartment during transfers from one salinity to another.

4. Osmoregulatory powers of juvenile salmon (smolts) and fresh-run adults are good, but spent fish (kelts) returning from fresh water to sea water, osmoregulate with difficulty or not at all.

The material used for the physiological studies reported here has been obtained principally from natural sources from many different parts of Britain. Without assistance from the various River Boards and other authorities this would have been impossible, and I would like to thank all those who have been concerned. In particular, I am most grateful to Messrs. G. Common, Northumberland and Tyneside River Board; H. Evans, Gwynedd River Board; H. Gavin, Aberdeen Harbour Board; B. C. Lincoln, Scottish Hydro Electric Board, Invergarry; and L. Stewart, Lancashire River Board.

REFERENCES

ANDERSON, D. W. & FELLERS, C. R. (1952). The occurrence of trimethylamine and trimethylamine oxide in freshwater fishes. *Food Res.* 17, 472–4.

AUVERGNAT, R. & SÉCONDAT, M. (1941). Influences des variations de salinité sur la pression osmotique des alévins vésicules de saumon migrateur (*Salmo salar*). *Bull. Inst. océanogr. Monaco*, no. 805, 17 pp.

BEATTY, S. A. (1939). Studies of fish spoilage. III. The trimethylamine oxide content of the muscles of Nova Scotia fish. *J. Fish. Res. Bd. Can.* 4, 229–32.

BENDITT, E., MORRISON, P. & IRVING, L. (1941). The blood of Atlantic salmon during migration. *Biol. Bull., Woods Hole*, 80, 429–40.

BLACK, V. S. (1957). Excretion and osmoregulation. In *The Physiology of Fishes*, I, pp. 163–99. Ed. M. E. Brown. New York: Academic Press.

BUSNEL, R. G. (1943). Recherches de physiologie appliqués à la pisciculture: à propos de la migration de la truite arc-en-ciel. *Bull. franç. Piscic.*, no. 127, pp. 45–67.

BESNEL, R. G., DRILHON, A. & RAFFY, A. (1946). Recherches sur la physiologie des Salmonides. *Bull. Inst. océanogr. Monaco*, no. 893, pp. 23.

CONWAY, E. J. (1957). *Microdiffusion Analysis and Volumetric Error*, pp. 464. London: Crosby Lockwood.

DRILHON, A. & PORA, E. A. (1936). Regulation minérale du milieu intérieur chez les poissons stenohalines. *Ann. Physiol. Physicochem. Biol.* 12, 139–68.

FIELD, J. B., ELVEHJEM, C. A. & JUDAY, C. (1943). A study of the blood constituents of carp and trout (*Salvelinus*). *J. Biol. Chem.* 148, 261–9.

FONTAINE, M. (1951). Sur la diminution de la teneur en chlore du muscle des jeunes saumons (smolts) lors de la migration. *C. R. Acad. Sci., Paris*, 232, 2477.

FONTAINE, M. (1954). Du déterminisme physiologique des migrations. *Biol. Rev.* 29, 390–418.

FONTAINE, M. & BARADUC, M. (1954). Influence d'une thyroxination sur l'euryhalinité d'un salmonide, la truite arc-en-ciel (*Salmo gairdnerii*). *C. R. Soc. Biol., Paris*, 148, 1942–4.

FONTAINE, M. & BOUCHER-FIRLY, S. (1934). Recherches au la réserve alcaline du sang des poissons. Ses variations au cours des changements de salinité. *Bull. Inst. océanogr. Monaco*, no. 646, pp. 1–12.

FONTAINE, M. & CALLAMAND, O. (1940). Influence de la temperature sur l'elimination chlorée de l'anguille. *C. R. Acad. Sci., Paris*, 211, 488–9.

FONTAINE, M. & CALLAMAND, O. (1948). Nouvelles recherches sur le déterminisme physiologique de l'avalaison des poissons migrateurs amphibiotiques. *Bull. Inst. Mus. Hist. Nat.* pp. 317–20.

FONTAINE, M. & HATEY, J. (1954). Sur la teneur en 17-hydroxycorticosteroids du plasma de saumon (*Salmo salar*). *C. R. Acad. Sci., Paris*, 239, 219–31.

FONTAINE, M., LACHIVER, F., LELOUP, J. & OLIVEREAU, M. (1948). La fonction thyroidienne au cours de sa migration reproductrice. *J. Physiol. Path. gén.* 40, 182.

FONTAINE, M. & LELOUP, J. (1950). L'iodémie du saumon au cours de sa migration reproductrice. *C. R. Acad. Sci., Paris*, 230, 1216.

FONTAINE, M. & LELOUP, J. (1950). L'iodémie du jeune saumon (*Salmo salar*) en eau douce. *C. R. Acad. Sci., Paris*, 231, 169–71.

FONTAINE, M. & LELOUP, J. (1952). L'iode thyroidein du jeune saumon au cours de sa smoltification. *C. R. Acad. Sci., Paris*, 234, 1479–80.

GORDON, M. S. (1959a). Ionic regulation in the brown trout (*Salmo trutta* L.). *J. Exp. Biol.* 36, 227–52.

GORDON, M. S. (1959b). Osmotic and ionic regulation in Scottish brown trout and sea trout (*Salmo trutta* L.). *J. Exp. Biol.* 36, 253–60.

GREENE, C. W. (1926). The physiology of the spawning migration. *Physiol. Rev.* 6, 201–41.

HOAR, W. S. (1951). Some aspects of the physiology of fish. I. Hormones. *Univ. Toronto Biol. Ser.* no. 59, 1–51.

HOAR, W. S. (1952). Thyroid function in some diadromous and land-locked teleosts. *Trans. Roy. Soc. Can.* 46, 39–53.

HOAR, W. S. (1953). The control and timing of fish migration. *Biol. Rev.* 28, 437–52.

HOUSTON, A. H. (1959). Osmoregulatory adaptation of steelhead trout (*Salmo gairdnerii* Richardson) to sea water. *Canad. J. Zool.* 37, 729–48.

HOUSTON, A. H. & THREADGOLD, L. T. (1961). An electron microscope study of the 'chloride-secretory cell' of *Salmo salar* L., with reference to plasma-electrolyte regulation. *Nature, Lond.* (in the Press).

IDLER, D. A. & TSUYUKI, H. (1958). Biochemical studies on sockeye salmon during spawning migration. I. Physical measurements, plasma cholesterol and electrolyte levels. *Canad. J. Biochem. Physiol.* 36, 783–91.

IDLER, D. A., RONALD, A. P. & SCHMIDT, P. J. (1959). Biochemical studies on sockeye salmon during spawning migration. VII. Steroid hormonesia plasma. *Can. J. Biochem. Physiol.* 37, 1227–1238.

KEYS, A. B. (1933). The mechanisms of adaptation of varying salinity in the common eel and the general problem of osmotic regulation in fishes. *Proc. Roy. Soc.* B, 112, 184–99.

KOCH, H. J. & EVANS, J. C. (1959). Sodium regulation in the blood of parr and smolt stages of the Atlantic salmon. *Nature, Lond.,* 184, 283–4.

KROGH, A. (1939). *Osmotic Regulation in Aquatic Animals*, pp. 242. Cambridge University Press.

KUBO, T. (1953). On the blood of salmonid fishes of Japan during migration. I. Freezing-point of the blood. *Bull. Fac. Fish. Hokkaido Univ.* 4, 138–48.

KUBO, T. (1955). Changes of some characteristics of blood smolts of *Oncorhynchus masou* during seaward migration. *Bull. Fac. Fish. Hokkaido*, 6, 201–7.

NISHIDA, H. (1953). The cytohistological observations on the gland cells of the branchial epidermis with the comparison of two types of *Oncorhynchus masou*, land-locked and sea-run forms. *Sci. Reps. Hokkaido Fish. Hatch.* 9, 33–7.

OKAMURA, H. (1935). Über auf Blut des Lachses der Laichzeit. *Japan. J. Med. Sci.* II, 3, 85.

PARRY, G. (1958). Size and osmoregulation in salmonid fishes. *Nature, Lond.* 181, 1218.

PARRY, G. (1960). The development of salinity tolerance in the salmon, *Salmo salar* L., and some related species. *J. Exp. Biol.* 37, 425–34.

PHILIPS, A. M. & BROCKWAY, D. R. (1958). The inorganic constituents of brown trout blood. *Progr. Fish. Cult.* 20, 58–61.

PICKFORD, G. E. & ATZ, J. (1957). *The Physiology of the Pituitary Gland of Fishes*, pp. 613. New York: New York Zool. Soc.

PYEFINCH, K. A. (1955). A review of the literature on the biology of the Atlantic salmon (*Salmo salar* L.). *Freshwater and Salmon Fisheries Research, Scottish Home Department*, no. 9, pp. 24.

RAMSAY, J. A. (1949). A new method of freezing-point determination for small quantities. *J. Exp. Biol.* 26, 57–64.

RAMSAY, J. A. & BROWN, R. H. S. (1955). Simplified apparatus and procedure for freezing-point determinations upon small volumes of fluid. *J. Sci. Instrum.* 32, 372–5.

SCHOLANDER, P. F., VAN DAM, L., KANWISHER, J. W., HAMMEL, H. T. & GORDON, M. S. (1957). Supercooling and osmoregulation in Arctic fish. *J. Cell. Comp. Physiol.* 49, 5–24.

SHAW, J. (1958). Osmoregulation in the muscle fibres of *Carcinus maenas*. *J. Exp. Biol.* 35, 920–9.

SPALDING, in CHESTER-JONES, I. (1956). Adrenal cortex and salt-electrolyte metabolism. *Mem. Soc. Endocrin.* 5.

SWIFT, D. R. (1955). Seasonal variations in the growth rate, thyroid gland activity and food reserves of brown trout, *Salmo trutta. J. Exp. Biol.* **32**, 751–64.

SWIFT, D. R. (1959). Seasonal variation in the activity of the thyroid gland of yearling brown trout, *Salmo trutta* L. *J. Exp. Biol.* **36**, 120–5.

VICKERS, T. (1958). A study of the cytology of secretion, with special reference to the chloride secretory cells of fish gills and the Golgi apparatus of epithelial cells. Ph.D. Thesis, University of Cambridge.

Roles of the Rectal Gland and the Kidneys in Salt and Water Excretion in the Spiny Dogfish[1]

J. WENDELL BURGER

Trinity College, Hartford, Connecticut, and the Mount Desert Island Biological Laboratory, Salisbury Cove, Maine

INTRODUCTION

Knowledge that the rectal gland of the spiny dogfish, *Squalus acanthias*, is a salt gland (Burger and Hess, 1960) introduces another parameter into the problem of the regulation of the internal environment of elasmobranch fishes. This report continues a previous study (Burger, 1962) and deals specifically with (1) the long term effects of removal of the gland, (2) comparative effects of salt-loading in fish with or without a gland, (3) the ability of fish with or without a gland to defend against external dilution, and (4) the effects of feeding on plasma osmolarity.

MATERIALS AND METHODS

The surgical, maintenance, and analytic methodology used previously (Burger and Hess, 1960; Burger, 1962) was employed in this study. In addition, a Fiske Osmometer, model G-61, was used. The individual experiments are described in context.

RESULTS

NORMAL VALUES

Table 1 gives the range in composition of the fluids appropriate to this study, both for fish confined to laboratory live cars (see Smith, 1931; Maren, 1962) and for fish sampled immediately after capture. Laboratory confinement induces no special state like the "laboratory chloruresis" found in marine teleosts. Many live-car fish have abnormally low hematocrits due to hook wounds. Data on normal volumes of rectal-gland fluid and urine are given in Burger (1962) and below.

EXCISION OF THE RECTAL GLAND

In normal dogfish the rectal gland tends to be active day after day. This presumably indicates a persistent influx of salt. It is of interest to observe what happens over a long period if the gland is removed. Three lots of six fish each were kept for separate 14-, 17-, and 21-day periods. In each lot three fish had the rectal gland removed surgically and three had dummy operations. Urine was sampled by temporary catheters as it was not feasible to catheterize permanently the rectal gland for such long periods.

The data for the 21-day experiment are found in Table 2. These data are representative also for the 14- and 17-day experiments. Without a rectal gland and receiving no food, dogfish can maintain normal plasma osmolarity and chloride for 3 weeks without a rise in urinary osmolarity and chloride. Previous experiments (Burger, 1962) for shorter periods with obstructed rectal glands gave urine whose chloride was above that of the plasma.

---

[1] This research was supported by Grant GM 07458-03 from the National Advisory Health Council, National Institutes of Health. The assistance of Bruce Thayer is also acknowledged.

TABLE 1 Normal composition of some fluids

Fluid[a]	Hematocrit (%)	Osmolarity (milliosmols/liter)	Cl⁻ (mmole/liter)	Na⁺ (mmole/liter)
Wild plasma	17–32 (11)[b]	996–1030 (6)	228–245 (6)	233–240 (6)
Live-car plasma	6–33 (27)	948–1036 (27)	222–262 (27)	253–262 (4)
Wild urine	—	700–850 (10)	60–350 (10)	165–367 (11)
Live-car urine	—	445–833 (27)	60–354 (27)	310–390 (11)

[a] Live-car rectal-gland fluid has a chloride range of 440–540 mmoles/liter and is isotonic to plasma. "Wild" fluids were taken minutes after capture from the sea. "Live-car" fluids were taken from fish in shallow live cars up to 14 days after capture.

[b] Numbers in parentheses are the number of fish sampled.

This was interpreted to mean that in the absence of the rectal gland the kidneys substituted for the gland. The present experiments show that this is not true; plasma chloride can remain stable in the absence of the gland without a concentrated urine.

To explore further, six fish, three controls and three made glandless, had total urines collected for 11–12 days. The average of the terminal plasma chlorides of these fish with the 14-, 17-, and 21-day fish shows slightly higher plasma chloride in the glandless fish (245 mmole/liter) than in the controls (235 mmole/liter). The frequency distribution is congruent with the average. This small accumulation of internal chloride is not progressive with time.

In the above six fish there is a difference in *urinary* loss of water and chloride between intact and glandless fish. In controls urine volume ranged from 5.9 to 11.7 ml/kg per day, with a chloride loss of 0.73–2.1 mmole/kg per day. In glandless fish urine volume ranged from 12.2 to 28.5 ml/kg per day, with a chloride loss of 3.8–6.6 mmole/kg per day. One of each type of fish had identical terminal urine chlorides (238 mmole/liter), but through higher urine flow in the glandless fish, three times as much chloride was lost as in the intact fish. While in glandless fish urine chlorides substantially above plasma levels may be encountered, there seems to be no specific renal mechanism for *regularly* excreting salt at above plasma concentrations. More commonly there is a greater urinary loss of salt through increased urine volume (*see* "Discussion").

EFFECTS OF SALT-LOADING

Injected sodium chloride stimulates rectal-gland secretion (Burger, 1962). To test how glandless fish handle a salt load, six control fish catheterized for rectal-gland fluid and urine and six glandless fish catheterized for urine were given subcutaneous or intramuscular injections of 50–100 ml of a 1 M sodium chloride solution.

Four to five hours after injection, plasma chlorides rose by about 20–30 mmole/liter; the rise in plasma osmolarity was lower, 10–15 mmole/liter. All fish with a rectal gland had plasma chloride return to preinjection levels within 48 hr. There was no change in urine chloride and osmolarity. For example, a 3.4-kg fish receiving 50 ml of the salt solution had preinjection urine chloride of 150 mmole/liter with a 406 osmolarity. A 3-hr urine sample 24 hr later had a chloride of 154 mmole/liter, with a 1,022 osmolarity. Rectal-gland fluid volume was 75% of urine volume. In no control fish did urine chlorides and osmolarities rise sharply.

In fish without a rectal gland, plasma chloride did not return to preinjection levels within 48 hr. A 4.2-kg fish receiving 60 ml of the salt solution had a preinjection plasma chloride of 238 mmole/liter. Four hours after injection it rose to 262 and for successive 24 hr samples it was 262, 262, 254, 250 mmole/liter. In another fish, plasma chloride rose from 226 to 251 mmole/liter and remained at 246 5 days after injection; there was no sharp rise in urine chloride. In this fish, preinjection urine chloride was 230 mmole/liter.

TABLE 2   Comparison of control and rectal-glandless dogfish kept 21 days

	PLASMA			URINE			
FISH	Osmolarity (millios- mols/liter)	Cl⁻ (mmole/ liter)	Hemato- crit (%)	Osmolarity (millios- mols/liter)	Cl⁻ (mmole/ liter)	Mg (mmole/ liter)	Ca (mmole/ liter)
Control:							
Initial	998	238	20.0	727	200	20	9
Terminal	1000	232	11.1	605	214	12	6
Control:							
Initial	1021	240	21.8	804	208	35	11
Terminal	1013	232	19.8	724	212	28	5
Control:							
Initial	993	236	23.8	712	169	44	12
Terminal	978	240	18.0	630	252	26	9
Glandless:							
Initial	1024	242	18.3	710	270	25	15
Terminal	1014	246	6.6	793	160	18	15
Glandless:							
Initial	999	234	22.0	810	232	38	17
Terminal	988	238	19.4	a	210	a	a
Glandless:							
Initial	1010	248	20.1	660	210	31	16
Terminal	999	244	10.6	578	216	20	5
Sea Water	−	−	−	932	500	50	9

[a]Sample lost.

During 5 days subsequent to injection it varied from 194 to 266 mmole/liter. In general, in all fish without a gland, urine chlorides clustered around the plasma concentration, only rarely falling below 200 mmole/liter. There is a marked tendency when the rectal gland is active for urine chloride to be low. It is clear that, when faced with a salt load, glandless fish can make no specific renal response to concentrate chloride above plasma levels, that is, the kidneys can not serve as a substitute rectal gland.

DILUTION OF THE EXTERNAL MEDIUM

Burger (1962) reported that short periods up to 24 hr in 87%–95% sea water did not change plasma chloride. Here eight intact and three glandless dogfish were kept 3–9 days in running sea water diluted with running tap water. It was not possible to keep a steady mixture, but, for the most part, the sea water was in the 72%–82% range with excursions up to 6 hr to 60% and 92%. The object was not to make comparisons between various dilutions but to test a general response to a substantial dilution. After dilution all fish were returned to full sea water for 2–3 days.

It takes about 2 days of dilution to affect fully the internal composition, which argues for a low permeability to water. There is increased hydration as judged by the fall in the hematocrit. In five fish whose hematocrits returned to predilution values when they were returned to full sea water, and in which one can assume no blood loss, the hematocrits fell 16%–20%. This presumably is a measure of the increase in internal hydration.

With the dilutions used, plasma osmolarity fell 10%–15% but retained the normal pattern of marked hypertonicity to the external medium. Plasma chloride is resistant to dilution. In a few fish it did not fall, but more commonly it fell to about 220 mmole/liter especially in the intact fish. For at least 9 days dogfish can stabilize their plasma composition.

The most surprising observation was that under conditions of dilution when plasma

TABLE 3 Comparison of normal and rectal-glandless dogfish in dilute sea water

	Osmolarity (milliosmols/ liter)	Cl⁻ (mmole/ liter)	Mg⁺⁺ (mmole/ liter)	Ca⁺⁺ (mmole/ liter	Volume (ml/24 hr)
Initial normal in sea water (4.1 kg):					
Plasma	1,030	260	—	—	—
Urine	713	134	20	3	—
After 8 days dilution:					
Plasma	887	220	—	—	—
Urine	382	72	8	4	82
Rectal-gland fluid	888	478	0	0	134
Returned 2 days to full sea water:					
Plasma	964	254	—	—	—
Urine	522	76	20	4	20
Rectal-gland fluid	962	514	0	0	74
Initial experimental in sea water (2.6 kg):					
Plasma	1,013	237	—	—	—
Urine	514	198	20	1	—
Glandless, 5 days dilution:					
Plasma	870	246	—	—	—
Urine	530	198	3	1	168
Returned 2 days to full sea water:					
Plasma	964	256	—	—	—
Urine	592	212	4	2	68
Dilute sea water	675–768				
Sea water	932–944				

chloride and osmolarity are lowered, the rectal gland is active. It was found to be secreting during the initial phases of dilution, for up to 9 days of dilution, and during the return to full sea water. During dilution secreted rectal-gland fluid was not below 7 ml/kg per day and reached over 30. It was suggested (Burger, 1962) that the stimulus for activating the rectal gland contains a volume component. Here, with an active gland associated with lowered plasma osmolarity and chloride but with increased hydration, the volume effect seems clear.

In Table 3 representative responses to dilution are given for intact and for glandless fish. There was a diuresis which subsided after return to full sea water. While intact dogfish in full sea water rarely have urine volumes of 30 ml/kg per day, here intact fish had volumes up to 65 ml/kg per day, and glandless fish up to 80 ml/kg per day. For both types of fish the urine was dilute (a chloride range of 46–198 mmole/liter), being more dilute in osmolarity and chloride in the intact fish.

An idea of the magnitude of the effect of dilution on salt and water loss can be gained from the following. In full sea water intact dogfish lose chloride through both the rectal-gland fluid and the urine in the 6–12 mmole/kg per day range, with a water loss rarely as high as 40 ml/kg per day. During the last 2 days of dilution the intact diluted fish in Table 3 lost chloride and water at 18.2 mmole/kg per day and 68 ml/kg per day, respectively. The water loss was divided into 36 ml of urine and 32 ml of rectal-gland fluid. These fluids had a composite chloride concentration of 266 mmole/liter. During the last 2 days of dilution, the glandless fish lost chloride through the urine alone at 11.2 mmole/kg per day, with a 183 mmole/liter concentration, and lost water at 61 ml/kg per day. Both in full and in diluted sea water, rectal-glandless fish have greater urine volumes than do intact fish. The total fluid loss seems to be of about the same order of magnitude for both types of fish.

EFFECTS OF DIET ON PLASMA OSMOLARITY

It is well known that the hypertonicity of elasmobranch plasma results from high concentrations of urea and trimethylamine oxide added to a saline plasma. The following experiment was performed to see if diet modified plasma osmolarity. Five dogfish (3.3–4.3 kg) selected for low plasma osmolarity (920–960 milliosmols/liter) and unfed for 5 days, were force fed with approximately 250 gr of fresh herring and refed 3 days later. It was determined that the herring were not regurgitated. Hook wounds were sutured to prevent bleeding.

Post mortem examination, 6 days after the first feeding, showed the herring to be digested completely. After 6 days no rise in plasma osmolarity or change in plasma chloride was found. Apparently the 500 gr of herring was not converted massively into urea. The rate of genesis and the origin of osmotic organic moieties is a problem of some interest.

DISCUSSION

The current data and that of Burger (1962) can be generalized into the following picture. In its environment, physical gradients direct sodium chloride and water toward the dogfish. Assuming that amount of the urine and rectal-gland fluid is a measure of net influx, there seems in the intact, unfed, unstressed dogfish an influx of a saline solution whose concentration lies between that of plasma and that of sea water. The kidneys, which form a hypotonic urine containing appreciable salt, cannot make a specific response to a salt load by raising urinary chloride to above plasma levels, even though such high urine chlorides do occur at times. The kidneys can make a specific response to a water load. Their role seems to be the control of water, the excretion of multivalent ions and certain organic substances, and the conservation of osmotic moieties. The rectal gland is a specific regulator of sodium chloride and uniformly concentrates salt. Its variable but persistent activity reflects a persistent saline influx from the external medium. At least one stimulus for increasing the activity of both organs is an increased volume of body fluid.

In the absence of the rectal gland, a plasma composition comparable to that of intact fish can be maintained both in full and in dilute sea water. This seems to be accomplished by decreasing the uptake of salt so that the influxing solution is at or below the plasma concentration. It is likely that humors not yet defined for the dogfish modify the action of the uptake and excretory sites.

LITERATURE CITED

BURGER, J. W. 1962. Further studies on the function of the rectal gland in the spiny dogfish. Physiol. Zoöl. 35:205-217.

BURGER, J. W., and W. N. HESS. 1960. Function of the rectal gland in the spiny dogfish. Science 131: 670-671.

MAREN, T. H. 1962. Ionic composition of cerebrospinal fluid and aqueous humor of the dogfish, Squalus acanthias. I. Normal values. Comp. Biochem. Physiol. 5:193-200.

SMITH, H. W. 1931. The absorption and excretion of water and salts by elasmobranch fishes. II. Marine elasmobranchs. Amer. J. Physiol. 98:296-310.

Additional Readings
CHAPTER 10

CONTE, F. P. 1969. Salt secretion. Chapter 3, pp. 241-292, in W. S. Hoar and D. J. Randall, eds., Fish Physiology, Vol. 1. New York: Academic Press.

HICKMAN, C. P., Jr. and TRUMP, B. F. 1969. The kidney. Chapter 2, pp. 91-239, in W. S. Hoar and D. J. Randall, eds., Fish Physiology, Vol. 1. New York: Academic Press.

HOLMES, W. N. and DONALDSON, E. M. 1969. The body compartments and the distribution of electrolytes. Chapter 1, pp. 1–89, *in* W. S. Hoar and D. J. Randall, eds., *Fish Physiology*, Vol. 1. New York: Academic Press.

LUTZ, P. L. 1975. Adaptive and evolutionary aspects of the ionic content of fishes. *Copeia* 1975(2): 369–373.

MACFARLANE, N. A. A. 1974. Effects of hypophysectomy on osmoregulation in the euryhaline flounder, *Platichthys flesus* (L.), in sea water and in freshwater. *Comp. Biochem. Physiol.* 47A: 201–217.

MAETZ, J. 1969. Seawater teleosts: evidence for a sodium-potassium exchange in the branchial sodium-excreting pump. *Science* 166:613–615.

MAETZ, J. 1971. Fish gills: mechanisms of salt transfer in freshwater and sea water. *Phil. Trans. Roy. Soc. Lond.* B 262:209–249.

MUNZ, F. W. and MCFARLAND, W. N. 1964. Regulatory function of a primitive vertebrate kidney. *Comp. Biochem. Physiol.* 13:384–400.

POTTS, W. 1968. Osmotic and ionic regulation. *An.. Rev. Physiol.* 30:73–104.

POTTS, W. and PARRY, G. 1964. *Osmotic and ionic regulation in animals.* Oxford: Pergamon Press.

POTTS, W. and EVANS, D. 1966. The effects of hypophysectomy and bovine prolactin on salt fluzes in fresh-water adapted *Fundulus heteroclitus. Biol. Bull.* 131:362–368.

POTTS, W. and EVANS, D. 1967. Sodium and chloride balance in the killi-fish, *Fundulus heteroclitus. Biol. Bull.* 133:411–424.

POTTS, W.; FOSTER, M.; RUDY, P.; and PARRY-HOWELLS, G. 1967. Sodium and water balance in the cichlid teleost, *Tilapia mossambica. J. Exp. Biol.* 47:461–471.

11

Reproduction

The Reproductive Cycle and its Environmental Control in the Pumpkinseed, *Lepomis gibbosus* (Pisces: Centrarchidae)

John R. Burns

The seasonal cycle of gonadal development was studied in pumpkinseed, *Lepomis gibbosus*, subject to natural temperatures and day lengths in a local pond. During late May, 1972, gonadal recrudescence in both males and females occurred, as indicated by an increase in the gonosomatic index and the appearance of spermatocytes in the testes and active vitellogenesis in the ovaries. During this time the pond temperature rose above 12.5 C, while the day length was near 15 hours.

Laboratory experiments with fish exposed to controlled temperatures and photoperiods were performed. The results showed that a minimal temperature between 11.5 and 14.0 C was necessary for recrudescence in males, while one between 14.0 and 16.5 C was necessary for the females. However, the seasonal study indicated that the critical temperature for females is probably lower than 14.0 C. The critical photoperiod for both males and females was probably between 12.0 and 13.5 hrs. Since the critical day length was reached sooner than the increase in pond temperature above the critical level, it appears that temperature is the environmental factor controlling the timing of recrudescence in the spring.

During the early post-spawning period temperatures and day lengths were still above the critical levels. However, no renewed gonadal activity was observed at this time, suggesting the existence of a post-spawning refractory period.

SEASONAL cycles of gonadal development have been described for many species of teleosts. Such cycles are most readily observed in fishes of temperate regions, where substantial variations in temperature and day length may occur over the course of a year. However, studies on the modulation of reproductive cycling by environmental factors are relatively few.

In nearly all of the species studied, the environmental factors which exert the greatest influence upon the initiation of gonadal development are temperature and day length. In many fishes gonadal recrudescence appears to depend upon the attainment of both a certain temperature and day length. Included among fishes with this type of gonadal regulation are *Phoxinus laevis* (Bullough, 1939, 1940; Harrington, 1959), *Oryzias latipes* (Yoshioka, 1963; Kasuga and Takahashi, 1971), *Gasterosteus aculeatus* (Baggerman, 1957), *Culaea inconstans* (Reisman and Cade, 1967), *Lepomis cyanellus* (Kaya and Hasler, 1972) and female *Enneacanthus obesus* (Harrington, 1956, 1959).

In the present investigation, seasonal changes in the gonads of male and female pumpkinseed, *Lepomis gibbosus*, held under natural conditions in a local pond were studied. Further studies were performed in the laboratory with fish exposed to controlled temperatures and photoperiods in order to establish more precisely the interaction of temperature and day length in the initiation of gonadal development in the spring.

MATERIALS AND METHODS

Lepomis gibbosus were collected from ponds in the area of Amherst, Massachusetts, and transferred to a holding net which floated in a pond near the university campus. A continuous yearly record of the pond temperature, measured at a depth of about one meter in the holding net, was provided by means of a recording thermometer.

Male and female *L. gibbosus* were removed from the holding net each month from January, 1972, to February, 1973. Weights of all fish were recorded, and both gonads were removed, weighed, and placed in Bouin's fixative. Gonosomatic indices (gonad wt·100·gm⁻¹ body wt) were calculated for all specimens. Fixed gonads were dehydrated, embedded in paraffin, sectioned at six micrometers, and stained with Weigert's iron hematoxylin and eosin. Stages of gonadal development were determined from these sections.

From *Copeia* 1976(3):449–455. Reprinted by permission.

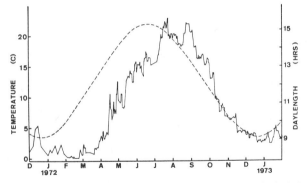

Fig. 1. Seasonal changes in temperature (solid line) and day length (dashed line) encountered by pumpkinseed, *Lepomis gibbosus,* in a holding pond at Amherst, Massachusetts (Lat. 42° 22′ 30″ N, Long. 72° 31′ West of Greenwich).

During the winter and spring of 1973, two sets of laboratory experiments were carried out in which *L. gibbosus* were maintained at controlled temperatures and photoperiods. These experiments were designed to see what temperatures and day lengths must be reached before gonadal maturation can proceed in the spring. Eleven to 15 fish were kept in each of four 75-l tanks fitted with light-tight hoods. In each tank, lighting was provided by two 15 watt, cool-white fluorescent bulbs and one 25 watt incandescent bulb located about 30 cm above the water surface, and controlled by an electric timer. Temperature regulation was accomplished with submerged cooling coils, thermostatically controlled, and an immersion heater controlled by a thermoregulator. In most cases the temperature was maintained $\pm$ 0.3 C. Fish were fed daily with TetraMin flake food.

In the first set of experiments, which began on January 14, 1973, samples of 11–13 fish (males and females) were maintained at four different temperatures (9.0, 11.5, 14.0, 16.5 C) under identical 15-hour photoperiods. In the second set, begun 30 March 1973, samples of 13–15 fish (males and females) were kept on four different daily photoperiods (9.0, 10.5, 12.0, 13.5 hrs) at the same temperature of 17.5 C. After 47–48 days under these controlled conditions all fish were weighed and sacrificed, and the gonads removed and treated as above.

Results

The seasonal changes in natural day length and holding pond temperature are shown in Fig. 1. The seasonal changes in the gonosomatic indices (GSI) of male and female *L. gibbosus* are shown in Fig. 2. The changes in the GSI's of males and females closely paralleled one another. From January to early May, 1972, the gonads of both sexes remained small. Beginning in late May and early June, however, the testes rapidly increased in size. The ovaries also began to increase in size during this time. By late June and early July the gonads of both sexes reached their maximum size, and decreased by mid-August, indicating that spawning had been completed. The GSI's of both sexes remained low from August through the fall and winter.

Seasonal histological changes in the gonads of the fish correlated well with the changes in the gonosomatic indices. The histological changes observed in the testes follow:

a) February to early May, 1972—seminiferous lobules collapsed; mostly secondary spermatogonia present.

b) Late May, 1972—initiation of active spermatogenesis; spermatocytes appeared, however, free spermatozoa were not yet present; seminiferous lobules were still collapsed.

c) Early June, 1972—all of spermatogenesis stages present; free spermatozoa began to fill the lumina of the lobules.

d) Mid-June to early July, 1972—further expansion of the lobules with free spermatozoa; all stages abundant.

e) Late July, 1972—seminiferous lobules totally distended with free spermatozoa; other stages scarce.

f) Late August, 1972—spermatozoa still present in many lobules, however, most lobules were collapsed; primary and secondary spermatogonia lined the lobule walls.

g) September, 1972, to February, 1973—spermatozoa became scarce until only occasional residual cells were observed; lobules collapsed; secondary spermatogonia increased in proportion to primary spermatogonia.

Only three major histological stages could be defined in the ovaries:

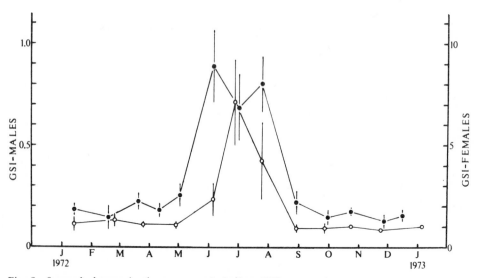

Fig. 2. Seasonal changes in the gonosomatic indices (GSI = gonad wt·100·gm⁻¹ body wt) of male (closed circles) and female (open circles) pumpkinseed, *Lepomis gibbosus*. Vertical bars indicate plus and minus two standard errors of the mean (95 percent confidence limits).

a) February to early May, 1972—largest oocytes 0.25 mm in diameter or less; very little yolk present.
b) Late May to early June, 1972—active vitellogenesis began; largest oocytes reached 0.35 mm in diameter.
c) Mid-June to late July, 1972—oocytes reached their largest size; yolk was extensive.
d) Late August, 1972, to January, 1973—essentially the same as "a" above.

Therefore, it appears that the first sign of gonadal recrudescence in both males and females occurred during late May in 1972. From Fig. 1 it can be seen that this period corresponded to a rise in pond temperature above 12.5 C, or so. The day length at this time was around 15 hrs, which was close to the yearly maximum.

The results of the laboratory experiments in which *L. gibbosus* were kept at different temperatures and a photoperiod of 15 hrs for 48 days are shown in Fig. 3. With regard to the males, Student's t-tests were performed on the GSI's between adjacent points from Fig. 3 and in no case were the values significantly different from one another. However, a trend toward increasing gonad size was seen between the fish kept at 11.5 C and those at 14.0 C. Since only two males from the 16.5 C group were available, little can be said concerning them.

A much clearer distinction was observed between males kept at 11.5 C or below and those at 14.0 C or above when the histology of the testes was considered. Stages later than second-ary spermatogonia were found in all but one of the testes from fish kept at temperatures of 14.0 C or above. Males maintained at 11.5 C or lower showed no signs of gonadal maturation, since the most advanced stages in their testes were only secondary spermatogonia. Therefore, in male *L. gibbosus* a critical temperature lying between 11.5 and 14.0 C apparently must be reached before spermatogenesis can proceed beyond the secondary spermatogonia.

Student's t-tests were also performed between adjacent points for the females in Fig. 3. The only significant difference was obtained between the females kept at 14.0 C and those kept at 16.5 C. The histological data indicated that the largest oocytes of females exposed to 14.0 C or lower reached only 0.22 mm in diameter, while the largest oocytes of those kept at 16.5 C reached 0.27 mm in diameter. Furthermore, active vitellogenesis was observed only in ovaries from fish maintained at 16.5 C. These results suggest that a critical temperature for oocyte development may lie between 14.0 and 16.5 C.

Fig. 4 shows the results of the experiments where fish were exposed to four different photoperiods at 17.5 C. With regard to the males, Student's t-tests showed that while all adjacent samples were significantly different from one another, there was no significant difference between the 9.0 and 12.0 hr groups. Although no explanation is available for the low values obtained for the 10.5 hr sample, it is clear that the GSI's of males kept on 13.5 hr photoperiods were significantly larger than those of males

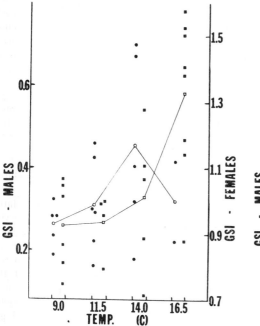

Fig. 3. Gonosomatic indices (GSI) of male (closed circles) and female (closed squares) pumpkinseed, *Lepomis gibbosus*, exposed to four different temperatures under a 15-hr daily photoperiod for 48 days. Open circles and squares represent the mean values for the groups.

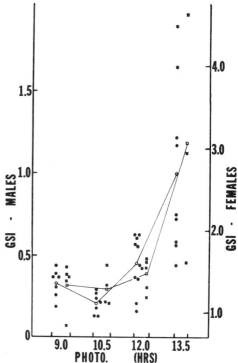

Fig. 4. Gonosomatic indices (GSI) of male (closed circles) and female (closed squares) pumpkinseed, *Lepomis gibbosus*, exposed to four different photoperiods at a temperature of 17.5 C for 47 days. Open circles and squares represent the mean values for the groups.

kept on 9.0, 10.5 or 12.0 hr photoperiods.

The histological changes in the testes of these samples were not as clearly defined. In all but one of the males (all groups) at the end of this experiment, free spermatozoa were found in the lumina of the seminiferous lobules, indicating that spermatogenesis had gone to completion during the course of the experiment. However, a noticeable reduction in the later spermatogenetic stages (spermatocytes and spermatids) occurred in most fish exposed to photoperiods of 12.0 hrs or less. In only one fish kept on these photoperiods (12.0 hr group) were the later stages present in abundance. On the other hand, in six of the nine males in the 13.5 hr group the later stages of spermatogenesis were abundant. This point will be discussed further.

With the females, Student's t-tests indicated that adjacent samples in Fig. 4 were not significantly different from one another. However, a definite increase in the size of the gonads of the females kept on 13.5 hr photoperiods over the other samples was evident. In the 13.5 hr group the size of the largest oocytes reached 0.58 mm in diameter and more, while in the other three groups it attained no more than 0.20 mm in diameter. Furthermore, active vitellogenesis occurred only in the 13.5 hr group.

These results suggest that a critical photoperiod between 12.0 and 13.5 hrs is necessary for gonadal recrudescence in female *L. gibbosus* in the spring.

Although the spawning period for both sexes was completed by late August, a recrudescence of gametogenesis (later stages) did not occur at this time even though the pond temperature was still very high and the day length longer than 13 hrs. This supports the concept of a post-spawning refractory period in *L. gibbosus* during which the environmental stimuli which caused gonadal recrudescence in the spring fail to cause a similar activation of gonadal maturation.

DISCUSSION

The seasonal study of the reproductive cycle of *Lepomis gibbosus* showed that in the spring gonadal recrudescence in both sexes began after the pond temperature rose above 12.5 C, with the day length at this time having been about 15 hrs. The results of the first set of laboratory experiments indicated that a critical temperature between 11.5 and 14.0 C was apparently required for testicular maturation. This is consistent with the results of the seasonal study. However, a critical temperature between 14.0 and 16.5 C was indicated for ovarian development. Thus, for the females a contradiction exists between the results obtained from the laboratory study and those from the seasonal study. Perhaps if the laboratory experiment were run for a longer period of time, maturation of the ovaries at a temperature lower than 16.5 C might have occurred.

In the first set of experiments the final GSI's in all groups of males tended to be higher than those of the initial controls. All the experimental temperatures were well above the pond temperature at the start of the experiment (about 2 C). Perhaps these experimental temperatures accelerated the development of the earlier spermatogenetic stages, whereas only a temperature above the critical level permitted development of the later stages. With the exception of the 16.5 C group, the final GSI's of the females tended to be equivalent to those of the initial controls in the first set of experiments.

In the second set of experiments it was found that males subject to a 13.5 hr photoperiod had significantly higher GSI's than those subject to photoperiods of 12.0 hours or less. However, histological examination revealed that free spermatozoa were present in nearly all testes. This experiment was begun on 30 March when the pond temperature had not yet exceeded 5.9 C but the day length had already reached 12.7 hrs. A possible explanation for these results is that the 12.7 hr day length was above a critical level for gonadal development. Once the temperature was raised to 17.5 C in the laboratory experiments, spermatogenesis went to completion in all groups until the effect of the imposed photoperiods became evident, which in those cases where it was below some critical level prevented further development of the later spermatogenetic stages. This hypothesis is supported by the result that a noticeable reduction in the later spermatogenetic stages (spermatocytes and spermatids) occurred in all but one fish exposed to photoperiods of 12.0 hrs or less, while in six of the nine males in the 13.5 hr group the later stages of spermatogenesis were abundant. Thus, a minimum photoperiod between 12.0 and 13.5 hrs seems likely for testis development.

The results with the females indicated that a minimum photoperiod between 12.0 and 13.5 hrs was necessary for ovarian development. The results for both males and females are consistent with the seasonal study where gonadal recrudescence in both sexes did not occur until late May, when the day length was already near 15 hrs.

In the second set of experiments the GSI's of males tended to be higher in all groups than those of the initial controls. Again, this may have been due to a general acceleration of early spermatogenesis by the higher experimental temperature. The GSI's of the females were also slightly higher than initial controls in all groups but the 13.5 hr group, where they were substantially higher.

A long day, high temperature regime begun in mid-January (Fig. 3, 16.5 C group) had much less of a stimulatory effect on both sexes than one begun in late March (Fig. 4, 13.5 hr group). This difference was especially evident in the ovaries. A 15 hr, 16.5 C regime initiated on January 14 and run for 48 days produced oocytes with a maximum diameter of 0.27 mm. A 13.5 hr, 17.5 C regime begun on 30 March and continued for 47 days resulted in oocytes of maximum diameter 0.58 mm and greater. The initial controls in both cases were essentially equivalent. This indicates that a seasonal difference in the responsiveness of the sunfish to similar environmental stimuli may exist. While a warm temperature, short photoperiod regime begun in March inhibited gonadal development, the effect of such a regime initiated in January was not tested.

Because the critical day length was probably reached nearly two months before the pond temperature rose above the critical level, it appears that temperature, and not day length, was the environmental factor that triggered the initiation of the spring reproductive development in *L. gibbosus*.

Similar results were found by Kaya and Hasler (1972) for the green sunfish, *Lepomis cyanellus*. In this species, initiation of gonadal development during the spring was also dependent upon the attainment of a critical temperature and day length. The critical day length for both sexes was between 10 and 15 hrs. While the critical temperature for males was between 10 and 15 C, that for females was between 15 and 20 C. Again, as with *L. gibbosus*, this difference may have been due to termination of the experiment too soon for the occurrence of a recognizable maturation of the ovaries at a lower temperature. The environmental trigger for gonadal recrudescence in *L. cyanellus* also appears to be temperature, rather than photoperiod (Kaya and Hasler, 1972).

In another sunfish, *Enneacanthus obesus*, stimulation of the later stages of oogenesis required high temperatures and long photoperiods (Harrington, 1956, 1959). Similarly, recrudescence of spermatogenesis (at high temperatures) in males of this species required long photoperiods (Harrington, 1956, 1959). *Phoxinus laevis* (Bullough, 1939, 1940; Harrington, 1959) and *Oryzias latipes* (Yoshioka, 1963; Kasuga and Takahashi, 1971) also required both high temperatures and long photoperiods for the initiation of gonadal development in both sexes.

Spermatogenesis would not proceed beyond the secondary spermatogonia in *Lepomis cyanellus* unless the temperature and photoperiod were above critical levels; critical levels of temperature and photoperiod also had to be reached before oocyte growth and active vitellogenesis occurred (Kaya and Hasler, 1972). Similar results are indicated in the present study for *L. gibbosus*.

The spawning period in *L. gibbosus* was completed by late August, 1972. Although the day length at this time was still longer than 13 hrs and the temperature above 20 C, a second period of gonadal recrudescence did not follow. This observation suggests that immediately after spawning a refractory period exists during which further stimulation of gonadal development by long days and high temperatures is not possible. Similar post-spawning refractory periods have been observed in *Lepomis cyanellus* (Kaya, 1973), *Oryzias latipes* (Kasuga and Takahashi, 1971), and *Gasterosteus aculeatus* (Baggerman, 1957).

Acknowledgments

This work was submitted in partial fulfillment of the requirements for the degree of Doctor of Philosophy at the University of Massachusetts, Amherst, and was supported in part by a Biomedical Sciences Support Grant to the University of Massachusetts, FR 07048 (NIH/NIMH). Thanks are extended to J. L. Roberts, M. V. Edds, Jr., L. Edds, G. A. Wyse, D. J. Klingener, J. G. Snedecor, W. B. O'Connor, D. Fairbairn, C. F. Cole, R. Reed and D. Noden.

Literature Cited

Baggerman, B. 1957. An experimental study of the timing of breeding and migration in the three-spined stickleback (*Gasterosteus aculeatus* L.). Arch. neerl. zool. 12:105–318.

Bullough, W. S. 1939. A study of the reproductive cycle of the minnow in relation to the environment. Proc. Zool. Soc. Lond. Ser. A 109:79–102.

———. 1940. The effect of the reduction of light in spring on the breeding season of minnow (*Phoxinus laevis*). *Ibid.* 110:149–157.

Harrington, R. W., Jr. 1956. An experiment on the effects of contrasting daily photoperiods on gametogenesis and reproduction in the centrarchid fish *Enneacanthus obesus* (Girard). J. Exp. Zool. 131:203–224.

———. 1959. Photoperiodism in fishes in relation to the annual sexual cycle, p. 651–667. *In*: Photoperiodism and related phenomena in plants and animals, R. B. Withrow, ed. AAAS, Publ. No. 55, Washington, D. C.

Kasuga, S., and H. Takahashi. 1971. The preoptico-hypophysial neurosecretory system of the medaka, *Oryzias latipes*, and its changes in relation to the annual reproductive cycle under natal conditions. Bull. Fac. Fish., Hokkaido Univ. :259–268.

A, C. M. 1973. Effects of temperature and ιotoperiod on seasonal regression of gonads of een sunfish, *Lepomis cyanellus*. Copeia 1973: 9–373.

—, and A. D. Hasler. 1972. Photoperiod and nperature effects on the gonads of green sunfish, *Lepomis cyanellus* (Rafinesque), during the quiescent, winter phase of its annual sexual cycle. Trans. Amer. Fish. Soc. 101:270–275.

Reisman, H. M., and T. J. Cade. 1967. Physiological and behavioral aspects of reproduction in the brook stickleback, *Culaea inconstans*. Amer. Midl. Nat. 77:257–295.

Yoshioka, H. 1963. On the effects of environmental factors upon the reproduction of fishes. II. Effects of short and long day-length on *Oryzias latipes* during spawning season. Bull. Fac. Fish., Hokkaido Univ. 14:137–151.

Department of Zoology, University of Massachusetts, Amherst, Massachusetts 01002. Present Address: Departamento de Biología, Universidad de El Salvador, San Salvador, El Salvador, Centro América. *Accepted 11 March 1975.*

PHEROMONAL STIMULATION AND METABOLITE INHIBITION OF OVULATION IN THE ZEBRAFISH, *BRACHYDANIO RERIO*[1]

Lo-chai Chen and Robert L. Martinich[2]

ABSTRACT

Female zebrafish, *Brachydanio rerio*, would not ovulate in the absence of males in waters previously inhabited by the fish. Chemical presence of males and fresh, dechlorinated tap water each induced ovulation in about half of the trials. Application of the two factors in combination gave 100% ovulation. These results suggest that in the zebrafish a pheromone released by the males stimulates ovulation and that metabolites produced by the fish repress ovulation. It is postulated that metabolites restrict spawning of the fish to the rainy season and that the pheromone functions in synchronizing reproductive readiness between sexes or in conserving courtship energy expenditure.

In a study concerning egg size, incubation period, and growth in the zebrafish, *Brachydanio rerio* (Hamilton-Buchanan), we encountered the problem of having to strip eggs from the females to synchronize the fertilization of the eggs artificially. We tried the method described by Hart and Messina (1972) without successes. We have regularly been able to induce natural spawning by introducing ripe individuals of both sexes from their holding tanks at 27°C together into a bowl of fresh, dechlorinated tap water at 21°C. Some of the changes associated with this introduction, such as the chemical presence of the males (pheromone), the physical presence of the males (visual, auditory, tactile, and lateral line), fresh tap water (absence of accumulated metabolites), and temperature shock (from 27° to 21°C), may be capable of inducing ovulation.

The roles of these factors in controlling reproduction in fishes have been well documented. Some of the examples are:

Pheromones—Aronson 1945; Tavolga 1956; Amouriq 1965; Gandolfi 1969; Rossi 1969; and Chien 1973.

Visual—Aronson 1945, 1965; Tavolga 1956; Rossi 1969; and Chien 1973.

Auditory—Tavolga 1956; Brawn 1961; Gray and Winn 1961; and Myrberg and Spires 1972.

Tactile—Egami and Nambu 1961.

Metabolites—Swingle 1956; and Greene 1966.

Temperature—Harrington 1959; Aronson 1965; and de Vlaming 1972a, b.

Much of the information in the literature, however, does not clearly distinguish between gonad development, ovulation, and spawning. The present study was undertaken to single out such ovulation-inducing factors.

MATERIALS AND METHODS

Female zebrafish were kept at 27.0 ± 1.0°C in 40- or 60-liter aerated aquaria subdivided into three or four compartments by perforated plastic dividers, one female per comparment to enable identification. Male zebrafish were isolated in aerated 20-liter aquaria at room temperature (21.0 ± 1.0°C). No visual contact was permitted between sexes. All individuals were subjected to 12 h of light per day and were generously fed "Tetramin"[3] in the morning and frozen brine shrimp in the evening. To ensure fertility, each fish was initially permitted to spawn naturally. This was done by introducing the fish into fresh, dechlorinated tap water at room temperature in a 20-cm finger bowl with another individual of the opposite sex. A total of 27 fertile females and 19 fertile males were used.

Eight experiments were designed to test the relative contribution of each factor individually, and in combination, on ovulation in the zebrafish (Table 1). In experiments 1 to 7, a female was transferred from the holding compartment into the experimental chamber for 12 to 18 h in nearly all the trials but for only 4 h in several instances in experiment 2, and then stripped by applying gentle pressure onto the abdomen. The release of ripe ova indicated that the fish had completed ovulation. Failure to give eggs, or the release of immature or ruptured eggs, was considered a negative response. Ripe ova are nearly translucent, round, and about 0.8 mm in diameter before taking on any water, and are not attached to each other. Immature ova are often opaque, may be undersized and irregularly shaped, and are often in clumps. In experiment 8, the female was stripped immediately upon removal from the holding compartment.

After successful stripping, the female was immediately permitted to spawn naturally with a male in order to assure release of all ovulated ova. After approximately 4 to 8 h, the male was

---

[1] The data in this paper were extracted from the master's thesis of R. L. Martinich.
[2] Department of Zoology, San Diego State University, San Diego, CA 92182.
[3] Reference to trade names does not imply endorsement by the National Marine Fisheries Service, NOAA.

From *Fish. Bull., U.S.* 73(4): 889–894. Reprinted by permission.

TABLE 1.—Design and results of experiments to test factors suspected of influencing ovulation in the zebrafish. Symbol " + " indicates presence of the factor and symbol "0" indicates absence of the factor. The chi-square values are for comparing results of any experiment with that of the control (experiment 8), and the 0.01 level critical limit is 6.63.

Item	Experiment								
	1	2	3	4	5	6a	6b	7	8
Factors:									
Pheromone	+	+	+	+	0	0	0	0	0
Temperature shock	0	+	+	+	+	+	+	0	0
Fresh tap water	+	+	+	0	+	+	+	+	0
Visual image of male	0	0	?	0	+	0	0	0	0
Auditory and/or lateral line stimulation	0	0	+	0	0	0	0	0	0
Number of females used	18	14	19	14	9	19	18	16	14
Results:									
Trials eggs obtained	20	15	21	8	5	17	10	7	0
Trials no eggs obtained	0	0	1	8	5	18	13	10	17
Chi-square	33.1	28.1	31.4	8.7	7.4	10.2	7.7	6.5	—
% positive responses	100	100	95	50	50	49	44	41	0

removed, and the female was returned to her compartment the following day. Between experiments each female was allowed to rest for 8 to 12 days, and males 4 to 6 days.

After an unsuccessful attempt of stripping eggs, the female was presented with either male pheromone and/or fresh tap water, whatever was lacking originally in the experimental chamber, and then stripped again 4 to 18 h later. If the second stripping failed again, then the female was permitted to spawn naturally with a male. In cases where natural spawning failed, data pertaining to that female were rejected. This procedure assured that an unsuccessful attempt at stripping a female of eggs was due to the subjected treatment and not due to an unripe condition of the female.

Trials of different experiments were alternated randomly without any definite chronological sequence.

The experimental chambers in experiments 1, 2, 5, 6, and 7 were 5-liter all-glass aquaria. In experiment 3, 20-liter aquaria were used and were partitioned into two halves, one the experimental chamber and the other the male chamber. The partitionings were done with 1-mm thick opaque plastic divider perforated with holes 1.5 mm in diameter and 3 mm apart. In experiment 4, a 60-liter aquarium was used and was partitioned into nonperforated black plastic dividers into a 30-liter metabolite chamber, a 15-liter male chamber, and a 15-liter experimental chamber. Water was circulated from the metabolite chamber into the male chamber, and then to the experimental chamber and back to the metabolite chamber by means of pumping and siphoning.

The presence of the male pheromone in experiments 1 and 2 was established by air lifting into the experimental chambers water from a 5-liter aquarium into which a male was introduced simultaneously with the introduction of the female into the experimental chamber, the water then was siphoned back into the male aquarium. In experiments 3 and 4, male pheromone was provided by placing, during the experimental period, a male into the male chamber which was chemically continuous with the experimental chamber

because of the perforations or water circulation.

The presence or absence of temperature shock was established by maintaining the experimental chamber respectively at room temperature ($21.0 \pm 1.0°C$) or at the temperature of the holding compartments ($27.0 \pm 1.0°C$).

The absence of metabolites in experiments 1, 2, 3, 5, 6, and 7 was attained by filling the experimental chamber and the male chamber with fresh, dechlorinated tap water. In experiment 4, metabolites were presented by conditioning the system for at least 2 wk with 75 mature zebrafish of both sexes in the metabolite chamber which is chemically continuous with the experimental chamber because of the water circulation.

Visual stimuli from a male were provided in experiment 5 by allowing the test female to be in visual contact with a mature male in a separate, chemically discontinuous all-glass aquarium. In experiment 3, the perforations of the divider partitioning the male chamber and the experimental chamber provided questionable visual stimuli from the male. In all other experiments (1, 2, 4, 6, and 7), visual stimuli from males were screened by visually isolating the experimental chambers with cardboard or black plastic sheet.

Possible auditory and lateral line stimuli from male were allowed in experiment 3 through the perforated condition of the partition separating the experimental chamber from the male chamber.

In experiment 6a, the experimental chamber was a simple 5-liter all-glass aquarium, whereas in experiment 6b a current similar to that in experiments 1, 2, 4, and 7 was provided by air lifting and back-siphoning of water between the experimental chamber and a vacated 5-liter aquarium.

Prior to each experiment, the glass aquaria and hoses were scrubbed, soaked, and thoroughly rinsed with tap water. Experiments testing the pheromonal responses utilized a different set of hoses from those used in experiments lacking the male pheromones. Different nets were used for netting males and females as a precaution against contacting a test female with the slime of a male.

RESULTS

The number of positive responses (trials eggs obtained) and negative responses (trials no eggs obtained) are given for each of the eight experiments in Table 1. The results of each experiment were compared with those of experiment 8 and the chi-square value was calculated. The percent of trials resulting in a positive response is also given for each experiment.

It is apparent from the results that presence of pheromone and absence of metabolites are the two most influential factors stimulating ovulation in the zebrafish. Experiments 1, 2, and 3 in which pheromone was provided and metabolites were absent invariably gave nearly 100% ovulation. Experiments 4, 5, 6, and 7 in which either pheromone was provided or metabolites were absent gave 40-50% ovulation. However, in experiment 8 in which pheromone was absent and metabolites were present, no ovulations were observed. The roles of metabolites and male pheromone are further indicated by the fact that females which initially responded negatively in experiments lacking the male pheromone and/or fresh tap water (experiments 4, 5, 6, and 7) gave eggs in the second stripping in all cases upon being presented with the missing factor(s).

None of the other factors tested, including temperature shock and auditory and/or lateral line stimulations seem important in controlling ovulation, as in no cases did their presence or absence significantly alter the results. The influences of water movement between the experimental chamber and the male chamber were insignificant, as there is no difference between results of experiments 6a and 6b.

Successful stripping was recorded at all times over the morning, afternoon, and early evening. After the stripping, without exception, a pair would commence natural spawning immediately upon introduction regardless of the time of day.

DISCUSSION

In the absence of the male pheromone and the presence of the metabolites, females consistently failed to ovulate (experiment 8). Under similar condition, Eaton and Farley (1974) also failed to strip eggs from isolated females. Histological studies of zebrafish ovaries by Hisaoka and Firlit (1962) indicated that oocytes are not released from the ovarian stroma into the central lumen and oviducts (ovulation) until stimulated by males during the breeding process. Eaton and Farley (1974) were able to obtain ripe ova from isolated females in the morning only after a brief (7 h) introduction of a male into the female's tank on the previous day. They suggested that the vigorous chasing behavior exhibited by the male toward the female might have provided the stimulus, although no supporting data were provided.

The results of the present study clearly establish that a male pheromone stimulates ovulation of the female. Little is known about the nature of the male pheromone. It appears not to be species specific since circulation of water between aquarium containing male *Brachydanio albolineatus* and aquarium containing female *B. rerio* elicited ovulation in the female in four out of four trials. Intrageneric interspecific effectiveness of sex pheromone has also been demonstrated by Rossi (1969) in *Colisa lalia* and *C. labiosa*. In this case a female pheromone can induce nest building in heterospecific males.

As to the chemical nature of piscine sex pheromones, Amouriq (1965) identified an estrogen as the pheromone inducing hyperactivity in male *Lebistes reticulatus*, and Tavolga (1956) identified the internal fluid of the ovary as the source of the chemical stimulus eliciting courtship behavior of male in *Bathygobius soporator*. In the present study, of six trials consisting of placing test females into fresh tap water previously occupied for 24 h by a male, only four positive responses were recorded. Since the metabolites produced by a male in 24 h are far below the threshold level for inhibiting ovulation, as we have experienced and as Greene (1966) has reported, the two failures out of six trials in the above experiment suggest either that the male pheromone is short lived or that less male pheromone was released in the chemical absence of the female.

The selective advantage of an ovulating pheromone in the zebrafish is not clear. Although Hart and Messina (1972) claimed to be able to obtain sperm from male zebrafish at all times under laboratory conditions, we often encountered unsuccessful milking of males. If both sexes are not sexually ready at all times, it would be advantageous to synchronize sexual readiness between sexes. If release of the ovulating pheromone corresponds with male readiness, synchronization would be guaranteed. However, males appeared to release the pheromone quite regularly, even while in the presence of metabolites as suggested by the 50% ovulation in experiment 4. Yet, it is possible that while the metabolites may repress testicular development or spermiation and the release of the pheromone by the males, the test male introduced at the same time as the test female into the two small chambers of experiment 4 was often already sexually ready at that time and would thus release the pheromone regardless of the presence of metabolites.

Such a pheromone, if functioning in synchronization, would be advantageous for a species with a long spawning interperiod. Although female zebrafish can spawn every 1 or 2 days under laboratory conditions (Eaton and Farley 1974), the spawning interperiod in the native habitat is not known.

In some fishes, it is possible that the active chasing of the female by the male prior to spawning takes part in stimulating ovulation. An ovulating pheromone would conserve such chasing energy and therefore, be selectively advantageous.

The inhibitory effect of metabolic wastes on fish reproduction has been reported by Greene (1966) who found that an increase in metabolite concentration resulted in a decrease in the number of successful natural spawnings in the zebrafish. Lin (1935) observed that grass carp, *Ctenopharyngodon idellus*, would spawn only after a rise in the river water due to rain. Similar observations confirming the coincidence of heavy rain and spawning have been made by von Ihering and Wright (1935) and Lake (1967). Lake suggested that the stimulatory effect of rain on fish spawning was through addition of soil elements through runoffs. However, according to Swingle (1956), draining a pond crowded with goldfish or largemouth bass and refilling it subsequently with new water could induce spawning in the pond fish. One of us (Chen) had observed on numerous occasions that goldfish spawned during or after rain in outdoor concrete tanks. In these cases, spawning occurred without input of soil elements. Swingle (1956) suggested that the effect of rain was to dilute a spawning repressive factor. It is obvious from the present experiment that this repressive factor is metabolites.

Tang (1963) noted that the testes of silver carp, *Hypophthalmichthys molitrix*, would develop only after the volume of the reservoir had been increased by rain, thus suggesting that maturation of testes may be retarded by waste products from fish and that new water, or dilution of these wastes, is necessary for sexual development. It is possible that removal of the metabolites can also induce the release of the pheromone by the male zebrafish, indirectly stimulating ovulation in the females. In the present study, however, removal of the metabolites apparently had a direct effect on the females, as mere exposure of the females to fresh tap water resulted in ovulation in nearly half of the trials (experiment 7). Tang (1957) reported that female common carp inhibited from spawning by metabolic wastes would release eggs in the absence of males upon introduction of new water

The chemical nature of the inhibiting metabolites is not known. Greene (1966) believed that they were ammonia. From the observation made by Swingle (1965) that crowding of bluegill inhibited spawning in the largemouth bass in the same pond, the inhibiting metabolites cannot be species specific.

As discussed earlier, many of the freshwater fishes in the tropics spawn only in the rainy season. During this period, there is an addition of flooded lowland suitable for the deposition of eggs, an increase in the dissolved oxygen favorable for embryological development, and an increase of organic and inorganic nutrients which promote growth of food plankton. Rain would also dilute any metabolic wastes accumulated during the dry season. In this context, metabolites may serve as a controlling factor, repressing ovulation until the rainy season when environmental conditions are more favorable for both embryo development and larval growth.

The results of the present study clearly indicate the stimulatory effect of the male pheromone and the inhibitory effect of metabolites on ovulation in the zebrafish. As gonadotropin is known to be effective in inducing ovulation in fishes, either directly, or via stimulating the synthesis of corticosteroids and/or progesterone (Donaldson 1973; de Vlaming 1974), the action of the ovulating pheromone and the metabolites is probably to activate or to deactivate the hypothalamus-pituitary-gonad axis. A pheromonal facilitation of gonadotropin-induced ovulation has been reported in mouse (Zarrow et al. 1973). Further studies are needed to clarify the route of action of the pheromone and the metabolites.

Aronson (1965) cited numerous examples in fishes in which gonadal development and subsequent spawning were stimulated by either an increase or a decrease in temperature. An increase in temperature has been reported to affect the gonadal response to treatment with gonadotropin in *Lepomis cyanellus* by Kaya (1973) and in *Gillichthys mirabilis* by de Vlaming (1972c). In the present study, a sudden decrease in temperature alone does not seem important in stimulating ovulation in the zebrafish.

In the zebrafish, visual or auditory and lateral line stimuli between sexes do not seem important in enhancing ovulation, although some of these factors may be pertinent in eliciting the proper behavior during the actual spawning act.

The onset of light alone is not sufficient to stimulate ovulation, as demonstrated by the complete failure to strip eggs during the morning hours from females tested directly from their holding compartments (experiment 8). Furthermore, these females were stimulated to ovulate later that day, after exposure to the male pheromone and fresh tap water. Ovulation and natural spawning were induced regardless of time of day. One of us (Chen) has observed natural spawning of zebrafish to commence at midnight in darkness and continue for hours. These observations conflict with all previous accounts that the onset of light is important to trigger ovulation and spawning in the zebrafish (Legault 1958; Hisaoka and Firlit 1960; Eaton and Farley 1974).

LITERATURE CITED

Amouriq, L.
    1965. Origine de la substance dynamogene émise par *Lebistes reticulatus* femelle (Poisson Poeciliidae, Cyprinodontiforme). C. R. Acad. Sci. (Paris) 260:2334-2335.

Aronson, L. R.
    1945. Influence of the stimuli provided by the male cichlid fish, *Tilapia macrocephala*, on the spawning frequency of the female. Physiol. Zool. 18:403-415.

1965. Environmental stimuli altering the physiological condition of the individual among lower vertebrates. *In* F. A. Beach (editor), Sex and behavior, p. 290-318. Wiley and Sons, N.Y.

BRAWN, V. M.

1961. Sound production by the cod (*Gadus callarias* L.). Behaviour 18:239-255.

BREDER, C. M., AND D. E. ROSEN.

1966. Modes of reproduction in fishes. Natural History Press, Garden City, N.Y., 941 p.

CHIEN, A. K.

1973. Reproductive behavior of the angelfish *Pterophyllum scalare* (Pisces: Cichlidae). II. Influence of male stimuli upon the spawning rate of females. Anim. Behav. 21:457-463.

DE VLAMING, V. L.

1972a. Environmental control of teleost reproductive cycles: A brief review. J. Fish Biol. 4:131-140.

1972b. The effects of temperature and photoperiod on reproductive cycling in the estuarine gobiid fish, *Gillichthys mirabilis*. Fish. Bull., U.S. 70:1137-1152.

1972c. The role of the endocrine system in temperature-controlled reproductive cycling in the estuarine gobiid fish, *Gillichthys mirabilis*. Comp. Biochem. Physiol. 41A:697-713.

1974. Environmental and endocrine control of teleost reproduction. *In* C. B. Schreck (editor), Control of sex in fishes, p. 12-83. Va. Polytech. Inst. and State Univ.

DONALDSON, E. M.

1973. Reproductive endocrinology of fishes. Am. Zool. 13:909-927.

EATON, R. C., AND R. D. FARLEY.

1974. Spawning cycle and egg production of zebrafish, *Brachydanio rerio*, in the laboratory. Copeia 1974:195-204.

EGAMI, N., AND M. NAMBU.

1961. Factors initiating mating behavior and oviposition in the fish, *Oryzias latipes*. J. Fac. Sci. Univ. Tokyo, Sect. IV, Zool. 9:263-278.

GANDOLFI, G.

1969. A chemical sex attractant in the guppy, *Poecilia reticulata* Peters (Pisces, Poeciliidae). Monit. Zool. Ital. 3:89-98.

GRAY, G. A., AND H. E. WINN.

1961. Reproductive ecology and sound production of the toadfish, *Opsanus tau*. Ecology 42:274-282.

GREENE, G. N.

1966. A reproduction control factor in the cyprinid fish, *Brachydanio rerio*. FAO (Food Agric. Organ. U.N.) Fish. Rep. 44(4):86-92.

HARRINGTON, R. W., JR.

1959. Effects of four combinations of temperature and daylength on the ovogenetic cycle of a low-latitude fish,

Fundulus confluentus Goode & Bean. Zoologica (N.Y.) 44:149-168.

HART, N. H., AND M. MESSINA.

1972. Artificial insemination of ripe eggs in the zebra fish, *Brachydanio rerio*. Copeia 1972:302-305.

HISAOKA, K. K., AND C. F. FIRLIT.

1960. Further studies on the embryonic development of the zebrafish, *Brachydanio rerio* (Hamilton-Buchanan). J. Morphol. 107:205-225.

1962. Ovarian cycle and egg production in the zebrafish, *Brachydanio rerio*. Copeia 1962:788-792.

KAYA, C. M.

1973. Effects of temperature on responses of the gonads of green sunfish (*Lepomis cyanellus*) to treatment with carp pituitaries and testosterone propionate. J. Fish. Res. Board Can. 30:905-912.

LAKE, J. S.

1967. Rearing experiments with five species of Australian freshwater fishes. I. Inducement to spawning. Aust. J. Mar. Freshwater Res. 18:137-153.

LEGAULT, R.

1958. A technique for controlling the time of daily spawning and collecting of eggs of the zebra fish, *Brachydanio rerio* (Hamilton-Buchanan). Copeia 1958:328-330.

LIN, S. Y.

1935. Life history of waan-ue, *Ctenopharyngodon idellus* (Cuv. & Val.). Lingnan Sci. J. 14:271-274.

MYRBERG, A. A., JR., AND J. Y. SPIRES.

1972. Sound discrimination by the bicolor damselfish, *Eupomacentrus partitus*. J. Exp. Biol. 57:727-735.

ROSSI, A. C.

1969. Chemical signals and nest-building in two species of *Colisa* (Pisces, Anabantidae). Monit. Zool. Ital. 3:225-237.

SWINGLE, H. S.

1956. Determination of balance in farm fish ponds. Trans. North Am. Wildl. Nat. Resour. Conf. 21:298-322.

TANG, Y. A.

1957. The effect of the "repressive factor" on fish reproduction. [In Chin.] China Fish. Mon. 57:2-3.

1963. The testicular development of the silver carp, *Hypophthalmichthys molitrix* (C. & V.), in captivity in relation to the repressive effects of wastes from fishes. Jap. J. Ichthyol. 10:24-27.

TAVOLGA, W. N.

1956. Visual, chemical and sound stimuli as cues in the sex discriminatory behavior of the gobiid fish, *Bathygobius soporator*. Zoologica (N.Y.) 41:49-64.

VON IHERING, R., AND S. WRIGHT.

1935. Fisheries investigations in northeast Brazil. Trans. Am. Fish. Soc. 65:267-271.

ZARROW, M. X., B. E. ELEFTHERIOU, AND V. H. DENENBERG.

1973. Sex and strain involvement in pheromonal facilitation of gonadotrophin-induced ovulation in the mouse. J. Reprod. Fertil. 35:81-87.

Social Control of Sex Reversal
in a Coral-Reef Fish

D. R. ROBERTSON

Smithsonian Tropical Research Institute
Balboa, Canal Zone

ABSTRACT

Males of *Labroides dimidiatus* control the process of sex reversal within social groups. Each group consists of a male with a harem of females, among which larger individuals dominate smaller ones. The male in each harem suppresses the tendency of the females to change sex by actively dominating them. Death of the male releases this suppression and the dominant female of the harem changes sex immediately. Possible genetic advantages of the system are considered.

Sex reversal is widespread in a number of tropical fishes included in the families Labridae, Scaridea, and Serranidea [1, 2]. In this report I describe the pattern of protogynous sex reversal in the labrid fish *Labroides dimidiatus.* The species is a member of a small but widespread genus, the species of which are termed "cleaner fish" because they remove ectoparasites from the skin of other fishes [3]. Choat [2] established that the species is protogynous, with far more females than males, and that probably all the males were secondarily derived from females.

The basic social unit is a male with a harem of usually three to six mature females and several immature individuals living within the male's territory. At Heron Island, Great Barrier Reef, detailed field records were kept on 11 groups for up to 25 months; 48 sex reversals were recorded in these and another eight groups. Individual adults were recognized by unchanging variations in their color patterns.

All individuals exhibit territoriality, but its expression varies with age and sex. The largest, oldest individual is the male, which dominates all the females in the groups. Larger, older females of the group dominate smaller ones, which usually results in a linear dominance hierarchy. Thus territoriality is only fully expressed in males and is directed mainly toward other males. Usually there is one dominant female in each group, but sometimes two equal-sized females are codominant and can successfully defend their territories against each other. The dominant female lives in the center of the male's territory, with the other females scattered around. The male is socially very active. It makes frequent excursions throughout its territory both to the feeding areas of the females and to points on the territory border where the male is likely to meet neighboring males. During these excursions the male feeds in the females' areas and actively initiates aggressive encounters with them and other individuals. Females, on the other hand, are more sedentary and passive. When a male meets a female of the same group, the male frequently performs a distinctive aggressive display toward the female. This display has not been seen in encounters between males and only very rarely in encounters between females, when it was given by dominant females.

Some males and large females have maintained nearly the same territories and feeding sites for almost 2 years. Small adults and large juveniles are more mobile. Deaths of individuals high in the hierarchy result in more marked changes in the distribution of other high-status individuals than do deaths of low-status individuals. With the death of a high-status female, the vacated area may be incorporated into the territory of an individual of

---

equal status or taken over by an individual immediately below the deceased in status, the lower status female deserts its own territory in the process. This shift can result in the immediate redistribution of three or four high-status females.

Sex reversal frequently occurs as a part of the reorganization of the group following the death of the male. The success of an initiated reversal depends upon both inter- and intragroup social pressures. Intergroup social pressures take the form of territory invasion and takeover attempts by neighboring males, and if these pressures are successfully resisted by the dominant female it changes sex. Groups with codominant females sometimes divide when both dominants change into males. In all, 26 cases of single dominant females reversing sex were observed (five naturally occurring and 21 experimentally induced by removing the male), and four cases of reversal of pairs of codominants were also seen (all induced by removing the male).

Observations of five dominant females after the removal of their males have shown that the first behavioral signs of sex reversal appear rapidly and that the behavioral changeover can be completed within a few days. For approximately half an hour after the death of the male the dominant female continues to behave aggressively as a normal female. This simple female aggression then wanes to more neutral reactions to nearby subordinate females. Approximately 1½ to 2 hours after male death, maleness appears in the form of the special male aggressive display that the new "male" starts performing to the females of its group. The assumption of the male aggressive role can be virtually completed within several hours, when the "male" starts visiting its females and territory borders. The switchover to male courtship and spawning behavior takes somewhat longer but can be partly accomplished within 1 day and completed within 2 to 4 days. Other individuals also respond within a couple of hours to the altered social situation created by male death; low-status females take over vacant female territories, and neighboring males invade and attempt to take over the territory and harem.

The death of a male does not necessarily lead to a sex reversal within the group. In 11 cases intergroup pressures were apparently too great, and neighboring males invaded the territory, taking it and the female group over. In four of these cases the dominant female had started to behave like a male before the invasion but reverted to female behavior after the completion of the takeover and remained as a fully functional female. In all these successful takeovers the invading male was considerably larger than the incumbent dominant female and was able to dominate relatively easily. In one interrupted sex reversal observed, the dominant female was under the control of a slightly larger invading male for about 2 weeks after the death of the original male. During this period the female behaviorally went through the series $♀ → ♂ → ♀ → ♂$, the final change being a successful one.

Five observed sex reversals were not associated with male death. Before reversal all five individuals were medium-large females of high status; four were subdominants and one was a codominant. The area of each individual was away from the main areas of social activity of the dominant male, which visited the female relatively infrequently. Consequently each female had much less social contact with the male than did females of comparable status within the same group.

Histological examinations were made of the gonads of 29 females and 35 males. The ovaries of 28 of the 29 females contained small spermatogenic crypts located close to sites of early oogenesis in the ovarian lamellae, and in 15 of these 28 females some crypts contained sperm or spermatids. Free sperm were not detected, and the spermatogenic crypts appeared to be completely enclosed. The gonads of 28 males of known "age" (age from the start of reversal) have been examined. From the small series of "young" males examined, it appears that sperm can be released 14 to 18 days after the start of reversal.

These data demonstrate social control of sex reversal in this species, with males regulating the production of males. Probably all females are capable of changing sex, and most (probably all) have testicular elements within perfectly functional ovaries. The tendency of any female to change may be actively suppressed by more dominant individuals

Females	Male aggressive acts		
	SA	HD	LD
Dominant	54	94	371
Large subdominant	36	8	48
Small subdominant	20	1	22

Table 1. Aggressive acts by males against three hierarchical classes of females [three types of aggressive acts—simple attacks (SA), high-intensity male aggressive display (HD), and low-intensity male aggressive display (LD)]. The data represent eight males and their harems. Hierarchy subdominants have been arbitrarily divided into two classes. The distribution of aggressive acts did not differ significantly between the eight social groups [goodness-of-fit test, G (5)]. The data from all groups were therefore pooled. The same method demonstrated significant heterogeneity among the three classes of females ($G = 69.085$, d.f. = 4, $P<.01$).

in the hierarchy. Non-dominant females have aggression by both sexes directed at them; the dominant female is the object of only male-type aggression and is dominated by only a single individual. Death of the male means that the female of highest status becomes totally dominant with the group, and the tendency to change sex is no longer suppressed. The rapidity with which a new male behaviorally assumes its role is a reflection of the presence of male elements in all females and the necessity for a new male to consolidate its position quickly in the face of constant intra- and intergroup pressures. Subdominant females are also potential males and must be inhibited if the group structure is to be maintained. Neighboring males must be excluded if a harem is to be maintained. Males direct their aggression differentially toward females of different status in their hierarchies. The male is more aggressive toward those females most likely to change sex and threaten his position—that is, larger females, especially the dominant one (Table 1). The aggression directed at these higher status females is also more characteristically male. Incomplete control of high-status females such as those most peripheral in the male's territory, can result in sex reversal. High-status females probably suppress females lower in the hierarchy; the latter evidently need less male control.

Field experiments with seven isolated females (the other members of naturally isolated groups were removed) indicate that the presence of a harem is not necessary for sex reversal to be accomplished, although the process may be slower. Experiments with six males similarly isolated without harems demonstrated the continuance of sperm production for up to 26 days in functional males.

Many Labridae and Scaridae are protogynous hermaphrodites with female-biased sex ratios [2], and in some species social control of sex reversal may operate in a similar manner to that in *Labroides dimidiatus*. In other species, especially schooling forms, a well-defined social structure based on individual relationships might not be possible, and sex reversal may be controlled more by endogenous factors. Male control of the production of males has been demonstrated in the laboratory in a protogynous serranid fish, *Anthias squamipinnis* [4].

At the present, discussion of the biological significance of protogyny remains speculative. Arguments have been put forward to explain protogyny and the biased sex ratio in terms of population growth, with the predominance of females increasing fecundity [4]. Choat [2] advanced the idea that the biased sex ratio, maintained by protogyny, could be considered as an inbreeding mechanism because it reduced the number of genotypes available for recombination, and this would permit adaptation to specific local conditions.

My observations on the pattern of sex reversal in *L. dimidiatus* support this idea of genetic advantages for the system. The genotypes of the males are those which are maximally recombined, because each male spawns regularly with the females of its group and each female spawns, in the main, with the dominant male only. The male genotype is the genotype best adapted to local conditions because the male is derived from the oldest female of the group. Individuals enter the group and gradually move up within it, with only the best adapted females eventually being able to reverse sex. Thus the social organization is a framework within which the selective process works. The social group is a self-perpetuating system which ensures the maintenance of the biased sex ratio by controlling sex reversal. Social control of sex reversal both maximizes the genetic advantages of the process and imparts considerable flexibility to it. Males are produced only when they are needed, and this method overcomes the possible precariousness of a strongly biased sex ratio maintained by endogenously controlled sex reversal.

1 June 1972

REFERENCES AND NOTES

1. J. W. Atz, in *Intersexuality in Vertebrates including Man,* C. N. Armstrong and A. J. Marshall, Eds. (Academic Press, London, 1964), pp. 145–232; R. Reinboth, *Zool. Jahrb. Abt. Allg. Zool. Physiol. Tiere* 69, 405 (1962).
2. J. H. Choat, thesis, University of Queensland (1969), part 1; R. Reinboth, *Z. Naturforsch. B* 23, 852 (1968).
3. J. E. Randall, *Pac. Sci.* 12, 327 (1958).
4. L. Fishelson, *Nature* 227, 90 (1970).
5. R. R. Sokal and F. J. Rohlf, *Biometry: The Principles and Practice of Statistics in Biological Research* (Freeman, San Francisco, 1969).
6. I thank R. Bradbury, A. Cameron, J. Choat, J. Connell, D. Dow, and J. Kikkawa for criticizing a draft of the manuscript; the Great Barrier Reef Committee for the use of Heron Island Research Station facilities; and the University of Queensland for financially supporting this research.

Latimeria, the Living Coelacanth, Is Ovoviviparous

C. Lavett Smith
American Museum of Natural History,
New York 10024

Charles S. Rand
Department of Biology, Long Island
University, Zeckendorf Campus,
Brooklyn, New York 11201

Bobb Schaeffer, James W. Atz
American Museum of Natural History

Abstract. *Dissection of a specimen of* Latimeria chalumnae *in the American Museum of Natural History revealed that it is a gravid female containing five advanced young, averaging 317.8 millimeters long. Each has a large yolk sac with no apparent connection to the surrounding oviducal wall. We conclude that* Latimeria *is ovoviviparous.*

Latimeria chalumnae Smith is the only living representative of a distinctive and once widespread group of lobe-finned fishes (*Coelacanthini*) first known from rocks of Devonian age and long believed to have become extinct in the Late Cretaceous. The capture of a living representative off the coast of South Africa in 1938 triggered an extensive search for additional specimens. It was not until 1952, however, that a second specimen was collected, this time off the Comoro Islands. Since then, more than 80 specimens have been taken by Comorean fishermen, at the rate of three or four a year.

Despite the number of specimens available for study, the mode of reproduction of *Latimeria* has remained unknown. The anatomy of the urogenital system and orifices of adult males and females was described by Millot and Anthony (*1 4*), but the scarcity of mature females and the absence of any obvious copulatory organ in males left unanswered the key question of whether *Latimeria* lays eggs or gives birth to living young. On the basis of a female found with eggs in her oviduct, Millot and Anthony (*2*) concluded that *Latimeria* is oviparous. Another female containing 19 apparently ripe eggs (8.5 to 9.0 cm in di-

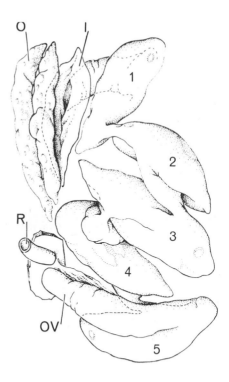

Fig. 1. Reproductive tract of gravid *Latimeria chalumnae*. Abbreviations: *O*, ovary; *I*, infundibulum of the oviduct; *OV*, distal part of the oviduct; *R*, rectum; *1–5*, yolk-sac young in expanded portions of the oviduct.

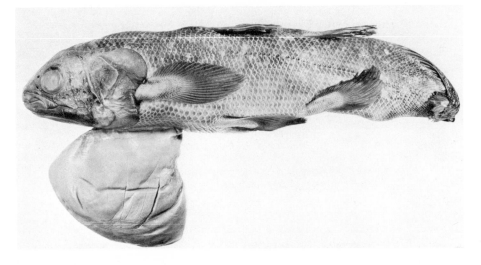

Fig. 2. Yolk-sac young of *Latimeria chalumnae*, the second of five found in a female 1.6 m long at the American Museum of Natural History. Unretouched photograph shows fins and tail as compressed by oviducal walls. Total length, 322 mm.

ameter) confirmed these authors' point of view (*3, 5*). Griffith and Thomson (*6*), however, believed that osmoregulatory requirements would make it impossible for such a shell-less egg to survive outside the body of the female and they concluded that *Latimeria* must be ovoviviparous.

With regard to the paleontological evidence, Watson (*7*) described two small skeletons of the Jurassic coelacanth *Undina* (= *Holophagus*) found inside the body cavity of a much larger specimen of the same taxon. He suggested that *Holophagus* was viviparous. More recently, Schultze (*8*) described several isolated larvae of the Pennsylvanian coelacanth *Rhabdoderma* with preserved yolk sacs and, noting that coelacanths lack any fins in the form of intromittent organs, he postulated that these fishes were oviparous. Schultze interpreted Watson's specimen as a case of cannibalism.

The specimen of *Latimeria* in the American Museum of Natural History measures 1.6 m in total length; its weight at the time of capture was reported to be 65 kg (*9*). The anatomy of the head of this specimen has been investigated (*10*), but its viscera were not dissected until recently, when samples of hemopoietic tissues were taken. During the course of the dissection, five advanced young were discovered lying free in the right oviduct. Millot and Anthony (*1,*

2) have observed that only the right oviduct is functional in *Latimeria*. As indicated in Fig. 1, all of the young were situated with their heads directed away from the urogenital orifice.

The following observations were made on four of the young that were removed from the oviduct, the fifth having been left in situ. The young resemble miniature adults, differing most noticeably in the possession of a yolk sac, the relatively larger eyes, and a more declivous profile (Fig. 2). Total length ranges from 301 to 327 mm, with an average of 317.8 mm. The maximum diameter of the yolk sac ranges from 80 to 129 mm; the largest fish has the smallest yolk sac, and vice versa. The yolk-sac stalk is broad, extending from the base of the pectoral fins approximately two-thirds of the distance to the base of the pelvic fins. Scales and fins appear to be fully developed in all four young, but they lack the denticles (odontodes) of the adult.

The gravid female under discussion was caught in January, the same month in which females with ovulated eggs have been taken. This suggests that gestation may require more than a year not an unexpected length of time in view of the tremendous size of the ripe egg.

Millot and Anthony (*1*) showed that the male of *Latimeria* possesses a cloaca which contains a urogenital papilla and is flanked externally by two pairs of erectile caruncles. Since internal fertilization of the female must occur, it seems likely that the cloaca functions as an eversible copulatory organ, in a manner reminiscent of the situation in some birds and gymnophiones (*11*). The caruncles perhaps serve as claspers. Similar suggestions have been made by Griffith and Thomson (*6, 12*).

Paleoichthyologists usually consider the coelacanths to be most closely related to the Paleozoic rhipidistians, and the latter in turn to be the fishes most closely related to the tetrapods (*13*). Nothing is known about reproduction in the rhipidistians, and there is no way of knowing whether the ovoviviparous condition in *Latimeria* is unique or whether it is shared by other crossopterygians and primitive tetrapods. Among other major groups of bony fishes, living lungfishes are oviparous, as are all living actinopterygians except 11 families (less than 5 percent) that exhibit viviparity or ovoviviparity as a derived condition or specialization. Although the ovoviviparity of *Latimeria* sheds no light on the reproductive mode of primitive osteichthyans, including crossopterygians, it does indicate that all the information we now have about reproduction in the fossil coelacanths is consistent with the hypothesis that they were ovoviviparous.

References and Notes

1. J. Millot and J. Anthony, *Bull. Mus. Natl. Hist. Nat. Ser. 2* **32**, 287 (1960).
2. ———, *C. R. Hebd. Seances Acad. Sci.* **251**, 442 (1960).
3. J. Anthony and J. Millot, *C. R. Hebd. Seances Acad. Sci. Ser. D Sci. Nat.* **274**, 1925 (1972).
4. J. Millot and J. Anthony, *ibid.* **276**, 2447 (1973).
5. ———, *Sci. Nature Environ. No. 121* (1974), p. 3.
6. R. W. Griffith and K. S. Thomson, *Nature (Lond.)* **242**, 617 (1973).
7. D. M. S. Watson, *Proc. Zool. Soc. Lond.* **1927**, 453 (1927).
8. H. P. Schultze, *Nat. New Biol.* **236**, 90 (1972).
9. The specimen, which is specimen 26 in the summary table of coelacanth captures prepared by J. Millot, J. Anthony, and D. Robineau [*Bull. Mus. Natl. Hist. Nat. Ser. 3* (No. 53), 533 (1972)], was caught off Mutsamudu, Anjouan Island, in 1962. G. W. Garrouste, a physician then living in Anjouan, arranged for its acquisition by the American Museum of Natural History. In the same table specimen 65 is incorrectly recorded as having also been sent to the American Museum.
10. For example, by G. J. Nelson, *Bull. Am. Mus. Nat. Hist.* **141**, 475 (1969); *Copeia* **1970**, 468 (1970); *Zool. J. Linn. Soc.* **53** (Suppl. 1), 333 (1973).
11. S. B. McDowell, personal communication.
12. In the light of the present discovery, Griffith and Thomson also may have been correct in suggesting that the isolated yolk-sac larvae described by Schultze were prematurely released from a stressed female. Such behavior is often seen in ovoviviparous sharks, rays, and teleosts.
13. J. A. Moy-Thomas and R. S. Miles, *Palaeozoic Fishes* (Saunders, Philadelphia, ed. 2, 1971).
14. We thank C. G. Schleifer for the drawing, C. Tarka for the photograph, and Dr. G. J. Nelson for his cogent comments on the manuscript.

29 September 1975

Oxygen Consumption of Embryos and Parents, and Oxygen Transfer Characteristics Within the Ovary of Two Species of Viviparous Seaperch, *Rhacochilus Vacca* and *Embiotoca Lateralis*

P. W. WEBB* AND J. R. BRETT**

*School of Natural Resources
Resource Ecology Program
University of Michigan at Ann Arbor

**Fisheries Research Board of Canada
Pacific Biological Station, Nanaimo, B. C.

Oxygen tension and content of intraovarian fluid were measured for the viviparous pile perch, *Rhacochilus vacca*, during middle and late gestation. Oxygen tension decreased with increasing demands of the brood, reaching a minimum of 13.7 mm Hg just prior to parturition. Total oxygen content of the ovarian fluid decreased to a minimum of 22 mg O_2, rising thereafter to 54 mg O_2 at parturition as the volume of ovarian fluid increased. The in vitro oxygen consumption of the young per unit weight increased 2.5 times during gestation reaching 222 mg O_2/kg/hr at birth (mean weight 3.8 g).

Oxygen consumption of two pregnant striped seaperch, *Embiotoca lateralis*, was fairly constant at 70 mg O_2/kg/hr early in gestation, increasing later to approximately 107 mg O_2/kg/hr at parturition.

An oxygen dissociation curve was determined for ventricular blood of pregnant pile perch. The $p50$ was 12.5 mm Hg. Along with other parameters, this was used to estimate the oxygen transfer characteristics of the brood-ovary exchange system, maximum possible oxygen consumption, and ovarian blood flow rate. The capacity of the system to meet the increasing requirements of the young decreased during gestation, reaching limiting conditions at parturition. It was concluded that transfer of oxygen to the young would be controlled by, and ultimately limited by, ovarian blood flow rate. The brood-ovary system is compared with the mammalian placenta.

The comparative anatomy and histology of embryonic and ovarian structural adaptations to viviparity in teleosts have received considerable attention (Hoar 1969). For embiotocids, these adaptations have been summarized by Webb and Brett (1972) with particular reference to the supply of metabolites to the developing intraovarian young. Elaboration of highly vascularized embryonic fins greatly increases the surface area for oxygen uptake, constituting the most important single adaption in these fish.

In comparison with the anatomy, the physiology of exchange of metabolites between the ovary and prenatal young has largely been neglected. Quantitative measurements of the relation between the weight and brood-ovary morphometrics in striped seaperch (*Embiotoca lateralis*) and pile perch (*Rhacochilus vacca*) were considered in relation to the structural barrier to the diffusion of metabolites (Webb and Brett 1972). It was concluded that supply would be limited by such factors as blood flow rather than structural attributes. The purpose of the following study, therefore, was to estimate the overall oxygen exchange performance of the brood-ovary system. It was anticipated that the oxygen demand of the brood and the oxygen characteristics of the intraovarian environment would be subjected to various physiological constraints influencing oxygen transfer. In

From *Journal of the Fisheries Research Board of Canada* 29:1543–1553. Reprinted by permission.

the absence of such information for other viviparous fish, the brood-ovary system has been compared with the mammalian placenta. The latter system has evolved to meet the same sort of oxygen supply problems as the brood-ovary system and, consequently, its physiology serves to emphasize the importance of limiting exchange parameters.

MATERIALS AND METHODS

FISH

Experiments were performed on the same fish as used in the preceding study. Most measurements were made on pile perch, *R. vacca,* but a few are reported for striped seaperch, *E. lateralis.*

Pregnant females were dissected in a darkened room to expose the ovary and remove the young through an incision in the ovarian wall.

OVARIAN FLUID AND MATERNAL BLOOD

The ovarian fluid oxygen tension was measured at 12 C for six pile perch. Two samples were drawn from each ovary into an air-free syringe, and injected into a thermostated microcuvette containing a Radiometer (Copenhagen) oxygen electrode.

An oxygen dissociation curve was constructed for a mixed sample of ventricular blood from two pregnant pile perch. Blood was collected in heparinised syringes and equilibrated with air and nitrogen, free from carbon dioxide, at 11 C. The dissociation curve was established by the microliter methods of mixtures at the same temperature; oxygen content of the blood and of ovarian fluid was measured using microliter methods (Tucker 1967).

OXYGEN CONSUMPTION OF THE YOUNG

Two samples of 2–10 excised young were immediately transferred to two 500-ml bottles used as respirometers. Initially, air-saturated 10‰ sea water (mean isosmotic) was run through each bottle. Two 150-ml water samples were siphoned from the bottom of each bottle during the flushing for oxygen determinations using the unmodified Winkler method (American Public Health Association et al. 1965). The bottles were then sealed, wrapped completely in black polyethylene, and immersed in a temperature-controlled water bath. After 1 hr, the bottles were inverted several times to mix the water. This induced the young to swim, facilitating uniform mixing, after which oxygen content was determined for two 150-ml water samples from each bottle. The young were removed, blotted with a moist cloth, and weighed to the nearest 0.001 g. Some measurements of the oxygen consumption of the young kept in 10‰ sea water were made 24 hr after removal from the ovary. Temperatures were controlled at the ambient temperature of the holding tank for the adult perch. It increased during the experiment from 10 C in the middle of May to 18 C at the end of August.

The young always settled at the bottom of the bottles, as observed under dim red light. They made occasional respiratory movements of the branchial apparatus, but did not swim, except as a result of the strong stimulus on mixing the water at the end of an experiment.

OXYGEN CONSUMPTION OF PREGNANT FEMALE

Two pregnant striped seaperch were held at 15 C in 180-liter "growth-metabolism" tanks (Brett et al. 1971). Their oxygen consumption was determined by sealing the tank and measuring the decrease in oxygen content after 2–3 hr.

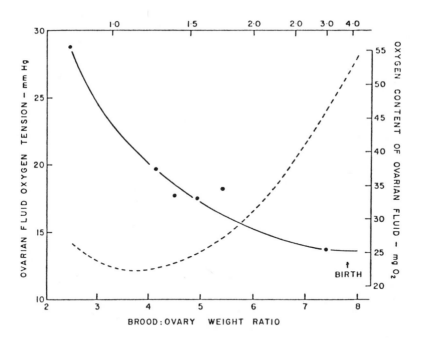

Fig. 1. Relation between the intra-ovarian oxygen environment of pile perch (*Rhacochilus vacca*) and the increasing load on the ovary, expressed as the brood: ovary weight ratio, during gestation. Ovarian fluid oxygen tension is shown by solid circles and solid line. Oxygen content of the ovarian fluid (dotted line) was calculated from this curve, the oxygen capacity, and volume of ovarian fluid (Webb and Brett 1972), which increased during gestation.

RESULTS

OVARIAN OXYGEN CONCENTRATION

Ovarian fluid oxygen tension (P_{fO_2}) is indicative of the extent to which oxygen supply by the ovarian blood stream is matched with the load imposed on the ovary by the brood. Changes in P_{fO_2} during gestation are best shown as a function of the brood-ovary weight ratio, since this is a measure of the load where the brood and the ovary both increase in weight during gestation (Webb and Brett 1972).

P_{fO_2} was highest early in the gestation period (Fig. 1). Extrapolating to an embryonic weight of 0.5 g, when structural transfer capacity was highest (Webb and Brett 1972), the peak P_{fO_2} was 36 mm Hg. The P_{fO_2} decreased exponentially as gestation proceeded, to reach a minimum value of 13.7 mm Hg towards term. Most increase in embryonic weight, from 2.0 to 3.8 g at term, occurred during the last 20–30 days of gestation. During this period, the brood-ovary weight ratio only increased from seven to eight while P_{fO_2} only decreased from 14.9 mm Hg to 13.7 mm Hg.

The ovarian fluid oxygen capacity was found to be about the same as that of 10‰ sea water, indicating the absence of any respiratory pigments. The total oxygen content of the fluid was calculated from P_{fO_2}, oxygen capacity, and ovarian fluid volumes from Webb and Brett (1972) (Fig. 1). As a result of rapidly falling P_{fO_2} as the young increased in weight, without any large increase in ovarian fluid volume, the oxygen reserve (content) decreased early in the gestation period to a minimum of 22 mg O_2 at a brood-ovary weight ratio of 3.8. Subsequently, the reserve increased towards term, reaching a maximum of 54 mg O_2, because of a rapid rise in ovarian fluid volume.

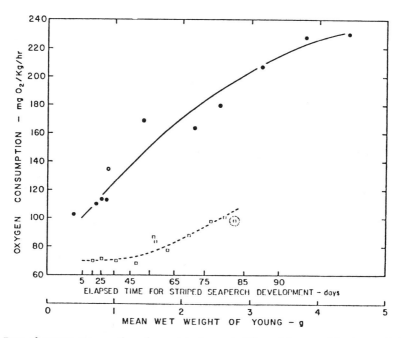

Fig. 2. Rate of oxygen consumption of prenatal pile perch (*Rhacochilus vacca*) in vitro, and of pregnant adult striped seaperch (*Embiotoca lateralis*) at normal ambient temperatures increasing from 10 to 18 C during gestation. Solid line shows oxygen consumption of young as a function of weight. Solid circles indicate values obtained for pile perch; the open circle, for striped seaperch. Open squares and dotted line, show rate of oxygen consumption of parents as a function of time. The two scales were fitted by the regression equation relating the weight of striped seaperch young during the development time from Webb and Brett (1972). The point ringed for oxygen consumption rate of adults was calculated from the minimum expected rate for the female without young, added to the expected rate of oxygen consumption of the brood.

OXYGEN CONSUMPTION OF YOUNG

The metabolic rate of the young measured immediately after removal from the ovary was not significantly higher than that recorded 24 hr later, permitting pooling of the data.

Oxygen consumption increased from 103 mg O_2/kg/hr for the earliest measured young at 0.389 g to a maximum of 230 mg O_2/kg/hr at 4.410 g (Fig. 2). The mean weight of the young at parturition was 3.8 g, when the oxygen consumption was 222 mg O_2/kg/hr; at 0.5 g, when structural transfer capacity was highest, the value was 105 mg O_2/kg/hr.

OXYGEN CONSUMPTION OF PREGNANT STRIPED SEAPERCH

The metabolic rate of the parents remained constant at 70 mg O_2/kg/hr during the period of gestation when the mean weight of the young increased to approximately 1.5 g. The metabolic rate of the parents was thus about two-thirds of that of the young. As the young continued to increase in weight, the metabolic rate of the parent also increased, reaching 107 mg O_2/kg/hr at parturition, when the oxygen demand of the young was 192 mg O_2/kg/hr. The final total weight of the brood was 22% of the total body weight of the parents.

MATERNAL BLOOD DISSOCIATION CURVE

The oxygen dissociation curve for mixed adult ventricular blood had a $p50$ of 12.5 mm Hg (Fig. 3). The haematocrit was 25 vol.%, and the oxygen capacity 10.0 vol.% (14.3

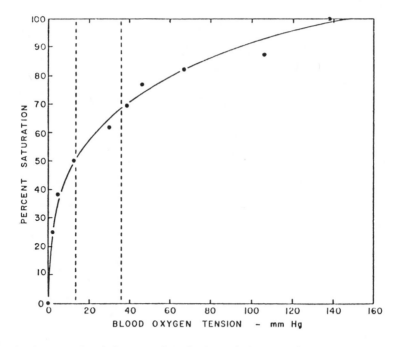

Fig. 3. Blood oxygen dissociation curve for mixed ventricular blood from two pergnant pile perch (*Rhacochilus vacca*) adults. The hematocrit was 25 vol.%, carbon dioxide tension 0 mm Hg. Vertical dotted lines indicate the range of ovarian fluid oxygen tensions expected during the gestation period.

mg O_2/100-ml blood). Because of using zero carbon dioxide levels, the dissociation curve will be most representative of arterial blood entering the ovary and for oxygen loading at the maternal gills.

DISCUSSION

VALIDITY OF IN VITRO MEASUREMENTS OF OXYGEN CONSUMPTION OF PRENATAL YOUNG

Oxygen consumption was measured under conditions of temperature and darkness similar to those in the ovary. Although 10‰ sea water was used instead of ovarian fluid, this was within the range of osmotic tolerance found for shiner perch (*Cymatogaster aggregata*) embryos by Triplett and Barrymore (1960). The behavior of the young, blood distribution to external exchange surfaces, and ventilatory activity of the branchial system was typical of that in the ovary. However, metabolic rates were measured within an oxygen tension range of 100–30% air-saturation, above the range found in the ovary. Standard oxygen consumption rates of fish tend to be independent of oxygen tension in the normal ambient range, but would become dependent at oxygen tensions found in the ovarian fluid (Fry 1957).

A measure of the validity of in vitro oxygen consumption measurements can be made by comparing measured metabolic rates of pregnant adults and calculated rates based on the separate oxygen consumptions of the brood and the parent-less-brood (Table 1). The measured metabolic rate of intact pregnant females at term was 107 mg O_2/kg/hr, compared with a calculated value of 97 mg O_2/kg/hr. The agreement between these values may be considered good, particularly since several factors that would increase adult oxygen consumption related to support of the young are not included; for example, increased ovarian blood flow and adult gill ventilation, together with longer feeding periods and food absorption costs.

TABLE 1 Calculations for the oxygen consumption of two pregnant striped seaperch (*Embiotoca lateralis*) adults from the oxygen consumption of the brood, and the female minus the brood.

Wet Weights		
Total wet weight of pregnant female (g)	628	569
Total weight of brood (g)	99	161
Oxygen Consumption		
Oxygen consumption of brood (mg O_2/hr)	18.1	32.5
Oxygen consumption of female excluding brood (mg O_2/hr)	37.0	28.6
Mean oxygen consumption of female plus oxygen consumption of brood (mg O_2/kg/hr)	97	
Measured oxygen consumption (mg O_2/kg/hr)	107	

Vertebrate viviparity is usually accompanied by mechanisms designed to enhance oxygen supply to the young. For example, in mammals there is usually a high safety margin in structural factors, and oxygen transfer depends on placental blood flow. A similar conclusion was reached for supply of materials to the seaperch brood (Webb and Brett 1972). The blood oxygen capacity of larval and foetal blood is usually higher than that of adult blood and is saturated at very much lower oxygen tensions (Manwell 1958). In addition, a double Bohr shift tends to be greater in young fish (Manwell 1958; M. A. Giles personal communication). Indications of the presence of similar mechanisms were noted by Eigenmann (1892) in viviparous seaperch. It is therefore likely that maternal and embryonic physiological factors would operate to meet the maximum requirements of the young up to birth.

It is therefore concluded that in vitro measurements of oxygen consumption are representative of intraovarian rates. Until intraovarian metabolic rates are measured, in vitro rates must be considered as maximum values.

OXYGEN TRANSFER BETWEEN THE BROOD AND OVARY

The factors relating to the exchange of oxygen between the ovary and brood are shown by Fick's diffusion equation:

$$Q_{O_2} = \Delta P_{O_2} \cdot k \cdot A/L$$

where Q_{O_2} is the rate of mass transfer of oxygen in mg O_2/hr (per unit mass, as required). Units of mass transfer will be used rather than volume transfer, since gaseous exchange as such is not involved at the respiratory interfaces (Brett 1972). ΔP_{O_2} is the difference between mean oxygen tensions in ovarian and embryonic blood streams, k is the diffusion coefficient for oxygen, A the exchange surface area, and L the diffusion distance. These latter three factors, expressed as $k \cdot A/L$, give the structural transfer capacity as determined by Webb and Brett (1972).

Values for the factors for Fick's equation are calculated for mean brood conditions during gestation for embryonic mean weights up to 4.0 g. The mean brood size was 49 young and the mean weight of the parents, 834 g (Webb and Brett 1972).

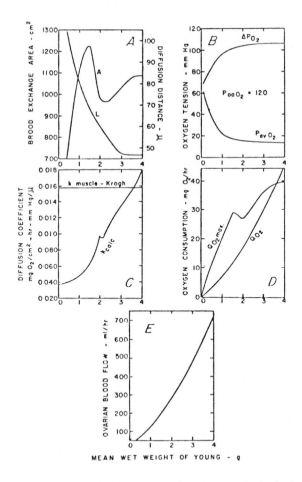

Fig. 4. Diagrams summarizing factors affecting rate of oxygen transfer in the brood-ovary exchange system, during gestation, shown as functions of the mean wet weight of the young. A) Relations between the area, A, effective for the exchange of oxygen for the brood, and the diffusion distance, L, with wet weight (Webb and Brett 1972); B) Deduced oxygen tensions, P_{oaO_2} and P_{evO_2}, respectively, and oxygen tension difference between ovarian and embryonic blood streams, assuming a perfect system; C) The oxygen diffusing capacity of the brood-ovary system, k_{calc} was calculated from Fick's diffusion equation, from data for the oxygen consumption rate of the brood, A, L, and deduced oxygen tension gradients. k_{calc} is compared with the value for muscle from Krogh (1919); D) Rate of oxygen consumption of the brood. Q_{O_2} are values measured for the brood, Q_{O_2max} are maximum values possible with the observed values of A, L, deduced oxygen tension gradients, and the muscle diffusion coefficient, calculated by means of Fick's diffusion equation; E) Calculated minimum blood flow rates required to supply the oxygen requirements of the brood, on the basis A to D, and the blood dissociation curve in Fig. 3.

Structural transfer capacity—The limiting exchange area, A, is that of the vascularized surface of the brood (Webb and Brett 1972). Up to a mean embryonic weight of 2.1 g, this is mainly the area of body and fins but, after that weight, only the area of fins and gills. The diffusion distance, L, is the effective distance between ovarian and embryonic blood streams. The total distance depends on convection in the ovarian fluid. Convection is unlikely in early gestation when the diffusion distance will be the combined thickness of ovarian epithelium, ovarian fluid, and embryonic epithelium. In late gestation, convection will result in similar oxygen tensions at ovarian and embryonic exchange surfaces; the diffusion distance will then be equal to the combined thickness of ovarian and embryonic epithelia. Values for A and L (Fig. 4A) were taken from Webb and Brett (1972).

Values for k have mostly been measured for nonrespiring tissue slices by Krogh (1919). The value for muscle, 0.0158 mg O_2/cm^2 hr-mm Hg/μ, is likely to be most similar to the exchange epithelia. For the ovarian fluid, k would be about three times higher. However, the magnitude of the fluid diffusion barrier is difficult to assess throughout gestation because of convection effects. Therefore, in subsequent calculations, Krogh's value for muscle will be used for the total diffusion distance. As a result, the magnitude of the structural transfer capacity is likely to be underestimated in early gestation, but not later, as term approaches.

It should be noted that k for live tissue could be 6 to 30 times greater than for non-respiring tissue (Steen 1971).

Oxygen tension gradient—No measurements were made of oxygen tensions in embryonic or ovarian blood streams, but ΔP_{O_2} can be estimated from P_{fO_2} values and the published physiology of oxygen uptake in fish.

The effectiveness of blood oxygenation at the gills is of the order of 95–100% in air-saturated water, for which arterial oxygen tensions are about 120 mm Hg (Randall et al. 1967; Cameron and Davis 1970). These values are assumed for the adult pile perch. The ovarian arterial oxygen tension, P_{oaO_2}, will therefore be taken as 120 mm Hg, and the ovarian arterial blood content, 9.5 vol.% (Fig. 3).

Embryonic and ovarian blood streams exchange oxygen with the ovarian fluid; there is no particular spatial relation between the streams. The exchange system is functionally similar to the postulated "pool" system of some mammals (Metcalfe et al. 1967). Ovarian and embryonic venous blood oxygen tensions would tend to reach equilibria with P_{fO_2}. Writing these venous tensions as P_{ovO_2} and P_{evO_2}, respectively, the following applies:

$$P_{ovO_2} \rightarrow P_{fO_2} \leftarrow P_{evO_2}$$

The difference between P_{fO_2} and P_{evO_2} will be small because the embryonic diffusion distance is small, the exchange surface large, and well vascularized. The difference between P_{fO_2} and P_{ovO_2} will be greater than between P_{fO_2} and P_{evO_2} for, although vascularization is as good, and the exchange surface greater for the ovary than the young, the diffusion distance is also greater. However, in the following analysis, the system is assumed to be perfect with $P_{ovO_2} = P_{fO_2} = P_{evO_2}$, and ΔP_{O_2} calculated from the difference between 120 mm Hg (P_{avO_2}) and P_{fO_2} (Fig. 4B). The assumption that the difference between mean oxygen tension in ovarian and embryonic blood streams is $P_{avO_2} - P_{evO_2}$ will tend to give high values for ΔP_{O_2}. However, the assumption will be offset to some extent by taking the mean embryonic blood oxygen tension equal to P_{fO_2}, and the likely double Bohr effect facilitating exchange.

Diffusion coefficient—The assumed value of k is the maximum probable value for diffusion of oxygen between embryonic and ovarian blood streams. This can be compared with the diffusion coefficient, k_{calc}, that would be required for the system to meet the oxygen requirements of the brood. Values for A, L, ΔP_{O_2} (from Fig. 4A and B), and Q_{O_2} (from Fig. 2) were used to calculate values for k_{calc} during gestation (Fig. 4C). Initially, k_{calc} was lower than Krogh's muscle value for k, but increased during gestation, reaching the same value at the stage in gestation when the mean embryonic weight was 3.6 g. The low values for k_{calc} earlier in gestation reflect the large safety factor in A/L and low oxygen demands of the brood.

Oxygen consumption—Values for A, L, ΔP_{O_2}, and Krogh's value for k (Fig. 4A, B, and C) can similarly be used to calculate maximum values for oxygen consumption, $Q_{O_2 max}$, consistent with the morphometrics and estimated oxygen tensions of the system. As expected, $Q_{O_2 max}$ was higher than the measured oxygen consumption for most of the gestation period, approaching and exceeding these latter values after the young had reached 3.6 g (Fig. 4D).

These calculations of k_{calc} and $Q_{O_2 max}$ further emphasize the hypothesis that there is a large structural safety factor early in the gestation period, and that oxygen supply to the brood will be limited by ovarian blood flow, rather than any other factor. They further suggest that the transfer limit of the system is just reached at term. The results of calculations, compared with observed values as term approaches, gives some confidence in the assumptions made.

OVARIAN BLOOD FLOW

The amount of blood required to supply the oxygen demands of the young can be estimated from assumed ovarian arterial and venous oxygen tensions, and the amount of oxygen that would be released from the blood for the oxygen tension differences. The same qualifications in assuming $P_{ovO_2} = P_{fO_2}$ must apply. Although the blood dissociation curve (Fig. 3) was determined for ventricular blood, it was purged of CO_2 and consequently values given are more likely to apply to arterial blood. The estimations of the amount of oxygen released are therefore likely to be low under venous conditions with higher CO_2. This, however, will tend to further offset the limitations involved in the assumptions made.

The estimated ovarian blood flow increased during gestation as expected. At a stage where the mean embryonic weight was 4.0 g, the required blood flow would be highest, at 714 ml/hr (Fig. 4E), and the utilization efficiency of arterial blood oxygen would then be 46%. In reviewing several cardiovascular parameters affecting metabolism, Brett (1972) considered that a representative cardiac output for fish would be 120 ml/kg/min. Assuming no change in cardiac output during gestation, the ovarian blood flow would represent 12% of the cardiac output. This is similar to the proportion of the cardiac output supplied to the mammalian pregnant uterus (Metcalfe et al. 1967).

These calculations on blood flow in particular are at present conjectural, being based mainly on estimated exchange parameters. In addition, the oxygen demands of the ovary are neglected but, if it consumed oxygen at the same rate as the brood, and was an eighth of the weight of the brood at term, blood supply would only need to be increased to about 14% of the cardiac output. Nevertheless, the estimates of blood physiological factors affecting exchange clearly show that they will ultimately dictate Q_{O_2} for the brood, and that exchange is limited by these factors at that stage of development at which parturition occurs in nature.

OVARIAN FLUID OXYGEN RESERVE

The oxygen contained in the ovarian fluid represents a substantial reserve that could make the brood relatively independent of maternal oxygen supply for short periods. This might be necessary should there be a temporary shut-down of the maternal system; for example, when the parent was temporarily stressed in any way. The large safety factor in the morphometrics for most of gestation would contribute to the use of such a reserve system by facilitating return to normal ovarian conditions after any shut-down period. The reserve of oxygen was lowest at 22 mg O_2 when the mean embryonic weight was about 1 g. Then, the metabolic rate of the brood would have been about 6.3 mg O_2/hr; if all the oxygen in the ovarian fluid was available to the young, it could support the brood for 200 min. A similar calculation for the brood, just prior to parturition, shows that the oxygen reserve would still support the young for a maximum of 78 min.

The ovarian fluid therefore has two main functions. It acts as a storage for brood requirements providing a buffer against temporary shortages. This buffer includes a food reserve (Blake 1867) as well as an oxygen reserve. In addition, the fluid facilitates exchange of metabolites by its convection.

COMPARISON OF THE BROOD-OVARY AND MAMMALIAN PLACENTA

No information comparable with that for the embiotocid brood-ovary system is available for other viviparous fish; the only physiological comparisons possible are the generalizations suggested by comparative anatomy, as discussed by Webb and Brett (1972). However, the mammalian placenta is functionally similar to the brood-ovary system, posing many of the same problems. Moreover, placental exchange has been extensively studied. The comparative physiology of the two systems is therefore of value, not only as a check on the conclusions for the brood-ovary system, but also to give additional insight into the interpretation of such exchange systems and to bring emphasis to the limiting factors in oxygen exchange.

Oxygen transfer in the placenta has been summarized in detail by Metcalfe et al. (1967) and Steen (1971). The following discussion is based on these reviews. The brood-ovary and placental systems are compared in tabular form in Table 2.

The structure of the brood-ovary is most similar to an epitheliochorial placenta, in which the greatest number of tissue layers separate maternal and foetal blood streams. The blood flow pattern in the brood-ovary is functionally most similar to mammalian pool types, but in other respects blood flow patterns differ. In the placenta, some blood is shunted away from the exchange surfaces, while the brood-ovary seems to be designed for uniform distribution of all blood to the exchange surfaces. In any case, shunts in the brood-ovary would be of little use, as they would reduce the effectiveness of oxygen transfer on approaching limiting conditions at term.

A different sort of shunt is present in the brood-ovary. Some portion of nutritional requirements are shortcircuited by secretion by the ovarian epithelium, and subsequent partial absorption in the gut of the young. In fact, this nutritional function of the ovarian epithelium is probably of greatest importance, for its thickness does not provide for good oxygen transfer.

Of the factors relating to oxygen transfer, the most important difference between the two systems is the diffusion distance. For the placenta, this varies between 1 and 100 μ, compared with 33 and 450 μ in the brood-ovary. Representative distances are 3.5 μ and 47 μ, respectively, at term. The very much greater ΔP_{O_2} in the brood-ovary reflects this difference in diffusion distance. Otherwise, differences are small. Limiting exchange area in the human foetus, for example, is a little smaller than in the brood-ovary, but oxygen consumption is higher. Blood supply (as a percentage of cardiac output) and percentage utilization of arterial blood oxygen are similar, although mammalian blood oxygen capacities are higher.

The magnitude of these differences and similarities in terms of the efficacy of the system for oxygen exchange is most clearly shown by the oxygen diffusing capacity, in mg O_2/hr-kg-mm Hg. For placentas with a pool-type blood flow, diffusing capacities range from 19.7 to 42.9 mm O_2/hr-kg-mm Hg, compared with 3.6 mg O_2/hr-kg-mm Hg in the brood-ovary. The higher placental diffusing capacities show that this system would be able to adjust far more rapidly to changing demands than could the brood-ovary. However, in the latter case, changes would be temporarily met by the ovarian fluid oxygen reserve.

This, then, is the important difference. Structural improvements in placental design, reflected in the high diffusing capacity, make the system capable of meeting the requirements of the foetus throughout gestation, and always with a high safety factor. The brood-ovary only maintains a reasonable safety factor early in gestation, and none at all as term approaches.

TABLE 2   Comparison between structural and physiological parameters affecting the exchange of oxygen in the mammalian placenta and seaperch brood-ovary at term. Information on the mammalian placenta taken from Metcalf et al. (1967).

	Mammalian placenta	Species	Seaperch brood-ovary
Wet weight of foetus or brood at term (*gm*)	3.3×10^3	Human	1.96×10^2

Structure

	Mammalian placenta	Species	Seaperch brood-ovary
Tissues supplied by maternal blood	Placental membrane Uterine muscle Supporting structures		Ovarian surfaces
Blood shunts outside exchange surface	Uterine and umbilical blood streams		?
Blood flow pattern	Counter-current Multivillous Pool	Rabbit Sheep Human Monkey Goat	Pool type
Tissue layers separating blood streams	Maternal capillary endothelium Connective tissue Placental epithelium Placental epithelium Connective tissue Foetal capillary endothelium Foetal capillary endothelium	Horse (Epitheliochorial) Rabbit (Hemoendothelial)	Ovarian capillary endothelium Connective tissue Ovarian epithelium Convecting fluid Embryonic epithelium ? Embryonic capillary endothelium
Diffusion distance μ			
Range	1–100		33–450
Representative	3.5		47
Limiting area	Foetal capillary area		Embryonic fins and gills
cm^2	1.2×10^4	Human	2.7×10^3
cm^2/gm	364		580

Physiology

	Mammalian placenta	Species	Seaperch brood-ovary
Oxygen consumption mg O$_2$/100 gm–hr	63–103 63	Various Human	44
Oxygen tension difference between maternal and foetal or embryonic blood streams (mm Hg) (Pool flow pattern)	20–35		106
Oxygen diffusing capacity mg O$_2$/hr–kg foetus or brood–mm Hg	19.7–42.9 31.7	Various Human	3.6
Blood flow, percentage of cardiac output	5–20 10	Various Human	12
Percentage utilization of arterial blood oxygen	28–50 30	Various Human	46
Maternal blood oxygen capacity (vol. %)	15.5	,,	10
Foetal blood oxygen capacity (vol. %)	20	,,	?
Maternal blood $p50$ (mm Hg) at venous pH.	27 ·	,,	12.5

TABLE 2   Comparison between structural and physiological parameters affecting the exchange of oxygen in the mammalian placenta and seaperch brood-ovary at term. Information on the mammalian placenta taken from Metcalf et al. (1967). − *(Continued)*

	Mammalian placenta	Species	Seaperch brood-ovary
Foetal blood p50 (mm Hg) at arterial pH.	19	,,	?
Maternal hemoglobin content (gm/100 ml blood)	11.6	,,	?
Foetal hemoglobin content (gm/100 ml blood)	14.9	,,	?
Double Bohr shift	Present		?

ACKNOWLEDGMENTS

This work was completed during the tenure of a National Research Council of Canada postdoctorate fellowship by P. W. Webb and facilities were provided by the Fisheries Research Board of Canada, Pacific Biological Station, Nanaimo, B. C. He would like to thank these two organizations for their generous support.

The authors are indebted to Dr. J. C. Davies of the Pacific Environmental Institute, West Vancouver, B. C., for his assistance in constructing the blood dissociation curve, and for the use of his facilities for measurement of dissolved oxygen parameters of blood and ovarian fluid.

AMERICAN PUBLIC HEALTH ASSOCIATION, AMERICAN WATER WORKS ASSOCIATION, AND WATER POLLUTION CONTROL FEDERATION. 1965. Standard methods for the examination of water and wastewater. 12th ed. New York, N.Y. 769 p.

BLAKE, J. E. 1867. On the nourishment of the foetus in Embiotocid fishes. Proc. Calif. Acad. Sci. 3: 314–317.

BRETT, J. R. 1972. The metabolic demand for oxygen in fish, particularly salmonids, and a comparison with other vertebrates. Resp. Physiol. 14: 151–170.

BRETT, J. R., D. B. SUTHERLAND, and G. D. HERITAGE. 1971. An environmental-control tank for the synchronous study of growth and metabolism of young salmon. Fish. Res. Board. Can Tech. Rep. 283: 27 p.

CAMERON, J. N. and J. C. DAVIS. 1970. Gas exchange in rainbow trout (*Salmo gairdneri*) with varying blood oxygen capacity. J. Fish. Res. Bd. Canada 27: 1069–1085.

EIGENMANN, C. H. 1892. On the viviparous fishes of the Pacific coast of North America. Bull. U.S. Fish. Comm. 12: 381–478.

FRY, F. E. J. 1957. The aquatic respiration of fishes, p. 1–64. *In* M. E. Brown [ed.] Physiology of fishes. Vol. 1. Academic Press, Inc., New York, N.Y.

HOAR, W. S. 1969. Reproduction, p. 1–59. *In* W. S. Hoar and D. J. Randall [ed.] Fish Physiology. Vol. 3. Academic Press, Inc., New York, N.Y.

KROGH, A. 1919. The rate of diffusion of gases through animal tissues with remarks on the coefficient of invasion. J. Physiol. (London) 52: 391–408.

MANWELL, C. 1958. A "fetal-maternal shift" in the ovoviviparous spiny dogfish *Squalus suckleyi* (Girard). Physiol. Zool. 31: 93–100.

METCALFE, J., H. BARTELS, and W. MOLL. 1967. Gas exchange in the pregnant uterus. Physiol. Rev. 47: 782–838.

RANDALL, D. J., G. F. HOLETON, and E. D. STEVENS. 1967. The exchange of oxygen and carbon dioxide across the gills of rainbow trout. J. Exp. Biol. 46: 339–348.

STEEN, J. B. 1971. Comparative physiology of respiratory mechanisms. Academic Press, Inc., New York, N.Y. 182 p.

TRIPLETT, E. L., and S. D. BARRYMORE. 1960. Some aspects of osmoregulation in embryonic and adult *Cymatogaster aggregata* and other Embiotocid fish. Biol. Bull. (Woods Hole) 118: 472–478.

TUCKER, V. A. 1967. Method for oxygen content and dissociation curves for microleter blood samples. J. Appl. Physiol. 23: 410-414.

WEBB, P. W., and J. R. BRETT. 1972. Respiratory adaptations of prenatal young in the ovary of two species of viviparous seaperch, *Rhacochilus vacca* and *Embiotoca lateralis*. J. Fish. Res. Bd. Canada 29: 1525-1542.

Additional Readings

CHAPTER 11

BALON, E. K. 1975. Reproductive guilds of fishes: a proposal and definition. *J. Fish. Res. Bd. Canada* 32(6):821-864.

BALON, E. K. 1975. Terminology of intervals in fish development. *J. Fish. Res. Bd. Canada* 32(9): 1663-1670.

BLAXTER, J. H. S. 1969. Development: eggs and larvae. Chapter 4, pp. 177-252, *in* W. S. Hoar and D. J. Randall, eds., *Fish Physiology*, Vol. 3. New York: Academic Press.

BLAXTER, J. H. S., ed. 1974. The early life history of fish. *Proc. Symp., Oban, Scotland,* May 1973. New York: Springer-Verlag.

BREDER, C. M. and ROSEN, D. E. 1966. *Modes of reproduction in fishes.* New York: Natural History Press.

CLARKE, E. 1959. Functional hermaphroditism and self-fertilization in a serranid fish. *Science* 129: 215-216.

GINZBURG, A. S. 1972. Fertilization in fishes and the problem of polyspermy. *Israel Program for Scientific Translation, Jerusalem.* U.S. Department of Commerce, Washington, D.C.

HARRINGTON, R. W. 1961. Oviparous hermaphroditic fish with internal self-fertilization. *Science* 134:1749-1750.

HOAR, W. S. 1955. Reproduction in teleost fish. *Mem. Soc. Endocrinol.* 4:5-24.

HOAR, W. S. 1969. Reproduction. Chapter 1, pp. 1-72, *in* W. S. Hoar and D. J. Randall, eds., *Fish Physiology*, Vol. 3. New York: Academic Press.

HUBBS, C. L. and HUBBS, L. C. 1932. Apparent parthenogenesis in nature, in a form of fish of hybrid origin. *Science* 76(1983):628-630.

LILEY, N. R. 1969. Hormones and reproductive behavior in fishes. Chapter 2, pp. 73-116, *in* W. S. Hoar and D. J. Randall, eds., *Fish Physiology*, Vol. 3. New York: Academic Press.

MEAD, G. W.; BERTELSEN, E.; and COHEN, D. M. 1964. Reproduction among deep-sea fishes. *Deep-Sea Res.* 11:569-596.

MOSER, H. G. 1967. Seasonal histological changes in the gonads of *Sebastodes paucispinis* Ayres, an ovoviviparous teleost (family Scorpaenidea). *J. Morphology* 123(3):329-353.

PIETSCH, T. W. 1976. Dimorphism, parasitism and sex: reproductive strategies of deep-sea ceratioid angler fishes. *Copeia* 1976(4):781-793.

SCHULTZ, R. J. 1973. Unisexual fish: laboratory synthesis of a "species." *Science* 179:180-181.

WARNER, R. R. 1975. The reproductive biology of the protogynous hermaphrodite *Pimelometopon pulchrum*. *Fish. Bull., U.S.* 73(2):263-283.

YAMAMOTO, T. 1969. Sex differentiation. Chapter 3, pp. 117-175, *in* W. S. Hoar and D. J. Randall, eds., *Fish Physiology*, Vol. 3. New York: Academic Press.

12

Behavior and
Other Adaptations

Some Aspects of the Organization of Fish Schools

JON C. VAN OLST

Project Director, Aquaculture, San Diego State University

JOHN R. HUNTER

Bureau of Commercial Fisheries, Fishery-Oceanography Center
La Jolla, California

The objective of this study was to describe the organization of schools of the pelagic marine fishes *Scomber japonicus*, *Trachurus symmetricus*, *Engraulis mordax*, *Atherinopsis californiensis*, and *Atherinops affinis*. Organization was studied in larval through adult stages by analysis of spatial and angular relations among fish in dorsal photographs of schools.

In all species, schools of young fish, larval and juveniles, were typically less compact and showed greater differences in angular headings than did schools of adult fish. The rate at which school structure changed with size varied among species; it was rapid in *Scomber* and the atherinids and slower in *Engraulis* and *Trachurus*. School organization differed among species at the adult stage. Schools of *Scomber* were typically the most compact and organized; *Trachurus* and *Engraulis* schools were intermediate in their organization and *Atherinops* schools were the least organized.

Spatial and angular measurements were also used to develop inferences regarding the "following reaction" in four of the species. The similarity in angular headings between fish was used as the criterion of following. These analyses showed that the similarities in headings between two fish in a school decreased with the distance they were apart. The headings most alike between adjacent fish in a school were between those in file. These results suggested that the neighbor directly ahead of a given fish in a school is used more frequently as an angular reference for the following reaction than ones to the side.

Analysis of the distances between neighbors in the four species indicated that fish were closer to adjacent neighbors in the file than they were to ones in rank. This suggested that spacing in the horizontal plane might be related to tail movement.

Received April 3, 1970

INTRODUCTION

THE PRINCIPAL CHARACTERISTICS of the organization of fish schools are that the individuals stay together, tend to head in the same direction, maintain even spacing, and the activities of individuals tend to be synchronized. The mechanism for the cohesion and synchronization of a school is considered to be the "following reaction," a concept used by Crook (1961) and others to describe bird flock organization and later applied to fish schools by Hemmings (1966). Cohesion and synchrony of movement develop gradually during early growth (Shaw, 1960) and vary among schooling species at maturity. The purpose of this study was to compare and describe these aspects of school organization for certain pelagic marine fishes at different stages of development by analysis of spatial and angular relations.

Angular differences were used to estimate the extent of the following reaction because when a fish failed to follow it was headed in a direction different from the rest of the fish. Measurement of angular differences also provided an estimate of the cohesion and synchrony of movement of the groups because these characteristics are dependent on the following reaction. Measurements

From *Journal of the Fisheries Research Board of Canada* 27:1225–1238. Reprinted by permission.

of interanimal distances were made to determine if the distances between fish in the schools were species-specific and to determine the extent interanimal distances changed during development. Additional spatial and angular measurements were made to evaluate several hypotheses regarding the mechanism of following.

The species studied were *Scomber japonicus* (Pacific mackerel), *Trachurus symmetricus* (jack mackerel), *Engraulis mordax* (northern anchovy), and two atherinids, *Atherinopsis californiensis* (jacksmelt), and *Atherinops affinis* (topsmelt). *Atherinops* was used in all work with postlarval and larger size classes of atherinids but larval *Atherinops* could not be separated from larval *Atherinopsis* without a postmortem vertebral count and consequently groups of larvae contained both species.

All of these species are schooling pelagic marine fish and all would be considered obligatory schoolers (Breder, 1967). Nevertheless, field observations suggested that even among these comparatively strong schooling fish, differences in school organization existed.

METHODS

Larval fish (21–40 mm) were captured at sea under a night-light, held in large seawater troughs, and fed *Artemia* nauplii at the marine aquarium of the Bureau of Commercial Fisheries Fishery-Oceanography Center, La Jolla, California. Juveniles were captured at sea, held in 4-m diam plastic pools, and fed live or frozen adult *Artemia*. Adult fish were purchased at a bait receiver, held in an 8-m diam pool, and fed frozen adult *Artemia* or chopped anchovy.

Measurements of the spatial and angular relations among fish in schools were taken from two-dimensional dorsal photographs of groups of six fish. To obtain proper photographic resolution and to avoid constriction of the schools, container size varied with the size of the fish photographed. Larvae were photographed in 48 × 60-cm oval or rectangular tanks and adult fish in a plastic pool, 8 m in diameter. Sea water temperature varied seasonally (20 ± 5 C). The 8-m pool was outdoors; the rest of the experimental tanks were placed in soundproof white rooms and were surrounded by tungsten lamps and given a 12-hr light cycle.

Groups were acclimatized in test containers for 2 days and filming of each group began on the 3rd day. Photographs were taken at 1-min intervals from 9:00 AM to 4:00 PM and the fish were fed at 12:00 AM–1:00 PM. We analyzed 50 or more of the photographs taken of each group. In each photograph the X–Y coordinates for head and tail of each of the six fish were determined and the mean distance to nearest neighbor and mean angular deviation of the school were calculated from the coordinate data.

The *mean distance to the nearest neighbor* is the average of the distances from each fish in a school to its nearest neighbor. The measurement is made between the two closest points on the midline of the bodies of the two fish, regardless of their orientation. The same measurement is used twice if two individuals are closer to each other than to any other individual in the school.

The *mean angular deviation* is a measure of the differences in orientation among fish within a school. To calculate the index, the heading of each fish, in degrees, is determined. Then the resultant direction of the school is computed by assigning each fish a value of one and adding the headings vectorially. The number of degrees each fish deviates from the resultant direction of the school is determined and a mean calculated. This value is the mean angular deviation.

Additional indices to be described in a later section were used to evaluate several hypotheses regarding the following reaction in fish schools.

In juvenile *Trachurus* schooling behavior has been reported to change during periods of hunger and food searching (Hunter, 1966). To account for and measure this possible source of variability in all groups, we analyzed 25 photographs taken 2 hr after feeding and 25 taken after a 24-hr deprivation period. In three out of four groups of juvenile *Trachurus* (< 70 mm standard length (SL)) the interanimal distances decreased after feeding (lower distance to nearest neighbor values — Mann-Whitney U test — $P = .05$) in accordance with Hunter's data. However, larger *Trachurus* and all size groups of *Scomber*, *Engraulis*, and the atherinids showed no consistent pattern. For adult *Scomber* additional data were taken. Two groups of adult *Scomber* (350 mm SL) were tested over deprivation periods of 2–9 days, but no relation between food deprivation and distance to nearest neighbor or mean angular deviation was found. Schools of *Scomber* after 9 days of food deprivation were the same as ones recently fed. Thus the effects of food deprivation on school structure were limited to small juvenile size classes of *Trachurus*. Consequently, in the following sections we have combined the data from before and after feeding to increase our sample size.

CHANGES IN SCHOOLING WITH SIZE

The objective of this analysis was to compare school structure among different size classes of fish varying from larvae to adults.

The data were segregated into size classes of 20 mm SL on the basis of the mean length of the fish in each group. The numbers of groups of six fish and the numbers of photographs analyzed for each of the size classes are shown in Table 1. Mean angular deviation and mean distance to nearest neighbor were

TABLE 1.   Number of groups tested and photographs analyzed for each length class.

Genus	Length class (*mm*)	No. groups	No. photographs analyzed
Scomber	41–60[a]	2	100
	61–80	1	50
	81–100	1	50
	101–120	1	50
	350	2	450
Atherinops & *Atherinopsis*	21–40[a]	2	100
Atherinops	41–60	2	100
	61–80	1	50
	121–140	1	50
Trachurus	41–60	2	100
	61–80	2	100
	81–100	4	200
	101–120	2	100
	121–140	1	50
	250	2	150
Engraulis	21–40[a]	2	100
	61–80	4	300
	81–100	1	100
	101–120	2	150

[a]Larval fish.

calculated for each photograph analyzed. To facilitate comparisons between fish of different lengths the mean distance to nearest neighbor was divided by the mean body length of the group and is presented as the number of body lengths between nearest neighbors (Breder, 1954).

In all species the mean angular deviation of the school and the mean number of body lengths between nearest neighbors were less in schools of large fish than in schools of small ones (Fig. 1). Thus, schools of large juveniles and

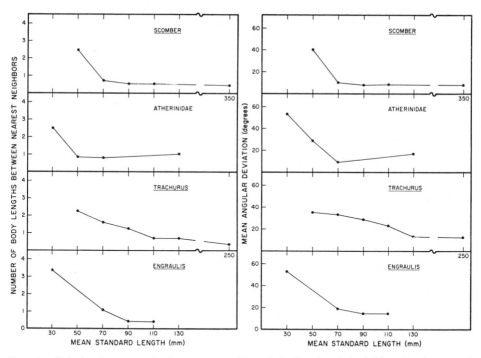

FIG. 1.   Relation between school structure and length in *Scomber*, Atherinidae, *Trachurus*, and *Engraulis*. Left, distance between nearest neighbor in body lengths, and right, mean angular deviation of the school. Midpoints of each length class are shown on abscissa, each point is the median of the values from all photographs analyzed for the particular length class. The number of photographs analyzed per length class are shown in Table 1.

adult fish were more compact and less variable in the directional heading among individuals than were schools of larval and small juvenile fish. The rate at which schooling changed with size differed among species. It was more rapid in *Scomber* and in the atherinids than in *Trachurus* and *Engraulis*. In *Scomber* for example, the schooling indices from groups in the 70-mm size class were the same as those for adults, whereas in *Trachurus* schools in the 70-mm size class were less compact, and the individuals were less uniformly headed than were adults.

Comparisons of the frequency distributions of mean angular deviation and mean distance to nearest neighbor to random distributions showed in all species that the schooling indices were nonrandom (chi-square median test, $P = 0.01$). Thus, the earliest stages of the development of schooling (see Shaw, 1960) had already occurred in the youngest specimens photographed. These data, therefore, do not document the entire development of schooling but only the later portion of it. They clearly show, however, that the development of the compact and integrated school of adult pelagic fish is a gradual process that may extend through a considerable portion of juvenile life.

That well-integrated schools occur late in the development of some of the species, for example *Trachurus*, does not imply that their younger stages could not also form well-integrated schools. Under certain circumstances such as disturbances near or in the tank, fish of all sizes momentarily formed well-integrated schools. For example, we filmed one group of *Trachurus*, 64 mm SL, when a predator was in the same tank. The median mean angular deviation for 25 photographs was 10° and the median distance to nearest neighbor was 0.25 SL. Thus, the presence and movements of a predator temporarily produced in a school of 64 mm *Trachurus* structural characteristics normally associated with the schools of adults. In the experiments presented in this section photographs were taken over relatively long periods and minor disturbances that led to the brief formation of well-organized schools probably had little or no effect on the medians. Thus, our measurements of spatial and angular relations provided an estimate of the typical level of school organization for a given size class under monotonous laboratory conditions. That schools of young fish were less organized than schools of adult fish implies that young fish did not typically follow the movements of their schooling companions as consistently as did older ones.

Differences in experience or maturation of organ systems might explain the differences in the following tendency and in interfish distances among juvenile and adult fish. We are more inclined to believe, however, that these differences were an adaptation to the higher food requirements of juvenile fish. Owing to the energy required for growth and to lower energy reserves, young fish must feed and search for food more often than adults. The nearly continuous maintenance of uniformly headed, compact schools as occur in the adult stage probably would not be adaptive in younger fish because it would probably interfere with feeding and food search. In sum, obligatory schooling fish (Breder, 1967) appear to pass through a facultative schooling stage, the adaptive significance of which may be to allow more flexibility and time for feeding and food search than is possible in the more rigidly controlled obligatory condition.

SPECIFIC DIFFERENCES IN SCHOOL STRUCTURE

The distances separating adult individuals were not species-specific but some differences existed. The medians of the mean distance to nearest neighbor in adult *Scomber*, *Trachurus*, and *Engraulis* were the same, 0.4 SL, whereas the median for adult *Atherinops* was 1.0 SL and was different from the other three species (chi-square test, $P = 0.01$). Interfish distances in fish schools have been measured by a number of other authors (Table 2) but their techniques and numbers of observations varied so widely that it is not possible to separate specific differences from differences in technique and accuracy of measurement. The values given by Breder (1954, 1967) are lower than other values probably because they are, according to the author, the "minimum normal swimming distance between side-to-side fishes." The most precise measurement of interfish distance was made on schools of *Harengula* by Cullen et al. (1965) who used a three-dimensional analysis. Their estimate of mean distance to nearest neighbor of 4.4 cm (measured between heads), estimated by us to be about 0.6 body length, is relatively close to our value of 0.4 SL determined for adult *Scomber*, *Trachurus*, and *Engraulis*, especially when one considers that our measurements are biased downward because of the omission of the vertical plane and because our measurements were made between the nearest points on the midlines of the body whereas theirs were made between heads. Considering all sources of variability the measurements for mature pelagic marine fish are surprisingly close. We suspect that the mean distance to nearest neighbor

TABLE 2.   Interfish distances for schools of various genera of fishes.

Genus	Fish length (*mm*)	Distance between nearest neighbors (*body lengths*)	Author and date
Menidia	7–10	18.0–72.0	Shaw (1960)[a]
Tilapia	11	1.3	Dambach (1963)[b]
Menidia	11–12	0.7–2.5	Shaw (1960)[a]
Menidia	12–16	0.4–2.0	Shaw (1960)[a]
Ameiurus	18	0.20	Breder (1954)[c]
Mugil	25	0.17	Breder (1965)[c]
Atherina	51	0.18	Breder (1954)[c]
Jenkinsia	58	0.25	Breder (1954)[c]
Harengula	75	0.6	Cullen et al. (1965)[b]
Trachurus	68	.25	Frightened by predator; current study
Engraulis	101–120	0.4	Current study
Atherinops	121–140	1.0	Current study
Sardinella	150	0.16	Breder (1954)[c]
Trachurus	250	0.4	Current study
Scomber	350	0.4	Current study
Sarda	570	>1.0	Magnuson & Prescott (1966)[a]
Thunnus	1800	0.5	Breder (1967)[c]

[a]Estimated value.
[b]Three dimensional analysis.
[c]"Minimum normal swimming distance between side-to-side fishes" Breder (1954).

for most pelagic schooling fish under monotonous conditions is generally about half a body length.

In the current study the median mean angular deviation for adult *Scomber* was 8°, *Trachurus* 12°, *Engraulis* 15°, and *Atherinops* 17°. The frequency distributions of mean angular deviation for *Trachurus* and *Engraulis* were not statistically different from each other but both were different from *Scomber* and from *Atherinops* (chi-square test, $P = 0.01$).

A ranking of the four groups by their mean angular deviation would agree with our subjective impression of the relative extent of school integration in the four groups. All the species used in this study formed well-integrated schools but their schools differed in general appearance. They also differ in the kinds of habitats they most frequently occupy in the ocean. Atherinids most commonly occur near the shore in shallow water, *Trachurus* and *Engraulis* occur in these areas but also commonly occur offshore, and *Scomber* occurs offshore. Ranking of these species or related ones by visual pigment absorption maxima also indicates that *Scomber* and *Trachurus* are adapted to blue offshore water whereas the atherinids and possibly *Engraulis* are adapted to green inshore water: *Scomber* 491 mμ; *Anchoa compressa* 507–508 mμ (a species in the same family as *Engraulis*); *Trachurus* 495 mμ; and *A. affinis* and *A. californiensis* 508 mμ (Munz, 1957). These relations suggest that the tendency not to stray from the school appears to be more strongly developed in fish adapted to the offshore environment. This conclusion is consistent with similar conclusions drawn by Breder (1967) and others, that, in general, schooling is more strongly developed in species that inhabit offshore environments.

Few measurements of the angular deviation of fish in schools exist: Clark (1963) estimated from aerial photographs that the greatest angle of deviation of individual rays (probably *Rhinoptera bonasus*) from the general direction of the school was 42°; Cullen et al. (1965) found that 44% of their measurements of mean angular deviation of schools of *Harengula* were 5° or less; Hunter (1966, 1968) measured the mean angular deviation of juvenile *Trachurus* and obtained values similar to the ones presented here; and Shaw (1969) considered an angular difference of 26° or less to be typical for schools of "parallel-oriented" *Caranx*. The lack of angular measurements is unfortunate because our results suggest that measurement of angular differences is a more useful criterion of specific differences in school organization than are inter-animal distances.

ASPECTS OF THE FOLLOWING REACTION

The object of this analysis was to develop inferences regarding the mechanism of the following reaction in fish schools from spatial and angular relations within the school. The following reaction in moving fish schools involves an angular component and a velocity component. A fish would be unable to school either if it failed to increase velocity when other fish did or if it failed to execute a course change when others did. Because this analysis was of still photographs of schools only the angular component could be examined. The velocity component has been examined using cinephotography in another study (Hunter, 1969).

In this analysis 450 photographs of *Scomber* (350 mm mean SL), 200 photographs of *Atherinops* (80 mm mean SL), 300 photographs of *Engraulis* (68 mm mean SL), and 700 photographs of *Trachurus* (117 mm mean SL) were used. The data for the first three species were drawn from those used in the preceding section (see Table 1) but the data for *Trachurus* was taken from a previous study (Hunter, 1968) and reanalyzed with the current objectives. The conditions under which *Trachurus* schools were photographed in the former study were the same as in the present one except photographs were taken at dawn under dim illumination as well as during the day but only the daytime photographs were used in the current analysis.

Two new indices were used in the analysis, separation angle and direction to nearest neighbor. *Separation angle* was considered to be a measure of the angular component of the following reaction. It was assumed that the extent of similarity in heading between two fish in the school was related, to the extent that one used the other as an angular reference for the following reaction. *Direction to nearest neighbor* is the angular position of the nearest neighbor relative to the position of the considered fish. The angular measurement was made between the tips of the snouts of the two fish, the heading of the considered fish was made equal to a compass heading of 0, and the position of the neighbor was calculated relative to this heading. Values greater than 180° were subtracted from 360°. If the neighbor was directly in front of the considered fish the direction to nearest neighbor was 0°, if directly behind it was 180°, and if their snouts were perfectly aligned side by side it was 90°.

The first question asked was whether or not a given fish tended to adjust its heading in relation to the nearest fish or adjusted its heading in relation to that of the group as a whole. For each fish in the group of six the separation angle between the fish and its nearest neighbor was compared with the average heading of the remaining five fish taken as a group. In all species except *Trachurus* the separation angle between the considered fish and its nearest neighbor was lower than that between the considered fish and the average of the headings of the other fish in the school (Table 3). In other words a greater similarity

TABLE 3. Average separation angle between nearest neighbors and the average separation angle between an individual fish and the mean direction of the rest of the school taken as a unit.

Genus	Separation angle between nearest neighbors (*degrees*)	Group separation angle (*degrees*)
Scomber	14	16
Atherinops	31	33
Trachurus	26	22
Engraulis	29	36

existed between the heading of a given fish and its nearest neighbors than between a fish and the average heading of the group. These data suggested that a fish nearby had more effect on the angular adjustment of a given fish than did more distant ones, and that a fish did not respond to all members of the group equally.

To discover the extent to which distance between fish influenced separation angle, we segregated the distance between fish into classes of 0.1 body length and calculated the mean separation angle for each distance class. In *Trachurus* the deviation in heading between two fish was correlated with the distance between them, that is the closer together the fish were in the school the more similar were their headings (Fig. 2). Scatter plots for *Engraulis* and *Scomber* were similar to the one for *Trachurus* and all yielded significant Spearman r_s correlation coefficients (*Trachurus* 0.57, *Engraulis* 0.47, and *Scomber* 0.81), but the data for *Atherinops* was insufficient to make a meaningful comparison. An interesting trend in the scatter plot for *Trachurus* and one that also occurred in the plot for *Scomber* was that at interanimal distances of 0.1–0.2 length the mean separation angle appeared to increase. This could be interpreted to mean that fish tended to avoid interanimal distances of less than 0.2 body length.

The objective of the next step in the analysis was to determine whether or not an individual fish showed any directional preference in the fish used. Differences in separation angle were used as the criterion for directional preference. In this analysis we measured the direction to nearest neighbor, the separation angle between nearest neighbors, and the distance in body length between nearest neighbors.

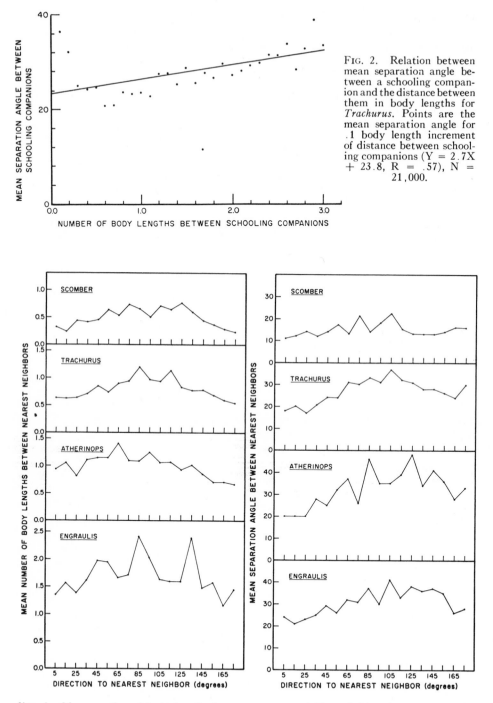

FIG. 2. Relation between mean separation angle between a schooling companion and the distance between them in body lengths for *Trachurus*. Points are the mean separation angle for .1 body length increment of distance between schooling companions (Y = 2.7X + 23.8, R = .57), N = 21,000.

FIG. 3. Mean number of body lengths between nearest neighbors (left) and mean separation angle between nearest neighbors (right) as a function of the direction to the nearest neighbor. Lines connect the means for each 10°-interval of direction to nearest neighbor. The range of N per 10° interval was 65–248 for *Scomber*, 134–376 for *Trachurus*, 39–97 for *Atherinops*, and 40–178 for *Engraulis*.

In all species the mean distance and mean separation angle to nearest neighbors were less when the neighbor was in front of or behind the considered fish than when the neighbor was to the side of the considered fish (Fig. 3). For statistical comparison we grouped the raw data into three 60°-categories of direction to nearest neighbor. Chi-square comparisons of distance and separation angle to nearest neighbor among the three categories of direction to nearest neighbor showed that the front (0–60°) and rear positions (121–180°) were different in distance and separation angle from the side positions (61–120°) ($P = 0.01$). Thus, fish approached more closely the neighbor that was ahead of them and maintained a heading more similar to that fish. These data suggest, therefore, that the neighbor ahead of a given fish in a school tended to be used more frequently as an angular reference for the following reaction than did neighbors to the side, and that fish tended to swim closer to the neighbor ahead of them.

As a final step in the analysis we wished to determine whether or not any particular angular position of fish in the schools of six fish occurred with any greater frequency than other positions. For this analysis we determined for each fish in a photograph the direction to every schooling companion. These data were summarized by calculating the frequency in percent that neighbors occurred in each of 18 angular classes of direction to schooling companions (Fig. 4). If a school were circular in the horizontal plane the numbers of neighbors occurring in each angular class would be expected to be equal. Schools of *Scomber*, *Trachurus*, and *Atherinops* did not differ from a circular shape although there existed a slight tendency for more neighbors to occur at diagonal positions. *Engraulis* schools, on the other hand, were not circular (chi-square test, $P = 0.05$). In the *Engraulis* schools more neighbors occurred in the front and the rear of the school so that they tended to be slightly elongated in the direction of movement.

DISCUSSION

Our approach in the last section was to search for broad trends in the data. Most important of these was that the heading of a fish in a school was more similar to that of fish swimming ahead or behind it than to that of fish swimming to the side. The implication is that fish ahead of a given fish are more frequently used as an angular reference for the following reaction than are ones to the side. It would be unrealistic to propose, however, that the fish in front of a given fish was the only one used as an angular reference. This would mean that angular changes by only the fish in the front rank of a school could affect the actions of the rest of the school, which is certainly not true. Other experiments (Hunter, 1969) have shown that *Trachurus* will respond to a speed increase by any fish in visual range. Similarly we believe that a fish can respond to a course change by any fish in visual range, but they tend to rely more frequently on the headings of the fish directly ahead. This interpretation seems reasonable because small changes in direction in the horizontal plane are more readily detected when a fish is viewed from behind than when they are seen laterally and also because the fish in front would often be within the binocular field of the viewer.

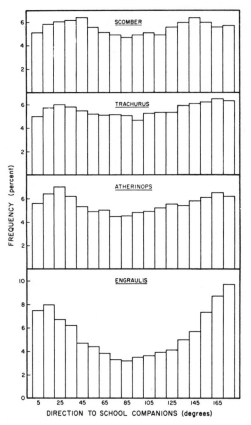

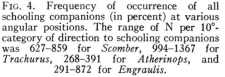

Fig. 4. Frequency of occurrence of all schooling companions (in percent) at various angular positions. The range of N per 10°-category of direction to schooling companions was 627–859 for *Scomber*, 994–1367 for *Trachurus*, 268–391 for *Atherinops*, and 291–872 for *Engraulis*.

Another trend in these data was that fish were closer to the neighbor in front than to the one to the side. This trend suggests that interanimal distances in the horizontal plane may be related to tail movement. In a moving fish school more space would be needed to the side than in front of a fish because space to the side must be sufficient for movement of the tail in the horizontal plane whereas a fish could approach the fish ahead more closely without interfering with the swimming of that fish. This interpretation rests on the assumption that our measurements of spatial arrangements in the horizontal plane were not distorted too greatly by differences in vertical spacing. We limited this source of error by use of shallow containers and small groups of fish. The fish in the school were usually spaced out in the horizontal plane and were not beneath one another but the extent of the difference in vertical position among fish was unknown. Nevertheless, we feel it is of value to consider some of the relations that might exist between tail movement and interfish distance.

The minimum space in the horizontal plane that could exist between the sides of schooling fish would be a function of tail beat amplitude and the relative angular position of the fish. The minimum possible lateral space between neighbors to the side would be lower if the fish consistently occupied diagonal positions than if they were perfectly aligned because the areas of tail movement would not overlap. In the fish we studied, however, the tendency to occupy diagonal positions in the horizontal plane was slight if it existed at all. The distributions of angular positions except in *Engraulis* did not differ from a circular distribution. This was not surprising because typically school structure is dynamic, all positions are in flux, and fish freely change position. To allow for frequent position changes in the direction of movement lateral spacing in the horizontal plane must be sufficient for free movement of the tail regardless of the angular position of the fish. Thus the amplitude of the tail beat may be the most important variable in determining the minimum lateral space.

Tail beat amplitude is the maximum extension of the tail on both sides of the body axis measured perpendicular to the axis to progression and is usually expressed as a proportion of the total length of the fish. During steady swimming at nearly all velocities tail beat amplitude is a constant proportion of body length (L) and appears to vary little among species. The mean amplitude for dace is 0.183 L, for trout 0.174 L, for goldfish 0.202 L (Bainbridge, 1958), for *Scomber* 0.221 L, for *Trachurus* 0.235 L, and for *Engraulis* 0.185 L (J. R. Hunter, unpublished data). Thus, if minimum lateral spacing in schools were a function of amplitude, one would expect it to be nearly the same in all fish schools, that is the minimum lateral space between body axes would be about 0.2 L.

The average lateral space in the school of *Trachurus* frightened by a predator was about 0.23 total length, which seems close to the tail beat amplitude since an average value would be expected to be higher than the minimum. The values presented for average minimum distance between parallel swimming fish given by Breder (1954) ranged from 0.16–0.25 L. If one assumes the maximum width of the fish studied to be 0.1 L, the range of lateral space between body axes would be 0.26–0.35, which again seems close to the tail beat amplitude during steady swimming.

Other than the one measurement on the frightened school of *Trachurus* the spacing measurements presented in this study were considerably above the minimum of 0.2 total length. The average lateral space in fish schools probably approaches this minimum value only when the school is stimulated by a predator or other fright-inducing stimulus. Under typical conditions the mean distance to the nearest neighbor, an average of interfish distance at all angular positions, was 0.4 SL for adult *Scomber*, *Engraulis*, and *Trachurus*. In adult *Scomber* the number of observations was sufficient to make separate estimates at different angular positions. When *Scomber* were nearly parallel (separation angle = 85° in Fig. 3), the mean space between fish adjusted from standard to total length (TL) was 0.55 TL or roughly twice the tail beat amplitude during steady swimming. Tail beat amplitude does not remain constant during acceleration, however, but increases (Gray, 1968). When *Trachurus* or *Scomber* accelerate they execute a few very high amplitude beats and then gradually decrease amplitude to the level used for steady swimming. In *Scomber* these initial beats are 0.4–0.5 TL (J. R. Hunter, unpublished data). Thus, lateral spacing in adult *Scomber* and possibly also in adult *Trachurus* and *Engraulis* may be adapted to accommodate the high amplitude tail movements required for sudden acceleration. It follows from this line of reasoning that if lateral space in the horizontal plane were less than that needed for acceleration, the school might not be able to accelerate without a loss of integration.

The relations we have suggested that may exist between tail movement and spacing are speculation but sufficient evidence exists perhaps to warrant their examination. Of particular interest would be the study of changes in spacing, and the rate of change of angular positions during steady swimming, during acceleration, and while the school is responding to a predator. The study would be greatly improved if a simple and rapid method could be developed for measurement of spatial relations simultaneously in three planes. Three-dimensional measurements of schools have been made (Cullen et al., 1965) but the methods appear to be too cumbersome for an extensive study on spacing in fish schools.

ACKNOWLEDGMENTS

C. M. Breder Jr., D. Kramer, and E. Shaw read the manuscript and made helpful suggestions. The computer programs used in the section "Aspects of the following reactions" were written by A. Good.

REFERENCES

BAINBRIDGE, R. 1958. The speed of swimming of fish as related to size and to the frequency and amplitude of the tail beat. J. Exp. Biol. 35: 109–133.

BREDER, C. M., JR. 1954. Equations descriptive of fish schools and other animal aggregations. Ecology 35: 361–370.
   1965. Vortices and fish schools. Zoologica 50: 97–114.
   1967. On the survival value of fish schools. Zoologica 52: 25–40.

CLARK, E. 1963. Massive aggregations of large rays and sharks in and near Sarasota, Florida. Zoologica 48: 61–64.

CROOK, J. H. 1961. The basis of flock organisation in birds, p. 125–149. *In* W. H. Thorpe and O. L. Zangwill [ed.] Current problems in animal behaviour. Cambridge Univ. Press, London.

CULLEN, J. M., E. SHAW, AND H. A. BALDWIN. 1965. Methods for measuring the three-dimensional structure of fish schools. Anim. Behav. 13: 534–543.

DAMBACH, M. 1963. Vergleichende Untersuchungen über das Schwarmverhalten von *Tilapia*-Jungfischen (Cichlidae, Teleostei). Z. Tierpsychol. 20: 267–296.

GRAY, J. 1968. Animal locomotion. Weidenfeld and Nicolson, London. 479 p.

HEMMINGS, C. C. 1966. Olfaction and vision in fish schooling. J. Exp. Biol. 45: 449–464.

HUNTER, J. R. 1966. Procedure for analysis of schooling behavior. J. Fish. Res. Bd. Canada 23: 547–562.
   1968. Effects of light on schooling and feeding of jack mackerel, *Trachurus symmetricus*. J. Fish. Res. Bd. Canada 25: 393–407.
   1969. Communication of velocity changes in jack mackerel (*Trachurus symmetricus*) schools. Anim. Behav. 17: 507–514.

MAGNUSON, J. J., AND J. H. PRESCOTT. 1966. Courtship, locomotion, feeding, and miscellaneous behaviour of Pacific bonito (*Sarda chiliensis*). Anim. Behav. 14: 54–67.

MUNZ, F. W. MS, 1957. The photosensitive retinal pigments of marine and euryhaline teleost fishes. Ph.D. Thesis. University of California, Los Angeles, Calif. 171 p.

SHAW, E. 1960. The development of schooling behavior in fishes. Physiol. Zool. 33: 79–86.
   1969. The duration of schooling among fish separated and those not separated by barriers. Amer. Mus. Novitates 2373: 13 p.

Why Do Fish School?

D. H. CUSHING and F. R. HARDEN JONES

Fisheries Laboratory, Lowestoft

ABSTRACT

Studies of fish behaviour suggest that the habit of schooling, whatever its mechanism, is an advantage to potential prey.

The survival value of the habit of fish schooling is the subject of a recent article by Dr. C. M. Breder[1], who has written a great deal about the social aspects of schooling. He has worked in streams, lakes and hatcheries in fresh water and in the sea off Bimini and off the west coast of Florida. His photographs of fish schools are brilliant[2], but they were taken in shallow or inshore well-lit waters. As fisheries biologists, we work on this problem in the open sea or in the deep ocean with acoustic equipment.

Breder[1] defines a school as "a large number of fish swimming together" all orientated in the same direction, and considers that "the group is permanent except . . . on extraordinarily dark nights"—permanent because it is a common observation that shoaling fish are all of the same length. But echo sounder records show that schooling fish tend to disperse into masses of individuals at night and to gather again into schools in daytime. Magnuson and Prescott[3] have suggested that the leaning behaviour of tuna in the early dawn allows them to use their silvery sides (Denton and Nicol[4]) to aggregate from extreme visual ranges. Because fish cruise at three lengths a second, a short period of activity in the early morning should segregate the fish into schools of specific sizes quite readily. Consequently, it seems unlikely that schools are permanent or need to be permanent. Spawning or pre-spawning schools may endure for longer than a day, because they do sometimes retain their identity at night (herring[5,6], cod[7]).

An earlier analysis by Breder[8] treats a fish school as being held together by attractive forces and repulsive forces, by analogy with centrifugal and centripetal forces, but the forces are not defined. The mathematical model was not fully developed and the survival value of schooling remained a subject for speculation.

There are now three articles which present models of schooling behaviour. The first, by Brock and Riffenburgh[9], emphasizes the importance of schooling as a factor in reducing predation. These authors define two probabilities—the first that of a single prey being sighted by a predator, and the second that of a predator sighting a school. The expectation of the number of prey being eaten depends on the number of predators, the number of prey and the distance at which the predator sights the prey. The expectation for prey randomly distributed is E_1 and that for schooled prey is E_2; when schooling is of advantage to the prey, $E_2 < E_1$. This treatment has the advantage of being independent of time and of prey density. Furthermore, the expectations can be readily expressed as simple volumes.

Let us assume that there are r^1/c prey along the radius (r^1) of a spherical school. Then the number of prey

$$nf = \frac{4\pi}{3}\left(\frac{r^1}{c}\right)^3$$

From *Nature*, 218:918–920. Reprinted by permission of MacMillan Journals Limited.

If the prey is to obtain any advantage in schooling, the quantity eaten by each predator

$$n_e \ll \frac{r^3 n_f}{\left[r + c \left(\frac{3 n_f}{4\pi} \right)^{\frac{1}{3}} \right]^3}$$

where r is the sighting range of the predator.

Brock and Riffenburgh tabulate the numbers of consumed prey needed to violate this inequality for different values of sighting range and prey numbers. The numbers of prey eaten are very great at sighting ranges greater than the distance between prey and at high numbers of prey. In other words, the schooling advantage is readily nullified at short ranges. Therefore we would expect fish to disperse at night and in turbid waters. Numerous experiments have been cited by Breder to show that schooling depends on a visual response.

A later article by Olson[10] has reached similar conclusions based on a theory of search (Koopman[11]) developed for anti-submarine warfare. The probability, P_a, of finding a single prey in the area A, swimming at random at constant speed V, for time t, is given by $P_a = 1 - \exp(-2r\, Vt/A)$ where r is the sighting range of the predator. The probability, P_s, of finding a shoal of radius r^1 is given by $P_s = 1 - \exp[-2(r + r^1)\, Vt/A]$. Let $P_s = 0 \cdot 5$, then $2(r + r^1)\, Vt/A = 0 \cdot 7$; let $r = 10$ m and $r^1 = 50$ m, then $Vt/A = 0 \cdot 0058$. Hence $P_a = 0 \cdot 11$. In a school, $P_s(m_e/m_f)$ is the probability of being eaten, P_e where m_e is the number of fish eaten by a predator and m_f is the number of fish in the school. Let $m_e = 20$; let $m_f = 20,000$, then $P_e = 0 \cdot 0005 \ll P_a$. So with a quite different model, Olson reached the same conclusion as Brock and Riffenburgh. Similar calculations show that the advantage is less when the probability of detection is low. To increase the probability of detection, the swept patch $2R$ should be increased and so it is perhaps an advantage to predators to school rather loosely. Magnuson and Prescott[3] have described a signalling system between tunas when bars appear on the sides of the fish as they sight food which implies a rather loose schooling. But this possible schooling of predators is really a function of their short sight range underwater. In air, with a long sight range, predators, like hawks, should never find the need to school.

The theory of search was extended by Saila and Flowers[12] at the recent FAO symposium on fish behaviour in relation to fishing gear and tactics. They showed that the number of prey, N_0, entering a circle of radius R about an observer is given by $N_0 = (4RN/\pi)$ $(u + v)E(\sigma)$, where N is the number of prey/unit area, u is the prey speed, v is predator speed, and $E(\sigma)$ is the elliptic integral of the second kind. So the greater the speed of prey, the more come in range than escape. Therefore, a predator should operate during periods of prey activity, for example, at dawn or dusk. It may be significant that some species (for example, herring, Muzinić[13]) feed heavily at dawn and dusk. Conversely, prey, to survive, should move at minimal speeds. Saila and Flowers further examined the case restricting search to a sector in the direction of travel. The probability of detecting prey at a restricted angle ahead increases with the ratio v/u from about $0 \cdot 25$ to a maximum just about 2. So the predator should search ahead and need only cruise at about twice the speed of the prey. These two principles could explain the idle behaviour of prey and predator underwater, as so remarkably shown by underwater films of tuna taken from the bow chamber of R. V. Townsend Cromwell (of the Bureau of Commercial Fisheries Laboratory, Honolulu).

The development of models based on theories of search shows that there could be an advantage to prey in schooling and, perhaps, to predators. The advantage increases with the probability of detection. The observed dispersal at night is expected and so are the apparently idle movements of prey and predator underwater. The models, when properly used as working hypotheses, serve to highlight those areas where critical observations and experiments are required. This, indeed, is their real purpose.

Breder[1] notes that "obligate schooling forms generally have a large geographic range, produce large numbers of young and commonly show migratory movements", and suggests that the formation of "great schools" may exercise a regulatory role in the gene flow of the species. One can enlarge on this line of thought. Nikolsky[14] argues, convincingly, that migration is an adaptation towards abundance. There is a limit to the weight of fish a given area can support, but, with separate feeding grounds for the younger and older stages, food can be concentrated from a wide geographical area to support a large population. It is therefore no accident that species of commercial importance are migratory: they are of commercial importance because they are abundant, and abundant because they are migratory. In temperate and arctic waters there are seasonal variations in the production cycle (Cushing[15]) and, if the young fish are to survive, spawning must be timed so that the eggs hatch when food is available. Furthermore, the spawning grounds need to be strategically sited in relation to the nursery grounds towards which the young are carried, passively, with the current. Within the area over which it is distributed a species may have several spawning grounds, but during a given period the bulk of the population would be recruited from only one or two grounds. The young fish would grow up in separate nursery areas and in different environmental conditions and there could be differences between the survivors from each spawning ground with regard to morphometric and meristic characters, growth, year-class strength and natural mortality. This is the biological origin of the stock.

During the period of larval drift the loss rate due to mortality and diffusion is high. The mortality rate is probably density dependent, sharply so in conditions of food shortage, and mildly so in conditions of food abundance. Here is a possible mechanism by which the numbers in each stock, and thus in the population as a whole, are regulated. A return of the survivors to the parent ground provides a means by which favourable conditions may be exploited. Migration and homing are thus complementary and further consideration of the interaction between them suggests that in temperate and arctic waters the fully adapted and successful species should be migratory and should home to its parent spawning ground; and that each stock should spawn on a fixed and restricted ground, and at a fixed and restricted season. It is the spatial and temporal separation of spawning grounds and spawning seasons that provides the reproductive isolation between stocks. As environmental conditions change on a long term basis, so the dominance swings from one spawning group to another. Thus the capacity to meet change lies, not in the flexibility of each stock, but in the multiplicity of stocks: there are stocks for all seasons, as Cushing[16] argues for the North Atlantic herring.

A fixed and restricted spawning season demands that the whole mature stock comes together within strict spatial and temporal limits to form the "great schools" to which Breder[1] refers. These schools can be very large indeed: in 1951, schools of spawning herring were continuous in the Straits of Dover for 17 miles; similar schools have been described by Runnström[17] for the Norwegian spring spawning herring; and the greater part of the mature cod of the Arcto-Norwegian stock gather within the arm of the West Fjord to spawn every spring. The means by which fish may mix freely on a common feeding ground and yet assemble with such precision and regularity on their different spawning grounds remains one of the outstanding problems of fish behaviour, to which further studies on schooling could make a significant contribution.

1. Breder, jun., C. M., *Zoologica, NY*, 52, 25 (1967).
2. Breder, jun., C. M., *Bull. Amer. Mus. Nat. Hist.*, 117, 393 (1959).
3. Magnuson, J. J., and Prescott, J. H., *Anim. Behav.*, 14, 54 (1966).
4. Denton, E. J., and Nicol, J. A. C., *J. Mar. Biol. Assoc. UK*, 46, 685 (1966).
5. Dragesund, O., *J. Cons. Perm. Intern. Explor. Mer.*, 23, 213 (1958).
6. Jones, F. R. Harden, *J. Cons. Perm. Intern. Explor. Mer.*, 27, 52 (1962).
7. Bostrom, O., *Atsberetn. Norg. Fisk.*, 1957, No. 9, 49 (1958).
8. Breder, jun., C. M., *Ecology.* 35, 361 (1954).

9. Brock, V. E., and Riffenburgh, R. H., *J. Cons. Perm. Intern. Explor. Mer.*, 25, 307 (1960).
10. Olson, F. C. W., *J. Cons. Perm. Intern. Explor. Mer.*, 29, 115 (1964).
11. Koopman, B. O., *Ops Res.*, 4, 324 (1956).
12. Saila, S., and Flowers, J. M., *FAO Conference on Fish Behaviour in Relation to Fishing Techniques and Tactics, Bergen*, Paper E.9 (1967).
13. Muzinie, S., *Ber. dt. Wiss. Kommn Meeresforsch.*, 6, 62 (1931).
14. Nikolsky, G. V., *The Ecology of Fishes* (English translation) (Academic Press, London, 1963).
15. Cushing, D. H., *Fishery Invest., Lond.*, Ser. 2, 22, No. 6 (1959).
16. Cushing, D. H., *J. Mar. Biol. Assoc. UK*, 47, 193 (1967).
17. Runnström, S., *Fisk Dir. Skr., Ser. Havundersok.*, 6, No. 8 (1941).

Internal Behavior in Fish Schools

WILLIAM N. McFARLAND* AND SANFORD A. MOSS**

*Section of Ecology and Systematics,
Cornell University,
Ithaca, New York 14850

**Department of Biology,
Yale University,
New Haven, Connecticut 06520

ABSTRACT

Structural changes within fish schools correlate with declines in environmental oxygen. The changes may result from the responses of individual fish to the environmental consequences of group metabolism. Individual behaviors are adaptive to the school in that they tend to maintain stability between school members and their environment.

During late fall in North America striped mullet, *Mugil cephalus*, form dense reproductive schools and migrate from bays of the Gulf Coast and southern portions of the eastern seaboard into the open sea. Since the mullet are large (20 to 40 cm), often school at the surface, and usually must migrate through passes into the ocean, extended observation of school structure is possible. We have accumulated data on types of schools and their alterations. When viewed from above the schools resemble geometric figures, such as circles, discs, ellipses, triangles, wedges, crescents, and lines. Internal structure is often modified within seconds or minutes, causing school shape to change in a kaleidoscopic fashion. Normally the schools are composed of a large proportion of polarized individuals. Change in school shape may or may not involve disruption of this parallel orientation, but if it does, disruptions are transient or localized within areas of the school. Individual members of a school continually exchange positions through slight alterations of swimming speed or direction even if school shape is not altered. Similar behaviors have been noted in other schooling species.

Several factors may cause school structure to change. Nonenvironmental factors, such as variation in individual tendencies to associate or disassociate, could result in the described group behaviors. The importance of these and other innate tendencies are difficult to assess. Environmental factors that might operate include temperature, light, salinity, water currents and waves, predation, feeding, bottom topography, and water chemistry. Of these factors we believe that levels of temperature, light, salinity, and water movement are too homogeneous in marine environments to be responsible for the continuous changes observed in behavior. School structure changes in response to acute predation but it is usually recognizable as a radiating eruption of portions of the school from the water surface [2]. It bears no resemblance to the slower and continuous modifications of school structure described here. The constant shifting in position of individuals within mullet schools, however, could function in feeding. Positional shifts would place fish in a forward and, presumably, a favorable position for feeding even if the position were maintained for only short periods. But it seems unlikely that all of the school shapes and transitions observed can be solely ascribed to feeding behavior. Examination of the stomach contents of 20 mullet taken from migrating schools in November 1966 revealed that these fish had

TABLE 1. The effect of size on the reduction of environmental oxygen in schools of striped mullet. The observations were made over an 8-year period.

School	Longest dimension (m)	O₂ (mg/liter)		Oxygen reduction (%)
		Outside	Inside	
Small schools				
a*	4	6.80	6.50	4.4
b	7	7.20	6.95	3.5
c	9	7.20	7.08	1.7
d	4	7.60	7.20	5.3
Medium schools				
e*	18	7.12	6.36	10.7
f	15	7.70	6.90	10.4
g	30	7.40	6.85	7.4
h	30	7.00	6.50	7.2
Large schools				
i†	150	7.30	5.20	28.8
j†	75	7.70	7.00	9.1
k†	240	8.00	6.70	16.3
l	300	7.60	6.00	21.0

*Winkler procedure. All other values by oxygen electrode.   †pH measured. No difference detectable inside schools with the exception of j.

not been actively feeding for some time before being caught. In general, striped mullet feed in loosely associated groups and not just before spawning [3].

The most obvious chemical factors that may be involved include soluble gases and dissolved organic substances of inter- or intraspecific origin. Of these factors only respiratory gases (oxygen and carbon dioxide), dissolved substances such as organic wastes, and perhaps specific organic secretions (pheromones) of intraspecific origin seem likely candidates. Only the respiratory gases, however, can be easily and rapidly analyzed in the field.

If we assume that respiratory gases may effect certain changes or characteristic "postures" in school structure, then the following sequence of events may take place. Reduction of dissolved oxygen and increase of carbon dioxide from school metabolism may be sensed by individual fish. This detection of altered environmental-gas concentration could induce modified behaviors such as changes in direction (orientation), spacing, and swimming velocity. The overall result would be the observed tendency toward continuous variability in group behavior. This hypothesis implies that individual physiological and behavioral response is transferred into social behavior in such a manner that it shortens the exposure of individual fish to less favorable conditions (low oxygen, high carbon dioxide and low pH, or both). Individual responses would function to distribute or average the effects of group metabolism to all members of the school. According to this metabolic model of the fish school, gradients of respiratory gases should exist in the water with increased changes associated with increased size and with increased density of schools.

To demonstrate these gradients we measured oxygen and pH both outside and inside migrating mullet schools. Specific procedures for oxygen included collection of water samples followed by standard Winkler analysis or, more commonly, the use of a portable oxygen electrode floated through a school. The latter method provided a continuous record which could be correlated with internal school behavior. The Winkler method was less versatile but did allow direct determination of oxygen. The pH of the water was measured with a portable meter, the electrode being floated through the school [6].

The metabolic effect of a variety of different types of striped mullet schools expressed as the percent reduction of environmental oxygen is presented in Table 1. Reduction of environmental oxygen was detectable within all schools and correlates with school size, large schools producing greater reductions. Although a reduction in oxygen perhaps should be expected, its magnitude and its gross correlation with school size are surprising.

The effect of metabolic carbon dioxide on the environment is far less dramatic than the effect of oxygen, due to the high buffer capacity of sea water. In all instances where pH was measured, changes were not detectable, except for one large school measured on 20 November 1965 (j, Table 1). The pH decline did not exceed 0.02 units and was, in fact, only detectable as a definite and reproducible downward deflection of the meter needle upon entry into the school. We have calculated a theoretical pH decline based on the environmental oxygen reduction of 9.1 percent and an assumed average respiratory quotient of 0.8 for a school of mullet. The expected environmental pH decline was obtained from a direct carbon dioxide titration procedure which relates pH decline to carbon dioxide added [7]. The calculation yields an expected change of 0.025 pH units, a value in excellent agreement with our field measurements. It is unusual, therefore, that slightly greater pH changes were not detected within the larger schools of mullet where oxygen reductions were higher (i and k, Table 1), but this may have been due to the limitations of our equipment. Our results do reveal, however, that sea water is an effective buffer for the amounts of carbon dioxide actually produced by a dense school of mullet.

It is possible to ascribe many of the observable changes in schools and even specific types of structures (varied shapes, spacing, and the like) to the effect of school metabolism. These behaviors may be adaptive in that they lessen the metabolic impact of the school on individual members of the group. However, it is difficult to demonstrate that the intensity of school metabolism is actually sufficient to modify school structure. Demonstrations of exactly how group metabolism might affect structure is even more difficult. And, even if a given school shape, spacing among fish, or a change in structure lessened the effects of group metabolism on individuals, the behavior could result from nonmetabolic as well as metabolic causes. In this case a direct correlation between metabolism and structure could not be demonstrated since a direct cause and effect relationship would not exist.

Our field data provide positive correlation between oxygen gradients within schools and drastic modifications in school structure. The most dramatic example is represented in Fig. 1. Fish in the front half and along the sides of the school were dense and highly polarized. Toward the center the fish were less polarized and swam slowly in various directions. In the back one-third of the school the fish were extremely dense, often in actual contact, completely unpolarized, and actively roiling the surface of the water. Individual fish appeared to rise to the surface and then retreat below. This activity constantly mixed the entire rear of the school, producing a turnover in the position of its members. Oxygen reductions of 22.6, 24.7, and 28.8 percent were obtained from three traverses through the school. In each instance the oxygen declined abruptly rather than gradually from the front to the back of the school. When we had completed the first oxygen profile and while the electrode was still at the back of the school, an unusual event took place. The entire rear portion of the school broke into several small schools and swam off in several directions (see inset, Fig. 1). While most of these small schools rejoined the large school during the next few minutes, at least one group did not. We conclude that the disruption of school behavior resulted from the abrupt and severe metabolic reduction of environmental oxygen and also an increase in the amount of carbon dioxide or, at least, from some undetected consequence of this metabolism [possibly release of a substance akin to "schrechtstoff" (8)]. Avoidance of low oxygen has been demonstrated, however, for a number of species of fish [9]. Field tests reveal that schooling alewives (*Alosa pseudoharengus*), when presented with a choice, consistently enter water with the least free carbon dioxide, if the difference presented exceeds 0.3 part per million [10]. While these results

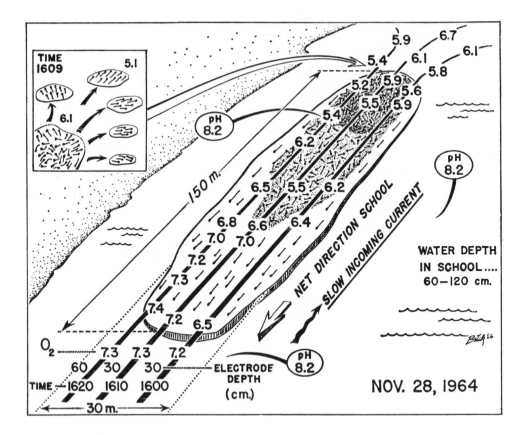

Fig. 1. The relation of school structure and behavior to metabolic modification of environmental oxygen and pH. The dot (head) and line (body) signify the orientation of individual fish in various parts of the school. Fish were dense throughout the school, but greatest density occurred in the rear, as indicated by stippling. Fish in the back of the school were actively roiling the water surface. The inset indicates breakup of the rear portion of the school into individual groups. Oxygen reported in milligrams per liter.

do not conclusively demonstrate that the behavior of fish can be influenced by reasonably small gradients of respiratory gas concentrations, the results are consistent with our hypothesis. Not all structural changes in the school can be expected to result from group metabolic effects. For example, the constant slow interchange of position between individual fish in mullet schools is probably not caused by the effects of group metabolism, although metabolic effects may enhance the rate of interchange. That the interchanges are not the result of group metabolism is shown by the experimental demonstration that isolated schooling fish alter position relative to a moving visual field even though orientation to general movement of the field is maintained [5]. This seems to represent an innate optomotor response which may be species specific. One functional result of this type of behavior is school turnover or mixing. We consider interchange adaptive, perhaps preadaptive to the formation of large dense schools, in the sense that it acts to equalize the time of exposure of each member of a school to the full metabolic impact of the group.

Whether the hypothesis may be generalized to other species must be demonstrated. It seems reasonable to expect, however, that dense schooling species as represented by many herrings and anchovies must change environmental gases through group metabolism. It is important in this regard that the hypothesis suggested here was first formulated from our limited observations of the behavior of small schools of the northern anchovy, *Engraulis mordax*, and not from our study of striped mullet.

Position within a school can expose a fish to a considerable reduction in oxygen. This condition can alter the physiology and behavior of a fish so that its chance for survival, relative to other members of the school, may be diminished if corrective action is not taken.

REFERENCES AND NOTES

1. C. M. Breder, *Bull. Am. Mus. Natur. Hist.* **117**, 397 (1959).
2. ——, *Zoologica* 50, 97 (1965).
3. J. M. Thomson, *Australian J. Marine Freshwater Res.* 6, 328 (1955); *Oceanogr. Mar. Biol. Ann. Rev.* 4, 301 (1966).
4. G. P. Whitley, *Proc. Roy. Zool. Soc. New South Wales* 13, 17 (1945/46); V. I. Eibl-Eibesfeldt, *Z. Tierpsychol.* **19**, 165 (1962).
5. E. Shaw and A. Tucker, *Animal Behav.* **13**, 330 (1965).
6. Oxygen electrode manufactured by Precision Scientific Co.; pH meter manufactured by E. H. Sargent Co.
7. R. J. Beyers, J. L. Larimer, H. T. Odum, R. B. Parker, N. E. Armstrong, *Publ. Inst. Mar. Sci. Univ. Tex.* 9, 454 (1963).
8. K. von Frisch, *Z. Vergleich. Physiol.* **29**, 46 (1941).
9. J. R. E. Jones, *J. Exp. Biol.* 29, 403 (1952); V. E. Shelford and W. C. Allee, *J. Exp. Zool.* 14, 207 (1913); C. M. Whitmore, C. E. Warren, P. Doudoroff, *Trans. Am. Fisheries Soc.* **89**, 17 (1960).
10. G. B. Collins, *U.S. Fish Wildlife Serv. Fishery Bull.* **52**, 375 (1952).
11. Supported by Office of Naval Research contract Nonr 401(52). We thank the staff of the Institute of Marine Science, University of Texas, Port Aransas, Texas, for their generous assistance.

27 January 1967

A Blind Fish Can School

T. J. PITCHER
*School of Biological and Environmental
Sciences, New University of Ulster,
Coleraine, Northern Ireland*

B. L. PARTRIDGE
*Department of Experimental
Psychology, South Parks Road,
Oxford, England*

C. S. WARDLE
*Marine Laboratory, Post Office
Box 101, Aberdeen, Scotland*

Abstract. *Vision is not required in order for fish to school. Five individual saithe,
Pollachius virens, were able to join schools of 25 normal saithe swimming in an annular tank, while blinded with opaque eye covers. Test fish maintained position within
the school indefinitely and responded to short-term movements of individuals within
the school, although quantitative differences in reaction time and schooling behavior
were noted. Five fish with lateral lines cut at the opercula were unable to school
when wearing opaque eye covers. Although it is unlikely that blind saithe could
school in the wild, the constraints of the apparatus permitted a demonstration of a
role of the lateral line organ in schooling.*

Vision has long been considered a vital
sensory component of schooling behavior (*1–3*) not least because fish usually
stop schooling at low light intensities (*4*).
Individual blind fish sometimes turned toward normal members of their own species (*1–3, 5, 6, 7*) and have occasionally
been observed to swim parallel to a control school for a few seconds (*3*) but have
never been observed to maintain position for longer. We report here that adult
saithe, *Pollachius virens*, wearing
opaque eye covers (blinders) were capable of maintaining position indefinitely
in a school of normal saithe swimming at
approximately two body lengths per second, although their behavior within the
school was quantitatively different from
that of normal fish.

Underwater motion pictures taken in
the wild (C.S.W.) show that saithe swim
in polarized and synchronized groups,
thus meeting Shaw's (*3*) definition of
schooling. The film suggests that saithe
are one of the strongest facultative
schoolers (*7*) among the gadoid fishes.

Twenty-five newly caught saithe between 25 and 35 cm long were individually freeze-branded and introduced into
an annular channel 1.5 m wide in the 10-
m diameter gantry tank at the Marine
Laboratory, Aberdeen, Scotland. A rectangular pool of light was projected onto
the floor of the annular channel from
spotlights on the counterclockwise rotating radial gantry; superimposed on it was
a random speckled light pattern. The
school of saithe were trained during a period of 4 days to swim above this moving
background and, thereby, to remain in
roughly the same area relative to the gantry (*9*). A continuous record of fish
schooling in this area was provided in
plan view by a television camera
mounted on the gantry and linked to a
videotape recorder. A saithe from the

trained school was anesthetized and fitted with opaque blinders, which completely covered both eyes. After the fish had partially recovered from the anesthetic, it was returned to the channel, where it soon swam slowly about in a restricted area. (The rest of the school was swimming continuously around the tank.) The fish with blinders avoided swimming into the walls of the channel (5). After about an hour it began to respond to the school, turning toward the leading fish as they passed on each circuit of approximately 69 seconds. The test fish soon began to follow and then swim with the school for increasing distances, until after about 3 hours, it was able to school indefinitely (Fig. 1). After experiments lasting an additional 3 to 4 hours, we caught the test fish, removed the eye covers, and returned it to the tank, where it immediately rejoined its fellows and behaved quite normally. Three more fish tested in the same manner were each found capable of schooling while effectively blind.

In order to be certain that these fish were unable to see, we fitted blinders lined with a smooth layer of aluminum foil to another test fish. This saithe took longer to begin schooling again (about 6 hours), but once it had started, its behavior in the school was similar to that seen in the other four blind fish experiments. Further evidence that all the test fish were unable to see objects is that although hand-netting normal saithe from the channel was very difficult none of the temporarily blinded fish avoided the mouth of nets placed in their path, even in bright light. In addition, the test saithe soon became dark in color (Fig. 1); this response is typical of blind fish, who match their skin color to their visual assessment of the surroundings (10).

When the school was startled by one of the experimenters suddenly reaching over the side of the tank, blind fish responded only if their neighbors were less than one body length away (Fig. 2) and only after these adjacent fish had accelerated. For six cases in which the fish with

blinders did startle, the average lag from the acceleration of their nearest neighbor was 0.4 second (20 frames on the video record). The average lag for normal fish was 0.045, but this value is not strictly comparable since sighted fish may have responded directly to the stimulus (1). When startled, blinded fish tended to bump into the walls of the tank and into other fish, whereas sighted fish rarely did this. On no occasion did we observe a test fish collide with the walls of the tank or other objects when approaching them at normal speed. Very occasionally they swam into others in the school, but only when the latter were executing some rapid maneuver [see also (5)].

Fish wearing blinders did not school normally but appeared to change position within the school far more often than their sighted fellows did. In order to test this, we superimposed a square grid on the video image and recorded the frequency with which test fish and controls crossed the grid lines. Since the camera was moving at the same speed as the school, most fish remained fairly stationary within the video image so that (for our camera orientation) the frequency with which a fish crossed horizontal and vertical lines of our grid gave measures of, respectively, side-to-side and fore-and-aft motion within the school. For each of the five blind fish experiments, five sequences of behavior were analyzed frame by frame on the videotape ($\bar{X}$ = 15.5 seconds, at 50 frames per second). Test fish crossed horizontal grid lines more than four times as often as randomly selected control fish from the school (Wilcoxon one-tailed test, $P < .01$). This difference resulted partly from a tendency of the temporarily blind fish to swim straight ahead, tangentially to the circular track, while fish in the accompanying school must have made a series of small turns to steer an apparently smooth circumferential course in the channel. Course corrections by blind fish were made less frequently and were of greater magnitude. They also showed greater latencies than their sighted neigh-

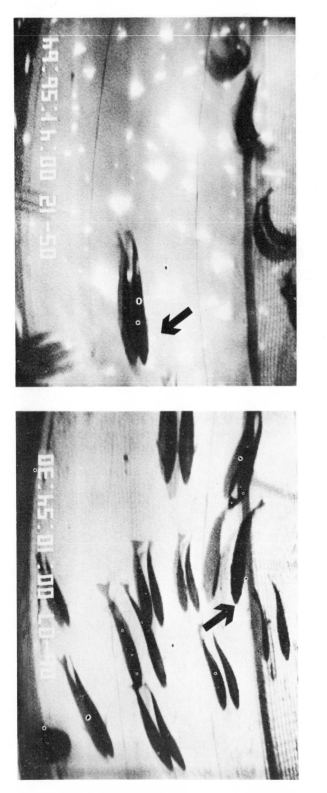

Fig. 1 (left). The blind fish (arrow), appearing darker than its fellows, is almost in the center of the school in this photograph of a single video frame. The eye covers, which are just visible, were made of overexposed photographic film further blackened with waterproof marker and lined with aluminum foil. Although the random pattern of projected light spots has been turned off, the fish are continuing to school. The orientation of the blind fish is slightly different from that of the rest of the school as it lags behind in a turn. The distance between the images of each fish and its shadow is used to calculate the height of each fish in the water (17).   Fig. 2 (right). Photograph of a single frame from videotape. Members of the school are seen responding to the experimenter's hands appearing over the side of the tank (upper left) but the blind fish (arrow) is not responding. The speckled light pattern that the fish followed around the tank is visible.

bors in responding to changes in velocity of fish in the school, both for minor accelerations and in the startle experiments.

The quantitative differences in schooling were not caused by irritation produced by the blinders, since fish wearing blinders with a hole cut out for the pupil or clear eye covers schooled immediately when they were reintroduced into the tank and did not show the same degree of lateral displacements as the fully blind saithe. Several potential test fish whose blinders fell out schooled normally immediately thereafter; they therefore control for the effects of the fitting operation.

In order for a blind fish to school it must (i) locate and join a moving group of fish and (ii) respond to short-term movements and changes in velocity of individuals within it. A blind fish might be able to do the first and not the second if, for example, it merely responded to the sound of the motor driving the gantry or to the light to dark boundary of the moving pool of light by way of the pineal body. This was not the case since, on the few occasions when the control school was absent from the spotlit area (so that only sound and light cues were present), test fish failed to turn and swim with the moving boundary. In contrast, the videotapes show a number of instances in which turns were an unequivocal response to the leading fish of the school (12).

We have no evidence that sound, light, or olfactory cues could account for the observed adjustments in position and velocity of the blind fish, once they had joined the school. For example, pattern recognition necessary for responding to other fish in the school could not occur by way of the lensless, unorganized mass of photoreceptors in the teleost pineal body (1, 2, 13). There are reports that bioelectric fields can be detected by teleosts with no special electro-receptors (14). Although such sensory receptors might account for the schooling of our test fish, they could not account for the ability of isolated blind saithe to avoid inanimate objects in the tank.

We believe that the sensory input used by blinded fish to maintain position within the moving school is the lateral line organ. Experiments on tuna separated by transparent barriers have indicated that the lateral line organ plays a role in the maintaining interfish spacing (15). We were unable to induce schooling in five blind saithe in which the lateral lines were cut at the operculum. However, five saithe with lateral lines cut, but with normal vision, showed apparently normal schooling (16); thus, later line information, like vision, is not necessary for schooling to take place.

Like the blind fish, the fish with blinkers and lateral line cuts could respond to bright light, probably by way of the pineal body. Although three of the five fish with lateral line cuts refused to swim at all while wearing blinkers, two could be induced to swim around the tank in front of a pole hanging from the moving gantry. Even when they were "poled" up into the school, however, they did not respond to movements of neighbors, and, if the pole was removed from the water, they immediately fell back out of the school and stopped swimming.

Two previous studies have failed to demonstrate schooling in temporarily blinded fish. When Keenleyside (1) fitted small rudd, *Scardinius eryopthalmus*, with aluminum foil blinkers, three blind fish would not school with three sighted fish, but did make schooling turns toward them. A single blind saithe probably had a much greater opportunity and motivation to school than Keenleyside's rudd since (i) it had been trained previously to swim around the tank, (ii) the school met the test fish once a minute at each circuit of the tank, and (iii) one test saithe had 25 normal schooling fish to respond to. If we allow for the different experimental procedures, Keenleyside's findings do not seem incompatible with our own. Parr (2) found that seven chub mackerel, *Scomber colias*, temporarily blinded with a mixture of lamp black and Vaseline applied to both eyes, failed to join a milling school of normal fish and collided repeatedly with them.

We do not know whether the differences between our results and those of Parr are consequences of technique or whether they reflect real differences between the two species; the extent of arousal may also be important. Parr's fish showed panic reactions which increased the more they collided, whereas the test saithe recovered very gradually from handling and anesthesia while being repeatedly presented with the school. Finally, none of our blind saithe showed any reaction to the school within the time scale of Parr's experiment. It is therefore likely that the present technique allows more chance for a blind fish to school.

References and Notes

1. M. H. A. Keenleyside, *Behaviour* 8, 183 (1955).
2. A. E. Parr, *Occas. Pap. Bingham Oceanogr. Coll.* 1 (1927); A. Schaifer, *Zoologica* 27, 75 (1942).
3. E. Shaw, in *The Development and Evolution of Behavior*, L. R. Aronson *et al.*, Eds. (Freeman, San Francisco, 1970), p. 452.
4. J. R. Hunter, *J. Fish. Res. Board Can.* 25, 393 (1968).
5. E. S. Bowen, *Ecol. Monogr.* 1, 1 (1931).
6. K. R. John, *Copeia* 2, 123 (1957).
7. B. K. Noble and B. Curtis. *Bull. Am. Mus. Nat. Hist.* 76, 1 (1939).
8. C. M. Breder, *Zoologica* 52, 25 (1967).
9. C. S. Wardle and P. D. Anthony, *Int. Counc. Explor. Sea. Coop. Res. Rep. Ser. B* 22 (1973).
10. P. Rasquin, *Bull. Am. Mus. Nat. His.* 115, 1 (1958).
11. See also J. R. Hunter, *Anim. Behav.* 17, 507 (1969).
12. During 3.5 hours of videotaping, there were no occasions in which a test fish appeared to adjust its position to a light speckle; on many occasions it responded to another fish changing position within the school. An olfactory cue is unlikely as well. To give information accurate to 1 meter, any pheromone would have to decay detectably in less than 2.5 seconds since a revolution took 69 seconds.
13. P. R. T. Pary, *Am. Zool.* 5, 682 (1965); E. Dodt, *Experientia* 19, 642 (1963).
14. V. R. Protasov, B. M. Basov, V. I. Krumin, A. A. Orlov, *Zool. Zh.* 49 (5) (1970), cited by D. V. Radakov, *Schooling in the Ecology of Fish*, H. Mills, Trans. (Wiley for Israel Program for Scientific Translations, New York, 1973); R. C. Peters and T. van Wijland, *J. Comp. Physiol.* 92, 273 (1974); Ad. J. Kalmijn, in *Handbook of Sensory Physiology*, A. Fessard Ed. (Springer-Verlag, Berlin, 1974), vol. 3, p. 147; E. Schwartz and A. D. Hasler, *Z. Vgl. Physiol.* 53, 317 (1966). Experimental evidence that bioelectric fields are used in orientation has come from catfish, which have specialized electro-receptor pits, whereas gadoids do not have this type of pit.
15. P. H. Cahn, *Lateral Line Detectors* (Indiana Univ. Press, Bloomington, 1967); *U.S. Fish. Wildl. Serv. Fish. Bull.* 70, 197 (1972).
16. There may be quantitative differences in spacing and velocity adjustment. A full analysis of the exact three-dimensional position of saithe in these experiments is in progress.
17. J. M. Cullen, E. Shaw, H. A. Baldwin, *Anim. Behav.* 13, 534 (1965).
18. We thank the Marine Laboratory, of the Department of Agriculture and Fisheries, Aberdeen, Scotland, for the use of the gantry tank and ancillary facilities and R. S. Batty and W. Mojsiewicz for practical help. J. M. Cullen, A. Macfadyen, R. Dawkins, and A. Cook criticized the manuscript. This work was supported in part by a New University of Ulster research grant to T.J.P.

6 May 1976; revised 8 July 1976

Evidence for a Home Site and Homing of Adult Yellowtail Rockfish, *Sebastes flavidus*

H. Richard Carlson and R. E. Haight

National Marine Fisheries Service
Auke Bay Fisheries Laboratory, Auke Bay, Alaska 99821, USA

Existence of a home site and homing ability was established for adult yellowtail rockfish, *Sebastes flavidus* (Ayres). Fish returned to the home site from as far as 22.5 km, some after displacement to other schools of the species and some after 3 months in captivity. Stretches of deep open water appeared to pose a hindrance to homing. Intensive fishing of a localized adult stock could cause a long-term decline in its abundance.

THE yellowtail rockfish, *Sebastes flavidus* (Ayres), is a common demersal species along the western coast of North America and is utilized in both sport and commercial fisheries. Observations by sport fishermen and scuba divers indicate a disjunct distribution of schools of adult yellowtail rockfish in southeastern Alaska. If these schools are discrete, as has been found in California for the blue rockfish, *S. mystinus* (Miller et al. 1967), such discreteness would be important in management of the fishery.

In this study, we consider the two closely related questions of a home site and homing for adult yellowtail rockfish. Home site is defined as the particular locality to which an animal displays attachment or association (termed "localization" by Scott 1958), and homing is the return of an animal to a place formerly occupied rather than to other equally probable places. We use homing and home site in the same sense as has Gerking (1959), but also agree with Green (1971) that homing implies some navigational ability.

Homing (in the sense we use it) has been demonstrated for only six species of demersal marine fishes. These were tidepool or reef fishes, however, and the distances they traveled were generally less than 100 m.

To investigate the discreteness of adult schools of yellowtail rockfish, we tagged fish taken from (what we supposed to be) a discrete school inhabiting the wreckage of a large vessel at Lena Point in Favorite Channel, near Juneau, Alaska (Fig. 1). We displaced some of the fish to locations as far as 35 km away, released others at the wreck as controls, and then attempted to recover the tagged fish. We selected release sites that would enable us to compare the ability of fish to return from sites along the same coastline and sites across open water, and also to test the inclination of fish to return from two sites inhabited by other schools of adult *S. flavidus*.

lature of each fish. The tags were serially numbered and were color coded so that divers could identify them.

Between August 1969 and September 1970, 337 fish were tagged and released (Table 1). Twenty-four were released at Lena Point, and 313 were displaced to 11 other sites. Three of the sites were along the mainland coast and eight were across open water (Fig. 1). The fish were transported to the release sites by skiff and were held en route in covered 114-liter plastic barrels filled with sea water. They were released over depths of 7 – 18 m (similar to the depths of capture). The distances between Lena Point and the other release sites ranged from 2.4 to 35.0 km.

About half of the fish were released on the day they were tagged, and the others were released later. The later releases included 127 fish that had to be held until the weather moderated enough for us to reach the most distant release sites in a small boat (3–13 days), 34 that were held at the Auke Bay Laboratory for 3 months to enable us to assess tag retention, and four that were held for 1 month so that we could evaluate a late-season release (November).

We did not attempt a random recovery effort of tagged fish throughout the general area because the schools of yellowtail rockfish were known to inhabit only certain sharply defined locations. Our main tag recovery efforts were at the wreck site, using hook and line. We also fished with hook and line at Point Terese, Point Stephens, and Barlow Cove and fished with trammel nets at Aaron Island. Auke Bay Laboratory scuba divers looked for tagged fish in the yellowtail rockfish schools that inhabited the release sites at Point Terese, Point Stephens, and Vanderbilt Reef. Many sport and commercial fishermen use the study area, and their fishing effort (although not measured) greatly exceeded ours in both time and distribution. A tag reward of two dollars was publicized in a local newspaper, on a radio program, and on posters at marinas in the area.

We made most of the tag recoveries, but some were made by sport and commercial fishermen. Although most of the recoveries were from hook and line fishing, laboratory divers captured some tagged fish with spears and made visual identification of others.

Materials and Methods

The fish for tagging were captured by hook and line. They ranged from 280 to 411 mm in fork length (average 355 mm) and from 7 to 16 years of age (average 9 years). Analysis of scales from 283 specimens showed that the school comprised mainly fish from two year-classes (1960 and 1961) during the 2-year period of the study. A Floy FD-67 anchor tag of vinyl plastic "spaghetti" tubing 7.6 cm long was inserted into the dorsal muscu-

Results

Of the 337 tagged fish released over a 15-month period, 74 (22.0%) were recaptured at the wreck site at Lena Point (Table 1). Only two fish (0.6%) were recaptured away from Lena Point, one at Vanderbilt Reef and the other near Barlow Point. Half of the control fish released at the wreck site were recaptured there; individual fish were recap-

From *Journal of the Fisheries Research Board of Canada* 29:1011–1014. Reprinted by permission.

TABLE 1. Release and recovery information for tagged yellowtail rockfish (*S. flavidus*) from the Point Lena wreck site which were displaced from or released at that site between August 1969 and September 1970.

Release site	Km from wreck site	Time of release	Fish released	Time until first fish recovered (days)	Fish recovered (%)	
					Wreck site	Other sites
Lena Point (wreck site)	–	October 1969, June 1970	24	11	50.0	0.0
On mainland coast						
Point Stephens	2.4	September 1970	12	10	50.0	0.0
Point Terese	8.0	November 1969, May 1970	39[a]	28	41.0	0.0
Auke Bay	8.0	August 1969	34[b]	19	47.0	0.0
Total	–	–	109	–	45.9	0.0
Across open water						
Shelter Island	2.4	May, June 1970	11	4	36.4	0.0
Aaron Island	4.8	May 1970	30	17	33.3	0.0
Barlow Point	8.0	June 1970	27	38	11.1	3.7
Outer Point	10.4	June 1970	33	41	9.1	0.0
Scull Island	19.3	August 1970	32[c]	42	3.1	0.0
Vanderbilt Reef	22.5	August 1970	33[c]	31	9.1	3.0
West Lynn Canal	22.5	August 1970	33[c]	–	0.0	0.0
Point Couverden	35.0	August 1970	29[c]	–	0.0	0.0
Total	–	–	228	–	10.5	0.9
Grand total	–	–	337	–	22.0	0.6

[a]Includes four fish held in captivity for 1 month before release.
[b]Fish held in captivity for 3 months before release.
[c]Fish held in captivity for 3–13 days before release because of poor weather.

tured (and subsequently released) as many as five times over time spans of up to 9 months.

The highest percentages of tag returns were from fish released at the point of original capture (Lena Point) and at other sites on the mainland coast. Returns from sites across open water were much lower. Among the highest returns were those for fish displaced to locations inhabited by schools of yellowtail rockfish (Point Stephens and Point Terese) and fish held in captivity for 3 months before release.

The time interval between release and recapture of the first fish from each group ranged from 4 to 42 days. The longest time at liberty for any fish was 428 days, a fish released at Auke Bay in August 1969 and recaptured at Lena Point in October 1970.

Discussion

Clearly, the yellowtail rockfish we studied have a home site and homing ability. That the wreck at Lena Point is a home site is evidenced by recaptures of different fish from the same release over successive years and of the same fish several times (up to five times) at this location.

We believe that yellowtail rockfish demonstrated a marked homing ability. Nearly half (45.9%) of the fish displaced along the mainland coast were recaptured at the wreck site (including 12 by sport and commercial fishermen, and none were recaptured elsewhere. If the displaced fish had moved randomly, the sport and commercial fishery effort (which was more or less randomly distributed) should have produced recaptures from many locations other than the wreck (home) site. Thus, we

feel that the fish directed their movement toward the home site, i.e. they could navigate. Additionally, we have preliminary evidence (unpublished data) from electronic tracking experiments and scuba diver observations of displaced fish which indicates that their movement was directed (quite precisely in some instances) and was not random or haphazard.

The strength of association with a home site may be measured by the high returns from releases at the two sites known to be inhabited by other schools of yellowtail rockfish and by the memory shown by returning fish held in captivity before release. Returns from the Point Terese and Point Stephens release sites (where the presence of yellowtail rockfish demonstrates the suitability of the locations) suggest that association with a specific home site is not due merely to accessibility or suitability. The high returns of fish held captive for 3 months before release at Auke Bay indicate a lasting memory for the home site.

A partial barrier or hindrance to homing may exist in the form of open stretches of deep water. The percentage of recaptures of fish displaced to sites along the mainland coast was over four times that of fish displaced to sites across open water where depths were in excess of 100 m (45.9% vs. 10.5%). These sharply contrasting rates of recapture may be due to the hazards of traversing open water or to disorientation if visual contact with the substrate is lost. Quast (1968) discusses the dependence of certain California demersal fishes on visual contact with fixed objects in order to remain in a selected locale.

This study adds another group of fishes (the Scorpaenidae) to the few types of demersal fishes in which a home site and homing have been demonstrated.

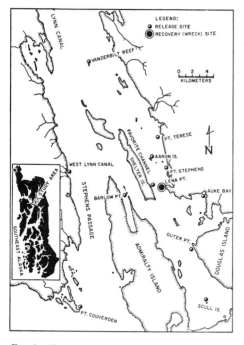

Fig. 1. Sites near Juneau, southeastern Alaska, where yellowtail rockfish were released and recaptured.

Homing in the sense we use the term was observed in displacement studies of the gill-finned goby, *Bathygobius soporator*, (Beebe 1931); the juvenile opaleye, *Girella nigricans*, and the wooly sculpin, *Clinocottus analis*, (Williams 1957); the tidepool sculpin, *Oligocottus maculosus*, (Green 1971); and the Nassau grouper, *Epinephelus striatus*, and the red hind, *E. guttatus*, (Bardach 1958). These studies involved homing only short distances (ge-

nerally less than 100 m), in contrast to our study in which yellowtail rockfish returned to their home site from as far as 22.5 km.

In view of the yellowtail rockfish's association with a specific site and the slow growth and great longevity of the species (Phillips 1964), it is apparent that an intensive localized fishery on an adult stock could easily cause a long-term decline in its abundance.

Acknowledgments

The authors wish to thank the biologist scuba divers of the Auke Bay Fisheries Laboratory for their assistance, particularly L. M. Barr and R. J. Ellis.

BARDACH, J. E. 1958. On the movements of Bermuda reef fishes. Ecology 39: 139–146.

BEEBE, W. 1931. Notes on the gill-finned goby, *Bathygobius soporator* (Cuvier and Vallenciennes). Zoologica 12: 55–65.

GERKING, S. D. 1959. The restricted movement of fish populations. Biol. Rev. 34: 221–242.

GREEN, J. M. 1971. High tide movements and homing behaviour of the tidepool sculpin *Oligocottus maculosus*. J. Fish. Res. Bd. Canada 28: 383–389.

MILLER, D. J., M. W. ODEMAR, AND D. W. GOTSHALL. 1967. Life history and catch analysis of the blue rockfish (*Sebastes mystinus*) off central California, 1961–65. Calif. Dep. Fish Game MRO 67–14.

PHILLIPS, J. B. 1964. Life history studies on ten species of rockfish (genus *Sebastodes*). Calif. Dep. Fish Game Fish Bull. 126: 70 p.

QUAST, J. C. 1968. Fish fauna of the rocky inshore zone, p. 35–56. *In* W. J. North and C. L. Hubbs [ed.] Utilization of kelp-bed resources in southern California. Calif. Dep. Fish Game Fish Bull. 139: 264 p.

SCOTT, J. P. 1958. Animal behavior. University o Chicago Press, Chicago, Ill. 281 p.

WILLIAMS, G. C. 1957. Homing behavior of California rocky shore fishes. Univ. Calif. Publ. Zool. 59: 249–284.

Territory Boundaries, Courtship, and Social Behavior in the Garibaldi, *Hypsypops rubicunda* (Pomacentridae)

Thomas A. Clarke

Adult garibaldi defend bottom territories throughout the year. Boundaries are usually respected by other garibaldi, and intraspecific aggression is uncommon. Jaw-locking between adjacent neighbors was observed. This behavior is probably a ritualized form of boundary fighting observed in other territorial pomacentrids.

Garibaldi occasionally aggregate and mix above the bottom without obvious agonism, ignoring territory boundaries below. During aggregation, pairs of garibaldi perform activities similar to those observed during courtship. It is proposed that aggregation above the bottom is a form of preliminary, communal courtship whereby neighboring fish can mix without evoking territorial aggression.

INTRODUCTION

THE garibaldi, *Hypsypops rubicunda*, is a brilliant orange pomacentrid fish found over rocky bottom between 0–20 m depths off Southern and Baja California. Adults are strongly territorial. I reported elsewhere the results of a study on the ecological effects of territorial behavior (Clarke, 1970). This report presents and discusses behavior related to maintenance of territory boundaries and to courtship.

Most of the observations reported here were made in two areas, Boomer Beach and Quast Rock, located about 170 m and 650 m, respectively, NW of Point La Jolla, California. The bottom in these areas, depths 8 m and 20 m, was high relief, sculptured sandstone. There were about 115 adult garibaldi in the Boomer Beach area (1570 m²) and 70 in the Quast Rock area (1000 m²). Territories were contiguous and ranged from 10 to 20 m² in area. Nest sites or shelter holes of about half the adults at Boomer Beach and all at Quast Rock were marked and regularly censused. About 30 adults in both areas were captured and tagged with numbered dart tags. Observations were also made at similar areas at the Coronados Islands, Baja California.

MATERIALS AND METHODS

Observations were made using SCUBA, mostly during the morning hours. There was no evidence that behavior was different during the afternoon. General observations, those made in the course of other work, were made from 1965 to 1967. Series of timed observations were made in November 1966 and July 1967. A total of 34 adult garibaldi were watched for 10–15 min each, and all activities recorded using an underwater tape recorder. The total observation time was 397 min. I observed no color changes or dimorphism and found, contrary to Limbaugh (1964), no reliable method of distinguishing sexes on the basis of external characteristics. I was thus able to distinguish only nest-guarding fish as males; others could have been either females or bachelor (nonbreeding) males.

TERRITORIAL AND SOCIAL BEHAVIOR

The life history of the garibaldi has been briefly described by Limbaugh (1964) and in greater detail by Clarke (1970). Garibaldi are active only during the day. They feed exclusively on benthic animals, mostly siliceous sponges, coelenterates, and Bryozoa. Adults are territorial all year, the males being more strict in defense of their territory. The territory defended includes the grazing area, shelter, and, for some males, the nest site. The nest is a small patch of red algae cultured by the male. The same nest is used by a male over a period of several years. Spawning will be described below. Eggs are present in nests from late spring to early fall. The male guards the eggs until hatching. The larvae leave the nest and disperse into the plankton. Juveniles settle out in shallow water ($\leqslant 5$ m) and remain close to shore until they assume adult coloration. Garibaldi mature at age 5–6 years and may live 12 or more years.

From *Copeia* 1971(2):295–299. Reprinted by permission.

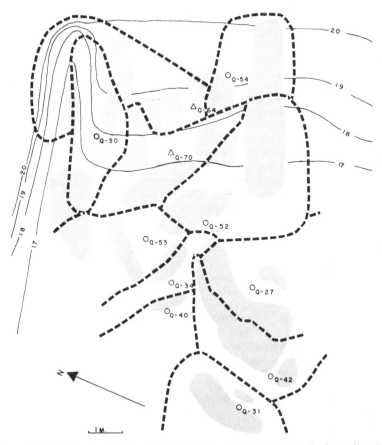

Fig. 1. Map of the territories of 11 garibaldi (Q–27, *etc.*) at Quast Rock, La Jolla, California. Movements of each fish were recorded for about 15 min; dashed lines define the limits of movement. Nest sites of the nine nesting males are indicated by circles; shelter holes of the other two individuals are indicated by triangles. Contours are in meters; large rocks ($\geqq 0.5$ m high) are shaded.

Garibaldi territories were usually contiguous (Fig. 1) except where their density was very low. Boundaries were not obviously related to topography, but were well-defined by restricted movements and rarely violated by neighbors. Agonistic encounters at the boundaries were unusual. Neighbors were frequently observed grazing near a mutual boundary only 10–15 cm apart with no sign of agonism or attempts to cross or expand boundaries. As a consequence, most aggression by garibaldi was against other species (mostly wrasses or embiotocid seaperches) that did not recognize or respect territory boundaries. Even though other species were not invariably attacked, interspecific encounters accounted for a total of 79 attacks, as opposed to eight intraspecific attacks, during the series of timed observations.

One particular sequence appeared to be related to boundary determination or maintenance. When two adjacent neighbors met near their mutual boundary, they frequently, but not invariably, approached each other until they were only a few centimeters apart. They sometimes remained facing each other head on for several seconds, beating the caudal fin back and forth rapidly. This ceremony often ended at this point, but about one-third of the time, the fish came together and physically locked jaws. They remained locked for up to 15 sec, separated, and sometimes locked again. During these actions, there was no obvious tugging or shaking. After cessation of jaw-locking, the two slowly backed away and resumed their usual activities. This sequence, or parts of it, was recorded twice during the timed observations and on several other occasions during the year.

Interactions on the bottom, boundary encounters or spawning, involved only two individuals, but adult garibaldi occasionally formed aggregations above. This behavior was initiated when one or two fish rose 2–3 m above the bottom over their territories. Others in the area then joined them, forming rather close aggregations with individuals only 20–30 cm apart and ignoring territory boundaries below. As many as eight fish, including both males with nests and others, participated. The aggregations typically lasted for several minutes with some fish leaving or entering during that time. When the aggregation dissolved, all the fish involved returned straight to their territories almost simultaneously.

Aggregations were observed throughout the year but more frequently just before and during the breeding season. They appeared to occur generally in areas more densely populated by garibaldi. In July 1967, three were recorded during a total of 45 min of observing the group of fish shown in Fig. 1. These aggregations were initiated by different fish each time. Fish Q-53, -52, -64, and -34 participated in all three, Q-40 in two. Fish Q-30, -54, and -70 sometimes turned and watched from the bottom but never participated. Definite identification of participants and nonparticipants were not made in other areas, but generally aggregations did not appear to involve all the fish in an area.

During aggregation, pairs of fish often associated more closely with each other than with other participants, the paired fish remaining within 20–30 cm of each other for extended periods while the other fish milled around and approached several individuals. Similar pairing was also observed separate from aggregations but always well above the bottom. When identities of the paired fish could be determined, invariably one of them was a male with nest site and the other was not. Frequently during pairing, one of the fish (when the individuals could be identified, it was always the male with nest) would tilt or turn completely sideways, approach the other head first, and attempt to bite or butt it on the side near the anal area. The latter fish either swam slowly, allowing the male to continue, or avoided the approach by swimming faster. When avoidance occurred, the male often became aggressive,

snapped his teeth, and chased the other fish, sometimes biting its fins.

If aggregating or pairing fish came within about 1 m of the bottom over the territory of a fish that was not participating, they were attacked. Such intrusions by a pair of fish provoked five intraspecific attacks by one other garibaldi during observations at Boomer Beach. This accounted for over half the intraspecific attacks recorded during the entire series of timed observations.

REPRODUCTIVE BEHAVIOR

The males trimmed the nest sites and removed other organisms in March. Spawning did not begin until water temperatures reached about 15° C, usually in May in shallow areas such as Boomer Beach and in August in deeper areas such as Quast Rock. In both areas the spawning season ended in September–October, a month or two before bottom temperatures dropped below 15° C.

During the spawning season, the aggregations described above persisted much longer; in some areas at Boomer Beach, fish were above the bottom almost continuously for over 2 hr. Males with nests singled out one fish, presumably a female, and repeatedly approached her. Sometimes the male attempted to side-bite or chased the female and bit her fins. Once I observed a male attempt to herd a female toward the nest by swimming parallel and slightly behind her and forcing her to spiral towards the nest. Males also approached the female head on, turned in front of or slightly below her, and returned slowly to the nest. This behavior is similar to courtship displays in other pomacentrids (see review by Reese, 1964) but was not observed frequently enough to make detailed comparisons.

The female consistently returned to the same general area and stayed above the bottom a few meters away from the nest. Unfortunately I did not observe the actual acceptance sequence. Females occasionally approached the nest but were always driven away. Limbaugh (1964) reported that immediately before spawning, the female approached the nest repeatedly and was finally accepted by the male when she came within about 30 cm of the nest.

Spawning was observed about 25 times. In each case the female pressed her genital area closely to the nest and deposited eggs, while the male darted back and forth rapidly (Fig.

Fig. 2. Photographs of spawning garibaldi. a) Female, lower fish (on side and facing camera), depositing eggs in nest (vertical rock face) while male, upper fish, hovers above. b) Male skimming nest after female has deposited eggs (lighter patch adjacent to males ventral surface).

2a). The male occasionally joined the female and rubbed his genital area over the nest, but usually remained above the nest. Any fish, regardless of species, was attacked immediately if it approached the nest. The female laid eggs for 10–15 min. When she was finished, the male drove her away and returned to the nest immediately. He continued to rub his genital area over the nest (Fig. 2b) for several minutes afterward, interrupting this behavior only to challenge and attack other fish.

DISCUSSION

My observations indicate that garibaldi recognize and usually respect territory boundaries. Furthermore, the boundaries are maintained with little intraspecific aggression, such behavior being directed mostly against other species. The jaw-locking sequence observed between neighboring gari-

baldi is likely related to maintenance of boundaries and is probably a ritualization of agonistic behavior. Jaw-locking has been reported in another pomacentrid, *Abudefduf abdominalis* (Helfrich, 1958) but accompanied by violent thrashing after the jaws are locked. Myrberg *et al.* (1967) reported momentary jaw-locking in *Chromis multilineata* along with other ritualized, but clearly agonistic, behavior during territorial encounters.

Since jaw-locking occurred rather infrequently, it is possible that other more subtle sequences are involved in boundary maintenance. Whatever the case, the suppression of aggression is not surprising in view of the garibaldi's long-term defense of territory. Damaging or exhausting boundary encounters all year over the many years a male defends his territory would undoubtedly be detrimental.

The aggregation behavior described for the garibaldi is not likely related to territory defense since boundaries are ignored. During the behavior, adult garibaldi (some of which would otherwise never come in contact) mix without apparent agonism. Since the garibaldi fulfills its obvious needs on the bottom—food, shelter, nest site, etc.—the function of the mixing is not clear.

One possibility is that aggregation is related to sexual recognition and perhaps represents a form of communal courtship that begins well before the breeding season. Both sexes are involved and some of the elements of actual courtship—pairing and side-biting—occur then. In addition, the incidence of aggregation increases during the breeding season. Complex behavior may be necessary for pair formation because the sexes are not clearly distinguished on the basis of color, morphology, or even nonbreeding behavior. Complex discriminative interactions also occur in those species of cichlid fishes with little or no sexual dimorphism (Baerends and Baerends-van Roon, 1950).

Aggregations above the bottom have been reported during courtship of two other pomacentrids, Chromis chromis (Abel, 1961) and C. multilineata (Myrberg et al., 1967). In both species females leave or are attracted from the aggregation to spawn with territorial males below. Myrberg et al. also noted that occasionally pairs of C. multilineata left the aggregation to spawn. Laboratory observations of communal spawning by Dascyllus aruanus (Fishelson, 1964) suggest that this species may also court and spawn communally in the field.

The general ecology and nonbreeding behavior of other pomacentrids studied in the field is different from that of the garibaldi. Chromis punctipinnis (Turner and Ebert, 1962), A. abdominalis (Helfrich, 1958), and Dascyllus albisella (Stevenson, 1963), like the species mentioned above, school and mix while feeding on plankton above the bottom. Also only part of the males are territorial at a given time, and then only part of the year. Thus mixing can occur without any radically (or noticeably) different behavior. It would be interesting to see if other species whose ecology is similar to that of the garibaldi, i.e., solitary bottom-grazers, also retain some means of mixing or a basis of contact other than territorial encounters.

ACKNOWLEDGMENTS

This work represents part of my Ph. D. research at the Department of Oceanography, University of California, San Diego. During this time, I was supported by a National Science Foundation Graduate Fellowship. I sincerely appreciate the assistance and guidance of E. W. Fager and R. H. Rosenblatt. I also thank A. O. Flechsig for technical assistance, E. S. Reese and G. S. Losey for review of the manuscript.

LITERATURE CITED

ABEL, E. F. 1961. Freiwasserstudien über das Fortpflanzungsverhalten des Monchfishes Chromis chromis Linne', einem Vertreter der Pomacentriden im Mittelmeer. Z. Tierpsychol. 18 (4):441–449.

BAERENDS, G. P. AND J. M. BAERENDS-VAN ROON. 1950. An introduction to the study of the ethology of cichlid fishes. Behavior, Suppl. 1, 242 pp.

CLARKE, T. A. 1970. Territorial behavior and population dynamics of a pomacentrid fish, the garibaldi, Hypsypops rubicunda. Ecol. Monogr. 40(2):189–212.

FISHELSON, L. 1964. Observations on the biology and behavior of Red Sea coral fishes. Bull. Sea Fish Res. Sta., Haifa, No. 37, pp. 11–26.

HELFRICH, P. 1958. The early life history and reproductive behavior of the maomao, Abudefduf abdominalis (Quoy and Gaimard). Ph.D. thesis, Univ. Hawaii, Honolulu, Hawaii.

LIMBAUGH, C. 1964. Notes on the life history of two Californian pomacentrids: garibaldis, Hypsypops rubicunda (Girard), and blacksmiths, Chromis punctipinnis (Cooper). Pac. Sci. 18(1):41–50.

MYRBERG, A. A., JR., B. D. BRAHY, AND A. R. EMERY. 1967. Field observations on reproduction of the damselfish, Chromis multilineata (Pomacentridae), with additional notes on general behavior. Copeia 1967(4):819–827.

REESE, E. S. 1964. Ethology and marine zoology. In: Oceanography and marine biology, annual review H. Barnes, ed., 2:455–488. George Allen and Unwin Ltd., London.

STEVENSON, R. A. 1963. Life history and behavior of Dascyllus albisella Gill, a pomacentrid reef fish. Ph.D. thesis, Univ. Hawaii. Honolulu, Hawaii.

TURNER, C. H. AND E. E. EBERT. 1962. The nesting of Chromis punctipinnis (Cooper) and a description of their eggs and larvae. Calif. Fish Game 43(4):243–248.

HAWAII INSTITUTE OF MARINE BIOLOGY, UNIVERSITY OF HAWAII, P. O. BOX 1067, KANEOHE, HAWAII 96744.

Agonistic Display in the Gray Reef Shark, *Carcharhinus menisorrah*, and its Relationship to Attacks on Man

RICHARD H. JOHNSON AND DONALD R. NELSON

An agonistic display directed primarily toward divers was observed on 23 occasions in *Carcharhinus menisorrah* at Eniwetok Atoll, Marshall Islands, during January, 1971. This display was filmed in normal speed and slow motion and found to consist of two locomotor elements: [1] laterally exaggerated swimming and [2] rolling and/or spiral looping, and four postural elements: [1] lifting of the snout, [2] dropping of the pectoral fins, [3] arching of the back and [4] lateral bending of the body.

This behavior was found to occur under approach-withdrawal conflict situations, and rapid diver approach was shown to be a releasing stimulus. It was a graded phenomenon with the most intense displays occurring when there was maximum escape-route restriction and when diver aggression was initiated while the shark was approaching rather than lateral or departing.

Under the circumstances in which it was observed, this display probably expressed defensive threat. It appeared ritualized in nature and is likely to be of value in normal social encounters. This display has been related to attacks on man and may indicate a motivational basis other than feeding for such attacks.

IN a paper entitled "Shark Attack; Feeding or Fighting?" Baldridge and Williams (1969) presented a case for attacks on man motivated by factors other than the desire to feed. This paper was the first to seriously question the basic premise upon which most shark deterrent research has been based, pointing to social interactions as a possible motivating factor in certain cases of shark attacks on man. Some evidence for this view can be found in the elasmobranch literature. The most significant incidents include at least five attacks by the gray reef shark, *Carcharhinus menisorrah*, which were prefaced by a display apparently identical to the one described in this report (Church, 1961; Fellows and Murchison, 1967; Randall, pers. comm.; and McNair, pers. comm.). Moreover, Limbaugh (1963) reported an unprovoked attack by the shovelnose guitarfish, *Rhinobatos productus*, possibly related to inter-ference with courtship and unprovoked attacks by the Pacific electric ray, *Torpedo californica*, of possible agonistic origins.

The literature relating to true aggression in sharks is slight and (with the exception of the first two studies cited) is based primarily on incidental observations. Intra-species dominance was shown in the smooth dogfish, *Mustelus canis*, by Allee and Dickinson (1954) where larger individuals, i.e., those at least 6.7% longer in total length, dominated smaller individuals. Myrberg and Gruber (in prep.) have quantitative evidence indicating straight-line size-dependent dominance in a group of captive bonnethead sharks, *Sphyrna tiburo*. Similar intra-species dominance, based on size, has been mentioned by Limbaugh (1963) in the galapagos shark, *C. galapagensis*, and by Matthiessen (1971) in the great white shark, *Carcharodon carcharias*. Springer (1967) suggested that

From *Copeia* 1973(1):76–84. Reprinted by permission.

"feeding schools of small sharks give way to individuals or schools of larger sharks." Intraspecies dominance based on sex (male dominating female) was noted by Clark (1963) in a pair of adult lemon sharks, *Negaprion brevirostris*, of similar size.

Inter-species dominance has also been indicated. Limbaugh (1963) described a "nip order" where the silvertip shark, *C. albimarginatus*, was dominant over *C. galapagensis* while the blacktip shark, *C. limbatus*, was subordinate to both when individuals were of similar size. Cousteau and Cousteau (1970) described the oceanic whitetip shark, *C. longimanus*, as dominating *C. albimarginatus* while gray sharks (species not clearly stated) were subordinate to each. Likewise, Springer (1967) described *C. longimanus* as dominating the silky shark, *C. falciformis*, where individuals were of similar size. He also suggested that "hammerheads have a special status, because sharks of other species tend to stay a distance from them even when no great disparity in size exists."

Territoriality (defense of an area) as distinct from home range (usually frequented area) although suggested by some has not been established. Cousteau and Cousteau (1970) reported quantified data indicating home range and stated "In the course of all our studies, we have often verified this idea of distinct territories." Although this conclusion is non-quantitative and apparently based on incidental observations, they reported intraspecific aggression where a shark (dominant only on a specific area of the reef) charged and struck another presumably in defense of its territory. Underwater photographers Giddings and Bergman witnessed "sentinals" leaving a pack of *C. menisorrah* to confront approaching divers, which they considered possible territorial defense (Giddings and Bergman, pers. comm.; Baldridge and Williams, 1969). Limbaugh (1963) and Randall (1963) reported an incident where two nurse sharks, *Ginglymostoma cirratum*, after being closely approached (within 0.5 m) left a cave (one which they frequented routinely) and aggressively pursued the diver to the surface. This incident may indicate defense of either an individual distance or a fixed geographic territory.

Distinct body movements or postures have been noted in certain sharks which do not appear necessary for nondisplay swimming.

Herald (pers. comm.) has noted a peculiar head-shaking, dubbed "shimmy dance," in *Sphyrna* sp. and Eibl-Eibesfeldt (1965) described head-shaking and jaw movements in *C. menisorrah*. Both of these behaviors bear certain resemblances to the posture described in this report, and the possibility of communicative function for them must not be overlooked.

A third and very distinct behavior (the subject of this paper) has been reported in *C. menisorrah* by several observers: Church (1961) at Wake Island, Hobson (1964) at Eniwetok Atoll, Fellows and Murchison (1967) at Johnston Island, Read (1969) in the eastern Caroline Islands, Nelson and Johnson (1970) at Rangiroa Atoll, Bergman and Giddings (pers. comm.) at Rangiroa Atoll, Randall (pers. comm.) at Eniwetok Atoll and McNair (pers. comm.) at Eniwetok Atoll. This same behavior has also been noted in *C. galagapensis* by Hobson (1964), Starck (pers. comm.) and McNair (pers. comm.) Church (1961) originally described this unusual display as follows: "the shark started a small circle just opposite us and as he came around his body started turning and twisting and rolling back and forth in the water as he swam." "The whole body was being used to swim with, his head moving back and forth almost as much as his tail." "He trimmed himself with his pectoral fins."

Of great significance is that in at least five incidents this behavior prefaced attacks in which men were involved. The incident reported by Church (1961) occurred after a shark passed from a confined location against a reef between the two divers toward open water. The divers made moves toward the shark as it passed, apparently initiating the display quoted above. Immediately upon termination of the display the shark rapidly dashed at one of the divers, Jim Stewart, who received two severe bites just above the elbow. The display reported by Fellows and Murchison (1967) occurred after Murchison chased the shark. Again, immediately upon termination of the display the shark attacked. In this case, however, the shark's charge was successfully repelled and no injury resulted. In another incident described by Randall (pers. comm.) a shark displaying between the diver and a reef face was shot with a spear gun. The shark terminated displaying, shook out the spear, and immediately attacked and vigorously bit the

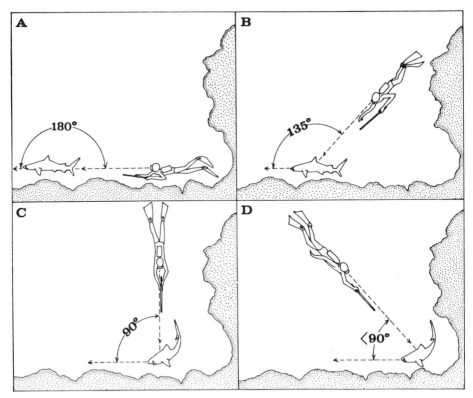

Fig. 1. Escape-route restriction as recorded during test trials in which divers charged sharks: A. (R^0) = escape-route angle 180° (minimal restriction), B. (R^1) = escape-route angle approximately 135°, C. (R^2) = escape-route angle approximately 90° and D. (R^3) = escape-route angle substantially less than 90° (maximal restriction).

nearest object, which in this case was the boat's anchor line.

Since the present study, two attacks by *C. menisorrah* have occurred on a two-man wet submersible at Eniwetok. In one case, after four minutes of following a shark in intense display, the shark "suddenly whirled and bit the plexiglass hood" directly over the heads of divers W. Starck and R. McNair (McNair, pers. comm.).

It is apparent there is much to be learned about the role of display behavior in the ethology of sharks. It is also apparent such behavior relates to the problem of shark attack, especially in *C. menisorrah*, and should be investigated where conditions permit.

Methods and Materials

We encountered considerable numbers of *C. menisorrah* of about 1 to 2 m total length while on a research visit to the Eniwetok

Marine Biological Laboratory, Eniwetok Atoll, Marshall Islands in January of 1971. During our initial underwater encounters we observed several incidents of the above described display. Consequently, we initiated a preliminary two-fold investigation of this behavior including: (1) a thorough description of the display, documented with normal (24 frames/sec) and slow motion (64 frames/ sec) cinematography and (2) an experiment to determine the possible role of diver behavior as a releaser for this display.

Ten test trials were conducted (no further were attempted due to the danger involved) which consisted of a diver rapidly swimming at a shark coming in on an initial approach. The diver remained stationary until the shark closed to within approximately 6.5 m at which time the charge was initiated. Six specific control trials were conducted, where the diver remained stationary upon the initial approach of a shark. However, during the earlier phases of this study many other encounters were recorded which contained the essential elements of the control trials. Where possible, the various parameters relating to the response of the shark were estimated and recorded. The intensity of display was coded as follows: 1) = mild, 2) = moderate,   and   3) = intense.   Various degrees of escape restriction, i.e., the degree to which the shark was cornered or it's escape route restricted by the position of reef structures, were defined (Fig. 1), and the data were recorded accordingly.

RESULTS AND CONCLUSIONS

Figure 2 illustrates display and normal swimming in lateral view. The display consisted of two locomotor (Fig. 3) and four postural elements (Fig. 4). The locomotor elements include: 1) laterally exaggerated swimming motion and 2) rolling (later tilting of the body, Fig. 2B and Fig. 3C, 2) and/or spiral looping (spiral up and down movement through the water, more pronounced in the anterior region, Fig. 3C, 1–6). Rolling, although often seen independently of spiral looping, appears indistinguishable from the initial phase of the latter, and both are frequently followed by a resumption of laterally exaggerated swimming (the most common display mode). The postural elements include: 1) lifting of the snout, in its most intense form resulting in a distinct bend between the chondrocranium and the spinal column and in a slight opening of the jaws, 2) relatively prolonged and at times severe dropping of the pectoral fins, 3) arching of the back and 4) lateral bending, often more pronounced at the posterior end of the body cavity.

Comparison of pectoral fin positions (Fig. 5) during normal swimming, startle responses (abrupt locomotor movements elicited by unexpected stimuli) and display posture, indicated severe pectoral fin depression is not necessary for quick turning or abrupt increase of speed. In the normal swimming position the angle between the pectoral fins varied from about 140° to 180°, while in the startle response shown in Fig. 5B, they dropped lower to about 130° apart. In the agonistic display the pectoral fin drop was variable, going from somewhat lower than natural to an extreme low of 20° to 30° between the pectorals. Moreover, in display the pectoral fin drop was sustained, while in the startle

Fig. 2. Photographs of the gray reef shark, *Carcharhinus menisorrah*: A. agonistic display, laterally exaggerated swimming mode; B. agonistic display, rolling mode and C. non-display swimming. From 16 mm motion picture frames.

response the pectoral fin drop was very brief lasting only long enough to initiate maneuvering and provide an initial burst of speed. Because *C. menisorrah* is capable of initiating abrupt turns and rapid increases of speed without extreme pectoral fin drop, and since in display posture they have exag-

Fig. 3. Comparison of normal and display locomotor swimming modes in the gray reef shark, *Carcharhinus menisorrah*: A. normal swimming; B. display, laterally exaggerated swimming and C. display, rolling (1-2-1) and spiral looping (1-6). Rolling, although similar to the initial phases of spiral looping, is distinct in that the shark returns to a level display attitude without entering into the up and down path seen in spiral looping.

gerated pectoral fin drop, it would appear pectoral fin depression is a significant component of display.

In each of the ten test trials a display was elicited (Table 1). These displays varied between 15 and 60 sec. (mean duration of 34 sec.) and occurred when the diver-shark distance had closed to an average of 4 m. No displays occurred during the six control trials and only one display was seen during the many similar encounters, even though the sharks closed to within an average distance of 2 m. It is, therefore, clear that rapid diver approach (as described) is an adequate releasing stimulus for this display. Altogether 23 occurrences of this behavior were observed under the following conditions: 1) during test trials when divers charged sharks (10

occurrences); 2) during or immediately after experimental playback of low-frequency sounds (7 occurrences, 5 apparently directed at the submerged speaker and 2 at the observer on the surface) and 3) other circumstances (6 occurrences: 4 toward divers, 1 at the boat anchor and 1 when a diver entered the water with a loud splash).

TABLE 2. INTENSITY OF DISPLAY IN THE GRAY REEF SHARK, *Carcharhinus menisorrah*, WITH RESPECT TO: DEGREE OF ESCAPE-ROUTE RESTRICTION AND B. ORIENTATION OF SHARKS (ON INITIAL APPROACH) TOWARD DIVER. DISPLAY INTENSITY CODED: 1 = MILD DISPLAY, 2 = MODERATE DISPLAY AND 3 = INTENSE DISPLAY.

	Mean Display Intensity	Number of Trials
A. Degree of restricted exit:		
$R^0 = (\cong 180°$ escape angle)	1.5	3
$R^1 = (\cong 135°$ escape angle)	2.2	3
$R^2 = (\cong 90°$ escape angle)	2.5	2
$R^3 = (< 90°$ escape angle)	3.0	2
B. Orientation of shark toward diver at point of charge:		
Departing	2.0	2
Lateral	2.1	5
Approaching	2.5	3

TABLE 1. OCCURRENCE OF DISPLAY DURING TEST TRIALS (WITH DIVER AGGRESSION) AND CONTROL TRIALS (NO DIVER AGGRESSION) IN THE GRAY REEF SHARK, *Carcharhinus menisorrah*.

	Display	No Display
Test Trials	10	0
Control Trials	0	6
Other Encounters*	1	$\cong 40$

* Six specific control trials were conducted; however, other encounters occurred during the study which contained the essential elements of control trials.

DISPLAY NON - DISPLAY

Fig. 4. Comparison of non-display and display postures in the gray reef shark, *Carcharhinus menisorrah*. Arrows denote: 1) lifting of the snout, 2) bend between chondrocranium and spinal column caused by lifting of the snout, 3) pectoral fin depression, 4) arching of the back and 5) lateral bending of the body.

The display was found to be a graded phenomenon, and it's intensity was possibly related to at least two factors: 1) the degree of escape restriction and 2) the orientation of the shark with respect to the diver prior to diver charge, i.e., whether it was approaching, lateral or departing. The intensity of display was greatest (3.0) with max- imal restriction (R^3) and least (1.5) with minimal restriction (R^0) (Table 2). Likewise, the intensity of display was greater (2.5) when the shark was charged head-on (on it's initial approach) then when charged after it had begun to depart (2.0). Because of the small number of trials further data would be desirable to confirm these relationships.

Fig. 5. Comparison of pectoral fin positions in the gray reef shark, *Carcharhinus menisorrah*: A. non-display swimming (relatively little pectoral fin depression), B. startle response (brief, moderate pectoral fin depression) and C. agonistic display (prolonged, moderate to extreme pectoral fin depression). From 16 mm motion picture frames.

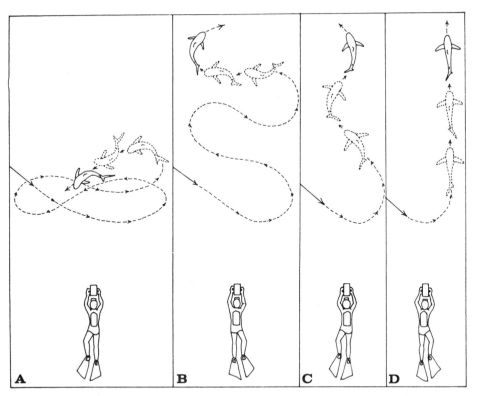

Fig. 6. Comparison of swimming paths under varying degrees of display intensity and during non-display swimming in the gray reef shark, *Carcharhinus menisorrah*: A. intense display, B. moderate display, C. mild display and D. non-display swimming.

Also related to intensity of display was reluctance of the shark to retreat upon approach by the diver. Fig. 6 compares typical paths taken by posturing sharks, at different intensities of display, with normal swimming. Sharks in mild display swam an elongate S-shaped path which effectively increased the diver-shark distance. Sharks in intense display swam a compressed S-shaped path or figure-eight pattern with the shark doubling back upon its previous course. This resulted in little or no retreat and the shark holding ground with respect to the diver. Sharks often developed a distinct anterior-up inclination of the entire body axis at this time. We also received the impression that sharks which had been in sight for a while, i.e., sharks not on an initial approach, were less likely to respond or would respond with less intensity when charged by a diver. The initiation and intensity of display appeared unrelated to water depth or number of sharks present.

A total of 14 displays were recorded on film, nine of which were probably by males (seven definite) and five of which were probably by females (three definite). Of the five maximum-intensity displays three were by males and two by females.

DISCUSSION

The various functions previously ascribed to this behavior in *C. menisorrah* all seem plausible to some extent. Certain authors advocate sensory advantage while others favor involvement of agonistic behavior. Hobson (1964) commented on the function of this behavior, stating it permits the maintaining of visual contact with an object directly behind the shark. Such an advantage may be obtained by posturing sharks in certain instances. However, we observed this posture in sharks in virtually every position with respect to the diver, e.g., approaching, lateral and departing; therefore, this sensory advantage would appear to be secondary to a more significant function. Underwater photographers Giddings and Bergman have called this display pre-attack behavior, inferring a communicative function indicating imminent attack. This interpretation seems valid only if it connotes threat display, i.e., an agonistic behavior, and not a signal to forewarn potential prey of intention to feed. Although their conclusions were based on a single incident, Fellows and Murchison (1967) have probably made the clearest and most accurate assessment of the function of this behavior. They suggested the display in *C. menisorrah* was a defensive behavior provoked by pursuit in a confined area, possibly signifying intention of attack.

Our observations indicate that display occurs during new or novel situations which seem to place the shark under approach-withdrawal conflict. Indeed, the latter element of conflict, i.e., where opposing motivations are approximately in balance, appears common to every observed or reported incidence of this behavior. In our test encounters the approach motive was thought to be investigation while the withdrawal motive was thought to be fear of the charging diver. During concurrent studies of shark attractions to low-frequency sounds (Nelson and Johnson, in press) agonistic displays occurred where sharks completing a rapid initial approach to the transducer, hesitated, turned away, and then began to display. These displays appeared triggered by a conflict between approaching the source of sound (feeding motivated) and withdrawing from the unfamiliar apparatus (escape motivated).

When the components of the display are compared to similar behaviors in other animals, they appear agonistic in nature—specifically representing threat. Display of finnage (dropping pectoral fins), lateral orientation, and slow distinctive movements are elements of threat display in many fishes, e.g., the Siamese fighting fish, *Betta splendens* (Simpson, 1968). Moreover, opening of the mouth (with teeth exposed) and the extreme muscular tenseness during intense display are also generally indicative of threat.

The displays we observed were stereotyped, distinct, and contained exaggerated movements. Such characteristics suggest a ritualized communicative function which we believe to represent threat. Since in the context of diver-shark encounters displays occurred in response to rapid diver approaches, which

are essentially aggressive, this behavior is considered defensive in nature. Although display during interactions with man appears relevant, its development certainly seems dependent upon broader usage under natural conditions. It would, therefore, seem likely that this behavior plays a significant role in the shark's normal social encounters—possibly in dominance, territoriality or courtship (if such exists).

The number of shark attacks prefaced by display and our demonstration that diver behavior can release display confirms Baldridge and Williams (1969) postulation of non-feeding attacks on man. We speculate that in diver-shark encounters such apparently defensive attacks are elicited by violation of some type of boundary determined by the interaction of time and distance. Indeed, the close and persistant approach prior to the attacks (McNair, pers. comm.) involving W. Starck and R. McNair (both of whom were aware of the present study) apparently support this view. Because this display is known in at least two species of sharks and is suspected in several others, agonistic motivation must be considered a potentially widespread cause of shark attacks on man.

ACKNOWLEDGMENTS

We are grateful to the personnel of the Eniwetok Marine Biological Laboratory, especially P. Helfrich and P. Allen, for personal assistance, material and financial support which made this study possible. Our gratitude is extended to Mrs. Loraine Peterson for preparing the drawings in this article. The authors also wish to acknowledge the assistance of the Department of Biology, California State, Long Beach, and the Office of Naval Research through contract N00014-68-C-0318 under project NR-104-062, for supporting the program of shark-behavior research of which this study is a part.

LITERATURE CITED

ALLEE, W. C., AND J. C. DICKINSON. 1954. Dominance and subordination in the smooth dogfish, *Mustelus canis* (Mitchill). Physiol. Zool. 27:356–364.

BALDRIDGE, D. H., JR., AND J. WILLIAMS. 1969. Shark attack: feeding or fighting? Military Medicine 34:130–133.

CLARK, E. 1963. The maintenance of sharks in captivity, with a report of their instrumental conditioning, p. 115–149. *In*: Sharks and survival. P. W. Gilbert, ed. D. C. Heath and Company, Boston.

CHURCH, R. 1961. Shark attack. Skin Diver Mag. June: 30–31.

COUSTEAU, J., AND P. COUSTEAU. 1970. The shark: splendid savage of the sea. Doubleday and Company, Inc. Garden City. New York.

EIBL-EIBESFELDT, I. VON. 1965. Land of a thousand atolls. (Transl. by Gwyne Vevers). The World Publishing Company. Cleveland.

FELLOWS, D. P., AND E. A. MURCHISON. 1967. A noninjurious attack by a small shark. Pacific Sci. 21:150–151.

HOBSON, E. S. 1964. Sharks increasing visual field. Underwater Naturalist. 2:29.

LIMBAUGH, C. 1963. Field notes on sharks, p. 64–94. *In*: Sharks and survival. P. W. Gilbert, ed. D. C. Heath and Company. Boston.

MATTHIESSEN, P. 1971. Blue meridian: the search for the great white shark. Random House, Inc., New York.

NELSON, L. R., AND R. H. JOHNSON. 1970. Acoustic studies on sharks, Rangiroa Atoll, July 1969. Office of Naval Research, Tech. Rep. 2.

RANDALL, J. E. 1963. Dangerous sharks of the western Atlantic, p. 339–361. *In*: Sharks and survival. P. W. Gilbert, ed. D. C. Heath and Company. Boston.

READ, K. R. H. 1969. Pacific reef sharks. Aquasphere 4:12–16.

SIMPSON, M. J. A. 1968. The display of the Siamese fighting fish, *Betta splendens*. Anim. Behav. Monogr. 1:1–73.

SPRINGER, S. 1967. Social organization of shark populations, p. 149–174. *In*: Sharks, skates and rays. P. W. Gilbert, R. F. Mathewson and D. P. Rall, eds. Johns Hopkins Press, Baltimore.

DEPARTMENT OF BIOLOGY, CALIFORNIA STATE UNIVERSITY, LONG BEACH, CALIFORNIA 90840.

The Ecological Importance of Cleaning Symbiosis[1]

George S. Losey, Jr.

The removal of most of the cleaner fish, *Labroides phthirophagus*, from a reef resulted in an increase in cleaning behavior by the remaining cleaners and changes in the behavior and distribution of the host fish. After the removal of all of the *L. phthirophagus* there was no increase in the ectoparasitic infestation of the host fish as compared with a similar control reef. The form of the behavioral changes and the lack of change in ectoparasites suggest that although the adaptive value of cleaning is probably ectoparasite removal, the proximate causal factors are not related to ectoparasites. Thus, in some areas, the relationship of the cleaner to the host may become commensal or even parasitic.

INTRODUCTION

CLEANING symbiosis is defined as the removal and subsequent ingestion of ectoparasites, diseased and injured tissue, and unwanted food particles by cleaning organisms. The cleaner removes and ingests material from organisms termed hosts. Cleaning behavior is seen in various types of animals, but is most common in marine reef fishes (see Feder, 1966, Losey, 1971, for review). In the ideal situation, the host fish displays or poses for the cleaner at a specific location on the reef termed the cleaning station. The cleaner swims close and inspects the host and picks at its body surfaces. The cleaner may even enter the host's mouth or gill chamber.

The gut contents of cleaner fishes include ectoparasites, in addition to fish scales and other material (e.g., see Feder, 1966, Youngbluth, 1968, Hobson, 1971). Several workers have hypothesized that cleaning symbiosis is a vital ecological relationship that reduces the level of parasitism in marine fishes (see Feder, 1966). Limbaugh (1961) removed all of the cleaning organisms from a patch reef in the British West Indies. Within two weeks he noted an apparent decrease in the number of fish on the reef and an increase in the infection of those fish that remained. Even though Limbaugh criticized his own lack of controls and lack of quantification, this work has frequently been cited as evidence of the ecological importance of cleaning symbiosis (Feder, 1966, Faulkner, 1965, Stroud and Jenkins, 1962, and others).

Youngbluth (1968) removed all but one of the *Labroides phthirophagus* Randall (the most specialized cleaning organism in Hawaii) from a patch reef in Kaneohe Bay, Hawaii. He observed no change in the number of interactions with the remaining cleaner. He removed all of the *L. phthirophagus* from a similar reef and noted no changes in either the number of fish on the reef or the degree of ectoparasitic infestation. Youngbluth suggested that the greater isolation of his reefs may have prevented emigration from the reef and that the common ectoparasite, a caligoid copepod, might not cause irritation. The number-of-interactions statistic which he used as a behavioral measure might also be too insensitive to reveal changes (Losey, 1971). Despite these qualifications, Youngbluth's results cast additional doubt on the popular interpretation of Limbaugh's results. *L. phthirophagus* appears to be an obligate cleaner (Randall, 1958, Youngbluth, 1968) and the major cleaning organism in Hawaii. If cleaning symbiosis is of such dramatic importance as has been supposed (Feder, 1966), the removal of these cleaners should produce some observable changes either in terms of host condition or supplemental cleaning relationships.

MATERIALS AND METHODS

Experimental rationale.—In order to understand the behavior and ecology of cleaning symbiosis it is necessary to resolve the apparent contradictions in previous work on cleaner removal. The removal or reduction of the number of cleaning organisms should be viewed as a perturbation of the ecosystem that can lead to several types of changes:

---

[1] Contribution no. 400 of the Hawaii Institute of Marine Biology, University of Hawaii.

---

1. The host-parasite balance might be disturbed and lead to abnormal infection and disease with possible emigration of the reef fishes.
2. The cleaning guild function or "work load" of ectoparasite removal might be assumed by the remaining cleaners.
3. Organisms that clean occasionally or not at all might take over the cleaning function.

If none of these effects are observed, the purported ecological significance of cleaning symbiosis must be reexamined.

All of the possible changes listed above may be quantified, but it is crucial to employ sufficiently sensitive measures in order to detect small changes in each one. Cleaning is a unique type of symbiosis in that it involves a large number of species. It is necessary to record species-specific interactions and not merely cleaner-host interactions (Losey, 1971). The changes suggested above might vary between species and thus mask the overall effect if all of the species are considered together. The emphasis of this study is placed on behavioral changes as sensitive and easily sampled parameters of cleaning symbiosis.

Behavioral parameters.—The behavior patterns of cleaners and hosts have been described in detail (Wickler, 1963, Youngbluth, 1968, Losey, 1971). A brief sketch of the pertinent action patterns is given here.

Labroides phthirophagus actions:

Inspect: (= inspect + pursue of Youngbluth, 1968) Swimming close and orienting to the body of another fish. It may include cleaning and contact by the cleaner's fins.
Clean: (= feed of Youngbluth, 1968) Picking at the body surfaces of the host.

Host fish actions:

Pose: The fish assumes a more or less species-specific orientation (head-stand, tail-stand, etc.), swimming pattern, and/or coloration that is usually seen only in cleaning interactions. Pose may vary widely both between and within species (Losey, 1971) but is usually easily discernible to the practiced observer.

A detailed analysis of the interactions between cleaner and hosts may be found in Losey (1971) and is outlined below in sufficient detail for present purposes.

1. Host-pose and cleaner-inspect are communicative behavior patterns. They form a mutually reinforcing system in that the occurrence of either action increases the probability of the other's occurrence.
2. Occurrences of pose and inspect also depend on the visual stimulus of the cleaner or host, respectively. Hosts apparently learn to recognize cleaners through tactile reinforcement (Losey, MS.).
3. The apparent threshold for posing behavior is lowered when hosts are deprived of cleaning in the laboratory. This results in an increase in pose behavior.
4. Inspecting behavior by the cleaner decreases in duration with repeated performance.
5. Factors no. 3 and 4 above contribute to an increase in the ratio of pose to inspect duration when hosts that have been deprived of cleaning are subsequently exposed to a cleaner.

The change in the pose to inspect (p/i) ratio may be used as a sensitive behavioral indicator of the degree of cleaning deprivation in hosts, but it has not as yet been possible to show any relationship between the pose to inspect ratio and the degree of parasitic infestation of the hosts.

Study sites.—The two small (about 30 m diameter) patch reefs in Kaneohe Bay, Hawaii, that were utilized by Youngbluth (1968) in 1966, were again used in this study (Fig. 1). The reefs are separated by about 500 m of 15 to 18 m deep water. These truncate platforms are awash at extremely low tide. The substratum is primarily coral rubble covered with the green alga, *Dictyosphaeria cavernosa*, with occasional living corals, predominantly *Porites compressa*, *Pocillopora damicornis* and *Montipora verrucosa*.

Observation equipment and technique.—Behavioral observations were made by a scuba diver lying near the top of the reef over the cleaning station (Fig. 1c). After 8 months of diving on the reef prior to behavioral observations, the underwater blind which had been placed on the reef (see Losey, 1971) proved to be unnecessary as the fish seemed to be little disturbed by the motionless diver.

A spoken commentary was recorded on a Hydro Products underwater tape recorder and the occurrence of various action patterns was recorded on an underwater event recorder. The event recorder consisted of a RustRak, 8-channel recorder in an underwater housing. The recorder was activated by a manually operated keyboard of either magnetically operated reed switches potted in resin, or microswitches in an oil immersion. The two recorders were used simultaneously during the behavioral observations. The channels of the event recorder were divided into four "pose-channels," one "inspect-channel" and one channel reserved for any chasing or signs of agonistic or predatory behavior between symbionts. The channels were kept "on" as long as the respective behavior occurred. A simultaneous voice recording of the species that were interacting was later intercollated with the event record. This provided a species specific interaction record which could include up to four hosts and one cleaner simultaneously, and an unlimited number of species.

Distributions of *Labroides phthirophagus* were surveyed by marking all apparent cleaning stations with small underwater buoys and then slowly swimming around the reef on subsequent days and noting the number and location of cleaners. Such buoys have no visible effect on the cleaning station (Youngbluth, 1968).

Distributions of host fishes were done by sitting quietly on each cleaning station for approximately 5 minutes and counting the number of each species present. Although this method leads to an inflated estimate of the population densities due to recounting individuals, it provides an estimate of the relative density of fishes on the cleaning stations.

Host fish were trapped and speared for ectoparasite assay and were immediately sealed in plastic bags. Ectoparasites were assayed in the laboratory by examining the body and gill cavity of the fish and the residue filtered from the contents of the plastic bags with a dissecting microscope at 240 ×. This insured that the many ectoparasites which drop off the host after spearing will be recovered (Hobson, 1971).

Experimental calendar.—The experimental design was strongly influenced by the availability of manpower and time and is best illustrated by the calendar presented in the next column.

Jan.–Aug., 1970: survey cleaner distributions on reefs 1 and 2.

Aug.–Sept., 1970: survey cleaner distributions on reefs 1 and 2 and make behavioral observations on reef 2.

Aug. 21–Aug. 24, 1970: spear all but two *L. phthirophagus* from reef 2. (It was intended to leave only *L. phthirophagus* adult no. 1 on station 3 but one young adult persisted after being wounded and was seen regularly on station 1. He could not be approached or observed due to a fright reaction shown to all divers.)

Sept.–Oct., 1970: survey cleaner and host distributions on reefs 1 and 2 and make behavioral observations on the remaining *L. phthirophagus* on station 3, reef 2.

Nov., 1970: remove both remaining *L. phthirophagus* from reef 2.

Nov., 1970–June, 1971: continually remove any incoming *L. phthirophagus* on reef 2 and conduct host ectoparasite assay.

Three young and one juvenile *L. phthirophagus* were removed from reef 2 between Dec., 1970 and June, 1971. All had presumably settled on the reef as juveniles.

RESULTS

Preliminary distributional surveys.—The surveys of *L. phthirophagus* conducted before the removal of cleaners revealed a maximum of 8 on each reef. The mean daily count and 95% confidence limits (by "t" approximation) are: 5.3 ± 0.6 for reef 1, and 5.3 ± 0.8 for reef 2 (21 samples). The removal of fish from reef 2 confirmed the presence of 8 *L. phthirophagus*.

The similarity of the two reefs was additionally established by observing the location of the *L. phthirophagus* on them. The frequency distributions for the occurrence of the cleaners on each of the stations (Fig. 2) were calculated by assuming that when one or more of the 8 *L. phthirophagus* that were present on the reef were not counted, there was an equal probability that they might have been on any one of the stations but not observed. This calculated "error" percentage was added to the actual percent of the fish observed on each station. For example, one count for reef 2 was 6 individuals, so 2 individuals were not seen and could have been on any one of the 6 stations. The resulting percentage of individuals assigned to each station was:

$$\frac{\dfrac{\text{number of fish not counted}}{\text{number of fish on reef}}}{\text{number of stations on reef}}$$

$$\times 100 +$$

$$\frac{\text{number of fish on this station}}{\text{number of fish on reef}}$$

$$\times 100$$

or for station no. 1 where one individual was counted:

$$\text{\% cleaners for station } 1 = (2/8/6) \times$$
$$100 + (1/8) \times 100 = 16.7\%$$

Since low counts frequently occurred on days with restricted underwater visibility, all observations were discarded where fewer than 5 cleaners were counted per reef.

The calculated distribution of *L. phthirophagus* on reef 2 is indicated as nonrandom (p < 0.05, by Kuiper modification of Kolmogorov-Smirnov method, see Batschelet, 1965) and is biased toward the ENE portion of the reef, or roughly the windward side. Although reef 1 appears to show the same trend, the distribution is not different from random (p > 0.10). The distribution on reef 1 is not different from that on reef 2 (p > 0.10).

The four individuals removed from reef 2 between Dec., 1970 and June, 1971 were all on the eastern portion of the reef, near, but not directly on, station 3.

The median number of *L. phthirophagus* observed per cleaning station on reef 2 (1.2 individuals) appears less than that for reef 1

(0.8 individuals) but the difference lacks significance (p = 0.091 by Mann-Whitney, Rank Sum method, Tate and Clelland, 1959).

Preliminary behavioral surveys.—The daily observation records were divided into 5.1-minute intervals. A total of 13 intervals, or 66.3 minutes of observation were made over four, nonconsecutive days. The duration of the action patterns was calculated as the sum of the individual bout lengths over each 5.1-minute interval. The median inspect duration (expressed as percent of observation time) and the median ratio of the pose duration to the inspect duration[1]) are shown for 5 *L. phthirophagus* in Figs. 3 and 4. Table 1 includes the median inspect durations, pose to inspect ratios, and plankton feeding times for the same 5 *L. phthiorphagus* as compared with comparable data for *L. dimidiatus* in Eniwetok (Losey, in prep.). Note that *L. dimidiatus* commonly feeds on plankton and has been observed to spend up to 91% of its time in plankton feeding activities (11.8 out of 13 minutes of observations on one individual). Although plankton feeding is rarely seen in *L. phthirophagus*, it may occur in some individuals at levels similar to those for *L. dimidiatus*.

Behavioral changes after removal of

---

[1] If either pose or inspect did not occur during any 5.1-minute interval, its duration was made equal to 0.5 seconds, the smallest duration possible with these methods. This was done since the occurrence of one in the absence of the other was a pertinent event.

TABLE 1. OBSERVED PARAMETERS OF SELECTED ACTION PATTERNS DURING INTERACTIONS OF CLEANERS WITH ALL SPECIES OF HOSTS. DURATION IS PRESENTED AS PERCENT OF THE TOTAL OBSERVATION TIME. WHEN MORE THAN ONE ESTIMATE IS AVAILABLE, THE VALUE PRESENTED IS THE MEDIAN.

Cleaner observed	Behavioral parameter			Location
	Pose / Inspect	Inspect duration	Plankton feeding	
Labroides phthirophagus				Kaneohe Bay, Hawaii
Adult #1	1.44	22.6%	0	Reef #2, station #3
Adult #2	1.69	3.5%	35.4%	Reef #2, station #3
Adult #3*	0.62	8.7%	0.7%	Reef #2, station #4
Adult #4	1.43	26.0%	0.4%	Reef #2, station #5
Adult #5	1.98	17.3%	0	Reef #2, station #6
Labroides dimidiatus				Eniwetok, Marshall Islands
Adult #1	0.62	14.6%	46.3%	Deep lagoon pinnacle
Adult #2	0.64	5.1%	11.2%	Deep lagoon pinnacle
Adult #3	0.73	10.0%	48.0%	Shallow fringe reef
Adult #4	0.64	27.1%	0.1%	Shallow fringe reef
Adult #5	0.81	25.0%	9.4%	Shallow fringe reef

* Indicates doubtful observation due to poor visibility.

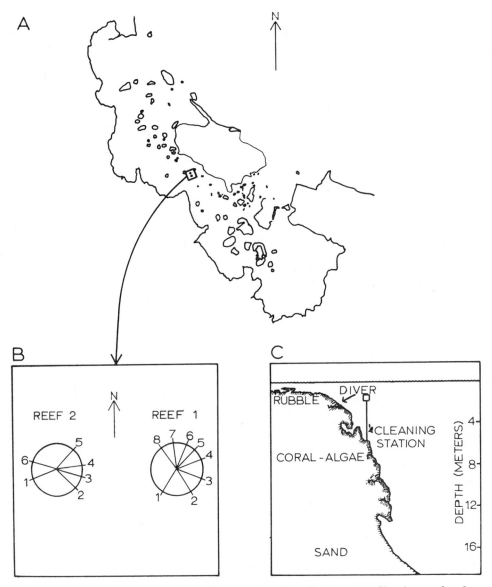

Fig. 1. Study reefs number 1 and 2 in Kaneohe Bay, Hawaii. Inset B: Cleaning station locations and compass bearings taken from the center of the reef. Inset C: A typical reef cross section showing approximate depths for observer, cleaning stations, coral-algae zone, and sand and silt zone to the bottom of the bay.

cleaners.—After the removal of all but two *L. phthirophagus* from reef 2, the behavioral interactions of the remaining adult no. 1 on station 3 were altered (Figs. 3, 4, Tables 2, 3). The cleaner remained on station 3 throughout the observations. All of the changes discussed later are in the interactions of adult no. 1 and its host fish on station 3.

The amount of time that was spent inspecting all host fish and the ratio of the total duration of host-pose behavior to the total duration of cleaner-inspect behavior (p/i ratio) increased after the removal of cleaners. The sequential distributions of cleaner-inspect behavior were compared by examining the duration of the intervals be-

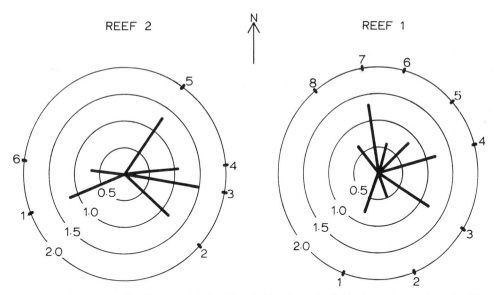

Fig. 2. The average distribution of *Labroides phthirophagus* individuals on the study reefs. The density at each cleaning station is indicated as distance from the center of the circles as the mean number of individuals. The location of the stations and their corresponding vectors are plotted as to their compass direction and indicated by the station numbers at the edge of the outer circle. Number of observations = 14.

tween inspect bouts. The mean interval length was reduced after removal. The temporal distribution of bouts was aggregated both before and after removal (p < 0.005 by chi square) with a trend toward less aggregation after removal ($S^2/\bar{x} = 22.8$ and 13.2 respectively).

The sequential distribution of host-pose

TABLE 2. VARIOUS STATISTICS FOR THE INTERACTIONS OF *L. phthirophagus* ADULT NO. 1 WITH ALL SPECIES OF HOSTS BOTH BEFORE AND AFTER THE REMOVAL OF OTHER CLEANERS.

Variable	Representative statistic	Before removal	After removal	Probability of Difference
Time spent inspecting as % of total time	median	25%	62%	< 0.03
Total pose to inspect ratio	median	1.45	1.96	< 0.02
Number of hosts posing per 3.7-second interval	mean ($S^2/\bar{x}$)	0.53 randomly distributed	1.56 evenly distributed	< 0.01
Number of seconds between successive inspect bouts	mean ($S^2/\bar{x}$)	9.1 aggregated distribution	4.5 aggregated distribution	< 0.05
Diversity of interactions based on inspect duration	$\hat{H}$	2.94 S.E. = 0.12	3.67 S.E. = 0.07	< 0.05
Diversity of interactions based on number of inspect bouts	$\hat{H}$	3.19 S.E. = 0.08	3.16 S.E. = 0.05	> 0.2

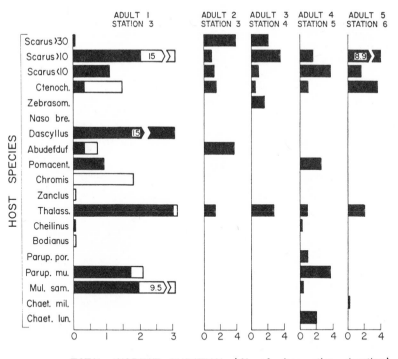

TOTAL INSPECT DURATION (% of observation duration)

Fig. 3. The median duration of inspect behavior by *Labroides phthirophagus* during interactions with various host species. Duration is presented as percent of each 5.1 minute observation period. Black areas indicate the level of activity before the removal of all but adult 1 on station 3. White areas indicate the level of activity after removal for adult 1 only. Abbreviations for the host species are:

Scarus > 30 = *Scarus* spp. > 30 cm st. 1.
Scarus > 10 = *Scarus* spp. > 10 cm st. 1., < 30 cm st. 1.
Scarus < 10 = *Scarus* spp. < 10 cm st. 1.
Ctenoch. = *Ctenochaetus strigosus*
Zebrasom. = *Zebrasoma* spp.
Naso bre. = *Naso brevirostris*
Dasycyllus = *Dasycyllus albisella*
Abudefduf = *Abudefduf abdominalis*
Pomacent. = *Pomacentrus jenkinsi*

Chromis = *Chromis ovalis*
Zanclus = *Zanclus canescens*
Thalass. = *Thalassoma duperrey*
Cheilinus = *Cheilinus rhodochrous*
Bodianus = *Bodianus bilunulatus*
Parup. por. = *Parupeneus porphyreus*
Parup. mul. = *P. multifasciatus*
Mul. sam. = *Mulloidichthys samoensis*
Chaet. mil. = *Chaetodon miliaris*
Chaet. lun. = *Chaetodon lunula*

behavior was approximated by counting the number of individuals that were posing in each 3.7-second interval. The numbers of individuals posing increased after removal. The distribution of the number of hosts posing was randomly distributed before removal ($S^2/\bar{x} = 0.94$, p > 0.2 of randomness) and evenly distributed after removal ($S^2/\bar{x} = 0.66$, p < 0.003 of randomness).

When the host species are considered separately, the results are different. Of the 14 host species which were commonly observed, 10 showed significant increases in the median p/i ratio after the removal of cleaners (p < 0.05 by Rank Sum method), 3 species showed

insignificant increases in the median p/i ratio and one showed an insignificant decrease. The observed alterations in the p/i ratio reflect a variety of behavioral changes (Table 3). The total duration, bout length and number of bouts for posing and inspecting show different combinations of increase, decrease, or no change at all. The sums of the "+" and "–" scores in Table 3 give an indication of the consistency of the changes in each variable. The p/i ratio is by far the most consistent, followed by bout length, total duration, and finally, number of bouts.

The diversity of the interactions of the cleaner was approximated by an information-

TABLE 3. TRENDS OBSERVED IN THE CHANGES OF SELECTED BEHAVIORAL MEASURES. SYMBOLS ARE: + = INCREASED AFTER CLEANER REMOVAL (p > 0.05), ++ = INCREASED (p < 0.05), − = DECREASED AFTER CLEANER REMOVAL (p > 0.05), —— = DECREASED (p < 0.05), 0 = NO TREND INDICATED, ? = INSUFFICIENT OBSERVATIONS TO SHOW ANY TREND. N = TOTAL NUMBER OF INTERACTIONS.

Species	Duration of actions			Bout length		Bout number		N	Remarks
	Pose								
	Inspect	Inspect	Pose	Inspect	Pose	Inspect	Pose		
Scarus > 300*	++	?	+	?	0	0	0	9	no *inspect* after removal
Scarus > 100*	++	++	++	++	++	++	++	132	
Scarus < 100*	++	——	—	+	++	——	——	97	
Ctenochaetus strigosus	+	+	+	++	+	0	+	54	
Zebrasoma flavescens	++	0	+	0	++	0	0	17	
Naso unicornis	++	0	0	?	?	0	0	8	no *pose* before and no *inspect* after removal
Dascyllus albisella	++	——	——	—	——	——	——	84	
Abudefduf abdominalis	++	+	++	++	+	+	++	75	
Pomacentrus jenkinsi	?	——	——	?	?	——	——	11	no interactions *after* removal
Chromis ovalis	?	++	++	?	?	++	++	91	no interactions *before* removal
Zanclus clanescens	+	++	++	+	0	++	++	30	
Thalassoma duperrey	++	+	+	++	++	—	0	74	
Cheilinus rhodochrous	++	0	——	—	+	——	——	24	
Bodianus bilunulatus	+	0	0	—	+	0	0	16	
Parupeneus porphyreus	?	0	0	?	?	0	0	4	no pose or inspect before removal
Parupeneus multifasciatus	++	+	0	+	+	0	0	10	
Mulloidichthys samoensis	—	+	0	+	++	0	0	18	
SUM OF ±	+22	+ 5	+ 5	+ 9	+13	− 2	+ 1	754	

* These categories include *S. dubius* and *S. sordidus* which are subdivided as to estimated total length. "*Scarus* < 100" are less than 100 mm st. l., "*Scarus* > 100" are between 100 and 300 mm st. l. and "*Scarus* > 300" are greater than 300 mm st. l.

theoretical method (Lloyd, et al., 1968). This method assumes that the sample is a random portion of the individual's repertoire. The diversity increases with both the number of species interacting, and with the equitability with which the cleaner's services are divided up amongst the species. When the diversity index (H) is based on the number of seconds that each host species was inspected by the cleaner, H increased after the removal of cleaners. But when H is based on the number of inspect bouts that were received by each host species, there was no change in diversity.

Inspecting and cleaning by occasional cleaners was observed only in adult *Chaetodon miliaris* before the removal of *L. phthirophagus* (1 second out of 72 minutes). After removal, 92 minutes of observation included 28.3 seconds of inspecting by juvenile *Bodianus bilunulatus*, 1 second by an adult *C. miliaris* and 1 second by a young

Scarus sp. (about 100 mm st. l.). The variability of the data renders this increase insignificant (p > 0.1). But it is important to note that in the many hours of informal observation before removal, no additional cleaning by other species was observed. The amount of cleaning by other species (0.6% of the total time) however, was far less than that previously accomplished by *L. phthirophagus*. Two evening dives (2100 to 2330) were made after removal to check for nocturnal cleaning, particularly by shrimps as observed by E. S. Hobson (pers. comm. 1971) in Kealakakua Bay, Hawaii. One instance of cleaning by a small, translucent shrimp on *C. miliaris* was observed. None of the numerous boxer shrimp, *Stenopus hispidus*, was observed cleaning.

Host density distributions after removal of cleaners.—In order to compare the distributions of host fish around the two reefs, the census samples were standardized as to the

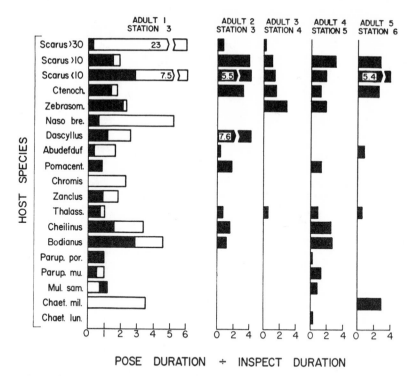

Fig. 4. The median pose to inspect ratio for *Labroides phthirophagus* during interactions with various host species. Black areas indicate the ratio before removal of all but adult 1 on station 3. White areas indicate the ratio after removal for adult 1 only. For abbreviations of host species see legend of figure 3.

compass bearings of the cleaning stations. This was necessary since many fish aggregate on the windward or ENE portion of the reef (as evidenced by the non-random distribution of cleaning stations) and face into the wind driven current. Reef 2 was divided into 6 sectors, equidistant between the 6 cleaning stations. When the resulting sectors were projected over the distribution of the stations on reef 1, only the sector that surrounded station number 2 did not include a station on reef 1. Consequently, this sector was divided in the center and lumped with the sectors on either side. As a result, both reefs were divided into 5 sectors (342°–65°–93°–135°–265°–342°). When sectors included more than one station on reef 1, the census counts for these stations were averaged.

Comparisons for each host species show that the distributions of *Scarus* spp. < 300 mm, > 100 mm st. l., *Dascyllus albisella* and three species of mullids differed between the reefs and were skewed toward station 3 on

reef 2 where the remaining cleaner was located ($p < 0.05$ by Kendall's Measure of Concordance, Tate and Clelland, 1959). *Zanclus canescens* appeared to show the same trend but the difference lacked significance ($p > 0.1$). None of the other species showed any clear trends.

Ectoparasite assays.—The ectoparasite assays showed no significant differences between the reefs (Tables 4 and 5). There appeared to be slightly more frequent infections by small monogeneid trematodes and caligoid copepods on reef 2 and slightly more frequent occurrence of lernaeid copepods on reef 1. No differences in the overall condition of the fish on reefs 1 and 2 were noted while diving. It is interesting to note the specificity of certain types of parasites, particularly the lernaeid copepods, and the overall scarcity of ectoparasites.

DISCUSSION

The removal of cleaner fish from a reef produces significant changes in the behav-

TABLE 4. THE PERCENT OF HOST FISH INFECTED BY AT LEAST ONE ECTOPARASITE ON REEF 1 (WITH CLEANERS) AND REEF 2 (WITHOUT CLEANERS). N = NUMBER OF HOST FISH SAMPLED.

| Host species | Location | N | Monogeneid trematodes | | Caligoid copepods | Lernaeid copepods | Cymothoid isopods |
			< 1 mm	> 1 mm			
Chaetodon miliaris							
	Reef 1	11	18%	9%	36%	0%	0%
	Reef 2	10	40	0	60	0	0
Chaetodon lunula							
	Reef 1	3	0	0	33	100	33
	Reef 2	5	0	0	0	60	20
Chaetodon auriga							
	Reef 1	3	0	0	0	67	0
	Reef 2	1	100	0	0	0	0
Ctenochaetus strigosus							
	Reef 1	6	33	17	0	0	0
	Reef 2	7	57	0	0	0	0
Acanthurus xanthopterus							
	Reef 1	5	0	0	0	0	0
	Reef 2	3	0	33	0	0	0
Zebrasoma veliferum							
	Reef 1	2	0	0	0	0	0
	Reef 2	2	0	0	0	0	0
Zebrasoma flavescens							
	Reef 1	2	0	0	0	0	0
	Reef 2	1	0	0	0	0	0
Thalassoma duperrey							
	Reef 1	10	40	20	0	0	0
	Reef 2	11	9	27	9	0	18
All Species							
	Reef 1	42	19	10	12	12	2
	Reef 2	40	25	10	25	8	8

ioral ecology of both host fish and the remaining cleaner. But these changes need not be accompanied by any change in ectoparasitic infestation. All of the behavioral changes point toward an increase in the "work load" of the remaining *L. phthirophagus* and other, more occasional cleaners. Inspection by the remaining cleaner increased both in absolute amount and in the diversity of hosts serviced. This indicates that hosts that had formerly been serviced by the other cleaners were probably interacting with the remaining cleaner instead. But the total amount of inspecting was less than that previously accomplished by all of the cleaners on the reef (62% total time vs. an estimated 136%, respectively). Posing increased in total duration and bout length, and posing bouts were more closely spaced. Posing also increased in the amount given per unit of inspection, but the absolute amount of pos-

ing and inspecting varied widely between host species. While diving, the density of host fish on station 3 appeared to be greater than expected after the removal of the other cleaners, but quantitative analysis of the distribution as compared with a similar control reef showed that only a few species altered their distribution toward the remaining cleaner.

Youngbluth (1968) failed to observe any change in the number of interactions after the removal of all but one *L. phthirophagus*. My results indicate that number of interactions is the least consistent indicator of the behavioral changes which occur (see Table 3). His manipulation of the reef may have produced similar changes which were not detected due to the insensitivity of the measurement.

The lack of any change in the level of ectoparasitic infestation indicated by Young-

TABLE 5. THE MEAN NUMBER OF ECTOPARASITES PER HOST FISH ON REEF 1 (WITH CLEANERS) AND REEF 2 (WITHOUT CLEANERS). N = NUMBER OF HOST FISH SAMPLED.

| Host species | Location | N | Monogeneid trematodes | | Caligoid copepods | Lernaeid copepods | Cymothoid isopods |
			< 1 mm	> 1 mm			
Chaetodon miliaris							
	Reef 1	11	0.2	0.2	0.6	0	0
	Reef 2	10	0.4	0	0.8	0	0
Chaetodon lunula							
	Reef 1	3	0	0	0.3	9.3	0.3
	Reef 2	5	0	0	0	1.6	0.2
Chaetodon auriga							
	Reef 1	3	0	0	0	3.7	0
	Reef 2	1	1	0	0	0	0
Ctenochaetus strigosus							
	Reef 1	6	0.3	0.2	0	0	0
	Reef 2	7	1.7	0	0	0	0
Acanthurus xanthopterus							
	Reef 1	5	0	0	0	0	0
	Reef 2	3	0	0.3	0	0	0
Zebrasoma veliferum							
	Reef 1	2	0	0	0	0	0
	Reef 2	2	0	0	0	0	0
Zebrasoma flavescens							
	Reef 1	2	0	0	0	0	0
	Reef 2	1	0	0	0	0	0
Thalassoma duperrey							
	Reef 1	10	1.1	0.4	0	0	0
	Reef 2	11	0.1	0.7	0.3	0	0.2
All species							
	Reef 1	42	0.4	0.2	0.2	0.9	0.02
	Reef 2	40	0.5	0.2	0.3	0.2	0.08

bluth (1968) agrees with present findings. It is difficult to explain the previous conclusion that the removal of cleaners leads to a drastic increase in ectoparasitism (Limbaugh, 1961) unless the rate of ectoparasitic infestation was much higher in his Caribbean study area, or the lack of quantification and control led him to unwarranted conclusions.

These results pose several questions:

1. If ectoparasitic infestations did not increase in the absence of cleaners, what caused the behavioral changes?

2. Why did the host species respond so variably to the removal of the cleaner?

3. What is the relationship between the density of ectoparasites and predation on ectoparasites by cleaner fish?

4. What is the ecological function of cleaning symbiosis?

Several lines of experimental and observa-tional evidence suggest a hypothesis as to the causes and function of cleaning symbiosis. It is best to develop the hypothesis by examining each of the questions in sequence.

1. What Causes the Behavioral Changes?

This question may be subdivided into the causation of posing and inspecting behavior. As outlined above, the probability of inspecting is increased by pose behavior and recognition of host fish, particularly preferred hosts (those with low p/i ratios) such as large *Scarus* spp. But inspecting is also subject to decremental effects which decrease the probability of its repeated occurrence (Losey, 1971). Some cleaners may also be attracted by prospective food items on the host (Wickler, 1968, E. S. Hobson in Losey, 1971).

The probability of posing is increased by inspecting and recognition of cleaners. The probability that a fish will pose is increased when they are deprived of cleaning (Losey, 1971).

The above factors account for the increase in the p/i ratio and the overall amount of inspecting. In general, deprived hosts show more pose behavior which releases more inspecting, but the p/i ratio increases due to a decrement in inspecting. It appears clear that the increase in posing did not depend on increased ectoparasitic infections but this relationship has not yet been shown by experimental analysis.

2. What Causes the Variability in Response?

One more factor is needed to explain the variability of the increase or decrease in posing for the various host species. Host fish will pose for a model of a cleaner fish (Fricke, 1966, Losey, 1971). When a moving model is used, the host fish position themselves so that they receive tactile stimulation from the model. This tactile stimulation serves as a positive reinforcement for posing in *Chaetodon auriga* as shown by classical and instrumental conditioning techniques (Losey, MS.). They appear to learn to recognize cleaners through tactile reinforcement. When *C. auriga* is deprived of tactile reinforcement, the pose response to the model and to other conditioned stimuli extinguishes. This phenomenon may prove to be widespread in fishes and is suggested by Abel (1971) who found a correlation between chafing and posing movements in freshwater fishes. Learning of recognition signals is also suggested by the exact resemblance of the cleaner mimic, *Aspidontus taeniatus* (Wickler, 1963).

Nonpreferred hosts interact with the cleaners at normally high p/i ratios and thus receive less inspection and, conjecturally, receive less tactile stimulation per unit of pose than do preferred hosts. On this basis nonpreferred hosts might be expected to extinguish the pose response at high p/i ratios. Extinction of response is even more likely in interactions with a living cleaner since the cleaning process may also result in negative tactile reinforcement due to biting and scale removal (Losey, 1971). Three of the hosts which showed a reduction in the duration of pose after cleaner removal are nonpreferred hosts (*Scarus* < 100 mm st. l., *Dascyllus albisella* and *Cheilinus rhodochrous*) as determined by previous observations (e.g. see Losey, 1971, p. 52); the remaining species

(*Pomacentrus jenkinsi*) is highly territorial and at least not strongly preferred.

In summary, one explanation of the variable changes in behavior is the extinction of the pose response in individuals of nonpreferred species due to a lack of tactile stimulation. The motivational basis for posing is not thoroughly understood, but it may be more closely related to tactile reinforcement by the cleaner than to irritation by ectoparasites.

3. Ectoparasite Density and Predation by Cleaners

The results suggest that there may be little relationship between the density of fish ectoparasites and predation by *L. phthirophagus*. These results might be expected if the fish populations of these reefs were primarily migratory. Wass (1967) removed all of the fish from a similar reef in Kaneohe Bay and monitored the subsequent repopulation of the reef. A few species, particularly small *Scarus* spp., evidenced frequent migratory behavior as reported by Bardach (1958) for this group in Bermuda. But the adults of most species were slow to repopulate the reef. Thus while some species might be cleaned on other reefs, frequent migration alone cannot explain the general lack of any increase in the number of ectoparasites.

While the gut contents of cleaners include ectoparasites, they may also include large numbers of fish scales (Youngbluth, 1968) with associated dermal and epidermal tissues, and some individuals may also feed on plankton. Their cleaning behavior with large fish which have a plentiful supply of mucus such as scarids, acanthurids and labrids is highly suggestive of mucus grazing as suggested for *Runula azalea* by Hobson (1969). In short, ectoparasites may form only a small portion of the diet of some cleaners. This limited predation pressure may be insignificant when compared with other sources of ectoparasite mortality. It is crucial at this point to gain some information as to the standing crop of ectoparasites available to cleaners in Hawaii.

Data on the number of ectoparasites found on fishes in California (Hobson, 1971) suggest that the standing crop of ectoparasites is far greater than in Hawaii. In addition, he found that the garibaldi, *Hypsypops rubicunda*, became more heavily parasitized during the reproductive period when cleaner fishes were not allowed in their territory.

4. What is the Function of Cleaning?

Discussion of the function of a symbiosis may be approached in many ways depending on the degree to which the association appears to be commensal, parasitic, mutualistic, etc. Physiological dependency (Cheng, 1967), population success (Odum, 1959), and selective advantage (Allee et al., 1949) are commonly used indicators of the type of symbiosis. Communication between symbionts should reflect the selective alvantage of the association and may be used as an indicator of the type of symbiosis. For example, commensalism or parasitism is suggested when only one member of the association responds to signals in a manner which initiates or maintains the symbiosis. Mutualism is suggested when both of the parties respond to signals in this manner. Mutualism is particularly likely when both parties also appear to generate signals which function only in the symbiosis and appear to have evolved for this purpose. Cleaning symbiosis might be appraised from all of these standpoints.

Physiological dependency.—L. *phthirophagus* has been listed as an obligate cleaner (Randall, 1958, Youngbluth, 1968). My experiences support this contention in that most individuals do not exploit any non-symbiotic food source to any appreciable degree, and when held without host fishes, they usually refuse alternate food supplies and die from starvation. But this does not mean that they are dependent on a diet of ectoparasites, necrotic tissue and "unwanted" food particles. They appear to be physiologically dependent on the host fishes as a substratum for grazing, whether they feed on ectoparasites, scales and associated dermal and epidermal tissues, or mucus.

The results of this study suggest that, at the levels of parasitism encountered in Kaneohe Bay, the host fish are not physiologically dependent on L. *phthirophagus*. Thus, with physiological dependency as the sole indicator, cleaning behavior in Kaneohe Bay would be classified as a parasitic association according to the guidelines suggested by Cheng (1967).

Population success and selective advantage.—Although there is no direct evidence allowing an assessment of these factors, we might surmise that the symbiosis in Kaneohe Bay contributes to the success of L. *phthi-*rophagus, but that it has little effect on the host population. According to the classification suggested by Odum (1959), cleaning would be ranked as commensalism.

Communication.—Both cleaners and hosts respond to signals in a manner that initiates and maintains the association (inspecting and posing, respectively). They also generate signals which appear to be unique to the symbiosis (inspecting, dancing, Wickler 1963, and posing). Such "cooperation" is an indication of possible mutualism.

Removal of ectoparasites is certainly the most obvious possibility for the adaptive function of the symbiosis and the reason for its widespread occurrence and ecological success. But this function need not form the causal basis of the interaction in terms of motivational and stimulus-response relationships, and it may not be active over the entire geographic range of the symbiosis. The mutualistic nature of the communication system could be maintained by the tactile reinforcement of the hosts and the physiological dependency and adaptive value of the association to the cleaner. In areas where there is a high rate of ectoparasitic infestation, the adaptive function of ectoparasite removal may be important to the host fish in terms of physiological dependency, population success and survival value. But in areas with a low rate of ectoparasitic infestation, the adaptive function may be minimized. The relationship would be of little selective disadvantage to the hosts since the cleaners probably remove little material from each individual and predation on posing host fish has never been observed (see Feder, 1966).

If the scale of this experiment was expanded, it is possible that the level of ectoparasitic infestation would show some increase. For example, if most of the cleaners in all of Kaneohe Bay were removed, the populations of ectoparasites might increase. Additional time might also reveal an increase in ectoparasites, but this appears less likely since the present study lasted for nine months, and Hobson (1971) found evidence of an increase in ectoparasitic infestation over shorter periods in California. There may also be considerable variability in the number of ectoparasites between years since Clarke (1970) found far fewer ectoparasites on *Hypsypops rubicunda* than Hobson (1971) in the same study area.

Conclusions

The hypothesis as to the function of cleaning symbiosis involves a separation between adaptive or ultimate factors and proximate causal factors. Cleaner fishes are adapted to feeding on the surfaces of other fishes. Some ectoparasitic fishes feed primarily on skin, scales, and mucus, but cleaners also feed on ectoparasites. Some cleaners feed primarily on inanimate substrata or on zooplankton and only occasionally on fishes. While the removal of skin and scales presents negative tactile stimuli to the host, cleaners also provide positive tactile reinforcement through contact with their fins and body. Tactile stimulation leads to posing and seeming cooperation and soliciting behavior in *Chaetodon auriga* and possibly other hosts. Such tactile stimulation may be similar to grooming in many higher vertebrates and might otherwise be obtained through chafing and rubbing movements in fish. Tactile stimulation might also be important in behavior such as "glancing" in some young cichlid fishes (Ward and Barlow, 1967). The adaptive value of ectoparasite removal has probably favored the response of host fishes to this stimulation and has perhaps shaped the form of the pose response and the associated learning system in the evolution of the host species.

Cleaning symbiosis must satisfy the requirements of a mutualistic relationship over at least a portion of its range. But due to an evident lack of any direct connection between the adaptive function of ectoparasite removal and the proximal causal factors, cleaning may exist in a form which at least approaches a commensal or even parasitic relationship.

Acknowledgments

This work was supported by NIH Postdoctoral Fellowship 1-F2-GM-38,866, AEC Contract No. AT(29-2)-226 and a U. H. Intramural Research Grant. I thank Mr. Peter Rosti for his help throughout the project and Dr. Edmund S. Hobson and Mr. Marshall Youngbluth for their suggestions and discussion.

Literature Cited

ABEL, E. F. 1971. Zur Ethologie von Putzsymbiosen einheimischer Süsswasserfische im natürlichen Biotop. Oecologia (Berl.) 6:133–151.

ALLEE, W. C., A. E. EMERSON, O. PARK, T. PARK, K. P. SCHMIDT. 1949. Principles of animal ecology. W. B. Saunders, Philadelphia.

BARDACH, J. E. 1958. On the movements of certain Bermuda reef fishes. Ecology 39:139–146.

BATSCHELET, E. 1965. Statistical methods for the analysis of problems in animal orientation and certain biological rhythms. Amer. Inst. Biol. Sci.

CHENG, T. C. 1967. Marine molluscs as hosts for symbioses. Adv. Marine Biol. 5.

CLARKE, T. C. 1970. Territorial behavior and population dynamics of a pomacentrid fish, the garibaldi, *Hypsypops rubicunda*. Ecol. Monogr. 40:189–212.

FAULKNER, D. 1965. Finned doctors of the deep. National Geographic, 128:867–873.

FEDER, H. M. 1966. Cleaning symbiosis in the marine environment, p. 327–380. *In:* Symbiosis, ed. S. M. Henry, Academic Press.

FRICKE, H. 1966. Zum Verhalten des Putzerfisches, *Labroides dimidiatus*. Z. Tierpsychol. 23:1–3.

HOBSON, E. S. 1969. Comments on generalizations about cleaning symbiosis. Pacific Sci. 23: 35–39.

————. 1971. Cleaning symbiosis among California inshore fishes. Fishery Bull., 69:491–523.

LIMBAUGH, C. 1961. Cleaning symbiosis. Sci. Amer. 205:42–49.

LLOYD, M., J. H. ZAR AND J. R. KARR. 1968. On the calculation of information-theoretical measures of diversity. Amer. Midland Nat. 79:257–272.

LOSEY, G. S. 1971. Communication between fishes in cleaning symbiosis, p. 45–76. *In:* Aspects of the biology of symbiosis, ed. T. C. Cheng. Univ. Park Press.

ODUM, E. P. 1959. Fundamentals of ecology. W. B. Saunders Co.

RANDALL, J. E. 1958. A review of the labrid fish genus *Labroides*, with descriptions of two new species and notes on ecology. Pacific Sci. 12:327–347.

STROUD, R. H., AND R. M. JENKINS. 1962. Saltwater parasite pickers. Sport Fisheries Inst. Bull. 129:1–3.

TATE, M. W., AND R. C. CLELLAND. 1957. Nonparametric and shortcut statistics, Interstate Printers and Publishers, Inc.

WARD, J. A., AND G. W. BARLOW. 1967. The maturation and regulation of glancing off the parents by young orange chromides (*Etroplus maculatus*: Pisces-Cichlidae). Behaviour 29: 1–56.

WASS, R. C. 1967. Removal and repopulation of the fishes on an isolated patch coral reef in Kaneohe Bay, Oahu, Hawaii. M.S. thesis, U. of Hawaii.

WICKLER, W. 1963. Zum Problem der Signalbildung, am Beispiel der Verhaltensmimicry zwischen *Aspidontus* und *Labroides* (Pisces, Acanthopterygii). Z. Tierpsychol. 20:657–679.

————. 1968. Mimicry, World Univ. Library, N. Y.

YOUNGBLUTH, M. J. 1968. Aspects of the ecology and ethology of the cleaning fish *Labroides phthirophagus* Randall. Z. Tierpsychol. 25: 915–932.

UNIVERSITY OF HAWAII, DEPARTMENT OF ZOOLOGY AND HAWAII INSTITUTE OF MARINE BIOLOGY, P.O. BOX 1067, KANEOHE, HAWAII 96744.

The nature of the symbiosis between Indo-Pacific anemone fishes and sea anemones

R. N. MARISCAL

Department of Biological Science, Florida State University; Tallahassee, Florida, USA

Abstract

Under the general heading of symbiosis, defined originally to mean a "living together" of two dissimilar species, exist the sub-categories of mutualism (where both partners benefit), commensalism (where one partner benefits and the other is neutral) and parasitism (where one partner benefits and the other is harmed). The sea anemone-fish (mainly of the genus *Amphiprion*) symbiosis has generally been considered to benefit only the fish, and thus has been called commensal in nature. Recent field and laboratory observations, however, suggest that this symbiosis more closely approaches mutualism in which both partners benefit to some degree. The fishes benefit by receiving protection from predators among the nematocyst-laden tentacles of the sea anemone host, perhaps by receiving some form of tactile stimulation, by being less susceptible to various diseases and by feeding on anemone tissue, prey, waste material and perhaps crustacean symbionts. The sea anemones benefit by receiving protection from various predators, removal of necrotic tissue, perhaps some form of tactile stimulation, removal of inorganic and organic material from on and around the anemone, possible removal of anemone "parasites", and by being provided food by some species of *Amphiprion*.

Introduction

Past attempts to characterize or study, systematically, the nature of symbiotic associations has been hampered, due, in part at least, to the confusing terminology used in various parts of the world. In his foreword, HENRY (1966) touches upon these problems, many of which can be traced back to a misinterpretation of DE BARY's original definition of symbiosis. DE BARY (1879) apparently intended the term symbiosis to mean simply a "living together" of two dissimilar organisms, regardless of whether this association was parasitic or commensal in nature. It is this more general definition of symbiosis which I shall follow, and under which will be placed the sub-categories of mutualism, commensalism and parasitism. Mutualism is here used to define a symbiotic association in which both partners benefit: commensalism is a situation in which one partner benefits and the other is neither harmed nor benefited: parasitism exists when one partner is benefited and the other is harmed by the association (ALLEE, et al., 1949; NOBLE and NOBLE, 1964; HENRY, 1966).

The symbiosis between tropical pomacentrid fishes, mainly of the genus *Amphiprion*, and giant stoichactiid sea anemones from the Indo-Pacific has attracted the interest of zoologists for many years. Until recently, however, relatively little serious study has been devoted to analyzing the nature of this symbiosis and the behavioral interactions of its participants. Generally, this symbiotic association has been described as commensal in nature, without the benefit of supporting field or laboratory evidence. The usual supposition is that such small, brightly colored fishes must find protection from predators among the nematocyst-laden tentacles of their anemone hosts, and that no obvious advantage accrues to the latter from such an association. The present paper presents the results of field and laboratory observations and experiments which indicate that rather than commensal, the pomacentrid

fish-sea anemone symbiosis is probably best characterized as mutualistic, with both partners benefiting.

Materials and methods

Field and laboratory studies were conducted on 15 species of fishes from the family Pomacentridae (including 12 species of *Amphiprion*, 1 *Premnas* and 2 *Dascyllus*). The tropical sea anemone hosts studied were *Radianthus ritteri*, *R. koseirensis*, *R. kuekenthali*, *R. malu*, *Stoichactis kenti*, *S. giganteum*, *Physobrachia ramsayi* and *Cryptodendrum adhesivum*. Field studies were conducted in the following areas: Oahu Island, Hawaiian Islands; Tutuila Island, E. Samoa; Viti Levu Island and Great Astrolabe Reef, Fiji Islands: Vanikoro Island, Santa Cruz Islands: Guadalcanal Island and Bougainville Island, Solomon Islands: New Britain Island and New Guinea, Territory of New Guinea; Green Island, Great Barrier Reef, N. Queensland, Australia: Tahiti Island, Society Islands; Kenya, E. Africa: Mahé Island, Seychelles Islands: Malé Atoll, Maldive Islands: Ceylon: Pipilek and Pipidon Islands, W. Thailand.

Experimental studies and observations were conducted using both the shipboard aquaria aboard the R. V. "Te Vega" and in specially constructed 20 gallon (75 l) Plexiglas laboratory aquaria in California, USA. Most laboratory studies were conducted with *Amphiprion xanthurus*, and the common tropical anemone *Stoichactis kenti*.

Results

Benefit to the fishes

Protection

Diurnal predators. Protection from predatory fishes has been long thought to be the primary advantage gained by *Amphiprion* in its association with sea anemones, and there are field and laboratory experiments which support this idea. For example, SLUITER (1888) found that aquarium *Amphiprion percula* were unharmed in the presence of larger predatory fish so long as the anemones were present. Upon removal of the anemones, however, *A. percula* were eaten by predators. VERWEY (1930) and COATES (1964) have reported similar aquarium observations, while EIBL-EIBESFELDT (1960) and the author have observed this in the field.

In field experiments off W. Thailand, I found that *Amphiprion percula* when removed from their *Radianthus ritteri* anemone and released up to 10 m away, were often eaten by larger predatory fishes in the vicinity. Even small non-predatory fishes of several species, including a school of small yellow pomacentrids, immediately surrounded and attacked the bright orange *A. percula* when away from their anemone. If no predatory fish were in the vicinity, the *A. percula* seemed able to make their way back to their anemone in about 5 to 15 min. However, small groupers lurking among the coral heads devoured 5 of the smaller *A. percula* out of the 15 tested, while the remainder managed to return to their anemones. When released at the surface, the *A. percula* immediately dived to the bottom, some 8 feet (2.4 m) down, and remained bobbing in place as if attempting to orient in the unfamiliar location. They then set off, remaining together, usually in the general direction of their anemone, although the latter was always shielded from view. ABEL (1960 b) and MARISCAL (in press) have both commented on the well-developed spatial orientation of *Amphiprion* to features in the vicinity of the anemone, and it may be that this underlies the fairly successful returns of the fish to their anemones. *A. percula*, however, were such poor swimmers that they had great difficulty in even making headway against the current over the reef at the time. This tends to argue against the idea that this *Amphiprion* species may be found free-living, something I have never observed throughout the Indo-Pacific. Some species of *Amphiprion* (e.g. *A. xanthurus*) however, are relatively strong swimmers, and may be found up to several meters from their anemones, thus giving the illusion of being free-living. In addition, the anemones are often well camouflaged and difficult to see among the coral until the *Amphiprion* are pursued into them.

In both the field and the shipboard aquaria, what appeared to be attacks on *Amphiprion* were broken off when the latter retreated into the tentacles of the host anemone. For example, off Funidu Island in the Maldives, whenever a specimen of *Amphiprion xanthurus* ventured too far from its anemone, it was attacked by a larger *Pomacentrus* sp. These attacks forced *A. xanthurus* back onto the anemone's disc, with the *Pomacentrus* closely following. However, the latter approached no closer than several centimeters from the tentacles, whereupon the attacks ceased.

In the shipboard aquarium, a relatively large *Pomacentrus tripunctatus* paid no attention to several Seychelles *Amphiprion akallopisos* when in their *Radianthus ritteri* anemone. However, when one of the *A. akallopisos* left the anemone, or if an isolated *A. akallopisos* was introduced, it was immediately attacked until it found shelter among the anemone's

Fig. 1. Electronic flash photograph showing the nocturnal coloration of a dark-adapted *Amphiprion xanthurus* in the tentacles of its *Radianthus* anemone. Note the faded color of both the body and white bars

tentacles. When the *A. akallopisos* were among the tentacles of their anemone or near it, they were ignored by *P. tripunctatus*.

SAVILLE-KENT (1893) first made the interesting observation that *Amphiprion* had been seen entering the mouth or coelenteron of their host for protection. WEBER (1913) and HERRE (1936) have also reported such behavior. However, WHITLEY (1927, 1929, 1932), VERWEY (1930) and GOHAR (1934, 1948) have all reportedly looked for such behavior in the field and have never observed it, nor has the author. CUTRESS, however (personal communication), has captured *Amphiprion* in this fashion after they sought refuge in the coelenteron of their host.

Nocturnal predators. In addition to its diurnal protective function, the host anemone serves as a refuge for the anemone fishes at night. At dusk, *Amphiprion* in both shipboard and laboratory aquaria settle into the tentacles of their anemone and become immobile. The fish also change color, becoming very pale so that their body color and previously contrasting white bars blend to nearly match the background color of the anemone's lighter tentacles (Fig. 1). This would seem to be an obvious adaptation to reduce the chances of a predator plucking the inactive fish from among the anemone's tentacles. This color change has been observed for *A. akallopisos, A. nigripes, A. percula*, and *A. xanthurus*. As soon as such fishes are exposed to light, they immediately begin reverting to their normal diurnal coloration (Fig. 2). No change in the anemone's color was observed at night.

Fig. 2. Electronic flash photograph of the same dark-adapted fish shown in Fig. 1 about 2 min after turning on light. Note that the normal diurnal coloration of black body and white bars has nearly returned, following exposure to the artificial light source

Other pomacentrids which associate with sea anemones such as *Dascyllus trimaculatus* and *D. albisella* as well as *D. aruanus* (a non-anemone symbiont) also showed a distinct blanching of the black portions of the body as well as a fading of the white-pigmented areas, thus reducing overall contrast at night. The white bars of the various *Amphiprion* species studied also underwent a pronounced fading which caused them to take on a grayish appearance, thus matching rather well their faded black or orange body color.

In the case of anemones which contract at night, the *Amphiprion* settled into the depression formed by the withdrawn tentacles.

The nocturnal behavior of *Amphiprion xanthurus* isolated from sea anemones was remarkably similar to its behavior when kept with anemones. Instead of settling into the anemone at night, however, the isolated fish settled into holes which they had dug in the bottom gravel, or leaned up against the side of the aquarium or the filter tube where they remained motionless until dawn. Similarly, they also underwent a blanching in color as did those fish with anemones.

Tactile stimulation

Observations of anemone fish vigorously "bathing" among the tentacles and oral disc folds suggest that the fish are perhaps deriving some sort of tactile stimulation from the anemone. This idea, although difficult to prove, has received tentative support from observations on *Amphiprion xanthurus* kept isolated

Fig. 3. Two *Amphiprion xanthurus* isolated from any contact with sea anemones, which have begun bathing among bubbles from the aquarium air stone. The larger fish often backed completely into the air stream and allowed itself to be carried to the top of the aquarium as shown here

from contact with sea anemones. Such isolated fish adopt features of their aquarium which not only furnish concealment, but which also appear to provide a certain degree of tactile stimulation (MARISCAL, 1966b). These features include tufts of algae, holes in the bottom gravel, and bubbles from the air stone (Fig. 3).

Regarding the latter, it was observed that isolated *Amphiprion* often swam or backed into the air stream and allowed themselves to be carried to the top of the aquarium by the flow of bubbles, whereupon they would exit and repeat the same behavior. While backing into the stream of bubbles, the fish often turned slightly to one side, thus allowing a larger surface area to be contacted by the bubbles. During such behavior, the bubbles were easily observed to be deflected off the body of the fish. The fish also settled into tufts of algae and holes they had constructed in the bottom gravel and in general behaved towards these objects much as they did towards an anemone. Upon re-introduction of the anemone, the same fish

lost interest in such objects, and again directed their attention solely towards the anemone. It is thus possible that isolated fish adopt such features of the aquarium because they provide a certain amount of tactile stimulation lacking in the absence of the anemone.

Parasite removal

DE CRESPIGNY (1869) suggested that the sea anemone might be effective in removing ectoparasites from the fish. However, MARISCAL (1966b) and BOWMAN and MARISCAL (1968) report evidence to the contrary. They found that *Amphiprion akallopisos* in the Seychelles Islands were much more heavily infested with an ectoparasitic isopod of the genus *Renocila* than were any of the other reef fishes in this area (Fig. 4). At least 5% of the *Amphiprion* observed, photographed and collected in Port Victoria, Mahé Island, were found with this isopod, while only a single juvenile chaetodont (*Chaetodon zanzibarensis*) out of the hundreds of other fishes observed underwater or collected with rotenone, was similarly parasitized. Therefore, rather than the *Amphiprion* being relatively free of ectoparasites, they were selectively much more heavily parasitized than other species of fishes observed in this area. Although the reasons for this are unclear, it must be concluded that, at least in this case, the anemone provides no advantage to its symbiotic fish in inhibiting crustacean ectoparasites.

Amphiprion, however, seem to be much less susceptible to various common protozoan and fungous aquarium diseases when kept with sea anemones than when isolated. Whether this has a psychological or a physiological basis remains to be investigated.

The anemone as a food source

Nibbling of the tentacles of the host anemone by *Amphiprion* has been observed by many workers including the author (MARISCAL, 1966a, b). Although mucus, sloughed-off cell fragments, and zooxanthellae are probably ingested in this fashion, I have observed various species of *Amphiprion* tear off and ingest long pieces of tentacle as well. This has been observed in aquaria for *A. akallopisos*, *A. nigripes*, *A. xanthurus*, *A. percula*, and *A. ephippium* and, in the field, for *A. nigripes*.

In order to determine if *Amphiprion* was actually eating the tentacles, the stomach and gut contents of several freshly collected Seychelles *A. akallopisos* were examined microscopically. The stomachs contained many unfired (and some fired) basitrichous isorhiza and microbasic-b-mastigophore nematocysts as well as many zooxanthellae, all of which are found in the tentacles of the normal host anemone *Radianthus ritteri*. The remainder consisted of fat droplets and pieces of connective tissue. In the hind-gut, only a few recognizable nematocysts could be found, and the zooxanthellae appeared to be in an advanced state of digestion. Since the zooxanthellae were the major component of the stomach contents, it seems possible that these symbiotic algae could form at least a portion of the diet of *A. akallopisos*, in addition to whatever other food sources might be utilized.

Fecal analyses of aquarium *Amphiprion xanthurus* also revealed the presence of the same type of nematocysts as found in the tentacles of the host anemone *Stoichactis kenti*, again indicating that the tentacles were possibly being eaten by the fish.

The author has frequently noted, as have others, that many species of *Amphiprion* commonly bite at and ingest anemone waste material, mucus strands,

Fig. 4. Close-up photograph of the parasitic isopod *Renocila heterozota*, attached to the head of an adult *Amphiprion akallopisos* from the Seychelles. Note the damaged tissue posterior to the large female isopod. A smaller male was attached in this region

and anemone-captured food (SLUITER, 1888; VERWEY, 1930; YONGE, 1930; MOSER, 1931; GOHAR, 1934; KOENIG, 1960; MARISCAL, 1966b). The significance of such material in the diet of the fish is, however, unknown.

Another potential food source, that may inadvertently be provided the fishes, consists of the lichomolgid copepod, crab and shrimp symbionts found with these sea anemones (e.g. see HOLTHUIS, 1947, 1952; JACQUOTTE, 1964; HUMES, 1964; MARISCAL, 1966a, b). Several species of these minute copepods are commonly found with the stoichactiid anemones, and it is quite possible that these are preyed upon by *Amphiprion*. Several genera of shrimps, mainly *Periclimenes*, and a species of crab, *Petrolisthes ohshimai*, are often found with these anemones, and the juveniles could easily be ingested by the anemone fish.

Benefit to the sea anemones

Protection

Territoriality is well-developed in anemone fishes (see MARISCAL, 1966a, b). A by-product of a vigorous territorial defense by *Amphiprion* is that the host sea anemone may be "protected" from coelenterate predators. Various species of fishes (e.g. chaetodonts) are known to feed on sea anemones in both the field and aquaria (e.g. FISHELSON, 1965). I have observed reef fishes which were about to bite at the tentacles of a *Radianthus ritteri* anemone be chased off by the resident *Amphiprion akallopisos*. The same species of fish frequently attacked my hands or dip net as I attempted to collect the host anemone in the field. In other cases, this species sharply rapped the soles of my swim fins when the fins came too near their anemone. It seems likely that such territorial behavior might easily serve to deter predation on its host sea anemone under both field and aquarium conditions since some *Amphiprion*, at least, do not hesitate to attack objects many times their own size.

Tactile stimulation

Various workers have indicated that *Amphiprion* provides some form of tactile stimulation for its host sea anemone, in the absence of which the anemone may

be adversely affected and even die (DE CRESPIGNY, 1869; VERWEY, 1930; HERRE, 1936; GOHAR, 1948; KOENIG, 1960). However, apparently healthy host anemones may be found in the field, as well as in aquaria, without *Amphiprion*. Therefore, in the absence of any experimental evidence to the contrary, it must be assumed that the lack of fish does not adversely affect the host anemone. However, there is evidence that the host anemones may respond to the fish, when present (VERWEY, 1930; HERRE, 1936; GOHAR, 1948; MARISCAL, 1966b, in press).

For example, when a badly contracted anemone's column is rammed or struck by the symbiotic fish in quick succession over a short period of time, the anemone may expand, first on the side touched, and then completely. In some cases, I have been able to elicit expansion by gently kneading a contracted anemone's column with the fingers. Although it was assumed at the time that such observations could merely have been coincidental, recent evidence by Ross and SUTTON (1968) reveals that the symbiotic sea anemone *Calliactis* can be induced not only to expand rapidly when mechanically stimulated (by the host hermit crabs or inanimate objects), but also to detach its disc from the substrate. I have obtained similar results with Florida *Calliactis tricolor* and found that, in addition, stroking or tapping the pedal disc and column with the fingers and cotton-tipped applicators were effective in both rapidly expanding the anemone and causing it to detach from the substrate. Ross and SUTTON (1968) also found that this response could be elicited from *Calliactis* by means of electrical stimuli. It would be of interest to extend their experimental technique to other anemones including stoichactiids, both with and without *Amphiprion*.

Removal of anemone parasites

As mentioned earlier, it is known that some of the large tropical anemones harboring anemone fish, as well as others, are also hosts for copepods of the genus *Lichomolgus* (e.g. HUMES, 1964). I have collected several species of such copepods from both *Radianthus* and *Stoichactis* anemones. Although it has not been clearly established that they are parasitic on the anemones, it seems likely that the copepods may obtain food from the anemone in some fashion, since they are commonly found in the coelenteron, as well as on the oral disc and the tentacles. Due to the small size of such copepods, they are probably relatively unimportant in the diet of large adult *Amphiprion*. However, they could conceivably serve as a food source for juvenile fish which are often found deep among the tentacles or folds of the oral disc of the host anemones (MARISCAL, 1966b). In any case, it would be of interest to know if one function of the observed nibbling of a host anemone's tentacles is the capture of such copepods by *Amphiprion*.

Removal of necrotic tissue

DE CRESPIGNY (1869) and VERWEY (1930) have postulated that another possible benefit provided by the fish might be the removal of necrotic tentacle tissue. EIBL-EIBESFELDT (1960) and I have observed such behavior in the field, and I have also seen it under aquarium conditions; its significance to the anemone is, however, unknown.

Water and food circulation

Several authors have suggested that *Amphiprion*, through its normal swimming movements, might aid in the circulation of fresh oxygenated water (or removal of CO_2-rich water) as well as of food particles over its anemone (DE CRESPIGNY, 1869; SLUITER, 1888; VERWEY, 1930; HERRE, 1936). Although this could conceivably be of importance in shallow, slowly circulating portions of a reef, the areas observed by the author generally had an adequate circulation of water which would probably offset any contribution by the fish in this regard. Once again, experimental data are lacking and little more can be said regarding this idea.

Removal of organic material from the oral disc

VERWEY (1930), MOSER (1931), GOHAR (1948), EIBL-EIBESFELDT (1960), KOENIG (1960) and the author have all observed *Amphiprion* eating or removing organic wastes from the oral disc of the host anemone. Generally the normal body movements of the fish serve to keep the oral disc free of such material. However, almost any foreign object on the disc is subject to the attention of the *Amphiprion* and will be bitten at or nosed by the fish. Since there are many anemones which manage to survive adequately without the services of a symbiotic fish, the importance of the above behavior remains doubtful.

Removal of inorganic material from the anemone

Small pebbles, coral rubble or sand is often removed from the oral disc of the host anemone by the normal "bathing" behavior of the symbiotic fish among the tentacles. However, VERWEY (1930) reported that *Premnas biaculeatus* was observed to remove coral rubble and enlarge a hole around its anemone. I have similarly observed in an aquarium *Amphiprion xanthurus* pick up, and carry in its mouth, small pebbles which were deposited at some distance from the anemone. Although the bottom of the aquarium was covered with such pebbles, the fish seemed to select slightly larger or more irregular pebbles from that region of the substrate which was in contact with the margin of the anemone's oral disc. This behavior was repeated about 6 times over a 15 min period.

Feeding the anemone

The carrying of food to its anemone by *Amphiprion* has been observed by a number of authors (SLUITER, 1888; VERWEY, 1930; GOHAR, 1934, 1948; HERRE, 1936; LADIGES, 1939; KOENIG, 1960; GRAEFE, 1964). I have observed this several hundred times, either in the aquarium at Green Island on the Great Barrier Reef, or in shipboard and laboratory aquaria (MARISCAL, 1966 a, b). Any piece of material which was too large to be immediately swallowed by the fish was returned either to be spat out over the disc or pushed into the tentacles (Fig. 5). In some cases, when the object was released prematurely and began settling to the bottom, the fish dived down to again seize and return it to the anemone, where it was more forcefully pushed into the tentacles and held for several seconds before being released. On some occasions, the fish bit off and ingested small pieces before the food could be eaten by the anemone; in other cases, the anemone's tentacles so completely enveloped the food that there was no opportunity for the fish to approach it. Even small non-*Amphiprion* type fishes (both dead and alive) may be seized and pushed into the tentacles and ingested by the host anemone (GOHAR, 1934, 1948; MARISCAL, 1966 b).

Although it seems likely that the anemones in the

above cases can benefit from being "fed" by their symbiotic fish, the evolutionary significance of such behavior is somewhat uncertain, since not all species of *Amphiprion* engage in this behavior. For example,

Fig. 5. *Amphiprion xanthurus* depositing a piece of fish among the tentacles of its host anemone. Other pieces of food previously returned by this fish may be seen in the tentacles. The anemone was ingesting several pieces at the time of the photograph

every time *Amphiprion nigripes* and *A. xanthurus* were presented with food material, they returned these to their anemones, while *A. percula* never did. *A. ephippium* also may return organic material to its anemone, but much less frequently than the first 2 species mentioned above. Such differences have also been observed by other workers (e.g. VERWEY, 1930). Furthermore, apparently any drifting or floating object whether organic or not, will be seized by a "feeder" species of *Amphiprion* and returned to its anemone. Such objects include pieces of paper, cloth, and foil among others. One must be cautious, therefore, in attributing any great significance to such behavior in the absence of careful experimental studies.

SAVILLE-KENT (1893), in his classic work on the Great Barrier Reef, made the suggestion that perhaps the brightly colored *Amphiprion* acted as a lure or decoy to attract larger predatory fishes which might themselves become prey for the anemone. In fact, to this day, *Amphiprion* is commonly called the "decoy fish" in Australia. If this idea is valid, such behavior would obviously benefit the anemone and the *Amphiprion* by providing both with a source of food, with the latter probably feeding on the egested remains of the prey. It might also help to explain the often gaudy coloration of many *Amphiprion* species. However, so far as is known, such decoy behavior has never been observed as GOHAR (1948), ABEL (1960a) and EIBL-EIBESFELDT (1960) point out. In many hundreds of field observations spanning the Indo-Pacific, I likewise have never seen this. In addition, the normal territoriality of *Amphiprion* tends to argue against such behavior. Although a larger fish may approach an anemone closely, the *Amphiprion* rather than retreating and drawing a predator into the tentacles, will commonly dash out to attack and drive off the other fish (i.e. engage in territorial defense of its anemone). On the other hand, when released away from its anemone, a normally territorial species of *Amphiprion* displays no aggressive tendencies and may quickly fall prey to larger fish before finding its anemone, as mentioned earlier.

Discussion

It seems clear from the foregoing discussion that benefits accrue to both partners of the sea anemone-*Amphiprion* association. The fishes benefit by: (1) receiving protection from both diurnal and nocturnal predators, (2) perhaps receiving some degree of tactile stimulation, (3) by being less susceptible to various protozoan and fungous diseases when kept with anemones in the aquarium, (4) feeding on anemone tissues, anemone prey, waste material and perhaps crustacean symbionts.

The sea anemone benefits by: (1) receiving protection from various fish predators due to the vigorous territorial defense of the resident *Amphiprion*, (2) perhaps some form of tactile stimulation, (3) possible removal of anemone "parasites", (4) removal of necrotic tissue, (5) removal of inorganic and organic material from, on, and around the anemone, and (6) in some cases by being provided food by its symbiotic fish.

Although a good deal more experimental work will be necessary to clarify the significance of some of the above behavior, it would appear that the sea anemone-*Amphiprion* symbiosis is best categorized as a mutualistic one in which both partners benefit to some degree from the association. In view of the predation on isolated anemone fishes, and their invariably being found with sea anemones in the field, this symbiosis is probably obligatory for *Amphiprion*. However, the association is probably a facultative one for the sea anemones.

In addition to the fish, crab, shrimp and copepod symbionts, many sea anemones also maintain a mutualistic association with various unicellular algae which is now being investigated in some detail (e.g. SMITH et al., 1969). Thus, in recent years it has become clear that symbiotic organisms have the potential to provide behaviorists, physiologists and biochemists with a wealth of unique comparative information regarding the interactions of a number of diverse animal and plant species within a single system. It is felt that the *Amphiprion*-sea anemone association of vertebrates, invertebrates and plants should be especially promising in this regard.

Summary

1. The nature of the symbiosis between various tropical Indo-Pacific sea anemones and fishes (mainly of the genus *Amphiprion*) has been studied both in the field and laboratory.

2. The sea anemone-fish symbiosis is probably best characterized as mutualistic, in which both symbionts benefit to some degree from the association.

3. The fishes benefit by receiving protection from both diurnal and nocturnal predators, perhaps by receiving some form of tactile stimulation, by being less susceptible to various diseases, and by feeding on anemone tissue, anemone prey, waste material and perhaps crustacean symbionts.

4. The sea anemones benefit by receiving protection from various predators, perhaps some form of tactile stimulation, possible removal of anemone "parasites", removal of necrotic tissue, removal of inorganic and organic material from on and around the anemone, and by being provided food by some species of *Amphiprion*.

5. Although both partners benefit to some degree, this symbiosis is probably an obligatory one for the fishes (*Amphiprion*) but facultative for the sea anemones.

Acknowledgements. This work was carried out partly during Stanford University's R. V. "Te Vega" Cruise 5 (supported by NSF Grant G17465) under the direction of Dr. D. P. ABBOTT of Hopkins Marine Station, and partly in the Department of Zoology, University of California at Berkeley (supported by NIH predoctoral fellowship 5-F1-6M-22, 391-02). I would like to thank Dr. C. HAND and Dr. R. I. SMITH of that Department, and Dr. D. DAVENPORT of the University of California at Santa Barbara, for reading a preliminary draft of the manuscript.

Literature cited

ABEL, E. F.: Zur Kenntnis des Verhaltens und der Ökologie von Fischen an Korallenriffen bei Ghardaqa (Rotes Meer). Z. Morph. Ökol. Tiere **49**, 430—503 (1960a).
— Ein Beispiel für die räumliche Orientierung von *Amphiprion percula* (LAC.). Pyramide **3**, 78—79 (1960b).
ALLEE, W. C., D. PARK, A. E. EMERSON, T. PARK and K. P. SCHMIDT: Principles of animal ecology, 837 pp. Philadelphia: Saunders Co. 1949.
DE BARY, A.: Die Erscheinung der Symbiose, 243 pp. Strasbourg: Trübner 1879.
BOWMAN, T. E. and R. N. MARISCAL: *Renocila heterozota*, a new cymothoid isopod, with notes on its host, the anemone fish, *Amphiprion akallopisos*, in the Seychelles. Crustaceana **14** (1), 97—104 (1968).
COATES, C. W.: Safe hiding places moved while you wait. Anim. Kingd. **67**, 77—79 (1964).
CRESPIGNY, C. C. DE: Notes on the friendship existing between the malacopterygian fish *Premnas biaculeatus* and the *Actinia crassicornis*. Proc. zool. Soc. Lond. **1869**, 248—249 (1869).
EIBL-EIBESFELDT, I.: Beobachtungen und Versuche an Anemonenfischen (*Amphiprion*) der Malediven und der Nicobaren. Z. Tierpsychol. **17** (1), 1—10 (1960).
FISHELSON, L.: Observations and experiments on the Red Sea anemones and their symbiotic fish *Amphiprion bicinctus*. Bull. Sea Fish. Res. Stn Haifa **39**, 1—14 (1965).
GOHAR, H. A. F.: Partnership between fish and anemone. Nature, Lond. **134**, 291 (1934).
— Commensalism between fish and anemone. (With a description of the eggs of *Amphiprion bicinctus* RÜPPELL). Publs mar. biol. Stn Ghardaqa **6**, 35—44 (1948).
GRAEFE, G.: Zur Anemonen-Fisch-Symbiose, nach Freilanduntersuchungen bei Eilat/Rotes Meer. Z. Tierpsychol. **21** (4), 468—485 (1964).
HENRY, S. M. (Ed.): Symbiosis. Vol. I. Associations of microorganisms, plants and marine organisms, 478 pp. New York: Academic Press 1966.
HERRE, A. W.: Some habits of *Amphiprion* in relation to sea anemones. Copeia **1936** (3), 167—168.
HOLTHUIS, L. B.: The Decapoda of the Siboga Expedition. Part 9. The Hippolytidae and Rhynchocinetidae. Siboga Exped. **39 a** (8), 1—100 (1947).
— The Decapoda of the Siboga Expedition. Part 11. The Palaemonidae II. Subfamily Pontoniinae. Siboga Exped. **39 a** (10), 1—254 (1952).
HUMES, A. G.: New species of *Lichomolgus* (Copepoda, Cyclopoida) from sea anemones and nudibranchs in Madagascar. Cah. océanogr. ORSTOM **6** (Série Nosy-Bé), 59—130 (1964).
JACQUOTTE, R.: Notes de faunistique et de biologie marines de Madagascar. 1. Sur l'association de quelques crustacés avec des cnidaires récifaux dans la région de Tuléar. Recl Trav. Stn mar. Endoume **32** (48), 175—178 (1964).
KOENIG, O.: Verhaltensuntersuchungen an Anemonenfischen. Pyramide 8 (2), 52—56 (1960).
LADIGES, W.: Das Rätsel der Symbiose zwischen den Riesenseerosen der Gattung *Stoichactis* und den Fischen der Gattungen *Premnas* und *Amphiprion*. Wschr. Aquar.- u. Terrarienk. **46**, 669—676 (1939).
MARISCAL, R. N.: The symbiosis between tropical sea anemones and fishes: a review. *In*: The Galápagos, pp. 157—171. Ed. by R. I. BOWMAN. Berkeley: University of California Press 1966a.
— A field and experimental study of the symbiotic association of fishes and sea anemones. Doctoral Diss., University of California, Berkeley. Ann Arbor: University Microfilms 1966b.
— The symbiotic behavior between fishes and sea anemones. *In*: Behavior of marine animals — recent advances, Ed. by H. E. WINN and B. OLLA. New York: Plenum Publishing Corporation. (In press).
MOSER, J.: Beobachtungen über die Symbiose von *Amphiprion percula* mit Aktinien. Sber. Ges. naturf. Freunde Berl. **1931** (2), 160—167 (1931).
NOBLE, E. R. and G. A. NOBLE: Parasitology. The biology of animal parasites, 2nd ed., 724 pp. Philadelphia: Lea & Febiger 1964.

Ross, D. M. and L. Sutton: Detachment of sea anemones by commensal hermit crabs and by mechanical and electrical stimuli. Nature, Lond. **217**, 380—381 (1968).

Saville-Kent, W. S.: The Great Barrier Reef of Australia. 387 pp. London: W. H. Allen and Co. 1893.

Sluiter, C. P.: Ein merkwürdiger Fall von Mutualismus. Zool. Anz. **11**, 240—243 (1888).

Smith, D., L. Muscatine and D. Lewis: Carbohydrate movement from autotrophs to heterotrophs in parasitic and mutualistic symbiosis. Biol. Rev. **44** (1), 17—90 (1969).

Verwey, J.: Coral reef studies. 1. The symbiosis between damselfishes and sea anemones in Batavia Bay. Treubia **12** (3—4), 305—366 (1930).

Weber, M.: Die Fische der Siboga Expedition. Siboga Exped. **57** (1913).

Whitley, G. P.: The fishes of Michelmas Cay, North Queensland. Rec. Aust. Mus. **16** (1), 1—32 (1927).

— Some fishes of the order Amphiprioniformes. Mem. Qd Mus. **9** (3), 207—246 (1929).

— Fishes. Brit. Mus. (Nat. Hist.) Scient. Rep. Gt Barrier Reef Exped. **4** (9), 267—316 (1932).

Yonge, C. M.: A year on the Great Barrier Reef, 246 pp. London: Putnam 1930.

Author's address: Dr. R. N. Mariscal
Department of Biological Science
Florida State University
Tallahassee, Florida 32306, USA

Date of final manuscript acceptance: March 12, 1970. Communicated by G. L. Voss, Miami

Contrasts in Social Behavior between Central American Cichlid Fishes and Coral-reef Surgeon Fishes

GEORGE W. BARLOW

Department of Zoology and *Museum of Vertebrate Zoology,*
University of California, Berkeley, California 94720

SYNOPSIS. The social systems and related behavior of cichlid and surgeon fishes are compared in terms of (i) physical spacing, (ii) theoretical spacing (communication), (iii) castes, (iv) group composition, (v) open versus closed groups, and (vi) reproductive behavior.

Cichlids only recently invaded Central America. Despite the occurrence of about 100 species there, most are in one genus, *Cichlasoma*. Yet, they express a spectrum of feeding behavior, ranging from grazing herbivore through omnivore to predator, each of varying degrees of specialization. In contrast, their social behavior is remarkably conservative. There is a tendency for the generally found division of labor, with the female doing more of the direct caretaking of the eggs or fry and the male more of the defense, to lead toward polygyny. This is counterbalanced by the need for both parents to defend the fry. Communication is most accessible through a study of color patterns. While seemingly diverse, there is a common plan that entails the use of some or all of the same vertical bars and their central spots, and the appearance of yellow orange, red, or black ventrally.

The coral-reef community is one of the oldest in existence. Surgeon fishes are pantropical, especially in the Pacific Ocean, and have developed distinct generic groupings within a compact family of about 75 species. Most are herbivorous, with some more specialized than others. The species fall into guilds, within which there is broad overlap in diets. The social systems differ radically, both when breeding and when not, and can be understood as consequences of their strategies of obtaining food.

Wickler's classification of reproductive types within the Cichlidae is shown to be no advance over the previous dichotomy of substrate and mouthbreeding species. Poster coloration in surgeon fishes is apparently as important, or more, in extraspecific than intraspecific aggression, and poster-colored surgeon fishes show pronounced rapid color changes when fighting intraspecifically.

INTRODUCTION

An important service rendered by symposia is the identification of areas where work is needed. This paper will have made a contribution if it does nothing beyond creating an awareness of the relatively primitive understanding we have of fish social systems in relation to their environment. This stands in stark contrast to the progress made in recent years in studies of the social systems of birds and mammals (e.g., Crook on weaver birds, 1964, and primates, 1970; Estes, 1969, on wildebeest; Pitelka et al., 1973, on shorebirds; and Tinbergen, 1959, and his colleagues on gulls).

While there has been no shortage of behavioral studies on fishes, most of it either has been fragmented within groups, or has concentrated on certain species. Thus, the comparative studies on cichlid fishes by Wickler (e.g., 1966) and in the field by Lowe-McConnell (e.g., 1969) have been opportunistic rather than programmatic. Apfelbach (1969) concentrated on the genus

So many individuals have helped in ways large and small over the years that they are too numerous to list, but my thanks go to all of them. The manuscript was kindly reviewed by J. R. Baylis and K. R. McKaye. The cichlid work has been generously supported by the National Science Foundation, most recently through grants GB 13426 and GB 32192X.

N.S.F. also funded in part the research on the surgeon fishes. I am pleased to acknowledge substantial support from the Oceanic Institute of Hawaii, through its then Director K. S. Norris. The field trip to Eniwetok was arranged by P. Helfrich, Director of the Eniwetok Marine Biology Laboratory, with funds provided by the Atomic Energy Commission.

From *American Zoologist* 14:9–34. Reprinted by permission.

Tilapia although he studied but 4 of 11 species intensively. The emphasis has been on reproductive behavior, mostly as seen in the laboratory. (To date, the book by Fryer and Illes [1972] has not been available to me.) Obviously, the study of social systems in fishes calls for observing all types of social behavior, ideally in nature. Programmatic studies of this type are now being pursued by Myrberg (e.g., 1972) on pomacentrids and by Ernest Reese on chaetodontids. Okuno (1963) has attempted a synthetic overview.

Being terrestrial, man is ill equipped and reluctant to invade the aquatic realm to observe fishes there. This attitude has even carried over to easily observed stream and lakeshore species. With the advent of SCUBA it has become possible to watch fishes underwater, even at moderate depths. Unfortunately, the observer is usually limited to 1 to 2 hr per dive, and generally to not more than two dives per day. Water temperatures are such that even with good diving suits a human being experiences a serious heat loss when lying still. And preparation for a dive often consumes considerable time. This, plus the basically hostile environment, makes underwater observations unlikely, though not at all impossible, between about 5:00 PM and 9:00 AM, when much of the most interesting behavior is occurring. Finally, even those who have become good divers have been trained mostly by ichthyologists who have never been underwater. Consequently, the problems inherited by students have usually been formulated by a terrestrially bound professor with more conventional views of fish biology.

Students embarking on a study of fish behavior would be best advised to read beyond the fish literature, studying particularly the recent work done on birds and mammals that lies at the interface of behavior and ecology. These ideas can be tested on fishes and reformulated. Fishes, after all, are the oldest, most diverse, most species-rich, and, in some instances, the most observable of all vertebrates. The ability of the observer literally to fly about in their environment creates possibilities unheard of in the terrestrial realm.

In what follows I attempt to bring to-

gether some of my thoughts on the social systems of freshwater cichlid fishes (Cichlidae) and marine surgeon fishes (Acanthuridae). I have been working on cichlids for about 14 years, but mostly in the laboratory. During the last 7 years I have made a number of field trips to Central America where my students and I have observed cichlid fishes underwater, primarily in Nicaragua. We have also watched these fishes in Panama, Costa Rica, El Salvador, and British Honduras.

The involvement with surgeon fishes is more recent but more intense and overtly comparative. I spent 7 weeks at Kealakekua Bay, Hawaii, in 1971, and then 3 weeks at Eniwetok Atoll with Ken McKaye in 1972. Prior to my interest in this group I made incidental underwater observations on their behavior in places ranging from the Gulf of California through the Galápagos Islands and numerous Pacific Islands from Oahu to the Philippines.

Two important points need to be made about the work that follows. It is a premature summary with relatively little documentation. Often there will be noncontrasting information on the two families of fishes, and there will be gaping holes in the story. This summary should be regarded as much a proposal of hypotheses as a declaration of a state of affairs. I anticipate that many of the conclusions here will be replaced as our knowledge grows.

BACKGROUND INFORMATION

Cichlidae

Cichlids are the most successful percoid fishes in fresh water. They are especially species-rich in Africa and South America, and also occur in tropical Asia. In those areas they are a well-established component of the mature fauna and have reasonably well defined genera; often there are many locally sympatric species.

Apparently the cichlid fishes invaded Central America recently from South America as the Panamanian Isthmus emerged, probably during the late Pliocene (Myers, 1966; Miller, 1966). At the time of their entry, Central America had a depauperate fish fauna dominated by poeciliids, that is, the mollies, swordtails, and their allies (Myers, 1966). The advancing cichlids radiated into the different water systems giving rise to nearly 100 species. Reflecting their recency, almost all the species have been placed in *Cichlasoma,* although several different lines obviously exist within that genus. Three other distinct genera, with but six nominal species, have been described.

Geographical isolation has been a decisive factor. Each water system is separated from the next by a land barrier, restricting the movements of both young and adults. One consequence is the apparent re-evolution of similar types in separate drainage systems. While some species are widely distributed, there is a high degree of endemism. In no water system is there an excessive number of sympatric species; the modal number of species appears to be around 10. The extensive Rio Asumacinto system contains 44 known species, but there is endemism within its boundaries (Miller, 1966). Thus, each faunal assemblage in each river system may be thought of as a replicate experiment with some endemic and a few ubiquitous species.

One of the most well-studied aspects of cichlid biology is reproductive behavior, probably because of the ease with which they breed in aquaria and their well-developed parental care. Generally, the male and female form a pair, prepare a nest site, and spawn. The eggs are then tended and fanned, as are the larvae that are kept in prepared places. Protective care continues for some weeks after the fry have become free swimming.

A major variation on this theme is the development of mouthbreeding in at least four different lines; these are represented by a number of genera that can be grouped with *Tilapia* and with *Haplochromis* in Africa, and by *Geophagus* and by *Aequidens* in South America. The other variation is polygyny, a harem society with one male and several substrate breeding, parental females, shown in the genus *Lamprologus* (Wickler, 1965) in Africa and *Apistogramma* (Burchard, 1965) in South America. Both mouthbreeding and polygynous species were derived from species that had joint parental care. Furthermore, mouthbreeding in the New World genera is less well developed than in the African forms.

Fundamental to understanding the adaptiveness of the social system of any animal is a knowledge of its feeding behavior. Unfortunately, there is little precise information available from the cichlid fishes in Central America. Mostly, it is based on watching the fish feed in nature, often under circumstances that preclude a confident knowledge of what is being eaten. Nonetheless, some differences are obvious, such as those between the herbivores and piscivores. Feeding adaptations, moreover, are correlated with morphological differences and with the habitat in which the species occurs. Hence the feeding habits can also be judged from morphology and occurrence.

The fry of all cichlid fishes start as carnivores. Most feed on plankton at first but soon take benthic microfauna as well. The young of many species in the New World nibble mucus from the parents' body. Virtually nothing is known about this type of feeding behavior in nature, however, except for the observations made by us in Nicaragua (Noakes and Barlow, 1973).

Within the juvenile and adult cichlids of Central America one finds almost all general feeding types. The most commonly occurring type is the omnivore. These fishes may eat Aufwuchs, plants, invertebrates, and fishes. Within this category there will doubtless prove to be varying degrees of specialization on different kinds of invertebrates, for example, snails, as well as cichlids that take more of one kind of material than of another. Most species in this group are middle sized, relatively deep-bodied fishes with small to modest gapes such as *Cichlasoma citrinellum, C. beani, C. maculicauda, C. octofasciatum,* and *C. cyanoguttatus* (see Fig. 1 for some of the species mentioned here).

Many species are largely herbivorous, such as the small monotypic *Herotilapia multispinosa,* the middle sized *Cichlasoma synspilum,* and the large *C. tuba.* These species, nonetheless, can be omnivorous.

A much smaller group is represented by the piscivorous large bass-like species such as *Cichlasoma dovii, C. managuense, C. motaguense, C. friedrichsthalii,* and *Petenia splendida.* These species take a variety of fishes, including other members of their

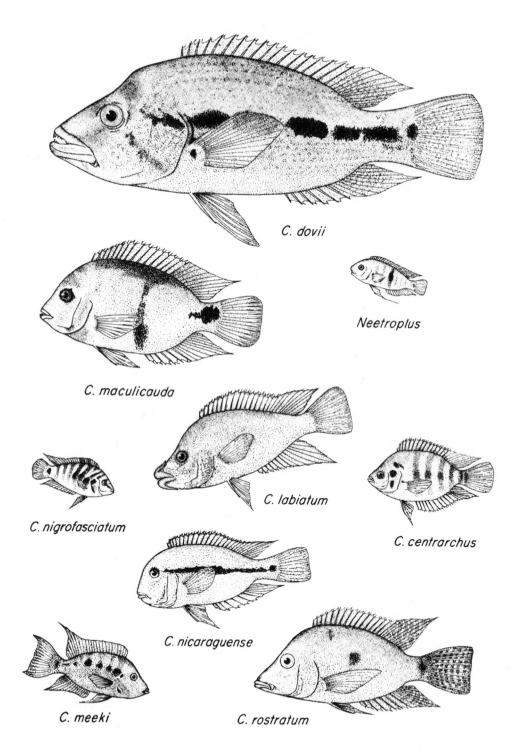

FIG. 1. Eight species of *Cichlasoma* plus *Neetroplus nematopus*. The relative sizes have been estimated. Color patterns are from live specimens; the *C. labiatum* was totally red.

own family, but prefer unarmored fishes such as atherinids.

Another group, perhaps more numerous than the piscivores, are the substrate sifters. Many omnivores sometimes sift the substrate for food, as does *C. citrinellum,* but some species are specialized in this regard. Included here are members of the subgenus *Thorichthys* (the firemouth group, e.g., *C. meeki*) and *C. longimanus.* These are small- to medium-sized species with relatively elongate faces. The most extreme development is seen in *C. longirostris;* this medium-sized fish has a long pointed snout that it plunges into the bottom; it bears an uncanny resemblance to South America cichlids of the genus *Geophagus.*

Close to the sand sifters is the distinctive *Cichlasoma nicaraguense* (usually labelled as its junior synonym *C. spilotum* by aquarists). It occurs in mixed rock and sand habitats. Its feeding behavior is unknown, although it probably takes algae, detritus, and invertebrates while engaging in sand sifting or scraping Aufwuchs. It is a moderate-sized species with a distinctively rounded shape to its head. In many ways, its morphology is intermediate to the next cichlid, *Neetroplus.*

One of the most highly specialized feeding types is that of the Aufwuchs scraper *Neetroplus* (three nominal species). This small, slender species has a down-turned mouth and can be seen rasping the Aufwuchs from rocks. On occasion, however, they can be carnivorous. For instance, they follow under schools of spawning atherines eating the falling eggs. They also prey on the fry of other cichlids.

The next feeding type is one largely inferred from morphology. *Cichlasoma labiatum* is a slender species of medium size that has enormous puffy lips. These evidently act as a gasket when the mouth is pushed into crannies (Baylis, personal communication), facilitating the extraction of detritus and small invertebrates.

The cichlids of Central America thus present a broad spectrum of feeding adaptations. But these adaptations are not profound, for the herbivores will feed as carnivores when suitable prey are presented to them. Even the most carnivorous species will readily take inanimate laboratory food.

Nonetheless, the different feeding adaptations are reflected in the size and body shapes of the fishes. And while the most common feeding type is the omnivore, specializations exist. The most highly specialized of these have given rise to the three genera, other than *Cichlasoma,* with but five species.

Acanthuridae

Surgeon fishes occur throughout the tropical seas where coral or rocky reefs provide the appropriate shallow-water habitats. To an ichthyologist they are a refreshingly compact family, consisting of about 75 species in six well-defined genera. While they are an advanced group of percoid fishes, they are members of the oldest continually existing community, that of the coral reef (Newall, 1971). They must, therefore, interact and compete with large numbers of other types of fishes.

There is some element of instability, however, since they have pelagic eggs and larvae that are variously vagile. The more widely distributed species must, in particular, be sufficiently adaptable to cope with the complex of species where they find themselves, for once the specialized Acronurus larva has descended to the reef, it is tied to that habitat. Open water forms a barrier to the adults.

Little is known about the spawning behavior of surgeon fishes. I will return to this later.

In contrast to the cichlids, the feeding biology of adult surgeon fishes is relatively well known, at least for the species that occur in Hawaii (Jones, 1968). The planktonic larvae are presumably carnivorous. But as soon as they settle to the reef and metamorphose, most become herbivorous. As they mature, they can be assigned to one of the feeding guilds. (Some representative species are shown in Fig. 2.)

Among the species tied to the hard reefs are the detritus feeders, all of the genus *Ctenochaetus.* Mostly these are small to medium in size. One species, however, the Hawaiian endemic *C. hawaiiensis,* is moderately large.

Perhaps the largest guild, in number of species, is the reef grazers (Jones considered the reef and sand grazers collectively,

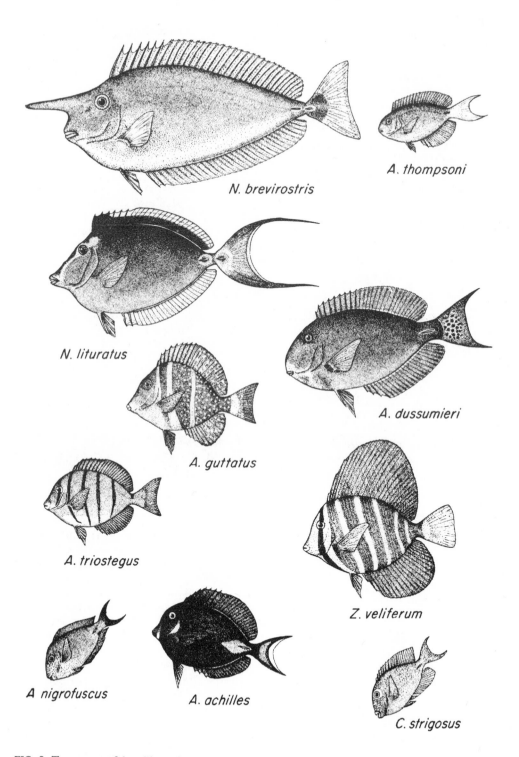

FIG. 2. Ten surgeon fishes, illustrating representatives of the feeding guilds (see text). The relative sizes have been estimated. Color patterns are from a combination of preserved and live specimens and may not be complete or correct in all details.

but they are better treated as separate groups). Most of the reef grazers are in the genus *Acanthurus*. These species are small to medium in size and seem to feed almost continuously by scraping at the reef with their mouths. There is broad overlap in the species of algae they consume (Jones, 1968).

Some division of resources is effected among the reef grazers by some of the species exploiting certain parts of the environment more than others. For example, atop the reef flat *A. guttatus* advances and recedes with the tide, as does *A. triostegus*. Being a smaller species, *A. triostegus* is often further shoreward and less in the surf line. At the edge of the reef flat and where the water surges a great deal one is more apt to encounter *A. achilles*, *A. glaucopareius*, and *A. lineatus*. Just off the reef flat, but still in the surgy area, are schools of *A. lucopareius*. Just below the rough water, and more intimately associated with the substrate, one finds *A. nigrofuscus* and *A. nigroris*. Here, and moving deeper, the detritus feeders become more abundant. At Eniwetok one species, *A. pyroferus*, is generally not seen until depths of at least 10 m have been reached; it is not clear what it is feeding on, however. None of these species is restricted to one place in the environment; it is common to find them feeding together, and in different areas.

Jones placed the two species of *Zebrasoma* within the grazing guild because of the species of algae found in their guts. But their long snouts suggest access to other types of food. The high rate of feeding, small size, and lack of mobility of *Z. flavescens* suggest that it is indeed a reef grazer. But the larger *Z. veliferum* spends less time feeding and it ranges over wide distances on the reef, suggesting that it is a browser (see below) not a grazer.

The next important guild is the sand grazers. All are in *Acanthurus*. They tend to be large mobile species, such as *A. dussumieri* and *A. mata*, who refuge (Hamilton and Watt, 1970) at selected places on the reef, or range widely among patch reefs. Their strategy is to take refuge on the reef when danger threatens and, when not, to move to nearby sandy areas where they ingest sand. They have a large muscular gizzard in which they remove diatoms and

algae from the sand grains (Jones, 1968). These fishes regularly move in schools of mixed species, and each species strongly resembles the others. While often busy with feeding, they seem to have much time available for other kinds of behavior.

Some species are intermediate between reef and sand grazers. *Acanthurus olivaceus* fits this category since it both grazes on the reef and ingests sand. It is intermediate in size, trophic anatomy, color pattern, and behavior. *Acanthurus gahm* may also be of this type.

Browsers are surgeon fishes who feed on relatively leafy algae that is apparently patchy in occurrence but quickly and easily ingested. All spend relatively little time feeding and have much free time. Most browsers are in the genus *Naso* and are large, highly mobile species. They are frequent where reefs drop to depths, such as off headlands, or at pinnacles in atoll lagoons. Two species favor shallow water. One is a typical gray *Naso*, *N. unicornis*. The other is the atypical *N. lituratus*. *Acanthurus bleekeri* shares many features with these *Nasos*, and may be a browser. *Zebrasoma veliferum*, as noted, may also belong here.

The most exceptional feeding guild within the surgeon fishes is that of the plankton feeders. This type of behavior has appeared in at least two different genera. *Acanthurus thompsoni* is a small typical *Acanthurus* except for its more terete shape. It feeds in schools in deeper water, say 10 to 20 m, off the face of cliffs and pinnacles. *Naso hexacanthus* is a large *Naso* that is said to feed on plankton (Jones, 1968). As is typical of this genus, it is a large highly mobile species. It has, however, a more streamlined shape, and the pair of knives on each side of its caudal peduncle have been reduced to rounded scutes.

These herbivores, then, may be split into guilds within which there is broad overlap in diet. The chief consequences of membership in a guild are size and mobility, time free from feeding, and extent to which competition exists.

The detritus feeders and reef grazers are mostly small busy feeders with time for little else. The reef grazers also compete with many species. All these fishes tend to remain in a relatively small area, although some of them, such as the reef-flat invaders, roam considerably.

At the other extreme are the browsers, large mobile species who feed quickly and have much open time. Competition between the species seems minimal.

The sand grazers are in many ways intermediate between the reef grazers and the browsers. They are large, but generally not as large as the browsers, and they are mobile. They seem to have an intermediate amount of free time, and they often travel and feed in mixed species groups. There is probably no competition for sand since it is available in boundless amounts *if* the fish dare range far enough from the protective reef. To do this, they join company with other species feeding in the same way.

SOCIAL SYSTEMS

Anyone having experience with the recent literature in social systems will be aware that the term means different things to different investigators. For that reason, I will briefly outline what I consider the essential dimensions. Some will not be applicable to certain species, and some are better treated together than separately, as occurs when discussing patterns of spacing and group composition below.

1) *Physical spacing:* A convenient and unambiguous method of describing social systems is to measure the spacing between its units. On the one hand, this will consist of measuring the spacing between solitary animals or groups that can be considered the social units. On the other hand, distance between individuals within a group constitutes a direct description of the social structure of that group. Home range and territoriality are included here.

2) *Theoretical spacing (communication):* Two approaches are conventionally used, the more common being dominance-subordinance relationships. The other measure of theoretical spacing or distance can be the rate of exchange and the consequences of communication between individuals. If these are signals communicating dominance and subordinance relationships, then the approach is identical to the conventional dominance-subordinance hierarchy. However, communication networks extend beyond that into the exchange of signals bearing other types of information. In what follows I will be considering theoretical spacing primarily in the context of approaching and withdrawing.

3) *Castes:* Social systems may consist of groups in which all individuals are basically the same, that is, of one caste, as in certain schooling fishes. Often, however, individuals differ. The two principle differences are age and sex. But caste can be distinguished even within these, particularly in reference to the phase of reproductive cycles, such as courting, parental, and so on. Taken together, age, sex, and reproductive state define an individual's caste (*sensu* McBride, 1971).

4) *Group composition:* Social systems can be defined by the number of individuals, by caste, of which they are composed. For example, one social system in cichlid fishes is the harem (one-male) group, as in *Lamprologus*. Another social system, as in *Tilapia*, consists of territorial males in a group receiving females who come individually, thus a lek society.

5) *Open versus closed groups:* If animals may join and leave a group with relatively little disturbance to that group, it is said to be open. If animals in a group resist the joining of that group by another individual, and if the individuals in that group tend to stay together, the group is said to be closed.

6) *Special attributes of reproduction:* To round out or make intelligible the description of a social system, and in particular to appreciate its adaptiveness, it is often necessary to take into consideration the special attributes of reproductive behavior. In some species of cichlid fishes, for instance, there would be no difference in social system as defined in the foregoing. Yet one species might be a substrate breeder, and the other a mouthbreeder. Sometimes, too, it is more convenient to consider attributes such as open versus closed (pair bonding) and communication in the context of reproducing individuals as opposed to those who are not.

Cichlidae

Physical spacing. In all species so far investigated, the fry form a dense school of closely spaced individuals which stays close to the parents. As juveniles, they tend to form aggregations, but information is scanty here. The nonbreeding adults of all species are also inclined to congregate, but there are detectable differences in this behavior.

The small species living in well-articulated environments, such as among rock slides or submerged branches, congregate where such environments exist, then space themselves there. They rely on the environment for protection and do not form conspicuous groups, although they do sometimes move about in groups. *Cichlasoma nigrofasciatum,* as one example, can sometimes be observed moving in groups while feeding. Individual *Neetroplus,* as another, are generally well spaced while associated with the bottom. However, I have seen them in dense schools, numbering perhaps 10,000 individuals, hovering over rocky outcrops at depths of 10 to 15 m in Lake Jiloá, Nicaragua. McKaye (personal communication) has observed them moving in groups over the bottom while feeding.

The medium-sized species that live within an articulated environment are more mobile and more apt to travel in schools. But when not moving, they generally spread out in weakly defined groups or as individuals.

Medium-sized species found in sandy or open areas, such as over beds of *Chara,* are apt to maintain group cohesion both while moving and feeding (e.g., *C. longimanus, C. nicaraguense,* and *C. maculicauda*). However, some of these species also tend either to be isolated (*C. rostratum*), or to move in the company of other species. Occurring over open bottom, therefore, tends to promote continual cohesion, even to the extent of interspecific associations.

The large piscivorous species are inclined to live well spaced, solitarily or in pairs, as seen particularly in *C. dovii* and *C. managuense.* Even these may form small schools or groups as adults (*Petenia splendida,* personal observation; *C. dovii* in rivers of Costa Rica, Meral, personal communication; and *C. dovii* in Lake Jiloá, Baylis, personal communication).

In no case is there adequate information to make conclusive statements about home range. Incidental observations suggest, nonetheless, that some individuals remain in the same general area for a period of at least some days or weeks.

Territoriality in nonbreeding adults is generally transitory and difficult to recognize. It is most commonly seen in one fish feeding on the bottom who, through aggression, maintains space around it free of other individuals. At least one species may have a cave or crevice which has been dug out and in which an individual may seek refuge when threatened with danger (*C. citrinellum*); however, no defense of this retreat has been seen, nor obvious avoidance by another potential occupant.

Large predators such as *C. managuense* and *C. dovii* may hold territories as pairs the year around. It is not clear whether they actually do, and whether they are going through one breeding cycle after another (Bleick, 1970). Adult *C. dovii* are said not to hold territories in the nonbreeding season in Lake Jiloá (Baylis, personal communication).

Theoretical spacing. Dominance-subordinance *hierarchies* are easy to demonstrate in the laboratory for a variety of Central American cichlids. This problem has not been explored in nature, however, since no fishes were marked so they could be recognized as individuals. However, I doubt the occurrence of stable dominance hierarchies in nature because groups change their composition so readily; they appear to be open groups, not closed. Dominance-subordinance *interactions,* in contrast, are obvious in the field.

It is more profitable to treat these approach-withdrawal relationships in the context of communication. In so doing, it is necessary to consider the three plausible sensory modalities.

It is now known that some communicate acoustically (Myrberg et al., 1965; Schwarz, unpublished). These signals consist of pulsed low-frequency sounds, emitted mostly during aggression, whether between rivals or within pairs. While it is too early to assert with confidence, acoustical signals seem to show little differentiation between species or between the sexes within the species after size differences have been taken into account.

There is even less information about the use of chemical signals. It is known, nonetheless, that some cichlid fishes can recognize not only larvae or fry of their own species, but that they can discriminate between the odor of their own young and that of other young of their own species and of the same age (Kühme, 1963; McKaye and Barlow, unpublished). Since in so many species there is virtually no sexual dimorphism, other than the size relationship *after* pairing, it is likely that sexual discrimination is chemical. I also suspect that chemicals may be the most important signal for species recognition in reproductive behavior.

When considering visual signals it is convenient to divide them into three types: (i) the movements performed, (ii) the shape of the individuals, and (iii) their color patterns. Considering first the relatively stereotyped movements, called here Modal Action Patterns or MAP's (Barlow, 1968), the similarity between the different species is striking. It is possible to use the descriptions in Baerends and Baerends-van Roon's (1950) monograph to deal with most of the species. There are clearly some statistical differences, however, in the frequency of occurrence and sequencing of the various MAP's. And there are some patent but small differences in the MAP's used by different species. For instance, *Neetroplus* sometimes lies on its side in frontal display. And *C. meeki* threatens frontally with greatly extended opercles and branchiostegal membrane. There are also small differences between the species in the degree to which the median fins are raised or closed, and when. Nonetheless, the general conclusion holds that there is no trenchant differentiation among the MAP's in the Central American cichlids. In fact, they differ little from their African substrate-breeding counterparts.

There are obvious differences in shapes between the different species (Fig. 1). However, the general plan of the omnivore is so widely distributed that there is consequently much similarity between many of the species. Several show sexual dimorphism in shape and size with increasing age, or

just during the breeding season: Males may develop a large nuchal hump, sometimes together with swelling of the throat (e.g., *C. citrinellum*, *C. parma*, and *C. dovii*). In some species, the nuchal hump is schematized into an almost wart-like protuberance, as in *C. nicaraguense* and in *Neetroplus*. In some species, such as *C. macracanthum* and *C. nigrofasciatum*, the trailing edges of the dorsal and anal fins are more protracted in the male than in the female. And in freely mated pairs, the male is invariably larger than the female; the difference may be appreciable (e.g., *C. maculicauda*) or slight (e.g., *Petenia*).

It is when considering coloration that the richest material is found. There is appreciable divergence among the species, but it is not as profound as the initial impression might convey. In particular, the black markings on the body are conservative. These start on the fry as a series of blotches along the top and sides of the body. With development, the blotches break up into a series of eight vertical bars. As they are being elaborated, a distinct black spot develops in the middle of each bar. With further development, the now juvenile fish demonstrate the ability to turn on either the bars or the spots, and to combine the spots into a median stripe running the length of the body (see Fig. 25 in Baerends and Baerends-van Roon, 1950).

The adult thus has available to it a selection of spots, bars, and a stripe of varying length. For convenience, each bar and its spot can be enumerated (Fig. 3).

In a large number of species, the adults have a "neutral" color pattern dominated by a few spots. Two are usually especially well developed, a small black spot at the base of the tail, and another (often number five) just posterior to the center of the body (Fig. 4).

Within a given species the pattern of spots or bars varies (Fig. 4) according to the behavior and environment. In general, the more the fish finds itself in open water, often schooling, the greater the tendency to develop the row of spots into a stripe. While up in the water but over rocks, particularly hovering in groups, the general pattern is for the appearance of the mid-body and base-of-tail spots. When the fish move closer to the bottom, often passing

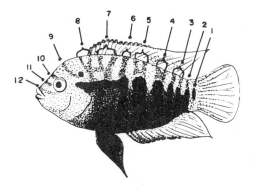

FIG. 3. *Herotilapia multispinosa* in breeding coloration (from Baylis, 1974). The major bars, with visible central spots, are numbered one to eight from rear to front; the head bars are also numbered. Note, too, the black ventral region.

in and out among holes or submerged tree branches, one sees a combination of spots and bars with softly developed edges.

Of more interest to the theme being developed here is the considerable variation in deployment and number of bars and/or spots among the different species. *Cichlasoma citrinellum* is typical of those species that develop the characteristic pattern of one spot at the base of the tail and one spot just to the rear of the middle of the body, plus a few others, while moving about in groups. In contrast, *C. maculicauda* has a pattern in which the mid-body spot is combined with the ventral half of its black bar, giving the fish a vertical slash in the middle of its body; there has also been a fusion of the tail spot with the one or two ahead of it to create a horizontal slash at the base of the tail (Fig. 1). As an extreme example, *Neetroplus* sometimes shows weakly developed barring, but the fish generally have a slaty gray body with but one vertical black bar, number 5 (Fig. 1).

The various species seem consequently to be utilizing an essentially digital code of black spots and/or bars. Not all combinations are seen, and some combinations are favored. No analysis has yet been done on the degree to which sympatric species use different patterns, and allopatric species the same. One of the difficulties is that interspecific communication may be important. For instance, the simple two-spot pattern, or longitudinal stripe, may facilitate interspecific schooling. More critical

to species isolation are the color patterns manifested during breeding (see below).

There is similarly a certain conservatism in the use of colors on the body as a whole. The first general conclusion is that when yellow, orange, or red are present, it is commonly found on the ventral surface of the body. Red is especially characteristic of eyes. Those species that have an appreciable area colored yellow, orange, or red are generally found in more turbid waters. Hues of these longer wave lengths penetrate murky water better than do blue or green. An excellent example of a yellow fish in murky water is *Herotilapia*, which occurs in swamps (Baylis, 1974). Another is the appearance of totally yellow, orange, or red morphs in *C. citrinellum* and *C. labiatum* in the perpetually murky Great Lakes of Nicaragua. On the other hand, *C. salvini* is brilliantly yellow when breeding yet occurs in clear waters in British Honduras; it is also an extremely aggressive species. Other brilliantly colored species occur in those clear waters, such as *C. synspilum* which is a gaudy and variable combination of orange, yellow, and red with black markings. Likewise, *Petenia* occasionally has brilliant yellow or orange morphs in the clear waters of British Honduras. Such correlations between coloration and the spectral properties of the water are difficult to make because of the diverse waters occupied by many species.

The use of blue or green tones in the body seem to characterize those species that generally occur in clearer waters (e.g., *C. urophthalmus*). These species also often have brilliant blue vermiculations on the face, as seen in *C. dovii*, *C. octofasciatum*, and *Aequidens coeruleopunctatus*. In Nicaragua, the large *C. dovii* tends to occur in the clearer bodies of water and has a decidedly blue and green cast, whereas its counterpart *C. managuense* resides in the murkier areas and has a yellowish tone to its body.

Some species have blue or green on their tops and sides but are orange or red ventrally. Good examples are *C. longimanus*, which occurs in relatively turbid waters, and *C. maculicauda*, which appears both in clear and murky waters.

Many cichlids have pearl-like flecks on their body or fins. This occurs in fishes

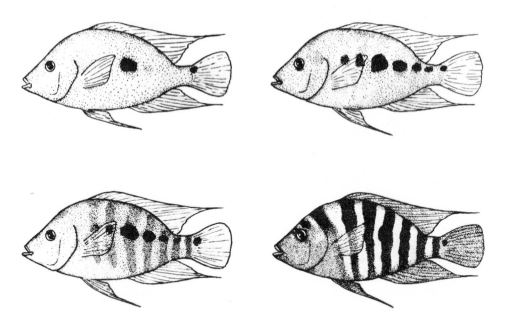

FIG. 4. Four color patterns seen in *Cichlasoma citrinellum* (explained in text).

that dwell in open areas, particularly out over the sand or in midwater. Doubtless they are showing a partial "mirroring" (Denton and Nicol, 1966) to facilitate camouflage. Examples are *C. rostratum* and *C. macracanthum*, and the species of *Geophagus*.

Finally, I need mention the recurring development of black areas on the ventral surface of some species. It appears during breeding (see below) in a variety of species (*C. spilurum, C. macracanthum, C. maculicauda, C. centrarchus, Herotilapia*). This is inverse countershading, which makes the parental fish more conspicuous (Albrecht, 1962; Baylis, 1974).

Breeding colors. One of the most commonly recurring changes during breeding behavior is the intensification of the normal pattern of vertical bars. Contrast is enhanced by making the bars very dark with sharp edges while the interspaces between bars become pale (Fig. 4). There are interesting species differences. One species drops the barring on the head and the first one on the body (*C. macracanthum*). Other species display the bar that connects the eyes dorsally (*C. beani; Herotilapia*) (Fig. 3). Yet another species emphasizes the hori-

zontal body stripe (*C. longimanus*). Other strategies may also be involved. For instance, *C. citrinellum* and *C. nigrofasciatum* show similar black barring when breeding and they are sympatric; however, *C. citrinellum* is a much larger species than *C. nigrofasciatum*, and the female of *C. nigrofasciatum* develops a large orange blotch on her side. Yet another tactic is shown in *Neetroplus:* When the fish breed they merely reverse the color pattern from a gray body with one black bar to a black body but now with the bar white.

It is again early to say with confidence, but there seems to be a correlation between the use of bars versus the stripe and the physical environment. Those species breeding among rocks generally wear bars. Those breeding more in the open favor the stripe, or some combination of spots plus part of the stripe.

There is also a general intensification and spreading of colors, especially yellow, orange, or red, or black, from the ventral surface up the sides (Fig. 3). Many species, moreover, make the eye more conspicuous, particularly by producing a pale eye against a dark face (e.g., *Neetroplus, C. macracanthum*).

Thus, despite the diversity of color patterns in the cichlid fishes of Central America there is a common theme. Mostly it consists of a simple recombining of the spots and/or bars on the body, together with the manipulation of colors yellow to red, or black, ventrally, and blue or green dorsally. There are, of course, also some remarkable exceptions. For instance, *C. tuba* displays a large patch of white when breeding (G. H. Meral, personal communication). And many species show interesting details such as red margins on the fins (*C. alfaroi*).

Castes. There is no noteworthy differentiation into castes. One can distinguish age castes, such as larvae, fry, juveniles, and adults. However, the juveniles are little more than small nonbreeding adults. And there is not much to distinguish between adult males and females when not breeding. Even in breeding pairs, dimorphism is often expressed only as the male being somewhat larger than the female (see below).

Group composition. Group composition in nonbreeding fishes has been described in the section on spacing. Generally, groups are open and highly variable in numbers. Males and females in nonbreeding groups are indistinguishable in their behavior.

Reproductive behavior. In contrast to the diversity of feeding habits, habitats occupied, and morphological differences, the reproductive behavior of these cichlids is noticeably uniform. The typical pattern starts with pair formation. We are least certain as to how pairs form in relation to the holding of a territory. We now suspect that either the female attracts the male to a territory which they then defend (as in *C. nigrofasciatum;* Meral, personal communication), or that the pair forms away from the territory and then captures one for themselves (*C. citrinellum;* McKaye, personal communication). The two fish alternately court in the territory, which is for reproduction, not feeding. The eggs are placed in a chamber. The larvae are similarly hidden away in cavities or pits.

In most species the female is clearly smaller than the male, being about 80 to 90% of his weight, and of a similar color pattern. Females develop full breeding coloration faster than do males, and once having developed it, are less apt to reverse it.

There is also appreciable differentiation of roles. The female does most of the direct care of the eggs and larvae, though not all of it in most species, and is more persistent in remaining near the offspring when danger threatens. The male spends more time patrolling the territory and driving off conspecifics.

When the fry become free swimming they form a large, coherent and ball-shaped school. Both parents vigorously defend these against predation; if the parents are chased away, the fry are eaten within minutes by other fishes which are constantly in attendance.

Not only do the parents defend the fry, but in many species they also help provide food. In some species the parents turn over leaves for the offspring (*C. nigrofasciatum;* G. H. Meral, personal communication), as do the Asian cichlid *Etroplus suratensis* (personal observation) and the African cichlid *Pelmatochromis guentheri* (Myrberg, 1965). When the fry are extremely hungry in almost any Central American species they will begin to graze on the mucus on the sides of their parents (*C. nigrofasciatum, C. spilurum, C. macracanthum, C. friedrichstahlii, C. beani, C. longimanus*). In *C. citrinellum* the response is apparent even when the fry are only modestly hungry (Noakes and Barlow, 1973), as is also true of *C. labiatum*.

The most noteworthy differences in breeding behavior between the different species are consequences of the physical environment. *Aequidens coeruleopunctatus* breeds in streams in Panama where there is little hard substrate on which they can deposit their eggs. The female selects a relatively rare rubbery leaf from among the litter on the bottom and carries it past the male during courtship. Later she spawns on the leaf (Fig. 5). When danger threatens she grasps the leaf in her mouth and pulls it back under the bank of the stream or into shallow water. If the leaf is turned upside down, she attempts to right it. This is obviously an adaptation both to the shortage of spawning sites and to the fact that they spawn in streams that are subject to periodical torrential flooding. Were the water

FIG. 5. A clutch of eggs of *Aequidens caeruleopunc-* Salud, Panama.
tata laid on a particularly rubbery leaf in the Agua

to suddenly become fast and high, the female could simply back into the quieter waters on the side of the stream, and return to the main stream as the water subsided.

The species *C. centrarchus* and *Herotilapia* both live in habitats where there is considerable vegetation. Both of these small species plaster their adhesive larvae on the plants, well off the bottom. *Petenia* and *C. synspilum* breed over sand bottom in dense vegetation in British Honduras. They expose the roots of these plants, upon which they spawn. The larvae are deposited in sand pits nearby.

Cichlasoma maculicauda breeds in Lake Gatun in Panama in areas where much of the bottom is either clay or covered with dense beds of *Chara*. The one nest John Mertz and I found in clay bottom was almost a perfect cylinder with a diameter equal to the body length of the female, and the depth about equal to twice her body length. The bottom was an enlarged chamber with many rootlets on one wall, presumably where the eggs had been laid.

About half way up the hole was a small antechamber in which the larvae had been placed (such a construction would simply never have been seen in the standard aquarium setting).

Cichlasoma nicaraguense is one species that is reasonably sexually dichromatic when breeding. Living in a mixed rock and sand habitat, it digs a remarkably deep hole in the sand by a rock. It lays extremely large but few eggs that lack adhesive threads (I thank the hobbyist Dick Stratton for calling this to my attention). The eggs are not only large but rather buoyant, bouncing around in the bottom of the nest. The absence of adhesive threads, large size, and buoyancy are adaptations to prevent loss of the eggs in the sand. While the female does some fanning of the eggs, she also does an inordinate amount of taking the eggs into her mouth and spitting them out (Stratton, 1968). Apparently this species is but one step away from becoming a mouthbreeder. When the fry swim, the male helps in their defense (personal observation).

There is also a trend toward polygyny in these cichlids. *Aequidens coeruleopunctatus* females are often found alone, caring for their eggs, larvae, or fry. I observed a male and female defending free-swimming fry in which the male ranged up to a meter away from the female, encountered another female, and began courting with her. Meral (personal communication) has made similar observations from one population of *C. nigrofasciatum* in Costa Rica. The often confirmed clearly stronger parental response in the female of most of the Central American cichlids suggests that the potential for polygyny is wide spread.

The general pattern of reproductive behavior within the cichlid fishes, in conclusion, is one of conservatism. Irrespective of other aspects of their biology, particularly their feeding behavior, they tend to have remarkably similar reproductive behavior. The most pronounced divergence in behavior is related to differences in the physical environment in which they breed. There is also a trend toward division of labor. This has meant size dimorphism with the larger male more apt to defend at the boundary of the territory and the female to stay with the offspring. This seems to have laid the ground work for the development of polygyny. The major pressure preventing the development of polygyny is doubtless the necessity of two adult fish to defend the fry against the many predators that lurk around them.

Acanthuridae

Physical spacing. Juvenile fishes have been observed in only a few species, so information about them is fragmentary. The pattern, insofar as known, is to establish solitary feeding territories after metamorphosis, as in *Acanthurus chrysosoma* (Okuno, 1963). Juveniles are sometimes differently colored than their adults, and this may be associated with their territorial way of life. However, the juveniles of some species look much like the adults and are also highly territorial: Randall (1961a) described well the early behavior of *A. triostegus*, and I have observed them in some detail. Evidently unique among the surgeon fishes, these juveniles occupy intertidal pools, and often at relatively high densities; individual territories are fiercely defended.

Among the adults there is a spectrum of patterns of spacing. In some species feeding territories are held by individuals or by pairs, and range from small to exceedingly large. Within these same species at another time, schooling behavior may prevail and territoriality be lacking.

It seems more appropriate to these fishes to discuss spacing from the point of view of territoriality than from the degree of schooling. Territoriality in these fishes is the securing of a feeding area. (Similarly, much of the grouping behavior can be explained as feeding strategy.) A difficulty in discussing territoriality here, as among non-breeding cichlids, is that feeding territories are often small and only briefly held, being given up for a new territory. This is not, therefore, the type of territoriality that students of bird and mammal behavior generally refer to when they use the term territoriality. But this behavior grades smoothly into well-defined, apparently persistent territoriality. In what follows, I will proceed from the species that are highly territorial to those that are less so, and on to those that seem to be nonterritorial.

There are many highly territorial small reef grazers, such as *A. nigrofuscus*, *A. achilles*, and *A. glaucopareius*. These fishes hold territories ranging from roughly 5-20 m^2. Whether these territories change in size, shape, or location through time is unknown.

More widely seen is the pattern found in many of the small reef grazers. This is one of holding territories briefly while feeding, driving away intruders, but then moving on. Frequently these species form schools while traveling from one place to another. Sometimes they feed together, but they are usually alone, as typified by *A. nigroris*. Included here also are *Zebrasoma flavescens* and possibly *Naso lituratus* (this is the smallest of the genus *Naso* and differs from the other *Naso* in many ways).

Many species are weakly, or not at all, territorial. These include a number of small to moderately large species adapted to invading the reef flats at high tide. Since they have to leave these areas as the tide ebbs, persisting territoriality would be disrupted by the tidal cycle. Included here is *A. guttatus*, a schooling medium-sized species.

Acanthurus triostegus is a smaller species that moves into the yet shallower areas on the reef flat, also in large schools. *Acanthurus lineatus* moves with the tide, but tends to frequent surge channels. *Acanthurus leucopareius* forms groups that move along the edge of the reef front and shows only sporadic if any territoriality. Interestingly, *A. achilles* and *A. glaucopareius* both hold territories on the tops of the reef flat near the front of the reef, yet individuals must forsake their territories at times; then they form schools adjacent to their uncovered territories.

The detritus feeders present some problems in classification, problems that could probably be resolved quickly by marking individuals. The smaller species are evidently territorial and may be living in groups in some species. They are closely bound to the reef and show a fair amount of aggression among themselves, as well as a considerable amount of toleration for members of their own species in close proximity. The large species, *Ctenochaetus hawaiiensis* appears to be a special case. Apparently it lives in groups which gather in numbers of, say, 3 to 20 at what appear to be refuges. Individuals or subgroups may leave and return from time to time. It remains to be determined whether these groups have exclusive use of territories.

Most of the weakly or nonterritorial species are highly mobile, moving about to more patchily distributed food. These are the larger species (plus the smaller reef-flat vagrants mentioned above). A transitional species is the large *Naso unicornis,* the only gray unicorn fish that feeds in the intertidal and just subtidal areas. Most of the gray *Naso* are large species that move in schools within a given area but show no territoriality. Possibly, however, the males in some *Naso* may be defending stations, off the pinnacles and cliffs where they occur, to serve a reproductive function (see below).

The sand grazers, as already described, refuge in mixed species groups on the reef and move out over the sand to feed in interspecific schools. The sand is essentially a limitless and indefensible resource, and not surprisingly these fishes show no territoriality. They do have a preferred refuge in many cases, and one can properly speak of home range.

One species, *Zebrasoma veliferum* seems exceptional. Unlike the territorial reef grazers, it roams considerable distances along the reef. Yet it also appears to be territorial in that it avoids the area occupied by other *Z. veliferum.* I have seen some displays occur when the fish meet at what might be the boundaries, but no overt aggression. I have also seen this species aggregate in as many as six to eight individuals, but at low tide in patch-reef situations where the animals may have been forced out of their territories.

Finally, it seems likely that the planktivorous *A. thompsoni* is not territorial. These animals live in schools and take refuge in the reef when danger threatens; conceivably, they could have individual holes to which they flee and defend, as does another planktivore, the black trigger fish *Melichthys buniva.*

Theoretical spacing. Dominance hierarchies have not been studied in the field, again because of the failure to mark individuals. They may exist, however, particularly if the species form closed groups. The most likely candidates would be those that most seem to live in groups, such as *Ctenochaetus hawaiiensis* and *C. strigosus.* Dominance hierarchies may also exist in the adult *Naso lituratus* one sometimes finds in groups and in which considerable fighting is seen. Much aggression is also expressed even by apparently nonterritorial reef grazers and by some browsers.

There are rather well-defined dominance-subordinance relationships *between* species. In some instances, the amount of aggression between certain species pairs is more than that seen within them. Thus, interspecific dominance relationships are an important factor in the social life of reef-dwelling surgeon fishes.

An appreciation of aggression interactions is the key to understanding the communication network of the social behavior of surgeon fishes. Almost all the obvious signals seem to be related to aggressive behavior.

The only sensory modality that will be considered in detail is the visual system. I have no knowledge of whether chemicals are used in communication. As for acoustical signals, the twitch-like displays of some of the species may be associated with the production of sound, but little more can be said.

All the surgeon fishes so far observed seem capable at some age of performing MAP's common to aggressive encounters as seen in most teleost fishes. For example, these fishes regularly show lateral display and tail beating. Also seen are vertical postures such as standing on the head or tail, and such overtly aggressive behavior as pursuit, ramming, and cutting with the caudal knife.

There are, nonetheless, some clear divergences in the MAP's employed in communication in the different species. *Acanthurus achilles* can often be observed in displaying pairs, swimming in parallel or in tight circles; one or the other fish may twitch all of the median and paired fins synchronously and repeatedly. *Naso lituratus* occasionally performs what looks like a tail waggle while standing in the parallel position with another of its species; this is obviously restrained tail beating, and often results in the two fish beating more at one another with their heads than with their tails; it is commonly terminated in one deep tail beat (an attempt to cut with the pair of knives) immediately followed by a chase. Another divergence is the pronounced "zooming" seen in *C. hawaiiensis*: These fish, particularly when one returns to the group, swim at high speed at one another as though to attack. Suddenly one fish turns off and glides through the water. *Acanthurus olivaceus* shows a similar behavior.

Although I was able to detect species-typical differences in behavior, all the species showed much the same kind of behavior when interacting interspecifically. That is, the species-typical behaviors appear to be restricted largely to intraspecific communication.

There is little differentiation in body shape within each of the various species. However, in the genus *Naso* sexual dimorphism in body shape and size seems more the rule. Several species have a median horn-like protuberance that extends straight ahead from the space above the eyes, which gave rise to the common name of unicorn fishes; only the males have this feature (Fig. 2). Some species lack a horn and have merely a pronounced hump where the horn

would otherwise be (*N. vlamingi*). *Naso lituratus* lacks even this nuchal hump, but the male has conspicuous streamers trailing out from the top and bottom margins of its caudal fin (Fig. 2). In all of the *Naso* that are sexually dimorphic (*N. hexacanthus* appears to be isomorphic), the male is usually larger than the female as well.

As with the cichlids, the most workable differences appear in the color patterns. But unlike the cichlids there is no obvious pattern for the group as a whole, with one exception: There is a pronounced tendency for either the caudal peduncle or the tail itself, or both, to bear a contrast-rich marking. Doubtless this is a consequence of the caudal peduncle being armored with a sharp, and perhaps poisonous knife (Randall, 1959; Yasumoto et al., 1971). In most species the knife is carried in a sheathed groove, one on each side of the fish. In *Naso* there are two knives on each side, and these are fixed out and thornlike.

Much of the differentiation in color patterns can be related to the feeding guild and thus to the environment. The planktivores and certain of the browsers spend much of their time out off the reef; all are principally gray through blue and protectively counter-shaded. The large *Naso* in this group commonly form interspecific associations when in open water (*N. brevirostris*, *N. hexacanthus*, *N. vlamingi*).

The sand-grazers are also a uniform group. When up over the reef these large fishes are generally black with conspicuous tail markings, such as a white band on the caudal peduncle. They also tend to have subtle markings, particularly yellow on the face, but also elsewhere, such as on the median, pectoral, or tail fin. They are thus much alike in the general pattern of a black fish with a pale tail mark. When out over the pale sand bottom their body coloration fades to gray. They so regularly school and feed together, that I am tempted to suggest that they are engaging in interspecific mimicry. To the observer underwater, these fishes are often difficult to distinguish at a distance because the resemblance is so great. The more subtle color markings are apparent only at close range and probably facilitate species identification.

Acanthurus olivaceus once again reveals

its intermediate nature between that of a sand and a reef grazer: Its body color varies between being all black or bicolor. The patch of orange color across its pectoral girdle is bright but relatively small, and it has subtle purple facial markings that are apparent only when up close.

Another form of intermediacy is seen in *N. lituratus*. It is basically black, like the sand grazers. It shares this characteristic not only with the sand grazers but with a goodly number of moderately large fishes that regularly hover up over the reef and take refuge in it, as does the highly mobile *N. lituratus*. But *N. lituratus* also has considerable ornamentation on the face and median fins; its caudal peduncle is brilliant orange, announcing the pair of formidable knives on each side. Thus, it is intermediate in color pattern between the sand grazers and the more colorful reef grazers that will be considered below.

The detritus feeders are usually drab. Most are dull brown with muted thin lines or blue dots on the body and inconspicuous orange dots on the face. Commonly only one species is found in a given place on the reef. In Hawaii, however, *C. strigosus* and *C. hawaiiensis* occur together. The smaller *C. strigosus* has a conspicuous orange ring around its eye. It sometimes chases the much larger *C. hawaiiensis*. The larger species is black with blue highlights. Interestingly, it spends much time well up from the reef. Thus, *C. hawaiiensis* resembles the sand grazers both in color and in this aspect of its behavior.

Among the reef grazers there has been a flowering of diversity in color patterns. Still, one can detect the tendency for tail markings that advertise the dangerous knife (although not always), as well as special and in some cases subtle facial markings. The types of coloration range from having the body a solid conspicuous color, such as yellow or blue, to marking the body with a variable number of vertical bars or with thin stripes. Some species have patches of color on the body, or polka dots. A common theme also is bright coloration on the pectoral fins or around the eyes.

In spite of this diversity and conspicuousness, there is evidence of protective coloration. For instance, *A. guttatus* is often found where the water is full of tiny bubbles from the surf, and it has numerous white spots. Further, the most common basic colors are inconspicuous, and most species are countershaded.

Many of these species conform to the concept of poster-colored fishes as advanced by Lorenz (1966), and since they range from highly aggressive to highly pacific, this seemed a good opportunity to test his hypothesis. It states that the color patterns associated with aggression are permanently turned on; no further change is necessary or possible. Further, the hypothesis predicts that poster-colored coral-reef fishes will direct their aggression only to members of their own species. A substantiating piece of evidence cited by Lorenz is that many damsel fishes (Pomacentridae) are drab and nonterritorial as adults (my observations on this correlation are to the contrary), whereas their poster-colored juveniles are strongly territorial.

The surgeon fishes have proved capable of extremely rapid and profound color changes, especially in connection with aggressive behavior. The basically black *C. hawaiiensis* sometimes develops a brilliant blue face while chasing. The extremely aggressive lavender tang, *A. nigrofuscus*, produces a dark profile around its head and body, leaving its center pale; *C. strigosus* and *C. striatus* show a similar change when fighting. The most remarkable color changes are shown by the most brilliantly colored species, *Naso lituratus*: When fighting, the forehead becomes brilliant canary yellow as do the pectoral fins. Sometimes during a fight the entire body becomes sky blue, only to change rapidly back to black. Extraordinary and rapid color changes are also seen in the nonposter colored, open-water *Nasos*. Depending on the species, these fishes turn on a brilliant blue-white vest, bib, or wedge just behind the head, with similar color changes on the tail (see *N. tapeinosoma* in Fig. 6b of Eibl-Eibesfeldt, 1962).

The remarkable fact in common to all these observations is that the color changes occur in intraspecific encounters. I have seen some changes in extraspecific threats, but only when a well-developed fight occurred (which is infrequent extraspecifically).

The one surgeonfish that was never observed to change colors when aggressive as an adult was *A. triostegus*. This is the least aggressive surgeonfish I have observed. Also, its caudal knife is greatly reduced and "unadvertised." However, the juveniles are aggressive and do show accompanying color changes. Thus, this is an example that is exactly contrary to the poster-color hypothesis: The least aggressive adult is characterized by the lack of change in coloration.

I observed what I believe to be prespawning behavior in *A. triostegus*, *C. striatus*, and *N. brevirostris*. In each instance the color changes were similar to those seen in aggressive behavior. In the case of *A. triostegus*, the color changes paralleled those noted for aggressive juveniles.

Surgeon fishes can also change their darkness to improve background matching and, thus, protection. The gray *Nasos* are pale up in the water but darken as they approach the reef to feed. Many of the reef dwelling *Acanthurus* and *Ctenochaetus* darken or fade as appropriate to their surroundings.

There are several conclusions that can be drawn from the analysis of color patterns in surgeon fishes. First, there is considerable species differentiation by color, but where the fish are constrained from dramatic coloration, as in the open-water species, some of this differentiation has been transferred to body shape. Also, there has been either convergence or mimicry in those species that move about together in a habitat that places constraints on the color patterns, i.e., off-reef *Nasos* and the sand grazers.

Diversification of color pattern can occur when the species are intimately associated with the reef that affords protection from predators (a similar view has been expressed by Hamilton, 1969). The diversification of color patterns here is probably a consequence of the abundance of species, since the communication involved in aggression is important in extraspecific encounters as well as in intraspecific hostile behavior. Recall that the reef-dwelling detritus feeders are drab in color when they usually face no competition from other acanthurid detritus feeders. This suggests that the diversity of colors among reef grazers serves to facilitate recognition of intra- versus extra-specific competitors for food. Their existence in the reef affords a measure of escape from predation. Thus, their relationship to predation is seen as permissive of the conspicuousness rather than causative.

There appears to have been selection for extremely rapid color change to communicate aggressive intent within species, even in the poster-colored ones.

Castes. The biology of juvenile surgeon fishes is poorly known. In a few cases, however, the young are clearly different from the adult, usually being solitary and territorial. In at least three widely unrelated species this is associated with the elaboration of bright yellow color. Nonetheless, in *A. triostegus*, in which the young are extremely territorial, the young show marked color changes in association with aggression.

Sex is difficult to distinguish externally in most species, especially in the genera *Acanthurus* and *Ctenochaetus*. Some species, however, live in pairs, suggesting a differentiation into sexual roles. Included here are the very similar *A. achilles* and *A. glaucopareius*. *Zebrasoma veliferum* lives in groups of one male and two females as well as in pairs; in each instance, the male is larger than the female. Randall (1961a) reported that *A. triostegus* may live in schools in which all individuals are male or all female.

In the *Naso* group, sexual dimorphism is often pronounced in shape and in color; the details have already been reported. In *N. lituratus*, while the unicorn is wanting its signal function appears to be served by the canary-yellow patch that is set off against a black background on the forehead during fights.

Group composition will not be discussed separately here, since all of the necessary information has been touched upon in the foregoing, or will be treated under reproduction.

Reproductive behavior. The reproductive behavior of surgeon fishes is poorly known. This is in large part because spawning probably usually takes place about dusk. The reef inhabitants count among their numbers many small planktivorous species that would devour the eggs if they were around much of the day. Releasing the eggs just before dark reduces to a brief period the time the eggs are exposed to predation from those planktivores, and it is also a time when many fish species are taking refuge in the reef (Hobson, 1972).

The reported cases of spawning (Randall, 1961*b*) involve *A. triostegus, C. striatus,* and *Z. scopas* (=*Z. flavescens*). All of those species were noted to aggregate toward sunset, and to move up in the water to spawn in small groups. The nonbreeding behavior in these species probably facilitates group spawning since each tends to live in groups, although *A. triostegus* is more apt to form large schools, and *C. striatus* to live in small aggregations. *Zebrasoma scopas* may sometimes live in pairs.

In spite of this lack of information, there is much suggestive evidence about the reproductive behavior of some of the species. For instance, those species that regularly move about in pairs probably also spawn in pairs, although this is not certain. *Zebrasoma veliferum* is a relatively uncommon species that is thinly distributed in its environment; it could profit by living in pairs. Its congener, *Z. flavescens,* lives in large loose aggregations where it is abundant, such as in Hawaii, but is sometimes seen in distinct pairs at Eniwetok where it is much less abundant. *Acanthurus achilles* and *A. glaucopareius* are clearly paired on the reef. *Acanthurus achilles* appears to form pairs as juveniles that may persist through life. In contrast to *Z. veliferum,* these two *Acanthurus* are often locally numerous and have small territories with several neighboring pairs visible to them. Furthermore, when disturbed they swim up from their territories and form schools. It is thus an open question as to whether they might spawn as pairs or within these larger groups.

One of the most interesting of all the surgeon fishes is *N. lituratus.* In some places, such as at Eniwetok, they exist as distinct pairs in the lagoon, but they form dense schools at low tide off the seaward reef. In Hawaii I have often observed one male with one, two, or three females. Occasionally, these animals tarry in nonfeeding groups in shallow water where the females appear to fight over the male.

The shallow-water unicorn fish, *N. unicornis,* seems to have a harem society. In Hawaii I have seen one male drive other males away from groups of presumably females that consisted of about 20 fish.

The other large *Naso* that live off the pinnacles and cliffs may have yet another reproductive strategy. *Naso brevirostris,* for example, is a highly dimorphic species in which one could anticipate sexual competition. While inconclusive, observations by McKaye and me suggest that males hold stations along the cliffs or pinnacles, much as do individuals in a lek society. *Naso vlamingi,* on the other hand is less dimorphic, having only a nuchal hump, which would suggest reduced sexual competition; nothing is known of its breeding behavior. *Naso hexacanthus* is not obviously dimorphic and is strongly schooling, probably in relation to its planktivorous way of life. The implication is that there is no sexual competition as a consequence, ultimately, of its feeding strategy, and that the fish therefore spawn in groups. Nonetheless, this is pure speculation since no information is available.

The evidence suggests a range of reproductive behavior from group spawning through harem formation and leks, and even enduring pairs. There are some suggestions of ecological correlations with breeding strategy, but the relationships are not clear.

DISCUSSION

To recapitulate, the cichlid fishes in Central America are products of a geologically recent radiation in the near absence of competition from other types of fishes. They have occupied almost the entire gamut of trophic types, but this division has not been profound. Interestingly, the least frequently encountered feeding specialization is that of the algal or Aufwuchs scraper. Only *Neetroplus* relies primarily on this food source. This may be because the poeciliid fishes preceded the cichlids into Central America (Myers, 1966), and many of these are specialized as Aufwuchs or algae feeders.

The surgeon fishes, in contrast, are a well-established family, having about the same number of species as do the cichlids in Central America. They exist in a complex, mature community with much trophic competition within and without the family. Other reef grazers include the parrot fishes (Scaridae), the damsel fishes (Pomacentridae), the siganids, and the kyphosids. Within their specialization of algal feeding there is a further division into guilds with narrow feeding habits. But within each guild there is considerable overlap in diet, and this is reflected in the social extraspecific interactions, the type depending on the guild. Thus, in the reef-grazing guild there is much aggressive interaction between species. But among the sand grazers and among the large *Naso* that live off the reef in open water, the fishes normally move together with little aggressive interaction between species.

I will quickly review the highlights of some, but not all, of the parameters of social systems as they apply to cichlid fishes and surgeon fishes.

The cichlid fishes space themselves either solitarily, in loose groups, or in well-defined schools. The more predatory they are, the more they tend to be solitary, while the more omnivorous, the more they tend to aggregate. But within any species, individuals may at some time be solitary and at others may move in close proximity to members of its species.

Within the surgeon fishes there is also a spectrum of patterns of spacing. Some species maintain relatively persistent feeding territories, others have only transient territories, and others appear never to be territorial.

Both in the cichlids and the surgeon fishes the smaller species that are more bound to the substrate are in general more inclined to be persistently territorial and spaced out. Thus, the small species that are territorial are the most aggressive members of the family.

Turning to the large species, in the Cichlidae these tend to be predators. They are generally well spaced and often territorial. In the laboratory they are exceedingly aggressive, especially *C. dovii*.

In contrast, the large surgeon fishes are generally highly mobile and gregarious species. While aggression is not common, it is seen among station-holding males, and regularly in the reef-dwelling *N. lituratus*.

Living in the open, as most of these large surgeon fishes do, has favored schooling as a maneuver to avoid predation. And when the species so engaged are not in competition for food, extraspecific schooling becomes a simple extension of that protective maneuver. Such behavior is facilitated by a close resemblance among the different species and by reduced aggression.

Something similar may be going on among the cichlid fishes that occur together and that feed over open bottom. In Nicaragua, the three species *C. longimanus, C. nicaraguense,* and *C. rostratum* bear a striking resemblance to one another when not breeding. They commonly school together. However, when feeding there is extraspecific aggression, with *C. longimanus* dominating.

The two families differ emphatically in the use of color in communication. Within the New World cichlids there is a common theme, almost a digital code, in the development of dark vertical bars and their contained black spots. There is also a recurrent pattern in the application ventrally of the colors yellow through orange and red, sometimes black, and blues or greens dorsally.

The only common theme in the coloration of surgeon fishes is the warning coloration associated with the dangerous knife at the base of the tail. Additionally, species that live away from the reef, and thus more exposed to predation, are colored for concealment. In the shelter of the reef, however, the color patterns tend to proliferate, especially among the reef grazers. The detritus feeders that live in the same environment are exceptional in that they are relatively conservative and cryptic in their coloration. This may simply reflect the fact that there are generally few sympatric species of *Ctenochaetus*.

Color changes in the surgeon fishes are more highly developed than in the cichlids of Central America in that they are so much more rapid. These conspicuous, contrast-rich, color changes emerge in the context of hostile encounters, predominantly intraspecifically, when even the most brilliant species change their signals. The drab surgeon fishes can also adopt striking color patterns.

Lorenz (1966) was extremely perceptive when he recognized the nexus between color patterns as signals, aggression, and the intense trophic competition on the coral reef. (It is not clear to me, however, how he decided which species to consider as being poster colored; to me they lie on a continuum of conspicuousness.) Lacking adequate information, Lorenz presumed perfect habitat partitioning among the poster-colored fishes, with no significant extraspecific competition.

In the reef-grazing surgeon fishes, extraspecific and even extrafamilial competition is an important reality. The conspicuous color patterns probably serve as broadcast signals, loosely addressed both to intra- and to extraspecific competitors. Color changes usually occur only during actual fighting where they are addressed to the object of the aggression. Since the more intense combats are largely reserved to intraspecific encounters, the signals emerging during such fights are primarily for intraspecific communication.

There is little worth commenting on with regard to the castes among cichlids and surgeon fishes. The cichlids are little differentiated when not breeding. Among the surgeon fishes a distinct juvenile caste is present in many species, and within *Naso* the sexes are usually recognizably different.

The problem of group composition has already been touched upon under the category of spacing. It bears repeating that the groups are variable and relatively nondifferentiated in the nonbreeding cichlid fishes. Furthermore, the groups seem to be open since their members leave and other join. Within the surgeon fishes the same situation prevails in many species. However, some species exist as pairs and even as threesomes, which are thus small closed groups. They may live in even larger groups that are closed, in other species, but this remains to be determined.

Generally the most interesting aspect of social organization is the reproductive behavior. Indeed, many writers equate it with social organization. It is here that it is most difficult to make contrasting comments because so little is known about the surgeon fishes. Fragmentary observations suggest that when their behavior is known we will have found a diversity ranging from group spawning through continuously maintained pairs, lek societies, and harems.

In contrast, more is known about reproduction in cichlids than about any other aspect of their social behavior. In Central America they have proved conservative in this regard. They follow the pattern of prolonged courtship with pair bonding, followed by parental care. The female does most of the direct parental care while the male guards the territory or remains nearby until the fry begin swimming. Then both sexes guard them. There is evidence of an inclination toward polygyny, but this is counteracted by selective pressure from predators, requiring both parents for protection of the fry. The greatest differences in reproductive behavior result from adaptations to differences in physical environment, particularly the suitability of the substrate as a spawning platform.

The only recent attempt to put the comparative study of reproductive behavior of cichlid fishes on a more solid footing has been that by Wickler (1962, 1966). He did an excellent job of analyzing the changes in behavior and egg morphology associated with increasing adaptation to spawning in holes. He attempted to relate the method of spawning and parental care to whether the species is monogamous or polygamous, and to whether it is sexually dimorphic or isomorphic. The previous classification divided the various species into substrate breeders versus mouthbreeders. Wickler, however, detected similarities between mouthbreeders and those substrate breeders that hide their eggs and larvae; these were called, collectively, "concealment breeders." The other cichlid fishes were termed "open breeders."

A number of difficulties arise when trying to use his more definitive statement (Wickler, 1966). First, he gave no criteria for clearly distinguishing when a fish should be classified as an open or a concealment breeder. His student Apfelbach (1969) later reclassified *Tilapia mariae* as a concealment breeder, whereas Wickler had considered it an open breeder, although both made the same basic observations. Likewise, we have found that *C. nigrofasciatum* is a hole (concealment) breeder, not an open breeder. In fact, my observations lead me to suspect that virtually all of the Central American cichlids are concealment breeders, which is not to be confused with breeding in the open, away from cover.

The second difficulty is that Wickler (1966) gave no workable criterion for deciding when a species is dimorphic as opposed to isomorphic. His definition was postulational: a species is dimorphic when the species itself can immediately recognize the sex of a conspecific. Evidently in practice he relied on the degree to which he could distinguish the sexes by color pattern. In so doing, he appeared to recognize small differences in the genus *Tilapia*, with which he is familiar. He overlooked pronounced differences in *Cichlasoma*: he tallied as isomorphic the obviously dimorphic and dichromatic *C. nigrofasciatum*.

I have taken the liberty of rearranging, simplifying, and summarizing Wickler's data (Table 1). The old classification is adjacent to the new. If the classification is an improvement, it should reduce the intra-category diversity present in the original classification. As can be seen, there was little if any gain. This is especially true when one considers that the category "open" may be nonexistent, that errors exist in the assignment to the categories, and that the criteria employed are almost impossible for another person to apply.

For analytical purposes the degree of dimorphism should be regarded as continuous rather than discrete. The same applies to the degree to which each species is adapted to a particular set of environmental conditions. In my experience Central American cichlids are all at least size dimorphic to some degree.

Wickler (1966, p. 137) has also commented on the direction of evolution in the reproductive behavior of cichlid fishes: "Evolution within this family leads away from the highly developed monogamy, and thus runs, to a degree, backward." This is a misreading of the evidence. In all known fishes that are parental, outside of the Cichlidae, the male is the parent. The evolutionary progression has been from (i) an exclusively parental male, to (ii) shared parental care by the male and female, to (iii) a division of roles with the female as the direct parent and the male as guardian, to (iv) polygyny (Barlow, 1964). This is clearly a forward progression resulting in a more efficient division of labor between the male and female.

Probably the main hurdle to the development of polygyny within the Cichlidae is that the school of fry requires the protection afforded by both parents. Polygyny would probably appear more often if predation on the fry were alleviated. This

could be done in a number of ways, such as the fry behaving differently. Wickler (1966) has shown one way in which this might proceed with the development of fewer larger eggs leading to larger, and more independent fry. Another adaptation would be for the fry to hug the bottom, thus avoiding many predators. Finally, the cichlids could breed in areas either ecologically or geographically distant from predators. It would be profitable in this respect to study the behavior in the field of the polygynous *Apistogramma* and *Lamprologus*. Of course it would also be necessary to take into consideration the problem of energetics. Polygyny would necessitate that many animals in the population be ready to breed at the same time. Often this is not the case in the tropics.

It is worthwhile to compare the reproductive strategies of the surgeon and cichlid fishes. The acanthurids require no special surface for spawning. However, those species that live as pairs are territorial reef dwellers. Apparently a physical center of activity promotes a continued association; it also enables a pair to exclude intruders.

Most likely all the surgeon fishes release vast numbers of eggs that become part of the plankton and are widely dispersed. Equally likely, they spawn repetitively, so that the number of gametes produced annually by each fish must be prodigious. With this simple and relatively primitive mode of reproduction, and a long time span, they seem to have produced a diversity of social systems.

The substrate-breeding cichlids, in contrast, require a particular surface on which to leave their eggs, and subsequently a place where they can put their helpless larvae in order to defend them. They then keep the few thousand or hundred vulnerable fry (a relatively small number) close to them, which makes their protection easier. One reproductive cycle takes about six to eight weeks; it is doubtless so energetically costly that it is not immediately repeated in nature. Such a mode of reproduction, however, must be advantageous or it would not have evolved. Yet it has been evolved at a cost. It ties the species, especially the smaller ones, to certain habitats and thus to a limited number of trophic situations. Remarkably, most substrate-

TABLE 1. *Species of cichlid fishes in each category of reproductive behavior, contrasting two systems of classification.*[a]

	Type of breeding			
	Original classification		Revised classification	
	Substrate	Mouth	Open	Concealment
Monogamous, Monomorphic	22 63%	2 20%	20 100%	4 16%
Monogamous, Dimorphic	9 26%	1 10%	0 0%	10 40%
Polygamous, Dimorphic	4 11%	6 60%	0 0%	10 40%
Polygamous, Monomorphic	0 0%	1 10%	0 0%	1 4%
Total species	35	10	20	25
H (Diversity)[b]	1.14	1.13	0	1.42
	1.84		1.71	

[a] Data from Wickler (1966).

[b] $H = \dfrac{1}{N} (\log_2 N! - \Sigma \log_2 n!)$.

breeding cichlids the world over have much the same social system. (One might have expected them to evolve closed groups from an extended family relationship.)

By evolving mouthbreeding some African genera appear to have broken away from previous constraints. The habitat requirements for spawning are minimal, and the fry are more advanced when released. Perhaps as a consequence, there has been a greater trophic radiation, as in the evolution of plankton filtering species.

In both the cichlids and surgeon fishes, nonetheless, the social systems are seen ultimately as consequences of their feeding behavior, but other factors have a profound and sometimes more proximate influence. In this paper, the physical environment and the effect of predation were seen as the most important proximate modulators of the reproductive behavior in the Cichlidae. In the Acanthuridae, timing of spawning was viewed as an adaptation to avoiding egg predators. But the basic social organization of surgeon fishes most clearly reflects their food habits and the physical environment in which they engage in feeding. Here the physical environment means essentially the degree to which they are exposed to predation. Another important variable should prove to be amount of open time, which is also a consequence of feeding behavior.

The social organization of these fishes is not, therefore, some happy accident of a capricious evolutionary machination, but rather it reflects an ultimate fundamental adaptation to the bioenergetics of the species.

REFERENCES

Albrecht, H. 1962. Die Mitschattierung. Experientia 18:284-286.

Apfelbach, R. 1969. Vergleichend quantative Untersuchungen des Fortpflanzungsverhaltens brutple-gemono- und -dimorpher Tilapien (Pisces, Cichlidae). Z. Tierpsychol. 26:692-725.

Baerends, G. P., and J. M. Baerends-van Roon. 1950. An introduction to the study of the ethology of cichlid fishes. Behaviour Suppl. 1:1-243.

Barlow, G. W. 1964. Ethology of the Asian teleost *Badis badis*. V. Dynamics of fanning and other parental activities, with comments on the behavior of the larvae and postlarvae. Z. Tierpsychol. 21: 99-123.

Barlow, G. W. 1968. Ethological units of behavior, p. 217-232. *In* D. Ingle [ed.], The central nervous system and fish behavior. Univ. Chicago Press, Chicago.

Baylis, J. R. 1974. The behavior and ecology of *Herotilapia multispinosa* (Pisces, Cichlidae). Z. Tierpsychol. (In press)

Bleick, C. R. 1970. The behavior of the Central American fish, *Cichlasoma managuense,* and the functions of its color patterns: a laboratory and field study. Masters Thesis, Univ. of California, Berkeley.

Burchard, J. E. 1965. Family structure in the dwarf cichlid *Apistogramma trifasciatum* Eigenmann and Kennedy. Z. Tierpsychol. 22:150-162.

Crook, J. H. 1964. The evolution of social organisation and visual communication in weaver birds. (Ploceinae). Behaviour Suppl. 10:1-178.

Crook, J. H. 1970. The socio-ecology of primates, p. 103-166. *In* J. H. Crook [ed.], Social behaviour in birds and mammals. Academic Press, New York.

Denton, E. J., and J. A. C. Nicol. 1966. A survey of reflectivity in silvery teleosts. J. Mar. Biol. Ass. U. K. 46:685-722.

Eibl-Eibesfeldt, I. 1962. Freiwasserbeobachtungen zur Deutung des Schwarmverhaltens verschiedener Fische. Z. Tierpsychol. 19:165-182.

Estes, R. D. 1969. Territorial behavior of the wildebeest (*Connochaetes taurinus* Burchell, 1823). Z. Tierpsychol. 26:284-370.

Fryer, G., and T. D. Iles. 1972. Cichlid fishes of the Great Lakes of Africa. Oliver and Boyd, Edinburgh.

Hamilton, W. J. 1969. Coral fish coloration. 91 p. (Unpublished manuscript)

Hamilton, W. J., and R. E. F. Watt. 1970. Refuging. Ann. Rev. Ecol. Syst. 1:263-287.

Hobson, E. S. 1972. Activity of Hawaiian reef fishes during the evening and morning transitions between daylight and darkness. Fish. Bull. 70:715-740.

Jones, R. S. 1968. Ecological relationships in Hawaiian and Johnston Island Acanthuridae (surgeonfishes). Micronesica 4:309-361.

Kühme, W. 1963. Chemisch ausgelöste Brutpflege- und Schwarmreaktionen bei *Hemichromis bimaculatus* (Pisces). Z. Tierpsychol. 20:688-704.

Lorenz, K. 1966. On aggression. Harcourt, Brace, and World, New York.

Lowe-McConnell, R. H. 1969. The cichlid fishes of Guyana, South America, with notes on their ecology and breeding behaviour. Zool. J. Linnean Soc. 48:255-302.

McBride, G. 1971. Theories of animal spacing: the role of flight, fright, and social distance, p. 53-68. *In* A. H. Esser [ed.], Behavior and environment. Plenum, New York.

Miller, R. R. 1966. Geographical distribution of Central American freshwater fishes. Copeia 1966:773-802.

Myers, G. S. 1966. Derivation of the freshwater fish fauna of Central America. Copeia 1966:766-773.

Myrberg, A. A. 1965. A descriptive analysis of the behaviour of the African cichlid fish, *Pelmatochromis guentheri* (Sauvage). Anim. Behav. 13:312-329.

Myrberg, A. A. 1972. Social dominance and territoriality in the bicolor damselfish, *Eupomacentrus partitus* (Poey) (Pisces: Pomacentridae). Behaviour 41:207-231.

Myrberg, A. A., E. Kramer, and P. Heinecke. 1965. Sound production by cichlid fishes. Science 149:555-558.

Newall, N. D. 1971. An outline history of tropical organic reefs. Amer. Mus. Novitates (2465):1-37.

Noakes, D. L. G., and G. W. Barlow. 1973. Ontogeny of parent-contacting behavior in young *Cichlasoma citrinellum* (Pisces, Cichlidae). Behaviour 46:221-255.

Okuno, R. 1963. Observations and discussions on the social behavior of marine fishes. Publ. Seto Mar. Biol. Lab. 11:111-166.

Pitelka, F. A., R. T. Holmes, and S. F. MacLean, Jr. 1974. Ecology and evolution of social organization in arctic sandpipers. Amer. Zool. 14:185-205.

Randall, J. E. 1959. Report of a caudal-spine wound from the surgeonfish *Acanthurus lineatus* in the Society Islands. Wasmann J. Biol. 17:245-248.

Randall, J. E. 1961a. A contribution to the biology of the convict surgeon fish of the Hawaiian Islands, *Acanthurus triostegus sandvicensis*. Pac. Sci. 15:215-272.

Randall, J. E. 1961b. Observations on the spawning of surgeonfishes (Acanthuridae) in the Society Islands. Copeia 1961:237-238.

Stratton, E. S. 1968. An ethogram of *Cichlasoma spilotum* (Pisces: Cichlidae). Masters Thesis, Univ. of California, Berkeley.

Tinbergen, N. 1959. Comparative studies of the behaviour of gulls (Laridae): a progress report. Behaviour 15:1-70.

Wickler, W. 1962. Zur Stammesgeschichte funktionell korrelierter Organ- und Verhaltensmerkmale: Ei-Attrappen und Maulbrüten bei afrikanischen Cichliden. Z. Tierpsychol. 19:129-164.

Wickler, W. 1965. Neue Varianten des Fortpflanzungsverhaltens afrikanischer Cichliden (Pisces, Perciformes). Naturwissenschaften 52:219.

Wickler, W. 1966. Sexualdimorphismus, Paarbildung und Versteckbrüten bei Cichliden (Pisces: Perciformes). Zool. Jahrb. Syst. 93:127-138.

Yasumoto, T., Y. Hashimoto, R. Bagnis, J. E. Randall, and A. H. Banner. 1971. Toxicity of the surgeon fishes. Bull. Jap. Soc. Sci. Fish. 37:724-734.

The Attitude of Fish Eye-Lines in Relation to Body Shape and to Stripes and Bars

George W. Barlow

The function of obliterative eye-lines has gained general acceptance, but no one has attempted to account for the variability shown in the inclination of the line. There is a clear relationship between the steepness of the line and (a) the body shape of the species, and also with (b) the angle of the forehead. Vertical eye-lines are associated with deep bodies and steep foreheads, while horizontal lines are characteristic of the more elongate species with low foreheads; exceptions prove of considerable interest.

An understanding of the adaptive significance of the attitude of the eye-line is aided by a consideration of the behavior and habitat of the fish in relation to the general color pattern. Longitudinal stripes occur on slender species that swim fast, whereas vertical bars typify deep-bodied fishes that turn sharply. The more closely a striped slender species is associated with the bottom, the more stripes it is apt to have. Barred species usually have deep bodies and live close to the substrate. Stripes or bars simultaneously serve as social signals and as antipredator markings.

Introduction

IN a classic treatment of the adaptive significance of color patterns in animals, Cott (1940) drew attention to the remarkable conspicuousness of eyes and eye-like markings. This led to a general discussion of color patterns that might camouflage eyes. While Cott gave many examples from the animal kingdom, only one passage dealt with the common occurrence of this phenomenon among fishes.

The eyes of bony fishes may be rendered inconspicuous in several ways (Longley, 1924). A complex pattern of reticulations or mottling causes the eye to blend into the head, as seen among sculpins, wrasses, and frog fishes, to name but a few (Fig. 1). A completely black eye disappears in a dark field; examples may be seen among the basslets, damsel fishes, wrasses, and trigger fishes. A prominent dark line through the eye, the most common stratagem, is the focus of this paper.

I noticed that the eye-line differs with the shape of a fish. Thus elongate fishes frequently have a line running straight back from the eye, whereas deep-bodied fishes more often have a vertical line crossing the eye. I hypothesized that the eye-line repeats the principle line of a nearby boundary. In deep-bodied fishes one expects the head to have a steep profile, and accordingly a nearly vertical eye-line. Slender fishes usually have a head with a low profile, however, so

one would predict a nearly horizontal line. Exceptions, such as long-bodied fishes with steep foreheads, should prove interesting test cases.

The primary objective of this paper was to analyze the attitude of the eye-line in relation to relative body depth, and also in relation to the slope of the forehead. I anticipated that significant correlations would be shown for both factors, and that exceptions to the model would pose further questions.

Materials and Methods

To obtain a sample, free of my bias, of species and their markings, I selected a book at hand that contained many illustrations of bony fishes. This was "The sea fishes of southern Africa" (J. L. B. Smith, 1950).

Some arbitrary decisions were made about the angle of the eye-line. I measured the most prominent line, if more than one, as judged by its length, width, and darkness. If two or more lines were equally prominent, which seldom happened, that species was not used. If the line ran all the way through the eye, as it usually does, I measured the angle made by the posterior or superior limb. The particular set of coordinates (Fig. 2) is not important.

The slope of the forehead was defined as the angle made by the intersection of a line that extended the long axis of the fish with a line tangent to the forehead at a point

From *Copeia* 1972(1):4–12. Reprinted by permission.

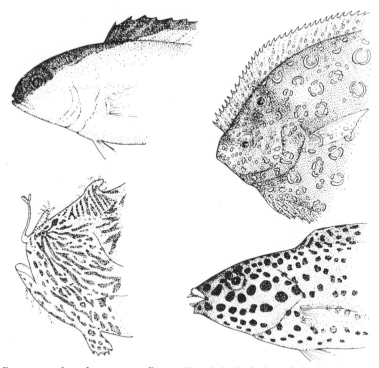

Fig. 1. Four examples of eye camouflage: *Top Left*—Inclusion of the black pupil in a black surround in the blackcap basslet, *Gramma melacarra*. *Top Right*—Mottling and partial rings to distract the observer from the eyes of the peacock flounder, *Bothus lunatus*. *Bottom Left*—Complex radiating lines in *Antennarius striatus*. *Bottom Right*—A field of roughly iris-size dark spots on the head of *Coris angulata*.

above the eye (Fig. 3). A fish with a rounded or broken profile was difficult to cope with, and the angle θ was estimated to the nearest 5° or 10°. If the decision proved difficult, the data were omitted.

The relative depth is expressed as a percentage. It was obtained by dividing the depth of the body by the standard length.

The data are shown in Figs. 4 and 6. They were analyzed with the Spearman rank correlation coefficient (Siegel, 1956). For the angle of the eye-line, rank ordering proceeded counterclockwise from the maxi-

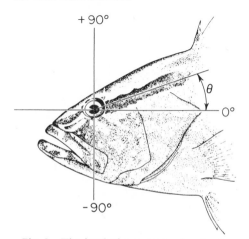

Fig. 2. The head of a grouper, showing how the angle of the eye-line, θ, is measured.

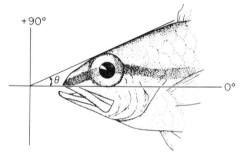

Fig. 3. The referants for measuring the slope of the forehead, θ, as illustrated in a cardinal fish.

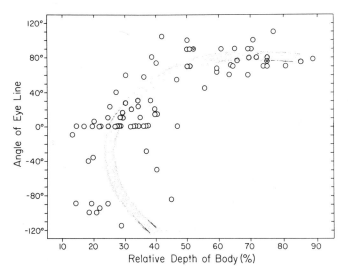

Fig. 4. Angle of the eye-line plotted as a function of the relative depth of the body. A double circle (⊚) indicates that more than one datum fell at the same place. The stippled curve was added merely to aid the eye in following the major trend.

mum negative angle through the maximum positive angle.

RESULTS

Attitude of eye-line and depth of body.— The Spearman correlation coefficient (r_s) between attitude of eye-line and body depth was 0.81 (p $\ll$ .001). Although not linear, the rank ordering of the angle made by the eye-line changes systematically with depth of body.

A closer examination suggests that at least three different relationships exist between the attitude of the eye-line and the depth of the body: 1) In deep fishes (depth 50%

Fig. 5. A male of *Blennius pavo* in its hiding place (after Fishelson, 1963). This species has the transverse eye-line running on above the eye, probably because of the crest on the head, a secondary sex character.

or more of length), the eye-line is nearly vertical and extends above or through the eye. 2) Among elongate fishes, (depth less than 30–40% of length), the eye-line often extends back as a longitudinal stripe along the body. (3) The third category contains transitional species (depth 30–50% of length) in which the attitude of the eye-line is progressively steeper with deeper bodies.

Plotting the angle of the eye-line as a function of depth immediately draws attention to exceptional cases. Most noteworthy are very slender fishes that have a vertical line usually extending ventrally from the eye rather than to the rear along the longitudinal axis of the body. Most of these species are blennies and gobies; they are predominantly forms with eyes high on the head and species that live on the bottom. Blennies in particular, but also gobies, commonly lie in a hole with the head protruding as far as the pectoral fins; thus the exposed part of the fish has a depth-length relationship appropriate to a deep-bodied fish (Fig. 5). A vertical eye-line would be appropriate for the exposed part of the fish. The converse does not exist: no deep-bodied fishes have the most prominent eye-line running through the eye as a horizontal stripe.

Furthermore, no species, irrespective of relative depth, has an eye-line extending forward from the eye onto the snout in the

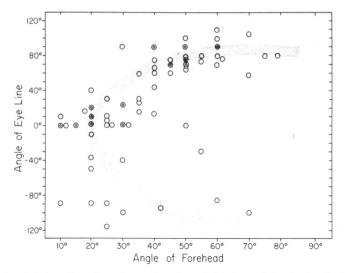

Fig. 6. Angle of the eye-line plotted as a function of the slope of the forehead. A double circle (⊚) indicates that more than one datum fell at the same place. The stippled curve was added simply to aid the eye in following the major trend.

absence of a line running to the rear. Some wrasses, in illustrations, approach this condition, *e.g.*, *Doratonotus decoris*, as do the anostomid fish *Leporinus fasciatus* and the loach *Noemacheilus barbatula*. All longitudinal preorbital stripes extend on through and to the rear of the eye. However, the stripe commonly starts at the eye and passes to the rear.

Attitude of eye-line and slope of forehead.—The attitude of the eye-line is positively correlated with the slope of the forehead ($r_s = 0.62$, $p \ll .001$). The relationship, however, is not as clear as that between the eye-line and the depth of the body; more scatter has crept in, especially for eye-line angles less than $0°$, indicating exceptions or departures from the rule. It is tempting to assume from this that the angle made by the eye-line is more strongly correlated with the depth than with the slope of the forehead. But caution is in order. The magnitude of correlation coefficients can depend greatly on the vagaries of sampling. It is also possible that the differences may have resulted from the criteria for, and precision of, measuring the slope of the forehead.

The general conclusion is that a steep forehead is associated with a tendency toward verticality in the eye-line. A low forehead is associated with a horizontal trend in the eye-line. Intermediate cases are common.

A few species bear an eye-line that runs diagonally down to the rear from the eye. Such a line is thus commonly disposed at a right angle to the slope of the forehead. But this line is frequently (not always) almost parallel to another boundary, the line of the jaw or the ventral profile of the head. Such a line is particularly, but not exclusively, found as a secondary eye-line in predaceous species (*e.g.*, *Polycentrus schomburgkii*, *Cichlasoma dovii*).

Slope of Forehead Relative to Depth of Body.—Deep-bodied fishes mostly have steep foreheads and, conversely, elongate fishes have low profiles ($r_s = 0.73$, $p \ll .001$; no figure).

There are exceptions. Some elongate fishes have steep foreheads, such as blennies and the dolphin. More unusual are deep-bodied fishes with a low forehead profile; these tend to be bottom dwelling fishes with large up-turned mouths (such as the frog fishes), surface-feeding deep-bodied fishes (*e.g.*, the Gastropelicinae), or odd-looking cyprinids with high, compressed bodies but pointed heads (*e.g.*, *Blicca* and *Chela*).

DISCUSSION

A major shortcoming of the foregoing analysis is that the data were derived from illustrations, mostly of preserved specimens. The trauma of capture and fixation may

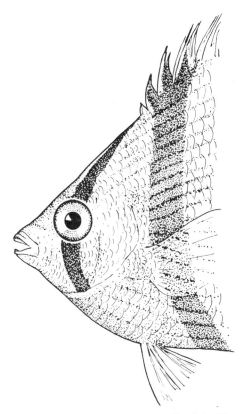

Fig. 7. The head of a butterfly fish, illustrating the tendency of the anterior-most bar to bend with the profile of the fish.

have caused changes in the color patterns, not to mention the direct chemical damage. Also, illustrators commonly render conspicuous eyes that are concealed as an aid to the reader, usually a systematist.

Nonetheless, the analysis led to three reasonably clear conclusions. First, the attitude of the eye-line is correlated with the relative depth of the fish: deep-bodied fishes have predominantly vertical lines whereas elongate fishes typically have longitudinal ones. Second, the eye-line is also correlated with the slope of the forehead. Finally, the exceptions, and the lack of them, aid in interpreting the results. For instance, an elongate fish with a vertical eye-line is most likely a bottom dwelling form, and typically exposes only its head from a burrow. Even more striking is the absence of deep-bodied fishes with a horizontal eye-line.

Why do such relationships exist? The answer may be sought initially with regard to the shape of the fish only. In a very elongate fish, the dorsal and ventral profiles consist of two long lines moderately close together. Thus the profile of the fish presents adjacent and parallel major boundaries. A longitudinal stripe through the eye, by repeating a nearby boundary line, may have a confusing effect on the receptor system of a potential predator.

Some elongate fishes have several stripes running their entire length. When these stripes extend onto the head, the upper and lowermost commonly (not always) bend toward the midline of the fish, converging on the snout. In so doing, the upper approximates the profile of the top of the head, and the lower that of the bottom profile, as in the black-striped cardinal fish, *Apogon novemfasciata* (see also Fig. 2).

For deep-bodied fishes the case is not so simple. In comparing progressively deeper fishes the profiles of the forehead usually steadily steepen. And the forehead profile is the major discontinuity close to the eye. The evidence for such a repetition of lines can also be seen in a more detailed examination of the trend of lines through eyes. For example, many butterfly fishes (Fig. 7) have a vertical line that nearly follows the dorsal profile above the eye, bending below the eye to flow with the ventral profile.

Of special interest are the markings on a few species that have a steep anterior profile together with an elongate body. The most noteworthy of these are the sciaenids *Equetus lanceolatus* (Fig. 8, top) and *E. punctatus*. Their more anterior markings are appropriate for a fish with a steep profile and/or deep body. But the vertical bar on the prominent dorsal fin bends to the rear to become a longitudinal stripe on the body, as befits a slender form. (The same relationship between shape and markings recurs on the unrelated roosterfish, *Nematistius pectoralis*.) However, the closely related *Equetus acuminatus* has a more recumbant forehead and a lower dorsal fin; it lacks vertical markings on the head, and horizontal markings prevail (Fig. 8, bottom).

A similar relationship can be demonstrated in the ontogeny of some species. For instance, the small juveniles of the porkfish, *Anisotremus virginicus*, are slender and have a sloping forehead; the trend of their markings is longitudinal. The body deepens with growth, however, and the forehead becomes steep; as this happens, the fish acquire the

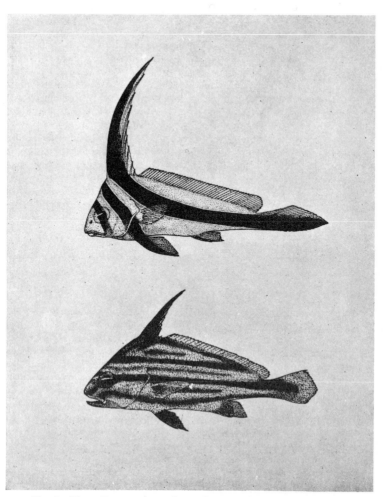

Fig. 8.   Top: *Equetus lanceolatus*. Bottom: *Equetus acuminatus*.

species-typical pair of nearly vertical black bars on the head, one through the eye (Walter A. Stark, II, pers. comm.).

Any discussion of the eye-line would be incomplete without taking into consideration the environment and the habits of the animals involved. Certainly an animal's ecology determines its form. And its environment, behavior, and shape mold the attitude of the eye-line. To appreciate this, one needs to see the eye-line as a part of the totality of markings borne by the fish. In the digression that follows, I will focus on a type of color pattern that is easy to treat because of its simplicity and recurrence in diverse species, and that is easy to relate to eye-lines. However, eye-lines accompany a much wider range of overall color patterns.

The first assertion is that the attitude of the eye-line is similar to the attitude of the main markings on the body. For example, both a vertical eye-line and vertical bars on the body are usually found on deep-bodied fishes. Horizontal stripes on the body, as well as the horizontal eye-line, more often characterize elongate fishes. (Vertical lines on fishes are conventionally called bars or bands, whereas horizontal lines are stripes.)

The number of stripes or bars on the body are determined in part by the interaction of mobility, type of movement, and relation to the bottom. Elongate fishes can be characterized as active species that swim rapidly but do not turn sharply. Those species that occur well up in the water are inclined to have either no stripes or perhaps one stripe the length of the body, often including the eye (an exception recurs in different jacks of the genus *Seriola*; these have an oblique eye-line paralleling the forehead, but lack a body stripe). Elongate fishes that are more closely associated with the bottom, such as poma-dasids, tend to be more deep-bodied and compressed; if striped, they usually have several extending the length of the body, and they associate with reefs or reef-like habitats.

Few deep-bodied fishes live in open water. Those that do are special cases such as occur among the plectognaths. Typically deep-bodied species are found just over the bottom, often closely associated with the substrate. The types of markings on the body may be diverse, as seen in the parrot and trigger fishes. But banding is common. Deep-bodied fishes with bands or bars are usually mobile, often gregarious fishes that are active just over or next to a complex substrate. They differ from elongate species in that they cannot sustain high speed, but they can turn sharply (Alexander, 1967).

Longitudinal stripes, beyond distracting from the profile, are probably of aid to a fish that is moving rapidly ahead; they should make it difficult for a predator to fix on a particular reference point, especially if the fish are schooling. Likewise, the bold dark-on-light banding on several deep-bodied fish turning rapidly doubtless confuses the predator.

Some elongate characins, such as the ano-stomids *Abramites microcephalus* and *Leporinus affinis*, have emphatic banding; but these are habitual "head standers" and thus behave unlike most elongate fishes (see Braemer and Braemer, 1958). A remarkable case is the elongate pilot fish, *Naucrates ductor*; the prominent bands on this slender fish must be related to its association with giant fishes, perhaps rendering it conspicuous to its large companion. Another exceptionally marked slender species is the banded pipefish, *Dunkerocampus caulleryi chapmani*.

Deep-bodied fishes with horizontal stripes are not known to me, unless one accepts those butterfly fishes having a number of lines running in several directions (but mostly following the outline of the fish).

Some species exhibit a gamut of color changes relevant to the arguments that have been raised here with regard to fishes of different shapes. Depending on circumstances, such as feeding or fighting, a fish of a given shape may have stripes at one time, bars at another (Albrecht, 1966; Magnuson and Prescott, 1966; Strasburg and Marr, 1961). Among cichlids in crater lakes in Central America, one elongate species, a not yet named *Cichlasoma*, is particularly adept at changing its basic color patterns. In open water, where it spends most of its time, it carries one long body stripe. When foraging over the bottom, however, that stripe separates into a number of spots. This species breeds on the bottom where its movements are confined to a small territory; then each spot is replaced by a vertical black bar set off against a pale background. Finally, when the parental fish enters the "breeding cave" it becomes totally black. Longley (1920:485) wrote ". . .that when any species has alternative patterns of longitudinal stripes (or self-color) and transverse bands, the former is shown when the fish that displays it is in motion, while the latter tends strongly to appear whenever it comes to rest." This has wrongly been too literally interpreted by subsequent writers who have equated at rest with motionless. Longley clearly meant here slowly milling fish holding station, as in schools of grunts that feed by night and congregate at a regular place during the day.

The tenor of this paper has been to argue that such markings conceal these fishes from the eyes of other fishes. Yet when this cichlid is wearing its stripe in midwater, others approach and aggregate with it, as occurs in some pomacentrids (Franzisket, 1959). When breeding, and showing the contrast-rich banded pattern, other members of its species avoid it. The chief markings on this species then can just as well be regarded as visual signals. Others have pointed out this paradox (Longley, 1917; Hemmings, 1966; Hamilton and Peterman, in press).

Eibl-Eibesfeldt (1962) recognized the general problem but in a slightly different form. He proposed that the markings usually shown are protective but that the signals are selectively revealed, as by raising fins or by briefly changing the color patterns. However, prominent species-typical marks, such as bands or stripes, or large ocelli at the base of the caudal fin, are important social signals that are almost always readily visible (Keenleyside, 1955). Note that in many species, especially solitary ones, the barred pattern is obviously an adaptation for crypsis: the bars and interspaces do not contrast strongly and their boundaries are indistinct. When clearly adapted as a signal, however, the contrast is great and the boundaries sharp (Barlow, 1963).

But even such emphatic patterns could have a protective function. Water is not a good medium for vision over a distance. At long range, at a distance greater than the flight distance of the prey fish, bold bands or stripes might by concealing. Cott (1940: 93 and fig. 39) pointed out that objects bearing black and white bars or stripes are conspicuous up close, but at some critical distance they blend into their grey surroundings. This might be especially applicable during crepuscular periods, when many predators are hunting (Hobson, 1965).

A fish that is by nature on the move just over the bottom, furthermore, could not afford to match the background closely because the background would differ depending on the relative positions of the viewer and the viewed. A simple disruptive pattern is one solution, and it can also serve in communication. Up close, at a distance permitted to members of ones own species, such markings are eye-catching and as such serve as social signals to maintain the cohesiveness of the group.

My underwater experiences suggest, however, that strongly barred or striped fishes are conspicuous over long distances during the day (see also Albrecht, 1966; Franzisket, 1959). Moreover, most fish predators attack from close range. Since boldly barred or striped species generally live in aggregations, the chief protective function of these markings probably lies in the visually confusing effect created when the fish rapidly mill and turn in escape, especially when seen against a complex background. An obliterative eye-line, repeating the major markings, would enhance that effect. The eye-line would also remove a cue important to the predator in leading the prey when attacking.

The attitude of the eye-line is but a part of a complicated chain of factors. It starts with the way the fish engages its environment. This determines the background against which the animal is viewed. The style of motion best suited to the feeding and escape behavior of the species will impose a particular shape to the head, body, and fins. And the more diurnally social the fish, the more important it becomes to communicate by means of color markings. Given an understanding of the complex interaction of these factors, it should be possible to predict the general nature of the chief markings, including the attitude of the eye-line when present.

ACKNOWLEDGMENTS

I am grateful to Catherine Bleick for her critical comments, and to Emily Read for preparing the illustrations. The writing was supported in part by a grant from the Committee on Research, University of California, Berkeley, and the cost of publication was borne by the National Science Foundation (grant GB 13426).

LITERATURE CITED

ALBRECHT, H.   1966.   Zur Stammesgeschichte einige Bewegungsweisen bei Fischen, untersucht am Verhalten von *Haplochromis* (Pisces, Cichlidae). Zeit. Tierpsychol. 23:270–302.

ALEXANDER, R. McN. 1967. Functional design in fishes. Hutchinson, London.

BARLOW, G. W. 1963. Ethology of the Asian teleost *Badis badis*. II. Motivation and signal value of the colour patterns. Anim. Behav. 11:97–105.

BRAEMER, W., AND H. BRAEMER. 1958. Zur Gleichgewichtsorientierung schräg stehender Fische. Zeit. vergl. Physiol. 40:529–542.

COTT, H. B. 1940. Adaptive coloration in animals. Methuen, London.

EIBL-EIBESFELDT, I. 1962. Freiwasserbeobachtungen zur Deutung des Schwarmverhaltens verschiedener Fische. Zeit. Tierpsychol. 19: 165–182.

FISHELSON, L. 1963. Observations on littoral fishes of Israel. I. Behaviour of *Blennius pavo* Risso (Teleostei, Blenniidae). Israel J. Zool. 12:67–80.

FRANZISKET, L. 1959. Experimentelle Untersuchung über die optische Wirkung der Streifung beim Preussenfisch (*Dascyllus aruanus*). Behaviour 15:76–81.

HAMILTON, W. J., III, AND R. M. PETERMAN. In Press. Countershaded colorful reef fish: adaptation to concealment, communication, or both. Anim. Behav.

HEMMINGS, C. C. 1966. Factors influencing the visibility of objects underwater, p. 359–374. *In*: Light as an ecological factor. B. Bainbridge, G. C. Evans, and O. Rackham, eds. Oxford, Blackwell.

HOBSON, E. S. 1965. Diurnal-nocturnal activity of some inshore fishes in the Gulf of California. Copeia 1965:291–302.

KEENLEYSIDE, M. H. A. 1955. Some aspects of the schooling behavior of fish. Behaviour 8: 183–247.

LONGLEY, W. H. 1917. Studies on the biological significance of animal coloration. I. The colors and color changes of West Indian reef-fishes. J. Exp. Zool. 23:533–601.

———. 1920. Marine camofleurs and their camouflage: The present and prospective significance of facts regarding the coloration of tropical fishes. Smiths. Inst. Wash. Ann. Rep. 1918:475–485.

——. 1924. Observations upon Tortugas fishes. Carnegie Inst. Wash. Yr. Book 23: 191–193.

MAGNUSON, J. J., AND J. H. PRESCOTT. 1966. Courtship, locomotion, feeding and miscellaneous behaviour of Pacific bonita (*Sarda chiliensis*). Anim. Behav. 14:54–67.

SIEGEL, S. 1956. Nonparametric statistics for the behavioral sciences. McGraw-Hill, N. Y.

SMITH, J. L. B. 1950. The sea fishes of southern Africa. Central News Agency, Capetown.

STRASBURG, D. W., AND J. C. MARR. 1961. Banded color phases of two pelagic fishes, *Coryphaena hippurus* and *Katsuwonus pelamis*. Copeia 1961:226–228.

DEPARTMENT OF ZOOLOGY AND MUSEUM OF VERTEBRATE ZOOLOGY, UNIVERSITY OF CALIFORNIA, BERKELEY, CALIFORNIA 94720.

BIOLUMINESCENCE OF LANTERN FISH (MYCTOPHIDAE) IN RESPONSE TO CHANGES IN LIGHT INTENSITY

J. F. CASE, J. WARNER,
A. T. BARNES AND M. LOWENSTINE

*Department of Biological Sciences,
University of California, Santa Barbara*

The characteristic ventral distribution of fish photophores suggests that their luminescence reduces the silhouette when viewed against a background of downwelling light[1-3]. This hypothesis is supported by demonstration of direct neural control of photophores in several species of myctophids and by morphological and behavioural indications that *Tarletonbenia crenularis* matches its luminescence to background illumination by visually monitoring a supraorbital photophore[4,5]. There is similar evidence for other taxa: shallow water leiognathids emit light in response to brief photic stimulation and mid-water squid have photosensitive vesicles which may participate in countershading[6-8]. Here we report photometric measurements of myctophid bioluminescent responses to light levels comparable with those occurring in their environment.

Symbolophorus californiensis (Eigenmann and Eigenmann) bears approximately 70 photophores of about 0.5 mm diameter on ventral and lateral surfaces. When immature, it lacks the brilliantly flashing luminous patches characteristic of many myctophids. It migrates daily from 600 m to or near the surface[9]. Immature specimens in good condition were netted at night by neuston net from RV Velero IV over the San Clemente Basin. They were transferred to containers of surface temperature seawater and held in darkness for experimentation within the next several hours aboard ship. Individuals were placed in a 1-1 cylindrical glass jar in an apparatus with which it was possible to continuously record bioluminescence against controlled background irradiance of up to 0.09 μW cm^{-2}. Background irradiance was generated by five Sylvania R1166 glow modulator tubes emitting white light onto a diffusing hemisphere above the specimen chamber. An EMI9781B photomultiplier, viewing the entire specimen chamber from below, detected bioluminescence. Interference from background irradiance was eliminated by pulsing the glow modulators at 180 Hz in synchrony with a rotating shutter over the photomultiplier tube. The 'on' period for the glow modulators corresponded to the period during which the photomultiplier tube was covered by the shutter. The photomultiplier signal was processed by a Kiethley 840 lock-in amplifier and displayed on a chart recorder with a bandwidth of 70 Hz. Background irradiance was measured with a United Detector Technology 40X radiometer. Tests of the performance of the apparatus showed that a photophore-sized light source, placed 10 cm from the photomultiplier, and producing an estimated irradiance of 5×10^{-5} μW cm^{-2}, could readily be detected against a 0.5-m^2 background producing an irradiance of 8×10^{-2} μW cm^{-2}. Because the 180-Hz glow modulator cycle exceeds the highest visual flicker fusion frequency reported for fish, the apparatus makes it possible for a subject to be exposed to perceptually continuous light while being monitored by a photomultiplier protected from dark current and sensitivity changes caused by excessive light exposure of the photocathode[10].

Six *S. Californiensis*, 26-30 mm standard length, responded similarly to repeated exposures to various background light regimes. Latency of bioluminescence initiation after switching on background lighting was as little as 0.5 s, with averages for four fish being 18.5 (four tests), 7.0 (one), 1.0 (four) and 2.0 s (six). 'Off' responses were similarly rapid but the data cannot be used for a precise measurement. In many instances a probable

From *Nature*, 265(5590):179–181. Reprinted by permission of MacMillan Journals Limited.

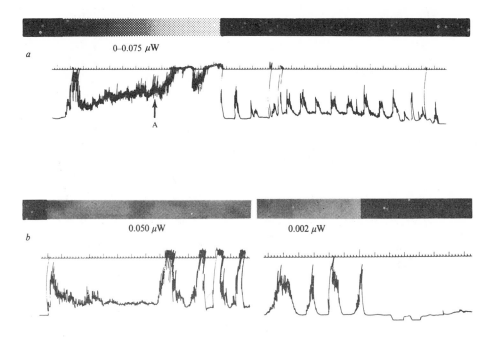

Fig. 1 Photomultiplier recordings of *Symbolophorus* bioluminescent responses to variation in background illumination. *a*, Probable alarm response and gradually increased bioluminescence in response to gradual increase in background illuminance, followed by diminished bioluminescence in darkness (point A equals 2 x 10^{-5} μW cm^{-2} at photomultiplier); *b*, probable alarm response followed by delayed onset of presumed countershading bioluminescence on sudden increase in background illuminance; *c*, sudden cessation of luminescence on cessation of low-level illumination. Records (*b*) and (*c*) were made with the same specimen. Time marks at 1 and 5 s, increasing bioluminescence indicated by upward deflection of traces.

luminescent startle response of 0.5–1.0 s latency, requiring an average of 4 s from half amplitude on to half amplitude off, precede initiation of sustained bioluminescence (Fig. 1*a* and *b*). Our data cannot be used to estimate how closely the fish match the background irradiance with their photophore emission because the position of the fish is indeterminate. The level of bioluminescence, however, is clearly directly related to background irradiance over part of the background irradiance range. When exposed to a ramp of increasing irradiance, ranging from near 0 to 0.008 μW cm^{-2} over 55 s, bioluminescence also increased in ramp-like fashion (Fig. 1*a*). Assuming a nominal position of 10 cm from the photomultiplier and maximum exposure of the ventral surface of the fish to the photomultiplier, point A in Fig. 1*a* corresponds to an irradiance of 2 x 10^{-5} μW cm^{-2} at the photocathode of the photomultiplier tube. Further evidence of proportionality of bioluminescence to background light intensity is seen in Fig. 1*b* and *c* where bioluminescence is off scale at 0.05 μW cm^{-2} background and considerably less at 0.002 μW cm^{-2} background. Bioluminescence is inhibited when the background reaches about 0.09 μW cm^{-2} and reappears when the background is reduced to 0.02 μw cm^{-2}, an effect that may be due to visual light adaptation because bioluminescence can be maintained to 0.08 μW cm^{-2} background irradiance when the background is cycled from dim to bright. During continuous background exposure, bioluminescence continues for at least 15 min, our longest test at a single background irradiance level. The short term peaks (roughly six to eight per min) coincide with the ship's motion. We believe they represent rotation of the free-swimming specimen with reference to the photomultiplier and that bioluminescence during exposure

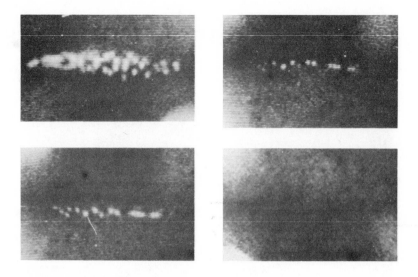

Fig. 2 Image intensified video recordings showing rapid onset of luminescence from ventral photophores of an approximately 5-cm standard length, unidentified myctophid. Interval between first and third frames is 116 ms, 676 ms for the entire series.

to light is uniform. A similar effect can be produced with an artifical light source in place of the fish. Photomultiplier records (Fig. 1*a*) and visual observations show some low level bioluminescence in darkness, often due only to the slow winking on and off of a single photophore.

Behaviournally-induced photophore responses of myctophids may be more rapid than the 0.5 s measured with the relatively poor time resolution of our recording system, as suggested in image intensified video recordings made according to the method of Barnes and Case[4]. Figure 2 shows video frames of an unidentified myctophid obtained by trawling in the Banda Sea. Within 677 ms all photophores in view have markedly increased their output.

These experiments demonstrate the presence of the requisite visual sensitivity linked with photophore control to facilitate bioluminescent reduction of the silhouette (countershading or counterillumination) in the typical light regime of lantern fish. Both the rapidity of photophore control and the demonstration of what may be a transient alarm response, however, argue that myctophid photophores have other roles.

This work was supported by the US Navy Office of Naval Research, the NSF and the Quantum and Marine Science Institutes of the University of California, Santa Barbara. The University of Southern California made available RV Velero IV. We thank Hans Stuber and Gerard Leaper for assistance.

1. McAllister, D. E., *J. Fisheries Res. Bd Canada*, **24(3)**, 537–554 (1967).
2. Jerzman, A., *Prezglad Zoologiczny*, **4**, 112–118 (1960).
3. Clarke, W. D., *Nature*, **198**, 1244–1246 (1963).
4. Barnes, A. T. and Case, J. F., *J. exp. mar. Biol. Ecol.*, **15**, 201–221 (1974).
5. Lawry, J. V., Jr., *Nature*, **247**, 155–157 (1974).
6. Hastings, J. W., *Science*, **191**, 1046–1048 (1976).
7. Young, R. E., *Pacific Sci.*, **27**, 1–7 (1973).
8. Young, R. E. and Roper, C. F. E., *Science*, **191**, 1046–1048 (1976).
9. Paxton, J., *Copiea*, **2**, 442–440 (1967).
10. Hanyu, I. and Ali, M. A., *J. cell. comp. Physiol.*, **63**, 309–322 (1964).

Additional Readings
CHAPTER 12

BAERENDS, G. P. 1971. The ethological analysis of fish behavior. Chapter 5, pp. 279–370, *in* W. S. Hoar and D. J. Randall, eds., *Fish Physiology*, Vol. 6. New York: Academic Press.

BARNES, A. T.; CASE, J. F.; TSUJI, F. I.; and REYNOLDS, G. T. 1972. Induction of bioluminescence in a nonluminous form of the marine teleost, *Porichthys notatus* by *Cypridina* (Ostracod) luciferin. *Am. Zool.* 12(4):683–684.

BEAMISH, R. J. and CHILTON, D. 1977. Age determination of lingcod using dorsal fin rays and scales. *J. Fish. Res. Bd. Can.* 34(9):1305–1313.

BREDER, C. M. 1967. On the survival value of fish schools. *Zoologica* 52:25–40.

CHAVIN, W., ed. 1973. *Responses of fish to environmental changes*. Illinois: Charles C. Thomas.

CHILDRESS, J. J. and NYGAARD, M. H. 1973. The chemical composition of midwater fishes as a function of depth of occurrence off southern California. *Deep-sea Res.* 20:1093–1109.

CLARKE, T. L. 1971. The ecology of the scalloped hammerhead shark, *Sphyrna lewina*, in Hawaii. *Pacific Science* 25(2):133–144.

CLARKE, W. 1963. Function of bioluminescence in mesopelagic organisms. *Nature* 198:1244–1246.

DENTON, E. J. and NICOL, J. A. C. 1966. A survey of reflectivity in silvery teleosts. *J. Mar. Biol. Ass. U.K.* 46(3):685–722.

DE VRIES, A. L. 1971. Freezing resistance in fishes. Chapter 3, pp. 157–190, *in* W. S. Hoar and D. J. Randall, eds., *Fish Physiology*, Vol. 6. New York: Academic Press.

DE VRIES, A. L. and WOHLSCHLAG, D. E. 1969. Freezing resistance in some Antarctic fishes. *Science* 163:1073–1075.

FRY, F. E. J. 1971. The effect of environmental factors on the physiology of fish. Chapter 1, pp. 1–98, *in* W. S. Hoar and D. J. Randall, eds., *Fish Physiology*, Vol. 6. New York: Academic Press.

FUJII, R. 1969. Chromatophores and pigments. Chapter 6, pp. 307–353, *in* W. S. Hoar and D. J. Randall, eds., *Fish Physiology*, Vol. 3. New York: Academic Press.

FUJII, R. and NOVALES, R. R. 1969. Cellular aspects of the control of physiological color changes in fishes. *Am. Zool.* 9:453–463.

GILBERT, P. W. 1962. The behavior of sharks. *Sci. Amer.* 207(1):60–82.

GLEITMAN, H. and ROZIN, P. 1971. Learning and memory. Chapter 4, pp. 191–278, *in* W. S. Hoar and D. J. Randall, eds., *Fish Physiology*, Vol. 6. New York: Academic Press.

HARDEN JONES, F. R. 1968. *Fish migration*. London: Edward Arnolds (Publishers) Ltd.

HASLER, A. D. 1971. Orientation and fish migration. Chapter 7, pp. 429–510, *in* W. S. Hoar and D. J. Randall, eds., *Fish Physiology*, Vol. 6. New York: Academic Press.

HASTINGS, J. W. 1971. Light to hide by: ventral luminescence to camouflage the silhouette. *Science* 173:1016–1017.

HOCHACHKA, P. W. and SOMERO, G. N. 1971. Biochemical adaptation to the environment. Chapter 2, pp. 99–156, *in* W. S. Hoar and D. J. Randall, eds., *Fish Physiology*, Vol. 6. New York: Academic Press.

JONES, B. C. and GEEN, G. H. 1977. Age determination of an elasmobranch (*Squalus acanthias*), by x-ray spectrometry. *J. Fish. Res. Bd. Can.* 34(1):44–48.

KETCHEN, K. S. 1975. Age and growth of dogfish *Squalus acanthias* in British Columbia waters. *J. Fish. Res. Bd. Can.* 32(1):43–59.

LOSEY, G. S., Jr. 1974. Cleaning symbiosis in Puerto Rico with comparison to the tropical Pacific. *Copeia* 1974(4):960–970.

MOSS, S. A. and McFARLAND, W. N. 1970. The influence of dissolved oxygen and carbon dioxide on fish schooling behavior. *Mar. Biol.* 5(2):100–107.

MYRBERG, A. A. and GRUBER, S. H. 1974. The behavior of the bonnethead shark (*Sphyrna tiburo*). *Copeia* 1974(2):358–374.

MYRBERG, A. A. and THRESHER, R. E. 1974. Interspecific aggression and its relevance to the concept of territoriality in reef fishes. *Am. Zool.* 14:81–96.

NICOL, J. A. C. 1969. Bioluminescence. Chapter 7, pp. 355–400, *in* W. S. Hoar and D. J. Randall, eds., *Fish Physiology*, Vol. 3. New York: Academic Press.

RAYMOND, J. A. and DEVRIES, A. 1977. Adsorption inhibition as a mechanism of freezing resistance in polar fishes. *Proc. Natl. Acad. Sci.* 74(6):2589–2593.

RUSSELL, F. E. 1969. Poisons and venoms. Chapter 8, pp. 401–449, *in* W. S. Hoar and D. J. Randall, eds., *Fish Physiology*, Vol. 3. New York: Academic Press.

SCHWASSMANN, H. O. 1971. Biological rhythms. Chapter 6, pp. 370–428, *in* W. S. Hoar and D. J. Randall, eds., *Fish Physiology*, Vol. 6. New York: Academic Press.

SIX, L. D. and HORTON, H. F. 1977. Analysis of age determination methods for yellowtail rockfish, canary rockfish, and black rockfish off Oregon. *Fish. Bull. U.S.* 405–414.

SPRINGER, V. G. and SMITH-VANIZ, W. F. 1972. Mimetic relationships involving fishes of the family Blenniidae. *Smithson. Contrib. Zool.* 112.

TAUBERT, B. D. and CABLE, D. W. 1977. Daily rings in otoliths of three species of *Lepomis* and *Tilapia mossambica J. Fish. Res. Bd. Can.* 34(3):332–340.

YOUNG, R. E. and ROPER, C. F. E. 1977. Intensity regulation of bioluminescence during counter-shading in living midwater animals. *Fish. Bull. U.S.* 75(2):239–252.

General References

ALEXANDER, R. McN. 1970. *Functional design in fishes.* London: Hutchinson and Company.

CURTIS, B. 1949. *The life story of the fish.* New York: Dover Publications, Inc.

GREENFIELD, D. W., ed. 1971. *Systematic ichthyology: a collection of readings.* New York: MSS Publishing Company, Inc.

LAGLER, C. F.; BARDACH, J. E.; MILLER, R. R.; and PASSINO, D. R. M. 1977. *Ichthyology*, 2nd. ed. New York: John Wiley & Sons, Inc.

LOVE, R. M. 1970. *The chemical biology of fishes.* New York: Academic Press.

MARSHALL, N. B. 1965. *The life of fishes.* London: Weidenfeld and Nicolson.

MARSHALL, N. B. 1971. *Explorations in the life of fishes.* Harvard Books in Biology, No. 7. Massachusetts: Harvard University Press.

NIKOLSKY, G. V. 1963. *The ecology of fishes.* New York: Academic Press.

NIKOLSKY, G. V. 1965. *Theory of fish population dynamics.* Edinburgh: Oliver and Boyd.

NORMAN, J. R. and GREENWOOD, P. H. 1975. *A history of fishes.* New York: John Wiley & Sons, Inc.

RICKER, W. E. 1971. *Methods for assessment of fish production in fresh waters.* IBP Handbook No. 3. Oxford: Blackwell Scientific Publications.

SHUL'MAN, G. E. 1974. *Life cycles of fish, physiology and biochemistry.* Israel Program for Scientific Publications. New York: John Wiley & Sons, Inc.

WEATHERLY, A. H. 1972. *Growth and ecology of fish populations.* New York: Academic Press.